D1187217

1156056 8

DAD'S ARMY

THE COMPLETE SCRIPTS OF SERIES 1–4

DAD'S

ARMY

Walmington Goes to War

The Complete Scripts of Series 1–4

Jimmy Perry & David Croft
Edited by Richard Webber

As far as possible we have tried to reproduce the original scripts of the television programmes. As you read the scripts you may, therefore, notice that changes did occur during the process of recording each episode.

First published in 2001
by Orion Books Ltd.
Orion House, 5 Upper St. Martin's Lane
London WC2H 9EA

Pictures supplied by: Radio Times

A CIP catalogue record for this book is available from the British Library.

ISBN 0-75284 153 X

Printed and bound in Italy

The Writing Process

'I think it's well documented that our working method was unusual. We would get together either at my place in Lansdowne Road, Notting Hill, or at Jimmy's flat at Morpeth Terrace in Westminster and, having set the world to rights for half an hour or so, we'd map out a couple of episodes. This would take us up to four days and the "map out" would consist of the main plot lines, the general shape of the scenes and a few comedy wheezes or incidents. Jimmy and I were from similar theatrical backgrounds and both well versed in farce, pantomime and summer season sketch comedy. We thought along the same lines.

'We would then go away and each of us would write up one of the episodes that we'd planned. I would then dictate my episode on to a Grundig or Phillips dictating machine which entailed rewriting any of my lines that did not transfer into spoken dialogue satisfactorily. Round about the end of week two we would get together again and read or play our episodes to each other. I never recall either of us rewriting our scripts.

'All the *Dad's* series were written in this way. The advantage was that we were each able to write at our own pace and at our own time. I preferred writing during the morning and early afternoon. Jim liked to write in the evening. It also, in a strange way, made us feel responsible for our own episodes.

'Rewrites just didn't happen and today I don't find it easy to identify which of us wrote a particular episode. Minor adaptations and the cutting of lines happened during rehearsals. Jimmy was inclined to watch the script closely and would draw the attention of the artistes to any variation that they introduced that we didn't approve.

'The scripts didn't change from the first draft to the second for the simple reason that there was never a second draft. All the characters were well and solidly established and their attitudes to any situation were plain to us. Therefore, there was no difficulty in writing for any character. I think the one exception to this was in the case of Mr Cheeseman, the character we used to make up the cast when Jimmy Beck died. He was a Welsh journalist. I think we made him irritating without being funny and I found the character a bit of a cliché. We stopped writing him after one series.'

DAVID CROFT

CATCHPHRASES

'So many people ask how the catchphrases in *Dad's Army* originated. Corporal Jones' "They don't like it up 'em!" was used by an instructor when in 1944 I was called up into the regular army and served in the Royal Artillery. Whenever he took us for bayonet practice he'd always finish with: "Just remember, lads, those Jerries don't like it up 'em, they can't abide it."

'"Permission to speak, sir," goes back to Victorian times. If a private soldier in the British army wished to address an officer, he'd always ask for permission. "Don't panic!" just happened. Clive Dunn slipped it in one day and it took off.

'"Put that light out!" was shouted by air raid wardens during the blackout in every town and village in the British Isles.

'"Stupid boy!" was what my father called me in exasperation when I told him that I was going to be a famous film star or a great comedian. And then, of course, there was John Laurie's "Doomed!" It was just one word in the script; John grabbed it by the throat and made it famous.'

JIMMY PERRY

THE ACTORS

THE ARTHUR LOWE–JOHN LE MESURIER RELATIONSHIP

'Actors don't necessarily have a close relationship with each other in order to work together successfully. I think this rule applied particularly to the chemistry between Arthur Lowe and John Le Mesurier.

'In the first place, they had quite different approaches to their work: John studied his part before coming to rehearsals. He had a photographic memory and on one occasion when he forgot the odd sentence I remember him saying to one of the stage managers: "Don't tell me – it's at the top of the next page after the bit in capital letters."

'Arthur, on the other hand, wouldn't even take his script home and used to shut it in his desk in the rehearsal room. After the first read-through of "Mum's Army", which Arthur initially didn't like, he remarked for all to hear: "If I'd read this script before I came to rehearsal I would have refused to do it." By Thursday he was saying: "This script – sheer genius."

'John found Arthur's attitude exasperating. He telephoned me one morning before we started a new series. "Can't you get him to learn the bloody thing?" he asked. I sent the scripts to Arthur enclosing two copies of each and a letter which said that the extra copy was sent with the suggestion that he would place it under his pillow in the hope that some of the words would filter through the feathers and penetrate to his sleeping mind. His only response was to say to Jimmy Perry, "David seems to be getting very crabby these days."

'The result with Arthur was two-fold. In the first place some of those heavenly pauses that he made were "what the hell do I say next?" pauses. The other factor was that Arthur would paraphrase lines. This kept everyone on their toes in case they had to rephrase their lines in order for them to make sense. I suppose that this accounted for some of the wonderful spontaneity of their playing. They watched each other intently. They both had acute ears for the audience reaction and never trod on a laugh. The expressions on Arthur's face in response to John's attitude to the impending invasion are a master class in comedy.

'It would be quite wrong for me to give the impression that Arthur and John didn't "get on". They both admired each other's playing enormously. They just didn't socialise.'

DAVID CROFT

JOHN LAURIE

'John Laurie rolled his piercing eyes and fixed me with a stare; the effect was quite mad. "You know you're almost illiterate, James, don't you?"

"Well, we can't all be perfect, John," I replied.

"Bah! You're a fool!" he hissed.

'In a strange sort of way I adored him; I suppose it's because I'm a bit potty myself. When David Croft and I were working on the pilot of *Dad's Army*, we wrote the part of "A Scotsman" in it. This was based on the fact that most small English seaside towns usually had several Scots in the community: they were either a doctor, dentist or solicitor and were treated with enormous respect by the English, who somehow felt that they were much cleverer.

'When Michael Mills, then Head of Comedy at the BBC, told us that he'd booked John Laurie for the part of "A Scotsman", David and I were slightly embarrassed and couldn't believe our luck. We thought back to all the great films he'd made: Alfred Hitchcock's 1936 version of *The Thirty-Nine Steps, The Four Feathers* and dozens of others. I remember one particular propaganda film made during the war; it was called *The Ghost of St Michael's,* with the fine comedy actor, Will Hay. John played a sinister butler in an old castle and he showed Will to his room with the words, "Keep your door locked during the night, and if you hear a scream it's only the wind."

'One day, he said to me: "Do you know, James, I've played all the great Shakespearian roles with Gielgud, Richardson and Olivier at the Old Vic, and it's no secret that I'm considered to be one of the finest verse speakers in the country today, but I have to wait till I'm 74 to become famous playing in this crap! I would never have considered playing the part of Frazer years ago; the work I did then had dignity and quality."

'"Oh, really," I said. "What about *Old Mother Riley Meets the Vampire*"? John just gave me one of his mad looks and I slunk away.'

JIMMY PERRY

CLIVE DUNN

'Back in 1948 when I first met Clive he was making frequent appearances at the Players' Theatre, underneath the railway arches at Charing Cross. He did a hilarious song called "The Ghost of Benjamin Binns". He was dressed as a sort of ghost and his gimmick was that his white-gloved hands were on the ends of two sticks. As he made his gesture he extended his arms until the hands were about twelve feet apart. The audience howled.

'We were both in London shows and so we saw a lot of each other. He was due to appear in a summer show on the end of the pier at Cromer – the show won the "Golden Bucket and Spade", which was the most coveted award for concert party shows. I wrote him a song in which he appeared in sou'wester carrying a three-foot plastic codfish. He was supposed to be a lifeboatman. The verse went:

> I think I'll resign from the lifeboats
> I've really had more than enough
> We never go out when it's sunny and smooth
> We only go out when it's rough.

'I frequently see him in Portugal, where at one time he ran a very successful restaurant with his two talented daughters and his wife, Cilla. He paints well and I have several of his paintings on my walls.

'Clive has total recall. He recounts incidents – never repeating himself – which results in us leaving his company weak having laughed so much. He was wonderful company during the *Dad's* years and I will always have the happiest memories of him and Corporal Jones.'

DAVID CROFT

JIMMY BECK

'Jimmy was exceedingly good company and when on location in Thetford we went around a lot together. He was a man of many talents. He did some very good sculptures and paintings which he was reluctant to allow anybody to see. He could do some hilarious impersonations of well known artistes.

'He first worked for me in *Beggar My Neighbour* with Reg Varney, Pat Coombs, June Whitfield and Peter Jones. He was very definitely my first choice for Private Walker having that cheeky self-assurance which was so valuable in the part. As a result of *Dad's Army*, his career began to take off and he was cast as the lead in *Romany Jones,* which turned out to be a popular series.

'It is now well known that Jimmy drank a lot, but in my opinion he was very far from being an alcoholic. Drink never affected his performance in any way either on the air or in rehearsal.

'I enlisted his help when I cast him in a pilot programme I was doing with Ronnie Fraser. Ronnie was a well-known tippler and was hilarious company when he got a bit lit. Jimmy knew about this so I asked him if he could help me keep Ronnie off the bottle during the pilot. Jimmy readily agreed. I then went to Ronnie and told him that Jimmy Beck was inclined to like the booze and it would be a great help if he would do his best to keep Jimmy away from temptation. Ronnie, who was a good friend, said: "Of course, David. You can rely on me." The conspiracy was entirely effective and it was not until a week later when they were having a drink together that they both confided in each other and discovered the plot. They had a good laugh and agreed that I was a devious bastard.

'Jimmy was taken to hospital with pancreatitis the evening before we went into the studio to record "The Recruit". Jimmy Perry and I had to make quick adjustments to the script to take Jimmy Beck out of the programme. In the event, what we wrote was rather poignant. Walker left a note in the place that he usually stood. It read: "Gone to the Smoke". He died three weeks later.'

DAVID CROFT

ARNOLD RIDLEY

'When David Croft told me he'd booked Arnold Ridley for the part of Private Godfrey, I was delighted. I didn't know him as an actor, but as an author I had done so many of his plays in weekly rep. At last I was going to meet the man responsible for one of the two classic popular plays that have gone into the English language: *Charley's Aunt* and *The Ghost Train.*

'Over the years, I've played the station-master in *The Ghost Train* at least half a dozen times, and I've never once known it to fail. David and I enjoyed writing inconsequential lines for Private Godfrey, and my favourite was this. The platoon is in a tight situation and Captain Mainwaring asks for comments. Everyone looks blank, trying to think of something to say. Suddenly, Godfrey pipes up: "The moving finger writes and having writ moves on." Mainwaring asks what that has got to do with the situation, to which he replies: "Nothing, I just thought I'd say it." This brought a close-up of Mainwaring and one of his wonderful reaction shots.

'I'm not sure if it's in the *Guinness Book of Records*, but not a single day goes by when there isn't an amateur production of *The Ghost Train* somewhere in the world, from the Kuala Lumpur Players to the Milton Keynes Dramatic Society. Unfortunately, when he was hard up, Arnold sold the amateur rights of *The Ghost Train* and lost a fortune.'

JIMMY PERRY

IAN LAVENDER

'My wife Ann knew that I was looking for a young actor to play Pike. She had seen Ian Lavender in a student production at the Bristol Old Vic and had been impressed by his performance and particularly with the effect he had on the young female element of the audience. She decided to sign him up to her agency there and then. It so happened that she had secured him an important part in a television play called *Flowers At My Feet.* Naturally she made sure that I watched it. I liked him, so I asked him to come to my office to read the part. Pike was supposed to be nineteen years old. Ian was twenty-one and looked nineteen so I cast him straightaway.

'It was interesting to see how he quickly settled amongst the very experienced members of the *Dad's Army* platoon. Arthur Lowe took to him at once and told him to stand beside him and he would take care of him. In fact the reverse was true. When Arthur tripped up or fell down, Ian would catch him and during the recovery process Arthur would re-arrange his spectacles so that they were on the skew and Ian would tilt Arthur's hat.

'Ian had a pleasant singing voice. We took advantage of this when we took *Dad's Army* into the theatre. He led a big musical production number singing "When Can I Have a Banana Again?" which was a popular song during the '39–'45 war. I also cast him in a singing part in a musical version of H G Wells' *Ann Veronica.*'

DAVID CROFT

FRANK WILLIAMS & EDWARD SINCLAIR

'When I first got the idea for *Dad's Army* I made a few sketchy notes in an old school exercise book. I wrote down "Old man, Young boy (a bit simple), Pompous man (perhaps a bank or building society manager) and Town vicar (Frank Williams)." I could never think of anyone else playing the Vicar but Frank.

'I first got to know him nearly 50 years ago when as a young actor I worked in the repertory company at the Palace Theatre, Watford. Some years later, I was producing at the same theatre and Frank came to me and asked if I'd put on a religious play, *The Substitute*, that he'd written. It was the story of the Crucifixion in modern dress.

I warned Frank of the perils of putting on your own plays, but he was so insistent that in the end I tried letting him off as lightly as possible: he would pay £300 for the week, which would include the whole production; this was in the days when actors were paid £12 a week. I would throw in playing one of the thieves, and the theatre would keep the bar and programme takings.

'"Would you like an agreement for me to pay a percentage if the play does well?" asked Frank, eagerly.

'"No, dear boy," I replied patronizingly, "just so long as we can all clear our expenses." Talk about a lamb to the slaughter, I thought, he's going to lose his shirt. I couldn't have been more wrong! Religious coach parties came from near and far; for six nights the theatre was packed to the rafters; we took a thousand pounds, a totally unheard of sum at that time.

'When it was all over, I said: "Frank, what are you going to do with the money?"

'He said: "I shall give it to the Church, of course, or perhaps I should let you have some to help the theatre funds."

"No, give it to the church," was my reply.

'Frank played the part of Reverend Farthing beautifully. Sometimes beaming with benevolence and others decidedly tetchy, the scenes he played with Edward Sinclair (the Verger) were a joy. I remember in "When Did You Last See Your Money?", Corporal Jones had mislaid some money. They were on night duty in the church hall and Frazer attempts to hypnotise Jones to help his memory. He's swinging a watch in front of Jones' eyes when the Verger sees him. He rushes up to the Vicar's room and wakes him up with the words: "Come quickly, your Reverence, there's a horrid black mass taking place in the hall."

"Black mass of what?" asks Frank.

'I always thought Teddy was a bit boring, although I was very fond of him. During one lot of filming, when for technical reasons we were forced to shoot "We Know Our Onions" down in Brighton, I remember we'd been hard at it all day and returned to the hotel worn out. I thought I'd take a quick nap before joining everyone down in the bar, and then as was our custom we'd go out for a meal. Unfortunately I overslept: my quick nap lasted two hours and when I got down to the bar, everyone had gone. Suddenly Teddy appeared. "Did you oversleep as well, Jimmy?" he asked.

'My heart sank. "Let's go out and get some fish and chips, I know a super little chippie just around the corner." And out we went.

'How wrong I was about Teddy – he wasn't boring at all. Not only that, we had some of the best fish and chips I've tasted for many a year. Yes, Teddy was great company and we chatted for hours. Sorry, Teddy, I was the one who was boring, you were a lovely man.' **JIMMY PERRY**

BILL PERTWEE

'For years Bill was my "warm-up man" in shows I was producing such as *Hugh and I* and *Beggar My Neighbour*. It is a thankless task but absolutely invaluable to the success of a television comedy. Bill did it wonderfully well. He has a warm, relaxed personality, which straight away put the audience at ease. He played parts from time to time. I first remember him as a customer in a cinema queue. Terry Scott was supposed to push in front of him but Bill's character would have none of it and pushed back. Terry was a good pusher so the resulting scene was very realistic.

'Bill was the ideal character to play Warden Hodges opposite Arthur Lowe. Their encounters became legendary and Bill was the perfect foil for the snobbish side of Mainwaring. His frequent appalled statement to Wilson, "The man's a green-grocer" was always a winner.

'Bill had a marvellous effect on the rest of the cast of *Dad's*. He was always upbeat and cheerful. If anybody ever had any doubts about a scene or line he would jump in with "What are you going on about – it's all going to be marvellous." And everybody believed him.

'John Le Mesurier leaned on him heavily – particularly in the later series when John was really very poorly. Bill used to collect him and deliver him to various places and was a wonderful friend to him and to us all. **DAVID CROFT**

REHEARSALS

BY HAROLD SNOAD

'It was customary – and still is – having recorded the previous week's episode in the studio, for the cast to have a day off before attending outside rehearsals for the next episode. In those days, the BBC didn't have a rehearsal block and, in common with other shows, outside rehearsals were generally held in various West London church halls or drill halls. These tended to vary over the years because either the one we'd used for the last series was occupied by another show or we'd found somewhere we liked better.

'On the whole, rehearsals for the material which was going to be recorded in the studio were very similar to any other comedy series. The location work, of course, had already been filmed: all location scenes required for the specific batch of episodes forming a series took place at the beginning in one session at Thetford before returning to London to rehearse and record the studio side of each episode.

'The first day of outside rehearsal for each episode started with a read-through. This usually

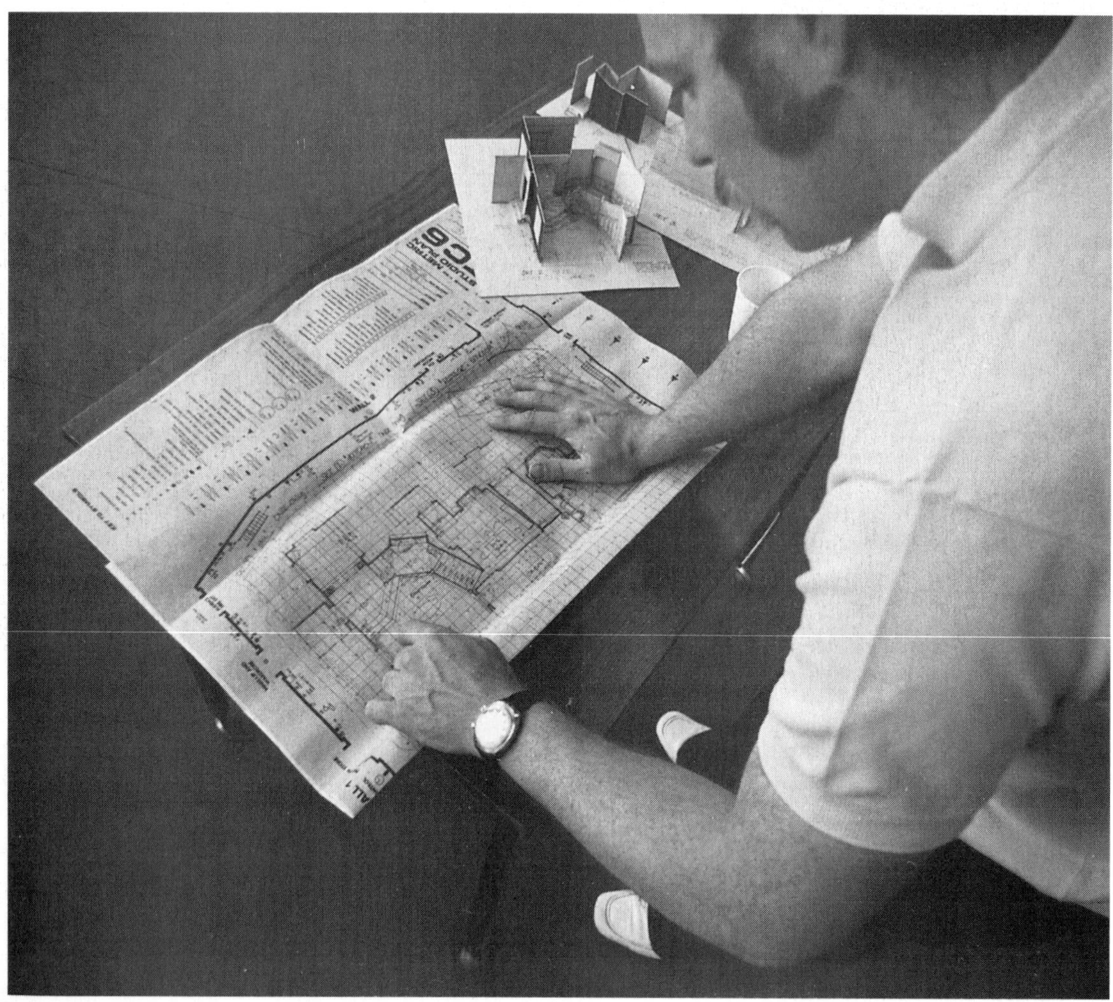

ABOVE The set is marked up on the rehearsal room floor, an exact scale representation of the floor plan.

LEFT Peter Fitton (assistant floor manager) studies the floor plan in the rehearsal room.

went well with the artistes enjoying themselves as they recognised and began playing on their established traits and relationships. There seemed to be a certain degree of "jealousy" between John Laurie and Arnold Ridley, and when a scene arose involving one of them, which was obviously going to create a lot of fun, there were several occasions when I noticed (and I doubt if I was alone in this) that the party who wasn't involved split his

Each set was marked out in the rehearsal room with different colour tape indicating individual sets.

time between looking rather miserable and shooting glances at the other one – especially if the reading of that element was creating a lot of laughs from the rest of the cast and members of the production team.

'The "blocking" (the director giving the artistes the moves and business) always went fairly smoothly. The cast usually watched the whole process even if they weren't involved in that particular scene, although sometimes when an artiste wasn't needed he would pop out for a quick cigarette; John Laurie or Arnold Ridley would sometimes also disappear for a few minutes because one was involved and the other wasn't!

'I remember it took John Le Mesurier rather longer than most of them to take on board moves and business, but he wasn't the most practical of people. As well as my pointing out one day that his watch had stopped and him asking me to wind it up for him, I experienced another example of his impracticality when I subsequently used his services whilst directing *The Dick Emery Show*. There was a film sequence involving John standing at the end of a bed pointing a revolver at Dick, who was in the bed, and asking him to hand over an item of jewellery. Whilst rehearsing the shot he demanded the piece of jewellery and then stopped, turned to me and said: "Wait a minute, I'm holding this

John Laurie and David Croft discuss the week's script.

revolver, how am I going to take the jewellery?" I replied: "Use your other hand!" He then looked down at his left hand which he'd obviously forgotten he had and said: "Oh, yes – of course."

'As rehearsals for *Dad's Army* progressed over the following two or three days the members of the cast gradually began learning their contributions for that particular episode and were able to put the script down. As has been reported in the past, Arthur Lowe, for some extraordinary reason – considering how professional his final contribution to any episode turned out to be – was extremely reluctant to take his script home after rehearsals in order to learn his lines, a perfectly normal element of any actor's life. When he "dried" during rehearsals he'd sometimes apologise and make the excuse of having accidentally left his script in the rehearsal room at the end of the previous day.

'On one occasion when he came out with this excuse I whispered to him a couple of minutes later that I'd seen him stuff it down the back of a radiator after rehearsals the previous day! He realised that he'd been rumbled, smiled, put his finger to his lips and mimed: "Sssh!".

'Unfortunately his method of taking on board the script for each episode rather late in the rehearsal period – which meant that he needed

The cast begins to work out all the moves in the scripts.

prompting quite a bit – began to affect the others who, perhaps subconsciously, started to be a bit more casual themselves about learning their lines. Jimmy Perry called me "the bravest man I know" because one day I actually said to the cast during a tea break: "Let's face it, some of you don't know your lines well enough." Although their initial reaction was to be stunned by this comment it appeared to work because from then on things seemed to get better.

'As in any show, the technical staff, plus the designer, wardrobe and make-up staff, would attend what is known as the technical run-through, which occurred each week two days before we were due in the studio. By this time, the director of the particular episode (in the early days David Croft or, sometimes, myself) would have worked out their camera script – how he planned to shoot the piece – which meant that the people who came in to see that run-through could be told where the cameras would need to be sited for each scene, where there would be recording breaks, set changes, etc. This was also, of course, the first time that these people had seen the rehearsals and, although there are only half a dozen individuals, their laughter is a great morale booster to any cast. This was certainly the case with *Dad's Army* and may well have served to

The first day begins with the read-through, a key part in the overall success of each episode.

make Arthur realise that the recording day was getting that much closer and he'd better have another look at the script!

'At the rehearsal stage of any television series the assistant floor manager, following the designer's set plan, would mark the sets out on the floor with sticky tape (generally using a different colour tape for each set). The cast would then have to make do with stand-in furniture and props – not the real items they would be using in the studio.

'I remember there was a slight deviation from this when it came to the episode, "Big Guns". In this the action required a lot of business involving a large artillery gun. As it was impossible rehearsals could be left until the recording day, I borrowed a gun from the Ministry of Defence. In fact, it was one of the guns that was used (and probably still is) for the Royal Salute at events featuring the Queen. Although the studio floor would cope with the huge weight of this gun, there was no way that the floor of the rehearsal room could and I had to arrange things so that rehearsals for this element were held in the car park of the London Transport offices in Wood Lane (just down the road from Television Centre) whose premises we were using at that time for outside rehearsals. Fortunately it was July and the weather stayed reasonable. (I still have a VHS copy of some film footage I shot at the rehearsals in the car park.)

'We then moved to the studio rehearsals and, of course, the actual recording. In those days the studios at Television Centre were always very busy. The set that had been required for whatever programme had been in our studio the day before was removed overnight and replaced by the set and props we required for that week's *Dad's Army* episode.

'Members of the cast generally arrived on time and we started camera rehearsals of the first studio scene at ten-thirty. This process involved each cameraman (usually four or five of them) working off a list of shots which the director needed him to offer at specific points in the scene.

'David Croft was an excellent director (I learnt a lot from him and he gave me my first chance to direct with an episode of *Hugh and I Spy*) and kept things fairly simple camera wise – not that there was any reason to do otherwise. For example, for the parade scenes, once you had set up a group shot of the platoon lined up with Mainwaring and Wilson at the far end, shots of specific members, a two-shot of Mainwaring and Wilson, and a single of Mainwaring to register his reaction to certain events, you more or less had the scene covered. The important thing was that the viewer should be seeing the correct shot at the right moment in the action. This was achieved by the vision mixer, who sat next to the director in the gallery, cutting from one camera to another at the point in the dialogue (or action) dictated by the director's camera script.

'It obviously helped enormously if the actors stuck rigidly to the script and, on the whole, the cast of *Dad's Army* always did so, although Clive Dunn was sometimes the exception. On many occasions his rendering of Jones' dialogue was not quite the same as written and, therefore, as it appeared on the camera script. He used to say what had to be said but often in a different way! This made life a little difficult at times.

'During rehearsals, David would sometimes have an extra idea which involved a member of the cast making a slightly different move or being given a new piece of business. When this involved John Le Mesurier, who as I've said wasn't the most practical person, John was often somewhat reluctant to make the alteration; he would say: "Do you think that's wise?" As fans of the series will know this observation was taken up by David and Jimmy, and sometimes used as part of Wilson's dialogue.

'Once the director was happy that the cameramen were conversant with the shots required at the dress rehearsal – and, again, at the recording in the evening – he moved on to the next studio scene. On the occasions when there was rather less location material than usual there could be quite a few studio scenes to rehearse, which was quite tiring for the artistes, especially in scenes where they had to stand about. We were always aware that Arnold tired fairly easily and he used to get looked after – much to the annoyance of John Laurie who would be heard to say: "What's all the fuss about, he's only one year older than me."

'By mid-afternoon we were generally ready to begin the dress rehearsal and having got through this we'd break for supper before recording the episode at eight o'clock in front of the studio audience. The cast were very professional and where a retake was necessary for some reason they happily

LEFT Rostra are often used to create extra height on the set.

RIGHT The assistant floor manager discusses the script with Jimmy Perry and David Croft.

LEFT Jimmy Beck, David Croft and Harold Snoad on location, with Paul Joel and Evelyn Lucas in the background.

BELOW Harold Snoad and John Laurie take a few minutes' rest from rehearsals.

BOTTOM The cast gather for a social occasion.

knuckled down and did it again. Arthur, for example, was fairly laid back and if something went wrong it didn't seem to worry him.

'After the recording, which generally finished no later than nine-thirty (although the episode only ran half an hour there were, of course, breaks for costume and scene changes) we'd often have a drink together in the BBC Club before going our separate ways. The cast had the following day off before starting all over again with outside rehearsals for the next episode.'

The Contributors

OLIVER BAYLDON

Oliver studied Fine Art and Design at Leicester before beginning his career at the Theatre Royal, Nottingham. He moved on to designing sets and costumes for the Royal Academy of Music, and designing television commercials. He joined the BBC as a design assistant, rapidly rising to designer on many award-winning films, serials and documentaries. He's won four BAFTA nominations and one BAFTA production design award. Since leaving the Beeb, he's been working freelance.

HUGH CECIL

Since the age of 11, Hugh has been performing magic and Punch and Judy shows, and he became a member of the Magic Circle at 18. He drifted into acting, appearing in sketches during summer seasons, beginning at Newcastle-upon-Tyne. He clocked up 50 episodes of *Dad's Army* as a member of the platoon's back row.

ALEC COLEMAN

Alec, one of the platoon's original members, turned to acting full-time after the war and it wasn't long before he was appearing on stage. His television debut was in *Z Cars* and he went on to appear in a myriad of other shows, playing small parts. Alec, who left the show after the second series, continues to act and appeared recently in two episodes of *Midsomer Murders*.

DESMOND CULLUM-JONES

For 63 episodes Desmond appeared in the platoon's back row. His lengthy list of credits includes appearances in shows like *Dixon of Dock Green; Father, Dear Father; Compact* and *Shoestring*. He's also led a busy film career. Desmond no longer actively seeks work and is enjoying retirement in Bournemouth.

PETER DAY

Peter was the visual effects designer on 20 episodes. After training in theatre design, he worked for several companies before joining the BBC in 1958 as a design assistant. Initially he worked on school programmes before concentrating on mainstream television. Peter retired from the organisation in 1985.

CLIVE DOIG

Clive, who joined the BBC in 1958, had worked with David Croft on several of his shows before joining the production team for *Dad's Army*. He was a vision mixer for seven years before turning his attention to directing. Clive left the BBC in 1981 and formed his own production company, Brechin Productions Ltd.

CLIVE DUNN

Clive, who made his professional stage debut during Christmas 1936 playing a dancing frog and a flying dragon, played Corporal Jones on television, radio, film and stage. Awarded the OBE in 1975, he divides his time between homes in London and Portugal.

ROSEMARY FAITH

Rosemary, who made three appearances in the sitcom, first worked for David Croft in *Beggar My Neighbour*. She worked in all mediums, including the last 12 episodes of *Please, Sir!*, before giving up acting in 1988. Today, she works in theatre administration in Worthing.

ARTHUR FUNGE

At 15, Arthur was appearing in musicals as an actor, but when he joined the BBC in the 1960s he started as a dresser in the Costume Department. In the 20 odd years spent at the Beeb, he worked on a myriad of shows and was John Le Mesurier's dresser for two years on *Dad's Army*. He left the Corporation in 1984 and retired from the business.

BILL HARMAN

After working on many BBC productions, Bill – who worked as an assistant floor manager on *Dad's Army* – left the Beeb in 1970. For five years he worked for WEA, the British record company, liaising with top British and overseas artists, before returning to the BBC in 1975 as a researcher on shows including *The Generation Game* and *All Creatures Great and Small.* He moved to Tyne Tees and reached the position of production manager before emigrating to New Zealand in 1981, where he continues to work in television.

BRIAN HILES

Brian chalked up 37 years with the BBC before leaving in 1992 and working as a freelance sound director. Throughout his extensive television career he worked on many top shows, including *Pennies from Heaven, Elizabeth R* and *Testament of Youth.*

PAUL JOEL

Paul, the designer on 52 episodes of *Dad's Army*, studied architecture in London and worked for several architects before moving into interior design. He joined the BBC in 1965 and was promoted to designer three years later. His career at the Beeb had spanned almost 30 years by the time he left in 1994. Paul, who occasionally works freelance, lives in Cornwall with his artist wife, Judy. Much of his time is now devoted to organising and designing art exhibitions.

EVAN KING

Evan was a solo ice-skating comedian for 13 years before joining the BBC in 1964 as a scene shifter. Within 17 months he'd transferred from Glasgow to London and was working as an assistant floor manager. During the 23 years he spent at the Beeb he worked on many shows, including *The Likely Lads, Last of the Summer Wine* and *Just Good Friends.* By the time he left the Beeb in 1987, after 23 years, he was a production manager. Evan took early retirement and now lives in Suffolk.

BARBARA KRONIG

Barbara, who was costume designer on the first six episodes of series four, joined the BBC in 1965. Although she did her fair share of light entertainment shows, she worked mainly on period productions and dramas. She left the Beeb during the 1980s and now works as a freelance costume designer.

IAN LAVENDER

After graduating from drama school at Bristol's Old Vic, Ian was offered a season playing juvenile leads at Canterbury's Marlowe Theatre. He made his television debut in an ATV play, *Flowers At My Feet,* the same year he was interviewed for the role of Pike. Ian remains busy today, particularly in the theatre.

CLAIRE LIDDELL

After studying at Glasgow's Royal Scottish Academy of Music, Claire won a scholarship to the Royal College of Music in London. Although her favourite instrument was the piano, she also studied composition. Claire, who's written a book on improvisation, is also a successful composer. Nowadays she regularly broadcasts and composes for her local radio station, BBC Scotland, and acts as musical director in theatre.

STEPHEN LOWE

Arthur Lowe's son, Stephen, moved to New Zealand in 1997. He's currently teaching multimedia at Aoraki Polytechnic in Timaru and Dundenin.

BILL McLEAN

A former actor, Bill, who's been an agent for over 30 years, represented Arnold's acting interests from 1968 to his death in 1984. After working for two other companies, Bill formed his own agency and remains busy in the industry today.

JIMMY PERRY and DAVID CROFT

Between them, Perry and Croft have formed one of Britain's most successful writing partnerships, penning not just *Dad's Army* but other classic sitcoms such as *Hi-De-Hi!, It Ain't Half Hot, Mum* and

You Rang, M'Lord?. In recognition of their service to television and the enjoyment they've given to millions, the writers were awarded the OBE.

BILL PERTWEE

Playing Hodges in 60 television episodes, the film, stage show and 33 radio instalments, Bill established a character who became the bane of Mainwaring's life. Since the series finished in 1977, he's remained busy, primarily in the theatre. He's also written several books.

PETER SINCLAIR PERRY

Peter, son of Gladys and the late Edward Sinclair, spent seven years in acting before forging a successful career in fine art publishing. He later entered the world of commercial radio, where he was founder and managing director of Radio Mercury, covering Surrey and West Sussex. He now works as a media consultant.

CARMEN SILVERA

Carmen, best known as Edith in *'Allo, 'Allo,* appeared as Mrs Gray in 'Mum's Army'. Her successful career has included many appearances in West End productions, including *Waters of the Moon* with Ingrid Bergman.

ROGER SINGLETON-TURNER

In the days of *Dad's Army*, Roger was an assistant floor manager at the BBC, but by the time he left the Corporation after 31 years' service, he was producing children's drama. He's now a freelance producer (among his many credits are two series of the children's drama, *Welcome to the orty-Fou* for Carlton TV) and lectures at the University of Leeds.

HAROLD SNOAD

Harold, who went on to direct a number of episodes, joined the production team at the show's inception. Post *Dad's Army*, he established a highly successful career, and at the age of 30 became one of the country's youngest producer/directors. He's worked with many of the industry's 'greats', and among the shows he's directed and produced are *Ever Decreasing Circles, Don't Wait Up, The Dick Emery Show* and *Keeping Up Appearances*.

DES STEWART

Over a period of three years, Des worked as an armourer on *Dad's Army*, before moving on and working in Health and Safety. After 24 years' service with the BBC, he left in 1997 and now works as a freelance health and safety advisor.

DAVID TAYLOR

After working as an accounts clerk in Television Accounts, David transferred to Television Production as a floor assistant. He went on to spend 32 years with the BBC and by the time he accepted early retirement in 1997, he was a producer in the Entertainment Department. David now does consultancy work for a media company.

FRANK WILLIAMS

For 39 television episodes, the Vicar was brought to life by Frank Williams, who made his name in *The Army Game*. On the big screen, his debut was in the 1956 film, *The Extra Day*, followed by more than 30 other pictures. Frank, who's a regular in panto, is also a playwright. Over the past few years, there have been successful productions of four of his thrillers.

Production Team

PRODUCER

David Croft

DIRECTOR

David Croft (all episodes, except Series 2, episodes 4, 5 & 6; Series 3, episodes 3 & 12; Series 4, episodes 2 & 5, which were directed by Harold Snoad)

PRODUCTION ASSISTANT

Harold Snoad (S1; S2, episodes 1–3; S3, episodes 1, 4–10, 12–14; S4, episodes 1, 3, 4 & 6)

Clive Doig (S2, episodes 4–6)

Steve Turner (S3, episode 11)

Jim Franklin (S3, episodes 2 & 3)

Donald Clive (S4, episodes 1–6)

Phil Bishop (S4, episodes 7–13; 'Battle of the Giants!')

PRODUCER'S ASSISTANT

Eve Lucas (S1, episode 1; S2, episodes 1–3)

Pat Parrish (S1, episodes 2–6; S3, episodes 1–7)

Ann Milford (S2, episodes 4–6)

Kay Johnson (S3, episodes 8–14; S4)

ASSISTANT FLOOR MANAGER (AFM)

Evan King (S1)

Tony George (S2)

Bill Harman (S3)

David Taylor (S4, episodes 1–6)

Roger Singleton-Turner (S4, episodes 7–13)

Bob Spiers ('Battle of the Giants!')

FLOOR ASSISTANT

Bernard Doe (S1)

Quentin Mann (S2)

Paul Cole (S3, episodes 1–7)

James Piner (S3, episodes 8–14)

Peter Fitton (S4, episodes 1–6)

Maurice Gallagher (S4, episodes 7–13)

STUDIO LIGHTING
(also known as Technical Manager 1)

George Summers (S1; S2, episodes 1, 2, 4 & 6; S4, episodes 7–12)

John Dixon (S2, episode 3)

Dennis Channon (S2, episode 5)

Howard King (S3; S4, episodes 1–6; 'Battle of the Giants!')

Technical Manager 2

Brian Fitt (S1, episodes 1 & 2)

John Farr (S1, episodes 3–6; S2, episodes 1, 2 & 6)

Dickie Ashman (S2, episode 3)

Reg Hutchings (S2, episode 4)

Tommy Claydon (S2, episode 5)

Fred Wright (S3, episodes 1–7, 9–14; S4, episodes 1–6)

Derek Slee (S3, episode 8)

Bob Warman (S4, episodes 7–13)

STUDIO SOUND SUPERVISOR

James Cole (S1 & S2)

Mike McCarthy (S3, episodes 1–11, 13 & 14; S4, episodes 2, 4, 6–13; 'Battle of the Giants!')

John Holmes (S3, episode 12; S4, episodes 1, 3 & 5)

TAPE/GRAM OPERATOR

(Job not listed on scripts after S3, episode 7)

Lance Andrews (S1, episodes 1–5)

Linton Howell-Hughes (S1, episode 6)

Dave Mundy (S2, episodes 1, 2, 5 & 6; S3, episodes 4–7)

Bob Stickland (S2, episode 3)

Malcolm Johnson (S2, episode 4)

Pat Tugwood (S3, episodes 1–3)

COSTUME SUPERVISOR

George Ward (S1; S4, episodes 7–13)

Marjorie Lewis (S2)

Odette Barrow (S3, episodes 1–7)

Michael Burdle (S3, episodes 8–14)

Barbara Kronig (S4, episodes 1–6)

Judy Allen ('Battle of the Giants!')

MAKE-UP SUPERVISOR

Sandra Exelby (S1)

Sheila Cassidy (S2)

Cecile Hay-Arthur (S3, episodes 1, 2, 5–14)

Jan Harrison (S3, episodes 3 & 4)

Cynthia Goodwin (S4)

Penny Bell ('Battle of the Giants!')

DESIGNER

Alan Hunter-Craig (S1)

Paul Joel (S1; S2, episodes 1, 3, 5 & 6; S3, episodes 1–7; S4; 'Battle of the Giants!')

Oliver Bayldon (S2, episodes 2 & 4)

Ray London (S3, episodes 8, 10, 12 & 14)

Richard Hunt (S3, episodes 9, 11 & 13)

VISION MIXER

Clive Doig (S1, episodes 1, 5 & 6; S4, episode 9)

Bob Hallman (S1, episodes 2, 3 & 4)

Dave Hanks (S2, episodes 1, 2 & 5; S3; S4, episodes 3–8, 10–13; 'Battle of the Giants!')

Bruce Milliard (S2, episodes 3, 4 & 6)

Dave Hillier (S4, episodes 1 & 2)

VISUAL EFFECTS

Peter Day (S3, episodes 4, 5, 6; S4, episodes 9 & 11)

John Friedlander (S4, episode 2)

Ron Oates (S4, episode 2)

Len Hutton ('Battle of the Giants!')

FILM CAMERAMAN

James Balfour (S3, episodes 1–3, 5–8, 10, 13, 14)

Stewart A. Farnell (S4, episodes 1–3, 5, 8, 10, 13; 'Battle of the Giants!')

FILM SOUND

Les Collins (S4, episodes 1–3, 5, 8, 10, 13; 'Battle of the Giants!')

FILM EDITOR

Bob Rymer (S3, episodes 1–3, 5–8, 10, 13, 14; S4, episodes 8, 10, 13; 'Battle of the Giants!')

Bill Harris (S4, episodes 1, 2, 3 & 5)

NO SMOKING
A.R.P.

THE SCRIPTS

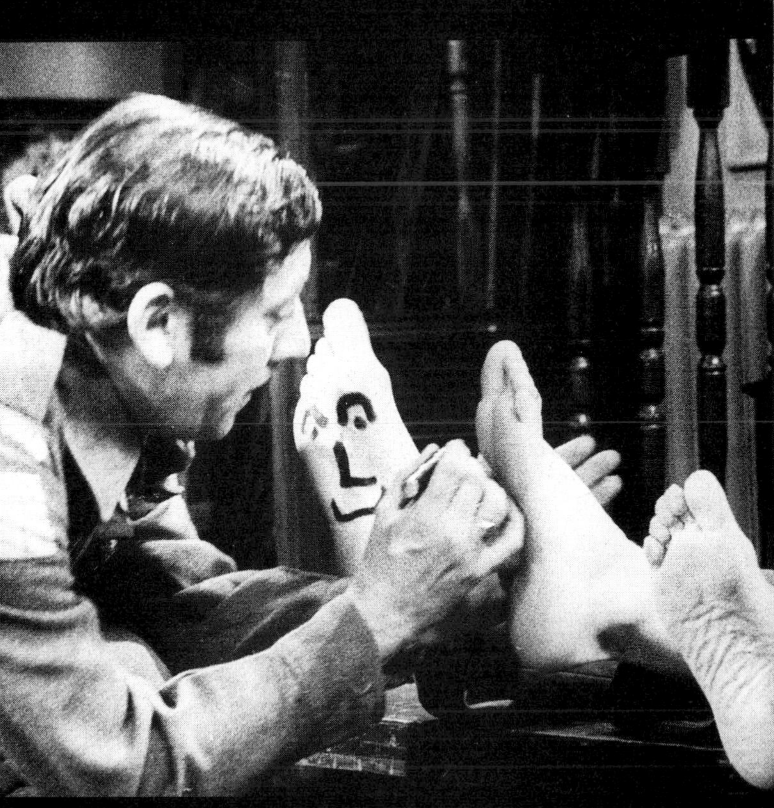

SERIES ONE **EPISODE ONE**

Recorded: Monday 15/4/68 (made in black and white)

Original transmission: Wednesday 31/7/68, 8.20–8.50pm

(This episode was originally planned for transmission on Monday 5/6/68.)

Original viewing figures = 7.2 million

ARTHUR LOWE .... CAPTAIN MAINWARING
JOHN LE MESURIER .... SERGEANT WILSON
CLIVE DUNN .... LANCE CORPORAL JONES
JOHN LAURIE .... PRIVATE FRAZER
JAMES BECK .... PRIVATE WALKER
ARNOLD RIDLEY .... PRIVATE GODFREY
IAN LAVENDER .... PRIVATE PIKE
JANET DAVIES .... MRS PIKE
CAROLINE DOWDESWELL .... JANET KING
JOHN RINGHAM .... BRACEWELL
BILL PERTWEE .... ARP WARDEN
NEVILLE HUGHES .... THE SOLDIER
GORDON PETERS .... CHIEF FIRE OFFICER
(SCENE WAS CUT PRIOR TO RECORDING)
PLATOON .... COLIN BEAN, RICHARD JACQUES, HUGH HASTINGS, ... CHRIS FRANKS, DAVID SEAFORTH, ALEC COLEMAN, ... HUGH CECIL, VIC TAYLOR, JIMMY MAC, PETER WHITAKER
OTHER EXTRAS .... JACK YEOMANS, BILL STRAITON, BRIAN NOLAN
(PLAYED FIREMEN DURING REHEARSALS, BUT SCENE WAS CUT PRIOR TO RECORDING)
DESPATCH RIDER .... JACK WRIGHT

THE MAN AND THE HOUR

• JIMMY PERRY REMEMBERS •

'As you can imagine, I was very nervous when it came to rehearsing and recording the opening episode. This was the first piece of work I'd written for television, so I was probably over-anxious about everything; it seemed to me, at times, as if no one was taking it seriously, they always wanted to finish early and go home! Arthur Lowe would often get stroppy, and others would mutter in corners.

'We'd start rehearsing at ten-thirty with the rehearsal room floor marked out with masking tape to represent the set. Proceedings appeared carefree and a bit sloppy, but we didn't need to make many changes and everything always came up trumps for the camera. I wasn't very happy with the first series, I wanted the performances sharper. In my view, there was too much "underwater" acting but, again, it all worked out okay.

'What an extraordinary bunch of people the *Dad's Army* team was. They became the characters they portrayed, and the characters became them.

'I remember in 1973, the team was invited to switch on the Blackpool illuminations. After a lot of cajoling and subtle threats they all agreed to do it. British Rail gave us a first class coach to ourselves and we were seen off from Euston by the stationmaster, complete in top hat. We were halfway through an excellent lunch when the train pulled into Crewe Station. Within minutes, dozens of faces were pressed against the windows of our carriage. They eagerly pointed at us, with cries of "Yes, it's them! There he is!" Arthur Lowe looked up, slowly put down his knife and fork, tapped on the window, and said: "Go away. Can't you see we're having our lunch?" The situation could have turned ugly, but fortunately the train started moving, pulling out of the station to the accompaniment of cries of "What a miserable old sod!" Arthur took a sip of wine, savoured it, and uttered the immortal words, "Take no notice."

'They were a bunch of tough old pros, but sadly most of them never lived long enough to see themselves become a legend.'

JIMMY PERRY

• DAVID CROFT REMEMBERS •

'The read-throughs during that first series – particularly for this, the opening episode – were tentative. I agree with Jimmy, the actors were inclined to do what we call "underwater" acting, where nobody puts much effort into it, perhaps because it's not the real thing. It was particularly worrying in the case of Arthur Lowe because he was mumbling a lot, not really playing the part at all. The cast made terrible mistakes during that first get-together, which was very concerning; but we needn't have worried because everything turned out fine for the actual recording.

'Using Eden's memorable speech worked well: I remember hearing it live on the radio, so it was interesting listening to it again. For many of us, rehearsing "The Man and the Hour" brought back lots of memories of the war years. When I heard the speech for real I was living in a tiny cottage in Bournemouth and it prompted me to try joining the local Home Guard. When they found out how old I was they decided not to accept me, believing I'd be called up to the regular army within six months, so I became a warden instead.'

DAVID CROFT

The award-winning writing partnership of Jimmy Perry and David Croft began with *Dad's Army*.

Prologue – Dad's Army

Section of long, hotel dinner table. Dinner-jacketed guests have concluded the meal. There is a large Union Jack on the wall and a slogan which reads 'I'm backing Britain'. As we track along the guests, the chairman (Wilson) is speaking. We see Walker – very smart and prosperous, Pike – clearly doing very well for himself now, Godfrey and Frazer – both very old indeed. Mainwaring – the guest of honour – is seated on the right of the chairman.

WILSON And so now, ladies and gentlemen – it gives me great pleasure to introduce our guest of honour – one of Walmington's most honoured citizens, and a man of many parts – Banker, Soldier, Magistrate, Alderman, Chairman of the Rotary Club and all round good fellow. Ladies and gentlemen – Alderman George Mainwaring.

Applause from guests as Mainwaring rises.

MAINWARING Mr Chairman, Mr Town Clerk, ladies and gentlemen. When I was first asked to be guest of honour tonight for the launching of Walmington's 'I'm Backing Britain' campaign, I accepted without hesitation. After all – I've always backed Britain.

Applause.

MAINWARING I got into the habit in 1940. Then, we all backed Britain. It was the darkest hour in our history – the odds were absurdly against us, but, young and old, we stood there – defiant – determined to survive, to recover and finally – to win. The news was desperate but our spirit was always high.

The Man and the Hour

NEWSREEL SHOTS

German troops advancing over the Low Countries, May 1940

Recorded voice of E.V.H. Emmett, commentator.

COMMENTATOR **(In E.V.H. Emmett style)** The massive Nazi war machine is pushing its way across Europe laying waste neutral countries with a savagery unmatched in history. Refugees clog the roads making our allies' task impossible. When Hitler comes up against British troops it's a different story – they fight him every inch of the way, giving as good as they get. It's a tough struggle – but is Tommy Atkins downhearted? We'll say he's not – why should he be with a leader like this:

Shots of Churchill inspecting troops

COMMENTATOR To make Tommy's task more difficult, a new menace has been added to an already brutal struggle. Hoards of parachutists descend from the skies trained to sabotage lines of communication and who knows, even our own shores may not long be spared this, the latest of Hitler's tricks. We all have our part to play. Every effort is being made to confuse the enemy.

SPECIALLY SHOT FILM – SIGNPOST SEQUENCE

Film: country lane – forked road. A signpost is seen. One arm reads 'To the sea'. The other 'To the town'. Jones pulls it up and changes it round. Another man appears on a motorbike, stops and looks at the sign, he turns down lane marked 'To the town'. There is a loud splash.

COMMENTATOR So look out, Adolf, every day our defences are strengthened, and if they do come let's give 'em a sharp welcome.

SPECIALLY SHOT FILM – STAKES SEQUENCE

Several nasty looking stakes are sticking upright in a field. Frazer, and three others are working on them. Frazer is finishing the last one. Close up as he touches the point with his finger, looks up and pulls a face.

Medium close up of bank sign – Swallow Bank Ltd

BANK MANAGER'S OFFICE

Mid shot of desk top showing desk calendar set at Tuesday 14th May. A hand comes into shot and takes a round ruler from the desk. We pan with it and see Mainwaring, the bank manager, who is putting down a pile of sandbags in front of the window. He uses the ruler to bash the top one down. Pike, the office boy, staggers in with another sandbag.

MAINWARING They've gone home. You can come out of the broom cupboard now, Miss King.

MAINWARING Well done, Pike. Well done.

He takes the bag from Pike and places it on top of the pile.

MAINWARING By Jove! These things are heavy.

PIKE **(Returning to door)** It's the sand being wet. If you'd waited for the tide to go out it would have been twice as easy.

MAINWARING Never mind, Pike, it will stop those Jerry bullets, that's the point – and don't be so long with the next one.

PIKE It's not my fault, sir, I've spent ten minutes picking the shrimps out of that lot!

Wilson, the chief clerk, enters with one more bag. Pike goes for another.

MAINWARING Thank you, Mr Wilson – just there, please.

Between them they place the bag in position. Mainwaring eyes the line of fire. Wilson squints over his shoulder.

WILSON It provides a reasonable field of fire, sir – covers the entire High Street.

MAINWARING Yes, I think we can safely say that Hitler's parachutists will be dead as mutton anywhere from Stead and Simpson to Timothy White's. We'll be covered down to the Pier Pavilion when that blasted woman gets out of the telephone box.

WILSON That's Mrs Hoskins calling her sister in Thetford. She'll only be three minutes.

MAINWARING Let's hope that Hitler will stay his hand until Mrs Hoskins gets the pips!

WILSON Let's hope he waits until you get a machine gun.

Pike enters, with one more bag.

PIKE That's the last one, sir.

MAINWARING What do you mean, the last one – it's not nearly high enough.

PIKE Sorry, sir, there's no more sand.

MAINWARING Nonsense, the beach is full of it.

PIKE The tide's in. The water's up to here by now – it came right over my Mum's wellingtons when I was getting the last lot. She won't half go on about it.

MAINWARING Pike, the dampness of your mum's wellingtons is of small consequence when all Europe is writhing under the Nazi heel.

PIKE My mum won't see it that way.

WILSON We can get some more at low tide.

MAINWARING Time is not on our side, Wilson. We must improvise. Tell me, how much copper have we got?

WILSON Copper, sir?

MAINWARING Yes, copper – pennies!

WILSON Say ten five-pound bags.

MAINWARING Pike, get 'em and stack them along here. (He indicates the top of the sandbags)

Pike goes.

WILSON I don't think you ought to do that, sir.

MAINWARING Why not?

WILSON We'll cause a penny shortage in the town.

MAINWARING Well?

WILSON It will be a considerable inconvenience.

MAINWARING Well, they'll just have to grin and bear it. Don't they know there's a war on?

WILSON I don't think Head Office is going to like it, sir.

MAINWARING This is no time for red tape, Wilson. At any moment hordes of Jerry parachutists may drop from the clouds – and they'll be using all sorts of disguises you know. A whole platoon of them could dress up as nuns and make their headquarters in that church over there and you wouldn't even notice.

WILSON I think I would, sir. It's the Presbyterian chapel.

Enter Pike with two bags of copper.

PIKE Two bags, sir.

MAINWARING Well done, Pike.

PIKE (As he puts the bags on the window) Cashier says will you sign for each one – like you was putting it in the vault, or shall we open an account in your name and give you an overdraft.

MAINWARING I'll talk to him later. (Door knock)

MAINWARING See who that is, Wilson, and tell them I'm not to be disturbed. Now take this paper, Pike. Lick it and stick it in crosses on the windows.

Pike starts to tear off lengths of paper, lick them and put them on the windows.

Wilson opens the door as Mainwaring starts to help Pike.

WILSON It's an Army dispatch rider from G.H.Q. Eastern Command, sir, and he's got a packet.

MAINWARING Poor devil, what was it – a sniper?

Wilson holds up a brown paper package.

WILSON It's for you, sir.

MAINWARING It's come – the moment I've been waiting for.

He tears open the packet and starts muttering to himself as he reads.

MAINWARING I've done it, I've pipped them at the post! A few weeks ago I sent a letter to G.H.Q. asking for instructions in case of an invasion. I pointed out that I held a commission, that I fought in the last conflict.

WILSON In the Orkneys, wasn't it, sir?

MAINWARING (Coldly) I was a commissioned officer and I served in France during the whole of 1919.

WILSON I thought the war ended in 1918.

MAINWARING Someone had to clear up the mess. And where were you during the war?

WILSON Mons, Passchendale, Gallipoli – Sergeant, R.A.

MAINWARING Well, there's no need to go into all that now.

MAINWARING (Reading) Dear Sir, In view of the grave danger of enemy parachutists landing in the Home Counties it has been decided to form a force of local volunteers to guard certain strategic points. This force will be known as the Local Defence Volunteers.

There is a knock at the door – Miss King enters in a state of some excitement.

MAINWARING What is it, Miss King?

MISS KING It's Anthony Eden, sir.

MAINWARING What, in person?

MISS KING On the wireless, sir. They say it's very important.

Mainwaring crosses swiftly to wireless set of period and turns it on. We hear the end of Anthony Eden's 'Local Defence Volunteers' announcement made lunchtime, 14 May 1940.

MAINWARING **(As he switches it off)** Back to work Miss King. There now, the main thing we've got to do is to form an invasion committee. Pike.

PIKE Yes, sir.

Pike is looking very green.

MAINWARING What's the matter with you, boy?

PIKE I feel sick, sir. It's licking all this paper.

MAINWARING Now, listen to me. Now we three are the invasion committee.

Wilson and Pike exchange looks. Mainwaring looks at the paper.

MAINWARING Now according to this, the next thing we've got to do is to appoint a properly appointed Commander.

WILSON A what, sir?

MAINWARING Appoint a properly appointed Commander. Now that's me – all right?

There is no answer.

MAINWARING You, Wilson will be my second in command.

WILSON Thank you, sir.

MAINWARING **(Looking at paper)** What next – ah yes – means of conveying instructions and information to the public, an information officer will be appointed. Pike – that's you.

PIKE Well, sir…

MAINWARING Now – **(He reads)** the information officer will be supplied with a megaphone. Now let me see – Wilson – hold this.

Mainwaring crosses to the fireplace, picks up the coal hod and empties it. Wilson hands him the tin opener. Mainwaring starts to open the bottom of the hod with the tin opener.

MAINWARING You will learn, Wilson, that in times like these improvisation is the keynote to success **(Mainwaring kicks hod, hands it to Pike)** That is your megaphone, lad. Now your first job will be to get on your bike and ride round the town with this message –

MAINWARING I'll show you. **(His voice booms out)** All Local Defence Volunteers report to the church hall at six o'clock tonight.

He lowers the megaphone and he has a big black ring around his face.

MAINWARING How was that?

WILSON Excellent, sir, I don't know how you do it.

MAINWARING History repeats itself, Wilson. Times of peril always bring great men to the fore – Wellington, Churchill –

PIKE Al Jolson.

CHURCH HALL

Fade up on a typical church hall. A large crowd of various men are all talking at once. The radio is playing the current Vera Lynn 'hit'. We do not see Jones or Walker. The men are gathered round a door that leads to a small ante room. The door is open, Wilson is addressing the crowd.

FRAZER **(The Scotsman, bearded, 50ish)** The meeting was called for six o'clock, it's now twenty past, where is he?

Mainwaring enters, and closes the door.

The crowd close round the door in a tight bunch. Mainwaring, followed by Pike – carrying papers both appear, through the door to the main hall. They try to push through the crowd.

BRACEWELL **(Very well dressed)** Here, who do you think you're pushing? Get back, we're waiting for the Appointed Commander.

MAINWARING I am the Appointed Commander.

BRACEWELL Oh, sorry!

They all break as Mainwaring and Pike open the door and go in. Cut to interior of small room.

SIDE ROOM

WILSON There you are, sir. Did you get the enrolment forms?

MAINWARING No.

WILSON Didn't they have them at the police station?

MAINWARING Yes, but they wouldn't let me have any without putting in an application form.

WILSON Well, why didn't you?

MAINWARING They hadn't got any! Anyhow we can use these. **(He takes papers from Pike and throws them on to the desk. Wilson picks them up)**

WILSON But these are paying-in slips, sir!

MAINWARING Don't keep putting obstacles in the way. Bring in the first man.

Wilson goes to the door and opens it.

WILSON Would you mind stepping this way, please?

MAINWARING Sergeant Wilson, come here. I intend to mould those men out there into an aggressive fighting unit. I'm going to lead them, command them, and inspire them to become ruthless killers, but I'm not going to get very far if you keep inviting them to 'step this way' – Quick march – is the order, Wilson.

WILSON I'm sorry, sir. (**To the man who is already standing at the table**) – Quick march.

FRAZER There's not much point – I'm here already.

MAINWARING Name please?

FRAZER James Frazer.

MAINWARING Occupation?

FRAZER I keep a philatelist's shop.

MAINWARING How d'you spell that?

FRAZER S.... H.... O.... P....

MAINWARING Thank you very much. From the look of you I imagine you have no previous army experience.

FRAZER No, none at all.

MAINWARING I thought not. We can usually tell, can't we, Sergeant? Once a soldier, always a soldier.

FRAZER I was a sailor – Chief P.O. Royal Navy, retired.

MAINWARING (**Hurriedly**) Sign here, please.

FRAZER (**Signs and then turns to Mainwaring fiercely**) Are you swearing?

MAINWARING I never said a word.

FRAZER You Army lot – don't you swear an oath of allegiance?

MAINWARING Yes, well – umph – we'll do that later. Wait outside.

Frazer goes out, muttering.

MAINWARING You'll have to watch him, Wilson – Bolshie lot, the Jack Tars. Bring in the next one.

Godfrey, a portly gentleman of about sixty, enters.

WILSON Quick march – halt.

GODFREY How do you do?

MAINWARING Name please?

GODFREY Godfrey – Charles Godfrey.

MAINWARING Occupation?

GODFREY Well, as a matter of fact, I'm retired. I was 25 years in the Civil Service.

MAINWARING Oh, were you – Indian or British?

GODFREY Civil Service Stores – men's wear.

MAINWARING Any pervious military experience?

GODFREY Well, I was in the Sports and Games Department. That, of course, covered archery and air guns.

MAINWARING Yes, well I'm sure that this knowledge in specialist fields will be very useful to us. Would you sign there, please?

GODFREY Yes, I'd love to. (**He signs**) Is that all?

MAINWARING For the moment, yes.

GODFREY Oh, I thought I'd get a receipt or something.

MAINWARING This is a fighting unit – not a drycleaners. Wait outside please.

WILSON Yes, you do that.

MAINWARING Wilson!

WILSON About turn, quick march.

As Godfrey walks out, Joe Walker slides into the room. He is wearing a smart chalk-striped suit with very padded shoulders, 22- inch bottoms and a hat. He has a small, toothbrush moustache.

WALKER Evening, gents.

MAINWARING Name please?

WALKER My card.

MAINWARING (**Copies from the card**) – Joe Walker, Wholesale Supplier. (**He looks up and sees the youngish face of Joe Walker**) I don't suppose you'll be with us long, think you're due for a call-up any time.

WALKER Oh no, guv'nor, I'm, you know, what's-'is-name. Reserved occupation.

MAINWARING How's that?

WALKER I'm a wholesale supplier, aren't I? I mean, I supply essential supplies.

MAINWARING Any military experience?

WALKER Well, my girlfriend's in the A.T.S.

MAINWARING Sign here, please.

WALKER (**As he is signing**) Oh, by the way, any time you gents require anything, just er... tip me the wink, you know.

MAINWARING Thank you. We'll bear it in mind.

WILSON About turn. Quick march.

WALKER Pardon.

WILSON Quick march.

WALKER You might wait till the ink dries.

As Joe goes, Jack Jones comes in. He is wearing his striped butcher's apron and his straw hat and is doing his own commands.

JONES Left, right, left, right – halt! Evening Mr Mainwaring. Evening, Mr Wilson. You know me, don't you?

MAINWARING Mr Jones, the butcher in the High Street, isn't it?

JONES That's right.

WILSON **(To Mainwaring)** Don't you think perhaps Mr Jones is a little old, sir?

JONES Old! Here, who are you calling old? Just let me get near some of them Jerry parachutists, I'll sort 'em out.

He gestures with a sharpener, hanging from his wrist.

MAINWARING There, you see, it's keenness that counts Wilson, not age.

JONES That's the ticket, sir. I'm as keen as mustard.

WILSON Any previous military experience?

JONES Ah, now you're talking. Signed on as a drummer boy, I did, in 1884, saw service later in the Sudan, them Fuzzie Wuzzies, they was the boys, they come at you with them long knives, zip you right open. **(He makes a ripping noise)** It soon shows if you've got any guts or not.

Close up of Wilson looking sick.

JONES Yeah, them Fuzzie Wuzzies – the only people who ever broke the British square not like them Jerries. Yeah, they couldn't punch puddin', they couldn't. They don't like the old cold steel, you see, they don't like it up 'em.

Jones has now worked himself up into a frenzy and is feeling faint.

MAINWARING I think you'd better sit down. Get him a chair, Wilson.

JONES Thank you, sir. **(Sitting down)** Not as young as I was you know. **(He realises his mistake and jumps up again)** Mind you, I can still give them the old cold...

MAINWARING Yes, yes quite so. I think you've proved your point. Sign there. When did you leave the Army?

Jones signs on table top.

JONES Nineteen fifteen, sir. Invalided out. The old minces, you know. Couldn't get the focus. **(He points to eyes)**

MAINWARING That, presumably, is why you signed the table.

JONES Not that they would have stopped me, you know, with the old bayonet – right up there with the old cold steel.

MAINWARING Yes, well, thank you very much, Mr Jones. That will be all.

JONES **(Putting a parcel on the table)** Oh, by the way, I've brought along a couple of pounds of steak – compliments of the house.

Mainwaring and Wilson look interested.

JONES Just one more thing, what about my stripe?

WILSON Your stripe?

JONES Yes, I mean I was a Lance Corporal for 14 years. I can keep it, can't I?

MAINWARING No, Jones, I'm afraid not.

JACK Well, in that case, I'll take the steak.

He picks it up.

MAINWARING No, wait a minute, we will be looking for N.C.O.s, you know, Wilson, and it could well be that Jones' past military experience could stand us in very good steak stead.

WILSON I think so too, sir.

MAINWARING That will be all then, Lance Corporal Jones.

JONES T.T.F.N. Right turn. Quick march. Left, right. Left, right.

Jones goes to the door, goes out only to return very quickly.

JONES Can I do you now, sir?
(As he gestures with his steel)

WILSON That's very good. We'll divide them up later.

Jones goes out. There is a disturbance outside. An A.R.P. Warden pushes his way into the room.

WARDEN Who's in charge here?

MAINWARING I am, why?

WARDEN Well, I must ask you to clear these premises at once.

MAINWARING Have you gone out of your mind? Do you realise that history is taking place in this hall.

WARDEN In five minutes time an A.R.P. Lecture is taking place in this hall.

MAINWARING I'm enrolling men for the L.D.V. and if you're not very careful I shall requisition this hall for military purposes.

WARDEN Well, you're too late, it's been requisitioned by the Civil Defence, for my purposes, so if you'd kindly clear this lot out of 'ere, I can proceed with my lecture.

MAINWARING Are you asking the Army to retreat?

WARDEN Why not? You've had plenty of practice lately.

WILSON That's going a bit far, isn't it.

MAINWARING Now, look here...

WARDEN Now, look, no offence, mate, but I've got my job to do, you've got yours, if you want to carry on in this office here you won't be in my way. But get this lot out of here, now.

The Warden goes out.

WILSON What are we going to do, sir? We've only enrolled four.

MAINWARING We shall just have to dispense with formalities, that's all. Pike – get 'em all in.

WILSON Right, in here – all of you – at the double!

They all swarm into the room. Mainwaring and Wilson are backed into a corner. The men pour into the small room until it is jammed tight. Mainwaring is right in the corner. The Scotsman's face is shoved right close into Mainwaring's and, try as he may, Mainwaring cannot get any room to address the crowd.

MAINWARING **(Starting his 'Agincourt' speech)** Men, today you have answered your country's call, and we are here to defend our homes and loved ones from a brutal enemy. I know you will not shrink from that duty.

Frazer is glaring at him on one side and he is face to face with Jones on the other side, who is hanging on every word.

MAINWARING We have no guns, we are naked, but we have one invaluable weapon in our armoury – ingenuity and improvisation.

FRAZER That's two.

MAINWARING Go to your homes, arm yourselves with whatever you can and be back here in an hour. From tonight, whatever the odds, we Englishmen **(He sees the Scotsman)** I mean – we Britishmen – I mean, we here can say 'Come on, Jerry – we're ready for you!' And don't forget your gasmasks. That's all.

BRACEWELL That was very nice.

CHURCH HALL

The men are lined up in two ranks, front rank consists of Lance Corporal Jones on the end in Boer War tropical kit with an assegai, Frazer, in Naval Commander's uniform with cutlass. Walker is in a suit carrying a pike. Bracewell is in a dinner jacket with golf club. Pike is in ordinary clothes with a broom and a knife tied to the end of it. Godfrey carries a shot gun; the rear rank have an assortment of pikes, pick helves, shillelaghs, one rolling pin, etc.

WILSON Squad – attention. Stand at ease. Squad, attention. **(Wilson salutes Mainwaring)** Men are all ready for inspection, sir.

Mainwaring walks down the line inspecting each one. He stops in front of Pike.

MAINWARING **(Pointing to the broom)** What's this supposed to be, lad?

PIKE Well, you said if we hadn't got anything else, we were to fix a carving knife on a broom handle.

MAINWARING Yes, but I didn't mean to keep the brush on the end of it, you stupid boy!

PIKE Well, you should've said.

MAINWARING And I don't want any insubordination either – take his name, Sergeant!

WILSON What's your name, lad?

PIKE You should know it by now – you've been a friend of my mum's ever since – before I was born.

WILSON Yes, well er... see it doesn't happen again.

MAINWARING **(To Godfrey)** Where did you get that gun?

GODFREY Eh?

MAINWARING The gun! Where did you get it?

GODFREY It belongs to my friend actually.

MAINWARING I see. **(He draws Wilson on one side)** He's got a friend – a gun.

WILSON Yes, I can see that, sir.

MAINWARING Well, I mean – I'm the officer, you're the sergeant. We should have it really for the machine gun post.

WILSON Yes, sir.

MAINWARING Well, you ask him for it.

WILSON Wouldn't it carry more authority coming from you, sir?

MAINWARING No.

Wilson reluctantly goes to Godfrey.

WILSON Mr Mainwaring wants your rifle.

GODFREY Who wants it?

WILSON Captain Mainwaring.

GODFREY Well, he can't have it.

MAINWARING Are you refusing to obey an order on active service? Do you realise that we could have you shot?

WALKER That would be a bit difficult – seeing as he's the only one with a gun.

MAINWARING **(To Walker)** Quiet.

Lance Corporal Jones takes one pace forward.

JONES Permission to speak, sir?

MAINWARING Permission granted, Jones.

JONES Why don't we take it in turns to have the gun.

MAINWARING Excellent idea. Draw up a rota, Jones, and put my name at the top. **(Stops at Frazer)** That's a formidable weapon.

FRAZER Yes, pull 'em in with that. Hit 'em with that.

He stops in front of Bracewell in the dinner jacket.

MAINWARING You needn't have bothered to dress you know.

BRACEWELL As a matter of fact, it's my wife's birthday, we are going on to a little dinner party tonight. Do you think you'll be much longer?

MAINWARING That's up to Jerry isn't it, but I wouldn't want to interfere with your social arrangements.

BRACEWELL That's all right – I'd ask you along too, but we haven't really been introduced have we?

MAINWARING **(Sarcastically)** No, we haven't, have we.

WILSON Well, we'll soon settle that. May I introduce Captain Mainwaring – I didn't quite catch your name.

MAINWARING That will do, Wilson. **(He draws him on one side)** What do you think you're doing?

WILSON Why, I thought he might ask me too.

While Wilson and Mainwaring are engaged in conversation, just out of the picture Walker nudges Bracewell.

WALKER Wife's birthday today, is it?

BRACEWELL Yes.

WALKER I suppose you got her a nice present.

BRACEWELL Well no, with all this confusion, I haven't had time.

WALKER **(Handing his pike to Frazer)** Here 'old that will you. **(He is wearing a double-breasted suit, he unbuttons it and swings back a flap inside – there we see hanging various watches)** Anything you fancy 'ere? **(He unhooks a watch)** 'Ere's a nice little thing – 15-jewelled, solid 18-carat, Swiss made, waterproof, shock proof, you can't get 'em anywhere these days. Ten quid and it's yours.

BRACEWELL Oh jolly good, thank you. **(He gives him the money and takes the watch)**

WALKER **(Taking his pike back from Frazer)** Ta, I don't suppose I could interest you in anything could I? **(Frazer glares at him)** No, I thought not.

Mainwaring comes back into the picture.

MAINWARING Stand at ease. Splendid turnout, men – splendid. If, in one hour, we can achieve this formidable fighting potential, think what we shall be able to do with a week's training. I have some good news for you. Our first consignment of firearms and uniforms should be here at any moment. We have no time to lose, the enemy may descend on us this very night, and we must learn how to deal with them. Now sit down on the floor and pay attention.

They move.

WILSON At the double.

MAINWARING How can they sit down at the double?

CHURCH HALL

The platoon are seated, at one end is a blackboard, on which is a large drawing of a German tank. Mainwaring is standing in front with a pointer.

MAINWARING Now, Sergeant Wilson here has very kindly drawn us this representation of a German tank. **(He looks at the drawing)** You will observe the following points – heavy armour in the front, usually four-inch plating, a 40, 50 or 60 millimetre repeating cannon, heavy machine guns here and here, light machine guns here – here, and here, a high pressure flame thrower at the front and, I'm told on very good authority, two grenade throwers. A very formidable opponent indeed. But we are going to tackle it.

Cut to the vacant faces of the platoon.

MAINWARING The question is, how?

JONES How about sugar, sir?

MAINWARING Sugar? What do you do with it?

JONES Stick it in the petrol tank,sir, and the engine fizzles out.

MAINWARING I think that's a good idea, don't you, Wilson?

WILSON Very good idea, sir. I'll make an application for an extra sugar ration.

MAINWARING We can always try it once, and if it doesn't work we'll use the rest in our tea.

JONES What about potatoes, sir?

MAINWARING Potatoes?

JONES You bung 'em on the exhaust – the gases can't escape and the engine stops.

MAINWARING Yes, I see. Well, unfortunately, Corporal Jones, these Nazi tanks have been designed with long, thin exhaust outlets.

JONES Well, we could get long, thin potatoes. Charlotte's Beauty. They're long and thin.

MAINWARING Yes, I suppose so.

WILSON Shall I order some potatoes, sir?

MAINWARING Yes, do that, Wilson.

PIKE If it doesn't work, we'll have some chips.

MAINWARING Your suggestions have stimulated a most interesting discussion, however, today we'll concentrate on my method. **(Pointing to a table on which are the various articles)** Now these, are our weapons – one blanket, one tin of petrol, one crow-bar, paraffin bombs and one box of matches. The procedure is as follows: we place ourselves under cover, carefully concealed from the enemy.

FRAZER Hear, hear!

MAINWARING We hear the tank coming – as it draws level, the first man pours petrol over the blanket, breaks cover and rushes up to the tank. Now for this job we want a young lad of the commando breed – that's you, Pike. The next man will then run out and set fire to the blanket.

JONES I'll do that, sir.

MAINWARING Very good, Corporal.

WILSON Do you think that's wise, sir?

MAINWARING Now are we all clear so far?

The platoon nod.

MAINWARING Good. You, Frazer, will prize open the lid of the tank with the crow-bar. Walker will have a petrol bomb in each hand. Lance Corporal Jones will light them, drop them into the aperture. Now are there any questions?

WALKER What will you be doing, sir?

MAINWARING I shall be observing from behind cover and deciding whether to send in the second wave. Now, before we start, the whole success of this operation depends on the decoy. Someone must take the attention of all those tank gunners to himself and away from us. You, Bracewell, will be the decoy. Right – now let's try it through by numbers. Back again to the wall. Pike, get down in that corner with the blanket and petrol. Frazer, Walker, stand by with the crow-bar and petrol bombs. Lance Corporal Jones, get ready with the matches, decoy – stand over there. (**He points to the privates**) Now, you four men are the tank, go to the end of the room and stand by. Sergeant Wilson will blow a whistle when you are to start.

They all get into position.

PIKE Hey, Sarge – d'you want me to put the petrol on the blanket now?

WILSON Of course not, this is a dummy run.

MAINWARING Right, stand by everybody. Off you go, Wilson – start them off.

Wilson blows his whistle. The four men who represent the tank link arms, two in front and two behind and start to shuffle down the room.

MAINWARING Right, decoy – attract the tank's attention now!

BRACEWELL (**Feebly**) I – oh I say. (**He waves a feeble arm**)

MAINWARING That's no good. You've got to make them angry and draw their fire. Do it again.

BRACEWELL I say you Fascist beasts…

MAINWARING Where's the blanket, Pike?

PIKE Sorry, sir. I didn't hear them coming.

MAINWARING (**To tank**) Start again, and this time make a noise like a tank.

The tank goes back to the end of the room.

WILSON All right, stand by. (**He blows the whistle**)

The tank starts again – Bracewell waves his arms.

BRACEWELL I say, you – er – you Fascist beasts…

Pike runs out with the blanket.

MAINWARING Well done, Pike, now light the blanket, Jones.

Jones lights the match and starts to run. As he runs the match goes out. He tries it a couple more times.

MAINWARING Oh, start again, you take over the matches, Pike.

JONES I'll have the blanket.

Wilson blows the whistle. Bracewell attracts attention. Jones is a bit slow with the blanket.

BRACEWELL (**Sings**) 'We're going to hang out the washing…'

MAINWARING Where's the flaming blanket?

JONES In me flamin' hands.

MAINWARING Well, get it up, man, get it up.

Jones rushes to the tank with blanket outstretched and falls over it when he reaches them. Tank collapses in heap.

MAINWARING That's it, put some beef into it. Frazer, get in there with the crow-bar – in with the petrol bombs, Walker.

Mrs Pike enters – she is a short widow, about 40, she comes into the middle of the room and looks at the heap.

MRS PIKE Frank, it's your bedtime!

She pulls Pike out of the heap.

PIKE I can't come now, Mum – we're blowing up a tank!

MRS PIKE Yes dear, well, you'll just have to blow it up tomorrow. (**To Wilson**) I'm surprised at you, Arthur, after all, you know what time he goes to bed.

Wilson looks embarrassed.

MRS PIKE Come on, Frank. (**She pushes him to the door, she is just going out as she turns to Wilson**) Will you be round later, Arthur, for your usual?

WILSON (**Purple with embarrassment**) Oh Mavis – please. Platoon fall in.

There is the sound of a lorry outside.

GODFREY It's the lorry, sir, from G.H.Q.

MAINWARING This is it, men, the moment I've been waiting for. Our first issue of uniforms and weapons.

A soldier enters and salutes.

SOLDIER Captain Mainwaring, sir?

MAINWARING Yes, that's right. I know what you've come for.

SOLDIER Just sign here, will you, sir?

Mainwaring signs.

MAINWARING Take the men outside, Sergeant, help to unload the weapons.

SOLDIER I don't think that will be necessary, sir. Here's the uniforms and there's the weapons.

Soldier hands Mainwaring a package, and L.D.V. arm bands.

MAINWARING **(Puzzled)** Open it, Sergeant Wilson.

Wilson quickly tears open the packet, inside are a dozen small packets.

WILSON It's pepper, sir!

MAINWARING Pepper?

WILSON **(Reading leaflet)** Pepper – enemy – for throwing in face of. Range – five feet.

MAINWARING Well, it's not quite what we expected, on the other hand, every addition to our armoury is one more nail in the enemy's coffin. Corporal, issue the armbands. They give us military status. Sergeant, issue the pepper.

Wilson starts to hand out the packets.

MAINWARING And men – take it with you wherever you go. If you see a parachutist – let him have it.

JONES That and the cold steel!

MAINWARING That's the spirit, Jones. We're making progress. A short time ago we were a disorganised rabble, now we can deal with tanks. We can kill with our pikes and make 'em all sneeze with our pepper. And after all, even the Hun makes a pretty poor fighter with his head buried in a handkerchief – but remember this, we have one other invaluable weapon on our side. We have an unbreakable fighting spirit, a bulldog tenacity that makes us hang on as long as there's breath left in our bodies. You don't get that with Gestapos and Jackboots, you get *that* by being British! So, come on, Adolf – we're ready for you.

The platoon cheer.

MUSEUM PIECE

SERIES ONE **EPISODE TWO**

Recorded: Monday 22/4/68 (made in black and white)

Original transmission: Wednesday 7/8/68, 7.00–7.30pm

(This episode was originally planned for transmission on Wednesday 12/6/68.)

Original viewing figures = 6.8 million

ARTHUR LOWE .... CAPTAIN MAINWARING
JOHN LE MESURIER .... SERGEANT WILSON
CLIVE DUNN .... LANCE CORPORAL JONES
JOHN LAURIE .... PRIVATE FRAZER
JAMES BECK .... PRIVATE WALKER
ARNOLD RIDLEY .... PRIVATE GODFREY
IAN LAVENDER .... PRIVATE PIKE
JANET DAVIES .... MRS PIKE
CAROLINE DOWDESWELL .... JANET KING
LEON CORTEZ .... HENRY, THE MILKMAN
ERIC WOODBURN .... GEORGE JONES, THE MUSEUM CARETAKER
MICHAEL OSBORNE .... BOY SCOUT

PLATOON .... COLIN BEAN, HUGH HASTINGS, RICHARD JACQUES, ... CHRIS FRANKS, DAVID SEAFORTH, ALEC COLEMAN, ... HUGH CECIL, VIC TAYLOR, JIMMY MAC, PETER WHITAKER

• PAUL JOEL REMEMBERS •

'The first episode of *Dad's Army* that I designed entirely by myself was "Museum Piece", so it has a significant place in my affections and career. Alan Hunter-Craig and I had co-designed the main (stock) sets – church hall, Vicar's office and Mainwaring's office at the bank – prior to the first series, after which we alternated on the design of the episodes, with Alan doing numbers one, three and five, and me two, four, six and the pre-studio filming sequences.

'Before filming for the first series started, a decision was made to use the West Tofts area near Thetford, and the MOD, who owned it, kindly agreed. The extensive acreage of rural land was ideal, providing us with fields, streams, forests and roads, all completely deserted, and no traffic or interested bystanders to worry about, so long as we avoided the military's "war games" weeks! Unfortunately there were very few useful buildings, as most were used for target practice and were, at least, partly demolished, so we searched farther afield for those. The choice of the fifteenth-century manor house, Oxburgh Hall, for the museum exterior sequences on film was an interesting one. The script called for a building of some historical interest, which offered an internal courtyard wide enough to allow the platoon to run a short distance with a battering ram to break down the entrance door. Oxburgh Hall – the "quintessential moated manor house" was old enough and near enough to our base in Thetford to be ideal.

'I was still a design assistant, temporarily promoted to designer status at the time, so was very eager to show the design department the extent of my talent, pouring my heart and soul into "Museum Piece". I designed not only the museum set in the studio to closely match the look and character of Oxburgh Hall, but also the special props for film and studio; the battering ram – which had to fall to bits when it struck the museum door; the boiling oil anti-siege weapon which poured cold water on the platoon; and the ancient Chinese rocket cannon. Later in the series, props such as these involving moving parts and pyrotechnics would be designed and built by visual effects experts, such as Peter Day, but for me at that moment in my career, it was a wonderful challenge. After researching some historical reference material, I decided on an approach of eccentric authenticity. The battering ram would surely be incomplete without a ram's head at the front, just like the Romans used; the anti-siege weapon should, at least, look capable of pouring boiling oil; and the ancient rocket cannon should possess several barrels and definitely be decorated with Chinese dragons.

'I stocked the museum set in the studio with old weapons on the scenery brick walls and columns from specialist prop suppliers, and designed display cases glazed with sugar glass for the platoon to smash without getting cut. The set was as real as I could make it – it had to be to help the comedy in the script. However, studio sets are notorious for being a bit flimsy, especially in situation comedies – you only have to watch *Auntie's Bloomers* to see what I mean! So I was quite pleased that the museum front door, designed to be on location and in the studio set, stood up to a great deal of abuse during filming, rehearsals and video-taping in front of a studio audience. It did not fall to pieces or trap Jones' dad's nose in the small opening panel; but I was embarrassed to see the toilet window wobble when Jones' dad fell into the loo – watch the artificial ivy, it wasn't a sea breeze that disturbed it! All through rehearsals it was sturdy; not until the recording did it wobble, which is Murphy's Law! David and Jimmy, I'm glad to say, overlooked this error and I went on to design most of the *Dad's Army* series. Great fun – I wouldn't have missed them for the world.'

PAUL JOEL
Designer

Museum Piece

LONG SHOT OF PLATOON

They are lined up for inspection carrying assorted weapons, civilian gasmasks and wearing civilian clothes.

NARRATOR May 15th is a very special day for Britain's Citizen Army, the L.D.V.

The platoon come to attention.

NARRATOR Though it's only a few days since they answered their country's call, they are already carrying out extensive manoeuvres like the seasoned troops they are.

Mainwaring and Wilson inspect the line.

NARRATOR After a brief inspection, the men move off to prepare an ambush for enemy armoured cars.

Platoon right turn and the men move off. Lance Corporal Jones remains facing rigidly front. The Sergeant collects him and he runs to catch up with the others.

NARRATOR Shortage of weapons is no handicap. Everything that can be used to harass the enemy is pressed into service.

The men are just finishing tying a garden roller to a tree, on the top of a slope. They hear the enemy coming. The Captain gives a signal. Lance Corporal Jones cuts the rope with his assegai, the roller starts to crash down the hill. Cut to men's faces as they follow it with their heads. There is a terrific crash. Cut to the road. The garden roller has been crushed under a huge steam roller.

NARRATOR The men are veterans of many campaigns, but now they are fighting for their homeland, and they know every street, every bush, and every inch of their own country.

Lance Corporal Jones is standing at the side of the road. An army dispatch rider comes up on a motorbike. He stops and beckons to Lance Corporal Jones. Dispatch rider unfolds the map, points to it and asks Jones the way. Jones scratches his head and shakes it.

NARRATOR For strenuous exercises like these the men must be really fit.

FILM OF RIVER CROSSING

Two men are swinging across on a rope and pulley. The first man is holding the pulley. The second man is holding the first man around the waist. The second man starts to lose his grip and claws at the top of the first man's trousers. They slowly start to come down.

NARRATOR Of one thing we can be sure. If Hitler tries any of his tricks here, Britain's Local Defence Volunteers will not be caught with their pants down.

Mix to sign: Swallow Bank.

MAINWARING'S OFFICE

Janet King is taking down the black-out screen, to reveal the paper-taped windows. The radio is playing a current hit and she is whistling to it. Frank Pike enters carrying papers.

PIKE Here's Mr Mainwaring's *Times.* And here's the one he reads.

He hands her the *Daily Mirror.* She looks at it.

JANET It doesn't look too good, does it?

Close shot of daily paper headline announcing the falling back of allied troops.

PIKE My mum was told last night that General Gort's letting 'em advance a bit so as to extend their lines of communication.

JANET What's the point of that?

PIKE Someone told my mum that when the time's right, he'll get 'em – right in the soft underbelly.

JANET Sounds awful. Here, the Manager's late isn't he?

PIKE We were out on L.D.V. manoeuvres all yesterday. Perhaps it was too much for them.

JANET You're just like a lot of kids playing soldiers.

PIKE Let me tell you...

The door opens, enter Wilson.

WILSON Good morning, Miss King. Morning, Pike. **(He looks at desk)** Did Mr Mainwaring sign the reconciliation?

JANET It's in the Out Tray.

WILSON Mr Mainwaring's mail is on my desk, Pike. Get it please.

PIKE Yes, sir.

He moves to door. Wilson sees the paper.

WILSON Oh dear, oh dear, oh dear.

MAINWARING **(In doorway)** We're not spreading alarm and despondency are we Wilson?

WILSON It doesn't look too good, sir.

MAINWARING **(Looking at headline as he takes off hat and coat)** You're right – it doesn't.

WILSON It's my theory that General Gort is just letting them Bosche extend their lines of communication and then bang. Right in the soft underbelly.

JANET That's funny. Someone told Mrs Pike that.

She goes.

MAINWARING **(To Wilson)** Sounds like another case of careless talk. Take a seat, Wilson. **(On sit)** I wanted to have a word with you about yesterday's manoeuvres.

WILSON Oh yes, sir.

MAINWARING I think we learnt a lot of valuable lessons.

WILSON I'm sure we did, sir.

MAINWARING At the same time, I don't think we received the unthinking obedience which we are entitled to expect, if we are to become an efficient fighting unit.

WILSON I wouldn't say that, sir.

MAINWARING Well I would. When I ordered the platoon to wade through the river, did I get unthinking obedience?

WILSON Well – some of them did have a thought or two about it, sir.

MAINWARING Precisely. And furthermore some of them put the thoughts into words.

WILSON **(Uncomfortable)** Did they, sir?

MAINWARING Unless I'm much mistaken, when I gave the command, 'Ford the river', somebody said 'Get stuffed'.

WILSON Probably that bolshie Scotsman.

MAINWARING The voice sounded English.

WILSON Yes. He's very crafty. I'll watch him.

MAINWARING **(Looking hard at Wilson)** The point is this, Wilson. Whoever said it, nobody crossed the river.

WILSON **(Embarrassed)** Some of us were wearing our best suits, sir.

MAINWARING You weren't wearing your best suit.

WILSON It was my father's, sir. He thought very highly of it. Young Pike tried – he fell flat on his face.

MAINWARING Be that as it may, I would have welcomed an example from you as my Second-in-Command.

WILSON I was first across the bridge.

MAINWARING I had already explained that the bridge was demolished.

WILSON But it wasn't, sir, was it?

MAINWARING You were supposed to pretend it was demolished.

WILSON But I did, sir. We all did. We all pretended it was demolished, and we just used it to help us to pretend to go splashing through the river without getting wet.

Mainwaring is temporarily baulked.

WILSON I am sure when we get uniforms you'll be able to send us charging like madmen through every river in the district with impunity.

MAINWARING I'll remember that, Sergeant Wilson.

WILSON Any news of the uniforms, sir?

MAINWARING Six weeks at the earliest. The same for the rifles.

WILSON Six weeks. So until then, we fight Hitler's parachutists with one shot gun, 15 carving knives and Lance Corporal Jones' assegai.

MAINWARING You left out Bracewell's Number Three Iron.

WILSON I'm sure he'd do better to take a Wood.

Pike knocks and enters.

PIKE The post, sir.

MAINWARING You seem to have recovered well after your ducking, Pike.

PIKE Yes, sir, as soon as I got in I wallowed in a hot bath.

MAINWARING Wallowed. That's not very patriotic is it? You're only supposed to have six inches of bath water, you know.

PIKE Well, sir, I worked it out that you can have seven 6-inch baths a week. That means that you can have 42 inches of water, but I do better than that. I make do with two 15-inch baths a week and save 12 inches of water.

MAINWARING You can save your mathematics for your work, Pike. That'll be all.

Pike goes. Mainwaring picks up the paper.

MAINWARING Oh dear, there's another account closed for the duration.

WILSON Which one's that, sir?

MAINWARING It's the Peabody Museum of Historical Army Weapons. It's from the Curator. He's joined the Navy. The Museum is closed for the duration, and he wants us to transfer all their funds to a deposit account till he returns. Make a note of that will you, Wilson?

WILSON Yes, sir. What's the name of it?

MAINWARING Peabody Museum of Historical Army Weapons.

WILSON Very well, sir, I'll attend to it right away. **(He walks to the door and then stops, he turns)**

WILSON Did you say weapons, sir?

MAINWARING **(Stands)** By Jove, Wilson, are you thinking what I'm thinking?

WILSON I doubt it, sir.

MAINWARING There might be something there we can use.

WILSON I don't think we should get too excited, sir. Their prize exhibit is a full scale replica of Boadicea's chariot.

MAINWARING But they go up to the Crimean don't they? And the Boer War?

WILSON Surely that sort of thing wouldn't be any use to us, sir.

MAINWARING Nonsense. The British Army hasn't changed its rifle since they threw out the flintlock. What do you think they used to relieve Ladysmith?

WILSON I've never given it much thought, sir.

MAINWARING Carbines. 303 Carbines, or I'm a Dutchman.

WILSON I'll draft a letter to H.Q. suggesting they look into it. (**On move**) Miss King, bring your notebook please.

MAINWARING Oh no, Mr Wilson. We're not writing for reams of bumph from G.H.Q. Before we see another dawn the sky could be black with parachutists. Those weapons will be in our hands today. Pike!

Pike enters.

PIKE Yes, sir.

MAINWARING Get a handcart.

PIKE A handcart, sir. Where from?

MAINWARING Builder, greengrocers, boy scouts. Use your initiative.

PIKE Yes, sir.

MAINWARING Move.

PIKE Yes, sir. (**He goes.**)

MAINWARING Sergeant Wilson. Parade the men at 16.00 hours, ready to move off.

WILSON The shops don't shut until 5.30, sir.

MAINWARING Well, they can be ready by six, can't they?

WILSON That's 18.00 hours, sir.

MAINWARING So it is. We'll parade them at 18.00 hours, for Operation Gungrab.

WILSON (**Going, then turns at the door**) One more thing, sir. If we just breeze along and take the guns, won't that be stealing?

MAINWARING There's a war on, Sergeant Wilson.

WILSON I'm fully aware of that, sir, but it still sounds very much like stealing.

MAINWARING I am an Army Officer, and I shall requisition anything I require for the defence of our homes and this town. Miss King, take this down. 'Under the emergency powers vested in me by His Majesty the King, I Captain George Mainwaring, hereby requisition… (**We fade on Wilson's worried face as Mainwaring continues to dictate his requisition**)

CHURCH HALL

Men are gathered round in a group waiting for the parade to start. Mrs Pike is talking to Frank Pike.

PIKE I wish you hadn't come down here tonight, Mum. It makes me look such a fool.

MRS PIKE I don't care. I'm not having you come home like you did Sunday, wet through. Wading through rivers indeed. I'm going to speak to Mr Mainwaring about it. He ought to be ashamed of himself.

PIKE Mum, please don't.

Joe Walker enters.

WALKER Good evening, gents, – oh, and lady. Now there's ten minutes before we start the parade and I've got a few items in scarce supply in case somebody's interested. (**He opens his case**) I've got chocolate biscuits, hairgrips, elastic. Here you are Mrs P. (**He stretches a length of elastic**) Five bob a yard. It's so long since it's been in the shops, some of you ladies must have been getting a bit desperate, eh?

Mrs Pike shows interest. Lance Corporal Jones enters. He has several small parcels.

JONES Evening all. Now there's chops for you, liver for you, oh, and sausages for you, Mr Godfrey.

He starts handing out the parcels and taking money. Both he and Walker are now conducting a brisk trade. Wilson enters and nobody takes any notice of him.

WILSON What on earth's going on here?

WALKER That's all right, Sarge. Just distributing a few supplies. (**He continues to trade**)

WILSON (**Looking around him**) Why, it's as bad as money-changers in the Temple. Stop it at once do you hear. (**He holds up his hand**) Stop it.

Suddenly the door bursts open. Captain Mainwaring rushes into the room, places half a brick in front of them.

MAINWARING (**Ad libs in German. He rushes out and slams the door. He yells from behind the door**) Bang. You fools, you're all dead. Every one of you.

Trading stops. The door opens and the Captain enters, walks slowly to the centre of the room, points to the brick on the floor.

MAINWARING That is a German grenade. I am a German parachutist and you're all dead. Now, why wasn't a sentry posted?

WILSON Well the parade doesn't start for another five minutes, sir.

JONES That's right. We weren't ready.

MAINWARING If you think the Nazi hordes are going to wait until you're ready, you've got another thing coming. **Mrs Pike who has watched all this with amazement, draws Mainwaring to one side.**

MRS PIKE Now, Mr Mainwaring, I am not having my Frank coming home wet through again. You're not going to wade through any more rivers, are you?

MAINWARING Not unless Hitler flings himself upon us, Mrs Pike.

MRS PIKE Well, if he does, that'll be different, of course. You expect it then, but you don't expect him to go jumping into water just to please you. I'm surprised somebody didn't tell you to…

MAINWARING They did, Mrs Pike, they did.

WILSON Shall I fall the men in, sir?

MAINWARING Thank you, Sergeant.

WILSON Would you mind falling in, in three ranks please.

MRS PIKE I'll be off then, Mr Mainwaring. Don't be late tonight, Arthur. **(She goes)**

WILSON At ease, everyone. Squad, 'shun. **(He salutes Mainwaring)** Men all present and correct, sir.

JONES No, sir, Bailey's not present and correct.

WILSON Why not?

JONES Bailey's counting the coupons. Otherwise, added to which had he not done so I wouldn't be present and correct. Coupon counting tonight. It's always coupon counting Mondays. Otherwise there's no meat next week.

MAINWARING Thank you, Corporal Jones. Stand the men at ease, Sergeant.

WILSON Yes, sir. Stand at ease you chaps.

MAINWARING Give it as an order. Platoon. Stand at ease.

WILSON They are at ease.

MAINWARING Stand easy. Now, men, I won't beat about the bush. As you know, we are desperately short of arms. So we are going to requisition what arms we need from the Peabody Museum of Army Weapons.

JONES **(Coming to attention)** Permission to speak, sir?

MAINWARING What is it?

JONES They won't let you 'ave nothing, sir.

MAINWARING I don't see why not. The Museum is closed for the duration. There's only some old fool of a caretaker in charge.

JONES That's my father.

MAINWARING Oh is it?

WALKER Your Dad – blimey! 'E must be getting on.

JONES No, he's only 88. Mind you he was very young when he had me. He got married again for the third time last year. Between you and me, I think he had to.

WILSON The point is, I shall make an official requisition and anyway he's too old to stop us.

JONES I wouldn't count on that, sir, he turns very ugly when he's roused.

WALKER It runs in the family.

JONES 'Ere, there's no call for that. Insubordination that is.

MAINWARING That'll do, Corporal Jones.

JONES I'll put 'im on a fizzer, that's what I'll do.

MAINWARING I don't think there's any need for that, Corporal Jones.

JONES Well, he's had it for offal.

WALKER I was only joking.

MAINWARING Silence in the ranks. Private Pike. Did you get the handcart?

PIKE No sir, but Henry's lending his horse and milk float.

MAINWARING Who?

PIKE Henry the milkman.

MAINWARING That's very generous of him, I'm sure.

PIKE He's come along himself, sir. **(As he indicates Henry the milkman)** He's over there.

HENRY That's right, cock. The horse won't shift for nobody else, sir.

MAINWARING Capital. Then we're all prepared. **(On turn)** Fall the men in outside, Sergeant and then quick march to the Peabody Museum.

Squad marching along behind a horse-drawn milk float. The Sergeant and Mainwaring march at the rear. The float stops. The squad closes in on the rear of the float. Wilson sees it.

WILSON Squad… Halt.

The squad halts. The float moves on.

WILSON Squad… Quick march.

The squad moves on. Very shortly the float stops again. The squad closes up.

WILSON Squad… Halt.

MAINWARING Double up and see what's happening, Sergeant.

Wilson runs to the front of the horse, where Henry is trying to get it to gee up.

WILSON Captain Mainwaring wants to know why we're having all these hold-ups.

HENRY Well, it's our regular round, you see. He always stops at every house. **(To horse)** Gee up, Flash. Go on, boy. Gee up, Flash. **(To Sergeant)** I think he's a bit upset. I usually have a basket of milk, you see. Go on, Flash. Gee up, boy.

EXTERIOR. MUSEUM

It is shaped like a medieaval tower. The turret of the roof is quite low. The front door is heavy studded oak and an openable panel is set in it. At the side of the door is a plate which reads 'Peabody Museum of Historic Army Weapons'. Over it is a notice saying 'Closed for the duration'. We hear the platoon singing in the distance and the sound of them marching. They come into the picture.

MAINWARING Squad, halt. Ring the bell, Sergeant.

The Sergeant pulls the bell pull. Nothing happens.

WILSON I think it's stuck, sir.

MAINWARING Well, give it a jerk.

Wilson jerks it. A long wire comes out. He pulls about three yards out and gives a final jerk. There is a faint tinkle.

JONES You'd better shove all that back, or he'll go beserk.

MAINWARING Shove it back, Wilson.

Wilson tries without much success.

JONES You've done it now.

Mainwaring starts to help him.

JONES I don't know what he's going to say when he sees that. It'll set him off properly.

WALKER He'll get ugly, won't he?

JONES Don't you start on me, you young whipper-snapper.

PIKE I can hear him coming.

JONES I think you'd better let me talk to him.

A small face-sized shutter opens in the door.

GEORGE What do you want?

JONES Hello, Dad. It's me. Young Jack.

GEORGE It took you long enough to come round.

JONES No need to be like that – there' s a war on.

GEORGE There's a what?

JONES There's a war on.

GEORGE I wondered what the noise was. How's Elsie?

JONES Well, it's 'er legs, you see.

GEORGE What?

JONES 'Er legs are troubling 'er a bit.

GEORGE They never troubled anybody else. Great fat bulging things like an elephant.

JONES There's no need for you to get personal about my Elsie. We never done you no 'arm.

GEORGE You never did me no good neither.

JONES You never deserved doing no good, you randy old drunk.

GEORGE Ah, you're getting ugly. You always did get ugly.

JONES It was you what got ugly.

MAINWARING Jones, I think I'd better take over. (**To George**) Now, Mr Jones, I've come to requisition some arms.

GEORGE Who are you?

MAINWARING My name is Captain Mainwaring. I'm the Manager of the Swallow Bank.

GEORGE Captains don't manage banks.

MAINWARING Anyone in the town will tell you that I'm the Manager of the Swallow Bank, and I've recently taken command…

GEORGE (**Interrupting**) Liar. I've been going to that bank for years. You've never served me.

MAINWARING I don't serve people. I'm in my office.

GEORGE Afraid to show your face, eh? Well, you're not getting nothing from me. Clear off. (**He slams the shutter**)

MAINWARING (**Shouting**) Open this door, Mr Jones.

JONES I told you he'd get ugly, sir.

MAINWARING By the powers vested in me by King George, I command you to open this door.

JONES It won't do you no good mentioning the King, he thinks Queen Victoria is the King.

MAINWARING All right, you asked for it. Men, gather round.

The men gather round him in a tight knot.

MAINWARING There's nothing else for it. We shall have to force our way in.

WILSON I say, sir. Do you think we should?

MAINWARING I am in command, Wilson. I accept full responsibility.

Pike and Walker come into the picture carrying a ladder.

PIKE Look what we found round the back, sir. It's a scaling ladder.

WALKER Yeah, there's all sorts of stuff round there. Battering rams, Norman siege catapults.

GODFREY I say, that's a good idea. Couldn't we catapult someone on to the roof.

MAINWARING Are you volunteering, Godfrey?

GODFREY Well I thought one of the young gentlemen might be more suitable.

MAINWARING We'll keep that as a last resort. Put that ladder up against the wall.

Pike and Walker run the ladder against the wall.

MAINWARING Wilson, you follow up. I shall lead the assault. Follow me. (**He puts his foot on the fourth rung. All** the rungs collapse. Mainwaring slowly picks himself up) (To Walker) Not very safe, is it?

WALKER Well, what do you expect for 300 years old.

MAINWARING Did you say there was a battering ram round the back?

WALKER Yes, that's right, sir.

MAINWARING Fall out men. Right men, follow your Commander.

EXTERIOR. MUSEUM

The men are standing in a grim line holding a battering ram. It is of medieval design with the head of a goat, with curled horns, on the front.

MAINWARING Charge!

They rush at the door. As the battering ram touches the door, it disintegrates.

EXTERIOR. MUSEUM

The men are once more in line. This time they have a much thinner, flagpole type of battering ram.

MAINWARING Charge!

The men rush at the door. The pole hits the shutter, which gives way and the pole disappears right through the door. The men stay outside.

EXTERIOR. MUSEUM

Once more the men are lined up outside, this time with a much thicker, heavier pole.

MAINWARING Charge!

They rush at the door. Just as they reach it, it flies open.

INTERIOR. MUSEUM

The men cannot stop. They charge through the museum, George running ahead of them. He opens the back door. As they all go through it, he shuts it after them. There is a terrific crash.

ROOF OF MUSEUM

George peering over the top of the ramparts. There is the sound of voices below. He starts to trundle a machine into position. Close up of museum plate on machine. It reads: 'boiling oil dispenser. Anti-siege weapon. Fourteenth century.'

George tries to light a little fire under the machine. It goes out.

GEORGE Never mind. They'll have to have it cold.

EXTERIOR. MUSEUM

They have got the ladder into position.

MAINWARING All right, Sergeant, um, take the men up. Charge!

They swarm up the ladder. They are half-way up when George empties the oil machine over them. It's full of water.

Cut to George's gleeful face.

CHURCH HALL

The Captain and Sergeant are in the centre of the group. It is now night. They are dressed in old clothes, possibly with blacked faces, for a commando-type raid.

Frazer is dressed as an A.R.P. Warden.

MAINWARING All right, men. We've tried force. Now we'll try cunning. So – here's the plan. We proceed to the Museum. We will then conceal ourselves by the front door. Private Frazer, disguised as an A.R.P. Warden, will knock until that silly old fool – I mean – Corporal Jones' father answers and then tell him he has a light showing. When he comes out to have a look, we will creep through the door, and lock it behind us.

WILSON Supposing he won't open the door, sir?

MAINWARING Well, we'll just have to make him open it.

WILSON I thought that's what we'd tried to do this afternoon, sir.

JONES Permission to speak, sir?

MAINWARING Yes, Jones.

JONES Show him half a bottle of whisky. That'll emolumate him and stop him getting ugly.

MAINWARING I'm sure it will. But where are we going to get half a bottle of whisky?

WALKER Hang on a tick.

He goes to the back of the hall, produces half a bottle of whisky from his suitcase.

WALKER Here you are. Thirty bob!

MAINWARING But it's only 15 shillings in the shops.

WALKER Yes, but you can't get it in the shops, can you?

MAINWARING Oh, all right. Hand it over.

He gives him the money, takes the bottle. Gives it to Frazer. Frazer licks his lips.

WALKER No, no. Don't worry. I'll put it on your account.

MAINWARING Don't look at it like that.

FRAZER I cannae help it.

MAINWARING Now don't drink it unless you have to. Just show it to him.

FRAZER You can trust me. I'll only drink it in the line of duty.

MAINWARING Now don't forget, Frazer, it's your job to keep George Jones busy while we help ourselves to whatever weapons we need. We will then load them on to the transport. Did you get the scout cart, Pike?

PIKE (**With a small boy scout standing beside him**) Yes, sir.

MAINWARING Who's that?

PIKE He's the patrol leader, sir. He's got to come with us. He says it's more than his job's worth to let it out of his sight.

Boy scout gives scout salute.

MAINWARING Synchronise your watches. The time is now 17… er, 19… is two whiskers past Mickey Mouse's nose. If all goes well, before the evening's out, this platoon will be fully armed.

JONES Fall in outside.

OUTSIDE MUSEUM

Platoon approach and gather round the doors.

MAINWARING All right, men. Keep the cart out of the way, and keep out of sight. (**To Frazer**) Now, tell him he's got a light showing.

Mainwaring and the rest of the platoon press up against the wall out of sight. Frazer bangs the door. As there is no answer, he bangs on the shutter. It flies open. George's head appears.

GEORGE What do you want?

FRAZER I'm an A.R.P. Warden. You've got a light showing.

GEORGE No I haven't.

FRAZER Well come out and see for yourself.

GEORGE I'm not opening the door in my night-shirt.

FRAZER I didn't know you had a door in your night-shirt.

GEORGE Funny man, eh? You should be in 'ITMA'… Buzz off!

Frazer holds the whisky bottle close to the shutter. He takes a drink.

GEORGE What's that, whisky?

FRAZER Yes, just a drop to keep the cold out. Want some?

GEORGE Yes, I'll have a drop.

FRAZER Well, you'll have to open the door.

GEORGE Hold on.

His face disappears. There's a rattle of chains and bolts. The door opens and George comes out.

GEORGE Well, where's the whisky?

Frazer hands him the bottle. George takes a swig.

GEORGE Now, where's this flaming light?

FRAZER You'll have to come over here.

They both move out of the picture. Mainwaring and the platoon creep through the doors and lock them behind them. Mainwaring pushes boy scout out of door.

MAINWARING Look after the cart.

GEORGE'S VOICE There's no light showing.

FRAZER There. Can't you see?

GEORGE No I can't. I'm going in.

George comes back in the picture. Goes to open the door, finds it's locked and gives a howl of rage.

GEORGE I can't get the door open. I'll catch me death of cold. (**Takes a swig at the whisky**) Flaming idiot you are. I'll have to try and get in at the lavatory window at the back. Come on, give me a hand.

INTERIOR MUSEUM

There are various display cases presumably containing weapons, display boards with flintlock pistols, etc.

Jones, Walker and Wilson come forward, Jones carrying a hurricane lamp. They come forward to the first case containing halberds.

JONES Eh, Sarge. Do you think we ought to take some of these halibuts?

WILSON No. Anyway, they're halberds.

WALKER Here, sir. Special elephant shooting musket, by Putt and Putt, Bond Street, 1835. Hm. Goes through an elephant. Probably go through a tank. (**He takes it down and swings it round. They all duck**)

MAINWARING Put it back, man, before you break something. (**Walker swings it round again and smashes a big glass display case**)

WALKER What d'yer say, sir?

MAINWARING Never mind. Put it back, Pike.

PIKE Yes sir. **(He takes it from Walker, swings it round, and smashes another cabinet)**

MAINWARING Here, give it to me. **(He snatches it from Pike and pokes it through a window)**

Cut to Jones who is examining a breastplate.

JONES Here, what's this?

WALKER It's a breastplate. Protects the top.

JONES How do you protect the bottom?

WALKER Don't turn your back on the enemy.

Cut to Godfrey examining the plaque on a case, with a match.

GODFREY This is it, sir. 303 Carbines. British Infantry Weapons during South African War.

MAINWARING How many are there?

GODFREY The case is empty, sir. Just a minute. There's another notice further down. **(He reads)** Requisitioned by ENSA. Five March 1940.

MAINWARING ENSA? What do they need rifles for?

GODFREY They have very difficult audiences sometimes.

MAINWARING Well that's it then, Sergeant Wilson. Time to withdraw. Back to base.

Cut to Jones and Walker who are examining another weapon.

WALKER **(Reads)** Chinese rocket gun, 1901. Used against the Boxers.

JONES They pay no heed to animals East of Suez.

WALKER Here, that'll brighten up manoeuvres a bit. **(He picks up one of the projectiles)** Here, look. It's got a sort of grenade on the end.

JONES Yellow fiends.

WALKER Cor, it could make a right mess of you, couldn't it? Lovely. Give us a hand.

Walker and Jones start to back it out.

Cut to small window rear of museum. Frazer is pushing George through the window rear first.

GEORGE Don't push too hard. I've got to find something to stand on. Hang on, I've put me foot on something. Pull me back, pull me back.

FRAZER What's the matter?

GEORGE I've got me foot stuck down the whatsit.

FRAZER Hang on. Grab hold of this chain.

Sound of a flush.

GEORGE **(Yells) (Comes up to window again)** That was very clever, wasn't it?

FRAZER Flushed you out, didn't it?

CHURCH HALL

Walker and Jones are examining the Chinese rocket gun. Mainwaring and Wilson are looking on.

WALKER Ah, I've got it. Look. The back end of the rocket stuck out there, and they laid a trail of powder, there, which fired each one in turn.

JONES **(Shaking a powder horn)** The fuse powder's in this horn here.

FRAZER And the spare rockets are down on the tray there.

WALKER That's it. And you lit it – there. **(To scout)** If you got busy with that hook thing on your pen-knife, young fellow, you could unbung those ports and have it working in no time.

JONES That's right. Get unbunging.

MAINWARING Walker, Jones, don't think your zeal and initiative are not appreciated. You have both displayed just the sort of spirit that's going to get Jerry on the run, but I feel this weapon is a little too antique even for us. So we'll return it in the morning.

WALKER We haven't got much else, have we, sir?

MAINWARING Even if it worked, I feel perhaps modern warfare has progressed way beyond the rocket.

WALKER Yes, sir.

MAINWARING I'd better talk to the men. I don't want them to lose heart over this little setback. Pay attention please.

WILSON Pay attention, everybody.

Jones and Walker are still working on the rocket gun.

MAINWARING Leave that, Walker, Jones. Now there's no doubt at all that H.Q. will rush weapons to us just as soon as they can get their hands on them. In the meantime we must press our ingenuity into service. On the march back, I had an idea and I give it to you as an example of the sort of thing we need. At the top of every hill we are going to station drums of old sump oil. At the first sign of emergency we're going to spread it all over the road. You can imagine the result. If the enemy transport can't get a grip on the road surface, his whole war effort will grind to a halt.

JONES Permission to speak, sir?

MAINWARING Yes, Jones.

JONES Tin-tacks – why don't we all have packets of tin-tacks to put on the road, as well.

MAINWARING Excellent, Jones. Punctured vehicles won't travel far, will they? Wilson get all the tacks you can lay your hands on.

JONES Permission to speak, sir?

MAINWARING Yes, Corporal.

JONES Woolworths have got them, sir.

WILSON Will you requisition them again, sir.

MAINWARING I think you might buy what we need Wilson. And one more thing, men. We're not leaving here until we've made a staunch effort to improve our arsenal. We're gong to set to and complete those petrol bombs. Walker's provided us with a fine selection of old wine bottles. You line them up and empty them, Frazer. You're in charge of the funnel, Jones. You pour the petrol, Wilson, and I'll supervise the string fuse and cork. Right, off we go.

Wilson picks up the can of petrol.

WILSON Excuse me, sir. The petrol can's empty.

MAINWARING Empty? Walker!

WALKER I had to use it in the car to fetch the bottles, didn't I?

The scout comes up and salutes.

SCOUT I've done it, sir.

MAINWARING Oh, er, thank you. What?

SCOUT Cleared the ports in the rocket gun.

MAINWARING Oh good, well done.

SCOUT The fuse powder's fizzing away beautifully.

MAINWARING Good. Now Walker. If we're to survive, it's very important that we get our priorities right.

It suddenly dawns on him what the scout's said.

MAINWARING What!

They run to the rocket gun which is now emitting sparks and smoke. Mainwaring takes off his hat and starts to try to douse the fuse.

Jones and Wilson dive for cover on the floor.

WILSON **(Over the din and smoke)** Fancy those rockets going off after all these years, sir.

MAINWARING Yes. Damn clever, these Chinese. Thank goodness they're on our side.

SERIES ONE **EPISODE THREE**

COMMAND DECISION

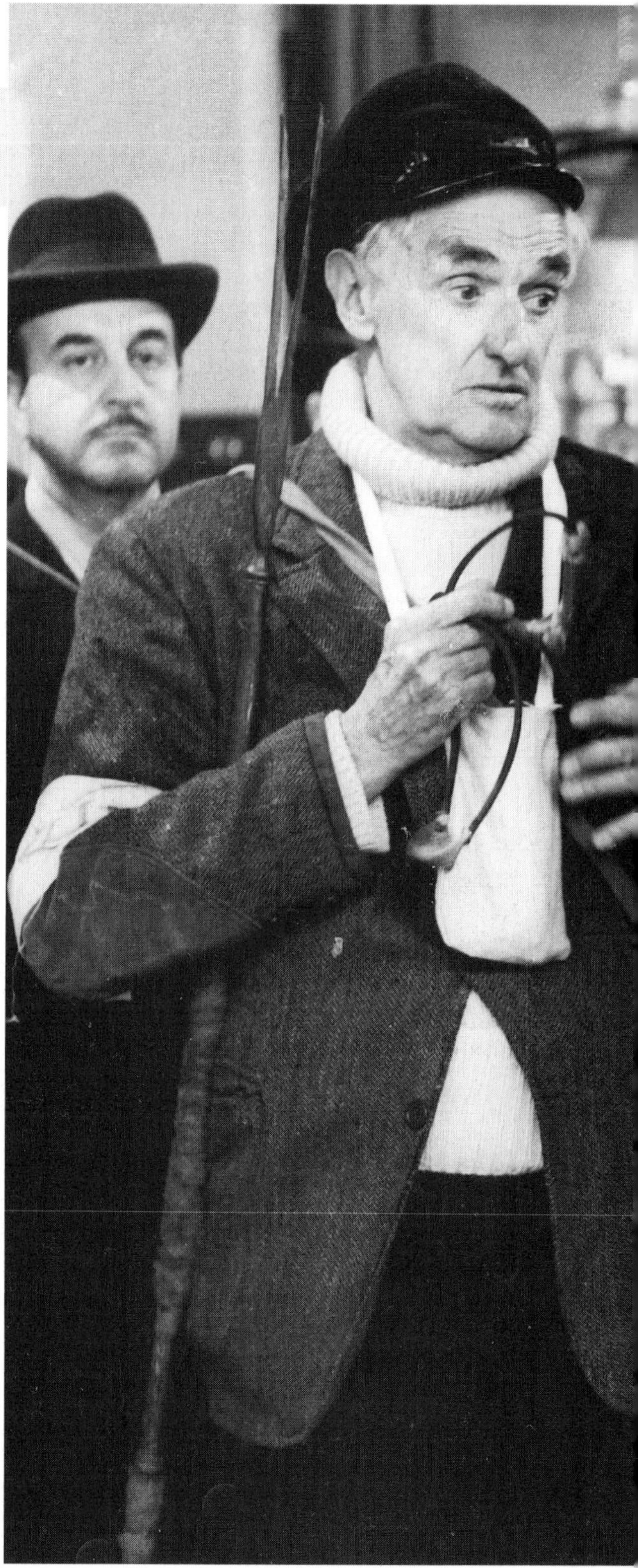

Recorded: Monday 29/4/68 (made in black and white)
Original transmission: Wednesday 14/8/68, 8.20–8.50pm
Original viewing figures = 8.6 million

ARTHUR LOWE .... CAPTAIN MAINWARING
JOHN LE MESURIER .... SERGEANT WILSON
CLIVE DUNN .... LANCE CORPORAL JONES
JOHN LAURIE .... PRIVATE FRAZER
JAMES BECK .... PRIVATE WALKER
ARNOLD RIDLEY .... PRIVATE GODFREY
IAN LAVENDER .... PRIVATE PIKE
CAROLINE DOWDESWELL .... JANET KING
GEOFFREY LUMSDEN .... COLONEL SQUARE
CHARLES HILL .... THE BUTLER
GORDON PETERS .... THE SOLDIER

PLATOON .... HUGH HASTINGS, RICHARD JACQUES, COLIN BEAN, ... CHRIS FRANKS, DAVID SEAFORTH, ALEC COLEMAN, ... HUGH CECIL, VIC TAYLOR, JIMMY MAC, PETER WHITAKER
SOLDIER (BURT) .... ALAN TRAVELL

• HAROLD SNOAD REMEMBERS •

'A sequence in this episode involved us filming outside a stables. During the recce I discovered a suitable building on the army battle area and, as usual, liaised with the very helpful commanding officer telling him when we would be there in order to gain his approval. On the agreed day we were halfway through filming the sequence when suddenly there was a rustle in the bushes alongside the camera and a young officer in full camouflage uniform, including a blackened face, informed me that he had orders to blow up the area in ten minutes. Everything stopped. I made an urgent telephone call to the CO and, as a result, the officer's attitude completely changed. "Oh, all right," he said, "we'll come back and blow it up tomorrow!" He then stood up, yelled out a command and another seventy or so soldiers appeared out of various bushes and from behind trees – all in camouflage gear – and gathered together before marching off.'

HAROLD SNOAD

Command Decision

TELECINE: BATTLESHIP FOLLOWED BY SHOTS OF BRITISH AEROPLANES

NARRATOR On sea and air the struggle continues to win back our civilisation.

TELECINE: MOTORCYCLE TROOPS AND SMALL TANKS

NARRATOR While our army continues to fight with all the gallantry of our great tradition, let us not forget the citizens who come home after a hard day's work and then go on parade as Local Defence Volunteers.

TELECINE: CIVILIANS STREAMING OVER BRIDGE

Shot of Frazer and Godfrey digging two holes in a field. They are wearing shirt sleeves and waistcoats.

NARRATOR Here they're preparing a few surprises for any unwelcome enemy visitors.

TELECINE: SHOTS OF IRON RAILINGS

NARRATOR They have an unbreakable will, and an iron resolve and if Adolf ever tries to set foot on this green and pleasant land he'll be chased right back into the sea.

Telecine same shot. The iron railings have disappeared, except for a single railing.

Cut to platoon running down street, brandishing the rails.

Cut to shot of statue holding sword.

Close shot of Jones removing sword from statue.

INTERIOR. CHURCH HALL

The platoon are drawn up in two lines. Wilson is drilling them. Mainwaring standing by watching. They are dressed in civilian clothes with L.D.V. armbands, they carry halberds. They wear an equal assortment of trilbies and caps.

WILSON Squad, 'shun!

They all come smartly to attention except Jones who is a beat late.

WILSON Stand at ease.

The squad stands at ease. Jones is again a beat late.

WILSON Squad, 'shun!

Repeat business.

WILSON Stand at ease. Squad, 'shun! Stand at ease.

Repeat business.

WILSON Squad, 'shun!

Repeat business.

WILSON **(Aside to Mainwaring)** I think it would save time if we settled for that, sir.

MAINWARING Go on to the next bit then.

WILSON Oh **(He salutes)** Squad present and correct, sir.

Mainwaring starts to inspect the squad. They are lined up in the following order, right to left: Jones, Walker, Pike, Frazer, Godfrey – the extras from the other rank.

MAINWARING **(Having inspected Jones)** Very smart, Jones.

JONES Sir.

MAINWARING **(To Walker)** Good, Walker. Very smart hat.

WALKER It fell off a lorry, sir.

MAINWARING Really. It stood up to it remarkably well.

He touches the blade of his pike.

MAINWARING That could do with sharpening, Walker.

WALKER It was all right when I carved the joint on Sunday.

JONES Where did you get a joint? I only served you with chump chops.

WALKER Mind your own business.

MAINWARING That'll do. We must look after our arms.

WALKER I'd rather look after our rifles.

MAINWARING We'll be receiving them very shortly – you can count on that. **(To Pike, who is wearing a scarf)** Pike, I told you yesterday, no mufflers on parade. You don't see the Grenadier Guards wearing mufflers do you, Wilson?

WILSON I've never thought to look, sir.

MAINWARING Well, of course you don't, Sergeant.

PIKE I've got a note from mother, sir.

Pike gets the note out of his pocket.

MAINWARING Note. I'm not interested in notes. You're in the army now, Pike.

WILSON Don't you think perhaps you should read it, sir.

MAINWARING Oh, very well.

He can't read it too clearly so he uses the magnifying glass on his watch-chain.

MAINWARING **(Reading)** Frank is starting with his chest

again. He ought to be in bed. If he can't wear his muffler he's to come home or he will catch his death. (**To Wilson**) I can't have him parading for inspection in that thing. It makes the whole platoon look ludicrous.

WILSON Perhaps he could wear it on patrol, sir. (**To Pike**) What time are you on?

PIKE Ten till twelve.

WILSON It's dark by then.

MAINWARING Oh, very well. Take it off in here and wear it on patrol. (**To Frazer, who is wearing a small linen bag slung over his shoulder**) What's this, Frazer?

FRAZER Stones, sir, for my catapult. (**He indicates the catapult which he is carrying in his breast pocket**)

MAINWARING This is war, Frazer. I think we should draw the line at catapults, pop-guns and other toys. In future ask the Sergeant's permission before you parade with any unauthorised weapons.

FRAZER I did, sir.

MAINWARING Did you?

WILSON I thought that in the absence of rifles it might be useful as a medium range weapon, sir.

FRAZER I was a dab hand with it as a boy, sir.

MAINWARING But that was some time ago, Frazer.

FRAZER I've just hit my target now sir, at a hundred yards. A Belisha beacon. Smashed to smithereens.

MAINWARING Great Scott. Well – er – keep it out of sight. (**To Wilson**) Good heavens, it'll be conkers next.

FRAZER Will we be having the rifles soon?

MAINWARING Very soon I hope, Frazer.

FRAZER Praise the Lord.

Mainwaring moves to Godfrey who nods and smiles.

MAINWARING Look to your front, Godfrey, and don't smile. This is a military inspection and not an advertisement for Odol.

Mainwaring returns.

MAINWARING Squad, stand at ease. I have one or two announcements to make before we continue with our unarmed combat. (**He takes some notes out of his pocket**)

FRAZER (**To Pike**) Unarmed combat, that's about our mark. Combat.

MAINWARING Mrs Samways, the Guide Mistress, has requested that when doing arms drill in the guide hut, the order 'slope arms' will not be given. It appears that the points of your halberds went straight through the felt roof and now when it rains she has to send half the troop home.

Reaction from platoon.

MAINWARING We must be very careful when dealing with other organisations, or for that matter, with the public, not to get ourselves a bad name. As an example of what I mean, Mrs Samways also mentioned that her Assistant, Miss Beckworth, was followed home last night by one of our men whom, she alleges, flashed an unobscured torch on her legs and was heard to say 'Look at them Gameroos'.

Reactions from Pike, Jones and Walker.

MAINWARING Now that's not the sort of thing I want to hear about my unit. Walker, Jones, Pike you were on patrol at that time. I'm not going to ask who it was but don't let it happen again.

JONES (**Coming to attention**) Permission to speak, sir?

MAINWARING Yes, Jones?

JONES I would like to confess, sir – it was me.

MAINWARING I'm surprised at you, Jones.

JONES I know, sir, I don't know what come over me.

MAINWARING I mean, it's most embarrassing for a young girl. And suppose it had been Mrs Samways.

JONES That would have been all right, sir.

MAINWARING Why?

JONES I wouldn't have bothered.

The platoon laughs.

WILSON Silence in the ranks.

MAINWARING Pay attention. One more thing. You'll be pleased to hear that the Spitfire Fund now stands at £3 9s 4d. Now on the word 'Move', the platoon will gather round for a further lecture on unarmed combat. MOVE!

They scramble to assemble themselves around the platform. Jones joins Mr Mainwaring.

MAINWARING Ah. Volunteering as the attacker yet again, Jones.

JONES Well, sir. We've got to do something, seeing as 'ow we've got no rifles.

MAINWARING Yes, Jones. Now you may remember, last night we were dealing with the counter-measures to be taken when assaulted by a man with a dagger. (**Jones whips a carving knife out of his belt and holds it menacingly for a blow**) (**Showing bandaged hand**) In view of last night's incident, we'll use something else. Wilson, the shillelagh (**Wilson hands a shillelagh to Jones and takes the knife**) Now having taken the blow below the knife on the left forearm, you recall that the next move is to twist your hand like this, and grab hold of the assailant's wrist. Is that right, Wilson?

WILSON Yes, sir. That's as far as we got before the doctor arrived.

MAINWARING Quite. The next step is to knock out the

opponent. This you can do with the flat of the hand to the throat, **(He demonstrates each position)** the knee in the groin, or two fingers jabbed into the eyes. **(Jones gives a slight stagger)** Stand behind him, Wilson, in case he falls backwards.

Wilson moves behind Jones.

JONES I won't fall. I won yesterday, didn't I?

FRAZER This jabbing in the eyes. What do you do if he's wearing glasses?

MAINWARING Good question. Now the Whitehall chaps who wrote this, thought of this, and they came up with a very smart alternative. They recommend that you shove your index and second finger right up his nose. Not a pleasant business, but this is war.

FRAZER What happens if he's wearing his gas mask?

MAINWARING Ah, ah, that's a very good question, isn't it Sergeant Wilson?

WILSON Very good indeed, sir.

MAINWARING What happens if he's wearing his *service respirator*? We must get into the habit of giving things their correct names, service respirator. Is there anything in the Manual, Sergeant Wilson?

WILSON Not in this one, sir.

MAINWARING Well there you are. Frazer's brought up a very good point which even the chaps in Whitehall haven't considered. Still, they're not front line fighting troops like we are. I tell you what we do. We improvise. Jones, put on your gas mask.

WILSON Service respirator.

MAINWARING Quite right. I forgot. I am subject to human frailties and weaknesses just like anyone else.

Jones has taken out his respirator and is removing a package from inside it.

JONES Hold this.

MAINWARING Your respirator is supposed to be at instant readiness, Corporal Jones.

JONES That's just the pieces for Mrs Foster's cat. She helps me count the meat coupons – I see her cat right. **(He puts on the mask)**

MAINWARING Well, it's no good trying to put our fingers in his eyes or up his nose. Which is no doubt why you've asked the question, Frazer. So what are we to do? Who's got a suggestion?

WALKER Breathe on his window.

MAINWARING Breathe on his window. An interesting suggestion, Walker. **(He tries it)** But it doesn't seem to work very well.

WALKER You blow, sir. You should have 'ughed.

Ad lib... Mainwaring tries it.

MAINWARING You try, Wilson.

WILSON Maybe it's this celluloid material, sir. It doesn't steam up.

JONES **(Inside the mask)** It's steamed up inside 'ere all right.

GODFREY Perhaps that's the answer, sir. Hold him there until he gets steamed up.

MAINWARING Well, it's a possibility, I suppose. I have it. Cut off his air supply. **(He puts his hand against the intake of Jones' mask)** Place the palm of the hand over the air intake, or in the case of the service respirator, of course, grab the air tube and close it. Now you know as well as I do that the biggest, toughest chap in the world, the Nazi storm trooper, the S.S. or just plain Fritz can't last for more than a few seconds without air.

Jones falls to the ground.

MAINWARING Get his mask off.

WILSON Service respirator.

MAINWARING Get it off.

Fade on Jones being revived.

SIDE OFFICE

Mainwaring and Wilson are bent over Jones who is sitting and being given a drink of water.

MAINWARING There now. Feeling better?

JONES Sorry, I was overcome.

WILSON It wasn't your fault.

JONES No I wouldn't have snuffed out like that normally, sir. It's just that my morale is all shattered. I try to hide it from the men but it's no use. I mean, what can you do with a shattered morale?

MAINWARING My dear fellow. I'm so sorry. I feel terribly responsible.

JONES No it's not you, sir. You see every morning I open my shop and all these women come in and try to get a bit on the side. I'd like to oblige them, sir, but I can't. What can I say to 'em? I'm used to joints, Mr Mainwaring. Topsides, sirloins, wing ribs, spare ribs, legs of mutton, legs of pork, every size and description. You name it, I've sliced it. But nowadays I've got to give 'em a one and tenpenny piece. You've no idea the precision of it. A slight shake of the hand, slap it on the scale, fourpence light – there's all hell let loose.

WILSON Well, we all have to put up with these things.

MAINWARING Yes, don't forget there's a war on.

JONES Sitting in my shop all day – with only two rabbits and a tin of corned beef in the window, that's bad enough, but when I've finished work, and had me tea, and take out me assegai and sharpen it up, I come down here for parade hoping there'll be a rifle for me, and there never is. **(He breaks down)** There never is.

Mainwaring draws Wilson to one side.

MAINWARING Our first casualty, Wilson. I never thought Jones would go like that.

WILSON I never did think he was the right type.

MAINWARING Nonsense, he just wants to have a go at Jerry like the rest of us.

WILSON I'm afraid if we don't get some rifles soon, our morale is going to drop to rock-bottom.

MAINWARING Well, we'll soon put a stop to that. Wilson, get the men on parade and tell them that I personally will see that they get some rifles before the week is out.

WILSON But sir.

MAINWARING Don't argue, Wilson. Go and do it.

Wilson goes.

JONES **(Shaking Mainwaring's hand)** What would we do without you, sir? You're our inspiration. **(He goes)**

MAINWARING **(Sticking his hand in his coat and looking in the mirror)** The hour, and the man.

MAINWARING'S OFFICE IN THE BANK

Mainwaring is at his desk signing a paper. Wilson stands beside him.

MAINWARING Anything else, Wilson?

WILSON Mr Adams the Music Shop has issued this cheque and there's nothing to meet it.

MAINWARING **(Looking at it)** He's not doing very well, is he?

WILSON He over-orders so terribly. He still has over 400 records of 'We're going to hang out the washing on the Siegfried Line' on his shelves.

MAINWARING He's not going to shift those now, is he? Couldn't he heat them up and turn them into nut bowls.

WILSON There's no nuts about, sir.

MAINWARING Poor fellow. But his spirit was right. We're slow starters in this country, Wilson. We don't like wars and bloodshed, but once we knuckle down to it, we finish up fighting better than anyone else in the world. He should hold on to his records. We *will* hang out the washing on the Siegfried Line, you know. Cash his cheque.

WILSON Yes, sir.

MAINWARING Any news from H.Q.?

WILSON Not a thing. I think you were a little hasty last night, sir, when you promised the men you would get them rifles before the week was out.

MAINWARING Well, I had to say something. Must keep their morale up somehow.

There is a knock on the door and Janet King enters with two cups of tea and two currant buns.

JANET As you were both busy I thought I would bring your cup of tea in here, Mr Wilson.

WILSON Yes, thank you, Miss King. Just put it down, will you? **(She puts the tray down on the desk and goes)**

MAINWARING **(Taking up his bun and breaking it in two)** Look at that. Not a single currant. Do you remember those buns we used to get before the war? Full of juicy fruit.

WILSON Yes, sir. **(He breaks his bun. It is full of currants)**

MAINWARING **(Staring at Wilson's bun)** You've got the wrong bun, Wilson.

WILSON No, sir. This is the one you left.

MAINWARING **(Chewing his own bun, it is very dry, and he sprays Wilson as he talks)** Well you might at least give me one of your currants.

WILSON I'm sorry, sir. **(He picks a currant out of his bun and hands it to Mainwaring. He goes to take it and it drops on the desk)**

MAINWARING You are clumsy, Wilson. Now you've dropped it.

WILSON Sorry, sir. **(He searches amongst the papers on the desk)** I can't find it, sir.

MAINWARING Oh, never mind, Wilson, I'll do without a currant. **(There is a knock on the door and Janet enters)** What is it, Miss King?

JANET Colonel Square to see you, sir. **(She gives Mainwaring card)**

MAINWARING Colonel Square. Marsham Hall.

WILSON Never heard of him.

MAINWARING **(Looking at card)** I wonder what he wants. Better send him in.

Before she has a chance, Colonel Square comes into the room. He is aged between 50 and 60 and is wearing a Macmillan type suit.

COLONEL Mainwaring. **(He pronounces it as spelt)**

MAINWARING Ah, Colonel, do sit down. Actually it's pronounced Mainwaring.

COLONEL Why the hell do you spell it Mainwaring then? Are you the L.D.V. fellas?

Janet is still at the door, giggling.

MAINWARING Yes.

COLONEL Well, I'll come straight to the point. The War House haven't found a job for me yet though heaven knows it shouldn't be difficult with a man of my experience. Four years in the desert you know. 1915 to 19. You've heard of E.L. Lawrence?

MAINWARING I beg your pardon, sir.

COLONEL E.L. Lawrence, man. E.L. Lawrence. What do you see in your mind's eye when I say that word. E.L. Lawrence?

MAINWARING I don't know, sir. What do you see, Wilson?

WILSON An ice cream, sir.

MAINWARING No, that's Eldorado.

COLONEL No, you fool. I'm talking about Lawrence of Arabia. I served with him. Ah. **(Suddenly he picks up a ruler, and brings it down on the table with a terrific crash)** Got it. Never miss. Always got a good eye for a fly, you know.

WILSON **(Picking up 'fly' and handing it to Mainwaring)** That's the one we lost, sir.

MAINWARING **(He takes it, and pops it into his mouth)** Thank you, Wilson.

COLONEL **(Staring at Mainwaring)** Do you always eat them?

MAINWARING Can't afford to waste them, you know, sir. Almost impossible to get in wartime.

COLONEL Extraordinary. Well now, when do you want me to take over?

MAINWARING Take over?

COLONEL Yes, take over the platoon, man. I mean, if I'm going to join your lot I've got to take over.

He points to his epaulette.

MAINWARING I'm afraid there's no establishment for another officer in the platoon. I am the Captain, Wilson here is the Sergeant. We might be able to fit you in as a Corporal.

COLONEL Corporal. Are you mad? Either I'm in full charge, or I don't join at all. I'm sure another platoon would welcome me with open arms, to say nothing of my rifles.

MAINWARING Your rifles?

WILSON Rifles?

COLONEL Yes. I've got about 20 rifles. Don't you want them?

MAINWARING Yes, of course we do.

COLONEL So do the Littleton platoon. I realise it's a bit of a blow to you. There's a lot of you chaps about. Want to be Generals overnight. But war is a serious professional business. This situation needs professionals trained in guerilla warfare like me. March your chaps over to my house at 6.30. **(He taps his visiting card to indicate the address)** I'll start making soldiers out of you all. Don't be late, we've a lot of work to do. **(He strides out)**

MAINWARING Damned impertinence. Did you ever hear anything like that?

WILSON No, sir. It makes it very difficult.

MAINWARING What do you mean, difficult?

WILSON For you, sir. It's a terrible decision to have to take.

MAINWARING I don't see where the decision comes into

it. We don't want old fools like that in command.

WILSON (**Tapping card**) He's got the D.S.O., sir.

MAINWARING I'm not saying he's not a brave old fool, I'm sure he is. He's got plenty of cheek too.

WILSON He's commanded guerillas.

MAINWARING In 1917 maybe. But what does he know about modern warfare?

WILSON What do any of us know?

MAINWARING Are you suggesting I should stand down, Wilson?

WILSON No. I wouldn't suggest that, sir. No, sir. Most certainly not. It would have to be entirely your decision.

MAINWARING Commanding our sort of unit isn't like commanding Arabs in the desert. These men are British. They have to be led not bullied. You have to have the right personality.

WILSON I do agree on that point, sir. Absolutely. The thing is, which is the most important weapon? Your personality, or his rifles?

CHURCH HALL

Jones, Godfrey and a few members of the platoon are sitting around disconsolate. Frazer pops his head round the door.

FRAZER Are they here yet?

JONES What?

FRAZER The rifles?

JONES What do you think? All we get is promises.

Frazer enters with his two-pronged halberd.

FRAZER Well I'm not marching through the streets with this thing any more. A gang of kids ran after me shouting 'Can I borrow your toasting fork?'.

GODFREY I know. One of them offered to lend me his cap-pistol.

JONES He offered it to me. (**Produces it**) I took it.

FRAZER At this rate we'll probably get 'em in time to fire the Victory salute. What's he doing about it?

GODFREY He's on the phone to H.Q. now.

INNER OFFICE

Mainwaring is on the phone. Wilson is watching anxiously over his shoulder.

MAINWARING I can't emphasise too strongly the urgency of the situation. Yes, of course I'll hold on. (**To Wilson**) He's talking to the Q.M.

Walker enters through outer door.

MAINWARING Yes, Walker?

WALKER I've just been on the blower to a geezer in the Smoke. I can get the rifles for you, sir. As many as you want. Eighteen quid a time.

MAINWARING I'm afraid that's out of the question, Walker.

WILSON Where do they come from?

WALKER Well, you don't ask, do you. But this geezer's a very good friend of mine. Very discreet and reliable. He used to knock 'em off for the I.R.A. (**Reaction from Mainwaring**) But seeing these are going to the home market he's prepared to chuck in ten rounds per magazine on a special offer.

MAINWARING I'm sorry, Walker.

WALKER (**To Wilson**) He's got a Lewis gun for a hundred quid.

WILSON A hundred pounds. That seems rather a lot.

WALKER I told him he was opening his mouth a bit wide. But he won't shift. But I look at it this way. There's a vault full of oncers at your bank. And who's going to count it except you two?

MAINWARING Walker, your proposition is quite outrageous. Kindly rejoin your platoon.

WALKER If you change your mind. (**He goes to the door and turns**) Mills bombs, pound each, deadly.

MAINWARING No, Walker.

Walker goes. Mainwaring returns to telephone.

MAINWARING Ah yes, good afternoon, sir. About this rifle situation. (**He listens**) But can't you let me have even half a dozen? There's division upon division of trained ruthless men, just across the water, and all I've got is pikes and pickhandles. (**Pause**) I see, sir. Very well. (**He puts the receiver down**) No luck I'm afraid.

Pike enters and gives him the evening paper.

PIKE Your paper, sir.

MAINWARING Look at that!

WILSON Rather attractive.

MAINWARING No, not that! Here – invasion barges moving down from the North. And my men unarmed.

WILSON Pity you made that promise.

MAINWARING It's not the promise that worries me. If Hitler kicks off, this town is going down in the annals of history as the place that stopped him. We can do it, but we must have guns. (**On rise**) Well, there's only one solution. My personal pride must not interfere with the defence of the realm. Call the men in, Sergeant. We march to Marsham Hall.

TELECINE: COUNTRY LANE

Men marching to military version of the signature tune.

FRONT DOOR OF MARSHAM HALL

Opened by butler.

MAINWARING No. 1 Platoon, D Company, Local Defence Volunteers reporting to Colonel Square.

BUTLER Oh! The Tradesman's Entrance is round the back.

COURTYARD

Platoon march in.

MAINWARING Halt. Right turn. Men, you may wonder why I've brought you here. I am placing this unit under the command of Colonel Square. I am doing this because he has not only the knowledge to form you into a fine fighting force but also the rifles, and I know that you'll find in him an officer of rare distinction and quality.

Cut to Colonel in distance on horseback.

COLONEL Charge! **(He charges the platoon brandishing a sabre. The platoon scatter)** Your first lesson, Captain. A mounted man is always superior to one on foot.

The platoon start to form themselves up again.

JONES If you ask me, he's a bit doolally.

MAINWARING You gave us a bit of a start, sir.

COLONEL Exactly, and we're going to give the Hun a start. Fast mobile mounted patrols, striking from the hills and disappearing into the night. Squad! Right turn. Quick march.

MAINWARING Did you hear that, Wilson. It's absurd. Cavalry went out with the ark.

WILSON We must humour him, sir. We need those rifles.

Long shot of stables (telecine still)

Medium length shot of Frazer leads a horse from the stables.

Cut to another stable door. Walker leads horse from the stable. Cut to another stable door. The horse comes out backwards leading Godfrey.

COLONEL These are your chargers. The horse is a noble, faithful and obedient animal. He has marched with man along the road to civilisation, proving himself a staunch and trusting friend.

Cut to Walker looking suspiciously at his horse.

COLONEL Wilson, Mainwaring, get 'em mounted, and walk 'em to the paddock.

WALKER Stand still or I'll turn you into glue.

Cut to shot of Walker endeavouring to mount a horse. The saddle slips.

Cut to Frazer being assisted by Wilson. Wilson turns the stirrup for Frazer. Frazer's foot goes into stirrup on top of Wilson's hand.

Cut to Jones being assisted by Godfrey. They are joined by Mainwaring for business of getting Jones into saddle.

Shot of platoon going through gateway of paddock.

Cut to Wilson, Mainwaring and butler.

WILSON Shall I ring for the ambulance now, sir?

MAINWARING The ground's pretty soft. We may be lucky. I must admit they're fine looking animals. **(To butler)** Did the Colonel breed them?

BUTLER No, sir. He's looking after them for the duration. They belong to Bailey's Circus.

High-angle long shot of horses going round in circle. On cue they peel off into small circles.

Long shot, another angle. In circle. Horses take six paces forward. Then six paces backwards. They all turn towards the centre.

Mid shots of individual members of the platoon coming forward.

Mid shots of members of the platoon on horses walking backwards.

COLONEL Now come on, sit up straight. You're like sacks of sherbet tied up awkward.

He goes up to Walker and hands him his sabre.

COLONEL You. Take this. **(Walker takes the sabre and grips it in his teeth, and continues to grip the horse with both hands)**

COLONEL What the hell are you doing, man? Get that sabre in your right hand.

WALKER **(Through his teeth)** I can't. I've got to hold on to my horse.

There is a low branch in the path of the platoon as they trot round the field. As each horse comes to it, the Colonel cries 'duck'. The first three horses come through ,the riders 'ducked'... the back of the horse, the fourth horse comes through without rider.

Cut to Jones hanging on overhanging branch.

JONES What was that?

Cut to Walker on his horse.

WALKER Don't worry Jonesey, I'll help you.

Walker takes his horse under the branch. In trying to help Jones, he is left hanging from the other side.

FRAZER I beg your pardon, sir. Some of us think we stand more chance against Hitler with you and the pikes, than wi' him and those four-footed dragons.

MAINWARING Thank you, Frazer, that's very loyal of you. I'm only allowing you to go through all this because we must have those rifles.

Pike and Butler come into shot carrying rifles. They are long Arabian or Moorish muzzle-loading muskets.

PIKE Here are the guns, sir. I think you ought to look at them.

Mainwaring takes one.

MAINWARING Great heavens. This is a war not the Desert Song. The man's a maniac. We've been hoodwinked. Wilson, fall in what's left of the platoon, and march them back to the church hall.

Telecine shot of the platoon marching back in great discomfort.

OFFICE. CHURCH HALL

Mainwaring is pacing up and down. He is alone. After a while he stops and listens at the door leading to the main hall. From outside can be heard loud angry voices. He crosses to the mirror.

MAINWARING If you can keep your head, when all around are losing theirs and blaming it on you.

The door opens suddenly. Wilson comes in. Loud voices from outside – he closes the door quickly.

WILSON The men are waiting, sir.

MAINWARING Now don't panic, Wilson. We must keep our heads.

WILSON It was so rash… If only you hadn't promised the men those rifles before the end of the week, sir.

MAINWARING A Commander in the field must take decisions, rash or otherwise. That's what makes him a leader.

The phone rings. Mainwaring and Wilson both rush to the phone. Mainwaring picks it up.

MAINWARING Captain Mainwaring here… Yes, sir… I see… Thank you, sir.

He hangs up.

WILSON **(Eagerly)** News of the rifles, sir?

MAINWARING I'm afraid not, Wilson. Just a message from G.H.Q. to say that we are no longer Local Defence Volunteers. In future we will be known as the Home Guard.

WILSON That's good news, sir.

MAINWARING Yes. I'm sure it will frighten the Germans to death, to know that they no longer have a bunch of unarmed Local Defence Volunteers to deal with. Instead they have got to face an unarmed bunch of Home Guards. Tell the men I'll be out in a minute.

WILSON What are you going to say to them, sir?

MAINWARING I don't know.

Wilson goes.

There is a timid knock on the back door. Mainwaring crosses to the door and pulls it open. An army driver comes in. He is a dreadful, scruffy little weasel of a man. He salutes.

WEASEL Captain Mainwaring, sir.

He pronounces Mainwaring as spelt.

MAINWARING Mannering, man.

WEASEL Well, I've got 500 armbands for you, sir.

Two men come in with two huge bundles of L.D.V. armbands and dump them on the desk.

MAINWARING **(Picking up one)** Local Defence Volunteers. You're a bit late.

WEASEL I got here from G.H.Q. as soon as I could. Sign here will you, sir? And here, sir. And here, and here. Once more, sir.

Mainwaring signs in despair. Pen into close up as he sits at his desk.

WEASEL'S VOICE Leave the rest of the stuff down here by the door. Goodnight, sir.

MAINWARING **(Faraway)** Goodnight.

There is the sound of things being dumped and the door closing. Mainwaring stares into space, then he turns slowly and looks at the door. There is a tinkling sound. Stacked by the door are five rifles. He crosses to them. The main door opens. Loud noise from men. Wilson comes in and closes the door behind him.

WILSON The men are ready, sir. They're waiting for you to talk to them.

Mainwaring picks up two rifles, puts the slings over one shoulder. He puts the other two rifles over the other shoulder, then picks up the last one.

Wilson stares with open mouth.

MAINWARING Very well, Wilson.

WILSON Have you decided what to say to them?

MAINWARING I will now thank the men, and show them that their faith in their leader was not misplaced.

Wilson opens the door, the men's voices are very loud. Mainwaring goes through followed by Wilson. The door closes. Silence. Suddenly there is a terrific cheer.

SERIES ONE **EPISODE FOUR**

Recorded: Monday 6/5/68 (made in black and white)
Original transmission: Wednesday 28/8/68, 8.20–8.50pm
Original viewing figures = 8.1 million

ARTHUR LOWE .... CAPTAIN MAINWARING
JOHN LE MESURIER .... SERGEANT WILSON
CLIVE DUNN .... LANCE CORPORAL JONES
JOHN LAURIE .... PRIVATE FRAZER
JAMES BECK .... PRIVATE WALKER
ARNOLD RIDLEY .... PRIVATE GODFREY
IAN LAVENDER .... PRIVATE PIKE
CAROLINE DOWDESWELL .... JANET KING
CARL JAFFÉ .... CAPTAIN WINOGRODZKI
DENYS PEEK & NIGEL RIDEOUT .... THE GERMAN PILOTS
BILL PERTWEE .... ARP WARDEN
DAVID DAVENPORT .... THE MILITARY POLICE SERGEANT

PLATOON .... COLIN BEAN, HUGH HASTINGS, RICHARD JACQUES, ALEC COLEMAN, HUGH CECIL, VIC TAYLOR, JIMMY MAC, PETER WHITAKER

OTHER MILITARY POLICE .... MICHAEL ELY, JOE SANTO, DENNIS BALCOMBE

THE ENEMY WITHIN THE GATES

• ALEC COLEMAN REMEMBERS •

'As well as playing a member of the Walmington platoon, I was asked to help gather the uniforms which Mainwaring and his men eventually wore. Having agreed a time and date, I attended Berman's theatrical costumiers' premises in Irvine Street, just off London's Leicester Square. There I met George Ward, the BBC wardrobe supervisor working on *Dad's Army*. After a lengthy discussion, we obtained the khaki LDV armbands, later to have the wording Home Guard, to be worn on the right sleeve.

'The denim-type battle dress was then sorted, together with the FS (Field Service) side caps, complete with the cap badge of the Royal West Kent Regiment. The serge khaki battle dress for later issue was also arranged, together with leather waist belts, bayonet frogs, anklets, service respirators (gas masks), army boots, ammunition pouches, haversacks, water bottles, army greatcoats, etc. Much later the shoulder/sleeve titles with battalion number and ID were added to the battle dress blouse.

'The ex-service members of the cast got into their battle dress quite easily. Others had a little difficulty, but we all worked together and the platoon was well turned out.'

ALEC COLEMAN

The Enemy Within the Gates

TELECINE

Newsreel shots of German planes in the air and crashed German planes on the ground.

NARRATOR Day after day the German Luftwaffe keeps up its attacks on our shores and day after day the R.A.F. takes its heavy toll. This beautiful summer of 1940 will be remembered as Britain's finest hour but let us not forget the men on the ground. Apart from the regular army there is Britain's citizen army – the Home Guard.

We see a motorcycle with a box-like construction made of corrugated iron covering the rider's position. There is a round hole in the top.

NARRATOR So far, they haven't been issued with tanks – but are they prepared to wait? Not Tommy Atkins –

The engine is running with much smoke issuing from the exhaust. Jones puts his head through the top and gives the thumbs up sign or Victory V.

NARRATOR – and what they lack in equipment they certainly make up for with ingenuity and British Bulldog fighting spirit.

Jones revs up. Jones, the motorcycle, the top and front piece of the contraption move off. The remainder of the iron box remains standing.

Lance Corporal Jones has a petrol tin strapped to his back. Attached to it is a petrol pump. He is holding a nozzle and a length of garden hose. This is also attached to the petrol tin. Private Pike is holding the pump.

NARRATOR Watch this – it's the latest thing in flamethrowers. A veteran of many campaigns demonstrates the deadly effect of this weapon. So, watch out, Adolf, we're on the home ground now and, what's more, we're preparing a warm welcome.

SWALLOW BANK

Mainwaring sat at his desk in the office.

Pike enters.

PIKE Bottoms.

MAINWARING I beg your pardon, Pike?

PIKE Bottoms. Bottoms. Bottoms. Oh, and tops.

MAINWARING What are you talking about, Pike?

PIKE Bottoms and tops have arrived, sir.

MAINWARING Why didn't you say so in the first place. **(On rise)** Where are they?

PIKE Mr Wilson is just signing for them, sir.

Wilson comes through the door with a parcel of field caps.

Pike starts to unpack.

WILSON I've signed for them, sir. There's 25 pairs.

MAINWARING Well, there's 17 of us. That means 1½ pairs each. How many caps?

PIKE Sixteen, sir.

MAINWARING We are one short. This could cause trouble, Wilson.

WILSON Perhaps we could give the one without a cap an extra pair of trousers, sir.

PIKE As we have only got five rifles, supposing we let the one without a cap have a rifle all the time.

MAINWARING That will only upset our rifle rota. What's more, the man who has a rifle doesn't have a water bottle, so – that in turn will mess up the water bottle rota.

WILSON I can't alter all the rotas.

MAINWARING I agree you've taken great pains with them, Wilson.

WILSON They take a lot of thought. It's about time someone else drew them up.

MAINWARING Take it in turns, you mean? Good idea. You'd better draw up a rota for it.

PIKE Look, sir, why don't you let me take back one of the extra pairs of trousers to G.H.Q. and swap it for a cap.

MAINWARING Good idea, Pike. It's nearly 5.30 in any case. Off you go.

Pike takes a pair of trousers and goes.

OUTSIDE OFFICE DOOR

Pike is just closing it. Janet King comes into the picture. Pike starts to put his cycle clips on.

JANET Where do you think you're going? It's only 5.15.

Wilson follows him through.

WILSON It's all right – you can go too, Miss King.

Mainwaring comes out from the office with two bundles of trousers. He puts them on the counter.

MAINWARING Pull the blinds down, Miss King, then we can sort these trousers out.

Janet pulls down the blinds.

JANET **(At door)** T.T.F.N.

WILSON Good night, Miss King.

PIKE Mind my bike, little girl.

They both go.

WILSON Do you think it's fair, sir, helping ourselves before the others get a chance.

MAINWARING It's not a question of helping ourselves, I just want to make sure of a good fit. They don't seem to be marked in any sizes. (**He sorts out two pairs**)

Wilson takes a pair of trousers. They are now standing side by side behind the counter. We only see them from the waist up. They take off their trousers and put on the others.

MAINWARING I think I've got 'em on back to front.

WILSON Yes, sir, mine are the same.

MAINWARING There's no fly.

WILSON They're at the side, sir.

MAINWARING That's not very convenient, is it?

Phone rings. Mainwaring goes to office.

BANK OFFICE

We see the trousers for the first time. They are very short and very tight and they look like toreador pants. Mainwaring picks up the phone.

MAINWARING What, sir? Yes, sir. I see, sir. Thank you. (**He hangs up**) There's been a slight mistake, Wilson. These trousers weren't meant for us.

Wilson coming through the gap.

WILSON Who were they meant for, sir?

MAINWARING The A.T.S.

CHURCH HALL

The men are lined up in two ranks. Six and six. The front rank has five rifles.

WILSON Platoon, attention. Slope arms.

The five with rifles slope arms and hand the rifles to the next five.

WILSON Slope arms.

The next five slope arms.

WILSON (**Saluting**) The men all ready for inspection, sir.

MAINWARING (**Out of the corner of his mouth**) You've left a rank out, Wilson.

WILSON Sorry, sir. Slope arms.

They do so.

WILSON They really *are* ready now, sir.

MAINWARING Order arms and stand at ease, Sergeant.

WILSON That was really rather a waste of time, wasn't it? Order arms. (**Those with rifles order arms – those without mime it**) Stand at ease.

MAINWARING Gentlemen, good news today. We have an issue of field service caps. Now, after the command fall out, collect your caps from Corporal Jones then gather round for a lecture. Platoon, fall out.

Fall out business.

Jones starts to dish out caps.

WALKER Six and seven-eighths, please.

JONES You'll be lucky – it's large or small.

WALKER In that case I'll take the large.

JONES Big head!

WALKER I'm the same.

Reaction from Jones.

GODFREY Small one please. Oh by the way, which side do you wear it on?

JONES You wear it on your right, Godfrey.

GODFREY What a pity –it's not my best side. (**He puts it on his head**) Does it suit me?

JONES Yes, if you're going to retreat and you've got it on back to front.

FRAZER Oh, you don't expect me to stick that on me head, do you?

JONES You can stick it where you like, mate. I'm just the man that gives them out.

Reaction from Jones and Frazer.

MAINWARING All right, gather round.

They all sit around.

MAINWARING Now then, men, let us sum up our situation. In spite of shortages we have built ourselves into a compact fighting unit. We have five rifles, we've ten rounds of ammunition for each rifle, four water bottles and a cap each, not to mention all the various items of equipment, of weapons which we have improvised for ourselves. Quite an advance on the early days eh? Now tonight, I want to deal with the subject of enemy agents. As you know, they are being dropped in all sorts of disguises – nuns, peasants, police – they might even be disguised as British Army Officers – come up to you and give you stupid instructions.

FRAZER (**To Walker**) How'd you tell the difference?

MAINWARING But don't worry, Frazer, if you keep your head, you can always tell if a man is really British.

Enter Army Captin. He speaks with a very thick European accent. There is a duelling scar on his cheek.

CAPTAIN Excuse, please. Is dis the H.Q. of the First Platoon, D Company, Home Guard?

MAINWARING That's right, sir. What can we do for you?

CAPTAIN I am from H.Q. Area Command. I should like to ask a few questions, please.

MAINWARING Certainly, sir. Lance Corporal Jones, carry on with rifle maintenance. Now, what do you want to know?

CAPTAIN I want to know exactly what weapons you have.

MAINWARING Well, we've got er…

WILSON Just a minute, sir. **(To Captain)** Would you excuse me, Captain? **(He drags Mainwaring away)** How do you know he's not a German spy, sir?

MAINWARING How can he be? He's got a British Army Officer's uniform on.

WILSON Yes, sir, but his accent doesn't go with that uniform.

MAINWARING Don't be a snob, Wilson. This is a democratic army. I mean, he doesn't have to be a public school man to hold a commission. This is 1940.

The Captain stands, glaring at them, just out of earshot.

WILSON But look at his cheek, sir – he's got a duelling scar.

MAINWARING There were some pretty rum goings-on at Oxford in the 20s, you know. But you could be right, Wilson. If you are, we'll soon put a stop to that little game. **(He crosses to the Captain)** So, you want to know what weapons we have?

CAPTAIN Dat is right.

MAINWARING **(Taking rifle from one of his men)** We've got this for a start. Get your hands up.

CAPTAIN But I don't understand.

MAINWARING All right, Corporal Jones, keep him covered. **(He does not know what to do now – there is an awkward pause. He crosses to Wilson)** Wilson! What do you think we ought to do now?

Wilson. I think we ought to have a general staff meeting, sir.

MAINWARING Good idea. Lance Corporal Jones. **(Jones is holding a rifle bayonet a few inches from the Captain's face, and is quivering with excitement)** Jones!

JONES Yes, coming, sir. If he moves as much as a eyelid, let him have it right up… He'll soon change his tune. The old cold steel never fails – they don't like it up 'em, you know.

MAINWARING Control yourself, Jones.

JONES I'm sorry, sir – it's going into action after all these years.

WILSON We had better make sure that he really is a Nazi before we hand him over to the authorities, sir.

MAINWARING There's only one thing for it – we must grill him.

JONES Yes, over a nice slow fire. That'll soon make him talk. We used to do that in the Sudan.

MAINWARING Pull yourself together Jones, we're not brutes. **(He takes a Home Guard Manual out of his pocket)** Everything will be done according to the Geneva Convention. **(He is thumbing his way through the pages)** Here we are – interrogation of enemy suspects. This is it. The pronunciation test. We'll try this. **(They cross to the Captain)** Now I want you to say after me just a few simple English words.

CAPTAIN A few simple English words.

MAINWARING I haven't started yet. Now say soothe.

CAPTAIN Sooze.

MAINWARING Wrong.

CAPTAIN Wrong.

MAINWARING Wretch.

CAPTAIN Wretch.

MAINWARING Rats.

CAPTAIN Rets.

MAINWARING No, rats.

CAPTAIN I said rets.

MAINWARING Those.

CAPTAIN Zose.

Reaction from Wilson.

MAINWARING Now, what would Mrs Mop say to you?

CAPTAIN She would say 'Can I do you now, sir?'.

JONES I got a good one – who won the boat race in 1938?

CAPTAIN Oxford.

JONES Blimey, he's right.

CAPTAIN It was raining at the time.

JONES Was it?

MAINWARING Who the hell are you?

CAPTAIN I am Captain Winogrodski of the Free Polish Forces attached to G.H.Q.

MAINWARING Well why didn't you say so?
We're very sorry, Captain, but it was an understandable mistake.

CAPTAIN I would call it a stupid mistake. As you know, many German airmen from crashed planes are landing everywhere. However the area commander is a little anxious in case any British pilots are shot by mistake. It has not happened so far but a stitch in time saves something....

MAINWARING Nine.

CAPTAIN Nein?

MAINWARING A stitch in time...

CAPTAIN ... So he has issued an order that lone parachutists are not to be shot down before they have a chance to disclose themselves. Furthermore a bounty of £10 will be paid for every Nazi airman captured alive and in good condition. That is all. **(He clicks his heels and hands a paper to Mainwaring)** Good day to you, Captain.

WALKER Blimey, did you hear that? A tenner a time for every Nazi airman. Here, Jonesey, you and I are on patrol tonight. Keep your eyes open – I should bring your reading glasses.

JONES Don't you start on me.

RIVER BANK

Walker, Jones and Pike come into the picture. Jones has his assegai. Walker and Pike a rifle each.

WALKER Blimey I must have a rest, my feet are killing me.

He starts to light a cigarette and Jones jumps on him.

JONES Put that light out. A sniper might see it.

WALKER Have you gone barmy or something? There's no snipers around here. You're not in the flippin' Sudan now you know.

JONES No, and it's just as well. You wouldn't last five minutes.

WALKER I could shoot Fuzzie Wuzzies the same as you, you know. Poor blighters only had spears.

JONES It wasn't only the Fuzzie Wuzzies, mate. There was flies, desert sores, malaria, dysentery, gippy tummy.

WALKER You should have packed it up then, shouldn't you?

JONES We didn't pack it up 'cause we were soldiers. There was a field marshall's baton in every knapsack.

WALKER You sound as if you'd have been better off with a bedpan.

The captain appears unexpectedly behind them.

CAPTAIN Put dem up.

They all jump.

WALKER Ah. Oh, it's you. **(He's very nervous)** You shouldn't do that. **(Indicating Jones)** You could frighten him to death at his time of life.

JONES I'm all right. It's you what jumped out of your trousers.

CAPTAIN I could have shot you – both. You are supposed to keep a lookout like soldiers, not talk like old women. You will be reported for slacking. Your names?

JONES Jones, sir.

PIKE Pike, sir.

CAPTAIN And you?

WALKER AND JONES **(At the same time)** Smith/Walker.

WALKER Oh, thanks very much.

CAPTAIN It is no use you try to give me falsies. I remember you all. **(To Pike)** You are the baby. **(To Jones)** You are the old grandpa. **(To Walker)** And you are the one who jumped out of his trousers. Wake your ideas up. **(He goes)**

WALKER There was no call for him to be like that.

JONES He shouldn't speak that way to an N.C.O. in front of his men. Against Queen's Regs that is.

WALKER King's Regs, you silly old muffin. What's the time?

PIKE Half past one.

WALKER Oh gawd another hour and a half. We might as well pack it up, there'll be no German planes over tonight.

The sirens start.

JONES Why don't you keep your big mouth shut.

PIKE Listen, can you hear a plane, Mr Jones?

JONES Yes. If he comes low enough I'll give him one right in the seat of his Heinkel. It's coming this way – you cowardly bastards.

WALKER It sounds like one of ours.

JONES Brave boys – good luck, mate.

We hear the whistle of the bomb. It flashes and explodes some distance away.

WALKER That wasn't one of ours.

JONES That dropped in Acock Wood, didn't it?

WALKER Here, the search lights are looking for him. **(He calls to searchlights)** You're a bit late, chum. He could have killed my friend and me with that bomb. **(Sound of machine gunning)** 'Ere, he's shooting at us.

JONES Machine gunning innocent women and children. They don't care.

PIKE No, it's one of our fighters gunning him.

JONES Give it to him, son.

There is another burst.

WALKER He'll head for home now.

JONES Yeah – one smell of our fighters and they're off. Cowardly Bosche.

PIKE (**Pointing up**) Look, Mr Jones, what's that white thing floating down?

WALKER Oh my gawd, it's a parachute.

PIKE Shall I fire, Mr Jones?

JONES No, you heard what the Captain said – we've got to let him expose himself. He might be one of ours.

There is a loud splash.

PIKE He's landed on the water.

JONES (**Calling out**) Surrender or we fire. (**No answer**) Say if you're German. Are you British? If so, say so.

No answer.

WALKER Can you see what it is?

JONES No it's too dark. Can you, lad?

PIKE Yes I can – it's coming towards us. I think I ought to fire, Mr Jones.

JONES (**Shouting**) I'll give you one more chance. Halt or we fire. (**No answer**) All right, lads let 'im have it.

Pike fires – there's a terrible noise which rises into the air.

WALKER Blimey, he's taking off again. It must be a secret weapon.

JONES That must have been his spirit rising up.

PIKE Look there's something white floating in the water. I think I've killed him.

WALKER There goes our ten quid.

JONES You'd better go in and get him.

WALKER Eh?

JONES Go fetch him.

WALKER That'll be nice.

Hold on Pike and Jones as we hear Walker splashing in the water.

WALKER Cor blimey.

PIKE What is it?

WALKER You shot a bleeding swan. (**He plonks it on the bank**)

PIKE Killing swans is against the law isn't it, Mr Jones?

JONES Yes, that's serious that is. All swans belong to the King, swans do.

PIKE What are we going to do with it?

WALKER I'm going to take it home, pluck it, dress it, hang it up for a few days and then I'm going to roast it with some potatoes and sprouts. Very tasty, very sweet.

PIKE What about the King?

WALKER He's always eating it, think he makes do on snook do you? Don't you want your share then?

JONES Of course.

WALKER You keep your mouth shut. I'm going to hide it, and then we can pick it up later. (**Picks up the swan and they go**)

JONES All right, come on... I still think...

Two German airmen enter. They are dressed in flying suits, each is carrying a small valise. They take off their flying suits and take a greatcoat out of their valise, put them on and bundle the suits back into the case. The greatcoats are quite plain. They speak in German – English subtitles at the bottom of the screen indicating what they are saying.

SECOND GERMAN (**Look at the time. Typical British inefficiency. It is now ten minutes since we have been shot down and nobody has captured us.**)

Mensch kuck mal die Zeit! Typisch britische Untüchtigkeit. Es sind nun schon zehn Minuten her, seit wir abgeschossen worden sind, und keiner hat uns gefangen – genommen.

FIRST GERMAN (**No wonder they are losing the war.**)

Kein wunder sie verlieren den Krieg.

SECOND GERMAN (**Ssh... what's that?**)

Ssh... was ist das?

There is a rustle in the bushes, they slowly part. We see Jones' black face, he is holding his assegai. He stares at them.

FIRST GERMAN (**My God. We took the wrong turning – we are in Africa.**)

Mein Gott, wir sind verkehrt abgebogen. Wir sind in Afrika.

SECOND GERMAN (**Don't be absurd. It is too cold. Don't you see the British are using Colonial troops, and armed with spears, how can they hope to win the war?**)

Sei nicht so blöd! Es ist zu kalt. Weisst du denn nicht, das die Engländer Kolonial truppen brauchen, die mit Speeren bewaffnet sind?! Wie können die denn hoffen, den Krieg zu gewinnen!

Jones comes through the bushes and points the spear at them.

JONES Who are you?

FIRST GERMAN Luftwaffe.

JONES Luftwaffe. Luft... I thought so! You're Jerries. Get back or I'll give it up you.

He waves his assegai at them. He is getting very excited and starts to dance up and down babbling to himself.

SECOND GERMAN (**Is he doing a war dance?**)

Führt der einen Kriegstanz auf?

JONES I've caught two Jerries. Go on get back or you'll have it up you.

Walker comes into the picture

WALKER What's the matter, Corp?

JONES I caught two Jerries.

WALKER Blimey, 20 quid's worth.

JONES What do you mean?

WALKER The bounty – £10 for every Nazi airman captured in good nick.

JONES I'd forgotten all about that.

WALKER Well I hadn't. How are we going to take them along?

PIKE Cut their trouser buttons off.

JONES Good idea. Hold that.

Jones gives spear to Walker. Advances on the Germans with his knife. They leap back.

WALKER Hang on, Jack. They're not sure how far you're going.

JONES That's cause I haven't made up my mind.

WALKER Don't do it, Jack. You're not in your butcher's shop now. Here you two (**He indicates the cases**) Pick 'em up and hold 'em over your heads. (**He mimes**) Over your head. Now you keep them covered, Pikey. March (**To Jones**) You go next – I'll feel safer.

SIDE OFFICE. CHURCH HALL

Wilson is at the desk. There is a knock at the outside door.

MAINWARING (**Off**) Are you there Wilson?

WILSON Yes, sir.

MAINWARING I'm coming in.

WILSON Good.

MAINWARING Well put the light out then.

WILSON Oh, sorry, sir. (**He crosses to the light and puts it out**) Come in. (**The door handle rattles**)

MAINWARING The damn door's locked.

WILSON Just a minute, sir. I'll unlock it. (**He bumps into something**) Ouch.

MAINWARING What's the matter?

WILSON I can't find the key.

MAINWARING Well put the light on – see where the key is, put the lights off and open the door.

WILSON Yes, sir. Ouch.

MAINWARING What is it now?

WILSON I can't find the light, sir.

MAINWARING This is ludicrous. It's by the wireless.

WILSON Ouch… I've found it. Ah…

The light goes on. He sights on the key of the outside door, puts out the light, and departs.

WILSON Coming, sir. (**There's a rattle of the key**) I've found the key, sir. (**He unlocks the door**) You can come in, sir. (**He opens the door, there is nobody there, he looks outside**) Are you there, sir?

MAINWARING (**By the door into the hall**) No, I'm here. I came in the other way.

Light on.

WARDEN (**Off screen**) Put that light out. (**Mainwaring puts out the light**)

Light off.

Wilson slams the door.

MAINWARING Is it shut?

WILSON Yes, sir. (**The light goes on**)

Light on.

MAINWARING We must fix up a light trap – blankets or something.

WILSON Anything happening, sir?

MAINWARING Search lights are still combing the sky. They don't seem to catch anything.

Enter Jones in great excitement from church hall. He salutes.

JONES Permission to speak, sir?

MAINWARING Carry on, Jones.

JONES We collared a couple of Bosches, sir.

MAINWARING You what?

JONES A couple of parachuters. They are in the hall. When they saw this they come quiet as mouses. They don't like it up 'em you see.

They go into the church hall. The two German prisoners are being covered by Pike and Godfrey.

Mainwaring sees Germans and crosses.

MAINWARING Keep 'em covered, Pike. You too, Godfrey.

The Germans mutter in German.

MAINWARING I don't know what you are talking about, but you're my prisoners. You will be properly treated but I must warn you not to get up to any of your Nazi tricks, or I can't answer for the consequences. (**To Wilson**) We must get on to H.Q. as quickly as possible. Keep them covered Pike and Godfrey. Walker and Jones you come with me and make a report.

They go into the office leaving Germans covered by Pike and Godfrey.

MAINWARING Fine night's work eh, Wilson? Well done, Jones and Walker. Well done indeed. You wait until H.Q. hears about this.

WALKER Don't forget to ask for our 20 quid, sir. (**Mainwaring takes up the receiver and jiggles the rest**)

MAINWARING It seems dead.

WILSON It is, sir. They cut it off.

MAINWARING Cut it off!

JONES **(Saluting)** Very good, sir. **(He moves to the door)**

WALKER Come back here, you silly old fool. I'll explain to him, sir.

WILSON The bill wasn't paid so they cut it off.

MAINWARING But don't they know there's a war on. They can't cut it off. We are a military unit. This is an emergency.

WILSON It's the Vicar's phone, sir, and he can't afford to pay it with this invasion scare. He has had to stop all his campanology.

MAINWARING Eh?

WILSON He can't ring his bells, sir.

MAINWARING What's that got to do with him not being able to pay the phone bill?

WILSON Well, sir, the Vicar is the editor of the Ring-a-Ding monthly and it isn't being published any more. His income has dropped.

MAINWARING But here I am in command of a unit with two valuable prisoners and my communications have been severed.

JONES Permission to speak, sir?

MAINWARING Yes, Jones.

JONES There's a phone at my shop. I'll ring 'em for you.

MAINWARING Well done, Jones. You go to it. **(Jones salutes)**

JONES Yes, sir. **(He goes out through outside door)**

WARDEN'S VOICE **(Off)** Put that bloody light off. **(Walker dives and puts the light out)**

WILSON It's too late now, man, put it on again. **(The lights are put on)**

Jones re-enters.

ALL Put that light out.

MAINWARING What's the matter, Jones?

JONES **(Saluting)** Permission to speak, sir?

MAINWARING Of course you have got permission, blast you.

WALKER There's no need to talk to him like that, sir, not at his time of life.

WILSON I'm sure Captain Mainwaring meant no offence.

MAINWARING What's the matter, Jones?

JONES I don't know the H.Q. number.

MAINWARING **(Writing)** Here it is – very sorry, Jones. You have done very well tonight. I'm very proud of you.

JONES **(Touched)** Thank you, sir.

MAINWARING With men like you this country has no need to fear for the future.

JONES Thank you, sir. You can have half a pound of liver when I come back.

MAINWARING Thank you, Jones. Now don't lose any time. **(Jones salutes and dives to the door)**

ALL Lights.

Irate Warden enters.

WARDEN Who's in charge here?

WILSON This is Captain Mainwaring.

WARDEN Oh, blimey, you again. If I have any more trouble from this place I am going to remove that bulb – understand?

MAINWARING I think you would be exceeding your authority if you as much as lay a finger on it.

WARDEN There's enemy aircraft circling overhead. They have already demolished several haystacks in this vicinity, and if I didn't know otherwise I'd say you were signalling to the enemy.

WILSON I'm sure we all have our jobs to do, Warden, but aren't you going a bit far?

MAINWARING It may interest you to know that we have two enemy airmen in the hall there.

WARDEN I don't care if you have got Goerring and Goebels. If I see that light on again I'm going to extinguish it.

MAINWARING I'm in the middle of an operational emergency. Get off my premises.

WARDEN I'm going, but I have warned you. **(He goes)**

ANOTHER VOICE **(Off)** Put that light out!

MAINWARING Now has anyone interrogated those two outside to see if there are any more roaming around the countryside?

WILSON I don't think so, sir. **(They go into the hall)**

Only Pike is there – Mainwaring sees empty hall.

MAINWARING Where are they?

PIKE Mr Godfrey has gone outside with them, sir.

WILSON Gone outside – what on earth for?

PIKE They wanted to tinkle, sir.

MAINWARING Tinkle?

PIKE Well, that's what my mum calls it.

WILSON When she says tinkle, sir, she means…

MAINWARING **(Interrupting)** I know very well what she means.

PIKE He went with them, sir, with his rifle. Expect they'll be back in a second or two. They've been gone quite a while.

Godfrey puts his head round the door.

GODFREY I say, have they come back?

PIKE No, Mr Godfrey.

GODFREY Rotters. **(He turns to go)**

MAINWARING Godfrey, come here. Get after them, Wilson. Take whoever is on guard with you.

WILSON Yes, sir.

MAINWARING Come here, Godfrey. Now, what happened?

GODFREY Well, sir, the foreign gentlemen wanted to wash their hands...

MAINWARING Why didn't you tell them to wait?

GODFREY Well, we are not beasts are we, sir?

MAINWARING Go on.

GODFREY So I took them to the outside convenience, sir. I shoved one down the spout.

MAINWARING One of the Germans?

GODFREY No, a bullet, sir. It was very dark but I stayed as close as I could in the circumstances.

MAINWARING You went in with them of course?

GODFREY No, sir. They locked the door.

MAINWARING Didn't you think that was suspicious?

GODFREY Not really, I usually lock the door myself, sir.

MAINWARING Go on.

GODFREY They seemed to be taking a long time so I coughed, sir – sort of dropping a hint as it were.

MAINWARING You should have done a damn sight more than that.

GODFREY I did, sir, I called out to them. When they didn't answer I went around to the window at the back.

MAINWARING And of course it was open.

GODFREY No, sir, it was closed and barred.

MAINWARING Then how did they get out?

GODFREY Well, while I was round at the little window at the back I can only conjecture that they must have slipped out of the little door at the front.

MAINWARING Holy suffering cats. **(Enter Wilson)** Did you find them, Wilson?

WILSON No, sir, I just remembered I haven't got a rifle with me. **(He takes one)** Will you excuse me, sir.

MAINWARING Get after 'em, man. You too, Pike. **(Pike and Wilson go)** Oh great Scott! The military police will be here in a minute to collect the prisoners – I'm going to look a right fool.

GODFREY I'm terribly sorry, sir.

WALKER What about if I ring up and tell them it was all a practical joke?

MAINWARING We are the practical joke I'm afraid –

CAPTAIN **(Outside)** Links Rechts, Links Rechts.

GODFREY Look, sir, they've come back.

The two pilots are marched in by the Captain.

CAPTAIN – Halt... I have just recaptured these two men who say they escaped from your custody. Is that correct?

MAINWARING I'm afraid so.

CAPTAIN I don't know what sort of an army you're in, Captain Mainwaring, but I don't think it is the same as mine. I have no difficulty in surprising your patrols – you still have no guard outside your headquarters – I have complaints from A.R.P.s that you are signalling to the enemy and you allow prisoners to escape. All this inefficiency will be reported. Furthermore, I shall claim the bounty for these men myself.

MAINWARING **(Trying to summon a little dignity)** I see. Well I find your attitude high-handed to say the least and if you have any further comments to make you'll find me in my orderly room.

CAPTAIN Good – it will leave me free to interrogate these men.

MAINWARING See they're well covered this time, Walker.

WALKER Sir!

CAPTAIN Huh. **(Mainwaring goes)**

Captain (in German) commences to interrogate them, asking them their names, their unit, their type of plane and how many in the crew, etc. They will only give rank and number. A Military Police Sergeant enters with three Corporals. Seeing the three talking German he turns to Walker.

SERGEANT You got some Jerry prisoners here, mister?

WALKER That's right, Sarge.

SERGEANT Blimey, three of them. The note only said two. Must have been a bad line.

WALKER **(Suddenly catching on)** Yeh, it must have been, Sergeant.

SERGEANT All right, you lot, outside in the van. **(They continue to talk)** Oi, outside in the van. **(To first Corporal)** Hey Bob, this one's dressed as a British Officer.

CAPTAIN I am a British Officer, you fool.

SERGEANT You don't sound like one, does he, Bob? **(To Walker)** Did he come with the other two?

WALKER As a matter of fact he did.

CAPTAIN Listen, I am a British Officer, attached to H.Q. Area Command.

SERGEANT Look out – he's got a gun. Have it off him, Bob.

The Corporal takes the gun out of the Captain's holster.

CAPTAIN What are you doing?

SERGEANT **(To Walker)** You shouldn't have let him keep it, you know.

WALKER Sorry, Sarge. I'm a bit new to this game.

CAPTAIN I am a British Officer. Here, look at my papers. Here's my identity card, my railway warrant to London for the leave tomorrow and a letter from the lady I am going to see in Golder's Green.

SERGEANT Look at these, Bob. What do you think?

WALKER **(Looking over his shoulder)** You have got to hand it to 'em, Sarge, they are very thorough.

SERGEANT You're dead right. In the van with him.

CAPTAIN **(As he is dragged off to van)** I protest, you are making a mistake. Can I do you now, sir? Cambridge won the boat race in 1938.

SERGEANT Don't know when they are beat, do they?

MAINWARING **(Enters)** What's all the commotion?

SERGEANT Just putting the Jerries in the van, sir. Now, there's your receipt. **(He hands him small piece of paper)** Pop along to your Brigade H.Q. with that and you'll get 30 quid bounty.

MAINWARING Thirty pounds?

SERGEANT That's right, three prisoners – £30 **(Salutes)** Goodnight, sir.

Mainwaring looks enquiringly at Walker.

MAINWARING *Three* prisoners?

WALKER We had a stroke of luck sir – another one turned up.

MAINWARING And how did you talk the captain out of his share?

WALKER He sort of talked himself out of it, sir.

Enter Jones with a parcel.

JONES There's your liver, sir, and I've chucked in a bit of kidney for good measure.

WALKER I'll round you up a couple of black market chops and you can have a mixed grill.

Enter Wilson, breathless...

WILSON They have vanished into thin air, sir.

MAINWARING Don't worry, Wilson, they are on their way to H.Q. plus another one that Walker managed to round up.

JONES Blimey, you're not getting *them* on the black market, are you?

The All Clear sounds.

MAINWARING Well, there they go – quite an eventful evening.

They walk through to side office.

SIDE OFFICE

MAINWARING I think as we have got an extra £10 we could afford to spend five on a celebration dinner for the platoon.

WALKER **(Taking out notebook)** Would you care to order now, sir?

MAINWARING What do you suggest?

WALKER Well, for a fiver, sir, I could do you a nice medieval dinner.

MAINWARING What's that?

WALKER Very rare luxury, sir. Roast swan.

Jones and Pike exchange looks.

SERIES ONE **EPISODE FIVE**

Recorded: Monday 13/5/68 (made in black and white)

Original transmission: Wednesday 4/9/68, 8.20–8.50pm

(This episode was originally planned for transmission on Wednesday 3/7/68)

Original viewing figures = 8.8 million

ARTHUR LOWE . . . . CAPTAIN MAINWARING
JOHN LE MESURIER . . . . SERGEANT WILSON
CLIVE DUNN . . . . LANCE CORPORAL JONES
JOHN LAURIE . . . . PRIVATE FRAZER
JAMES BECK . . . . PRIVATE WALKER
ARNOLD RIDLEY . . . . PRIVATE GODFREY
IAN LAVENDER . . . . PRIVATE PIKE
JANET DAVIES . . . . MRS PIKE
MARTIN WYLDECK . . . . MAJOR REGAN
PATRICK WADDINGTON . . . . BRIGADIER
EDWARD SINCLAIR . . . . CARETAKER
THÉRÈSE MCMURRAY . . . . GIRL AT THE WINDOW

PLATOON . . . . COLIN BEAN, HUGH HASTINGS, RICHARD JACQUES, ALEC COLEMAN, HUGH CECIL, VIC TAYLOR, JIMMY MAC, PETER WHITAKER, CHRIS FRANKS, DAVID SEAFORTH

TRAINING SERGEANT . . . . CHARLES FINCH

THE SHOWING UP OF CORPORAL JONES

• PETER SINCLAIR PERRY REMEMBERS •

'Edward Sinclair was a truly wonderful husband to Gladys and an equally wonderful dad to his two sons: Keith and myself. Maurice Yeatman, "The Verger", on the other hand, really was a miserable old devil. Yet, despite these contrary personalities, there were some very recognisable traits from "The Verger" in Edward "The Family Man".

'How could this be? It's surely to do with the lifelong process that gives an actor the tools to create the diversity of characters that is an actor's lot. An actor is like a sponge, soaking up the nuances of other people's personalities.

'Ted certainly started this process at an early age. As Gladys recalls, "Ted was a choirboy from the age of 12 at St Luke's Church in his hometown of Kingston. The church verger, Mr Hedges, was forever at the mercy of the choirboys who constantly drove him mad by the usual teasing and pranks that boys are so expert at. They argued that Mr Hedges deserved all he got for being such a miserable old devil.

'Indeed, in later life Ted often reminisced with Gladys that Mr Hedges was a role model for the characterisation of his *Dad's Army* portrayal of Maurice Yeatman. Keith and I also remember seeing a particular trait in both "The Verger" and our dad. It's fair to say that we weren't always perfect. Many parents of our era, when driven to despair by naughty offspring, would administer a clip round the ear, or sometimes even more forceful reproachments. Ted, however, never resorted to any such tactics but he did employ something that we would recall as being every bit as devastating: the look!

'As we got older, Keith and I remember reacting to this form of chastisement with humour rather than fear – somewhat defeating the objective. Fortunately, as the Sinclair household was always a fun place to be, it became increasingly difficult for Edward to maintain this facial weapon as a means of maintaining order. It must have come as a relief to Ted to be able to re-introduce "the look" with such devastating effect on the residents of Walmington-on-Sea.

'The Sinclair clan moved several times but, at each home, Ted was always the perfect neighbour – to an almost obsessional degree. He was always thoughtful of the neighbours' feelings and was anxious that his boys didn't encroach upon their space – both physical and auditory. He would regularly remind us to "keep the noise down" and "to park the bikes on our side of the drive". It didn't always work but this bossy trait was definitely evident in Ted's TV persona as "The Verger", albeit with a considerable degree more humour and warmth at home.

'Ted was the ever-generous host and the Sinclair homes were always places for friends of all ages to congregate. His interest in other people was deep rooted and he would spend hours with anyone needing a helping hand – very much the David Copperfield character of Barkis.

'"Barkis is willing" is a truism of the Charles Dickens character as well as Ted, unless it was to do any DIY – something he avoided at all costs. This aversion to DIY was, in part, due to his poor health that gave rise to breathlessness.

'However, being the consummate professional, he managed to hide this breathless condition well, throughout his life as an actor, as the show must go on. The whole family has inherited this attitude.

'One great advantage of having an actor around the house was that the family was generally able to spend more quality time with Ted than "normal" families could with their husbands/fathers. He was always the super optimist, turning even the most dreadful of domestic calamities into almost comic interludes. In this respect, perhaps Ted did bring his work home but it certainly made the Sinclair home an interesting place to be for anyone fortunate enough to cross the threshold.

'His untimely death was a great tragedy to us all, but his humour and zest for life has been carried on not only by all of us, but by our respective children as well. Like Ted, any excuse for a party and out comes the wine! He would have liked that.'

PETER SINCLAIR PERRY

The Showing up of Corporal Jones

TELECINE

Newsreel shots of civilians digging for victory.

NARRATOR All over Britain the civilian population are digging for victory. Every square inch of space that can be used for growing food is under intensive cultivation. Nothing is too small, nothing too humble. Every ounce of food grown at home means home security.

TELECINE

Close up of window with paper on. There is a window box underneath with carrot tops sticking out. The window opens. Little old lady waters the box with a watering can. Camera pans down to receive close up of Mainwaring and Wilson. They also have carrot tops in their steel helmets. They crouch against a wall. Water is poured over them.

TELECINE: ALLOTMENT

Jones and three others are digging for victory.

NARRATOR Here we see some members of the Home Guard working on their allotments. But all the time they are on the alert and they are always ready for a fair fight. That is to say, one Home Guard for four Germans.

Jones suddenly stops listening and points to the sky with a dramatic gesture. He calls to the others.

NARRATOR Hello, what's this! They've spotted a low-flying enemy plane.

The men grab their tin hats and rifles and take up positions with their rifles pointed in the air. They fire. Several birds fall.

NARRATOR A lucky escape for Jerry. But it's pigeon pie for supper for the boys of the Home Guard.

Jones and co. are waving the pigeons in triumph.

SIDE OFFICE. CHURCH HALL

Wilson – while glancing at the daily paper is idly switching on the radio.

From set: Lord Haw-Haw's Voice: 'Germany calling? Germany Calling? Germany calling? Here are the Reich stations, Hamburg, Bremen, Munich.'

Mainwaring enters. He listens for a few seconds.

MAINWARING Wilson!

WILSON (Quickly turns off radio) I – I just turned it on, sir. That's how it was tuned. It's the Vicar's.

MAINWARING Good Heavens!

WILSON It must be a mistake.

MAINWARING All the same, we'll have to watch him. That sermon of his on Sunday was pretty seditious.

WILSON I didn't notice anything, sir.

MAINWARING With Hitler just the other side of the Channel, he could have chosen a better subject than the parting of the waves. Wilson, Major Regan from Area H.Q. is paying us a visit. (He flourishes an order paper) I expect it's because the platoon's on coastal watch tonight. We're responsible for the section from Stone's Amusement Arcade to the west to The Jolly Roger Pier to the east. (He points to the pier on the map) That's our weak spot – that pier. Put our best man that end. Who's on first?

WILSON Godfrey and Frazer.

MAINWARING Who's the better of the two in your judgement?

WILSON In the ordinary way of things, Godfrey. Unfortunately he has this bladder trouble.

MAINWARING A little risky. The invasion might start while he had his back turned. Put Frazer that end.

Pike puts his head round the door.

PIKE Sir. They've arrived. The uniform tops. They're here.

MAINWARING By Jove that's good news, isn't it, Wilson? Bring them here and we'll unpack them.

PIKE (Out of vision) The men have unpacked them already, sir.

MAINWARING They've no right to. I'm the officer, you're the sergeant – we should have had first pick, Wilson. Let's see what they look like then.

JONES Permission to speak, sir?

MAINWARING Now now, Jones. Get the men fallen in. (As the men are falling in, Mainwaring turns to Wilson) They couldn't have come at a better time, Wilson. Just when we're going on coast watch.

WILSON Yes, sir. (Looking at his ill-fitting jacket) Instead of looking like partisans, we can look like Fred Karno's Army.

JONES Here, I didn't tell you to fall out – fall out!

MAINWARING Damn it. We should have been here first. They've left me the one without buttons.

WILSON Same here, sir.

MAINWARING Platoon, 'shun!

The platoon are lined up at attention. The jackets are done up at the belt – nobody has buttons.

JONES Permission to speak, sir?

MAINWARING Not now, Jones. Don't any of the jackets button?

SQUAD No, sir.

JONES That's what I wanted permission to speak about.

WALKER They usually have little rings – to 'old 'em in.

MAINWARING Well, this isn't going to stop us. We all have buttons at home, and this is the sort of occasion that brings out the very best in the women folk. We'll parade back here in 45 minutes and I know we're all going to have everything absolutely buttoned up, eh?

JONES All buttoned up.

WILSON Nice little joke, sir. Squad, 'shun.

Jones comes to attention the usual beat later.

WILSON Squad – stand at ease.

The same business.

WILSON Squad, 'shun.

MAINWARING **(To Wilson)** Leave him for now.

Mainwaring and Wilson look proudly at the squad.

MAINWARING Soldiers! That's what they look like, Wilson. Soldiers.

He inspects Jones and passes to Pike. Being large, his jacket is rather small.

MAINWARING **(He moves to Walker)** What's that cap badge you're wearing, Walker?

WALKER One and six, sir.

MAINWARING I beg your pardon.

WALKER If you want to fit out the whole mob, they'll come at 14 bob a dozen.

MAINWARING What regiment is it?

WALKER Anything you like. Coldstreams, Durham Light Infantry. Grenadiers, R.A.M.C. Tanks…

MAINWARING Don't you understand, Walker. Wearing a badge to which you are not entitled is an offence.

WALKER Well, I wouldn't have called it an offence. A liberty, yes.

WILSON Take it off.

Mainwaring passes to Frazer who has duffle coat wooden pegs in his denims.

FRAZER They came off my old patrol coat. I've not worn it since Jutland. The moths got to it.

MAINWARING Lucky you didn't get wood worm. **(He passes to Godfrey who has mother-of-pearl and diamante dress studs and cufflinks to replace the buttons)** A little flamboyant isn't it, Godfrey.

GODFREY My dress studs, sir. The best I could do on the spur of the moment. I'm afraid the diamonds are not real.

MAINWARING Stand at ease! I think you'll all agree this is a great moment. A great step forward in our progress towards fighting power. It's very well timed, because we take over the defence of a vulnerable stretch of our beloved land. Tonight we are responsible for England between The Jolly Roger Pier and Stone's Amusement Arcade. We have 15 minutes before we move off to the Guard Post at the Novelty Rock Emporium. I think we can well employ our time smartening ourselves up and checking our weapons. Fall the men out, Corporal Jones.

JONES Sah! Platoon 'shun! Fall out!

MAINWARING **(To Wilson)** I think we'd do well to check our weapons.

JONES I'll bring your bangers in a minute, sir.

SMALL OFFICE

MAINWARING Now let me see. Waterbottle, gas-mask, knife, knuckle-duster, bicycle chain, cosh, sandwiches.

Voices can be heard from outside the door. They belong to Frank and Mrs Pike.

MRS PIKE Now you keep it on, do you hear me? **(As they enter)**

PIKE But, Mum, it's such a silly colour.

MRS PIKE Nonsense, Mr Mainwaring won't mind.

Mrs Pike pushes Pike into the room. He is wearing a balaclava helmet with rabbit's ears on it.

MRS PIKE You don't think he looks silly, do you, Mr Mainwaring?

MAINWARING Well – the colour is a little startling.

MRS PIKE Well he must have something to keep him warm if he's here on coast watch all night. I made them just before the war for the Bunny Babe's Dancing Display. They make lovely balaclava helmets, don't you think?

WILSON Yes, excellent.

MRS PIKE I'm so glad you like them, because I've brought one for you, Arthur.

MAINWARING Ha! It should suit you admirably.

MRS PIKE And one for you, sir.

MAINWARING Oh no. Well, it's very kind of you, Mrs Pike, but I don't think the ears will fit under my steel helmet.

MRS PIKE Don't be silly. I'm going to cut the ears off. **(She produces scissors)** Now come on, try them on.

MAINWARING Really, I don't think –

MRS PIKE **(To Wilson)** Come on, put your ears on, Arthur. **(She hands them the helmets)**

WILSON Look – must I...

MRS PIKE I don't want you to have any more trouble with your chest. That time you went out on manoeuvres you were awake all night with your coughing – you said.

WILSON **(Quickly)** All right, I'll try it on. **(He quickly grabs the helmet and they both put them on)**

MRS PIKE Now we'll just snip those ears off.

She pushes the three of them into line and goes to cut the ears off Frank's helmet. But can't reach properly.

MRS PIKE It's no good. I can't see what I'm doing. You'll have to get down a bit. **(The three of them crouch down)** That's better.

There is a knock at the door. Frazer enters.

FRAZER Major Regan, sir. From Area Headquarters. **(Regan enters close behind him)**

MAJOR REGAN Good evening.

He sees the three rabbit-eared men.

MAINWARING She was just going to cut our ears off, sir.

MAJOR Really.

MRS PIKE You see, I made them for the Bunny Babes.

MAJOR I see.

MAINWARING But then she thought they'd make good balaclava helmets.

MAJOR Pink – with ears on?

MRS PIKE Well, you can take the ears off yourselves, can't you? I'll just run along.

FRAZER I'll away and put on my Winnie the Pooh set.

Mrs Pike turns to Wilson.

MRS PIKE Tuck it well in.

Mrs Pike goes. Pike follows her out.

The door closes.

MAJOR I'm sure they're very cosy. But I don't think pantomime hats are very good for discipline.

MAINWARING I assure you discipline here is absolutely first class, and...

Door bursts open. Walker comes into the room.

WALKER There you are, Mr Mainwaring. I nearly forgot. Half a dozen eggs and a half pound block of milk chocolate. And here's your fags, Sarge. **(He chucks the sergeant a packet)** You can settle up with me later. I'll just make a note. **(He jots in his notebook. Major taps him on his shoulder)**

MAJOR **(Grittily)** Haven't you forgotten something?

WALKER I'll take your order in a minute.

MAJOR You've forgotten to salute your Commanding Officer.

WALKER **(Seeing his rank)** Cor blimey! **(He salutes Mainwaring. Walker salutes Major. Mainwaring salutes Wilson)**

MAJOR Now look here, Mainwaring. What's going on here?

The door opens again and Jones enters. He slaps a large packet on the desk.

JONES There you are, Mr Mainwaring. Six pounds of sausages. There's enough there for the whole platoon. I brought a bit of fat, so's we can have a good fry-up about two o'clock in the morning.

MAJOR **(In Jones' ear)** Rank, man. Rank.

JONES I beg your pardon. Those were fresh this morning. **(He turns and sees the Major – he comes to attention and salutes)**

Jones exits.

MAJOR Perhaps you'd care to explain, Captain.

MAINWARING We're just getting ready for coast watch, sir.

MAJOR It looks as if you're getting ready for a damn party.

WILSON These little extras keep up their morale you know, sir.

MAJOR The best way to keep up morale is to have discipline and efficiency. The B.G.S. has appointed me to inspect training and battle drill in all our Home Guard Units in the Command, and I'm going to start with you.

MAINWARING You'll be most welcome. We're proud of our progress here, aren't we, Sergeant?

WILSON Yes, sir. What sort of things do you want to see?

MAJOR The lot. Use of weapons, aiming and firing, crawling, use of cover, map reading, first aid, bayonet fighting, physical fitness, unarmed combat...

MAINWARING Good. Anytime you like. We're ready for you.

MAJOR Now?

MAINWARING Ah. That would be a little awkward. We're just off on coast watch.

MAJOR Tomorrow morning?

MAINWARING Well, Wilson and I have to open the bank at 9.30. What about the rest, Wilson?

WILSON Well, Lance Corporal Jones, the butcher, sluices down his slabs at eight o'clock.

MAINWARING He's nothing to put on them, you understand. But old habits die hard.

WILSON Frazer, Locke and Wiper all have shops.

MAINWARING Godfrey has retired. You can inspect Godfrey.

WILSON Not tomorrow, sir. It's his pension morning.

MAJOR Tomorrow evening then.

MAINWARING Excellent.

MAJOR At 18.00 hours.

MAINWARING Eh?

WILSON Six o'clock, sir.

MAINWARING Six o'clock it is, sir. We shall look forward to seeing you. I think you might get quite a surprise.

MAJOR I very much doubt it. **(He goes)**

MAINWARING We'll have to watch him, Wilson, his eyes are too close together.

SIDE ROOM OF CHURCH HALL

Mainwaring is just putting the finishing touches to the flags in his map. Wilson enters.

MAINWARING Everything ready, Wilson?

WILSON As near as it can be in the time.

MAINWARING I hope they acquit themselves well. They're a grand bunch, but I have so much to do, there are serious gaps in their training.

WILSON I shouldn't worry too much, sir. While you've been planning the grand strategy I have been teaching them quite a lot in my own quiet way.

Enter Jones.

JONES Major Regan, sir.

Major Regan enters.

MAINWARING Thank you, Corporal. Good evening, Major. We're all ready for you.

MAJOR No bazaar trading today. Or is it early closing?

CARETAKER I'm the caretaker.

MAJOR Then get out of the way, this is a military inspection.

They move to three soldiers who are sitting on the floor in front of a chart of a Heinkel 111.

WILSON These men are studying aircraft recognition.

MAINWARING Try them out, sir.

MAJOR Do all the men learn it?

MAINWARING Oh, yes, definitely.

MAJOR Then we won't have any set pieces. **(To Pike, who is standing nearby)** You, boy. What plane's that?

PIKE A Heinkel 111, sir.

MAJOR Good. Show the next diagram.

WILSON It's the only one we have.

MAJOR What's the good of only recognising a Heinkel 111.

WILSON Well round here it usually *is* a Heinkel 111.

MAINWARING We asked your chaps for more charts and they couldn't help us.

MAJOR Well, of course these things are in very short supply.

Caretaker sidles up to the group.

CARETAKER I'm not used to being spoken to like that, you know.

WILSON It was all a mistake, Mr Harman.

CARETAKER If I tell the Vicar, he'll turf you all out.

MAJOR There's a war on you know.

CARETAKER That cuts no ice with His Reverence. The Vicar's not very happy about the church premises being used for war-like purposes.

WILSON We'll discuss it later, Mr Harman.

CARETAKER There was no need for him to go on at me like that. **(To Major)** Blimp!

WILSON Don't be cheeky.

Mainwaring pulls the Major quickly to one side where Frazer is leaning over a map with Pike.

MAINWARING Here we learn the rudiments of map-reading.

MAJOR **(Pointing to a sign)** What's that?

FRAZER A church without a steeple.

MAJOR Give the map references.

FRAZER 602391. It'll be Methodist, I expect.

MAJOR **(Pointing again)** What's that?

FRAZER A water-mill.

MAJOR And that?

FRAZER A railway cutting.

MAJOR And that?

FRAZER **(Looks)** A wee speck of dirt.

MAJOR **(Looking)** So it is. Not bad, not bad at all. **(To Jones, who is standing to one side)** You. Come here! **(Pointing to another sign)** What's that?

JONES A map.

WILSON **(Jumping in quickly)** Over here is First Aid Instruction, sir.

Godfrey is bandaging another soldier's arm.

GODFREY How do you do?

MAJOR How do you arrest arterial bleeding?

GODFREY Oh. A tourniquet to the pressure point. Here. Here. Or here.

MAJOR What do you have to remember about a tourniquet round the throat?

GODFREY It kills the patient.

MAJOR Eh!

GODFREY It's better to use the thumb and to relieve the pressure every five minutes. Is that what Sir had in mind?

MAJOR Yes, of course.

WILSON **(Leading Major to the next party)** These two are working on their unarmed combat, sir.

A private is making a gentle token knife attack against Walker.

MAJOR He won't come at you like that, you know. He wants to kill you. He's after your blood. Like this. **(The Major gives a yell and attacks Walker using his cane as a knife. Walker parries the blow and neatly throws him in a judo thrust. We see the stunned look on Mainwaring's and Wilson's faces as the major crashes off screen)**

WALKER 'Ere, that was a liberty. Lucky I didn't put the boot in, mate.

The Major rejoins the group.

MAINWARING Not bad, Walker. You're coming along well.

MAJOR There was no need to do that.

MAINWARING My men are very keen, sir. If you value your life, don't trifle with them.

WILSON Shall I fall them in for a more formal inspection, sir, while we get our breath back?

MAJOR Yes. Please do.

WILSON Fall in, in three ranks.

The men fall in with much bashing of feet and measuring of distance with arms, etc. Mainwaring takes Wilson aside.

MAINWARING Having regard to Jones' presence, go easy on the arms drill, Sergeant.

WILSON Don't worry, sir. Squad, 'shun.

There is a considerable pause.

Then the men come to attention perfectly.

WILSON Slope arms.

There is another pause. But again they perform the manoeuvre together.

MAINWARING Together! How did you do it?

WILSON Well they're all doing it to Jones' time. We couldn't beat him so we joined him.

MAJOR **(As he approaches the ranks)** I dare say you are wondering why I am here. Well the reasons are very simple. The Home Guard has got to become an efficient fighting unit. **(He stops in front of Pike)** There is no room in it for Mummy's darlings, **(He moves to Walker)** slackers, dodgers, spivs and drones, **(He moves to Frazer, Godfrey and Jones)** or elderly gentlemen amusing themselves. **(To Frazer)** How old are you?

FRAZER Fifty-eight.

GODFREY Fifty-nine.

JONES Sixty.

WALKER House!

MAJOR Sixty, eh? You've got a lot of medal ribbons. What are they? I don't recognise them.

JONES A bit before your time, sir. Look I'll show you. **(His rifle at the slope is hiding some of them, so he hands it to the Major)** Here, hold this. These – one, two, three, four, five and six, are all General Service medals – number seven, that's the Egyptian Campaign 1884 – to 1885 – number eight, that's the Caleph's Star.

MAJOR And what's number nine?

JONES We got that trying to relieve General Gordon. And there's this one...

MAJOR **(Pointing to number seven)** You must have been pretty young when you won that.

JONES Well, I didn't have me stripe, that I do remember.

MAJOR That's hardly surprising. You'd be six.

JONES Ah! Yes! Perhaps I have knocked off a year or two, but I'm as fit as anybody. That's the point. Just let me get at 'em with me cold steel. I'm fit enough for that. **(He makes a gesture of bayonet fighting with his rifle, and suddenly realises he doesn't hold it)** 'Ere, where is it? Oh, you've got it. **(Major hands it to him)**

MAJOR I don't suppose you've even fired it.

Jones takes it back – pushes the trigger and it fires.

JONES I have now.

MAJOR Right, let's see some of your fighting spirit. Order arms! Fix bayonets!

The squad fix their bayonets. Jones has great difficulty.

JONES They've given me the wrong one here.

Wilson crosses to him and fixes it.

WILSON For heaven's sake, mind where you point it.

MAJOR **(Taking Mainwaring on one side)** That man's making a shambles of your platoon.

MAINWARING He's very good as a rule, but you're making him nervous.

MAJOR I don't like nervous soldiers. Right. Now let's see what you make of bayonet fighting. Let's see you two.

(He indicates Frazer and Godfrey) And you. (He indicates Jones) (To Godfrey) You see that target? (He indicates the bayonet target)

GODFREY Yes, sir.

MAJOR Charge!

Godfrey makes a fair stab at it.

MAINWARING Not bad, eh?

MAJOR Fine, when you're fighting bags of straw. Let's see some guts. (To Frazer) You. Charge!

Frazer goes in with a blood-curdling highland leap and fierce yells. He circles back to his place.

MAJOR Good. You really thought you were doing that to a Nazi, didn't you?

FRAZER (Pointedly to the Major) No. Just someone I don't like over much.

MAJOR (To Jones) Now you, Corporal. That's a Nazi. Show us what you're going to do to him. Charge!

JONES (Standing and muttering) You dirty, heathen swine. Plunderer, looter, rapist, ravisher, despoiler of women. (He growls and then shouts) Ah! Aaaah! Aaaaaah!

MAJOR Well, go on. Charge!

JONES I can't. My glasses have steamed up.

MAINWARING Would you care to see a little grenade drill, sir?

MAJOR (To Pike) What are the rules of aiming?

PIKE Keep the tip of the blade of the foresight in the centre of the circle of the backsight and in the centre of the target.

MAJOR Good! (To Jones) You! The rules of aiming.

JONES Well he's just told you, sir! Er, tip the forething between the shoulder blade and in the 'U' of the backside and in the centre of… That wasn't quite right, was it? (Ad libs)

MAJOR No. I've seen enough. Carry on with your training.

MAINWARING Carry on, Sergeant.

JONES That was rude. I was talking to him.

Mainwaring and the Major go to one side.

MAJOR That man is making your platoon look ridiculous.

MAINWARING But he's keen as mustard. I think he's a marvellous example to the youngsters.

MAJOR I think he could be a positive danger. He's just not physically up to it.

MAINWARING It's the fighting spirit we need. I should hate to lose him.

MAJOR You may have to.

MAINWARING But surely that's up to us.

MAJOR (Pointedly) Not necessarily. However, I shall make my report on your unit to the Area Commander. You've a long way to go, but you've done well, remarkably well. Congratulations. Good show, Mainwaring.

We fade as the Major goes to the door and Mainwaring becomes ten feet tall.

SIDE OFFICE

MAINWARING There's no doubt about it, Wilson, we acquitted ourselves absolutely marvellously.

WILSON Yes, I must say I was very pleased.

MAINWARING Of course, no one man could take the credit. But it made all my hard work very worthwhile.

WILSON Yes. I don't know who was more surprised, Major Regan – or you.

MAINWARING Why do you have to go and spoil everything, Wilson. You can go.

WILSON Yes, sir. (He turns to the door. Mainwaring picks up a letter and reads it)

MAINWARING Rotten bastard.

WILSON (Turns with a look of horror) Sir?

MAINWARING (Still looking at the letter) Swine.

WILSON I know we've had our differences in the past, Mr Mainwaring, but there's no need to use such strong…

MAINWARING Listen to this, Wilson. It's from G.H.Q. … and in view of the fact that Lance Corporal Jones' records clearly show that he is over age, we feel that he should stand down. (He hands the letter to Wilson) It's that Major Regan. I said his eyes were too close together. He couldn't fault us for anything else so he had to pick on poor old Jones.

WILSON Wait a minute, sir. You didn't finish the letter. Listen to this… however in view of your strong personal views and the fact that Lance Corporal Jones has such a distinguished record of service, Major Regan has suggested that if Jones can complete the Divisional Assault Course in 15 minutes, he shall be allowed to remain with the platoon during the present period of emergency.

MAINWARING Fifteen minutes, that's a bit steep, isn't it?

WILSON They give the Infantry ten.

MAINWARING He'll never do it. Regan just wants to see Jones make a fool of himself.

They point to each other and both speak at once.

MAINWARING One of us is going to have to tell him.

Jones breezes into the room.

JONES Evening all. I saw you coming across. I just had to pop over. There's a pound of steak for you, Mr Mainwaring, and a pound for you, Mr Wilson. We showed him, didn't we?

MAINWARING Please sit down.

Sit business.

MAINWARING Jones. There's something I've got to tell you.

JONES Do you mean I'm going to get my second stripe, sir?

MAINWARING Well, no, not exactly, Jones. You see the fact is, I've had a letter from G.H.Q. and they say that – er, that – er...

JONES Yes, sir.

MAINWARING That – er – you're a little over age.

JONES Over age for what, sir. I'm only 70.

MAINWARING That's just the point, Jones. You see, they feel that 70 is a bit – er – over age.

JONES But that ain't fair, Mr Mainwaring. I can do everything that the other blokes can do. I bet it's that snooty Major. I wish he was registered with me for meat. I'd show him. He'd get his ration, but I'd cut it for gristle. I do you know, if I don't like 'em, then I sit at home Sunday lunchtime thinking of them trying to chew it.

MAINWARING I'm sorry, Jones, they want you to stand down.

JONES Stand down! Is there nothing you can do, sir?

WILSON What about the test, sir?

MAINWARING I don't know whether Mr Jones would be up to it.

JONES What test is that, sir?

MAINWARING To go over the Divisional Assault Course in 15 minutes.

JONES Oh, it'd be a bit of cake, that would.

MAINWARING I really don't think you could manage it, Jones.

JONES Manage it? You must leave it to me. I tell you what. We'll try it out this evening. As soon as we've finished Parade, we'll go down to the Assault Course and you'll see, Mr Mainwaring. They don't call me 'Up 'em Jones' for nothing.

ASSAULT COURSE. STUDIO

We are at the first obstacle, which is a wooden wall – made of substantial timber between six and seven foot high. Pike, Frazer, Godfrey and Walker are grouped together. Mainwaring and Wilson are talking to Jones. Walker has a stop watch.

MAINWARING Now don't forget, Jones. You've got 15 minutes.

WILSON Stand by with the stop watch.

WALKER You'd do better with a grandfather clock.

JONES I heard that.

MAINWARING Sergeant Wilson and I will come round with you. Before you start I have to give you a message. I can only say it once so listen carefully because when you've completed the course you have to repeat it back to us. Are you listening?

JONES Yes, sir.

MAINWARING The enemy is on the run so send reinforcements. Going to advance. Got it?

Jones nods.

MAINWARING Right. Let's go. **(He blows the whistle)** Over you go, Jones.

Jones takes a terrific leap and just manages to get a grip on the top of the wall. After a few struggles he relaxes his grip and falls in a heap.

JONES All right. Give him a hand over, Sergeant.

Wilson stands with his back to the wall, cups his hands in front of him. Jones props his rifle against the wall. Wilson and Mainwaring do not notice it. Jones goes back a few feet. He runs to the wall and goes to put one foot into Wilson's cupped hands. He gets his foot stuck down the front of Wilson's trousers. He's gripping the top of the wall.

MAINWARING Get him over, Wilson.

WILSON I cannot, sir. He's got his foot stuck.

Mainwaring tries to release Jones' foot. They both give a heave and Jones flies over the wall.

MAINWARING **(Seeing the rifle propped against the wall)** You've forgotten your rifle, Jones. **(No answer)** Jones, your rifle. Can you hear me, Jones. **(Shouts)** Jones.

Jones comes round the edge of the wall and stands just behind Mainwaring.

MAINWARING **(Shouts again)** Jones.

JONES Yes, sir.

MAINWARING You've forgotten your rifle. **(He throws it to him)**

JONES **(Taking it)** Thank you, sir. **(He starts trying to climb the wall again)**

MAINWARING We'll take it as done. Let's try the next one.

They go round the edge of the wall to the next obstacle. A tarpaulin about 16 foot long by 8 foot wide is fastened to the ground all round.

MAINWARING All right. Under you go, Jones.

Jones dives underneath. We can see his outline as he moves along. He suddenly disappears. Wilson and Mainwaring look at each other.

Wilson pulls up the edge of the tarpaulin.

WILSON Are you all right, Jones? (There is no answer) He's gone, sir.

MAINWARING He can't have gone. Go in and find him.

WILSON Don't you think it would have more authority coming from you?

Wilson goes under the tarpaulin. We can see his shape. Suddenly Jones' shape appears. The two shapes start to go round in a circle. Mainwaring steps on to the tarpaulin. He goes up to one of the shapes and prods it with his foot.

JONES (Pops up beside him) What's he doing under there?

MAINWARING He's looking for Jones.

Fade up on the wall. It is dark.

Pike, Frazer, Godfrey and Walker in a group.

PIKE How long have they been gone, Mr Walker?

WALKER (Looking at watch) Two hours, 15 minutes.

FRAZER Well if he can knock two hours off his time, it'll be all right.

PIKE I hope nothing's happened to him.

GODFREY Perhaps we'd better give them a shout, Mr Mainwaring.

There is no answer.

FRAZER I don't think he'll stand much chance with the real test, do you? (He says this to Walker)

PIKE I'm afraid it's hopeless.

GODFREY He's such a nice old chap. It's a pity to lose him.

FRAZER What do you say, Joe?

WALKER What are you all looking at me for?

PIKE Well, we thought perhaps you might be able to help.

WALKER How can I help? I mean I can nobble greyhounds, but that's a different caper, isn't it. I mean I can't make him run faster, can I? I can't doctor his oats can I? I can't make him…

We zoom in to his face.

WALKER Wait a minute. I've got an idea.

SAME PART OF ASSAULT COURSE, DAY

The platoon are lined up. In front are Mainwaring and Wilson, looking very miserable. Jones is standing with Major Regan. The Brigadier is looking on. Frazer and Godfrey are grouped behind. Walker, Pike and two younger members of the platoon are missing.

BRIGADIER Dashed sporting of you to do this, Lance Corporal Jones. Still, once an old campaigner, always an old campaigner, eh, Major?

MAJOR He's an old campaigner, all right. Jones, where's your helmet?

JONES No one said nothing about bringing a helmet.

Major turns to Training Sergeant who is wearing a white one.

MAJOR Sergeant, lend him yours.

Sergeant hands Jones a white helmet.

MAJOR Very often that's the straw that breaks the camel's back.

Jones puts on the helmet.

MAJOR Now we won't have any trouble spotting you, will we? I'll just give you the message and off you go. Remember you've got 15 minutes. Are you ready? (Jones nods his head) Here's the message, 'Send the following ammunition at once: fifty thousand rounds of 303, thirty-three thousand rounds of 300, forty-six Mills Grenades, two hundred 3.7 shells and two hundred and seventy-five Pull Throughs.

JONES Is that all, sir?

MAJOR Right, stand by. (He presses his stop watch) Go!

Jones starts off. Suddenly Frazer gives a cry and falls at the feet of the two officers.

GODFREY He's fainted. (The whole troop swarm round, blocking the view of the two officers. Jones runs up to the wall, an arm comes round the edge of the wall with a small ladder. Jones nips up it and is whisked away. The Major is pushing aside the men)

MAJOR Get out of the way, you fools. I can't see.

Cut to Jones on top of the wall. He gives a little wave and disappears.

BRIGADIER (To Major) Good heavens. That was quick.

MAJOR Yes, very quick. (He raises his binoculars)

Cut to Jones at tarpaulin. He dives under the end and we see his shape move along.

Cut to the edge of the tarpaulin. The edge lifts up. A white helmet appears. Walker's face is underneath. He runs out of shot.

Telecine: Long shot of Walker running to a clump of trees.

Close shot behind the trees. Walker changes hats with Pike.

Long shot of Pike in white helmet completing the next close up behind tree. Another member of the platoon is waiting. Pike changes helmets with him.

Long shot of other members of the platoon running to obstacle.

BRIGADIER By Jove, he's got some spirit.

This action is repeated once more.

Long shot of figure breaking cover. Runs towards camera and runs out of shot.

STUDIO

Tarpaulin. Figure in white helmet dives under the tarpaulin. The shape moves along, reaches the end and Jones emerges. He runs up behind the wall. Somebody appears on top and jumps down. He runs up to the Major and salutes.

Mainwaring, Wilson and the two officers are facing Jones.

BRIGADIER Well done, Jones.

MAJOR **(Angry)** The message, man. What's his message?

Godfrey and Frazer hold up cards with the message on it in large letters. Jones screws his eyes up and repeats it.

BRIGADIER Amazing. If I hadn't seen it with my own eyes I'd never have believed it. **(He shakes Jones' hand)** What was the time, Major?

MAJOR Thirteen minutes, sir.

BRIGADIER Fantastic. Well, I don't think we need worry about you any more, Jones. Carry on.

They all salute. Brigadier goes.

MAINWARING Well done, Jones. We're all proud of you.

The men gather round slapping Jones on the back.

MAJOR Just a minute. There's something fishy going on here and I mean to get to the bottom of it.

He goes round the wall over to the tarpaulin. Lifts up the edge and crawls under. We can see his outline as it moves along. Suddenly it disappears. The platoon all cheer.

SERIES ONE **EPISODE SIX**

Recorded: Monday 20/5/68 (made in black and white)

Original transmission: Wednesday 11/9/68, 8.20–8.50pm

(This episode was originally planned for transmission on Wednesday 10/7/68 at 8.20pm.)

Original viewing figures = 9.7 million

ARTHUR LOWE .... CAPTAIN MAINWARING
JOHN LE MESURIER .... SERGEANT WILSON
CLIVE DUNN .... LANCE CORPORAL JONES
JOHN LAURIE .... PRIVATE FRAZER
JAMES BECK .... PRIVATE WALKER
ARNOLD RIDLEY .... PRIVATE GODFREY
IAN LAVENDER .... PRIVATE PIKE
BARBARA WINDSOR .... LAURA LA PLAZ
JANET DAVIES .... MRS PIKE
CAROLINE DOWDESWELL .... JANET KING
MARTIN WYLDECK .... MAJOR REGAN
JIMMY PERRY .... CHARLIE CHEESEMAN
THÉRÈSE MCMURRAY .... THE GIRL AT THE WINDOW

PLATOON .... HUGH HASTINGS, RICHARD JACQUES, DAVID SEAFORTH, JIMMY MAC, VIC TAYLOR, HUGH CECIL, DAVID FRANKS, ALEC COLEMAN, COLIN BEAN

SHOOTING PAINS

• EVAN KING REMEMBERS •

'It was June 1940. I was ten years old. My father announced that due to the gravity of the war news detailing the collapse of our army in Europe, my sister and I could not go ice skating; we must stay close to home because invasion could be imminent. No ice skating, so I made a bow from a garden cane, carved some wooden arrows from an orange box and armed them with darning needles and broken propelling pencil tips. I was seriously ready to fight the invaders.

'In 1968, twenty-eight years later, I was assistant floor manager to David Croft, with the BBC comedy department. David, as always highly communicative, had a new production, *Dad's Army*, and said he wanted it to be "right". With the main location filming at Thetford over, we came to the last episode of the series, "Shooting Pains", and a crack shot had to be found, and who better than a music hall sharpshooter. To play the character, the wonderous, professional and absolutely no-nonsense Barbara Windsor was the inspired casting.

'The music hall sequence was filmed at the Richmond Theatre in Surrey, and Barbara's sharpshooting was done by a BBC armourer called Jack. Meanwhile, Jimmy Perry did his cheeky chappie stand-up routine, and when we discovered Arthur Lowe's period spectacles were missing, I matched them with a pair of sunglasses with the lenses removed.

'Outside rehearsals, studio rehearsals, recording with the audience at 8pm and my last day as an AFM. The dizzy heights of floor manager loomed. The designer had produced, in addition to the regular sets, a shooting range, on which Canadian Ross rifles firing blanks were used. It was hectic, especially when Harold Snoad was unable to take studio camera rehearsals because of flu. When a standby was suggested, David Croft said: "That daft Scottish bugger will do it." However, Harold, god bless him, arrived to take the recording. Now, 33 years on, I feel we definitely got it right.'

EVAN KING
Assistant Floor Manager

Shooting Pains

TELECINE

Stock newsreel shots of German staff officers looking across Channel, etc. Shots of general Home Guard training.

COMMENTATOR As the battle for our Homeland reaches its climax, the enemy is throwing everything he's got into the fray. Britain's citizen army, the Home Guard, jeeringly referred to as 'The Broomstick Army' by Dr Goebbels, is now fully armed. And if Mr Hitler does put his foot on our doorstep, the so-called 'Broomstick Army' will soon make a clean sweep of him. These men never spare themselves. They train day and night, every moment of spare time away from their civilian jobs is taken up with this one thought. In the words of Herbert Morrison 'Go To It'.

TELECINE: A BACK GARDEN. NIGHT

Close up of wall at bottom of garden. Three helmets appear, covered in leaves, etc. Close up of Walker looking very sinister. Figure climbs over wall.

Figures run from bush to bush up the garden, Walker reaches back door of house. He whistles. Female appears at window and throws down key. He opens door and goes in.

COMMENTATOR Loss of sleep is no obstacle to these men. After being up all night on manoeuvres they go straight to their offices and factories.

BACK DOOR OF HOUSE. MORNING

Door opens. Female kisses Home Guard. He goes.

COMMENTATOR They work hard all day and as soon as it's time to knock off, back they go to their training again. This leaves them no time whatever for any other activities.

INTERIOR. BANK OFFICE. DAY

Mainwaring is seated at his desk. He has a row of toy soldiers and a field gun that fires matches in front of him. He is holding a Home Guard Field Manual in one hand, he fires the gun, the first soldier falls back and knocks all the others over.

MAINWARING Just as I thought.

Tap on door.

MAINWARING Come in.

Wilson enters.

MAINWARING Here's a good point, Wilson. (**He stands the soldiers up again**) Now you know what I'm always telling the men about advancing in extended order. Now when I fire this gun it knocks the first man over and he in turn knocks all the others over. Now you see if this was a machine gun, they'd all be mown down.

WILSON Quite, sir.

MAINWARING Now watch. (**He fires the gun and the first soldier falls forward, the rest of the soldiers remain upright**) Well you get the general idea anyhow.

WILSON Yes – (**on move**) the weekly orders from G.H.Q., sir. There's your copy, sir. (**He hands one over to Mainwaring**)

MAINWARING Thank you, Wilson. I'll put them in my map-case, then I won't forget them. (**He suddenly goes very stiff in his chair, swings round and gets up with great difficulty and walks with a terrible limp over to his briefcase**)

WILSON Are you all right, sir?

MAINWARING Of course I'm all right. (**He puts the paper in his briefcase and swings round. He has a 45 revolver strapped to his left thigh**) Not bad eh, Wilson? Elizabeth made it for me. It's for a quick draw.

WILSON Oh, I see. It's a bit unorthodox, isn't it, sir?

MAINWARING (**Goes back to desk**) You know your trouble, Wilson, you've got a 'Blimp' mentality. Of course it's unorthodox, that's the whole point. If we're going to beat the 'Hun' we must be unorthodox, not stuck in a rut – we must be flexible. (**He looks at his watch**) Where's that girl with the coffee? She knows I like it sharp on the dot of 10.30 every morning. (**He sits**)

WILSON I'll go and tell her, sir.

MAINWARING No, don't bother. I can wait. (**He shifts in his chair**) It's no good, I'll have to take it off. I can't wear it sitting down. (**He places the 45 on the table**) That's better, have to keep it handy, never know when the enemy will be at our throats.

WILSON Yes, quite, sir.

MAINWARING Are we going to get a full turn out for target practice on Saturday afternoon, Wilson?

WILSON I hope so, sir.

MAINWARING To tell you the truth, I was a little ashamed at last week's shoot.

WILSON Oh, I don't know, sir. Some of the men didn't do too badly.

MAINWARING Yes, but I don't see how they could have mistaken the tyres of the Area Commander's staff car for the target.

WILSON Did they hit all four of them, sir?

MAINWARING No, five. They got the spare as well.

WILSON Well, he shouldn't have parked it so near the targets.

MAINWARING Yes, half a mile was a bit close. There's no getting away from it, Wilson, the standard of shooting in the platoon is very poor.

WILSON It's not really the men's fault, sir. We can't get any ammunition to practise with. I mean, we're never going to learn to shoot by just pulling the trigger and saying bang!

MAINWARING **(Crossing to briefcase)** Tell Miss King to hurry up with my coffee, Wilson.

WILSON Aren't you going to look at the orders? **(Opens door and calls out)**Bring in Mr Mainwaring's coffee will you, Miss King. **(He turns back into the room. Mainwaring is looking at the orders)**

MAINWARING **(Excited)** Listen to this, Wilson – 'the Prime Minister will inspect coastal defences in approximately ten days' time. For security reasons, date and time will not be released until last minute. In view of the fact that your platoon was the first to be formed in this area, you have been chosen to act as the Guard of Honour.'

WILSON That's wonderful news, sir.

MAINWARING You see, Wilson, in the end, real leadership will always be recognised.

WILSON But it says we've been chosen because we were the first platoon to be formed.

MAINWARING **(Acid)** That will be all, Wilson.

Wilson goes.

MAINWARING Pity he's got no imagination. I suppose I ought not to be too harsh with him. Some men are born to be leaders and others born to be led. Unorthodox. **(He picks up his revolver, puts it in his holster, tries a few quick draws)**

Janet enters.

JANET Oh… sir.

CHURCH HALL MAIN. EVENING

The men are drawn up on parade. Mainwaring is addressing them.

MAINWARING I'm not going to read you all the details out, but what it boils down to is this: during the Prime Minister's inspection of the coastal defences, we have been chosen to act as the Guard of Honour.

The men all cheer.

MAINWARING You will also be pleased to hear that ammunition is now more plentiful and we shall be having our second target practice on Saturday afternoon. We are very fortunate that Major Regan will be there to give us expert tuition.

WALKER **(Aside to Jones)** Blimey, I thought we'd seen the last of that basket.

A mutter through the ranks.

MAINWARING Now if any of you can't come, take one pace forward.

All take one pace forward.

MAINWARING Why can't you come, Walker?

WALKER I've got me stall in the market Saturdays.

MAINWARING What about you, Pike?

PIKE I'm playing football, sir.

MAINWARING Frazer?

FRAZER Fishing, sir.

MAINWARING But you weren't there last time.

FRAZER I did'na catch anything.

MAINWARING Godfrey?

GODFREY My day at the clinic.

MAINWARING Corporal Jones?

JONES My father's coming to tea.

MAINWARING I don't like this men. This is the first time you haven't shown one hundred per cent keenness. If it's Major Regan that's worrying you, I can assure you that he only has our interest at heart.

JONES Permission to speak, sir?

MAINWARING Yes.

JONES He hasn't got my best interests at heart – he said I was too old.

MAINWARING That'll do, Corporal. I intend to ignore what's just happened and I shall expect a full turn out on Saturday afternoon. Right, platoon attention. That's better. Very smart. When the Prime Minister walks down your ranks in ten days' time, I want him to say to himself: 'Of such stuff as this are Britons made'.

TELECINE: A COUNTRY LANE. DAY

The platoon are seen marching along. In the rear is the boy scout cart with the ammo, flags, marker and dummy.

RIFLE RANGE. EXTERIOR. DAY. STUDIO

Major Regan is standing waiting.

WILSON Squad, halt. Left turn. Would you mind putting your guns beside your boots.

MAINWARING Order arms. **(Salutes Major)** 1st Platoon, B Company Home Guard reporting, sir.

MAJOR Thank you, Captain. Stand the men at ease will you, Sergeant.

WILSON Platoon, stand at ease. Easy.

MAJOR Good afternoon, chaps. We're going to do a spot of shooting today. I gather your shooting is not all that it might be, but if you miss the target you can always fix bayonets and charge, what? Now first of all we need four chaps to go down into the pits as markers. That all right with you, Captain?

MAINWARING Yes, of course, sir. It's all arranged. Carry on, Sergeant.

WILSON Corporal Jones, fall out the markers.

JONES Follow me. Come on Pikey, get the phone.

Pike goes with Jones and Frazer. We are left with the remaining privates, Mainwaring, Wilson and the Major, who now starts to take charge.

MAJOR Squad, attention! For inspection, port arms!

The men port arms with much clicking of bolts. They stand ready with their rifles. The Major walks down the line pulling the rifles round and looking down the barrels. He stops at Godfrey.

GODFREY All right, sir?

MAJOR Where's your thumb?

GODFREY Eh?

MAJOR Where's your thumb?

Godfrey shows his thumb.

MAJOR When you port arms for inspection, you put your thumb in the breech, like that. **(He sticks his thumb in the breech) (Godfrey starts to close bolt)** Yieeeeee!... **(Major doubles up with pain)**

THE TARGET PITS. EXTERNAL. STUDIO. DAY

Two large army targets worked by counter-weights. When one is pulled down the other is exposed to fire. On the top of one is a large hook for hanging dummies.

Jones, Frazer and Pike come into the picture.

JONES The phone's ringing. **(Picks it up)** Lance Corporal Jones here.

WILSON We're ready to start shooting now, Jones.

JONES Okay, Mr Wilson.

WILSON Thank you, Jonesey.

JONES 'Ere lad, grab that flag and every time you hear a shot, wave it.

PIKE What's that mean, Corp?

JONES It means they've missed.

PIKE **(Picking up flag)** How do we know they've missed if we don't pull the targets down and look at them?

JONES They'll miss all right.

RIFLE RANGE

MAJOR Now gather round you chaps and I'll just fire a few shots so that you can get the idea. All right, blow the whistle, Sergeant.

Wilson blows whistle. Major lies down to fire. The rest gather round. He fires.

Flag waves in front of target.

Major looks very annoyed. Fires again.

Flag waves again.

Major, furious, fires again.

Pike is holding half the flag. The top has been shot off.

PIKE 'Ere, Corp. Someone's shot the top off me flag.

JONES They must be improving.

They all laugh. Phone buzzes like mad.

Jones picks up phone.

JONES Lance Corporal Jones 'ere.

MAJOR **(Livid)** What the hell's going on down there? Why do you keep giving me a miss? I've never missed a target in my life.

JONES Was that you firing, sir?

MAJOR Of course it was me, you fool. I'm coming down to the pit.

JONES Hey up! He's coming down. It was him firing.

This throws them into a panic.

PIKE Oh dear. Will I get into trouble?

WALKER No – we'll tell him it was Jonesey's fault.

Frazer climbs up and looks over parapet.

FRAZER He's nearly here, Corp, and Mr Mainwaring's with him.

JONES All right. Don't panic.

WALKER I'm not panicking – we're blaming you.

The Major and Mainwaring jump into the pit.

MAJOR Now what's happening here? Get that target down. **(They pull it down. There is a group of three holes in the centre of the target. The Major points to them)** What do those look like to you, Corporal?

JONES Well, I'd say they were holes, sir.

MAJOR **(Pointing to Walker)** You?

WALKER Yes. Definitely holes, sir.

MAJOR **(Pointing to Pike and Frazer)** You two?

PIKE AND FRAZER Holes, sir.

MAJOR And what do you think, Captain?

MAINWARING I'd say they were holes too, sir.

MAJOR Well I'm glad you cleared that up for me, Captain. **(Nasty)** Now listen to me, you lot. Just pull yourselves together, do you hear. You're sloppy, that's what you are, sloppy. Tidy this place up for a start. Now just get hold of yourselves. Come on, Mainwaring. **(He goes)**

MAINWARING Now look here you chaps, do try and…

MAJOR'S VOICE At the double!

Mainwaring goes.

WALKER Phew! That was a near one, Corp. How were we to know that flippin' Tom Mix was going to be the first one to fire?

JONES Crack shot 'e is. Sergeant told me last night he's shot at Bisley.

PIKE Did he kill him?

WALKER No, he wouldn't dare do that. I expect he was just trying to frighten him.

Jones double take. Phone buzzer goes. Jones picks up phone.

JONES Lance Corporal Jones 'ere.

MAJOR'S VOICE Are you men all ready?

JONES We certainly are, sir.

MAJOR'S VOICE Then we can start.

RIFLE RANGE

Privates are standing in a line. One is just getting up having fired his last shot.

MAJOR That's the lot I think. Thank you, Godfrey

MAINWARING Very seasoned man, sir.

MAJOR Well. You've each fired your five rounds and I must say the results are pretty sloppy. Now, before we get the other chaps up, I'm sure Captain Mainwaring and Sergeant Wilson would like to fire a few rounds. Eh, gentlemen?

MAINWARING It's all right, sir. No hurry.

MAJOR Oh, come now, Captain. Don't be modest. **(Nasty)** I say, that's a pretty holster you've got there. Why do you wear it so *low down* on your hip?

WILSON Well, sir, he thought it would be rather quicker to draw.

MAJOR Oh really! I think you've been seeing too many cowboy films. When did you last fire it?

MAINWARING Well I haven't really fired it yet, not intentionally that is.

MAJOR He hasn't fired it yet! Well, no time like the present. Sergeant, tell them to put the dummy up.

Wilson rings buzzer.

PITS

Pike is on the phone.

PIKE Yes, Right-oh, Sarge. **(Hangs up)** 'Ere, Corp. The Sergeant wants us to put up the dummy. The Captain's going to fire his revolver.

JONES All right, I'll do it. **(Grabs life-sized dummy which is stuffed with straw and hangs it on the hook)** Come on, you blokes. Give me a hand to pull it up.

Walker and Frazer pull it up.

Captain is standing with revolver in his hand. Major is standing just behind him.

MAJOR Now, are you all ready, Captain? Just bring your revolver up slowly, keeping your arm straight and squeeze the trigger.

Pan round on anxious faces of men. There is a bang. They all wince. Pan back to Mainwaring and Major on ground. Mainwaring is in Major's arms.

MAJOR **(Furious)** I haven't told you to fire yet.

MAINWARING I'm sorry, sir. It just went off. I didn't realise it had such a kick.

MAJOR Of course it's got a kick. It's not a damn water pistol. Now what are you laughing at, Sergeant? It's your turn next – five rounds rapid fire.

Pan on faces of others – they are all very close together. Shot rings out. They fling themselves to the ground. Close up of their faces on the ground. Three quick shots ring out, they all wait for the last one. There is a quick bang and the Major flings himself on top of them.

MAINWARING Was I on the target at all?

MAJOR You weren't even on the range. Let's see if you're any better, Sergeant.

MAJOR This is the Thomson Sub Machine Gun which will be issued to the platoon very shortly, and as the Platoon Sergeant you will carry it, Wilson. Now you can fire it from the hip or from the shoulder. We'll start off by firing it from the hip. All right, Sergeant?

MAJOR Now get hold of it man, nice firm grip with your left elbow well into your side. Here's the magazine, make sure it's fully home. **(Wilson is holding the gun and the Major clips it on)** Now all you've got to do is to cock it, take your right hand off the grip and pull back the bolt. Well, go on man. **(Wilson cocks the gun)** Right, now you're all ready to fire. **(The rest of the platoon press themselves back against the wall)** Just one more thing, these guns tend to pull to the left and down so I'll brace myself against your left shoulder. Now you have all that. And one more thing. The cartridges come out of the right-hand side, so get out of the way.

WILSON **(Nearly at the end of his tether, in faint voice)** Yes, sir.

MAJOR All right, stand by. **(He braces himself against Wilson's left shoulder)** Just one more thing. Shell cases come spewing out. Watch your face. Now, fire!

Pike throws dummy. Jones falls back against the target, the hook for the dummy catches him underneath his battledress collar. He shouts 'Hup' and the target flies up with Jones on it.

RIFLE RANGE

Close up of Major firing Tommy gun.

PITS

PIKE Pull it down, boys, Mr Jones is up there.

WALKER Blimey **(They pull him down, Walker and Frazer take him off the hook. Jones collapses on the ground. There is an outline of him in bullet holes on the target)**.

WALKER Talk about tear round the dotted line.

CHURCH HALL. INTERIOR. DAY

There is a trestle table in the centre of the room. On it are tea and sandwiches. Mrs Pike is pouring out the milk. The men come through the door, see the tea and crowd round.

JONES Hello, Mrs Pike. This is a surprise. Just what the doctor ordered.

WALKER Mrs Pike, you're a darling. Come on. Get stuck in, fellas.

MRS PIKE Oh no you don't. Where's Arthur and Mr Mainwaring?

PIKE They're just coming now, Mum.

MRS PIKE Well, you don't start till they get here.

Door opens and Wilson and Mainwaring come in.

MRS PIKE What's the matter? You both look worn out.

MAINWARING Al Capone here has had rather a shattering experience.

WILSON **(Icy)** I think what unnerved me most, sir, was your impersonation of Billy the Kid.

MRS PIKE Well, never mind, have one of my rock cakes.

JONES You don't want to worry about the men's shooting, Mr Mainwaring. Just so long as we can fix bayonets and charge. They don't like it up 'em... **(etc. etc.)**

MAINWARING Yes, thank you Corporal, I'm sure your fighting spirit is a great example to us all.

JONES I'm all right, sir, but I'm afraid this afternoon's little affair is going to shatter the men's morale.

FRAZER **(With a mouthful of cake)** As long as the men's morale is as firm as these rock cakes, we shan't have much to worry about.

MAINWARING Now, men, carry on drinking your tea but pay attention. Our shooting today wouldn't have killed many Nazis but on the other hand it would certainly have made them keep their heads down. All we need is a little more practice and then if Hitler does come knocking at the door he's going to find us very much at home. **(Loud knocking on door)** See who that is, Jones. **(Major storms in)**

MAJOR I want to talk to you. Over here at the double, man! Don't you salute a superior officer? You can forget all about being the Guard of Honour for the Prime Minister's visit. I told the Area Commander what a sloppy lot you were and that I thought the Eastgate platoon would make a better job of it.

MAINWARING I really must protest, sir!

MAJOR There's no need. The Area Commander is going to give you one more chance. Tomorrow afternoon there's going to be a shooting contest between you and the Eastgate platoon. So pick your three best shots and be on the range tomorrow afternoon at 13.00 hours. Any questions?

MAINWARING Yes. What time is 13.00 hours?

WILSON One o'clock, sir.

MAINWARING No questions.

MAJOR Carry on.

He goes.

MAINWARING It's absurd, Wilson. We can't possibly be ready by tomorrow.

WILSON It's only between the three best shots in the platoon.

MAINWARING But it's only young Pike who's any good at all.

WILSON Frazer says he thinks he can manage to hit the target, sir.

MAINWARING But we've never even seen him shoot.

WILSON I must say, it does look a bit grim.

MAINWARING Grim, it looks hopeless. **(Picks up teapot)** There's not even any more tea in the pot, what are we going to do? **(They both sit down side by side looking very miserable)**

Mrs Pike and Walker enter.

MRS PIKE Hullo, Mr Mainwaring, sorry you missed the tea, would you like me to make you some fresh?

MAINWARING No thank you very much, Mrs Pike.

MRS PIKE Well I must say you two do look miserable, you look as though you've been stuck against a wall to be shot.

WALKER Well they wouldn't have anything to worry about if our platoon was doing the shooting eh, Mrs P?

MAINWARING That's very amusing, Walker.

WALKER Look I got an idea, I usually go along to the Hippodrome Saturday nights, you know, little orders for the artistes. Why don't we make up a party and all go along and have a good laugh? Then I can nip round backstage and do my little bit of business in the interval.

MRS PIKE That's a lovely idea, Joe.

WALKER Charlie Cheeseman the Cheerful Chump is top of the bill.

MRS PIKE Charlie Cheeseman the Cheerful Chump, oh I love him, he always makes me laugh, doesn't he make you laugh, Arthur? **(Wilson looks desperate)** I'm sure he'll make you laugh. And you, Mr Mainwaring, he'll make you both laugh your heads off.

Close up of Wilson and Mainwaring.

HIPPODROME THEATRE

Charlie Cheeseman is on the stage and is just finishing his act.

CHARLIE ... so listen, the Air Raid Warden shouted out, 'ere missus you've got a chink in your bedroom. So she poked her head out of the window and said do what?, he said, you've got a chink in your bedroom, so she said, the liar, he told me he was a Japanese Admiral.

Laughter. Cut to audience, Walker and Mrs Pike are enjoying the show, Wilson and Mainwaring are not laughing. Mrs Pike nudges Wilson, he gives a terrible grin. Cut back to stage.

... I got home the other night and my wife was crying her eyes out. I said what's the matter?, she said I'm homesick. I said this is your home. She said yes I know, I'm sick of it. And she's a big woman my wife, a big woman, she weighs 18 stone, that's with her eyebrows plucked and her ears pierced. She's so fat, my wife, I have to put a bookmark in to remember where her mouth is. Anyhow, we're sitting there having our supper, a nice piece of cod, plenty of chips, bread and marg and a pot of tea. All of a sudden Lord Haw Haw comes on the wireless, have you heard him, Lord Haw Haw? He said this is Germany calling, everyone in England you're all starving. So I looked over to the wife and I said Blimey someone's telling a lie.

(Applause)

... and now customers, a little number dedicated to all fire-watchers entitled 'I can get over a girl like you, so turn out the light yourself'. Thank you, Professor **(Starts to sing 'I don't want to set the world on fire')**

Cut to audience. Wilson and Mainwaring are sitting side by side, Mrs Pike on Wilson's right and Walker is on Mrs Pike's right. Walker is in an expansive mood and smoking a cigar.

MRS PIKE **(To Wilson)** Isn't he a scream, Arthur?

WILSON Yes.

MRS PIKE **(Leaning over to Mainwaring)** Don't you think he's a scream, Mr Mainwaring?

MAINWARING Yes, a perfect scream.

MRS PIKE **(To Walker)** You know I do love the smell of a cigar, Joe. **(Mrs Pike and Walker are talking together)**.

MAINWARING I don't think this was a very good idea, do you, Wilson?

WILSON No, sir, I'm afraid not.

VOICE And now, ladies and gentlemen, from South America, the crack shot of the Pampas, Laura La Plaz!

STAGE

Laura La Plaz enters. She is in a spot. The rest of the stage is in darkness. She is a very pretty girl, about five foot high. She is dressed in tights and spangles. There is a table behind her with several rifles on it. She picks one of them up. Smiles at the audience.

AUDIENCE

Tight shot on the three faces. There is a drum roll. Six shots ring out. There are gasps and oohs from the audience and applause.

STAGE

Laura takes a bow, smiles and picks up another rifle. She raises it to her shoulder.

AUDIENCE

There are more shots and applause.

Close up of Walker's face. In the background there are more shots and applause. We see that his brain is beginning to work.

WALKER Excuse me, Mrs P. I've just got to nip out for a minute. See you after the interval.

He gets up to go.

INTERIOR LAURA'S DRESSING ROOM

The room is empty. Door opens. Walker pokes his head round the door, sees the room is empty and dodges in. Laura's act is just finishing. Applause and music in background. Walker looks around. Crosses to dressing table. A look of disgust comes on his face. He picks up a newspaper. Rolls it up and brings it down with a quick whack on the dressing table. He looks a little closer and picks up a false eyelash.

WALKER Blimey! I thought it was a spider.

The door opens and Laura comes in.

WALKER (In his best Spanish) Buenos Notches Senorita.

LAURA (In Cockney) 'Ere! Who the hell are you? How the hell did you get past the doorkeeper?

WALKER He's a friend of mine. I come round here every Saturday night.

LAURA Oh you do, do you? Well whatever it is you've got to sell, I'm not interested.

WALKER (Opening his case) 'Ere what do you think of these silk stockings?

LAURA (Weakening) How much?

WALKER I'll let you have 'em for nothing if you're interested in a little proposition of mine.

LAURA And if you're not out of here in two minutes I'll have you thrown out.

WALKER No, it's nothing like that.

LAURA What do you mean?

WALKER It's very simple. There's nothing to it. This is what I want you to do. Now tomorrow afternoon...

CHURCH HALL. DAY

Wilson and Mainwaring are alone.

MAINWARING Now, what is all this, Wilson? I couldn't make head or tail of your conversation on the phone last night.

WILSON I don't know, sir, Walker just said he had an idea to help us win the shooting contest this afternoon.

MAINWARING What's he going to do? Bribe the Major?

FRAZER Mr Mainwaring, sir, there's something I never had a chance to tell you.

Walker and Jones enter with Laura.

WALKER Good morning, gentlemen. May I introduce Miss Laura La Plaz from the Hippodrome Theatre.

LAURA Good morning, boys. (She opens her coat. Underneath she is wearing a very brief stage costume and tights) Now when do I start? (Mainwaring is shocked)

MAINWARING (To Walker) Have you gone mad?

WALKER No, sir, you don't understand. She's a ballistics expert.

MAINWARING I can well believe that.

WALKER No, sir. I mean she knows all about it.

JONES That's right. She's going to have a go with us on the range this afternoon.

MAINWARING That's enough. Young lady, cover yourself up and go home. What were you saying, Frazer?

FRAZER Something's driven it out of my head.

LAURA I'm not going home. What about my stockings?

WALKER Don't break into a trot, sir, you've got it all wrong. This young lady is the crack shot from the Hippodrome show we saw last night and she is going to shoot for us on the range this afternoon. (Goes upstage for equipment)

Pause.

WILSON But we'd never get away with it, sir.

MAINWARING (Looking at her bosom) I quite agree. What's more, it's downright dishonest.

Walker comes into the picture with a pile of equipment which he dumps on the floor.

WALKER Don't worry, sir. We'll soon make her look like a soldier. Here, try these on for size. (Hands her a battledress coat)

Wilson draws Mainwaring to one side. Close up of just the two faces.

WILSON This is madness, sir. We'll never get away with it.

MAINWARING I quite agree with you, Wilson.

WILSON If we're found out it will mean a court martial.

MAINWARING Of course it will.

WILSON I didn't even like her act.

Laura puts trousers on.

MAINWARING Don't keep staring, Wilson.

LAURA Thank you, Mr Jones.

WALKER There's something not quite right here, Jonesey. What is it? **(He hands her some boots)** 'Ere. Try on the daisy roots.

LAURA **(Putting boots on)** Haven't you got anything a bit smaller?

WALKER No, that's all we've got.

JONES What about her Barnet, Walker?

WALKER **(Holding out a tin hat with camouflage hanging all over it)** How about this?

He puts it on her head. They all stand back to admire the result.

MAINWARING The whole idea is ridiculous.

JONES She still looks like a girl to me.

WALKER How would you remember…

JONES Don't you start.

Walker sticks a moustache on her and a pair of thick pebble glasses.

JONES 'Ten, shun!

WALKER Try sticking your chest out.

She does so. Double take from Wilson and Mainwaring.

JONES I don't think it's going to work, sir.

WALKER Don't give up. Right turn, quick march!

JONES Left, right…

MAINWARING You've really gone too far this time, Walker.

Door suddenly opens. Major Regan comes in.

MAJOR Good afternoon, gentlemen. **(Walker slides into the background)** All ready for the shoot this afternoon? **(Sees Laura)** My God, what's this?

MAINWARING Er! A new recruit, sir.

WALKER He's shooting for us this afternoon.

MAJOR A bit puny isn't he? **(Slaps her in the stomach)** What's he doing with pebble glasses? How the hell can he shoot with those on?

MAINWARING He's very long-sighted, sir. He takes them off to shoot with.

MAJOR What's his name?

MAINWARING **(To Wilson)** What's his name, Sergeant?

WILSON Paderewski, sir.

MAJOR Can't he speak for himself?

JONES No sir. He's Polish.

WILSON He was with the Polish Cavalry.

MAINWARING That's why he's so short. He used to be a jockey.

MAJOR Glad to have you with us. **(Shakes hands. Suddenly he looks down and notices that Laura is wearing a very fancy diamond ring. He snatches his hand away in horror. Mutters to Mainwaring)** Did you see that diamond ring? Bit of a nancy boy, isn't he?

MAINWARING I haven't known him very long.

MAJOR Oh yes, quite. Well, see you this afternoon. **(Nasty)** Oh, by the way, I shall be there this afternoon to make sure that everything is above board. Right, carry on. Should be a very interesting afternoon.

MAINWARING Yes, very.

Salute business.

TARGET PITS. STUDIO. DAY

Pike is just firing his fourth shot. He fires.

MAINWARING Very good, Pike. Keep it up. One more.

Pike spits on his thumb and wets the foresight of his rifle.

MAINWARING What did you do that for, you stupid boy?

PIKE I don't know, sir. I saw Gary Cooper do it in a film.

MAINWARING Oh, get on with it.

WILSON I saw that film too, sir. It worked awfully well for Gary Cooper.

Pike fires.

MAINWARING Well, it hasn't worked very well for Pike.

MAJOR Level pegging so far, Mainwaring. Now let's see what your Number Two can do.

MAINWARING Come on, Private Shostakovitch.

MAJOR I thought his name was Paderewski.

MAINWARING That's right, sir – Paderewski-Shostakovitch. Very long names, these foreigners.

MAJOR Right, off you go.

Laura fires first shot.

MAINWARING Bull's eye!

She gets up and holds rifle upside down.

MAINWARING What are you doing? You can't do that!

LAURA All right, then.

She puts the rifle between her legs.

MAINWARING Get down!

LAURA Well, can't I have my mirror then?

MAINWARING No, you can't, get down!

MAJOR Hurry up, Mainwaring!

She fires four shots and misses each time.

MAJOR Four outers, not so good. That puts you four points down.

MAINWARING Frazer!

Frazer gets down.

MAINWARING **(To Laura)** What went wrong? I thought you were supposed to be a crack shot.

WILSON Perhaps we should have used clay pipes for the target, sir.

Bang.

WALKER Well, the first one was a bull's eye, anyhow.

LAURA 'Cos that was normal.

WALKER What do you mean, normal?

LAURA My routine. One normal, one upside down, one between my legs and one with a mirror.

MAINWARING Why can't you do it laying down?

LAURA 'Cos I can't get close to the ground.

Bang – Frazer fires his second shot.

JONES **(Leaping with excitement)** Sir! Frazer's got two bulls!

Mainwaring gets down beside Frazer. Frazer fires next shot.

MAJOR Bull!

MAINWARING Now steady, steady! Don't wave it about like that.

FRAZER Don't worry, I was in minesweepers during the war – I used to set off the mines.

He fires.

MAJOR Bull!

MAINWARING Why are you waving it about like that?

FRAZER It's the only way I can shoot. You see, this is the motion of the ship.

MAINWARING Do it whatever way you like then.

FRAZER Oh, get away – you're putting me off!

JONES Shall I get him a tot of rum, sir?

MAINWARING **(Heavily sarcastic)** Where are we going to get a tot of rum on a firing range?

WILSON Well, there's a NAAFI just down the road, sir.

MAINWARING Wilson!

Frazer fires his last shot.

MAJOR Bull!

Loud cheers.

MAINWARING Why didn't you say you were a crack shot, Frazer?

FRAZER You did'na ask me, sir.

MAINWARING Do you mean to say, you stood there while we were trying to make that stupid girl look like a man… You let us go all through that ridiculous pantomime and didn't say a word. Why didn't you speak, man?

FRAZER Well, sir, as soon as she started to take her clothes off, words failed me!

EXTERIOR. BRICK WALL. STUDIO. DAY

The men are drawn up on parade.

MAINWARING 1st Platoon, Brightsea-on-Sea Home Guard… present arms!

They present arms. Sergeant stands at end of line next to Fish. Rigidly to attention. The back of a figure with a cigar comes into the picture. He walks slowly down the ranks. The men swell with pride. Pan back to close up of Mainwaring and Wilson – there are tears in their eyes.

SERIES TWO **EPISODE ONE**

Recorded: Sunday 13/10/68 (made in black and white)
Original transmission: Saturday 1/3/69, 7.00–7.30pm
Original viewing figures = 13.9 million

ARTHUR LOWE .... CAPTAIN MAINWARING
JOHN LE MESURIER .... SERGEANT WILSON
CLIVE DUNN .... LANCE CORPORAL JONES
JOHN LAURIE .... PRIVATE FRAZER
JAMES BECK .... PRIVATE WALKER
ARNOLD RIDLEY .... PRIVATE GODFREY
IAN LAVENDER .... PRIVATE PIKE
JANET DAVIES .... MRS PIKE
JAMES COPELAND .... CAPTAIN OGILVY
SMALL BOY .... COLIN DANIELS

PLATOON .... COLIN BEAN, RICHARD JACQUES, FRANK GODFREY, ALEC COLEMAN, HUGH CECIL, JIMMY MAC, DESMOND CULLUM-JONES, VIC TAYLOR, DAVID SEAFORTH, RICHARD KITTERIDGE

HIGHLAND SOLDIERS .... ALEX DONALD, ROBIN WILLIAMS, DENNIS HALCOMBE, BARRY RAYMOND, BRUCE WELLS

PANTOMIME COW .... THE LYNTON BOYS

OPERATION KILT

• JIMMY PERRY REMEMBERS •

'People often ask if *Dad's Army* was realistic compared to my days in the real Home Guard, and I think it was. What we concentrated on mainly was the comedy of older men, even though the number of old men in the real Home Guard reduced as the years passed. People like Frazer and Godfrey were present in most units in the early days of the war, but gradually more and more younger men joined. Like me, they were in their teens and very fit. Within about 18 months, most units were well armed, quite disciplined and had formed an extremely useful auxiliary unit, taking over duties from the army.

'Everybody became frightened of fifth columnists, which was all rubbish because there weren't any, really, it was all a myth. But we didn't know that and thought they were behind every tree. As boys in the Home Guard we were stopping people. I remember approaching a couple of factory workers once and asking to see their identity cards. They refused because we were just boys in their eyes. I demanded to see them, so they gave in and cooperated, but before we'd finished with them, they said: "You're not checking them properly, you should check it like this." It was ridiculous.'

JIMMY PERRY

Operation Kilt

SIDE OFFICE. CHURCH HALL

Mainwaring is sitting at his desk, he is reading a newspaper. Wilson enters.

WILSON Ah, there you are, sir. You left the bank early, didn't you?

MAINWARING Yes, I had a lot of paperwork to get on with.

WILSON I see.

MAINWARING **(Rustling the newspaper)** I've finished it now.

WILSON I was just wondering why you left the bank by the back door.

MAINWARING There's no reason why I can't leave the bank by the back door is there, Wilson?

WILSON None whatsoever, sir, but I did just happen to notice that as you were leaving by the back door, Mr Green from Head Office was coming through the front door.

MAINWARING Really, what did he want?

WILSON Well, he seemed a bit cross, sir. He said this is the third time this week he's missed you. And he took a rather dim view of all those Ministry of Information posters in the bank.

MAINWARING Doesn't he know there's a war on?

WILSON Yes, sir, but he feels they rather clash with ours.

MAINWARING Oh, in what way?

WILSON Well, underneath one of our posters which says 'Let us invest your money' you've put one which says 'Trust no one, careless talk costs lives'.

MAINWARING Just an unfortunate coincidence.

WILSON I'm sure it was, sir. But you also put 'Don't be a squander bug like me' underneath the portrait of the founder of the bank.

MAINWARING Oh I can't be bothered with all that rubbish.

There is a yell from outside the door, and the sound of dustbins. The door flies open and Corporal Jones staggers in with his hat over his eyes, grasping his rifle. Wilson dives under the desk.

JONES Some fool put up a booby trap, sir.

MAINWARING That was me, Jones.

JONES Very good idea, sir.

MAINWARING What is it you want, Corporal?

JONES Well, I thought I'd be the first one to bring you the good news. The meat ration's gone up 1s 10d to 2s 2d.

MAINWARING Thank you, Corporal Jones, that's a great comfort.

JONES But I'm afraid your butter's gone down two ounces. But the fat ration's still at eight ounces, so that means you can have six of marg and two of butter, or four of marg, two of cooking fat and two of butter, or four of cooking fat, two of marg and two of butter or three of cooking fat, three of marg and two of butter, or four of marg and four of cooking fat or eight of marg.

WILSON Yes, thank you, Jones, you've been a great help. Oh, by the way, sir, this packet came for you at the bank just after you left. **(He hands Mainwaring a book)**

JONES **(To Wilson)** Of course if you felt like it you could have six of cooking fat and two of butter... **(He rambles on)**

MAINWARING **(Reading)** Listen to this, Wilson. In future, all H.G. units will do 15 minutes P.T. before parade. That will get rid of the excess fat.

JONES You can't have any excess fat, sir. I've told you, you can either have two of...

MAINWARING **(Shouting)** Jones! Listen to this, Wilson. In future all H.G. units will do 15 minutes P.T. before parade. Right, we'll start tonight.

WILSON **(On rise)** Tonight, sir. But who's going to take us?

MAINWARING I am, of course, here's all the instructions. **(He holds up handbook)** All right, Jones. Parade the men outside in the yard, there's nothing like plenty of fresh air when you're doing P.T. And, Jones, tell them to strip off.

JONES I beg pardon, sir.

MAINWARING Strip off. **(Jones starts to)** Not here, outside.

WILSON The men, Jones. Tell the men.

JONES Yes, sir. Sorry, sir. **(He goes)**

WILSON Wait a minute, sir. Captain Ogilvie of the Highland Regiment is due here at 1930 to brief us about the night manoeuvres on Saturday.

MAINWARING Nineteen thirty? **(Looks at watch)** That'll be in about...

WILSON Seven thirty, sir.

MAINWARING I know, Wilson. Well, it's only six thirty now, we've got plenty of time.

WILSON But don't you think you're being a bit hasty, sir. After all you don't know anything about P.T.

MAINWARING **(Coldly)** When we took arms in the hour of our country's need, we didn't know anything about a lot of things, Sergeant. But I've never let you down yet, have I?

WILSON Well, er...

MAINWARING That will be all, Sergeant. Outside and strip off!

THE YARD OUTSIDE THE CHURCH HALL

The men are drawn up on parade. Lance Corporal Jones is standing in front.

JONES Now look here – I'm giving you an order. Captain Mainwaring says you've got to strip off.

FRAZER Strip off, for what?

JONES The Captain's going to give us some P.T.

FRAZER **(Indicating Godfrey)** He can't strip off. It's only his clothes keep him from falling apart.

WALKER Well I'm not stripping off in this draughty yard. Besides, people can see us from the road.

JONES Look, I don't want any insubordination.

Mainwaring and Wilson enter.

JONES Squad, attention. **(He salutes)**

MAINWARING Why aren't the men ready, Jones?

JONES Well, sir. They er... **(He quickly starts to strip off)** Well I'm ready, sir.

MAINWARING Thank you, Jones. All right, stand them at ease, Sergeant.

WILSON Platoon, stand at ease. Easy!

MAINWARING Right now, pay attention men. If we're going to beat the Hun, we must be fit in every way, with clean bodies and clean minds. Now I've never asked you to do anything that I wouldn't do myself, so on the command strip, we shall all strip off together.

Jones is shivering.

JONES **(With his teeth chattering)** Per... per... per... mission to speak, sir?

MAINWARING What is it, Jones?

JONES It ain't half chilly out here. Can't we go inside?

MAINWARING Certainly not, if you're cold, start running on the spot.

JONES Yes, sir. **(He starts running)**

MAINWARING All right men, strip.

They all start to strip to the waist except Wilson. Frazer has several tattoos on his arm.

WALKER **(Pointing to tattoos)** I can see you're naval, Taff. **(He laughs)**

FRAZER It's nothing to laugh at, these cost me quite a few bob.

WALKER 'Ere what's this one? 'Will love you for ever, Mary'?

FRAZER I canna remember.

GODFREY **(To Mainwaring)** Excuse me, sir?

MAINWARING What is it, Godfrey?

GODFREY Do you want me to remove my binder?

MAINWARING Your what?

GODFREY My flannel binder. Shall I take it off?

MAINWARING Of course.

GODFREY Well would you mind holding the safety pin for a minute?

He starts to unwind.

MAINWARING Oh – keep it on – we shall be here all day.

KID'S VOICE **(Off)** Look at old hairy chest.

MAINWARING Who said that, Wilson?

WILSON It's some boys playing in the churchyard.

MAINWARING Well, tell them to go away at once.

WILSON Go away at once, you boys.

VOICE Why aren't you taking your clothes off as well, big bonce?

MAINWARING **(To Wilson)** Yes, why aren't you taking... I mean **(Shouts)** Clear off at once, you boys wouldn't be laughing at us like that if the Germans came.

VOICE No, but the Germans would.

MAINWARING If you don't go away at once I should clear the churchyard.

VOICE All right, Baldy, keep your shirt on.

They run off laughing.

MAINWARING We'll have a word with Miss Beckwith and have that ginger-haired one kept in after school.

Mrs Pike enters.

MAINWARING Now then – on the command 'Spring' – I want you all to –

MRS PIKE **(To Mainwaring)** I'm sorry to interrupt like this, Mr Mainwaring, but you see... **(She breaks off)** Why have you all got your clothes off?

WILSON Oh Mavis please, can't you see we're busy.

MAINWARING Well, Mrs Pike, what is it? We're just about to start some P.T.

MRS PIKE Oh I see, well don't let Frank stand around too long like that will you, Mr Mainwaring. I don't want him to start with his chest again.

MAINWARING Don't worry, Mrs Pike. He'll soon warm up.

MRS PIKE Why have you still got your shirt on, Arthur?

MAINWARING Yes, hurry up, Wilson.

WILSON I don't think it would be very good for discipline, sir.

MAINWARING What are you talking about?

WILSON **(Dropping his voice)** Well you see, sir, I'm afraid I've got rather a large hole in my vest.

MRS PIKE You didn't put that vest on again this morning did you, Arthur? I told you to leave it out for me to mend.

WILSON Please, Mavis, not so loud.

MRS PIKE **(In loud whisper)** Well take your shirt and vest off together, then no one will notice. You've got nothing to be ashamed of with your body, Arthur, you know. Mr Mainwaring, he's got a lovely physique when he strips off. Arthur take it off.

WILSON It's too cold.

MRS PIKE You're showing me up. Keep your hand over it.

Wilson quickly strips off and stands looking very sheepish.

MAINWARING What is it you want, Mrs Pike?

MRS PIKE Oh yes, I nearly forgot. **(She takes a rifle bolt out of her handbag)** I think this is part of Frank's gun, he left it behind. Is it important?

MAINWARING **(Taking it)** Yes, Mrs Pike, it is very important. **(He crosses to Frank Pike)** What's this, Pike?

PIKE It's a rifle bolt, sir.

MAINWARING I know what it is, you stupid boy. It belongs to your rifle.

PIKE I'm sorry, sir. I must have forgotten to put it back when I cleaned it.

MRS PIKE You left it on the draining board, Frank. I'm afraid I washed it up with the tea things. Anyhow, there's no harm done. I must be off now, don't let him stand around too long without his jacket on will you, Mr Mainwaring. **(She goes)**

MAINWARING **(Handing the bolt to Frank)** I'll talk to you later, Pike, now hold on to this and don't lose it.

Pike is wearing a thick woollen vest and he slips the bolt down the front of it.

Jones is still running on the spot.

MAINWARING That'll do, Jones. **(Jones stops)** Warmer now?

JONES Yes, sir. Dizzy, but warmer.

MAINWARING See he doesn't keel over, Walker. Now perhaps we can start. Give me the manual, Sergeant. **(Wilson hands it to him)** Here we are, deep breathing. 'Stand with your legs apart, hands on hips and chest out and breathe in through the nose, out through the mouth.' Well that's fairly simple. Have you got that?

They are all standing in the correct position with both hands on their hips, except Godfrey who only has one on his hip.

MAINWARING It's *both* hands on the hips, Godfrey.

GODFREY Oh I'm so sorry, sir.

MAINWARING Right men, are you ready? Now then, In, Out. **(He repeats this several times)**

WALKER **(Aside to Frazer) (He sniffs)** What's that funny smell?

FRAZER It's fresh air.

MAINWARING **(Reading from manual)** Now then, stand to attention. Jumping astride with the feet and arms at the same time like this. **(He shows them)**

WILSON Shall I hold the manual, sir?

MAINWARING Excellent idea, Sergeant.

Wilson takes the manual and holds it for Mainwaring to read while he is doing the exercise.

MAINWARING Are you ready? Go!

They all start the exercise except Wilson who is holding the book.

MAINWARING Don't joggle the book up and down like that, Wilson, I can't read the instructions.

WILSON If you don't mind me saying so, sir, it's not the book that's joggling up and down, it's you.

MAINWARING Platoon halt. Now I... I... **(He is gasping for breath)** I bet you feel better for that don't you, men? What's next?

WILSON Press ups, sir.

MAINWARING Ah yes. **(Wilson is still holding the book for Mainwaring to read)** Everyone face down on the floor. **(Mainwaring gets down on the floor, Wilson kneels down beside him still holding the book)** Now then, on the command one, you will slowly raise yourselves up, hold it and then lower yourselves to the floor. Right, one! **(Mainwaring tries to raise himself and fails)**

WILSON Allow me, sir. **(He grips Mainwaring by the back of his trousers and pulls)**

MAINWARING Thank you, Wilson, two. **(With Wilson's help he lowers himself again, he does this several times. Only a few of the rest of the platoon can raise themselves... the rest lie down)** One, two.

WILSON One...

MAINWARING All right, all right. Right on the feet, up. **(Wilson helps Mainwaring to his feet. The rest of the platoon struggle up)**

WILSON Circumrotary trunk movements next, sir.

MAINWARING **(Who is all in)** All right, Wilson, let them get their breath back. Some of these chaps are not used to it. **(The whole platoon is now on its feet with the exception of Jones who is still lying flat on his face)** What's the matter with Jones? (He crosses to him) Get up, Jones. (He kneels down and shouts in his ear) *Jones!*

JONES (Raising himself on his elbow) Oh I'm sorry, sir, I must have just dozed off. (He gets up)

MAINWARING Not bad men, not bad at all.

WILSON Circumrotary trunk movements next, sir.

MAINWARING (Icy) I shall decide what's next, Wilson, and now, men, I think we'll finish up with a simple exercise, touching our toes a half a dozen times. Right, begin. (Mainwaring raises his arms above his head and swings down to touch his toes. He gives a howl of agony, he is stuck)

WILSON Are you all right, sir?

MAINWARING It's my lumbago.

WILSON (To Jones) Quick, get a chair.

Jones rushes into the hall. The rest of the platoon break ranks and crowd round.

WALKER Shall I get the doctor, Sergeant?

FRAZER You'd be better off getting a new P.T. instructor.

Jones comes out with a chair.

JONES Here you are, Mr Mainwaring. (He puts the chair down)

WILSON Now then gently sit down, sir. (He lowers Mainwaring into the chair)

MAINWARING Ow! Get me up, it's agony, I must stand. (Wilson pulls him up again)

JONES What about brown paper and a hot iron, sir?

MAINWARING (Gasping) As long as I stay like this I'm all right. Just let me walk up and down for a bit. (Still bent double, he starts to walk up and down)

Captain Ogilvie enters, he is a tough Scot.

CAPTAIN Which is Captain Mainwaring?

MAINWARING I'm Captain Mainwaring.

CAPTAIN (Saluting) Oh! Captain Ogilvie, Highland Regiment.

MAINWARING (Returning the salute) How do you do? (He shakes hands)

CAPTAIN Are you in some sort of trouble, Captain?

WILSON Well you see, sir, it's his lumbago. He was showing us an exercise and he got stuck.

CAPTAIN Oh is that all? I'll soon fix that, now hold still. (He grips Mainwaring in a half Nelson, puts his knee in his back and gives a quick jerk. Mainwaring opens his mouth but no sound comes out) There, how's that?

Mainwaring mouths 'all right'.

CAPTAIN Good, then let's get down to business.

MAINWARING (In a faint voice) Fall the men in, Sergeant.

WILSON Right, fall in men.

They do so.

CAPTAIN Now then, Captain, I want you and your men to pay very careful attention. This is the scheme. A Sergeant and nine of my men will attempt to capture your headquarters. We shall start off from our H.Q. at Manor Farm which is three miles away, we will then infiltrate through the town and try to capture your H.Q. here. As you outnumber us three to one you shouldn't find it very difficult to stop us, on the other hand my men are highly trained professional soldiers, one hundred per cent fit. (He glares at Mainwaring) So watch out for yourselves. Now each side will have three lots of paint. Red paint for dead, blue paint for wounded, and white paint for a prisoner, they will then daub the enemy with the appropriate colour. If one of the enemy is wounded and taken prisoner as well, then you will daub him with a dash of blue and white paint. In the event of a dispute, you will call me, I shall be carrying a tin of pink and a tin of yellow paint. If I decide that he is wounded and not dead I shall add one daub of orange paint... if on the other hand I think he is dead instead of wounded I shall add two daubs of orange paint, but if I think that he is neither dead, wounded or a prisoner, I shall give him a daub of yellow paint which will cancel the whole thing. (He rattles this whole speech off at a terrific speed) Operations commence at 22.00 hours. Now are there any questions?

Mainwaring is doing frantic sums on his fingers, Wilson opens and closes his hand twice to signal ten o'clock. The Captain is looking at the men and does not see all this.

MAINWARING (Suddenly) Ten o'clock.

CAPTAIN (Fiercely) That's what I said, 22.00 hours. If you want to see me I shall be at my H.Q. at Manor Farm. You can carry on with your P.T. now Captain Mainwaring, and I must say by the look of your men they can do with it.

MAINWARING They're pretty fit you know, sir.

CAPTAIN Really. (Crossing to Pike) How old are you, lad?

PIKE Seventeen, sir.

CAPTAIN Well, in another year or so you'll be ready for the Army.

PIKE I want to go in the Navy, sir.

CAPTAIN You're very puny looking for your age, lad, and round shouldered too.

PIKE I'm very fit, sir.

CAPTAIN Are you now? Well I'll just see how fit you are, now clench your stomach muscles tight, I'm just going to give you a 'wee' blow to test you. Are you ready?

Pike screws his face up tight and nods, the Captain gives him a

nasty little jab with his right, there is a thud and the Captain doubles up with agony.

PIKE How's that, sir?

CAPTAIN **(Gritting his teeth)** Splendid, that will be all, Captain Mainwaring, carry on.

Mainwaring salutes, the Captain does his best to return the salute with his injured hand and goes.

MAINWARING Good gracious you took that well, Pike, anyone would think your stomach muscles were made of steel.

PIKE It's not my stomach muscles, sir, it's my rifle bolt. **(He reaches down into his vest and pulls out his bolt)**

MAINWARING Right men. Get dressed. Gather round. As you can see we are up against a pretty formidable opponent. Now are there any suggestions as to how we should tackle this problem?

FRAZER Well, sir, there's one thing that's worrying me.

MAINWARING What's that, Frazer?

FRAZER I feel a bit of a traitor, sir.

MAINWARING How's that.

FRAZER Well you see, sir, I'm a Highlander as well and I feel I'm fighting my own kith and kin so to speak.

MAINWARING Don't be absurd, Frazer, they're only acting the part of the enemy. After all, we're all British. I mean if Jerry comes, it won't make any difference whether you're wearing a kilt or trousers, he'll try to kill you just the same.

WALKER On the other hand, if it's a dark night and you're wearing a kilt he might get other ideas.

JONES Permission to speak, sir?

MAINWARING Yes, Jones.

JONES Well, sir, they're going to try and capture our headquarters, right?

Mainwaring nods.

JONES Well, why don't we move the headquarters, then when they get here, they won't know where it is?

MAINWARING I don't think that's quite the idea, Jones.

WILSON I know, sir, why don't we send someone into the enemy's camp, so to speak, to find out what their plans are?

WALKER That's a good idea, sir, all we've got to do is to dress Frazer up to look like a Scotsman.

FRAZER I am a Scotsman.

GODFREY As it's a farm, sir, why not dress someone up as a land girl.

FRAZER Are you volunteering, Godfrey?

WALKER It's perfectly simple, sir, all we've got to do is to disguise ourselves as something that won't look out of place on a farm.

MAINWARING And what do you suggest, Walker?

WALKER Leave it to me, sir.

FADE.

YARD. A LITTLE LATER

JONES Squad, 'shun. All present except Frazer and Walker, sir.

MAINWARING Where are they?

JONES They're involvulating a little scheme, sir.

Enter cow (Walker and Frazer inside).

MAINWARING It won't work, Walker. **(Cow turns its head towards Mainwaring)** I said it won't work, oh for goodness sake take that stupid head off, Walker.

Walker stands upright and takes off the head.

MAINWARING I wish you'd use your intelligence, Walker. How could you possibly pass for a real cow?

WALKER No, sir, you don't understand, my plan is to get mixed up with a flock of other cows.

MAINWARING It still wouldn't work, all right men – fall in inside the hall – put that thing back in the choir room. You'd no business to touch it. **(To Wilson as they go)** The Vicar would be furious if he found out. He practically lives for that scout pantomime. Jack and the Beanstalk this year, isn't it?

WILSON Yes, I must say His Reverence does make a simply marvellous dame.

MAINWARING Hm – a bit too life-like for my money. **(They go)**

Frazer's head pokes up, he is the rear end of the cow.

FRAZER What did he say?

WALKER Oh the usual, he says it wouldn't work.

FRAZER Well, how can we find out if we don't try?

WALKER That's the spirit, Taff, look I tell you what, you and me'll meet tomorrow night.

TELECINE

Cow trotting along country lane.

Cow looking round corner of farm building.

Cow trots up to gate in field, hand comes out from skin, opens gate, cow goes through gate, hand comes out again and closes gate.

Cow in field trots towards bunch of real cows, it gets in amongst them, kneels down cross legged, hand with a telescope comes out of skin. The telescope pans round the field.

Farm hand starts to drive cows across field. Panto cow follows, dog barks and snaps at its heels, cow kicks at dog.

Cow trotting across field, sound of a bull, cow looks round, starts to run, more bellows.

YARD. THE NEXT EVENING

There is a large blackboard with a map drawn on it. Mainwaring has a pointer. The rest of the men are standing round.

MAINWARING Now this is a rough plan of our position. Here is our H.Q. (**He points**) So you can see, the enemy can come on us from all sides.

WILSON It's going to be a bit of a job to cover all these points with only 17 men.

Walker and Frazer enter wearing the remains of the cow skin.

WALKER You were right, sir, it didn't work.

MAINWARING What happened?

WALKER Well, sir, we got up close to the farm and we were doing very well, then we crossed this field.

MAINWARING You mean someone spotted you?

WALKER Yes, sir, a bull, he was in the field as well.

FRAZER It was a terrible experience, sir.

WALKER It wasn't as bad as all that.

FRAZER You were in the front.

MAINWARING Well, Walker, I'll leave it to you to explain to the Vicar how you ruined his cow skin. Now where was I, Wilson?

WILSON We'd come to the conclusion we hadn't got enough men to go round, sir.

MAINWARING You're right, Wilson, we must find some way of getting into that farm. Now we must keep cool and think. What examples can we take from great military campaigns of the past? For instance what position would Napoleon take?

JONES (**Sticking his hand in his jacket**) He usually stood like this, sir.

MAINWARING Thank you, Jones, I'm well aware of how Napoleon stood.

WILSON What about the Trojan Horse, sir?

MAINWARING The Trojan Horse?

FRAZER Well, I'm not going to be the back legs of that.

WILSON Yes, you see, what I have in mind is this…

YARD. LATER

A small tractor with a truck loaded with hay is drawn up.

MAINWARING Well done, Wilson. How on earth did you manage to get this so quickly?

WILSON It came from Mr Gregg's farm.

MAINWARING Oh yes, I know him, he banks with us.

WILSON That's right, sir.

MAINWARING Well?

WILSON Well, you know he asked you for an overdraft, and you refused.

MAINWARING Yes.

WILSON Well, I told him you'd changed your mind.

MAINWARING You'd no right to exceed your authority like that, Wilson.

WILSON I'm sorry, sir. Well, my dear fellow. Who are we trying to help?

MAINWARING Well, now we've got it we might as well use it. Now we want someone to hide in the straw, then we drive it into the yard at Manor Farm and leave it there.

JONES (**Rushing forward**) Permission to speak, sir? I'll do that.

MAINWARING I think perhaps we ought to have a younger man. Pike you'd better do it and as you brought it here, Wilson, you'd better drive it. The trouble is they'll recognise you at once.

WILSON No they won't, sir. Excuse me a minute. (**He goes**)

MAINWARING All right, Pike get under the straw.

PIKE But, sir, I…

MAINWARING Don't argue, boy, do as I say. Come on, Godfrey, Frazer lend a hand.

They all push Pike under the straw.

MAINWARING There, that should do the trick.

Suddenly from under the straw there are three huge sneezes. Young Pike bursts out with his nose and eyes streaming.

MAINWARING What on earth's the matter with you, boy?

PIKE (**With his face buried in a hanky**) I kept trying to tell you, Mr Mainwaring, it's my hay fever. (**He gives another terrible sneeze**)

JONES (**Rushing forward again**) Permission to speak, sir? Let me go in, sir.

MAINWARING Oh, all right, Jones, seeing as you're so keen. Wait a minute, how are you going to breathe?

GODFREY What about a length of rubber tubing, sir?

MAINWARING An excellent idea, Godfrey, go into the Hall and get the stirrup pump.

Godfrey exits.

MAINWARING All right, now come on you men get him under the straw.

Godfrey enters with pump.

GODFREY Here you are Mr Mainwaring.

MAINWARING Thank you, Godfrey (He pulls the hose off the pump) Here you are Jones, stick this in your mouth.

Business getting Jones into straw.

MAINWARING That should be all right.

Wilson enters dressed in smock, felt hat and Farmer Giles beard.

MAINWARING Where did you get all that stuff, Wilson?

WILSON The same place as they got the cow skin from.

MAINWARING I don't know what the Vicar's going to say I'm sure. Now listen, if you're challenged, don't say anything. Just shake your head and say Ahhh!

WILSON All right, sir, I know.

MAINWARING Well, go on, try it.

WILSON Ahhh!

MAINWARING I suppose that will have to do. (He addresses the cart) Now listen to me, Jones, I want you to keep your ears open, and remember everything you hear, do you hear that, Jones? (Silence) Jones ,can you hear me? (He picks up the tube and shouts down it) Jones! (He pulls the tube and it comes away) He's got no air. He'll suffocate, quick get all that straw off the cart.

They all tear the straw off the cart, when the cart is empty there is still no sign of Jones.

MAINWARING Oh for goodness sake, where is he?

Jones taps Mainwaring on shoulder.

MAINWARING Jones, where have you been?

JONES I fell through the bottom of the cart.

TELECINE: FARM YARD

Long shot of hay cart and tractor are standing in the middle of yard.

Close up of top of Jones' head poking through the top of the hay.

Close up of clock on stable at nine.

Close up of Jones licking his lips.

Close up of clock at twelve.

VOICE All right, night manoeuvre section over here.

Sound of running feet.

Jones' head goes down.

Mid shot of back of cart.

CAPTAIN All right, Sergeant, fix the plan on the back of the cart here. (Sergeant fixes large plan on cart) Now pay attention, men, this is the plan. The scheme starts at 22.00 hours but we shall move off 21.00 hours. We shall skirt the town and move through these woods here, now we can't get out of the woods this side as we shall be spotted crossing the road. Now, at the bottom of the woods are cliffs which lead on to the beach, we shall descend the cliffs by means of ropes which we will carry with us. When we reach the bottom we will quickly move along the beach and rendezvous here under the pier, now at exactly 22.00 hours we shall move off up the street here and capture their H.Q. Now, as I've said before, the scheme starts at 22.00 hours, and five minutes later we shall be in their H.Q. Here. (He sticks in a flag with a large pin) and here. (He sticks in another flag)

Close up of Jones' face screwed up in agony.

WOODS. NIGHT

Mainwaring and Wilson are covered with foliage.

WILSON I only hope this idea of yours works, sir.

MAINWARING Well it worked all right in that Tarzan film I saw. The dirty rotters starting an hour early.

WILSON Well all's fair in love and war, sir. Besides, they're only getting into position a little earlier. I mean, they're not going to move off from their rendezvous until 22.00 hours.

MAINWARING Well, they won't even get into their rendezvous if I have anything to do with it.

Jones enters with the rest of the platoon.

JONES We've got all the paint, sir.

MAINWARING Thank you, Jones, now pay attention men. I'll just go over our plan again, now there are eight paths through the woods and every one is covered by a mantrap. Now what happens is this, the enemy comes running down the path, he puts his foot in that noose, the counterweights take his weight, then one of you pulls the rope and then up he goes feet first.

FRAZER Excuse me, sir have you ever seen it work?

MAINWARING Of course I've seen it work, I er...

WILSON In a Tarzan film.

WALKER 'Ere what about this paint then, sir?

MAINWARING Oh yes, now it's red for wounded.

WILSON No sir, it's red for dead, blue for wounded.

JONES No, no, you've got it all wrong, Mr Wilson, it's white for wounded and yellow for dead.

PIKE Why don't we give them a bit of each, sir, just to make sure?

MAINWARING Splendid idea, Pike, initiative, that's what I like to see.

PIKE I saw it in a Laurel and Hardy film, sir.

MAINWARING **(Looking at watch)** All right. Now we've got another hour before they're due to take up their positions. Walker. Jones. You will remain here to man this path. All right, the rest follow me.

They all go. Walker and Jones are left alone.

They pull the bushes round them and settle down.

Moon and clouds racing across sky.

Back to Jones and Walker.

JONES 'Ere, Joe.

WALKER What?

JONES Can you hear anything?

WALKER No.

JONES Neither can I.

WALKER What are you talking about, you silly old buffer?

JONES Well I thought perhaps you could hear something that I couldn't hear.

WALKER Well I can't.

Suddenly a whistle goes, followed by loud shouts.

JONES Blimey they're 'ere, stand by, Joe.

Dead silence.

JONES They've gone a bit quiet. **(There is a swishing sound and a cry)** That's the first trap. **(He chalks on a tree) (Two more cries)** number two and three. **(He marks the tree) (More cries)** Four, five, six, seven. **(He marks the tree)** We're next, stand by.

Silence.

WALKER Perhaps they've taken the wrong turning?

JONES Shush! I'm trying to listen.

Mainwaring and Wilson come through the bushes.

MAINWARING Good night's work, men.

Jones turns with a start.

JONES Oh, it's you Mr Mainwaring, you did give me a start.

MAINWARING What's happened?

WALKER Nothing yet, sir.

Frazer enters.

FRAZER We've got all the men taken prisoner, sir.

MAINWARING Quiet Frazer we're still waiting for the others.

WILSON Perhaps he doesn't know where the trap is, sir?

MAINWARING Well of course he doesn't know where the trap is, I mean if he knew where it was he wouldn't run into it would he?

JONES Permission to speak, sir?

MAINWARING Yes, Jones.

JONES Look, why don't I go out there, sir, get him to chase me, then I can decoy myself and they follow me. Then...

MAINWARING Then what?

JONES They fall into the trap.

MAINWARING Good idea, Jones.

JONES Right, sir, and if two figures come crashing through the bushes, let the first one go by, that will be me.

MAINWARING Right, off you go Jones, and good luck.

Jones goes.

MAINWARING There's no doubt about it, that man's got guts, Wilson.

WILSON Yes, sir, very gutsy.

MAINWARING All right, get your paint brushes ready men. **(They dip their brushes in the paint and wait)** And keep the paint off the uniform. **(There are loud shouts)** Stand by men, 'ere they come, and don't forget, let Jones go by first.

The first figure crashes across the path and into the bushes, he is followed by the second figure.

MAINWARING All right men, pull. **(The second figure flies in the air. Frazer and Walker slosh the paint on his face)** Stop! It's Jones. **(Jones is hanging upside down)** Get him down quick. Are you all right, Jones?

WILSON I don't understand at all, sir. Who was the first man?

CAPTAIN That was me. **(They all spin round, the Captain is standing behind them with a Tommy gun)** I must congratulate you, Captain Mainwaring, you almost outsmarted us.

MAINWARING Really, sir, I must protest!

CAPTAIN Don't, I'm afraid it's red paint on the boots for all, right, line up. **(To Frazer)** All right, hand me that brush and red paint, wait a minute, on second thoughts, I'll get it myself.

He steps forward, and puts his foot in the second noose, he flies up in the air and hangs upside down with his kilt hanging over his face. Close up of Mainwaring and Wilson. They quickly put their hands over their eyes then they slowly open their fingers.

WILSON Good Lord, sir.

MAINWARING Yes Wilson, now we really know what they wear underneath.

SERIES TWO **EPISODE TWO**

Recorded: Sunday 20/10/68 (made in black and white)
Original transmission: Saturday 8/3/69, 7.00–7.30pm
Original viewing figures = 11.3 million

ARTHUR LOWE	CAPTAIN MAINWARING
JOHN LE MESURIER	SERGEANT WILSON
CLIVE DUNN	LANCE CORPORAL JONES
JOHN LAURIE	PRIVATE FRAZER
JAMES BECK	PRIVATE WALKER
ARNOLD RIDLEY	PRIVATE GODFREY
IAN LAVENDER	PRIVATE PIKE
JANET DAVIES	MRS PIKE
AMY DALBY	DOLLY
NAN BRAUNTON	CISSY
BILL PERTWEE	ARP WARDEN
COLIN BEAN	PRIVATE SPONGE
PLATOON	RICHARD JACQUES, FRANK GODFREY, ALEC COLEMAN, HUGH CECIL, JIMMY MAC, DESMOND CULLUM-JONES, VIC TAYLOR, DAVID SEAFORTH, RICHARD KITTERIDGE

Designer Oliver Bayldon's illustrations of Godfrey's cottage and revolving summer-house reveal the meticulous planning that went into making *Dad's Army*.

THE BATTLE OF GODFREY'S COTTAGE

Originally titled, 'The Battle of Mon Repos'

• OLIVER BAYLDON REMEMBERS •

'I remember the poor buyer having trouble finding a suitable cockatoo parrot for this episode. The bird was delivered to the studio and it was placed inside a hired period cage. The trouble with parrots is that they don't understand cues; we'd been assured this one was silent, so that a voice could be dubbed over at a later date. However, this bird didn't understand the concept of camera rehearsals, and the bloody creature made repeated screeches, disrupting all the work. We had to cover the cage with several layers of blanket to plunge it into darkness until the recording, whereupon it was whipped off, the bird thrust into the spotlights, then quickly covered over again. After that experience, I never trusted parrots on the set!

'One of the items that I designed for this episode was a revolving summer-house for Godfrey's garden. A technical point always arose with floors, especially on scenes involving the garden. In this particular episode, the floor had to be smooth and clear wherever cameras ventured because they had mostly heavy pedestals on very low, highly mobile castors, surrounded by metal skirts which swept all before them. Anywhere cameras went could only be surfaced in something like painted lino to represent grass or gravel, while beyond in a sort of fringe was a border of grass, plants and bushes built upon sandbags covered with peat (no grit permitted because that would damage the camera wheels!). I remember the little circular summer-house had hidden castors, and one day a cameraman casually leant against it and it began revolving, depositing him on the ground!'

OLIVER BAYLDON
Designer

The Battle of Godfrey's Cottage

OUTSIDE NOVELTY ROCK EMPORIUM

The front of the shop is sandbagged in, and the door is boarded over. The name can still be clearly seen over the shop.

INSIDE NOVELTY ROCK EMPORIUM

Captain Mainwaring is alone, he is just putting the finishing touches to a large diagram which is fixed to the wall; he gives a little belch and thumps his chest. The shop bell rings and Wilson enters, pushing his bike.

WILSON Good evening, sir, you're early.

MAINWARING Yes, I wanted to finish this new battle plan. (**He gives another belch**) Unfortunately I had to rather rush my evening meal.

WILSON Oh, what did you have tonight, sir?

MAINWARING Woolton pie and treacle tart.

WILSON You had a real meal, eh, sir? But how did you get the treacle?

MAINWARING Well it wasn't real treacle, it's a new recipe my wife was trying out. The pastry is made from potato, and the treacle from grated carrot and saccharin.

WILSON What's it taste like?

Mainwaring thumps his chest again.

WILSON Indigestion, sir?

MAINWARING Just a touch of flatulence.

WILSON (**Handing him a little box**) Try one of these, sir.

MAINWARING Hmm! 'Calm-Tum tablets. Quick relief from all tummy upsets. Also combats air-raid strain.' What's air-raid strain got to do with the tummy?

WILSON Well it can be a bit embarrassing, you know, sir.

Shop bell goes, Jones and Frazer come in, pushing their bikes.

JONES Evening, Mr Mainwaring, Mr Wilson.

Frazer nods, Mainwaring shakes two tablets on to his hand and pops them in his mouth.

JONES What's that you're taking, Mr Mainwaring? (**He looks at the box**) You shouldn't have taken these you know.

MAINWARING Why not?

JONES Keep you on the run, sir.

MAINWARING Really? I thought they had the opposite effect.

JONES Touch of flatulence is it? 'Ere, try some of this.

He fishes a large medicine bottle out of his pack.

JONES There you are, the old bicarbonate of soda. I always carry it with me you know, got into the habit when I was in the Sudan. General Kitchener was very keen on it. 'Boys,' he used to say, 'always keep your bayonets sharpened and your bicarbonate of soda ready, then you won't get the wind up.' He had a very dry, subtle sense of humour you know, sir. That was 45 years ago, sir, and I've always carried this bottle of bicarbonate ever since. Mind you, it's not the same lot.

MAINWARING Thank you, Jones, but I think I'm all right now.

JONES (**Putting it back in his pack**) Well if you want it, sir, just let me know.

FRAZER It's going to be a bit crowded with the whole platoon in this wee shop, don't you think, Mr Mainwaring?

MAINWARING We shall just have to manage the best we can, won't we?

The shop bell is now going pretty hard as the rest of the platoon arrive. Most of them are pushing their bikes.

WILSON Don't you think we ought to remove that shop bell, sir? It's a bit of a nuisance.

MAINWARING Nuisance, where's your imagination Wilson? It will stop the enemy taking us by surprise.

The shop is now crowded out.

MAINWARING Oh really, Wilson, we can't have all these bikes in here, there won't be room to swing a cat. Tell them to put them outside.

WILSON Would you mind putting your bikes outside, please.

MAINWARING Give it as an order, Wilson. All bikes outside!! That goes for you too, Wilson, put your bike outside.

WILSON Yes, sir, shall I put yours out as well?

MAINWARING No, wait a minute, on second thoughts I think there's just room for two.

Walker enters.

WALKER Good evening, gents, what's this? Are you turning it into a second-hand bicycle shop, Mr Mainwaring? By the way, here's the tin of treacle I promised you.

MAINWARING Thank you, Walker. (**Thumping his chest**) I could have done with that earlier.

Pike enters, pushing his bike.

By now most of the platoon are outside the shop.

PIKE Why are all the men leaving, Mr Mainwaring? Is the parade over?

MAINWARING It hasn't started yet, you stupid boy, I told them to put their bikes outside. You'd better put yours outside too.

PIKE **(To Wilson)** Mum's not going to like me leaving my bike in the street you know, Uncle Arthur, it might get pinched.

MAINWARING That will do, Pike, put your bike outside at once. **(Pike goes, pushing his bike) (To Jones)** All right, Jones, fall the men in. Just a minute, Wilson, I want to talk to you.

JONES Platoon, fall in. **(The men fall in)**

Mainwaring and Wilson are talking right up close against the wall, they have their backs to the platoon.

MAINWARING **(Whispering)** Now look here, Wilson, I wish you'd stop young Pike calling you Uncle Arthur, it's bad for discipline you know.

WILSON I'm sorry, sir, it's not really my fault. You see when he was a little boy he used to call me something else, and Mavis, I mean Mrs Pike, told him to call me Uncle to stop him er... calling me something else.

MAINWARING What did he used to call you?

WILSON **(Dropping his voice right down)** Daddy.

MAINWARING What?

Wilson, frantic with embarrassment, mouths the word 'daddy'.

MAINWARING Well you're not really his Daddy, I mean, his father, are you?

WILSON Certainly not, sir.

During this, Jones has been falling the platoon in and checking them off.

MAINWARING Well you'll just have to tell him that in future...

JONES Platoon! Open order march.

The men open order and pin Mainwaring and Wilson to the wall.

MAINWARING What are you doing, Jones?

JONES I'm sorry, sir, I didn't realise the place was so small.

The front row of the platoon are standing jammed up against the wall.

MAINWARING **(Shouting)** Well put them back.

JONES Yes, sir, sorry, sir. **(In a panic)** Platoon, about turn.

The platoon about turn, the front row now have their backs to the wall and the back row have their faces to the wall.

MAINWARING Jones, pull yourself together.

JONES Sorry, sir. Platoon! Close order march.

They do so, they are now facing the wrong way round.

MAINWARING Put them in order, Wilson.

WILSON Platoon, about turn.

MAINWARING That's better. Who's missing, Jones?

JONES Godfrey, sir.

MAINWARING Oh well, we'll just have to carry on without him. All right men, on the command fall out, I want you to gather round the board here. Platoon, fall out!

They all sit in a tight circle around the board.

MAINWARING Now pay attention, men, this morning I received orders from G.H.Q. giving us our exact instructions in case the balloon goes up. Now I've asked you to parade here tonight at the Novelty Rock Emporium because in the event of an invasion, this shop will be our command post, our nerve centre.

The shop bell goes and an A.R.P. Warden comes in.

WARDEN **(Striding over the men)** Who's in charge here? **(He gives Wilson a push)**

WILSON **(Pointing)** Captain Mainwaring.

WARDEN Oh, it's you again is it? What are all those bicycles doing outside?

MAINWARING They belong to members of my platoon.

WARDEN I don't care who they belong to, get 'em shifted.

MAINWARING I don't think I like your tone.

WARDEN Oh, don't you, then I'll try it in a different tone. Get 'em shifted. How's that?

MAINWARING Don't you think you're rather exceeding your authority?

WARDEN The Defence of the Realm Act states – 'no vehicles or any other means of transport will be left unattended in a usable condition.' Don't you realise those bicycles could be used by enemy parachute troops?

MAINWARING What er... I am aware of the situation, and I shall take steps to see that it is attended to.

WARDEN You'd better, otherwise I shall have to let the tyres down, mate.

MAINWARING Don't you dare lay a finger on those machines. Now leave my shop, I mean my command post at once!

WARDEN I'm going, but don't say I haven't warned you, and you as well. **(To Wilson)**

He steps over the men and goes.

WILSON Just go away.

MAINWARING Corporal Jones, detail a man to stand guard over those bicycles.

JONES Yes, sir. **(He crosses to extra)** Private Sponge, outside and stand guard over those bikes, fix your bayonet, and if that Warden touches those tyres, let him have it right up.

Private Sponge goes through the door and Jones shuts it after him.

MAINWARING Jones, lock the door, I don't want that Warden trampling all over the platoon again.

Jones locks the door.

MAINWARING Now, men, as I was saying, in the event of an invasion this is the plan.

There is a knocking on the shop door.

MAINWARING All right, leave this to me, men.

He steps over the platoon and unlocks the door.

MAINWARING Now look here… **(It is Godfrey)** Oh, it's you Godfrey.

GODFREY Are you closed?

MAINWARING Why are you late, Godfrey?

GODFREY **(Still outside the door)** I'm sorry, sir, my bicycle had a puncture so I had to walk.

MAINWARING Well don't stand out there, man, come in. **(Godfrey comes in, Mainwaring locks the door and steps over the platoon and takes up his position by the board)** Now, as I was saying, as soon as you hear the church bells you will proceed at once to the Novelty Rock Emporium here. **(He points to the map)** I shall then divide the platoon into two sections. I shall take one half and Sergeant Wilson will take the other half. The first section will then move off to the crossroads here, one mile away. Now this is a vital strategic position. He who holds the crossroads, holds Walmington-on-Sea. Now we need to establish a machine gun post, and I think the ideal place would be your cottage here, Godfrey. You don't mind, do you?

GODFREY Mind what, sir?

MAINWARING Haven't you been listening? If we use your cottage as a machine gun post. You live with your two sisters, don't you?

GODFREY That's right, sir. The trouble is they might be in bed when the invasion comes, and as they're a little hard of hearing they might not let us in.

MAINWARING Well you've got a key, haven't you?

GODFREY Well no, sir, you see there's only one and they've got it. They did promise me one years ago, but nothing came of it.

JONES Permission to speak, sir? Why don't they leave it under a flower pot?

MAINWARING Excellent idea, Jones. See to it, Godfrey. So that's the plan, men. **(He stops)** Now from these two points **(He is starting to look very uncomfortable)** we shall send out patrols, and both **(He starts to talk very quickly)** points will keep in touch by the means of runners. **(Hissing to Wilson)** Have you got a penny on you, Wilson?

WILSON What on earth for?

MAINWARING **(Desperate)** Don't argue, give it to me now. **(Wilson hands him a penny, he snatches it and rushes to the door, tries to pull it open and finds it locked)** I can't get out. **(Wilson and Jones cross to the door)**

JONES Of course you can't, it's locked, sir.

MAINWARING Well unlock it then.

Jones unlocks door and Mainwaring rushes out.

JONES **(To Wilson)** I said he shouldn't have taken those tablets you know.

OFFICE AT BANK

Mainwaring is sitting at his desk. Mrs Pike is sitting facing him. There is a newspaper on the desk. Close up of headlines '50 Nazi Divisions Poised Across Channel'.

MAINWARING Yes, I think we should definitely dispense with the Channel Tunnel, Mrs Pike, and buy some war loans, they seem to be going well. **(He presses button)**

MRS PIKE I'm so grateful for your advice, Mr Mainwaring, you see being a widow, it's not always easy to know what to do for the best.

MAINWARING I quite understand, Mrs Pike, but don't worry, as your bank manager, I'm always here to help.

MRS PIKE You see, Mr Mainwaring **(Wilson comes in quietly and stands beside Mrs Pike)** what I miss is not having a man to look after. **(She turns and her eye is line with Wilson's jacket)** You've got a button missing, Arthur. Why didn't you tell me before you left this morning?

WILSON **(Aside to Mrs Pike)** Mavis, please. You sent for me, sir?

MAINWARING Yes, here are the details of Mrs Pike's shares I want you to sell, **(Hands him list)** Wilson. Anytime I'm not here, Mrs Pike, you'll find our chief clerk is perfectly equipped to handle your affairs.

MRS PIKE **(Blushing, looking down)** Yes, I'm sure. **(Getting up)** Well I'd better 'Go to it'. Mr Wilson's coming to supper with me tonight, aren't you, Arthur?

MAINWARING I'm afraid he won't be able to, Mrs Pike, he's taking a party of 18 to the cinema at Eastgate.

MRS PIKE A party of 18?

WILSON Home Guards.

MAINWARING It's a special showing for all H.G. units of the film, 'Next of Kin'.

MRS PIKE 'Next of Kin'. I've heard of that. Are you all going?

MAINWARING Yes, except me, I took my wife and her two sisters to see it last week.

WILSON Coals to Newcastle, eh, sir?

MRS PIKE Goodbye, Mr Mainwaring.

MAINWARING I'm glad I'm not coming with you tonight, Wilson, I've got a lot of paper work to catch up with down at H.Q. Well, I'm off now. I'll leave you to lock up. Oh look, Mrs Pike's forgotten her gloves, run after her. **(Wilson takes the gloves and goes. Mainwaring puts on his bowler hat, straps on his revolver and picks up his tin hat and gas mask, he sees a deed box on the desk)** I'd better put Mrs Pike's deed box back downstairs in the vaults. **(He picks up the box and opens the door to the vaults and closes it behind him. The office door opens, Wilson comes in)**

WILSON I Just caught up with her in time… oh, he's gone, funny I didn't see him, I expect he left by the back door.

Pike enters.

PIKE The rest of the staff have gone, sir. Do you want me for anything else?

WILSON No that's all, Pike. We haven't got much time, the coach leaves in 15 minutes.

PIKE I can't understand why they're taking us all to the pictures tonight.

WILSON G.H.Q. want all units to see the film, it deals with the effects of careless talk.

PIKE Who's in it then?

WILSON They didn't say. **(Church bells start to ring)** What's that?

PIKE Church bells, funny time of the day to ring them, perhaps someone's getting married.

WILSON It's the invasion signal.

PIKE Oh, Uncle Arthur, what are we going to do?

WILSON Well you can stop calling me Uncle Arthur for a start.

PIKE Shouldn't we go down to the Novelty Rock Emporium?

WILSON Yes, we should.

PIKE But the coach is waiting to take us to the pictures.

WILSON Well we shall just have to go another night. Get your rifle and gas mask and I'll lock up. **(He goes through the door)**

PIKE **(Following him through the door)** But, Uncle Arthur, don't you think we ought to tell Mum…

He closes the door behind him. The church bells have now stopped. The door from the vault opens and Mainwaring comes back in.

There is the sound of the front door of the bank slamming, Mainwaring goes out of the door into the bank.

MAINWARING Is that you, Wilson? He didn't waste much time, must have thought I'd gone, and as soon as my back's turned he makes off, he's getting a bit of a clock watcher, I must have a word with him about that too in the morning.

SIDE OFFICE. CHURCH HALL

Mainwaring is sitting at his desk, he is reading some papers.

The door bursts open and Frazer and Jones rush in.

JONES **(Gasping for breath)** They're here, sir, we're just on our way now to the Novelty Rock Emporium.

FRAZER We just happened to see your bike outside as we were passing. Come on, sir, there's not a moment to lose.

MAINWARING What are you talking about, Frazer?

FRAZER The church bells, sir, they've been ringing.

MAINWARING I've heard nothing. When was this?

FRAZER About 20 minutes ago, I was at home having my tea so I went straight round to collect Jones at his house and we're just on our way to the command post.

MAINWARING But this is terrible, the coach will be half-way to Eastgate by now. We've been waiting for six months for this moment, and now Hitler's at our throats and my platoon has gone to the pictures. By the way, why weren't you there?

JONES Coupon counting.

FRAZER Stocktaking. What are we going to do? There's only three of us left to defend the whole town.

MAINWARING Just a minute, let me think.

JONES **(Fixing his bayonet)** We'll fight to the last, that's what we'll do, sir, fight to the last, and when we run out of ammo we'll give 'em the old cold steel, they don't like it up 'em you see, sir, they don't like it up 'em.

MAINWARING Oh do pull yourself together, Jones.

JONES Sorry, sir, it's just that I've got the smell of battle in me nostrils, it gets me going you know. **(His bayonet is shaking)**

MAINWARING Do put that away, Jones, you'll hurt someone.

FRAZER It's going to be a bit difficult to defend with just three men you know, sir.

MAINWARING You're right, Frazer. We shall have to accept the fact that we three couldn't stop them landing. We shall have to change our plans. A commander in the field must always be flexible, make a snap decision.

JONES Don't take too long. They'll be here soon.

MAINWARING (**Crosses to cupboard**) The crossroads are a key position. Three determined men could hold up an army there. Deny the enemy their axis of advance. If we can hold out long enough, our regulars will have enough time to re-group for the counter attack. Might be the end of us, of course, but we are prepared for that, aren't we?

FRAZER Yes, sir.

DOLLY Do you know I had to queue up for 20 minutes this morning, just for that little bit of fish.

CISSY Aren't you parading with the Yeomanry tonight, Charles?

GODFREY No, dear, I have to go down to the clinic.

CISSY Oh, I see, well you'd better hurry up or you'll be late for parade.

• HUGH CECIL REMEMBERS •

'In this episode there was scripted dialogue between Percy the Parrot and Godfrey's sister Dolly, in the drawing room of their cottage. During rehearsals, knowing I could do quite a good parrot voice with the aid of a "Mr Punch" gimmick (Punch and Judy being one of my sources of income outside the TV studio), I asked who was to be the parrot on the night. The answer was Arthur Lowe. Nothing daunted, next day at rehearsal I was armed with a swazzle (the proper name for the gimmick in question) and in the bar at lunchtime I started practising. After lunch, Harold Snoad, the production assistant, came up to me and said: "Hugh, we're going to accept your offer; you can be the parrot and get paid accordingly."

'Unfortunately "The Battle of Godfrey's Cottage" is one of the missing episodes, so instead of having some really nice repeat fees, I'm still waiting for the tape to turn up!' **HUGH CECIL**

Since Hugh wrote this piece, the BBC have announced that this episode has been found.

Mainwaring takes a Lewis gun out of the cupboard.

MAINWARING We'd better take this with us. Jones, Frazer grab a magazine each.

JONES I don't think we're going to have much time for reading you know, sir.

Frazer grabs two magazines and gives one to Jones.

FRAZER Here.

JONES Oh, I see.

MAINWARING All right, men, at the double to Godfrey's cottage.

GODFREY'S COTTAGE

Olde worlde lattice windows, chintz curtains, padded chairs and a fringed pelmet round the mantelpiece. The place is crowded with Victorian knick knack. Godfrey is sitting having his tea with his two sisters, Cissy and Dolly, they are both in their 70s. There is a parrot in the corner of the room. They are all three rather hard of hearing

DOLLY Are you enjoying your nice bit of haddock, Charles?

GODFREY Yes, thank you, Dolly.

DOLLY Don't rush him, Cissy, I'm sure he's got time for another cup of tea and one of my upside-down cakes.

CISSY That reminds me, have a little word with that nice Mr Walker tonight will you, Charles, we need some more sugar.

GODFREY But I'm not going on parade tonight, Cissy.

CISSY Thank you dear, I'm sure he'll get them for you.

Godfrey gives up and carries on eating his tea. There is a loud squawk from the parrot.

DOLLY (**To parrot**) What is it, Percy, do you want your tea? How about a little bit of Dolly's upside-down cake? (**She crumbles some cake on a saucer and takes it to the parrot**) Here you are, Percy.

PERCY Ger, you silly old faggot.

DOLLY No, no, it's not maggots, it's one of my upside-down cakes.

There is a loud knocking on the door, Dolly goes to open it, there is the sound of muttering voices, she comes back to Godfrey.

MAINWARING Good evening, Mr Godfrey. May I come in? This is an emergency.

DOLLY Charles, dear, it's that nice bank manager Mr Mainwaring, he's got a big gun with him.

GODFREY I wonder what he wants. (**He quickly crosses to**

the door) Do come in, sir. (Mainwaring comes into the room with Jones and Frazer)

MAINWARING What are you doing here, Godfrey? I thought you'd gone into Eastgate with the rest of the platoon.

GODFREY No, it's my night for the clinic, sir.

FRAZER That makes one more of us anyhow, sir.

MAINWARING Well, hurry up and get your rifle and steel helmet, the invasion's on.

GODFREY What invasion, sir?

MAINWARING The Germans, of course. Didn't you hear the church bells?

GODFREY No, sir, I'm afraid not.

MAINWARING There's no time to go into it all now, we're setting up our machine gun post here. You did tell your sisters, didn't you?

GODFREY I'm afraid it slipped my mind, sir.

MAINWARING Well, you'd better tell them now. Good evening. We'll set the Lewis gun up here at this window, it gives us a clear line of fire. Give me a hand, Jones. (He puts the gun on desk)

GODFREY Would you mind putting this doyley underneath. Mind you don't scratch the top of that regency desk, sir. (Mainwaring gives him a glare)

JONES What we really need at this window is some sandbags, sir.

FRAZER What about cushions and pillows, sir?

MAINWARING Good idea, Frazer, go round the house and get as many as you can.

Frazer goes, the room is now a hive of activity. Mainwaring and Jones drag a settee up against the window. The two sisters are at the table still sipping their tea.

DOLLY (To Godfrey) Don't be so rude, Charles, offer your friends some tea.

GODFREY I don't think they want any just at the moment.

MAINWARING Come on, Godfrey, lend a hand.

GODFREY Yes, sir. (He has now got his rifle and is putting his steel helmet on)

CISSY It's that nice Mr Jones, the butcher from the High Street.

DOLLY Would you like a cup of tea, Mr Jones?

JONES Not just now thank you the Misses Godfrey, you see the Germans are coming. (He gets back to the window)

DOLLY Yes I know, so many people for tea, I think I'd better make some more.

She takes the teapot and goes to the door. As she opens it, Frazer comes in with an armful of cushions and pillows.

DOLLY Oh good afternoon, there's a gentleman here selling pillows. Better buy some. They match the ones upstairs. Cissy. Just wait there, will you? My sister will attend to you. (She goes)

FRAZER Here you are, sir.

MAINWARING Well done, Frazer. (He starts stacking them in the window) Have a look round the room, see if you can find some more. (He sees that Jones is still wearing his straw hat) Where's your helmet, Jones?

JONES Eh! (He takes off his hat) Oh blimey, sir, in all this confusion I'm afraid I forgot it.

MAINWARING You must have a steel helmet, man.

GODFREY Wait a minute, Mr Mainwaring I've got an idea. (He reaches out of the window, he unhooks an old German steel helmet which is hanging upside down with flowers in it)

MAINWARING Thank you, Godfrey, but I don't think putting a flower pot on his head is going to help.

GODFREY It's not really a flower pot, sir, it's an old German steel helmet. I brought it back from France in 1918 as a souvenir.

MAINWARING It's better than nothing. (He takes the helmet, empties the flowers and earth out of the door) Sorry about your geraniums, Godfrey, but this is war. Here you are Jones, put that on.

Jones takes the helmet and puts it on, the wrong way round, the neckpiece covers his eyes.

MAINWARING You've got it on the wrong way round, Jones.

JONES (Turning it round) Oh yes, sir, sorry, sir.

MAINWARING Hurry up with the rest of those cushions, Frazer.

FRAZER Coming, sir. (He has gathered up all the cushions in the room except the one Cissy is sitting on) Excuse me, Miss Godfrey. (He takes the cushion from underneath her, he crosses to the window) Here you are, sir, that's the lot.

MAINWARING (Taking the cushions) Well done, Frazer. Go and see if there's a position at the back window.

FRAZER Aye, sir.

JONES Oo er.

MAINWARING What is it, Jones?

JONES I've got a cold wriggly feeling down my spine, sir.

MAINWARING Pull yourself together, Jones, you've been into action before.

JONES Yes, but I've never had a cold wriggly feeling down me spine like this before. Ow. (He snatches off his helmet, and puts his arm down his back inside his shirt, he pulls out a worm)

CISSY **(Coming into picture)** Well if he will wear a flower pot on his head what else can you expect?

FRAZER This is the best line of fire.

MAINWARING Good man, Frazer. **(Picks up cushion)** Who put this here? They won't stop any bullets.

JONES Soon fix that, sir. Go on, Frazer. Fill them with something harder. **(He holds cushion and starts taking out feathers)**

CISSY We'll have to get some condition powder for Percy. He's moulting terribly.

FRAZER **(Returning with coal)** How about this?

DOLLY How many lumps?

FRAZER How many lumps?

JONES Put the lot in.

NOVELTY ROCK EMPORIUM

Walker and Wilson are looking up the street through slits in the sandbags.

WILSON I don't like it Walker, it's *too* quiet.

Oliver Bayldon's illustrations – including the Novelty Rock Emporium – provided an overall picture of content and mood.

WALKER It's funny you should say those words like that, Sarge.

WILSON Oh why?

WALKER Well that's what the Sergeant always says in those western films.

WILSON Really.

WALKER Yeh, you see this cavalry patrol are trotting along, they stop and the officer looks round through his field glasses. Then the Sergeant says, I don't like it, sir, it's *too* quiet.

WILSON Then what happens?

WALKER He gets a dirty big arrow in his chest. THUCK!

WILSON (**Raising his eyebrows**) I see.

WALKER Mind you, sometimes it's the officer who says it's *too* quiet. The Sergeant still gets the arrow. THUCK!

WILSON All right, Walker, that will do.

WALKER Here's young Pike.

The shop bell rings and Pike comes in with two extras.

WILSON Well, where's the Lewis gun, Pike?

PIKE It's not there, sir.

WILSON What do you mean, not there?

PIKE Well, Sarge we went back to the church hall to fetch it like you told us, and when we got there the cupboard was bare.

WALKER Blimey, perhaps the Germans have taken it, Sarge.

WILSON They wouldn't know where it was. I can't understand what's happened to Captain Mainwaring and the rest of the platoon.

PIKE Mr Frazer was the Lewis gunner, Sarge. Wherever he is, he's probably taken the gun with him.

WALKER If he's gone where I think he's gone, he couldn't have taken a gun with him, son.

WILSON Oh go and stand somewhere else, Walker. You're getting on my nerves.

WALKER There's not many places I can stand with all these flippin' bikes in here. (**He slides out of the picture**)

Wilson peers over the sandbags looking up the street.

PIKE Uncle Arthur, I mean Sarge, do you think Mr Mainwaring and the others are all right?

WILSON Yes, of course they are.

PIKE Well why aren't they here, then? I mean, Mr Mainwaring knows where to come, I mean he told us, he said if you hear the church bells, go at once to the Novelty Rock Emporium.

WILSON Oh do be quiet, Pike, I'm trying to think.

Silence.

PIKE Uncle Arthur.

WILSON What is it now?

PIKE I ain't half hungry.

WILSON Well you should have brought some sandwiches, you knew we were going over to Eastgate.

PIKE Well I thought I'd get an ice cream in the pictures, and have my supper when I got in.

Silence.

PIKE Uncle Sergeant.

WILSON What?

PIKE If anything happens to Mr Mainwaring, will they make you the manager?

WILSON (**Brightening slightly**) I don't know, I hadn't thought about it.

PIKE If they make you the manager perhaps they'll make me the chief clerk.

Walker comes into the picture with a cardboard box.

WALKER 'Ere look what I've found down in the basement. (**He pulls out some sticks of rock**) They must have been there since before the war. Shall I hand them out, Sarge? The platoon look as if they could do with a bit of nourishment.

WILSON Yes, all right, Walker.

WALKER Line up lads, get your rock 'ere, Walmington-on-Sea stamped right through it.

PRIVATE How much?

WALKER A sprazy will do. (**He takes money**)

PRIVATE 'Ere, this has got Clacton stamped on it.

WALKER Well what do you expect for a tanner, Ashby-de-la-Zouche?

WILSON Walker, what are you doing taking money for that rock?

WALKER Sorry, Sarge, they forced it on me.

WILSON Well give it back at once.

WALKER All right, Sarge. Do you want a stick?

WILSON No, thank you.

There is now silence except for everyone sucking rock.

WILSON I can't wait any longer for Captain Mainwaring, we've been here nearly two hours, we shall just have to carry out the battle plan without him. Pike, Walker, get your things together, we're going to establish a second command post at Godfrey's cottage. Private Sponge, you'll be in charge. Wait for half an hour and if we're not back, then send out a patrol to report to me at Godfrey's cottage. Got that?

PRIVATE Yes, Sarge.

PIKE Can I bring my stick of rock with me, Uncle Arthur?

WILSON No you can't. Put it away. (**He opens the shop door**) Come on.

GODFREY'S COTTAGE. DUSK

Mainwaring and Frazer are peering over the Lewis gun out of the front window, and Jones and Godfrey are peering out of the back. Dolly and Cissy are both knitting. The furniture is all piled against the doors and windows in a state of siege.

FRAZER **(Peering out)** I don't like it, Captain Mainwaring, it's *too* quiet.

MAINWARING Can you see anything?

FRAZER Not a thing, it will be dark soon.

MAINWARING I wonder where the rest of the platoon are?

FRAZER They probably had to leave the coach and walk back. All civilian vehicles have to be put out of action during an invasion alarm.

MAINWARING In that case they won't be back for hours. **(There is a terrible squawk from Percy)** Can't you keep that parrot quiet, Miss Godfrey?

DOLLY **(Coming over to Mainwaring)** Yes he is rather sweet, isn't he? He belonged to our father, you know. He's nearly a hundred years old, the parrot, not our father – he died at 92, five years ago. During the last year of his life he was confined to his bed, so we bought him the parrot to keep him company, and it was during that time that he taught Percy to speak. Percy, say 'here comes the Vicar, let's say our prayers'.

PERCY Take off your knickers, get up them stairs.

DOLLY There, you see, he was a very religious man, our father.

PERCY Take off your knickers, get up them stairs.

JONES **(Coming over to Mainwaring)** Permission to speak, sir?

MAINWARING What is it, Jones?

JONES Can I go outside for a minute, sir?

MAINWARING What! Oh yes. I'll come and cover you.

THE REVOLVING SUMMER-HOUSE
AT THE BOTTOM OF GODFREY'S GARDEN

It is now dark. Wilson, Pike and Walker come round the edge of the summer-house.

WILSON It doesn't look to me as if there's anyone at home.

WALKER Godfrey's two sisters are probably in bed, Sarge.

PIKE Shall I nip round the front and look under the flower pot for the key.

WILSON No, wait a minute, I don't like the look of this, it's *too* quiet. **(There is a sound of a flush)** What was that?

WALKER Sounded like the what's name.

PIKE **(Pointing)** Uncle Arthur, look, it's a German soldier coming out, look at his helmet.

WALKER Blimey, he's right.

WILSON Take cover in here. Prepare to fire.

WALKER Don't you think we ought to wait until Private Sponge gets here with the rest of the platoon?

WILSON There's no time. Take aim. FIRE!

INSIDE COTTAGE

Jones staggers through the door.

MAINWARING **(Dragging Jones through the door)** Quick, inside, Jones. Shut the door. They're here, keep down everyone.

Jones is trembling with rage and fixing his bayonet.

MAINWARING What are you doing, Jones?

JONES Heathen swine, I'm going to sort 'em out.

MAINWARING Get down on the floor at once. Frazer, cock the gun.

FRAZER Right, sir. Give me a hand, Jones.

Frazer and Jones bring the Lewis gun over to the rear window.

DOLLY What was that noise, dear?

CISSY I don't like to interrupt them, but we shall really have to ask them to draw the blinds and put the lights on. I can't see to knit.

FRAZER All ready, sir. Shall I fire?

MAINWARING *Wait a minute!* Where did those shots come from, Godfrey?

FRAZER From the direction of the revolving summer-house, sir.

GODFREY It's rather nice. You see you can turn it in whatever direction the sun's shining.

JONES The sun isn't shining.

MAINWARING Oh shut up, Jones. Have you got the range, Frazer?

FRAZER Aye, sir.

SUMMER-HOUSE

WALKER Did we get him, Sarge?

WILSON I don't know. We'd better keep under.

COTTAGE

Frazer with Lewis gun ready to fire.

MAINWARING Fire!

SUMMER-HOUSE

As the bullets hit it, it starts to revolve.

COTTAGE

DOLLY We'd better get these tea things cleared away. You take the tray out to the kitchen. **(Goes to window)**

CISSY Better not disturb them.

DOLLY I'll shake the cloth out of the window upstairs.

MAINWARING Cease fire.

SUMMER-HOUSE

PIKE What was that?

WALKER 'Ere, Sarge, the cottage has disappeared.

WILSON We're facing the wrong way round.

PIKE Look, I can paddle us round like this.

WILSON Keep down.

PIKE What are we going to do?

WILSON I think we'd better go somewhere else.

WALKER 'Ere, look at that, they're waving a great white cloth out of the window, they're surrendering. You'd better go in and accept it, Sarge.

WILSON No, you go, Walker, I'd better stay here and keep an eye on things.

WALKER Perhaps young Pike ought to go.

PIKE Well you're the oldest, Uncle, I mean Sergeant.

WILSON We'll all go.

COTTAGE

FRAZER Mr Mainwaring, sir, they're surrendering, three of them are coming out with handkerchiefs tied to their rifles.

MAINWARING Well done, men, we showed them, eh! They might be up to their tricks. I'll make them come right into the room. Keep 'em covered, Frazer. **(Shouting)** Come in ze here. Put the lights on so we can get a good look at them. **(Jones puts the lights on and stands trembling with his bayonet)** All right, come in ze here with your hands up. **(Wilson, Walker and Pike come in)** Good heavens, Wilson.

WILSON Mr Mainwaring.

MAINWARING You might have killed us!

WILSON No, you might have killed us!

MAINWARING I'm disappointed in you, Wilson. You surrendered. You should have fought to the last man.

WILSON But we thought you were Nazi soldiers.

MAINWARING That's no excuse. You should have kept on firing.

WILSON But we might have killed you.

MAINWARING That's beside the point. You'd no right to give in.

WILSON We didn't give in. You gave in first.

MAINWARING Oh, no we didn't.

Ad lib dialogue.

The A.R.P. Warden bursts into the room.

WARDEN Who's in charge here? Oh, I might have guessed. I'm going to get you good and proper this time, Light streaming all over the road, what's the idea, eh? Good job I was passing on my way home.

MAINWARING What are you going home for? There's an invasion on.

WARDEN What are you talking about?

MAINWARING The church bells, of course.

WARDEN That was a false alarm, we've been stood down for ages. Right, I'm going to book you all for flagrant disregard of blackout regulations.

MAINWARING All right, get on with it. **(To Wilson)** Now for the last time, Wilson, I did not surrender and I repeat, nothing would ever make me surrender.

Sound of shots.

MAINWARING What's that?

They all duck.

WALKER Blimey. It's Private Sponge.

MAINWARING Quick. Hang something white out of the window.

SERIES TWO **EPISODE THREE**

Recorded: Sunday 27/10/68 (made in black and white)

Original transmission: Saturday 15/3/69, 7.00–7.30pm

(The episode was initially planned for transmission on 20/1/69.)

Original viewing figures = 11.3 million

This episode is no longer available in the BBC archives.

ARTHUR LOWE . . . . . CAPTAIN MAINWARING
JOHN LE MESURIER . . . . . SERGEANT WILSON
CLIVE DUNN . . . . . LANCE CORPORAL JONES
JOHN LAURIE . . . . . PRIVATE FRAZER
JAMES BECK . . . . . PRIVATE WALKER
ARNOLD RIDLEY . . . . . PRIVATE GODFREY
IAN LAVENDER . . . . . PRIVATE PIKE
ANTHONY SHARP . . . . . BRIGADIER (WAR OFFICE)
DIANA KING . . . . . CHAIRWOMAN
PATRICK WADDINGTON . . . . . BRIGADIER
EDWARD EVANS . . . . . MR REED
MICHAEL KNOWLES . . . . . CAPTAIN CUTTS
GILDA PERRY . . . . . BLONDE
LARRY MARTYN . . . . . SOLDIER
ROBERT LANKESHEER . . . . . MEDICAL OFFICER
COLIN BEAN . . . . . PRIVATE SPONGE

PLATOON . . . . . RICHARD JACQUES, FRANK GODFREY, ALEC COLEMAN, HUGH CECIL, JIMMY MAC, DESMOND CULLUM-JONES, VIC TAYLOR, DAVID SEAFORTH, RICHARD KITTERIDGE

The Loneliness of the Long-Distance Walker

• JIMMY PERRY REMEMBERS •

'When it came to dreaming up ideas for all the episodes I'd often think back to old films and plays I'd seen. During the war years, I'd go to the cinema three or four times a week, and some of the films proved to be an inspiration; I also looked through back copies of the *Daily Mirror*.

'We also focused on issues that affected society during the war, such as rationing. We were all in the same boat, but it's been said that British people were never as healthy as they were during the war. We had plenty of potatoes, and the seas were full of fish. The trawlers didn't have to travel out too far either – not like today.'

JIMMY PERRY

The Loneliness of the Long-distance Walker

CHURCH HALL

The men are all drawn up on parade. Wilson is calling the roll.

WILSON Private Pike?

PIKE Here, Sergeant.

WILSON Private Frazer?

FRAZER Here, Sergeant.

WILSON Lance Corporal Jones?

JONES Here, Sergeant.

WILSON Private Walker?

There is no answer.

He calls again.

WILSON Private Walker? Has anyone seen Private Walker?

They all shake their heads.

WILSON Private Godfrey?

GODFREY Pardon?

WILSON Are you there?

GODFREY Yes.

WILSON Well, say so. Platoon atten… try to get it right, Jones… shun. (**He salutes Mainwaring**) Platoon ready for inspection, sir, bar one.

MAINWARING Wilson – you're supposed to be giving me a piece of military information, not calling the odds. Who's missing?

WILSON Private Walker, sir.

MAINWARING He's bringing me a bottle of whisky tonight. I hope he's all right.

WILSON So do I, sir. He's bringing me some cigarettes.

A murmur runs through the platoon.

FRAZER I don't like the look of this. I ordered a bottle of whisky.

JONES He promised me a bottle of gin.

GODFREY He's bringing me a box of fudge, for my sisters, you know.

WILSON Shall we carry on without him, sir?

MAINWARING Yes, of course.

WILSON Platooooon – open order – march!

JONES Sorry, I'm not my usual self.

WILSON Oh yes you are.

The door bursts open – Walker rushes in, in a terrible state. He staggers up to Mainwaring and salutes.

WALKER I'm sorry I'm late, but I've got to go, you know.

MAINWARING We all realise that, Walker. Fall in.

WALKER No, sir. You don't understand. I've got to go. It's the medical.

MAINWARING Well, you probably took too much of it. Are you all right now?

WALKER No, sir. It's my call up! I've got to go for my medical in ten days' time.

MAINWARING But I thought you were in a reserved occupation? What do you describe yourself as?

WALKER I put myself down as a banana salesman and a wholesale supplier of illuminated signs. D'you think that's where I slipped up?

MAINWARING This is very serious news. You'd better fall the men out, Sergeant.

WILSON Er, yes. Fall out, you chaps.

The men fall out and crowd round.

FRAZER This is terrible news, Joe, terrible! What about my whisky?

JONES And my gin?

GODFREY What about my sisters' fudge?

PIKE What about my Mum's elastic?

MAINWARING Don't be selfish, men. We mustn't think about ourselves. By the way – what about my whisky?

WALKER I've got it in my bag.

He opens his bag, takes out a bottle of whisky, gives it to Mainwaring.

MAINWARING Oh, that's good. Thank you. The point is, we really need you in the platoon. I mean, you're more important to us here than you would be there, eh, Wilson?

Walker hands Wilson his cigarettes.

WILSON Definitely more important, sir.

MAINWARING But you can't expect a lot of brass hats in Whitehall to know what the situation is. I mean, to them, Walker is just a cipher. (**Walker resents this**) But to us he's an important cornerstone in our organisation. Well, this is a time for action not words – don't you agree, Wilson?

WILSON I always think it a good idea to keep the words down to an absolute minimum, sir.

MAINWARING Precisely. We'll send a signal to the War Office pointing out that they've made a mistake and telling them that we're jolly well coming to sort it out for them. Well we'd better send a telegram. Take it down.

WILSON I'll just go and get a pencil and paper, sir.

Wilson goes to office.

JONES Look, sir – I know a few dodges that will stop him passing his medical. The best one is to drop some water in his ear 'oles. Plug 'em up with cotton wool.

MAINWARING Yes, what happens then?

JONES And that'll make him deaf just long enough not to pass his medical.

MAINWARING Jones! Are you suggesting that I should stoop to underhand tricks?

JONES No, sir – but it's the only way you'll do it.

MAINWARING Nonsense! I shall tell them straight that he's more important to us than he would be in the army. **(Wilson returns)** Now take this down, Wilson – 'To the Officer in Charge, Home Guard, War Office, London'. Message begins –

WILSON Message begins –

MAINWARING No, don't put that down. 'Desirable Walker not called up yet –'

WILSON Shall I put that down?

MAINWARING Yes, of course, that's the message. 'Request interview tomorrow at 5 pm'.

WILSON That's 17.00 hours.

MAINWARING Yes, exactly. That should do the trick! 'Signed – Captain Mainwaring Officer Commanding First Platoon, Walmington-on-Sea Home Guard'.

WALKER **(Handing him the money)** Here you are, Mr Mainwaring – have this on me.

MAINWARING That should do the trick. Thank you, Walker. Right, send that off will you, Wilson.

SMALL ROOM IN THE WAR OFFICE

The Brigadier is sitting behind a desk. He is a scholastic 'Joe Grimond' type. On the desk are several phones and three signal lights – one of them is flashing.

BRIGADIER **(On phone)** I don't give a damn – I want it seen to at once, d'you understand – you're not the only one who's been up all night. I haven't left this desk for 24 hours. **(He slams down phone as the Staff Captain enters)** These armchair officers get on my nerves!

CAPTAIN There's a Captain Mainwaring and a Mr Wilson to see you, sir. They have an appointment for 17.00 hours.

BRIGADIER Oh five o'clock. I'd forgotten all about them! It's all the fault of that damned brother-in-law of mine, he's C.O. of this P.T. outfit and he's a mad keen heel-and-toe merchant.

CAPTAIN Heel-and-toe merchant, sir?

BRIGADIER Long-distance walker. He won the London to Brighton race in '37. He wants to get together a crowd of fellows to make up a crack team.

CAPTAIN What's this got to do with the Home Guard, sir?

BRIGADIER Well, he thought that there'd be lots of fellows in the Home Guard Units waiting for their call-up, so he asked me to send out a round robin to various units asking if they'd got any champions – due to go to into the army.

CAPTAIN Did you have any luck?

BRIGADIER No good at all – didn't get a single answer. That was until this morning – then I got this. **(He hands telegram paper to the Captain)**

CAPTAIN **(Reads)** Desirable Walker not called up yet. Request interview tomorrow – 17.00 hours.

Captain crosses to the door and opens it.

CAPTAIN Come in, please.

Mainwaring and Wilson enter.

BRIGADIER Sit down, gentlemen. I can give you five minutes only. I'll just take down the details. What's this walker's name?

MAINWARING I beg your pardon, sir?

BRIGADIER The walker's name – man!

MAINWARING Walker, sir.

BRIGADIER I know that – I want his name.

WILSON His name's Walker, sir.

BRIGADIER D'you mean to say you've got a walker named Walker?

MAINWARING Yes, sir.

BRIGADIER That's unusual – eh, Cutts!

CAPTAIN Oh, I don't know, sir. I knew a butcher named Butcher once.

BRIGADIER Did you? Well – go on – what's his record?

MAINWARING His record, sir?

BRIGADIER He's got a record, hasn't he?

MAINWARING **(Aside to Wilson)** Has he got a record, Wilson?

WILSON I don't think he's ever been found out, sir.

MAINWARING No record, sir.

BRIGADIER Well – is he good?

MAINWARING Yes – very good, sir.

BRIGADIER How the hell can he be good if he hasn't got a record?

MAINWARING I don't think I follow you.

BRIGADIER Look – is he one of the London to Brighton walkers?

MAINWARING No, sir. I think he's one of the Walmington-on-Sea Walkers.

BRIGADIER Sea Walkers?

MAINWARING No, jay-walker, sir.

BRIGADIER Jay-walker!

MAINWARING Yes, Joe Walker – that's his full name.

BRIGADIER I know what his name is, but how d'you know he's a walker?

MAINWARING Because he told us so!

WILSON That's right – he said – 'I'm Walker'.

BRIGADIER Surely he said – 'I'm *a* walker'?

MAINWARING No, sir – not A Walker – He said 'I'm J Walker'.

There is a pause – the Brigadier clears his throat.

BRIGADIER When is he due for call up?

MAINWARING Very soon. He goes for his medical next week.

BRIGADIER Very well – leave it with me. I'll see what I can do. Good day.

MAINWARING Thank you very much, sir.

Mainwaring and Wilson start to go. One of the lights on the desk starts to flash.

CAPTAIN **(To Wilson and Mainwaring)** That's the yellow warning – air raid. You two had better go to the shelter in the basement. It's along the passage and down the stairs. Just follow the others. It's clearly marked.

MAINWARING Oh, thanks. Er... Good day.

They both go.

BRIGADIER A. Walker – J. Walker – those two are up the pole if you ask me. **(Tears up the paper)** If my brother-in-law wants any walkers, he's just got to get them himself.

CAPTAIN Hadn't we better beat it down the shelters, sir?

BRIGADIER What! With those two lunatics? You can go if you like – I'd rather take my chance up here.

SHELTER

WILSON Wake up, sir, the all-clear's gone.

MAINWARING Good heavens! Look at the time, we've missed our last train home. Come on, we must find a hotel for the night.

UNDERGROUND STATION

Close up of Mainwaring's head on pillow. Beside him is a pretty blonde. On the other side is Wilson's head.

MAINWARING Are you asleep, Wilson?

WILSON Not yet, sir.

BLONDE Are you sure you wouldn't like your friend to come and lie next to you?

WILSON No thank you, Madam. I'm quite comfortable where I am.

MAINWARING Jolly decent of you to make room like this – Miss – er?

BLONDE Just call me Judy.

MAINWARING Er... well, my name's Mainwaring. And this is Mr Wilson.

WILSON How d'you do?

MAINWARING Well, goodnight – er Judy. Goodnight, Wilson.

WILSON Goodnight, sir. Goodnight, Judy.

BLONDE Goodnight, boys.

The camera pans up the wall and we see an underground sign which says 'Trafalgar Square'. We pan along a row of sleeping figures.

MAINWARING'S OFFICE AT THE BANK

The office is empty. We hear voices – the door opens, Mainwaring and Wilson come in, they both look pretty scruffy, and could do with a shave. Pike follows them in.

MAINWARING Oh Pike – I want you to apologise to the staff for me for keeping them waiting. Tell them we were caught in an air raid and we had to wait for the first train back in the morning.

PIKE Nasty thing to happen, sir.

Pike picks a long blonde hair from Mainwaring's shoulder.

MAINWARING You see... we... er had to sleep in the Underground. Things got a bit mixed up.

PIKE Yes sir! Was there anything else, sir?

MAINWARING Of course there wasn't. Oh – I see what you mean. No thank you, Pike.

Pike goes.

MAINWARING You always were tone deaf, Wilson.

WILSON If you don't mind me saying so, sir, you seem a bit edgy this morning.

MAINWARING Edgy? Who wouldn't be edgy after a night in the Underground?

WILSON Didn' t you sleep, sir?

MAINWARING I do not find that someone shouting – 'MIND THE DOORS, LET 'EM OFF FIRST PLEASE' in my ear conducive to a good night's rest.

WILSON Well, I'll just pop off home to shave and change, sir. I haven't got much time – the Committee is meeting at 11.30.

MAINWARING What precisely do you do on this committee – inspect the drains?

WILSON It's the Military Service Hardship Committee, sir, for people with one-man businesses, who'll be ruined if they're called up.

MAINWARING Oh, I see. Draft dodgers.

WILSON Not all of them, sir. Some of them are quite genuine cases.

MAINWARING Well, I'm sure that… wait a minute… Walker! He's got a one-man business.

WILSON But if he's called up, he'll hardly be ruined.

MAINWARING No – but we shall be.

WILSON Ah – I'm sorry, sir, but I couldn't be a party to anything like that.

MAINWARING I'm not suggesting anything underhand, Wilson. There's nothing to stop him going before the Committee is there?

WILSON No I suppose not, sir.

MAINWARING And you'd be there to make sure he got a favourable hearing.

WILSON I must emphasise, sir, that I shall have to be absolutely impartial.

MAINWARING I shall expect you to be, Wilson. I shall expect you to be, and I know I can rely on you to banish from your mind the thought that if Walker goes – so will the cigarettes and whisky. You will decide the case solely in the light of the mortal blow dealt to his struggling one-man business and the threat to the security of this island if we lose one of the only able bodied men in our unit.

WILSON But he will be in the army, sir.

MAINWARING This is the place where Jerry is going to attack, Wilson – not Catterick. What does he have to do?

WILSON He fills in an application form.

MAINWARING Well, bring one back with you. We'll get it filled in tonight.

WILSON Then he must have someone to speak for him.

MAINWARING A lawyer?

WILSON No. Just a reliable citizen of some repute.

MAINWARING Can you think of any more suitable person than a bank manager like me?

WILSON Well…

MAINWARING That settles it, I shall represent him.

CHURCH HALL. DAY

The three members of the Committee are sitting at a table. The chairman is a J.P., a tight-lipped, efficient-looking lady. The trade union representative is a stroppy Welshman – the third member of the panel is Wilson. Mainwaring is addressing the tribunal, Walker sits beside him.

MAINWARING And in conclusion may I urge the tribunal, with respect, of course, but may I urge the tribunal to consider this is not a war in which gallant knights ride out to cross swords with the King's enemies – this is mortal combat – to the death – for every man with – whose veins course with British blood – every man Jack of us can throw out our chests and say – 'I'm a front line solder'.

CHAIRMAN Not only the men, Mr Mainwaring!

MAINWARING Precisely, er – Mrs Chairman – er Mrs Chairwoman. That is the point I am trying to make. Every man Jack and er… and every woman Jack… can throw out our… well you know the sort of thing I mean. And that Mr er… Madam Chairman – woman – and er… er… Gentlemen is my case, on behalf of Joseph Walker.

There is a pause. The three members of the tribunal put their heads together, whisper vigorously.

CHAIRMAN Before we continue, I'm sure we'd like to thank Mr Mainwaring for coming here and assisting us. Do you second that, Mr Wilson?

WILSON Oh yes – indeed I do. Mr Mainwaring has put Walker's case most ably, (**Looking at his watch**) if at some length.

CHAIRMAN Do you wish to say something before we go any further, Mr Rees?

MR REES Yes, Madam Chairman. Through the Chair, I would like to say that we have heard a very eloquent speech from Mr Mainwaring, but none of it was really to the point. What we are here today to decide is if Mr Walker is called up – would it ruin his business – and that and nothing else. The fact that Mr Mainwaring has extolled the virtues of Mr Walker has no bearing whatsoever on the case.

CHAIRMAN Thank you, Mr Rees. Have you anything else to add to that Mr Wilson?

WILSON I'm sure Mr Mainwaring would be the last person in the world to waste the time of the tribunal – deliberately – I think it was just ignorance of our procedure that led him to go – er – a little longer than was perhaps absolutely necessary.

CHAIRMAN Well, let's just get the details right. The address of your business Mr Walker is 1B, Slope Alley, just off the High Street? You know, I've lived in Walmington-on-Sea all my life and I still can't place where your business is.

MR REES Yes – through the Chair, I'd like Mr Walker to tell us where his business is.

WALKER **(Hoping to make a good impression)** Well, through the Chair, I'll tell you.

CHAIRMAN No, no Mr Walker – you don't go through the Chair.

WALKER Eh?

CHAIRMAN Mr Rees and Mr Wilson speak through the Chair, but you speak *to* me.

WALKER Oh!

CHAIRMAN You see, I am the Chair!

WALKER Oh – yeh – well, you go down the High Street just past Mr Mainwaring's bank – and carry on for about a hundred yards and Slope Alley is on your right. You go down it, about 20 yards and you come to a little green door – you go through that and you'll find yourself in a yard.

CHAIRMAN And that's where your business is?

WALKER No, not quite – that's where Sid Newman's business is – secondhand motor accessories – well you go through his yard – down at the bottom are a couple of old garages – that's where I am.

CHAIRMAN And how long has your business been established?

WALKER Oh – about a year. I started just after the war broke out, as soon as I realised that things were going to er... be in short... **(Mainwaring kicks him)** I mean, I was a bit short of money when I started it.

CHAIRMAN Mr Rees, have you any questions?

MR REES Yes – I see you describe yourself as a wholesale supplier – what exactly does that mean?

WALKER Well – it means that if you want something – I can get it for you.

MR REES Be specific.

WALKER **(Aside to Mainwaring)** What's he mean?

MAINWARING Tell him what you supply.

WALKER Oh I see. Well – it all depends what you want.

CHAIRMAN Haven't you got a relation – someone who could run your business for the duration?

WALKER No, I'm an orphan.

MAINWARING Poor fellow – he has no mother – or father.

CHAIRMAN We know what an orphan is, Mr Mainwaring.

WILSON I am sure Mr Mainwaring has no intention of casting any slur on the intelligence of the tribunal – it's just that when one talks as much as Mr Mainwaring does **(Mainwaring reacts)** averages – a certain amount of what he says is bound to be rather unnecessary.

Mainwaring reacts.

CHAIRMAN Have you any questions, Mr Wilson?

WILSON No, no.

The Committee put their heads together.

CHAIRMAN Well, before we come to any decision about your case, we'll have to see your books.

WALKER **(In panic)** Eh?

CHAIRMAN Your account books, have you brought them with you?

WALKER No – I didn't think you'd want to see them.

CHAIRMAN Until you produce your books, Mr Walker, we cannot proceed with your case. Is this the last appeal today, Mr Wilson?

Wilson nods.

CHAIRMAN Then, I'll be off – I'm late enough as it is.

She gathers up her things and sweeps out.

MR REES **(Getting up and crossing to Walker – all charm)** Oh, by the way, boyo, let me have your card, will you – might be able to do a bit of business before you're called up.

WALKER **(Handing him card)** Here you are, mate.

MR REES Thanks. **(He goes)**

MAINWARING I think we did very well, Walker. I think they were impressed with our case.

WALKER Do you, sir?

MAINWARING Well, of course, they'd be the last people in the world to allow their feelings to show.

WALKER I got the impression they thought we were a couple of right Charlies!

MAINWARING Well, I'm a pretty old hand at this game and let me assure you, you're quite wrong. All we have to do is bring your books along next week and everything will be all right.

WALKER I can't do that, Mr Mainwaring.

MAINWARING Why not?

WALKER I don't keep 'em.

MAINWARING D'you mean to say you run a business and you don't keep books? I've never heard anything like it.

WALKER Couldn't we cook up a set of books between us Mr Mainwaring, after all, you're a bank manager, you should know how.

MAINWARING How dare you suggest such a thing, Walker, in all my years in banking I have never heard anything so outrageous. I wash my hands of the whole affair, good day.

WALKER (**Appealing to Wilson**) What did I say?

CHURCH HALL. LATE AT NIGHT

Jones, Pike, Frazer, Godfrey and Walker are grouped together. In the picture is a small step ladder and a tin bath.

JONES There's only one way out of this Joe, we shall just have to make sure that you don't pass that medical tomorrow.

He and Pike pull the ladder into position.

JONES All right, Joe, get your shoes and socks off.

WALKER What for?

JONES You ain't got flat feet have you?

WALKER Course I ain't.

JONES Well you soon will have. All you got to do is keep jumping off this ladder and remember to land flat-footed.

WALKER I'm not doing that, it will hurt me.

JONES Only at first, you'll soon get used to it.

JONES Look, start from the bottom step, when you jump, you won't feel a thing.

GODFREY Like this. (**Godfrey coyly takes Walker's hand**) Not now, wait until he's up the ladder. Come on, Joe, get on with it.

PIKE I'll start counting.

Walker starts at the bottom run, and jumps off, every time he does he gives a little 'ow'. Pike counts one.

Recording pause. Run on. Fade up.

PIKE Four hundred and ninety-eight.

WALKER (**Jumps**) Ow, that's the lot, I'm not doing any more.

Jones pulls tin bath into position.

JONES All right, stick your feet in here. (**Walker steps in bath**) Now step on this newspaper. (**Walker steps on paper**) Now let's see the result. (**Walker steps off – close up of footprints**) There you are, flat as a pancake.

WALKER (**Pulling on his boots**) I can't get me boots on, me feet is all swelled. You're ruined me for life.

JONES Don't worry, lad, your feet will be as right as rain in a couple of days, just long enough for you to fail your medical. Now, let me see, you was in the last lot, Jock, can you remember anything else you did at your medical?

FRAZER I had to give a little cough.

JONES Show us.

FRAZER Ahem.

JONES Must be more to it than that.

FRAZER Yes.

JONES There must have been something else.

FRAZER I can't remember, it was a long time ago.

JONES I can't either, we'll skip that for the minute. Now pay attention, this is the plan for tomorrow, what time have you got to be at the medical board?

WALKER Nine thirty.

JONES Right you will leave your place at 9.00 sharp, young Pike will come with you. You will run right round the town until you reach the medical centre at 9.20. Keep running all the time. We shall be waiting for you round the back. By the time you get before that medical board you'll be fit for…. fit for nothing.

BACK OF MEDICAL CENTRE

Jones, Frazer and Godfrey are standing in a group waiting.

JONES Now, the whole thing depends on split second timing. (**Looking at watch**) It's 9.20, and here he comes.

Walker comes into the picture with Pike.

WALKER (**He is so out of breath he can hardly speak**) Blimey, I'm all in, let me sit down.

JONES You're not sitting down, mate, keep running. (**Walker runs on the spot**) 'Ere, eat this. (**He hands him a little bit of soap**)

WALKER What's it for?

JONES Make your heart beat faster. (**He pops it in Walker's mouth**)

WALKER If my heart beats much faster I'll take off.

Walker has started to foam at the mouth.

JONES All right, now, stand still a minute. (**He blindfolds him**)

WALKER What's this for?

JONES It will put your eyes out of focus. I'll take it off at the last minute. Don't stop, keep running, keep going. (**He looks at his watch**) 9.27, right, start spinning him round. (**They spin him round**) All right, mate, this is it, come on. (**Jones gets hold of Walker's hand and rushes him up to the door. He whips off the blindfold and pushes him through it, there is a loud crash**)

The others join Jones round the door.

JONES He'll be in there a good half hour, we'd better wait and see what happens.

Walker staggers out of the door.

JONES Blimey, that was quick, did they turn you down?

WALKER No they've cancelled it, it's not till tomorrow.

CHURCH HALL

The men are drawn up on parade.

WILSON Parade at 6.30 tomorrow night. Platoon, attention. Dismiss.

Walker comes over to Mainwaring.

WALKER They passed me A1 this afternoon, sir. That means I shall be leaving in about two weeks' time.

WILSON It's G.H.Q. for you, sir.

MAINWARING Who is it?

Split screen. Mainwaring: left of screen, Brigadier: right of screen.

MAINWARING Hullo.

BRIGADIER Mainwaring. What's all this I hear about Walker being called up.

MAINWARING I'm afraid it's true, sir.

BRIGADIER Who's going to take over our essential supplies?

MAINWARING Essential supplies?

BRIGADIER The whisky, man.

MAINWARING I'm afraid there'll be no more, sir.

BRIGADIER No more. But it's essential to the Home Guard war effort.

MAINWARING It does help to keep the lads all on their toes.

BRIGADIER Keep 'em on their toes? It's the only thing that keeps our chaps on their feet. My staff are all Boer War Veterans.

MAINWARING I'm afraid there's nothing we can do, sir.

BRIGADIER There's something I can do. You can take it from me that Walker will not be called up.

MAINWARING Thank you, sir. (Turns to Walker) It's all right, Walker. I've fixed it. I've had a word with the Brigadier and you can take it from me that you will not be called up.

TELECINE: BARRACK GATES

Notice 'Infantry Training Barracks'. Walker goes through them with small case. Voices can be heard shouting commands, sounds of men marching.

Walker under shower.

'Sideburns' being shaved off.

Clippers giving him a short back and sides.

Walker standing in his long woollen underwear.

VOICE Battle dress trousers two. Battle dress blouses two. Flannel shirts two. Woollen socks four. Greatcoat one. Boots two, etc. etc.

Each item is plonked into Walker's arms until he is loaded down.

TELECINE: SECTION OF TABLE IN MESS HALL

Two privates are eating. Poster on wall: 'We are not interested in the possibilities of defeat, they do not exist', Queen Victoria or 'Careless talk costs lives'. Walker sits beside them with his mess tin full of food. There is the most terrible clatter. The two other men are looking very glum.

WALKER (To man) First army meal, eh!

MAN What?

WALKER I said, oh never mind. (He is fed up. He starts to eat. He picks up a corned beef fritter on his fork) What's this then?

MAN Eh!

WALKER I said, what's this then? (He is holding his fritter on his fork)

MAN Don't you want it, ta! (He takes the fritter off Walker's fork and plonks it in his own mess tin) They're all right these corned beef fritters. (He has his mouth stuffed with food and he splashes Walker as he talks)

Walker, fed up, slowly starts on his remaining fritter.

WALKER 'Ere this ain't bad, you know, it's a funny thing but I've never tasted corned beef before.

MAN Eh!

WALKER Oh skip it. (He chews the rest of the fritter)

BARRACK ROOM

Walker climbs into his bunk. Bugle in distance plays. Lights out.

BARRACK ROOM WINDOWS

Lights go out.

CLOCK

Shot of clock on tower at ten. Last bugle notes fade away.

Hands on clock move round to two.

BARRACK ROOM WINDOWS

Lights all go on.

Feet hurrying along passage.

VOICE Get the M.O. at once.

BARRACK ROOM DOOR

Light goes on at bottom of door. Frantic knocking.

VOICE Come at once, doctor.

Lots of noise of hurrying feet.

BARRACK ROOM

Men are gathering round Walker's bunk. We do not see him. We just hear his groans.

VOICE Let the doctor through.

M.O. pushes his way through men.

M.O. My God, what is it?

Close up of Walker's face, it is swollen and has huge blotches on it. Groans.

CHURCH HALL

The men are drinking tea.

FRAZER Go easy with that sugar, there's not much left.

PIKE How are we going to get any more without Mr Walker?

JONES I don't know, son, we're going to miss him you know.

FRAZER I still can't believe he's gone.

Door bursts open, Walker enters.

WALKER All right, line up. I've got chocolate biscuits, hair grips and nylons.

Mainwaring and Wilson come out of office.

MAINWARING Good heavens, Walker, what are you doing here?

WALKER I've got me ticket! I'm out!

MAINWARING How?

WALKER Simple, I'm allergic to CORNED BEEF!!!

The platoon all gather round him, shaking his hand and laughing.

• JIMMY PERRY REMEMBERS •

'This is a lovely episode. Walker discovers he's got an allergy to corned beef. It was partly based on the fact that I was allergic to mustard pickle. If I ate it I'd swell up and have to be taken to sick bay. They didn't know a lot about allergies in those days.'

SERIES TWO **EPISODE FOUR**

Recorded: Friday 4/11/68 (made in black and white)
Original transmission: Saturday 22/3/69, 7.00–7.30pm
Original viewing figures = 13.6 million

ARTHUR LOWE .... CAPTAIN MAINWARING
JOHN LE MESURIER .... SERGEANT WILSON
CLIVE DUNN .... LANCE CORPORAL JONES
JOHN LAURIE .... PRIVATE FRAZER
JAMES BECK .... PRIVATE WALKER
ARNOLD RIDLEY .... PRIVATE GODFREY
IAN LAVENDER .... PRIVATE PIKE
JANET DAVIES .... MRS PIKE
GRAHAM HARBORD .... LITTLE ARTHUR
PLATOON .... COLIN BEAN, RICHARD JACQUES, FRANK GODFREY, ALEC COLEMAN, HUGH CECIL, JIMMY MAC, DESMOND CULLUM-JONES, ARTHUR MCGUIRE, DAVID SEAFORTH, RICHARD KITTERIDGE

SGT WILSON'S LITTLE SECRET

• CLIVE DOIG REMEMBERS •

'I worked with David Croft on a number of sitcoms as his vision mixer, and mixed the very first episode of *Dad's Army* and most of the first series for him. I then gained an attachment as a production assistant/floor manager to Light Entertainment and was lucky enough first to trail Harold Snoad and then floor-manage a couple of episodes in the second series.

'After five days of outside rehearsal for one of the episodes, we moved into the studio. We had a great number of straw bales on the set, as well as a couple of painted backcloths, showing Walmington-on-Sea through the windows, all of which I knew were potential fire hazards.

'The visit of BBC's fire officer to our studio was one which filled me with trepidation and fear. He was empowered to remove offending fire hazards and halt production accordingly until everything was fire safe. However, Paul Joel, the designer, had assured me the battered old backcloths and bales of straw were fire-proofed.

'In the studio, the fire officer took out his gas lighter which had the power of a blowtorch and applied it to the top bale of straw. It was as dead on the flammable front as a block of asbestos. But then he turned up the wick and lit the bottom of one of the cloths round the back of the set. I looked on in astonishment as the wispy bottom edge of the canvas caught alight and a huge flame and subsequent scorch mark flashed up the beautifully painted Walmington-on-Sea church. "Can't accept that," the fire officer announced with obvious glee. "Not properly treated. It will have to come down and be redone."

'"But we haven't time, rehearsals start in 15 minutes," I protested. "Anyway the cloth didn't catch light, it was your flame thrower that did that. You've ruined the church, burned it down."

'Paul Joel came to the rescue. Yes, it had been properly fire-proofed. He'd personally supervised both cloths in that application. The ensuing contretemps between us and the fire officer lasted until the start of rehearsal when all the actors were coming in. The "officer of inflammability" fortunately couldn't repeat any further flash fires with his massive lighter and finally accepted they were in order. I called in the standby scenic artist to repair the steeple scorch mark, with newly painted stone work, during the morning's rehearsal.

'In this episode the camera may never have seen the instantly rebuilt church through the window, well, not as to notice anyway, the action on the set was far more important.

'The cast were an absolute delight to work with: Arnold Ridley seated on his little canvas chair in the corner of the rehearsal room with his crossword, Jimmy Beck and Clive Dunn pacing the floor, arm in arm, in intimate anecdotal conversation, John Laurie shouting all his lines out, so that everyone flinched, until he was able to tone down his projection, and Arthur Lowe and John Le Mesurier immersed in their own separate thoughts. John never remembered my name, calling me Colin throughout.'

CLIVE DOIG
Vision Mixer and, later, Production Assistant

Sgt Wilson's Little Secret

CHURCH HALL

The platoon are drawn up on parade. Wilson is in charge.

WILSON Now, before we fall out, I've been asked to draw your attention to an item in yesterday's newspaper which states that a member of the H.G. in the Midlands was fined £5 for being drunk in charge of his rifle.

JONES Permission to speak, Mr Wilson.

WILSON Yes, Jones.

JONES I'm sure you don't think any members of this platoon would behave like that, Mr Wilson. I think it's a bit of an insult to our integrity.

Chorus of 'Yes it is' etc.

WILSON I'm sure no offence was intended, Mr Mainwaring just asked me to draw it to your attention so that we might all benefit from the lesson.

FRAZER What lesson?

WALKER Don't take your gun to a party.

FRAZER Well, all I've got to say is if Mr Mainwaring intends to insult us, he should do it to our faces instead of asking other people to do it.

Chorus of 'That's right' etc.

WILSON I'm sure Mr Mainwaring had no intention of insulting you.

FRAZER Well, why isn't he here?

WILSON He is here.

FRAZER What's he doing, hiding?

WILSON Yes, he is, in a way.

JONES I'm not surprised, after making out we're all a load of drunks.

PIKE Anyhow, my mum doesn't allow me to drink.

WALKER I mean I don't mind a drink now and then, but as Jonesey says, making out we're all a load of drunks, I think it's a bit of a liberty.

The whole platoon are now thoroughly upset.

WILSON Please, please calm down, Mr Mainwaring is going to give us a surprise lecture, so on the command 'fall out', I want you to gather in a semi-circle round the stage. Platoon, fall out.

The platoon fall out and gather round the stage muttering.

WILSON **(In stage whisper)** Are you ready, sir?

MAINWARING All right, just about, Wilson, you can announce me. **(Turns)**

WILSON Quiet please, now settle down. Captain Mainwaring is now going to show us something unusual.

FRAZER What's he going to do, give us a comic turn?

WALKER What's unusual about that?

Mainwaring comes through the curtains, camouflage all over him, he looks like a small tree.

MAINWARING Good evening, men, I expect you're all wondering why I'm dressed up like this.

FRAZER Aye, we are.

WALKER No, no.

MAINWARING Now men, seeing me like this, what do you think is going to be the subject of my lecture?

The platoon are puzzled.

GODFREY Pruning fruit trees, sir?

MAINWARING No, Godfrey, camouflage. Now, I require a volunteer to drop in the scenery.

JONES I would like to volunteer to drop in the scenery, sir.

MAINWARING Oh, I think not, Corporal. It's rather heavy.

JONES I'm quite used to this type of work, sir. Last year in the Vicar's pantomime I did the beanstalk. When you've done a beanstalk you're...

MAINWARING Oh, all right, Corporal. Stand over there on the side.

JONES Thank you, sir. We call it the wings.

MAINWARING Stand by the curtains, Wilson.

WILSON Yes, sir.

MAINWARING Now, men, camouflage is the art of merging with your background. Draw the curtains, Wilson.

WILSON Yes, sir.

MAINWARING You will observe how I stand out against a plain background. All right, Jones. Drop in the backcloth with the woodland scene on it.

JONES Right, sir. **(Jones starts to lower a cloth in)**

MAINWARING You will observe how I blend in with the background. Now can you suggest any way I could improve this camouflage?

WALKER How about disguising yourself as a lump of coal, sir.

MAINWARING What?

WALKER You're going to burn your bottom if you're not careful.

MAINWARING Jones, you've let in the wrong scene.

JONES What's that, sir?

MAINWARING I want the *woodland* scene.

JONES What, oh yes, sorry, sir. I remember that scene – that's the Baron's kitchen, where the pumpkin turns into a coach.

MAINWARING Yes, thank you, Jones. (Goes off)

JONES Of course, we had a lot of trouble with Shetland ponies though – just about where you are standing.

MAINWARING Corporal, will you get the woodland scene in?

There is a terrific crash as Jones lets in a French flat, it is 'outside the palace gates', there is a door in it. There is a howl of agony from Mainwaring. The flat has come down in front of Mainwaring about two inches in front of his face.

MAINWARING (Voice from behind flat) That was my foot, Jones. What, what do you think you're doing? Jones! (The door in the flat opens and Mainwaring comes through) Jones, where are you? (He walks into the wings calling. The door opens and Jones comes through it, he closes it behind him)

JONES (Calling) Where are you, Mr Mainwaring? (Wilson comes on to centre of stage) Where's Mr Mainwaring gone, Mr Wilson?

WILSON He went round the back. (He knocks on the door) Are you there, sir?

MAINWARING'S VOICE Of course I'm here, open this door at once.

WILSON (Shaking the door) It seems to be stuck, sir. (To Jones) Go round and help Mr Mainwaring to open the door. (Jones goes into the wings)

The door bursts open and Mainwaring comes through and slams it behind him.

MAINWARING Get that woodland scene in, Wilson. (Wilson goes, the door rattles)

JONES' VOICE I can't get the door open, Mr Mainwaring.

MAINWARING Well, hang on where you are. (The French flat flies up in the air, there is no sign of Jones)

MAINWARING Where are you, Jones?

JONES (From 'flies') I'm up here, sir, I went up with it.

MAINWARING Wilson, let it down at once, you are not much better at it than Jones.

WILSON Well I've never done a beanstalk, sir.

The flat with the door has come in. Jones comes through the door.

MAINWARING Take it away again – are you all right, Jones?

Flat up.

JONES Yes, thank you, sir. It makes a bit of fun.

MAINWARING Yes, well, go and sit down.

JONES Can you manage now, sir?

MAINWARING Yes, I think so.

MAINWARING Now men, what do you think of that?

WALKER I think it's the best turn I've seen for a long time.

The platoon all applaud.

WILSON (Coming on from the wings) Quiet please.

MAINWARING Thank you, Wilson. Now these are the points I want you to make a note of, men. First of all, the face. For this we shall need some corks. Champagne corks are the best. You cook them under a grill until they are burnt right through, and then… (Thumbs through book)

WALKER You serve them on toast, very tasty, very sweet. (They all laugh)

WILSON Quiet.

MAINWARING Walker, your life may depend on this one day. (Glaring at Walker) You grind them to a powder, mix with grease and keep in an old tin. This mixture is applied to the face. Now are there any questions so far?

FRAZER Yes, how are we going to get hold of champagne corks, sir? Don't forget there's a war on.

MAINWARING I'm well aware of that Frazer, as usual we must improvise.

JONES Permission to speak, sir?

MAINWARING Yes, Jones.

JONES What about getting a cork bath mat, sir, and cutting it up into lumps.

MAINWARING Excellent idea, Jones. Make a note of that, Wilson.

WALKER You're going to have a job getting one of them, Mr Mainwaring, very scarce they are.

MAINWARING Oh really.

WALKER It so happens I've got one only left in stock, seeing it's for the platoon, 30s – right?

MAINWARING Thank you, Walker. But I think we'll find some other source.

GODFREY What about medicine bottle corks? I'll ask at the clinic.

MAINWARING Excellent idea, Godfrey. Do that.

WALKER Blackleg.

MAINWARING Now, working from head to toe, we start with the helmet. You will notice the grass tucked under the net is kept fairly short, this is so that it will blend in with most backgrounds. Now if I had tall tufts of grass sticking out of my helmet, it might look a bit odd.

WALKER Especially if you was trying to hide on a bowling green.

WILSON Quiet.

MAINWARING You will observe that the rest of me is covered in foliage. Now are there any questions?

FRAZER Yes, what do you do in the winter, when you can't get any foliage?

MAINWARING That's a good question. Now, has anyone got any ideas?

JONES What about covering yourself in holly leaves, sir.

MAINWARING An excellent idea, Jones, you just cover yourself with holly leaves instead of foliage.

GODFREY Or mistletoe, sir.

Mainwaring reacts.

MAINWARING So don't forget, men, your main task is to break up your outline. Now I want you to parade back here in one hour's time and, bearing in mind what I've told you, I want everyone to camouflage themselves, is that clear? Off you go.

The platoon start to disperse. Sound of a dog barking.

MAINWARING What's that, Wilson?

WILSON Sounds like a dog, sir.

MAINWARING What? All right. Platoon dismiss.

Mainwaring runs off stage.

CHURCH HALL

The rear two ranks are marking time.

WILSON Quick march. Left, right, etc. (**The front rank march in**) Halt! (**They halt**) Turn left! (**They do so**)

MAINWARING Excellent turn out, men, don't you think so, Wilson?

WILSON Yes, absolutely first class, sir.

Mainwaring stops in front of the first man, he is covered from head to foot in hay.

MAINWARING (**Aside to Wilson**) Who's this, Wilson?

WILSON I haven't the faintest idea, sir.

Walker pulls aside the hay and pokes his head through.

WALKER It's me, sir. I'm a small haystack.

MAINWARING Good gracious that's good.

WILSON Awfully good, sir.

Suddenly there is a terrific sneeze from young Pike who is standing beside Walker. He sneezes again, his eyes are running and he is in a terrible state.

MAINWARING What on earth's the matter with you, boy?

PIKE I can't stand it, sir, it's my hay fever.

MAINWARING Well, don't stand next to him then, move to the end of the line.

PIKE Yes, sir.

He moves to the end of the line. Mainwaring moves on to Godfrey who is wearing a beekeeper's mask and veil which is full of holes, he is also wearing a lei of flowers round his neck.

MAINWARING What's this supposed to be, Godfrey?

GODFREY Well, I tried several things on, sir, and none of them really seemed to suit me.

MAINWARING But you're supposed to break up your outline.

GODFREY I thought it looked pretty broken up as it is, sir.

MAINWARING What's that you've got round your face?

GODFREY It's my apiaristic mask, sir.

MAINWARING Your what?

GODFREY Bee keeping.

MAINWARING But it's full of holes.

GODFREY It's all right, my bees are quite friendly.

MAINWARING (**Touching the 'lei'**) But why this? It looks as if you're going on a cruise to the South Seas.

GODFREY Well I got the idea from a film I saw at the Odeon last week, it was called 'South of Pago-Pago', it had Dorothy Lamour and Victor Mature in it.

FRAZER Was it good?

GODFREY Well, I liked it, but my sisters thought Miss Lamour was rather fast.

MAINWARING What's that got to do with camouflage?

GODFREY I don't know really, sir, I just thought it looked rather er... open air.

MAINWARING I see. (**He moves on**)

WILSON He's right you know, sir, it does look open air.

Mainwaring gives him a glare and stops in front of Frazer. He has a battered top hat on his head and a tatty bit of white sheeting round his shoulders like a cloak.

MAINWARING What have you been to see? The Phantom of the Opera?

FRAZER No, this is winter camouflage, sir, you wear it in the snow.

He crouches down, and turns the sheet so that it falls in front of him. It has three black buttons painted on it. On the back of his head he has a snowman mask which he turns round, he replaces top hat and sticks a pipe in his mouth.

MAINWARING Well done, Frazer (**He passes on to Jones who is wearing his butcher's outfit, straw hat and apron**) Why aren't you wearing camouflage, Jones?

JONES I am sir, I'm camouflaged as a butcher.

MAINWARING But you are a butcher.

JONES I know that and you know that, but Jerry doesn't, sir. Well, sir, I'm standing outside my shop, right.

(Mainwaring nods) A Jerry soldier comes along, he don't know I'm in the Home Guard, he thinks I'm a butcher, right. (Mainwaring nods) Then when he's not looking, whop! Right up with the old cold steel. And that's one thing they don't like, you know, sir.

MAINWARING Yes, thank you, Jones, I'm well aware of that fact.

He passes on to Pike who is wearing his uniform and no camouflage.

MAINWARING What's the meaning of this, Pike?

PIKE I've got a note for you, Mr Mainwaring, it's from my mum. (**He hands Mainwaring note, Mainwaring takes it and moves down with Wilson**)

MAINWARING (**Reads**) 'I'm not having our Frank covered in a lot of damp leaves, it will only set off his chest again.' Right, this is the finish, Wilson, I want to speak to you in my office as soon as the parade's over.

SIDE OFFICE

Mainwaring is sitting at his desk, Wilson is standing.

MAINWARING I've never heard anything like it in all my life, Wilson. The way Mrs Pike mollycoddles her son is absurd. Always sending notes and coming down here and interfering with the running of the platoon, I tell you Wilson, it's got to stop.

WILSON Yes, sir.

MAINWARING I mean, supposing all the other men arrived with notes from their mothers. It would look a bit odd, wouldn't it?

WILSON It certainly would, sir, at their ages.

MAINWARING The fact is Wilson, someone has got to talk to Mrs Pike, and as you're quite friendly with her I think it ought to be you. You are quite friendly with her aren't you, Wilson?

WILSON Well, I take her out to the cinema now and then. I quite often go round and have a meal with her, and that sort of thing.

MAINWARING What sort of thing?

WILSON Well, whatever she happens to be cooking at the time, sir.

MAINWARING Oh. I see.

WILSON You see she has my ration book and that makes things a lot easier.

MAINWARING Yes, I'm sure it does. The point is you've got to tell her, Wilson. I mean, I wouldn't even allow my *wife* to tell me how to run this platoon. She knows that a woman's place is in the home. (**He gets up from the desk and crosses the room to put some papers in a file**) And never for one moment would I tolerate her telling me what to do.

The phone rings.

WILSON (**Picking up the phone**) Hullo yes... Oh good evening, Mrs Mainwaring. It's your wife, sir.

MAINWARING (**Taking phone**) Hullo Elizabeth... Yes... Look, I'm very busy just at the moment, I'm afraid I shan't be home for another half hour. What's that... Yes Elizabeth... Yes Elizabeth... (**He hangs up and gives Wilson a sickly grin**) (**He gives a false laugh**) I'll leave you to lock up, and by the way don't forget to talk to Mrs Pike. Put your foot down, Wilson. (**He goes**)

WILSON Yes, sir, I'll do that.

MRS PIKE'S HOUSE. THE SITTING ROOM

Frank and Mrs Pike are having tea. Mrs Pike is reading a letter.

MRS PIKE Frank, that's your butter ration for the week. Oh dear.

PIKE What is it, mum?

MRS PIKE It's from the W.V.S., they want to know if we can take in one evacuee. I suppose we ought to do all we can to help. I think we could manage one all right, he can have that little room at the back. I'll write and let them know tonight.

PIKE Isn't Uncle Arthur supposed to be coming to tea today, mum?

MRS PIKE Yes, I expect he'll be here in a minute. You don't mind, do you?

PIKE No, mum, I quite like Uncle Arthur.

MRS PIKE No, I mean you don't mind us having a little evacuee to stay with us.

PIKE No, I don't mind.

Cut to outside door.

Wilson is just about to come into the room. The door is slightly open.

MRS PIKE'S VOICE The trouble is children grow up so quickly, still I must say it will be nice to have a little child about the house again.

Wilson freezes outside the door with his hand on the knob.

PIKE'S VOICE I wonder if it will be a boy or girl?

MRS PIKE'S VOICE Well, we shall just have to wait and see. (**Close up on Wilson's face**) You know Frank, it's going to be funny being a mother again after all these years. Oh, don't say anything to Uncle Arthur about it just at the moment, let me tell him in my own time.

PIKE'S VOICE Sure, mum.

Wilson, looking very faint, pulls himself together, pushes the door open and enters the room.

MRS PIKE There you are Arthur, you are late.

WILSON Yes.

MRS PIKE Well, hurry up and sit down or the tea will get cold. You look very pale, are you all right?

WILSON What... er, yes.

MRS PIKE He does look pale doesn't he, Frank?

PIKE You know what they say mum, pale and passionate. **(He laughs)**

MRS PIKE Now that will do, Frank, hurry up and finish your tea.

She pours out a cup of tea for Wilson.

MRS PIKE Don't you want anything to eat, Arthur?

WILSON What... no, not just now, thank you.

MRS PIKE Well, you must eat something. I know, I managed to get some of those nursery biscuits today. I'll fetch them. **(She starts to rise)**

WILSON Please don't bother, Mavis, I'm quite all right.

MRS PIKE But you like nursery biscuits, Arthur, they're your favourite, they've got icing on top with little children on them.

WILSON I know perfectly well what they look like, Mavis, and I don't want any.

MRS PIKE There's no need to snap like that, Arthur, especially after me using all my points to get them.

WILSON I'm sorry. I seem to have lost my appetite.

MRS PIKE Well, if I'd known I wouldn't have wasted my points on them. I've got to be very careful with everything on points you know.

PIKE It seems about the only thing you can have these days that's not on points, is a baby.

MRS PIKE Now Frank, don't be coarse, I'm sure I don't know where you get it from, unless it's from some of those rough men in the Home Guard. I think I shall speak to Mr Mainwaring about it.

WILSON Mavis, please.

PIKE Well, I'd better get into my uniform, mum, it will soon be time for parade.

He gets up and goes.

MRS PIKE I don't know what's the matter with you tonight, Arthur, it's not like you to look so miserable all the time.

WILSON Look, Mavis, I couldn't help overhearing what you were saying to Frank just now.

MRS PIKE Oh, about the addition to the family?

WILSON Er, yes.

MRS PIKE Well, why should you worry about it?

WILSON Of course I worry. I just can't understand why you're taking it so calmly, Mavis.

She starts to clear away the tea things.

MRS PIKE Well, what do you expect me to do? I mean it isn't as though I'm the only woman in this situation.

WILSON Couldn't you stay still for one moment? But I feel responsible, Mavis.

MRS PIKE I don't see why you should, after all I'm the one who decided to have the child.

WILSON But why?

MRS PIKE Why, because there's a war on, and we must all do our bit.

WILSON But what's the war got to do with it?

MRS PIKE Well, I wouldn't be having the child if there wasn't a war on, would I? **(As she is moving about clearing the table, he follows her about)** Oh, Arthur, do stop trailing about after me like a lost sheep, I'm trying to get on. You'd better go now or you'll be late for parade.

WILSON But Mavis...

Frank comes in, in his uniform.

PIKE Are you ready, Uncle Arthur... **(Glare from Wilson)** I mean Sergeant.

CHURCH HALL

The platoon are sitting on benches in a half circle. Mainwaring and Wilson are standing.

MAINWARING You have read on the notice board, we are starting a competition each month for the best suggestions for improvised weapons or means of defence. A prize will be awarded for the best idea which will be paid for out of platoon funds, and supplied by Lance Corporal Jones. What have you got for us, Jones?

JONES Two lamb chops and a quarter pound of chitterlings.

MAINWARING Do you hear, men, two lamb chops and a quarter pound of chitterlings. What are chitterlings?

JONES A secret part of a pig, sir.

MAINWARING Really, a worthy prize indeed. Now we have three entries, Sergeant Wilson, Private Frazer and Private Walker.

WALKER We'll go and get ours ready, sir.

MAINWARING Sergeant Wilson will demonstrate his idea first. Sergeant Wilson, carry on. **(Wilson does not hear, he is miles away)** Sergeant Wilson.

WILSON Yes, sir?

MAINWARING We're waiting for you to demonstrate your grenade-firing crossbow.

WILSON My what, sir?

MAINWARING Your grenade-firing crossbow.

WILSON **(Whispering)** I'm terribly sorry, sir, I'm afraid I've left it at home.

MAINWARING **(Drawing him to one side)** What on earth's the matter with you, Wilson? You've been in a day dream all the evening. You're not ill, are you?

WILSON No, sir.

MAINWARING Well, just pull yourself together, I'll speak to you after parade. In the absence of Sergeant Wilson's grenade-firing crossbow. **(He comes down to the men again)** Our next entry is Private Frazer who will demonstrate an anti-tank device.

Frazer steps forward with a pile of white dinner plates.

FRAZER Now, sir, this is the road. Right. I place a row of dinner plates upside down in a line right across it so. **(He lays the plates across the room)**

MAINWARING You did say this was an anti-tank trap, Frazer?

FRAZER Aye, sir. That's right.

MAINWARING Dinner plates.

FRAZER Yes, sir, dinner plates.

MAINWARING Please continue.

FRAZER **(Giving him a glare)** Now the enemy tank comes down the road, suddenly he sees the row of plates lying in his path. He doesn't know what they are, so he stops and opens his turret and gets out to have a look. Meanwhile, we're hiding behind cover and as soon as he gets out of his tank we let him have it – ping. How's that, sir?

MAINWARING Not bad at all, Frazer.

FRAZER Thank you, sir. **(Goes to seat)**

MAINWARING Our next entry is Private Walker.

Walker and Jones enter.

Walker comes into the picture with Jones who is wearing half an old tyre round his shoulders like a yoke.

WALKER Right, now, here we have the greatest invention since chain mail, etc.

MAINWARING You are not in the market place now. Just get on with the demonstration, Walker.

WALKER Right, now I'd like to demonstrate my 'All purpose shoulder protector'. You'll observe that it's made from half of an old rubber tyre. This will protect the shoulders from shrapnel or a blow from a weapon, so. **(He draws his bayonet and gives Jones a cut across each shoulder)**

JONES Didn't feel a thing.

MAINWARING Two excellent suggestions. Now, I think we'll settle this in a democratic fashion by a show of hands. Now hands up those who liked Frazer's idea. **(Six hands go up)** And now Walker's idea – 1, 2, 3, 4, 5 – **(Five hands go up)** Six, seven – Walker is the winner.

Frazer gives a black look and mutters.

WALKER **(To Frazer)** Don't take it to heart, Taff. I'll give you some of my chitterlings.

MAINWARING There's no doubt that Walker's idea is first class. I think we ought to equip the whole platoon. Let me see, there's 17 of us, that means we shall require nine old tyres.

WALKER There's just one snag about this idea, Mr Mainwaring.

MAINWARING What's that?

WALKER It's very difficult to get old tyres, rubber's like gold in war time.

MAINWARING Well, what did you want to suggest it for in the first place. You'd better give Frazer the prize.

FRAZER Aye. **(He goes to grab it)**

WALKER 'Old on a minute, I said they were *difficult* to get, I didn't say impossible.

MAINWARING What do you mean?

WALKER It so happens I've got a few old tyres in stock, I can let you have nine at 10s – each. How's that?

MAINWARING It's outrageous, besides we only need eight and a half tyres.

WALKER All right, I'll tell you what, I'll do you nine for four quid.

MAINWARING It's outrageous.

GODFREY My friend has some old tyres.

WALKER He bleeding would have, wouldn't he?

GODFREY You can have them for nothing.

WALKER Tell you what, I'll cut them up for half a crown a time.

MAINWARING Be quiet, Walker. Right, Jones.

JONES Yes, sir.

MAINWARING Dismiss the men. **(To Wilson)** Wilson, I want to see you in the office now.

WILSON Oh er… yes, sir.

Mainwaring crosses to the office, followed by Wilson.

JONES All right, fall in.

OFFICE

Mainwaring enters followed by Wilson. In the background we can hear Jones dismissing the men.

MAINWARING Come in, Wilson, and close the door.

WILSON Yes, sir. (**He closes the door**)

MAINWARING Now what's the matter, Wilson?

WILSON Matter, sir?

MAINWARING Yes, you've been in a day dream all night. Several times I've spoken to you and you haven't been listening, and on top of that you go and leave your grenade-firing crossbow behind.

WILSON Well, sir, it's a bit difficult.

MAINWARING You'd better sit down, Wilson. (**Wilson sits**) Now what is it, are you in some sort of trouble?

WILSON It's not me that's in the trouble, sir, it's er... Mrs Pike.

MAINWARING What do you mean, Wilson?

WILSON (**Shuffling his feet**) She's er... she's er.

MAINWARING Now look, Wilson. I'm not only your Commanding Officer, but I'm also your friend and you need have no hesitation in confiding in me. Now what's all this about Mrs Pike?

WILSON (**Blurting it out**) She's going to have a baby, sir.

MAINWARING Oh good, I expect her husband will be delighted and... but she's a widow, isn't she?

WILSON Yes.

MAINWARING Then how can she have a baby?

There is a silence – they both stare at each other.

MAINWARING I thought you said you only went round there for meals!

WILSON Well, I told you she had my ration card, sir.

MAINWARING Yes, and now she's got something else. I really can't believe my ears. I've come to the conclusion I don't know you, Wilson – you're a cad, that's what you are. How long have you known her?

WILSON Quite a number of years, sir.

MAINWARING Then why on earth haven't you asked her to marry you?

WILSON Well, sir, I've never really got round to it.

MAINWARING Well, you'd better get round to it now. You can't go about behaving like Errol Flynn, you know. What do you think the directors of the bank would say if they knew?

WILSON I've really no idea, sir.

MAINWARING Well I have. There's only one thing for it, you must do the honourable, decent thing and ask her to marry you.

WILSON Yes, I think you're right, sir. I'll have a word with her in the next few days.

MAINWARING You'll have a word with her tonight, Wilson. You don't seem to realise there's no time to lose.

WILSON But it's Tuesday, sir.

MAINWARING What on earth has that got to do with it?

WILSON Well she'll be in bed and asleep. She always goes to bed early on Tuesday, you see she gets terribly tired on Monday.

MAINWARING How do you know... I mean, you'll just have to wake her up. And when I see you at the bank at nine o'clock tomorrow morning, I shall expect to hear that it's all settled.

WILSON Very well, sir.

FRONT DOOR OF MRS PIKE'S HOUSE

Wilson comes into the picture, he gives a furtive look round and rings the door bell. Silence. He rings the bell again. There is the sound of a window opening above his head.

MRS PIKE'S VOICE Who's that?

WILSON (**Stepping back and looking up**) It's me, Mavis. I must speak to you at once.

MRS PIKE What on earth do you want at this time of night?

WILSON It's only ten o'clock, I must see you at once.

MRS PIKE Really, what will the neighbours think? All right, I'll come down. (**She closes the window**)

There is a dead silence, Wilson waits. Suddenly a figure comes out of the darkness.

WALKER Here, who's there? (**Wilson turns**) Oh, it's you, Sarge. I saw a figure in the doorway and I thought there might be something fishy going on.

WILSON Oh, no worry at all.

WALKER Locked you out, has she?

WILSON No, no, not in the least.

WALKER Lost your key?

WILSON No, I don't have a key.

WALKER (**Producing bunch**) Try one of these – 3s – each.

WILSON Oh, Walker, I wanted to remind young Pike about the parade tomorrow night.

WALKER But you will see him in the bank in the morning.

WILSON I wanted to remind him about that as well. **(Letter box opens and Mrs Pike calls through it)**

MRS PIKE Arthur, darling, are you still there?

WILSON **(With a glance at Walker)** Yes, I'm still here, Mavis.

MRS PIKE Good job you arrived when you did, I have only just got undressed. **(Wilson and Walker exchange glances)** Another five minutes, I should have been in bed asleep.

WILSON Mavis, please.

WALKER You can rely on my discretion, sir. We've all got our private lives to lead. Mum's the word.

WILSON Good night, Walker. **(He turns to the door)** Why on earth don't you open the door, Mavis?

MRS PIKE I can't, I've taken the blackout down, besides I've got my mother staying with me for a few days. What would she think?

WILSON But I want to talk to you.

MRS PIKE Well, you can talk through the letter box.

WILSON Oh really, this is absurd.

MRS PIKE What is it you want to say?

WILSON **(Hissing through the letter box)** Will you marry me?

There is a silence. Suddenly there is the sound of a bolt being drawn, the door flies open and Mrs Pike throws herself into Wilson's arms. The light from the hall floods out.

MRS PIKE Arthur, darling!

VOICE Put that light out!

CHURCH HALL

The men are drawn up on parade.

MAINWARING I'm dismissing you a little early tonight, men. As you know, Sergeant Wilson and Mrs Pike are getting married next Saturday and we are going to provide the guard of honour. Now I want to have a little rehearsal, so we'll assume that the door at the back of the hall is the entrance to the church. Now, on the command 'fall out', I want you to form two ranks each side of the door. Platoon, attention! Fall out.

They do so, get rid of their rifles and form into two ranks each side of the door.

MAINWARING On the appearance of the happy pair. **(Looks at Wilson)** I want you to draw your bayonets and form an arch, have you got that? **(They all nod)** All right, Wilson, take your place by the door.

WILSON Oh really, sir, is this necessary?

MAINWARING Of course it's necessary. We want to get it right, don't we? Go and take your place by the door. Wait a minute, we need someone to stand in for Mrs Pike, now who's about her height?

JONES Permission to speak, sir?

MAINWARING Mmm?

JONES I'd like to volunteer to be about her height, sir.

MAINWARING Good man, Jones, go and stand on Sergeant Wilson's left. Right, now get into position. **(They do so. Wilson is hating every minute of it)** Right, are you ready? Now, as they come through the porch. Take his arm, Jones. Guard of Honour present bayonets, not you Jones, take his arm. **(They do so, Wilson and Jones walk slowly between the ranks) (The platoon sing 'The Wedding March')** For goodness sake smile, Wilson. It's your wedding day.

JONES I expect he's a bit nervous, sir. **(The door opens and Mrs Pike rushes in)**

MRS PIKE Sorry to interrupt you, Mr Mainwaring, but Arthur, our little newcomer has arrived.

WILSON Good heavens!

MRS PIKE It's a dear little boy.

WILSON But that's impossible, when?

MRS PIKE About half an hour ago.

WILSON You are a brick.

MRS PIKE And you'll never guess, his name's Arthur too. **(She calls through door)** Come along, dear.

A little boy of about ten enters.

Mrs Pike takes his hand and leads him over to Wilson.

MRS PIKE This is the addition to the family, our little evacuee.

BOY **(To Mainwaring)** 'Ullo, are you my Auncle Arfer?

MAINWARING Ha, ha! No no, there's your Uncle Arthur and I'm sure he's very relieved to see you.

WILSON Yes, I'm very relieved to see you.

Mainwaring laughs.

Wilson laughs.

SERIES TWO **EPISODE FIVE**

Recorded: Friday 15/11/68 (made in black and white)

Original transmission: Saturday 29/3/69, 7.00–7.30pm

(This episode was originally planned for transmission on 27/1/69 at 7.30pm.)

Original viewing figures = 11.3 million

This episode is no longer available in the BBC archives.

ARTHUR LOWE .... CAPTAIN MAINWARING
JOHN LE MESURIER .... SERGEANT WILSON
CLIVE DUNN .... LANCE CORPORAL JONES
JOHN LAURIE .... PRIVATE FRAZER
JAMES BECK .... PRIVATE WALKER
ARNOLD RIDLEY .... PRIVATE GODFREY
IAN LAVENDER .... PRIVATE PIKE
GEOFFREY LUMSDEN .... CORPORAL-COLONEL SQUARE
JOHN RINGHAM .... CAPTAIN BAILEY
GORDON PETERS .... POLICEMAN
EDWARD SINCLAIR .... CARETAKER

PLATOON .... COLIN BEAN, RICHARD JACQUES,
.... FRANK GODFREY, ALEC COLEMAN, HUGH CECIL,
.... JIMMY MAC, DESMOND CULLUM-JONES, VIC TAYLOR,
.... DAVID SEAFORTH, RICHARD KITTERIDGE

A STRIPE FOR FRAZER

• CLAIRE LIDDELL REMEMBERS •

'John Laurie, the distinguished Scottish actor, was not given to gossip, unlike the character he played in each series.

'I first worked with John when the programme had become established as one of the nation's all-time favourites, so it was no surprise to me that he was instantly recognised everywhere we went between performances.

'It was lovely to see the number of young people who would approach our table rather shyly to ask for his autograph, which he always gave with grace, humour and a certain dramatic bravura. After he'd penned his distinctive signature, I was amused to observe them turning hesitantly towards me, wondering if I might be of some importance to be in such exalted company, then silently deciding, I suspect, that I must be some kind of "hanger-on" and therefore of no importance!

'Of course, it was not only the young who recognised John, but older people who were more inhibited, settling for nudges amongst themselves and sly glances in his direction. As far as I know, John remained unaware of being the focus of attention, but he quickly sensed atmosphere, especially if we were sitting in a particularly sedate lounge for, with a deft change in the conversation, he would raise his voice and enquire: "When are you going to bed with me, lamb?" All heads around us turned (how John loved to shock the prim and proper!) as I replied: "Tomorrow, John, tomorrow", in mock distress that it wasn't to be that very night!

'The romantic side of John's nature never made an appearance in *Dad's Army* but the use he made of his voice and expressive eyes (sometimes, in the series, rolling with innuendo), were well-loved by me, and his dramatic gestures off stage as well as on seemed fresh and spontaneous.

'Never once did he express regret about being in *Dad's Army*. On the contrary, it gave him a new lease of life and a new audience for his creative talent at a late stage in his career. He was sometimes sad, however, that his earlier stage work had not had more recognition – especially in his native Scotland – but, characteristically, he didn't dwell on that for long. It was a fleeting emotion, then over.

'Apart from referring to the blow he felt at "dear Jimmy Beck's death" and his dislike of Arthur Lowe's pomposity, John didn't indulge in talk about the show, although he did tell me he was a godfather to one of Ian Lavender's children. Frazer and Pikey, the old and the young, seemed a strangely fitting and fond friendship. Somehow, I felt any questions I might ask about *Dad's Army* would intrude on that part of himself which John kept private. I respected and loved him for that quality.'

CLAIRE LIDDELL
Composer, Pianist and Friend

A Stripe for Frazer

CHURCH HALL

The platoon is assembling with uniforms and with rifles. Wilson is drilling them. Mainwaring is in the side office.

WILSON Platoon, 'shun. Stand at ease. Platoon, 'shun. Stand at ease. I thought that whole movement lacked verve. Try and put a bit more sparkle into it. Platoon, 'shun! For inspection port –

Jones enters.

JONES Sorry I'm late, Sarge.

WILSON Fall in, Corporal Jones. Try to be on time in future.

JONES I wouldn't have been late now, Sarge, but you see the offal comes today and they haven't sent no suet.

WILSON Settle down. Platoon, for inspection port…

JONES Hang on, I haven't got my bundook.

WILSON Hurry up, Jones!

Jones goes to corner to get his rifle. Comes back with it.

JONES It's been one of those days, today!

WILSON Yes, Jones, but we have to get on with the parade you know, in spite of the absence of your suet.

JONES I promised it to Mrs Prosser of the W.V.S. you see, sir. (**To Frazer**) She was doing dumplings. She don't like the lads to go without their dumplings. As you can well imagine.

WILSON Be quiet, Jones! For inspection p——ort arms! As you were. Now, your left hands are coming up to catch the rifle far too soon. You should whip the left hand up at the very last second. Try again. For inspection, p——ort arms.

Godfrey doesn't catch his rifle and it falls to the ground.

GODFREY I left it a bit late, and er… the left hand wasn't there.

WILSON It's the noise I can't stand, Godfrey. Pick it up. Oh, Pike, pick it up for him. Now, let's try again. For inspection p——ort…

Mainwaring rushes in waving a rattle and wearing his gas mask. Everyone else stands transfixed. Mainwaring continues with the rattle and shouting 'Gas, Gas…' from inside his mask. Seeing no reaction, he stops and takes off his mask.

MAINWARING What are you all standing there for? You know what this is, don't you?

WALKER It's a rattle.

MAINWARING It's a warning that the enemy is attacking with gas – now what are you all waiting for?

FRAZER We're still at attention! It's up to him at the end there to take his finger out!

Indicating Wilson.

MAINWARING Enough of that, Frazer.

FRAZER Yes, sir.

MAINWARING (**On his turn**) Good. At the same time, Wilson, I think it is up to you to take your… to take some action.

WILSON Yes, sir. Right (**He shouts**) Gas attack – gas attack, on the command 'fall out' put on your gas masks. Fall o…ut.

General confusion as they all try to handle their rifles, hats and equipment and get the masks on. Walker does not move.

MAINWARING Come on – you'll have to be quicker than that, you know. You're all choking by now. Walker, what's the matter with you? Get that flap open and the face piece on. (**He goes up to Walker and starts to open the flap**) It's creeping into your lungs – you can't breathe. What's this? (**He sees something inside the gas mask case**)

WALKER Whisky, sir.

MAINWARING Whisky! Do you realise you could be court-martialled for this?

WALKER It's for the Sergeant.

MAINWARING Come over here.

Mainwaring takes him to one side.

MAINWARING Wilson! (**Wilson comes behind Mainwaring. He's wearing his gas mask**) Wilson, what have you got to say about this? (**He turns and sees Wilson**)

MAINWARING Take that damned thing off! (**He points to the four half bottles in the case**) Now – is this yours?

WILSON Well, it's not all mine, sir. Only one bottle.

MAINWARING I see. Who else is in this conspiracy?

Frazer, Jones and Godfrey put up their hands, they all wear masks.

MAINWARING Take their names, Sergeant.

WILSON That's rather difficult, sir – not being able to see their faces.

MAINWARING I never knew a man like you for finding excuses.

WILSON How would it be if you sounded the All Clear?

Fixing him with a stare, Mainwaring blows blasts on his police whistle.

MAINWARING Now, come forward and collect this damned stuff.

JONES How much was it, Joe?

WALKER A pound a time, Jonesey.

JONES (**Feeling in his pockets**) Here we are then.

MAINWARING We'll save the cash transactions until after the parade, Jones.

JONES Yes, sir. Sorry, sir.

GODFREY It's not for me – it's for my sister. Every time the siren goes, she has a funny turn.

MAINWARING Back to your place, Godfrey.

Frazer is getting his bottle.

MAINWARING Are you taking their names, Sergeant.

WILSON Jones, Godfrey, Frazer…

FRAZER Is there a regulation in the Army that stops a Scotsman buying a bottle of whisky?

MAINWARING Back to your place, Frazer. (**Indicating Walker's haversack**) What's that at the bottom?

WALKER (**Holding up box**) Your cigars!

WILSON (**Still writing**) Mainwaring…

MAINWARING Right, I'll take charge of that, Sarge.

MAINWARING Now, listen to me, you chaps. As soon as you hear this, those masks must be on in a flash. As soon as you hear this. (**He waves his rattle**) And they must stay on until you hear this. (**He blows the whistle again**)

Enter policeman with truncheon drawn.

POLICEMAN What's the trouble?

MAINWARING No trouble, officer.

POLICEMAN Somebody was blowing for assistance.

MAINWARING Aah! You mean this – it was for gas.

POLICEMAN Gas – Blimey! (**He starts to put on his mask**)

MAINWARING It's all right, officer, just a practice alert.

POLICEMAN Oh, I see. Ah, well, you can't be too careful these days, can you?

MAINWARING Just what I was telling my men.

POLICEMAN (**On the way out, he turns**) If you're doing any more whistling, you might tip me the wink first.

MAINWARING Certainly, officer, certainly.

POLICEMAN Otherwise, when I hear that whistle, I jump to it.

WALKER He'll have a job in those boots.

POLICEMAN Do you mind if I have a word with that man?

MAINWARING By all means, please do.

WALKER Sorry, I can't talk to you – I'm on duty.

POLICEMAN In that case, I'll have to get them somewhere else.

WALKER Wait a minute, Tosh.

MAINWARING Look to your front, Walker. I want you all to practise getting into your masks in double quick time, so that if Hitler does bowl this cowardly weapon at us, it will be a no ball. Carry on, Corporal Jones. Wilson, come into the office, leave Jones to lick them into shape. (**Mainwaring goes towards side office with Wilson**)

JONES Yes, sir. Of course, sir.

FRAZER (**Aside**) If he bowls, it'll be a no ball. What a lot of blether he comes out with.

JONES That will be enough of that, Frazer. Now, on the command 'Go', I want you to shove your 'mushes' smartly in the face piece.

SIDE OFFICE

Mainwaring and Wilson enter.

MAINWARING If I catch anyone else using their respirator for improper purposes, they'll be in trouble, I can tell you. (**He goes to shelf for hat**)

WILSON What's that, sir?

MAINWARING Just arrived. What do you think of it?

It is a 'cheese cutter' type of officer's hat. He puts it on.

WILSON Oh, I say, that's rather dinky.

MAINWARING Suits me better than the forage cap, don't you think?

WILSON Yes, sir. Your face doesn't look nearly so round and moonlike.

Mainwaring reacts.

WILSON Oh, yes, excellent. I think I'll get one.

MAINWARING Oh no, you won't. These are for officers only.

WILSON Ah, I might have guessed. (**He turns away**)

MAINWARING Anyway, it wouldn't suit you – the jauntiness of the forage cap offsets that craggy careworn face.

There is a knock at the door. Enter Jones.

JONES Permission to speak, sir?

MAINWARING Yes, Jones.

JONES They're getting on very nicely with the gas drill, sir, and there's that bit of steak I promised you.

MAINWARING (**Putting it away quickly**) Thank you, Jones. Er, back to your duty.

JONES (**At door**) Permission to make a personal remark, sir!

MAINWARING What is it, Jones?

JONES That hat – suits you a fair treat, sir!

MAINWARING Thank you, Corporal Jones. (**Knock at door. Jones exit**) Yes – what is it? Oh!

Enter Army Captain – Captain Bailey.

CAPTAIN BAILEY Captain Mainwaring?

MAINWARING That's right.

BAILEY Ah, I'm from Div. Ack and Quack.

They salute, Mainwaring remains seated.

MAINWARING This is my sergeant – Sergeant Wilson – Captain Ack and Quack.

WILSON How d'you do?

BAILEY That's not my name. It stands for Assistant Adjutant & Quartermaster General. I'm Staff Captain A. Brought a few bits of bumph round and the new standing orders.

MAINWARING Thanks very much.

BAILEY Good news for you on the establishment side. You can make somebody up to Corporal. That gives you a Sergeant, a Corporal and a Lance Corporal.

MAINWARING That is good news, isn't it, Wilson?

WILSON I suppose it is.

MAINWARING Well, of course it is. On Monday night when Jones is counting coupons, there's been no one to share the burden of command.

BAILEY Well, you can make 'em up as soon as you like. Just give the names to Adj.

MAINWARING He'll have them this pip. emma. We don't dally when it comes to decisions.

BAILEY Good. I'll cut along then. (**He salutes. Mainwaring salutes back**) Oh, and don't let the Old Man catch you saluting sitting down. Drives him right round the bend.

Mainwaring stands up apologetically.

MAINWARING Oh, oh – does it? I'll remember. (**Captain Bailey turns at the door**)

BAILEY He's a bit of a stickler about uniform too.

Mainwaring reacts.

BAILEY So, don't wear that hat with battledress – only with field service uniform.

MAINWARING But I don't have field service uniform.

BAILEY In that case, don't wear that hat!

Bailey goes.

MAINWARING Damned red tape!

WILSON (**Suppressing a laugh**) It is a pity, sir. Seemed to make you look more like an officer.

Mainwaring reacts.

WILSON You go on wearing it, sir. I'll get one of the lads to keep cavey – when the Old Man appears, you can do a quick switch.

MAINWARING There's no need to humour me, Wilson. Never mind about that for now, we have the question of these promotions to consider.

WILSON Yes – an extra Corporal – I suppose we give Jones another stripe.

MAINWARING Well, of course, he has the maturity – there's no denying that – and the experience – and the guts.

WILSON And the meat!

MAINWARING And the meat. Well, we have to disregard those sort of things, and decide this purely on the grounds of the national interest.

WILSON Of course, I realise that – only it's my turn for rump next week.

MAINWARING I think the wisest strategy would be to make up another Lance Corporal and see who shows the best potential. The question is who?

WILSON I favour one of the younger men.

MAINWARING Mrs Pike's boy for instance?

WILSON Well he is one of the younger ones.

MAINWARING He'll be called up in no time, and we'll be no further forward. We need someone who'll remain on the strength.

WILSON Walker?

MAINWARING No – he'd have access to the stores. Before we know where we are, he'd be flogging the bayonets for carving knives.

WILSON Well he did pinch them for us in the first place.

MAINWARING We need a man of integrity.

WILSON Godfrey? He's as honest as the day is long.

MAINWARING But could he lead men?

WILSON Well, not from the front. He couldn't keep up.

MAINWARING Then there's his bladder trouble.

WILSON Well, at least we'd know where to find him.

MAINWARING No, for my money, the man for the job is Frazer.

WILSON I don't think he'd be right, sir. If there's any grumbling it always seems to come from him.

MAINWARING It could be a case of the poacher turned gamekeeper. He was a Jack Tar, wasn't he?

WILSON I believe so.

MAINWARING One thing you can say for the boys in blue – they stand firm in the face of the enemy.

WILSON Well, there's nowhere to run on a boat, is there?

MAINWARING I pride myself I'm quite a good judge of character, Wilson. He's our man, mark my words. Call him in.

WILSON Very good, sir. (**He goes to door**) Frazer!

FRAZER What's up now?

WILSON Would you mind coming into the office.

MAINWARING It's an order, Wilson! (**He shouts**) Frazer! In here at the double!

FRAZER (**To the man next to him**) Regimental bastard! (**Frazer crosses to the office and ambles up to the desk and salutes**) Was there something you wanted?

MAINWARING (**Rises and salutes**) Yes. Stand easy, Frazer. Now, Sergeant Wilson and I have been watching you very closely in the last few weeks.

FRAZER Aye, well I'm sorry, but it's all this damned bull. I canna see the sense in it.

MAINWARING A smart soldier is a good soldier – Frazer – but I haven't called you in here to discuss spit and polish. We're looking for N.C.O.s, and if I'm any judge of a man – you have the necessary qualities of leadership, discipline and reliability. (**Frazer reacts**) You held N.C.O. rank in the Navy, didn't you?

FRAZER Aye, I did that. Chief Petty Officer. Before I was busted.

MAINWARING Busted?

FRAZER Aye, I hit the Officer of the Watch.

MAINWARING Did you?

FRAZER With a boat-hook.

MAINWARING Oh dear!

FRAZER The crooked end.

MAINWARING Well, I'm sure you must have had a very good reason.

FRAZER Oh, I had that.

MAINWARING (**To Wilson**) I thought so.

FRAZER I was drunk.

MAINWARING Well, that's all in the past. There's not much danger of that happening again – is there Wilson?

WILSON Not with a boat-hook, sir.

MAINWARING Do I take it you'll accept the stripe?

FRAZER Aye, I will. I like your hat, sir.

MAINWARING Thank you, Frazer. Sergeant Wilson – get Jones.

WILSON Yes, sir.

He opens the door. Jones, having been listening at the key hole, falls in.

JONES **Ad libs.**

Jones enters and approaches desk.

MAINWARING Jones, I want you to be the first to know that I'm making Frazer here up to Lance Corporal.

JONES Permission to speak, sir?

MAINWARING Yes, Jones.

JONES A very good choice.

MAINWARING We now have room on the establishment for a full Corporal.

JONES That's very good news, sir.

MAINWARING Now, as the Commander in the Field, I have to ensure that we get the right man with the best fighting potential.

JONES I've got that all right. Just you let me get at 'em, sir. I'll be in the front there, with my cold steel. They don't like it up 'em!

MAINWARING We will therefore select our Corporal from our two Lance Corporals.

JONES Ah – a competition like. Well, that seems fair.

FRAZER It will be if you stop bribing them with steak.

JONES Now look…

MAINWARING I can assure you, Frazer, that Corporal Jones' activities as a tradesman will in no way influence our decision.

Wilson reacts.

JONES Ah, well, I wouldn't want to take any advantage or put a forward conception on it, Mr Mainwaring, sir. (**To Frazer**) I'll tell you what, I'll hold up their supplies until they've given the stripe.

FRAZER Aye, I'd like that fine.

JONES And when they've decided, they can have it again (**To Mainwaring**) or not as the case may be.

CHURCH HALL

The men are in groups. Mainwaring enters hall from side office.

MAINWARING Now, men, I want you to bring those chairs up and gather round in front of the platform for a lecture. Move.

FRAZER (**Galvanised into action**) Come on now, look lively there. Gather round the platform at the double.

Jones gives the same commands a little later.

FRAZER (**Salutes**) Platoon present, sir, and ready for the lecture.

JONES (**Saluting**) Er… ready for the lecture.

MAINWARING Thank you, Corporals. (**Turns to Wilson**) Right, back to your place. Lots of keen N.C.O.s here, Sergeant.

WILSON Yes, haven't we just.

MAINWARING Now, I want you to pay particular attention to what I'm about to say.

FRAZER Pay attention there! You – Godfrey!

Godfrey suffers.

MAINWARING The fact that Hitler hasn't kicked off with his invasion doesn't mean to say that the whistle's gone for 'no side'. It's quite on the cards he'll put recce parties ashore from submarines to find out the disposition of our forces.

FRAZER That's right, you know. The Captain's right.

MAINWARING Thank you, Frazer. Such parties could strike at any time, before church bells were rung – while we were still in our homes – and shops.

FRAZER You might be in the bank, sir. Is that not so, sir?

MAINWARING Yes, quite right, Frazer. But we're going to be ready for them. Our watchword must be – 'they shall not pass'.

FRAZER Beautiful words. Beautiful words.

Mainwaring reacts.

MAINWARING So there we are, at home, probably without our guns, when suddenly a ruthless Nazi storm-trooper bursts through the door holding a Luger or a machine gun. There he stands, facing you. What are you going to do?

WALKER I'll have done it.

FRAZER That'll be enough of that. I've got his name, sir.

PIKE Hear that, he's got your name.

WALKER Yeah, I've got his whisky.

MAINWARING Now, I daresay you think this situation is pretty hopeless.

FRAZER Absolutely hopeless.

The platoon nod.

MAINWARING Well, it's not.

FRAZER It's not hopeless at all.

MAINWARING All you need is a clear head, steel nerve and a quick hand.

WALKER And a tank.

FRAZER That was Walker again, sir. I've got him, sir. Fall in, two men.

MAINWARING Back to your place.

WILSON Frazer, don't let's be too hasty.

WALKER **(Laughs)** We've created a monster, sir.

MAINWARING New brooms you know.

WALKER Oh, is that it?

MAINWARING You don't need a tank in a situation like this, Walker. You need guts. And know how. You've all got the guts and by the time you leave this hall I'll have given you the know how. Now, I want two volunteers.

Frazer and Jones leap forward.

MAINWARING Ah, two keen men, yes. I want one of you to be a storm-trooper. Take this. **(Mainwaring hands over his gun)** Now Jones, I want you to imagine that you're in your shop this afternoon, going about your normal business. Got that?

JONES Yes, sir.

MAINWARING Right. Now you, Frazer, enter from the door.

JONES Permission to speak, sir?

MAINWARING Yes, Jones.

JONES I wasn't in my shop this afternoon, sir.

MAINWARING Well, er… we'll imagine that you were.

JONES Today's early closing day, you see, sir.

MAINWARING Well, we'll ignore that for the time being. Frazer, you burst in – see Jones – and tell him to stick 'em up.

JONES Handy hoch.

MAINWARING What?

JONES Handy hoch. That's what they say, sir. That's Bosche parlez-vous for 'stick 'em up'.

MAINWARING Thank you, Jones. Go on, Frazer.

FRAZER Handies hoch Englander Sweinhund, etc…

MAINWARING Now, what are you going to do, Jones?

JONES Put my handies hoch, sir.

MAINWARING Quite right. No sense in antagonising him. The next thing to do is to fix him with a stare.

Jones, adjusting his glasses, does so.

MAINWARING When you have his attention, you can distract him. **(Mainwaring notices Jones)** Look at me, Frazer – look me in the eyes. Great Scott – look out.

Frazer looks behind him. Mainwaring whips up a chair and lunges, stopping just short of Frazer.

FRAZER It wasn't fair. I wasna ready.

MAINWARING No, Frazer – and the Bosche won't be ready either. Now I want you to take particular note of the way I used the chair. You must lunge with the legs – like that. **(He demonstrates)**

GODFREY Like a lion tamer, sir.

MAINWARING Er, yes – yes, that's right, Godfrey. It's no good swiping at it like this – you must lunge. Lunge, lunge, lunge. **(He demonstrates and bangs into Jones)** So there you are, you can deal with a storm-trooper with a gun.

JONES There's just one thing, sir.

MAINWARING Yes, Jones.

JONES I don't have no chairs in my shop.

MAINWARING Ah, don't you? Well I'm sure you could look round and improvise some other weapon.

WALKER Perhaps you could make him sit on the bacon slicer, Jonesey?

FRAZER Shall I take his name, sir?

MAINWARING Don't be facetious, Walker. It's a very real enemy that we have to deal with.

FRAZER Let me take his name, sir?

MAINWARING No thank you, Frazer.

WALKER He's going to have to go!

GODFREY Power corrupts, I'm afraid.

MAINWARING Right, we'll deal with your problem later, Jones. In the meantime, another couple can have a try.

JONES 'Ere, wait a minute, I 'aven't done the chair yet. I only fixed him a stare.

MAINWARING Oh, very well. One more volunteer.

FRAZER Walker!

WALKER I never said a word!

FRAZER You're volunteering.

WALKER Oh, am I?

FRAZER Jump to it.

WALKER All right.

MAINWARING Oh, good man, Walker. Take the gun, Jones, you're going about your business.

JONES I thought if you didn't mind, sir, that I'd be poking the fire.

MAINWARING Yes, Jones, anything you like. Now, in you come, Walker.

WALKER Handy hoch!

JONES Ah! (**He puts his hands up**) I'm fixing him with my stare. Ah, was ist das?

WALKER Eh?

JONES That's German for 'what's that?'.

WALKER What's what?

MAINWARING You're supposed to look round, Walker.

WALKER Oh, sorry, sir. Do it again, Jonesey.

JONES I think I'll poke the fire this afternoon.

WALKER Handy hoch!

JONES Was ist das?

Business with chairs.

WALKER I reckon you're dead, Jonesey.

JONES Well, it's like I said, sir. I wouldn't have a chair in the shop.

WILSON Excuse me, sir, but it's about time some of your men went on guard.

MAINWARING By Jove, so it is! Fall in your guard, Frazer.

FRAZER Fall in – the guard. Over here at the double.

Walker, Pike and Godfrey fall in.

FRAZER Smarten up your ideas there. Chin in, chest out, stomach in. Squad, 'shun. S…lope arms. Right turn. Guard… to the Command Post qui…ck march. Right wheel double. (**They double**) Right wheel.

He doubles them twice round the hall. Godfrey stops after the first circuit and catches up the last time. They go out of the door, giving eyes right on the way.

Mainwaring and Wilson exit.

MAINWARING (**To Wilson**) I think I've picked the right one there, Wilson.

WILSON Yes, sir. You've picked a right one.

SIDE OFFICE

A dust sheet covers the desk. A plank between two trestles stands against the book case over the desk chair. Enter Mainwaring. He looks round.

MAINWARING Wilson! Wilson!

Wilson enters from the main hall.

WILSON Yes, sir?

MAINWARING What the devil's going on here?

WILSON I gather the Vicar found a couple of tins of white-wash and he and the Verger decided to lighten their darkness.

He moves round in front of the chair and grabs the dust sheet.

MAINWARING Give me a hand to get this off.

WILSON Do you think we should? I mean, it is the Vicar's desk.

MAINWARING We'll have to get this situation with the church clarified. I mean all that confusion over the ammunition and the altar candles would have looked very bad if the balloon had gone up. (**He sits**) Shove it away for now. We'll put it back after parade. (**There is a knock at the door**) Come in. (**Enter Frazer. He salutes**) Ah, Corporal Frazer. (**He rises to salute and knocks his head on the plank**) This'll have to go, Wilson. All go well with the Guard last night?

FRAZER Aye, sir, it did. Here are the charge sheets.

MAINWARING Charge sheets?

FRAZER Aye, that's what I said. Charge sheets.

Mainwaring picks them up and reads them.

MAINWARING Private Pike deserting his post. Private Godfrey cowardice in the face of the enemy. Private Walker – mutiny. Those are rather serious charges, you know, Frazer.

FRAZER I ken that fine, sir. And I hope you'll make an example of these men, sir, by dealing with them with the utmost severity.

MAINWARING I see. Would you mind leaving us for a moment, Frazer. I'd like to talk to Sergeant Wilson about this.

FRAZER Certainly, sir. I'll have the prisoners and escort standing by. (**He salutes. Mainwaring stands to salute and bangs his head again**)

WILSON Shall I get some of the men to take these down, sir?

MAINWARING Never mind that now. What are we going to do about these?

WILSON I don't think we're allowed to put them on a charge.

MAINWARING Neither do I. What punishment can we give? I can't give Pike C.B. We're shorthanded at the bank as it is.

WILSON Couldn't we tell him C.B. means confined to bank?

MAINWARING Oh, don't be absurd! We can hardly dock their pay. They don't get any. And what's even worse – all these charges on active service are court martial offences carrying the death penalty!

WILSON Perhaps you could give them a good talking to.

There is a knock at the door.

MAINWARING Come in.

Enter Jones. He salutes. Mainwaring stands but remembers the plank.

MAINWARING Yes, Jones.

JONES Captain Mainwaring, sir. I got a serious complaint. Lance Corporal Frazer just put me on a fizzer!

Frazer, entering behind him.

FRAZER Aye, there it is – it's on the sheet, you've got to go through with it.

JONES He can't do that to me – I'm senior to him.

FRAZER He called me a stupid old – what it says on that paper – in front of the men.

MAINWARING Now, really, this has gone far enough. Get those other men in, Frazer.

FRAZER Yes, sir. Prisoners – caps off. Prisoners and escorts, quick march. Left, right, left, right, left, right – left wheel – halt! Right turn!

Godfrey and Pike, flanked by two privates, enter. They salute. Mainwaring returns salute and hits his head.

MAINWARING This is ludicrous. Get that plank out. Get all these escorts out of here. These aren't desperate criminals on the run. Get 'em out.

FRAZER Escorts, disss-miss.

The escorts push through the confusion to get back into the hall.

They remove the plank.

MAINWARING Now, first things first. Now, what happened last night, Pike?

PIKE Well, sir – I was in the slit-trench when a great big Alsatian came up and barked at me and he wouldn't go away so I went to the guard house to get a bone to placate him, sir.

FRAZER Deserting his post.

MAINWARING Godfrey?

GODFREY Well, Corporal Frazer told me to go and help like and I told him I didn't want to. You see dogs don't like me, even quite little dogs. I seem to bring out the worst in them, so I wouldn't go.

FRAZER Cowardice in the face of the enemy.

MAINWARING You can hardly call an Alsatian an enemy.

FRAZER A German dog, sir.

MAINWARING I see. Well – Walker?

WALKER Well, I told Taffy here, if he went on being so regimental we'd stop his whisky.

FRAZER Note that, sir – '*We'd* stop his whisky'. They'd conspired together – that's mutiny! And then, just now, Corporal Jones – in front of my men calling me a stupid old 'what's written on that piece of paper'.

JONES Oh no – I didn't. You said – I suppose you think I'm a stupid old 'what's on that paper'. I said yes.

The next three speeches are spoken together.

WALKER How can it be mutiny to stop him getting his whisky?

PIKE I didn't desert. I just went to get help from the guard room.

GODFREY I don't think it's very fair to go through this rigmarole just because dogs don't like me.

The Verger has been overhearing the last 30 seconds.

VERGER Can I be getting on with the ceiling? I won't disturb you more than necessary.

MAINWARING (**Rises**) Really, this is the last straw! Can't you wait ten minutes, blast you!

VERGER I'm going to have this out with the Vicar. If you ask me, you're the silly old – 'what's on that paper'.

He goes.

MAINWARING Now look here – I've had enough of this. I'm going to adjourn this case until I've had time to take legal advice. In the meantime, you all return to your duties which are to prepare yourselves to defend your homes from Nazi assault. Is that understood?

FRAZER Yes sir! Prisoners – about –

JONES Here – I'll do that. I'm the senior one. Prisoners...

MAINWARING Get out! All of you! Get out...

FRAZER AND JONES Yes, sir. (**Ad lib on exits**)

They all go.

MAINWARING Wilson – I'm a patient man, but I think I'm reaching the end of my tether.

WILSON Yes, isn't it exasperating?

SQUARE (Out of vision) Hold my horse. Mainwaring! (He pronounces it as spelt)

MAINWARING Great Scott! It can't be!

Enter Colonel Square.

SQUARE First lesson of warfare. Never leave your rear exposed. You remember me – Square. Square's the name.

WILSON Oh yes – you were with Lawrence of Arabia – Colonel Square.

SQUARE Corporal, Colonel Square.

MAINWARING Corporal Colonel?

SQUARE Of course – it couldn't be Colonel Corporal could it? I've been attached to you by H.Q. to train you in guerrilla warfare.

WILSON Ours is not to reason why.

MAINWARING Oh, I see. Good.

SQUARE It's good to be back in the saddle again, eh?

MAINWARING We're not going through all that business with the horses again, are we?

SQUARE Lord no! Got to get those old fashioned notions out of your head. (He sees the charge papers on the table) Good heavens! Two five two's – charge sheets. That takes me back. I haven't seen one of these since 1919. Got through five thousand of them in one month.

MAINWARING Five thousand charge sheets!

SQUARE Well – we were right out in the desert. We couldn't get anything else. What fool made these out?
Mainwaring reacts.

WILSON Why? Aren't they any good?

SQUARE Mutiny isn't section 40, neither is cowardice. Hah, playing at soldiers. You're all the same you chaps. Are your men on parade?

WILSON Yes, they're in the hall.

SQUARE Right, I'll start licking them into shape. (He crosses to door) By the look of those charges you need a bit of discipline around here. Oh, by the way, I've brought these for you. I know you are partial to them.

MAINWARING What are they?

SQUARE Flies. (He exits. Out of vision, we hear his voice) Right, fall in, in three ranks, etc. etc.

MAINWARING The whole thing is getting out of hand, Wilson. I shall be glad when today's over.

WILSON But if these charges aren't properly made out – you can drop them and that's the end of it.

MAINWARING Yes – as long as we can stop our N.C.O.s from making any more.

WILSON Oh, I don't think you need worry about old Jones.

MAINWARING We'd better talk to Frazer *now* – before anything else happens.

WILSON I'll get him in.

Frazer storms in.

FRAZER You've done this deliberately!

MAINWARING Frazer! What's the matter now?

FRAZER Yon maniac's put me on a bloody fizzer! (He goes)

MAINWARING Frazer! – Wilson – get Square in here.

SQUARE (Out of vision, we hear his voice) Prisoners and escort – quick march.

Godfrey, Pike and Walker are marched in. Jones is an escort, with his hat on. Prisoners have their hats off.

SQUARE Left wheel – halt. Right turn.

MAINWARING What in heaven's name is happening?

SQUARE Slackest rabble I've ever seen. They're all on two five two. Idle on parade, sir. And I'm charging that Scot N.C.O. of yours with insolence!

JONES (Enjoying it) Permission to speak, sir?

MAINWARING Yes, Jones.

JONES What he said was much worse than what was on that paper.

MAINWARING Oh really – this has got to stop. Wilson – get Frazer.

WILSON (At the door) He's gone, sir.

JONES Deserting his post! Shall I get the charge sheet ready, sir?

MAINWARING I want him back here at the double. We've all got to come to an understanding. I can't have all my time taken up with these petty fogging little charges.

WALKER I don't think Frazer will be long, sir. He's only gone round the corner.

MAINWARING What in heaven's name for?

WALKER He's gone for a boat-hook.

HALL

Frazer enters, brandishing a boat-hook.

FRAZER Where is he? Let me get at him. (He charges towards the office door)

MAINWARING Wilson – lock that door! Don't let him in.

We fade on Frazer as he starts to attack the door with the boat-hook.

SERIES TWO **EPISODE SIX**

Recorded: Wednesday 27/11/68 (made in black and white)

Original transmission: Saturday 5/4/69, 7.00–7.30pm

(This episode was originally planned for transmission on 3/2/69 at 7.30pm.)

Original viewing figures = 11.6 million

This episode is no longer available in the BBC archives.

ARTHUR LOWE .... CAPTAIN MAINWARING
JOHN LE MESURIER .... SERGEANT WILSON
CLIVE DUNN .... LANCE CORPORAL JONES
JOHN LAURIE .... PRIVATE FRAZER
JAMES BECK .... PRIVATE WALKER
ARNOLD RIDLEY .... PRIVATE GODFREY
IAN LAVENDER .... PRIVATE PIKE
JANET DAVIES .... MRS PIKE
GEOFFREY LUMSDEN .... CORPORAL-COLONEL SQUARE
JOHN RINGHAM .... CAPTAIN BAILEY
QUEENIE WATTS .... MRS KEEN
GLADYS DAWSON .... MRS WITT
ERNST ULMAN .... SIGMUND MURPHY
BILL PERTWEE .... ARP WARDEN
JUNE PETERSEN .... WOMAN
PLATOON .... COLIN BEAN, RICHARD JACQUES, FRANK GODFREY, ALEC COLEMAN, HUGH CECIL, JIMMY MAC, DESMOND CULLUM-JONES, VIC TAYLOR, DAVID SEAFORTH, RICHARD KITTERIDGE

UNDER FIRE

• OLIVER BAYLDON REMEMBERS •

'One of the reasons *Dad's Army* struck a chord with me was that, although I don't remember the Home Guard, I was brought up in a village in Rutland immediately after the war. Traces still lingered there, like those rotting straw sacks suspended in wooden frames that had been used for bayonet practice, and sandpits that were once firing ranges.

'We did a lot of research for *Dad's Army*. Much care was taken by all the design teams (sets, costumes and make-up) to be as authentic as possible; the scripts were so true there was no need to pastiche.

'As a designer, one had to furnish settings with what could be purchased and hired. Budgets were tightly controlled. Most of the dressing (furniture, ornaments, etc.) came from Old Times Hire, and later from Terry O'Docherty Hire. The sets, meanwhile, were all built in BBC workshops, although occasionally by a local firm called City Display. There was a kind of tyranny of the stock book, whereby items of flattage, doors, windows, arches, panels, fencing, etc., had to be booked in advance. And one rearranged items to suit one's design, thus keeping within the budget.

'One of my clearest memories is of Jimmy and David laughing. There was a wonderful atmosphere about their technical runs, everything so well thought out.

'One of the sets I had to design for this episode was a church tower from which Frazer and Godfrey spotted a light flashing from a house. The actors were very dubious about the scene on the roof. Someone complained they had no head for heights, so I had to explain it wouldn't be more than a few feet from the floor, and not 60 feet high – Jimmy Beck said he'd not risk a pint beforehand! The episode was shot in the studio, with bushes and everything else hired in. The design crew tweaked the branches of the bushes to represent light breezes because the big fans were too strong and affected the sound booms.

'We had to cheat with the roof of the church. It would only just fit in a corner of the studio because there were so many stock sets, hence the high walls behind – as if it were an extension – because there was no space for sky. Night exteriors were always far easier

Oliver Bayldon's illustration of the church roof.
The number of stock sets meant there was only room in a corner of the studio to build the roof.

than day exteriors when it came to lighting because you only needed to light the foreground – the camera did the rest.

'Something else I'll always remember about *Dad's Army* is how committed the so-called "extras" were in the platoon. They were an integral part of the show and not just the usual "walk-ons" like in other productions. The main cast knew their stock sets so well they would arrange the dressings themselves all in the cause of authenticity. They were a really nice group of men who forgot they were acting, and for those thirty-odd screen minutes became the characters they played.'

OLIVER BAYLDON
Designer

Under Fire

SIDE OFFICE. DAY

Enter Mainwaring in his tweed suit with the Sunday papers. He hangs up his tin hat and his gas mask. Takes off his muffler and jacket. We see he is in pyjamas. He takes his uniform out of the carrier bag and puts it on the desk. He removes his trousers, revealing pyjama trousers.

Enter Wilson.

WILSON Sorry, sir. Good Lord! Er, did you sleep here, sir?

Mainwaring is putting the buttons in his uniform jacket.

MAINWARING No, no. And more's the pity with those damned aircraft passing over all the time. Had a shocking night. Elizabeth, you know, very nervous type. As soon as the siren goes she's in the cupboard under the stairs. Wild horses wouldn't drag her out until the All Clear. Scared out of her wits.

WILSON Where were you then?

MAINWARING I don't like leaving her on her own, so I have to go too.

Wilson, having hung up his gas mask and helmet, helps with the buttons.

MAINWARING To make matters worse, we have Elizabeth's mother staying with us. She sat on my chair all night with her gas mask open on her lap, clutching her pension book. I was on a camp stool with my elbow on the gas meter, my head resting on a coat hook.

WILSON Dear oh dear. I spent the night under the kitchen table. **(He starts to undress. He is also in pyjamas)**

MAINWARING I didn't think you had a kitchen table.

WILSON I don't think I have any more. Oh, I was at a friend's house. There was so much shrapnel coming down from the ack ack guns that they wouldn't let me go home.

MAINWARING Huh, lucky they had pyjamas to fit you, wasn't it?

WILSON Yes, wasn't it?

Mainwaring starts to undo his trousers.

Enter Mrs Pike.

Mainwaring saves 'face' behind desk.

MRS PIKE **(She hands Mr Wilson his shirt and tie)** Oh really, Arthur. You'd forget your head if it wasn't screwed on.

WILSON **(Whispering)** Mavis! I didn't need it, and you were asleep.

MRS PIKE Afraid I might wake up, were you? **(He ushers up to door)** Good morning, Mr Mainwaring. **(She exits)**

MAINWARING Good morning. Hm. I had to leave mine as well. It was in the airing cupboard – in the bathroom. Elizabeth's mother was in residence. Extraordinary woman – she sits there for hours.

There is a knock on the door.

WILSON O, Lord! What does she want now?

Enter Colonel Square, he salutes.

MAINWARING Ah, good morning, Corporal Square.

SQUARE Corporal *Colonel* Square.

MAINWARING Of course. Good morning Corporal *Colonel* Square. We weren't expecting you quite so soon.

SQUARE So it seems. Come to prepare the morning's exercise. **(He crosses to the door, turns and looks again)** Extraordinary! **(He goes out)**

MAINWARING I think we had better get dressed as quickly as possible before the rest of the platoon start trooping in.

WILSON I quite agree, sir.

Mainwaring takes off his pyjama trousers to reveal long johns. Wilson is taking off his pyjama top.

MAINWARING I recommend you get a pair of these before the winter sets in, Wilson.

WILSON Funnily enough, I bought a pair last week, sir. **(Takes his trousers off revealing a similar pair)** I got them specially for when we are on guard. These denims aren't very thick. **(Admiring Mainwaring's long johns)** I must say those look awfully cosy.

MAINWARING **(Turning to show them off)** Twenty-two and six – Mrs Nolan's. Under the counter, of course. She has any amount of stuff hidden away, you know.

WILSON So it seems. It must be quite an Aladdin's cave.

MAINWARING Yes. Have a look at this double stitching.

Enter Bailey.

BAILEY Good grief! **(He salutes)** Good morning.

MAINWARING Ah, good morning.

BAILEY **(Not knowing what to say)** Ah! Well, er, shall I come back later?

MAINWARING No, no. We're just changing into our uniforms.

BAILEY Ah!

WILSON Can we help you at all?

BAILEY Ah, well, London took a bit of a pasting last night.

MAINWARING Did they indeed? Poor devils. We heard them going over all night.

BAILEY Well, of course, it may be your turn next. They are using enormous numbers of these incendiary bombs. The Old Man wants all units to put maximum strength on duty to help tackle them.

MAINWARING You can count on my men to give every support.

BAILEY Yes, well the main thing is to check on your sand and your water supplies.

MAINWARING Make sure that's done, Wilson.

BAILEY How's Square getting on with the guerrilla training?

MAINWARING Huh, a bit old fashioned if you ask me.

BAILEY He seemed full of ideas for harassing the enemy.

WILSON You must admit, sir, he's come up with one or two good wheezes. The stop-me-and-buy-one, for instance.

MAINWARING Filling choc ices full of Harpic? Hardly appropriate for modern warfare, Wilson.

SQUARE **(Out of vision)** Infantry, right – engage point. Infantry, left – engage point. Foot soldier, left – engage point, etc.

MAINWARING We'd better go and see what's going on.

HALL. DAY

They enter the hall. As they open the door, Square yells

SQUARE Charge!

Pike, Walker and Jones are mounted on bicycles. They pedal across towards Mainwaring and co., yelling as they go. Mainwaring, Wilson and Bailey dodge aside. Jones goes straight through the doorway and crashes into the desk.

MAINWARING Great Scott! What's going on?

They rescue Jones.

WILSON Are you all right, Jonesey?

JONES Sorry, Mr Mainwaring, sir. I had me sabre in me brake hand.

MAINWARING Lucky you didn't do yourself an injury, Jones.

JONES I'd have done those Jerries an injury. They'd have had my cold steel right up 'em, sir. They wouldn't have liked it, sir. Oh disaster!

MAINWARING What's the matter – have you broken something?

JONES Yes, my pump!

SQUARE No good at all. You're not on a Sunday School ride. You're killing Nazis.

WALKER Would it be more frightening if we rang our bells? **(He does so)**

SQUARE Back to your place, Walker.

WALKER Only a suggestion.

MAINWARING What's going on, Corporal?

SQUARE Forming a mobile striking force, sir. Swift and silent, sabre slashing – thrusting where the enemy least expects it – on bicycles. **(To men)** Now, let's have another go. Infantry, left – engage point. Infantry, right – engage point.

MAINWARING All right, that'll be enough of that. I want to address the men.

JONES Excuse me, Mr Mainwaring. I won't be able to do any more charging, sir, until I get me brakes fixed.

MAINWARING Yes, all right.

JONES I shall need a new valve rubber.

MAINWARING Yes, yes.

JONES And I shall have to get me pump fixed. Mind you, I could be first line of reinforcement, sir.

MAINWARING Jones, *please*. Fall the men in, Corporal Square.

SQUARE Corporal *Colonel* Square.

WILSON Fall in, in three ranks.

The men start to fall in. Mainwaring starts to move to his position. He suddenly becomes aware of Captain Bailey.

MAINWARING Don't let us keep you, Captain Bailey.

BAILEY No, that's all right. I'm in no hurry.

MAINWARING Oh, very well.

BAILEY We young officers at Area Command are always keen to see how you veterans operate.

Mainwaring reacts.

Walker is talking to Jones.

JONES You see, it's my private property, Joe.

WALKER Tell you what, I know a geezer get you a new front wheel – 17s 6d. Throw in a pump an' all.

MAINWARING Walker! When you've finished. Fall in.

WALKER Mind my bike, little girl. **(Throws bike down)**

BAILEY Chocolates, cigarettes, ices.

Mainwaring reacts.

MAINWARING Hurry up, Walker. Right, settle down. Squ-a-ad.

SQUARE Wrong.

MAINWARING **(Taking no notice)** Squ-a-ad.

SQUARE Wrong.

MAINWARING Is there something you wanted to say?

SQUARE You're giving the wrong command, Mainwaring. We aren't a squad, we're a platoon.

MAINWARING I'm sure what you say is correct, but these chaps here are fighting troops, not parade ground wallahs. Results are what we're after, not a lot of bull. Squad – er Platoooon, atten-shun.

They come to a ragged attention.

MAINWARING That was a very sloppy movement, Jones.

SQUARE It was a sloppy command.

Walker, Jones and Mainwaring react.

SQUARE You want to put some snap into it, man. Platoon, stand at ease.

Jones does nothing.

Mainwaring reacts.

SQUARE Platoon, atten-shun.

Jones again does nothing.

The same again.

SQUARE There you are, you see? When they hear a proper word of command, they jump to it. All together. **(Jones winks at Mainwaring, who winks at Bailey and reacts)**

MAINWARING I am sure we are all very grateful to you for your help, Corporal Square.

SQUARE Corporal *Colonel* Square.

WILSON **(Having edged close to Square, suddenly is prompted for the first and probably the last time in his life to behave like a Sergeant. He barks)** Silence in the ranks! **(Square looks round in surprise)** Look to your front. Did you shave this morning?

Square, completely surprised, looks round towards Wilson again.

WILSON Look to your front. Next time, stand nearer the razor.

In dead silence Wilson goes to Mainwaring and salutes.

WILSON Platoon ready for your inspection, sir.

MAINWARING **(Returning his salute, says almost under his breath)** Well done, Wilson.

WILSON That's nothing, sir. A little bit I picked up at Catterick. **(To Bailey)** Do you mind?

MAINWARING Now, pay attention, please. So far, Hitler has lacked the courage to come and scrap with us toe to toe. Instead he is using a new and cowardly weapon. Aerial attack with the fire bomb. Now, you all know how to deal with those, but we must check that our equipment is in tip-top condition. Frazer, you've been responsible for the stirrup pump. Is it in working order?

FRAZER Yes, sir. I'll bring it round after parade.

MAINWARING Good. Bring it round? Why isn't it here –

FRAZER I was using it for the 'Dig for Victory' campaign – in my garden. My apples had the blight.

MAINWARING This is a vital piece of military equipment. It must not leave our headquarters. I take it you didn't borrow the water as well?

FRAZER No, sir. Only the bucket.

Mainwaring reacts.

MAINWARING See they are returned, Wilson. **(Reacts to Bailey)** And Jones, check the sand buckets and the extinguisher. Oh, and the long-handled shovel.

Jones whispers to Walker.

MAINWARING Don't tell me that's been borrowed.

JONES Yes, sir. For the Command Post stove, sir.

MAINWARING I'm sure you don't need a 12-foot shovel for the Command Post stove.

WALKER You do for nicking the coal from the railway siding.

MAINWARING **(Turning to Sergeant)** Wilson.

WILSON I'll see they're brought back, sir.

BAILEY Well, I hope you won't get any action. But if you do, good luck.

MAINWARING You can rest assured that this unit will be one hundred per cent prepared by the time the sirens blow. We'll form a fire-fighting force and spotters will be posted on the church tower.

BAILEY Bully. **(He salutes and leaves)**

MAINWARING Bully?

WILSON He's only jealous, sir.

ROOF OF CHURCH TOWER

Frazer and Godfrey are on guard, tin-hatted. It is night. There is a heavy drone from the aircraft overhead. Searchlights probe the sky.

FRAZER My, there's a lot come over tonight.

GODFREY There must be hundreds.

FRAZER You're trembling like a leaf. Are you cold?

GODFREY No. Just frightened.

FRAZER **(Looking up)** Aye, I'm not blaming you.

GODFREY It's not them, so much, it's being up so high. I've always been the same. When I was in the Civil Service Stores I could have had a marvellous job in Accounts, but it was on the fifth floor. How much longer before we get relieved?

FRAZER Twenty minutes.

GODFREY I'll just pop down for a minute.

FRAZER Man, you've been down there three times already. Why don't you go over there by the gargoyle?

GODFREY Wouldn't that be sacrilege?

FRAZER Sacrilege? What would you do if a parachutist started coming down?

GODFREY Well, I hope he'd be too much of a gentleman to look.

FRAZER No, I mean you'd have to shoot him, wouldn't you?

GODFREY Oh, I couldn't do that. War doesn't suit me, I'm afraid. It's not that I'm a conscientious objector, or anything like that. I'm just not very good at it.

FRAZER **(Seeing something)** What's that over there?

GODFREY Where?

FRAZER That light.

GODFREY Oh. It's going on and off.

FRAZER Damn it, man, I believe they're signalling.

GODFREY Who would do a thing like that?

FRAZER Where is it?

GODFREY It's on the corner of Mortimer Street, near where the bomb dropped last night.

FRAZER We'll go and tell the Captain.

CHURCH HALL

Mainwaring is crossing the hall. He stops dead in his tracks. We see the poster he is looking at. It has been drawn on by a child.

MAINWARING Wilson! **(Wilson comes out of the side office)** Wilson. Look at this!

WILSON Rather good, sir.

MAINWARING Wilson! Have a word with Miss Beckwith. If this sort of thing carries on I shall have to keep those children out of here all together.

WILSON Right, sir.

FRAZER **(Out of vision)** Captain Mainwaring, sir. **(Frazer, followed by Godfrey, staggers up to Mainwaring)** There's a light going on and off in the town. It looks as if someone's signalling to the enemy.

MAINWARING Are you sure you're not mistaken, Frazer?

FRAZER Absolutely. We both saw it. It's on the corner of Mortimer Street.

MAINWARING I'll phone the police.

SQUARE Why waste time phoning them? You have the authority. You're on active service – attack.

MAINWARING I'll take the decisions here, Square. This is police business, don't you think so, Wilson?

WILSON I'm certain it isn't ours, sir.

SQUARE Isn't it? What if it's a Jerry paratrooper marking the target?

FRAZER Let's go and get him, sir.

MAINWARING Very well. When action is needed I'm the first to take it. You know where it is, Frazer. Lead the way. You stay here, Square. Come with me, Wilson.

GODFREY Er, er, could you give me a moment or two before we go?

MAINWARING Certainly not. Every second is vital.

GODFREY Yes, it is, sir.

MAINWARING Right. Lead on, Frazer.

EXTERIOR OF HOUSE

Cut to door of house. It should be the three-storey, Victorian terrace-type house. Beside the door are three bell buttons, indicating that the house is divided into three flats. There is a small overhanging porch overhead. Similar houses are seen in the background. Heavy ack ack fire and overhead bursts are heard. Enter Mainwaring and Wilson in great rush.

WILSON Heavens, did you hear that shrapnel falling? A lump missed you by inches.

MAINWARING I know. I heard it. Are Frazer and Godfrey all right?

WILSON **(Looking round)** Frazer's helping him. Godfrey's not very nimble on his pins, I'm afraid.

MAINWARING Top floor, wasn't it?

He rings the bell. Frazer and Godfrey arrive.

MAINWARING Come here, you two.

FRAZER My, it's coming down.

MAINWARING Are you sure this is the house, Frazer? **(He feels for a match)**

FRAZER Aye, this is it.

MAINWARING Let's see what the name is. **(He strikes a match)**

VOICE OF WARDEN **(Out of vision)** Put that light out, you bloody lunatic!

Mainwaring quickly puts the match out.

MAINWARING Damn. I didn't see it.

WILSON I did, sir. It was Murphy.

MAINWARING Murphy? That's suspicious. This could be a nasty business.

GODFREY Would you like my flashlight, sir? It's rather a nice one – it has **(he hands it over)** three colours. Green, red and white, you slide…

MAINWARING All right, Godfrey.

Mainwaring puts torch to letter box.

Murphy, on the inside, does the same thing. Then opens door. Mainwaring falls inside. Mainwaring reappears.

A short fat, Continental gent is revealed. He has a thick German accent.

MURPHY Yes, please?

MAINWARING Ah. Are you Mr Murphy?

MURPHY Vot is it you are vanting?

MAINWARING One of my men saw a light flashing on and off at your flat.

MURPHY Don't be so damned ridiculous. Who are you? **(He shines his torch in Mainwaring's face)**

MAINWARING I – I'm Captain Mainwaring, Home Guard. What's more to the point, who are you? **(He shines his torch in Murphy's face)**

MURPHY My name is Murphy. Sigmund Murphy.

WARDEN **(Out of vision)** Put that light out!

MAINWARING You're not English, are you?

MURPHY What are you talking about? I have lived here for 25 years.

FRAZER You don't sound like an Englishman.

MURPHY For that matter, my friend, neither do you.

WILSON I think he was born here, for some reason.

MURPHY No, I was born in Salzburg.

FRAZER That's Germany, isn't it?

MURPHY No, it is not. It is Austria, but I am a naturalised Englishman.

MAINWARING Well, why do you call yourself Murphy?

MURPHY With a war on, how would you like to be called von Schickenhausen?

WILSON I can see his point, sir.

MAINWARING **(Reacts)** Anyway, the point is, one of my men saw you flashing a light as if making a signal.

WOMAN'S VOICE **(Out of vision, as if from upper window)** He was doin' it last night and all.

MURPHY **(Shouting)** Why do you say such damned lies?

WOMAN Oh, yes you was. Just before the bomb dropped.

MURPHY Are you mad? Do you think I signal so they drop a bomb on me? **(To Mainwaring)** You don't want to take any notice of her. She is an interfering old cow. **(Shouts)** What about all those sailors that are visiting your flat, ha?

Mainwaring reacts.

WOMAN I'll have you for libel.

MURPHY And the entire Canadian Air Force.

WILSON Don't you think we ought to go inside before a scene develops?

MAINWARING Yes, I think it might be advisable. Take that woman's name.

HALLWAY OF HOUSE

They go inside into the hallway and close the door.

MAINWARING Now, Mr Murphy, what have you to say about this signalling?

MURPHY I tell you, I was not doing the signalling.

FRAZER You're a German though, aren't you?

MURPHY I'm as British as you are.

WILSON Don't start that all over again.

Godfrey whispers to Mainwaring.

MAINWARING What is it, Godfrey?

Godfrey whispers again.

MAINWARING Oh, not now, for heaven's sake.

FRAZER He's a German. I know damn well he's a German.

Mrs Keen, middle-aged blonde lady comes downstairs carrying a dachshund.

MRS KEEN Would you mind keeping your dog under control. He's been in my room again. **(She hands him the dachshund)**

FRAZER There, look. That's a German dog.

MURPHY Fritz, come here, you bad boy.

FRAZER He's even got a German name.

MRS KEEN Damn foreigners. You ought to be interned.

MURPHY Why don't you mind your own business?

Mrs Witt, a little old lady, emerges behind them from the cupboard under the stairs.

MRS WITT It's your moment of triumph, isn't it? Twenty-five years he's been plotting all this.

MURPHY Get back in your cupboard, you old hag.

MRS WITT He's a spy.

MURPHY Don't be so ridiculous.

MRS KEEN You ought to be done away with.

MAINWARING Oh, come, come, madam.

MRS KEEN He's in my room every night, eating my slippers.

MURPHY I think she is talking about my dog.

Woman comes in.

WOMAN OPPOSITE He was signalling last night, no matter what he says. Nazi!

MURPHY I am not a Nazi. I am British.

MRS WITT There's often a strong foreign smell coming from his kitchen – and he smells of garlic!

WOMAN OPPOSITE And he walks out of cinemas while they're still playing 'God Save the King'.

MAINWARING Does he indeed? The evidence against you looks pretty strong, Mr Murphy. I'm taking you into custody, so the police can investigate.

WILSON Do you think that's wise, sir?

MURPHY The world has gone mad!

MAINWARING I take full responsibility, Wilson. Fall in the guard. **(Godfrey and Frazer go to Murphy)** Bring him along to headquarters.

GODFREY **(To Murphy)** Before we go, do you think I could wash my hands?

MURPHY Certainly not.

MAINWARING By God. I think he is a German.

SIDE OFFICE

Square is at the desk, on the phone.

SQUARE Right. If there are any suspects I'll hold 'em until we can hand 'em over to the civil power… What are you worried about? I'm in command… Very funny… Right, well I'm coming back there as soon as I can hand over. You sound as if you need me… I don't see what a hole in the head has to do with it.

Mrs Pike enters the side office through the outside door.

MRS PIKE Frank forgot his balaclava. Where is he?

SQUARE He's fire spotting on the church tower.

MRS PIKE He'll get his death. I'm going to have words about this.

SQUARE Here, ma'am . You can't go out without a steel helmet. You'd better take mine.

MRS PIKE Thank you. You're an officer and a gentleman, Colonel.

SQUARE Not Colonel, ma'm. That was when I was in the regular army in the last lot – with Lawrence.

MRS PIKE Lawrence. Lawrence who?

SQUARE Lawrence of Arabia, ma'm. I'm only a Corporal in this mob.

MRS PIKE As an ex-Colonel it must come pretty hard taking orders from a Captain.

SQUARE I'm used to it. Had the same problem when I was only a Second Lieutenant. In the Jerusalem Campaign – siege of Jaffa… Not enough pips.

MRS PIKE Well, thank you, anyway. **(She exits)**

Pike enters.

PIKE Here, Corp.

SQUARE Corporal *Colonel.*

Effects: Ack ack guns.

PIKE Er, Corporal Colonel. It's getting a bit hot up there. There's lumps of shrapnel coming down like hail.

SQUARE Get back to your post, boy.

Effects: Distant explosion.

PIKE But if one of them pieces hits me, I'll be killed.

SQUARE **(Rises)** That's what soldiers are for. Get back.

Pike goes out through the outside door. There is a renewed sound of ack ack.

Mainwaring and Wilson rush in breathless.

WILSON I didn't care for that very much.

MAINWARING I quite agree, Wilson. Being brave is all very well, but it's damned frightening.

Mainwaring eyes Square and they change places.

MAINWARING Bring him in here, Frazer.

SQUARE Is this your prisoner?

MURPHY You'll be the laughing stock, that's what you'll be. The laughing stock.

SQUARE Sounds like a blasted Hun.

MURPHY I tell you I'm Breetish citizen.

SQUARE I've told Command. They're advising the civil power.

WILSON The who?

SQUARE The police, man. The police.

MAINWARING The point is, what do we do with him in the meantime?

SQUARE In the desert we used to bury them up to their necks in the sand and leave 'em.

MAINWARING Well, we can't do that here.

WILSON We could always take him down to the beach.

Mainwaring reacts.

SQUARE Well, work something out, Mainwaring. You have to stand on your own feet sooner or later. I've been called back to H.Q.

MAINWARING Have you? Then we'll *try* to manage without you.

SQUARE I wish I'd had you in the desert, Mainwaring. I might have made a soldier out of you. **(He crosses to the door, turns and looks him up and down)** Damn it, I don't believe even I could have done it. **(He goes out)**

MAINWARING Don't salute without your hat on! Damned

arrogance. I'm going to see the General about him.

GODFREY You won't be needing me for a minute or two, will you, sir?

Pike rushes in.

PIKE There's incendiaries coming down all over the place, sir.

There's a noise in the hall. Walker enters.

WALKER Blimey. There's one come in through the roof.

JONES **(Entering with them)** It's all lit up, sir. It's all lit up.

Mainwaring goes to door, and looks into hall.

Effects: Bomb hissing.

MAINWARING Frazer, give a hand outside. We'll deal with the one in the hall. Walker, get the pump. Wilson, you guard him.

JONES **(Running up and down)** Don't panic, anybody. Keep calm. Don't panic.

MAINWARING Jones, get more water.

JONES Permission to speak, sir?

MAINWARING Yes, Corporal?

JONES I wasn't panicking, sir.

MAINWARING Walker, you pump. Godfrey, feed the hose through. I'll take the nozzle.

WILSON Er, it's the jet for the fire, and the spray for the bomb, sir.

MAINWARING I know that.

Walker arranges the pump and a bucket. Godfrey gets down on his hands and knees to feed the hose through the door.

MAINWARING Where's the end?

GODFREY I – I – I'm trying to find it sir.

CHURCH HALL

Jones enters the main hall, he crosses under the gallery to where a fire bucket is hung, head high. He unhooks the handle from the bracket. The bottom of the bucket is supported by another metal bracket which tips the contents of the bucket right over him. He staggers, with the bucket, into the office door, meeting Mainwaring coming out.

JONES Who wired this up? **(Spurting out a mouthful of water)** It's empty, sir.

MAINWARING Well, fill it from the static water tank outside. **(Jones goes)** Jones!

Jones turns to run to the door. He slips and falls while doing so. He finally scrambles up and goes out. Mainwaring goes down on his hands and knees to approach the bomb.

MAINWARING **(Calling behind him)** Water on!

Walker starts to pump. Mainwaring is a long way from the bomb.

MAINWARING More hose, it's too far away.

Mainwaring crawls forward. Godfrey, Walker, the bucket and the pump follow, still pumping.

MAINWARING I need more hose, damn you.

Mainwaring tugs hard. It comes off the pump.

MAINWARING That's more like it. Water on.

WALKER **(Out of vision)** Right, sir. **(Walker pumps hard. Water spurts from the side nozzle of the pump, landing on Godfrey's backside)**

GODFREY Captain Mainwaring, sir. I wonder if I could possibly be excused for a moment or two?

MAINWARING Certainly not. Walker, why don't you pump, blast you?

WALKER I am doing, sir.

MAINWARING Do it harder.

Walker pumps harder and then sees what's happening.

WALKER Blimey, it's come off.

MAINWARING I don't believe it. **(As he rises and crosses, Jones runs in clutching a second bucket of water to his chest. He slips backwards on the wet part of the floor, drenching the second bucket over him. Mainwaring helps him up.**

MAINWARING What are you doing, Jones?

JONES **(Spurting out a mouthful of water)** Sorry, sir. **(He pours a few drops into the other bucket)** Every little helps. **(He goes half away and then comes back)** My old dad used to say that, sir. **(He goes for another bucket. Godfrey is trying to put the hose back on the pump)**

MAINWARING Hurry up and fix it, Godfrey.

GODFREY I'm trying. Has anyone got a little screwdriver?

WALKER **(Producing one)** Here you are, three and a tanner.

PIKE What about using the fire extinguisher on the stage, sir?

MAINWARING Good idea, Pike.

They cross the hall to the stage.

STAGE

MAINWARING Right, grab it, Pike.

Pike takes down the cone-shaped fire extinguisher from behind the proscenium. Note: This is a non-practical one. They are both now on the stage.

MAINWARING Now, strike the knob.

Pike turns it upside down and hits it with his hand.

MAINWARING Not like that. Strike it on the floor.

Pike raises it.

MAINWARING Not too hard.

Pike taps it gently.

MAINWARING Well, harder than that.

Pike taps it fractionally harder.

MAINWARING Oh, give it to me.

Mainwaring raises the extinguisher high and drives it down on the floor. It goes straight through the stage and disappears.

VOICES **(Godfrey/Walker: Out of vision)** Hurry up, sir. It's catching on.

Mainwaring plunges his hand into the hole after the extinguisher.

MAINWARING Give me a hand, Pike.

PIKE Can you feel it, sir?

MAINWARING No, get out of the light.

Mainwaring looks into the hole. A jet of foam, as if from the extinguisher, shoots into his face. Wilson comes up to Mainwaring.

WILSON Er, do you think you could hurry up, sir?

MAINWARING What do you think I'm trying to do?

WILSON It's just that I think it's spreading.

MAINWARING Well, get water, and get back and guard that Jerry.

Mrs Pike joins the group.

MRS PIKE Frank, I've been looking all over for you. Get this on. **(She has a balaclava with her)**

Jones enters with a bucket of water.

MRS PIKE Where's my Frank? I expect he'll need me.

MAINWARING Not now, Mrs Pike.

MRS PIKE He'll catch his death running around like this.

Jones runs to Mainwaring.

JONES Permission to speak, sir?

MAINWARING What is it, Jones?

JONES I brought another bucket of water, sir.

MAINWARING **(As the foam dies down)** Good. I think we'd better try the stirrup pump again.

As they cross, another member of the squad grabs the bucket and runs out via the office.

JONES Here, come back. That's my bucket.

Jones exits.

WALKER I know. The long-handled shovel.

MAINWARING Where is it?

WALKER Outside the office, sir.

They crowd into the office. Frazer enters with the long-handled shovel. It is *very* long.

FRAZER How about this, sir?

WALKER Great minds think alike, Taffy. Now, round here with it.

They try to get the shovel into the office and round through the door into the hall.

MAINWARING Er, er, take it further out. Now try it higher up.

There is a lot of ad lib toing and froing. Jones enters, trapping Mainwaring between the two doors.

JONES I found the bucket, sir. Where's Captain Mainwaring?

Mainwaring pushes the door into Jones. The bucket of water goes all over Jones.

MAINWARING Now push it. **(Murphy tries to help)** Don't you touch it!

WALKER Why don't we cut it in half?

MAINWARING Back it up a bit.

Mrs Pike enters, trapping Mainwaring as before.

MAINWARING Out of the way, woman. We are trying to deal with this fire bomb.

MRS PIKE It's out. I put it out.

MAINWARING It's what? How?

MRS PIKE It's out. I put a sandbag on it.

Enter the irate Warden through the outside door.

WARDEN Now look here. I've had a serious complaint from the Head Warden that someone's been signalling to those planes overhead.

MAINWARING Don't worry, Warden. We have apprehended the alleged culprit. My men spotted him. He was in the house at the corner of Mortimer Street.

WARDEN Oh, no. It's this door he's on about. It's been opening and shutting and showing a blinding light every time a fresh wave comes over. You've got a rotten apple in your barrel. Now, who is it? **(He looks round)** Hullo, Siggy. What are you doing here?

MAINWARING This is the man who was signalling, and what's more, he's German.

WARDEN Oh, no, he's not. He's a British subject and what's more, he was married to my Auntie Ethel.

MURPHY They told the whole street I was a spy.

WARDEN Oh no. This is where the spy is, mate. This is where the signal came from. You ask the Head Warden.

Pike rushes in from hall door and knocks his mother into Mainwaring's arms.

MRS PIKE Oh, Captain Mainwaring!

PIKE There's another stick of fire bombs, sir. They've fallen right across the street.

MAINWARING Right. Out you go, men. Grab the pump, Walker. Bring the water, Jones, and all the sandbags you can lay your hands on.

As they cross the hall, the front one slips on the wet patch and they all collapse in a heap. Murphy and Wilson are left in the office.

MURPHY You know, we Breetish are a vonderful people. We are brave, we have the great sense of humour, but I don't see *how* we are going to win the war.

WILSON Yes, I must say that thought does occur to me from time to time.

Fade on the mob trying to disentangle themselves.

SERIES THREE **EPISODE ONE**

Recorded: Sunday 25/5/69
Original transmission: Thursday 11/9/69, 7.30–8.00pm
Original viewing figures = 10.5 million

ARTHUR LOWE .... CAPTAIN MAINWARING
JOHN LE MESURIER .... SERGEANT WILSON
CLIVE DUNN .... LANCE CORPORAL JONES
JOHN LAURIE .... PRIVATE FRAZER
JAMES BECK .... PRIVATE WALKER
ARNOLD RIDLEY .... PRIVATE GODFREY
IAN LAVENDER .... PRIVATE PIKE
JANET DAVIES .... MRS PIKE
BILL PERTWEE .... ARP WARDEN
FRANK WILLIAMS .... VICAR
QUEENIE WATTS .... MRS PETERS
PAMELA CUNDELL .... MRS FOX
JEAN ST. CLAIR .... MISS MEADOWS
OLIVE MERCER .... MRS CASSON
NIGEL HAWTHORNE .... THE ANGRY MAN
HAROLD BENNETT .... THE OLD MAN
DICK HAYDON .... RAYMOND

PLATOON .... COLIN BEAN, FRANK GODFREY, RICHARD JACQUES, HUGH CECIL, DEREK CHAFFER, RICHARD KITTERIDGE, GEORGE HANCOCK, MICHAEL MOORE, VIC TAYLOR, FREDDIE WILES

ATS GIRL .... COREEN REED

SAILOR .... BRIAN JUSTICE

LADIES IN SHOP AND IN STREET .... PATRICIA MATTHEWS, ANNE EVANS, MARY POWER

THE ARMOURED MIGHT OF LANCE CORPORAL JONES

Originally titled, 'The Armoured Might of Jack Jones'

• FRANK WILLIAMS REMEMBERS •

'On 19 May 1969, I set out for the London Transport Training Centre, in which the BBC had a rehearsal room. At the time, I had no idea that this was the beginning of one of the longest and happiest chapters in my career. I was to rehearse in the first episode of the third series of a comedy programme. I had worked for the director, David Croft, on previous occasions and I knew his co-writer, James Perry, from the days when he was running the repertory theatre at Watford. I had not seen any of the previous two series, so knew little of what it was all about.

'The programme was *Dad's Army*. I had one short scene in which as the gullible vicar I allowed Frazer and Jones to take gas from my fire to fill the gas bag used to fuel the van. We recorded the episode on the following Sunday and as far as I knew that was the end of it; but, of course, it wasn't. The vicar was recalled for further episodes during 1969 and over the years for many more. The television series spawned a feature film, a radio series and a stage show.

'That episode, "The Armoured Might of Jack Jones" (later retitled substituting "Lance Corporal" for "Jack") was my introduction to a remarkable cast of actors. Edward Sinclair was one of the kindest of men and he and I became great friends. Bill Pertwee, the irascible air raid warden, was also to become a good friend and over the years, the three of us became a kind of unholy alliance both on and off screen.

'The platoon themselves were a marvellous bunch of characters. There was Ian Lavender, the stupid boy, who regularly did *The Times*' crossword. James Beck, who played the much-loved Private Walker, was about the same age as myself. He was a cheerful and good-natured man and would, I believe, have become one of our most popular character actors had he not died so tragically young. Arnold Ridley, Private Godfrey, had written the famous play, *The Ghost Train,* when he was a young man. He had sold the amateur rights, which over the years would have been worth hundreds of thousands of pounds, for £200. Amazingly, he felt no bitterness, saying that to a young and struggling actor/playwright £200 meant a great deal in those days. John Laurie had played all the great classical roles at Stratford between the wars. Tongue in cheek, he once reminded Jimmy Perry of this, adding: "And now I become a household name doing this rubbish of yours!" Clive Dunn was, of course, much younger than the character he portrayed. It was fascinating to see a comparatively young man create so convincingly the character of Corporal Jones. For me, some of the most joyous moments of the

series come when he embarks on one of his endless reminiscences while Captain Mainwaring listens with ever-increasing frustration.

'Arthur Lowe himself was often perceived as being rather like the character he played, but I feel this was an unfair assessment. He certainly did not suffer fools gladly and always knew his own mind, but he also had an ability to laugh at himself. Personally, I found him a most kind and generous man.

'What can one say of John Le Mesurier? He was a past master of vagueness, both on and off screen. When we were on tour, he once asked Teddy Sinclair and myself what we did about dirty washing. I said I found a laundry and Teddy said he used a launderette. John stared at him in disbelief. "You mean you sit there and watch it going round and round?" he asked, shaking his head in amazement.

"What do you do, John?"

"Well," he confided, "I just leave the washing around and some kind person always does it for me." Such carefully created helplessness, seemingly so innocent when combined with John's natural charm was, of course, irresistible.

'"The Armoured Might of Lance Corporal Jones" is significant for a number of reasons: it marks the debut of Mrs Fox (Pamela Cundell), it has the young Nigel Hawthorne in a cameo role and features the first appearance of Jonesey's famous van as the platoon's transport. For me, it was the beginning of a wonderful time with wonderful people in a programme that, 30 years later, is as popular as ever. Is it any wonder that I view the episode with such affection?'

FRANK WILLIAMS

The Armoured Might of Lance Corporal Jones

YARD OUTSIDE CHURCH HALL

The platoon are lined up with their gas masks on and gas capes. Mainwaring and Wilson are standing in front. They also have their gas masks on. Mainwaring is giving them a lecture on gas.

MAINWARING So, to summarise… the gases you'll have to contend with are mustard, phosgene, D.M. and chlorine. **(He takes his mask off)** That concludes my lecture on various types of gases that the enemy would be liable to use. Now, is there anything that's worrying you?

Jones comes to attention.

JONES **(Through his mask)** Permission to speak, sir?

MAINWARING **(To Wilson)** What did he say, Wilson?

WILSON **(Through his mask)** I couldn't quite catch it, sir.

MAINWARING What's that, Wilson?

WILSON **(Shouting through his mask in Mainwaring's ear)** I said, I couldn't quite catch it, sir.

MAINWARING I don't want to know what you said. I want to know what he said. Go and ask him.

Wilson crosses to Jones.

WILSON Captain Mainwaring wants to know what you said.

JONES What's that?

WILSON **(Right in Jones' ear)** The Captain wants to know what you said.

JONES **(In Wilson's ear)** I said – 'Permission to speak', Sergeant.

WILSON Thank you. **(He crosses back to Mainwaring and shouts in his ear)** He wants permission to speak.

MAINWARING Well, of course he's got permission to speak. Ask him what he wants to say.

Wilson nods and crosses back to Jones.

WILSON **(In Jones' ear)** What do you want to say?

JONES **(In Wilson's ear)** I wanted to say that I haven't heard a word he's said.

Wilson nods and crosses back to Mainwaring.

WILSON He says he can't hear a word you've been saying.

MAINWARING I can't hear. Take your respirator off, Wilson. **(Wilson takes it off)** Now what did you say?

WILSON He said he couldn't hear a word you've been saying, sir.

MAINWARING Do you mean to say that he never heard a word of that lecture I gave?

WILSON I'm afraid not, sir.

MAINWARING Did the rest of you hear?

They all shake their heads in unison from side to side.

MAINWARING Can you hear what I'm saying now?

They all nod their heads in unison.

MAINWARING All right, men. Remove your respirators and put them away. We'll continue this lecture tomorrow. Now then, I want to introduce you to a new weapon. **(He holds up a wire cheese cutter)** Can anyone tell me what this is?

JONES It's a grocer's cheese cutter, sir.

MAINWARING Correct, Jones. It's a harmless cheese cutter, but properly applied it can become a deadly weapon. I will tell you the story of how I got the idea for using this as a weapon.

WILSON Stand easy.

MAINWARING It's an example of improvisation at its best. **(Clears his throat)** A few days ago I went to get the week's rations for my wife and myself from the grocers. As he cut off our meagre ration of cheese, I thought: 'Why am I getting such a little piece?' And as the wire cut through the cheese and it dropped off the cutting board, suddenly, in my mind's eye, it turned into the head of a Nazi Paratrooper. That's it, I thought. Just the thing for dealing with enemy sentries. You creep up behind him – **(He demonstrates)** Then you lob it round his neck, so – **(Still demonstrating)** – and pull…

WILSON You all right, sir?

MAINWARING Yes, of course. Result… instant decapitation! He doesn't even know what's happened.

WALKER **(Aside)** Not until he nods his head.

MAINWARING What did you say, Walker?

WALKER I said, he'd be better off in bed, sir.

MAINWARING He would indeed. **(He gives the wire another savage jerk)** Instant decapitation!!

Pike comes to attention.

MAINWARING What is it, Pike?

PIKE Permission to be sick, sir.

MAINWARING Permission granted.

Pike rushes out with his hand over his mouth.

MAINWARING That lad wants toughening up, Wilson. Fancy feeling sick just because I mentioned decapitation.

WILSON It's not that, sir. He just doesn't like cheese.

MAINWARING Now pay attention, men. I have just received a communication from G.H.Q. saying there is not enough co-operation between the A.R.P. and the Home Guard, and that in future we must both work together for the common cause. They also say that the Chief

Warden will be calling on us tonight to discuss various means of cooperation. By the way, who is the Chief Warden?

WILSON It's that terrible common man, Mr Hodges.

MAINWARING You mean to say they've made him Chief Warden... he's a greengrocer!

WILSON That's right, sir. He's the one with the dirty fingernails.

MAINWARING How do you know he's got dirty fingernails?

WILSON I can see them when he pushes his takings under the grill.

FRAZER He keeps the shop next to me, sir, and ever since he's been made Chief Warden, there's been no holding him.

GODFREY He's become absolutely corrupted with power, sir.

JONES Nasty bit of work, he is, sir. You want to put your foot down, otherwise before you know where you are, he'll be taking over from you.

MAINWARING I should like to see him try.

Warden comes in.

WARDEN Now then. Who's in charge here?

MAINWARING You know perfectly well who's in charge here. Can't you see my insignia?

WARDEN Oh. It's Mr Mainwaring the bank manager.

MAINWARING I am Captain Mainwaring and this is Sergeant Wilson.

WILSON How do you do?

WARDEN As far as I'm concerned, you're still the bank manager and he's the chief clerk. I can't forget his face. Every time I go into the bank with my takings, he gives me a dirty look.

WALKER It matches his nails.

WARDEN **(To Mainwaring)** What did he say?

MAINWARING Nothing.

WARDEN Now I've had instructions that we're supposed to co-operate. So I'll just tell you once. I want this hall every Wednesday evening for an A.R.P. lecture. Got it?

MAINWARING I'm afraid that's out of the question.

WARDEN What are you talking about?

MAINWARING I have a parade here every Wednesday evening.

WARDEN That's your hard luck.

MAINWARING I have a long-standing arrangement with the Vicar.

WARDEN What goes on between you and the Vicar is entirely your affair. All I know is, I want this hall every Wednesday. **(Pokes his finger in Mainwaring's face)** Get it? That's all. **(He goes)**

MAINWARING You're quite right, Wilson. His nails are filthy.

JACK JONES' BUTCHER'S SHOP

Close up of six ladies' faces, assorted types. They all have a look of rapture, a couple of them give heavy sighs.

Close up of two ladies' faces.

MRS PETERS He does it beautifully, don't you think?

MRS FOX There's no doubt about it. He's an artiste.

MRS PETERS How can he make a little look so much. It's amazing.

MRS FOX He's a wonderful man for his age.

Camera pans back. For the first time we can see we are in a butcher's shop. Jones is just finishing slicing a small piece of corned beef into wafer thin slices.

JONES There you are, ladies. Now, who's next? Good morning, Mrs Peters.

MRS PETERS **(Pushing across ration books)** Good morning, Mr Jones. Now what can I have?

JONES **(Looking at books)** Well, you haven't got very much there, have you, Mrs Peters?

MRS PETERS Are you sure you're looking at them properly?

JONES I know my eyesight's not too good, but I can see you've only got a shilling's worth left on each book.

MRS PETERS Oh, dear. Is that all?

JONES Well, you shouldn't have had that joint on Friday.

MRS PETERS It's not my fault, Mr Jones. My husband will insist on his bit of brisket every weekend.

JONES I can let you have three lamb chops. **(He slaps them on the scale)** They come to 1s 8d. I'm afraid you'll have to have the rest in corned beef. **(He puts four slices on the scale)** That comes to exactly two bob. How's that?

MRS PETERS **(Leaning right across the counter, in Jones' ear)** Any sausages?

Jones hesitates, then suddenly whips two sausages from under the counter and quickly wraps them up. The next woman in the line, noticing this at once, whispers to the next woman.

NEXT WOMAN IN QUEUE He's got sausages!

Each woman in turn whispers down the line 'sausages'.

The word 'sausages' gets louder and the whole queue takes it up.

JONES All right, ladies, please. I can only let you have one with each book. **(He shouts to the woman in the cash desk)** Take 2s 4d please, Miss Mortimer.

Mrs Peters crosses to the cash desk. We cannot see who's behind it. A hand comes through the grill and snatches the ration books.

JONES (To next lady) Morning, Mrs Fox.

Mrs Fox is a very large lady with a bosom to match, which she thrusts in Jones' face.

MRS FOX Hullo, Mr Jones. I've got everything today. (She hands him two books)

JONES (Looking at books) You certainly have, Mrs Fox. You never bought any meat over the weekend.

MRS FOX I know. My hubby and I went away.

JONES Well, you've got your full week's ration here. 2s 2d on each book. What will it be?

MRS FOX A nice piece of steak, I think.

JONES A little Veronica Lake, eh? (Cutting off steak and weighing it) Comes to 3s 4d and the rest of your ration in corned beef. (Weighing corned beef) That's exactly 4s 4d. Do you want your sausages?

MRS FOX Of course.

Jones whips two more sausages from under the counter.

MRS FOX (In a whisper) Any kidney?

JONES Sorry, Mrs Fox.

MRS FOX (Pursing her lips) But surely you must have a little bit of kidney tucked away somewhere?

JONES Not a bit, Mrs Fox.

MRS FOX Well, I shall just have to make do with what I've got, shan't I? (She pushes a tin across the counter) For you, Mr Jones.

JONES Eh?

MRS FOX Your favourite tobacco... I shall be in again in a few days.

JONES Oh, thank you very much, madam. Take 4s 8d please, Miss Mortimer.

Mrs Fox gives Jones a hungry look and goes over to the cash desk. A hand comes through the grill and snatches her ration book. The next customer is Miss Meadows. A thin lady with earphone buns and glasses. She quickly pushes a small box across the counter.

JONES Good morning, Miss Meadows. What's this?

MISS MEADOWS Just a little cake I made for your tea, Mr Jones.

The whisper of 'she's brought him a cake' passes down the queue.

JONES Oh, thank you very much, Miss Meadows. I hope you didn't use up too many points making it.

MISS MEADOWS You can have my points any time, Mr Jones.

JONES Eh!

MISS MEADOWS What I mean is, you deserve looking after. No one can accuse you of not doing your bit. As a butcher, you look after our insides, and as a Home Guard you protect our outsides. (She laughs. The rest of the queue give her a cold look)

JONES (Embarrassed) Yes, quite. (He shouts through the door) Bring in the brawn, Raymond!

RAY'S VOICE Just coming, Mr Jones.

JONES What's it to be, Miss Meadows?

MISS MEADOWS I'll take it all in corned beef.

JONES Do you want your sausage?

MISS MEADOWS Oh, yes. I'll have my sausage.

JONES (Wrapping it up) I wish all my other ladies were as easy as you, Miss Meadows.

MISS MEADOWS Well, I try to please.

JONES Take 2s 4d please, Miss Mortimer.

Miss Meadows crosses to pay desk. Hand comes out of grill and snatches book. Raymond comes from the back of the shop with a large brawn. It is nearly all jelly, just a few tiny bits of meat in it.

RAYMOND Here's the brawn, Mr Jones.

The queue breaks into an uproar.

JONES Now take it easy, ladies. I can let you have two ounces with every book.

MRS CASSON Not much meat in it, is there?

JONES What can you expect? It's not on coupons. You don't want to look a gift horse in the mouth, you know.

MRS CASSON If it's horse, I don't want it.

JONES It's not horse. It's pork.

MRS CASSON But you said it was horse.

JONES I said 'You don't want to look a gift horse in the...' Oh, never mind.

Joe Walker pushes his way into the shop, pushes to the head of the queue, and cries of 'Why don't you take your turn', 'Who do you think you are', etc.

WALKER All right, ladies. Keep calm. It's only me. I'm here on business.

MRS CASSON We all know what your business is.

WALKER Now, I ask you. Is that nice?

JONES What is it, Joe?

WALKER I want to talk to you, Jonesey. It's urgent and private. (Glare from stroppy customer)

JONES In that case we'd better go into the cold room. Take over, Raymond.

RAYMOND Yes, Mr Jones.

They both go into cold store.

COLD STORE

WALKER Blimey. What do you want to bring me in here for? It's freezing.

JONES It's the only place we can't be overheard.

WALKER Listen, Jack, have you still got that old delivery van of yours?

JONES Yes. It's out in the back yard.

WALKER Does it go?

JONES Of course it does. I just can't get any petrol for it.

WALKER Look, I've got an idea. Why don't you offer it to Captain Mainwaring as platoon transport.

JONES Why?

They are now both starting to shiver.

WALKER Why? Well you see, it's like this. I sometimes have to transport certain things at night. Now, if I'm driving an ordinary van, I might get stopped. On the other hand, if I'm driving the official transport for the platoon, and I'm in uniform, I won't get stopped. Get it?

JONES I g… g… g… get it all r… right, but what do I get out of it?

WALKER I'll t… t… tell you. Do you have to have this place so cold?

JONES Yes, it's r… reg… regulations.

WALKER Now listen. If… if… if… you let them use your van, they'll have to give you the petrol coupons for it.

JONES But. I… I… thought you could ger… ger… get petrol.

WALKER I… I… can get per… per… petrol, it's the c… c… coupons, they're wer… wer… worth ter… ter… ter… ten bob each. Anything we mer… mer… make, I'll split fifty fifty. All right?

JONES It ser… ser… sounds a bit dodgy to me.

WALKER Ler… ler… look don't worry. Leave it to yer… yer… old pal Joe.

Their faces are now covered with frost.

JONES Oh… er… er… all right.

WALKER (Patting his face) That's my Jonesey. (He gives the waxed end of Jones' moustache a tweak. It breaks off)

WALKER (Holding up the end of the moustache) Oh, sorry mate.

YARD OUTSIDE THE CHURCH HALL

The butcher's van is drawn up. All the men are gathered round. Jones is in the middle with Mainwaring and Wilson.

MAINWARING Absolutely first class! This must be a proud moment for you, Corporal Jones.

JONES Yes, sir.

MAINWARING Thanks to your unselfishness, our platoon now has its own transport. (To men) Corporal Jones and Private Walker have worked on this vehicle non-stop for the past three days, and now Corporal Jones will show us the result of all their hard work.

JONES Before we start, sir. I am the official driver. That's all right with you, isn't it, Captain Mainwaring?

MAINWARING Yes, of course, Jones.

WILSON (Aside to Mainwaring) Do you think that's wise, sir?

MAINWARING Of course, we've got to let him drive it. It's his own van.

WILSON I'm not too keen on the idea, sir.

MAINWARING You're never too keen on anything, Wilson. Right, carry on, Jones.

JONES Right, if you'll just follow me, I'll show you the details. (Opening the doors) This is an all-purpose vehicle. It can be used as an armoured car (you'll observe the sandbags stacked along the side – that makes it bullet-proof). An ambulance (you'll observe the racks for the stretchers). Also – it is troop transport – you sit on the floor.

FRAZER (Pointing to the floor) It's going to be a bit cold, sitting on those marble slabs.

GODFREY It wouldn't do me any good sitting on those, Captain Mainwaring. My doctor says I mustn't sit on cold things.

PIKE My mum wouldn't like that, sir.

MAINWARING Quiet! What are those marble slabs for, Jones?

JONES They're out of my shop, sir. I put them on the floor in case we go over a landmine. Protection, you see, sir. Mind you, they've got to go back in the shop every morning.

MAINWARING Well, in that case, I think we'd better dispense with the slabs unless there is an actual invasion. Now, pay attention, men – what we've got to do is work out a drill so that the whole platoon can embark and disembark.

WILSON I've… er… already done that, sir.

MAINWARING What?

WILSON Perhaps you'd like to see it, sir.

MAINWARING (Testy) I certainly would, Wilson.

WILSON All right. Battle section line up. (Two files of five men line up at the back of the van) Right! Embark. (He gives a peep on his whistle) (The two files scramble aboard. This is done with terrific precision) Now, sir, I want you to imagine that the vehicle is going along the road.

JONES Well, I'd better be driving it then, Sergeant.

WILSON Very well, Jones.

GODFREY We ought to assume that the door is shut, sir.

Jones scrambles round to the front and pretends to be turning the starting handle.

JONES Right, Sergeant. I've started it. **(Gets no reaction – jumps out and runs to back of van)** Right, Sergeant, I've started it. **(He is now making a noise like an engine. He scrambles into the driving seat)** All ready, Sergeant.

WILSON Off you go.

Jones is now pretending to drive. He is still making a noise like an engine.

WILSON Now, sir. The men are inside and the vehicle is moving along the road.

MAINWARING Yes, I rather gathered that, Wilson.

WILSON Enemy on the left. Range one hundred yards, five rounds rapid fire. **(He blows whistle) (As if by clockwork, five rifles appear through holes in the side of the van. They come out straight. Then, as one, they turn to the left. From inside, come fire bans, chanted in unison. The rifles then withdraw)** ... out, two, three. Enemy on the right. Range one hundred and fifty yards. Five rounds rapid fire! **(He blows his whistle) (The whole business is repeated, this time the rifles turn to the right)**

WILSON Enemy dive-bomber overhead. Five rounds rapid fire. **(He blows whistle) (This time ten rifles come through the roof and the whole business is repeated again)** Disembark! **(He blows whistle) (The two files come out of the van. They halt, turn left, slope arms, and butt salute, all the time shouting out the numbers in unison)** How's that, sir?

MAINWARING You never cease to amaze me, Wilson.

WILSON You see I am keen, sir, I'm as keen as you are. It's just that I... er... **(Blurting it out)** have a terrible job showing it.

MAINWARING **(Placing his hand on Wilson's shoulder)** I understand, Wilson. **(Jones is still making engine noises)** All right, Jones. **(Jones takes no notice)** Jones!

JONES Yes, sir.

MAINWARING You can stop now. We're there, we've arrived.

Enter A.R.P. Warden.

WARDEN What's going on, here? I've never heard such a row. **(Pointing to hall)** This is Wednesday night, you know, and I'm trying to give a lecture in there.

MAINWARING Well, nobody's stopping you.

WARDEN How do you think I can make myself heard with you lot shouting 'Bang Bang Bang' all the time? What are you doing? Playing cowboys and Indians?

MAINWARING We were trying out our new ambulance/troop carrier.

WARDEN This is an ambulance? It looks to me like a butcher's van. What time's the horse coming?

MAINWARING I can assure you that this makes a very efficient ambulance indeed.

WARDEN Well, this is your lucky day, mate.

MAINWARING What do you mean?

WARDEN It so happens that we are having a large-scale air-raid practice next Saturday, and we need all the extra transport we can get our hands on. So, report with your ambulance and a party of six men to act as stretcher-bearers to Percy Street at two o'clock next Saturday afternoon.

MAINWARING That's 14.00 hours.

The platoon all do a take on Mainwaring.

WARDEN Yes, 14.00 hours. **(He goes)**

WILSON You've got it right, sir. Well done.

MAINWARING Thank you, Wilson. We'll soon show him how efficient we are.

WALKER Excuse me, sir. What about the petrol coupons? After all, we're going to use quite a bit of juice you know.

MAINWARING I'm glad you brought that up, Walker. It's going to be converted to gas.

JONES AND WALKER Gas!

MAINWARING Yes. I got on the phone to G.H.Q. earlier on, and told them all about it, and in order to save petrol, they want us to take it down to the R.A.S.C. transport pool and get it converted. You and Jones had better take it down there now. Then you can both collect it in time for the air-raid practice next Saturday.

Walker and Jones exchange looks.

TELECINE: VAN IS DRIVING ALONG A COUNTRY ROAD

The van has a huge gas bag on top of it. It backfires very loudly.

INSIDE CAB

Jones is driving, Walker is sitting beside him.

JONES 'I've got a good idea, Jonesey,' you said. 'Let the platoon use your van and then we can get some petrol coupons,' you said.

WALKER It's not my fault, is it? I mean, I'm not a clairvoyant, am I?

JONES Look what they've done to my van. What's this flippin' great thing?

He points to five- inch flexible pipe.

WALKER That feeds the gas through to the engine.

JONES I've never seen anything like it. There's a great sagging bag everywhere I look.

WALKER Can't you keep your mind off women for five minutes, mate?

JONES Oh shut up.

There is a section of gas pipe just behind their heads. Jones' rifle with the bayonet on it is between them. It keeps falling on Walker.

WALKER Oh blimey. What do you want to keep the bayonet on this for?

JONES Never know when we might need it.

WALKER 'You never know when we might need it.' Flippin' thing.

He jerks the bayonet off the rifle, the point of it pricks the gas pipe. There is a hissing sound.

WALKER You're bayonet mad, you are, mate. You're not going to meet any Fuzzie Wuzzies here, you know.

The hissing sound gets louder. Suddenly Jones gives a giggle.

WALKER What's the matter with you?

JONES I don't know. I feel all light-headed.

WALKER That's nothing new. **(Jones suddenly starts laughing)** What are you laughing at? **(Walker starts laughing too)**

JONES **(Singing)** I dreamt I dwelt in Marble Halls, with a little hot oil and a feather. **(Walker takes up the song. They are now both quite drunk)**

TELECINE: VAN MOVING ALONG THE ROAD

The van is swerving from side to side.

BACK IN CAB

They are both singing their heads off. Walker takes out a cigarette and sticks it in his mouth.

WALKER Got a light, Jonesey?

JONES 'Ere y'are.

He takes out a lighter with his left hand, Walker has veered away to the left and is staring out of the window. Jones lights the lighter over the hole where the gas is escaping. The gas ignites into a long thin jet. Jones puts away his lighter and is humming away to himself. Walker swerves his face round and lights his cigarette from the gas jet.

WALKER Thanks, mate.

JONES Don't mention it.

The jet is still coming out of the gas bag.

WALKER It's a bit hot in here. **(He mops his brow, sees flame. Does a take on it)** Blimey! We're on fire! Stop the van!

Jones pulls up with a jolt and tries to blow the jet out. Walker smothers it with his cap.

JONES There's a hole in the pipe. The gas is escaping. Quick. Do something.

WALKER What?

JONES I don't know. Do what the little Belgian boy did in Brussels.

WALKER What, here?

JONES No, stick your finger in the hole.

WALKER You're thinking of the Dutch boy. **(He sticks his finger in the hole)** You silly old duffer.

Jones starts off with a jerk.

YARD OUTSIDE CHURCH HALL

The van has just pulled up. The gas bag has lost quite a lot of gas, and is drooping all over the van. Jones jumps down from the driving seat, Walker still has his finger in the gas bag. Frazer comes running out of the door.

FRAZER There you are at last. Where have you been?

JONES We had a bit of trouble on the way. Where is everybody?

FRAZER Captain Mainwaring couldn't wait any longer. He's gone on down to Percy Street with the rest of the party. He left me here to tell you to follow on as soon as possible.

WALKER **(Calling from the van)** 'Ere, Jonesey. How much longer have I to keep my finger stuck in this hole.

JONES Until we've finished the exercise.

FRAZER That gas bag looks a wee bit empty to me.

JONES **(Seeing the half empty gas bag)** Blimey! We ain't half lost some gas, Joe. Whatever you do, don't pull out your finger. Just keep thinking of that little Belgian boy.

WALKER Dutch boy, you silly old fool.

JONES There's no call for you to get nasty, Joe. **(To Frazer)** We need some more gas in that bag you know, Jock.

FRAZER Wait a minute, Jonesey, I've got an idea. Why don't we take some gas from the Vicar's gas fire.

JONES And just how do you think we're going to do that?

FRAZER You'll see. **(He goes in through the door)**

JONES Captain Mainwaring will do his nut if we don't get there soon. It's all your fault, Joe.

WALKER I like that! Blaming me! If it hadn't been for your flippin' bayonet, all this would never have happened.

Frazer appears at the window with a stirrup pump hose.

FRAZER Here you are, Jonesey. (He hands him the end of the hose) Connect this up, and I'll turn the fire on.

JONES (Taking the hose) Good old Jock, what would we English do without the brains of the Scots? (He connects the hose) All right, turn her on.

Close up of window with hose pipe over the ledge. Vicar comes into picture and peers into room.

VICAR May I ask what you're doing here?

FRAZER Me? I'm looking out of the window.

VICAR (Peering into the room) Why have you got that hose connected to my gas fire?

FRAZER Oh – ay… well, you see it's like this, Your Reverence. (Pointing) You see that big bag of gas?

VICAR Yes.

FRAZER We did'ner know what to do with it, so we thought we'd fill up your gas fire.

VICAR (Beaming) Most charitable, my friend, most charitable.

PERCY STREET

Godfrey, Pike, Mainwaring, Wilson are standing on the pavement. Three people are lying down there in a small knot of onlookers. The Warden is pushing them back.

WARDEN All right. Stand back. There's nothing to see.

MAINWARING (To Wilson) Really, this is most embarrassing. Where's Jones with that van?

WILSON Perhaps he's run out of petrol.

MAINWARING It's been converted to gas, Wilson.

WILSON Oh, yes, of course.

WARDEN When are they going to get here with that ambulance, Captain Mainwaring?

MAINWARING They'll be here any minute.

WARDEN They'd better be. If this is a taste of your efficiency, I don't think much of it. (He turns on the crowd) I told you to stand back.

Mrs Pike pushes her way through the crowd and goes up to Wilson.

MRS PIKE I've been looking for you everywhere, Arthur. You forgot to give me the housekeeping money.

WILSON Oh, Mavis, please. Not now. Can't you see we're busy?

MRS PIKE I can't help that, Arthur. I've got to do my shopping.

WARDEN (To Mrs Pike) All right, lie down on the pavement beside that old man.

MRS PIKE Certainly not.

WARDEN You're one of the casualties, aren't you?

MRS PIKE No, I'm not.

WARDEN In that case, stand back out of the way.

WILSON Now look here. This lady's talking to me, and will not stand back until she has finished. Understand?

Warden glares at Wilson, but thinks better of it and turns away.

MAINWARING Well done, Wilson.

WILSON Will two pounds be enough, Mavis? (Hands her the money)

MRS PIKE Yes, of course. (To Mainwaring) You know he's a wonderful man, Mr Mainwaring. (She goes)

WARDEN I've never seen such chaos in all my life – utter chaos. (He pronounces it 'chos')

The van draws up.

WILSON Here they are now, sir.

MAINWARING Thank goodness for that.

WARDEN Right. Get this lot on the stretchers and load them in the ambulance. I'm going to see how they're going on in the next street.

Jones runs up and salutes. Frazer, who has been riding on the running board, comes into the picture.

JONES (Saluting) Sorry we're late, sir, – we had a bit of trouble.

MAINWARING That's nothing to what we've had here. All right – Godfrey, Pike, put that old man on the stretcher, and then put it in the back of the van. (He points to the old man lying on the pavement)

Pike and Godfrey roll the old man on to the stretcher.

MAINWARING Right! Lift!

Pike picks up his end of the stretcher, Godfrey cannot lift his end and the old man rolls back on top of him.

MAINWARING For goodness sake, lift your end, Godfrey. He's only a little old man.

GODFREY He's not as old as I am, sir.

MAINWARING Take over, Frazer. (Frazer picks up the stretcher with Pike) Right now, bring it back round the back of the van. (They rush the stretcher round to the back of the van) Open the doors, Jones.

JONES Yes, sir. (He tries to open the doors, they are locked) I'm afraid they're locked, sir.

MAINWARING What!!! Who locked them?

JONES I did, sir.

MAINWARING What on earth for?

JONES Well, I didn't want anybody getting at my marble slabs.

MAINWARING Well, unlock them at once.

JONES I can't, sir, I haven't got the key.

MAINWARING Oh, for goodness sake. Is there no end to all this? Where is the key?

JONES It's back at my shop, sir.

MAINWARING Go and get it at once. No, wait. **(Pointing to bike leaning against wall)** You'd better take that bike.

JONES Yes, sir. **(He grabs the bike and rushes off)**

FRAZER If I may make a suggestion, sir, there's a wee door at the back of the driving seat. We could get him into the van through there.

MAINWARING Good idea. All right, pick him up. You too, Wilson.

WILSON Yes, sir.

Frazer, Pike and Wilson carry him round to the front.

MAINWARING **(Seeing Walker)** What are you doing in there, Walker? Come on, get your finger out.

WALKER I can't, sir. I've got to keep me finger in the whatsit.

MAINWARING Put him in feet first.

Pike has the old man's feet. He climbs up into the cab on top of Walker. Wilson and Frazer have the bottom half. The old man's feet go into Walker's face.

WALKER Ger' out of it! Get him through here.

MAINWARING Feet first, feet first! No, no, no! Take him off the stretcher! Bend his legs round, Pike, bend them round!

PIKE They won't bend, sir.

Angry man comes into picture.

ANGRY MAN **(To Mainwaring)** Did you tell one of your blokes to take my bike?

MAINWARING Yes, I did. What about it?

ANGRY MAN What about it? You can't go round taking private property.

MAINWARING This is an emergency, and I am a Captain in the Home Guard. **(Shouting to Pike)** Bend him round, bend him round. **(To angry man)** Will you go away.

ANGRY MAN I certainly will not. What are you doing to that poor old man?

MAINWARING Mind your own business.

WILSON Wouldn't it be better if we took the seat out, sir?

MAINWARING Good idea. **(They start to take the seat out. Walker, Pike and the old man are now crushed up into the cab)** Wait a minute, get the old man out first. **(They start to pull the old man out)**

ANGRY MAN You leave that old man alone. **(He starts to pull at the old man)**

MAINWARING **(To angry man)** Don't you touch him. **(The angry man is now in the cab as well, pulling at the old man)** Frazer, Wilson – give me a hand. **(They all pull the angry man)**

Jones rushes up.

JONES I've got the key, sir.

MAINWARING What? All right, get him out again. Unlock the door, Jones.

They carry the old man round to the back of the van. The angry man follows, shouting

ANGRY MAN You're a bunch of raving lunatics. I'm going to fetch a policeman. **(He goes)**

Jones appears, opens the doors, they put the old man in the van.

WARDEN Hey! What do you think you're doing? You can't take him without a stretcher – now get him on there quick sharp. Driver, I'll give you the signal when I'm ready – two bangs.

JONES You give me the signal when you're ready – two bangs.

Warden reacts.

WARDEN We'll never get him in with this door flapping about, bloomin' thing.

Warden bangs.

MAINWARING Right, take it away, Jones.

Van pulls away.

MAINWARING Follow that van.

Ambulance drives along – back doors flapping – Warden and H.G. Private carrying old man on stretcher run to try and catch up with it. Eventually ambulance stops. Warden and H.G. Private put one end of the stretcher on to ambulance. Warden walks to side to shout at Jones.

WARDEN Hey!

JONES **(Sticks his head out of window)** What's up?

WARDEN That wasn't the signal, the door was stuck.

JONES Well, it sounded like the signal.

WARDEN You old fool! This is the signal. **(Bangs the side of the van twice)**

Ambulance drives off again – the stretcher falls to the ground. The Warden runs after the ambulance. The old man gets off the stretcher.

OLD MAN I'll walk to the flippin' hospital. **(He limps off into the distance)**

SERIES THREE **EPISODE TWO**

Recorded: Sunday 1/6/69
Original transmission: Thursday 18/9/69, 7.30–8.00pm
Original viewing figures = 11.4 million

ARTHUR LOWE .... CAPTAIN MAINWARING
JOHN LE MESURIER .... SERGEANT WILSON
CLIVE DUNN .... LANCE CORPORAL JONES
JOHN LAURIE .... PRIVATE FRAZER
JAMES BECK .... PRIVATE WALKER
ARNOLD RIDLEY .... PRIVATE GODFREY
IAN LAVENDER .... PRIVATE PIKE
ALAN TILVERN .... CAPTAIN RODRIGUES
ALAN HAINES .... MAJOR SMITH
COLIN BEAN .... PRIVATE SPONGE

PLATOON .... FRANK GODFREY, RICHARD JACQUES, HUGH CECIL, RICHARD KITTERIDGE, DESMOND CULLUM-JONES, GEORGE HANCOCK, MICHAEL MOORE, VIC TAYLOR, FREDDIE WILES

STUNTMAN .... JOHNNY SCRIPPS

EXTRAS .... RON HICKEY, DEREK CHAFFER, ANTHONY POWELL, PAT GORMAN, JAY NEIL

BATTLE SCHOOL

• BRIAN HILES REMEMBERS •

'I was a Sound Supervisor in BBC Television from 1964, which entailed all the processes involved in producing sound for telly programmes and a lot of music recording. In February 1968, I was given the task of recording the title music for *Dad's Army*; this was to be a four-hour session (2–6pm) in the Riverside Studios, London. Thanks to Ronnie Hazelhurst, I knew what was required: opening and closing titles to be recorded, the opening being a song by the near-immortal Bud Flanagan, to be arranged and balanced in a 1940s style – a fairly reverberation-free sound with a prominent vocal and stylistic tricks such as fiddles playing the tune and rhythm strictly on the beat – and a full-works, heartily stirring military band closing. The musicians were not to be drawn from the ranks of the usual army of session musicians we were used to, but from the real Army – no less than the Band of the Coldstream Guards, conducted by their Director of Music, Major Trevor Sharpe.

'Everyone, including Bud Flanagan, arrived at the studio by two o'clock. For the opening tune the studio was full of acoustic screens dividing the band into sections to produce the desired sound in the rather reverberant studio, while the vocal booth had been readied for Bud. After the usual pleasantries and getting everybody ready, including introducing Bud to his somewhat unnatural home for the next few hours and making sure he had his famous hat to hand to sing in, we started rehearsal with the band. Being used to session musicians when chat and jokes would break out at every stop, the discipline when the musicians were told to "sit at ease" and "sit easy" felt quite strange, but they were quickly note-perfect; Captain Sharpe had done a splendid job on the arrangement so that the desired sound developed fairly easily. We put Bud in the booth complete with hat and began to rehearse with the vocals. I have a treasured memory of looking through several layers of distorting glass into the booth and seeing straw-hatted Bud doing a full stage performance – a close-up of something I'd only previously seen at a distance from the gods at the Victoria Palace.

'Dear old Bud wasn't capable of singing the song unless he *was* giving a performance, and this extended to learning the words rather than having them written out in front of him. Unfortunately, his memory wasn't quite as sharp as he thought, so when the actual recording started we began getting new and different versions.

He got quite upset at the idea of having a board in front of him and so we just had to struggle on hoping that the right words would all appear in one take. The bit I remember giving the most trouble was the middle section: "Mister Brown goes off to town on the eight twenty-one", which would come out, *inter alia*, as "Mister Brown when he comes home on the one twenty-eight"; being the total old trouper that he was, the show had to go on and so he would improvise a rhyme to fit. For example, instead of "a ready with his gun" we would have "a-swinging on the gate".

'By four o'clock, we had well over 20 imperfect takes and as a photo-call had been booked, tea was declared with a view to trying to get it right after that. My tape-op and I were left alone in the cubicle, and in slight desperation began checking through what we'd got. Fortunately, the band had been so consistent in tempo that we realised we could cut between takes fairly freely, so we started cutting and assembling. It took bits from around 12 different takes, but we finished up with a viable version.

'Meanwhile, the band had changed into uniform for the photo-call and the photographers had re-arranged Bud, musicians, chairs and mics to get the shots they needed. What I didn't realise till much later was that they'd taken one of the trumpet mics, and turned it round for Bud to appear to sing into. As soon as the photograph was published in the national press those who knew (my eagle-eyed mates) spotted that he was apparently singing into the wrong side of a totally unsuitable mic.

'That over, David, Ronnie Hazelhurst, Trevor Sharpe et al came back into the control room and we played back the fruit of our labours. As we'd hoped, amazement and congratulations ensued, and we got Bud in to hear it. We played it through, the tape op standing in front of the machine so you couldn't see all the bits of editing tape whizzing through; there was a small silence and Bud said "Did I *really* sing that?" There was a chorus of "Yes, of course you did, Bud" accompanying the silent near-corpsing and knowing glances.

'So that was the opening, but by now it was getting on for five o'clock and we still had the closing, in several versions, to record in the remaining hour. I had intended, imagining a more controlled situation than the reality, to completely re-lay out the band (much augmented and with the string players of the opening now playing brass instruments of various sizes) and the mics in a way that would give me the desired sound and control over balance. However, after the photo-call, the musicians had (helpfully but misguidedly) moved everything out of the way, found themselves enough chairs and were all sat down in their accustomed order. I emerged from the control room after Bud had been seen safely off to a waiting cab, to be confronted by several dozen musicians, some in uniform, all waiting patiently to play. Hopes of getting them all to go away for a while whilst my assistant and I sorted out the chairs, put all the mics in the right places and got everybody settled again, vanished just by looking at the clock.

'And so the rehearsal for the closing titles became for me a time of great improvisation. Being inexperienced in recording military bands at that time, I shall forever be grateful to Ronnie Hazelhurst who sat next to me at the desk and told me very quietly and intensely what we should be hearing as the piece progressed. The bandsmen were in a far-from-ideal situation in a solid block; the only way I could achieve separation and definition was by adding extra mics as we went along. We got it all in the can by the skin of our teeth – well, with maybe just a teeny overrun, and I can remember the feeling of exhaustion tempered by elation when everyone had gone and we'd tidied up.

'Sadly, Bud died shortly afterwards; when the series became a success Pye Records issued "Who Do You Think You Are Kidding, Mr Hitler?" on a 45 and my version was the only usable one. I wish you got royalties for doing the balance!'

BRIAN HILES
Sound Supervisor

Battle School

FILM. DAY

Establishing shot of steam train.

INTERIOR RAILWAY CARRIAGE. DAY

The right-hand side of the carriage: at the far end in the corner is Wilson. Next to him, Mainwaring. Next Frazer, smoking large drop pipe, he is knitting socks. Next Godfrey, reading *The Tailor and Cutter.*

The left-hand side: at the far end is Pike, he is reading a copy of *The Hotspur* and he is sucking his thumb. Next to him is Jones and then Walker – they are both playing crib on Walker's supply suitcase. Next Private Sponge, who is reading a H.G. Handbook.

The train suddenly comes to a violent halt. Everyone is thrown about.

WALKER (Picking his cards up) Blimey, how many more times?

MAINWARING (To Wilson) It's too bad the way this train keeps stopping and starting. (Looking at watch) What time are we due at the weekend battle school?

WILSON Sixteen hundred hours, sir.

MAINWARING What?

WILSON Four o'clock.

MAINWARING I know, Wilson, I know. Four hours to do an hour's journey – it's absurd. If I'd known the journey was going to take all this time I'd have brought something to eat – I'm starving.

GODFREY Well, I hope we get there soon.

MAINWARING Why?

GODFREY Well, it's a bit awkward... I mean with no corridor on the train... I find it very awkward indeed.

MAINWARING Well, you'll just have to control yourself... this is war, Godfrey... we're on active service, you know.

JONES I've got an idea, Mr Godfrey. Why don't you recite a piece of poetry... that might take your mind off it.

GODFREY All right. The owl and the pussy cat went to sea. In a beautiful pea green boat. They took some... er.

WILSON Honey and plenty of money.

GODFREY Oh yes... honey and plenty of money. Wrapped up in a five pound note.

Suddenly there is a sharp jerk and the train stops. Godfrey is thrown into Mainwaring's arms. He looks up into his face.

GODFREY The owl looked up to the moon above...

MAINWARING (Pushing him off) Oh get off, Godfrey.

WILSON Look, sir, now that we've stopped, Godfrey can... er... nip outside.

MAINWARING Good idea. Go on, Godfrey, out you get. (He swings the door open and starts to push Godfrey out)

GODFREY It's very high up, sir.

MAINWARING Get on with it, man.

Sponge and Pike help Godfrey down.

GODFREY (His head level with the door) Would you mind closing the door, please.

Wilson pulls the door to.

WILSON (In unnatural voice) Spring appears to be a little late this year.

MAINWARING Why are you talking like that, Wilson?

WILSON I'm trying to be nonchalant... I don't want to put Godfrey off.

MAINWARING Rubbish. We're a fighting force on active service. Godfrey must learn to rough it.

The whistle goes and the train starts to move.

MAINWARING Quick! Get him in!

Wilson swings the door back and we see Godfrey's head... he is running to keep up with the train.

WILSON Come along, Godfrey... hurry up.

MAINWARING Pull him in, man.

PIKE I'm trying to, sir.

GODFREY (Panting) Mr Mainwaring, please. I can't keep up much longer.

Mainwaring and Wilson reach down and pull Godfrey in. Wilson closes the door. Jones helps Godfrey up.

JONES Are you all right, Mr Godfrey?

GODFREY I'm afraid not... er... The owl and the pussy cat went to sea in a beautiful...

TELECINE: COUNTRY HALT. DAY

Deserted country halt. All the place names are painted out.

The platoon are gathered on the platform. We can hear the sound of the train moving away.

MAINWARING Corporal Jones!

JONES Yes, sir.

MAINWARING Fall the men in.

JONES Come on, you blokes – fall in.

Mainwaring draws Wilson on one side.

MAINWARING I hope this is the right place, Wilson. It looks a bit deserted to me.

WILSON Well the guard did tell us to get out here, sir.

MAINWARING Yes, but it could have been a trick. I mean, how do we know he was the guard?

WILSON Because he was wearing a railway uniform, sir.

MAINWARING That means nothing. It could be a trap. I tell you, we must be on our guard at all times.

WILSON But our guard got back on the train.

MAINWARING Are you trying to be funny, Wilson?

WILSON No, sir, perhaps you're a little on edge. After all, you haven't had any lunch.

MAINWARING (**Gives him a glare**) I'd better open these sealed orders. (**He takes two packets out of his pouch. He looks at the first one. Reads**) Hmm. Sealed instructions for opening sealed orders. (**He opens the packet. Reads**) Break the seal on the sealed orders... and then destroy these instructions. (**He breaks the seal on the second packet and hands the first one to Wilson**)

MAINWARING Set light to that, Wilson.

WILSON (**Taking packet**) Yes, sir.

MAINWARING (**Opening second packet – it contains a map**) Now we shan't be long.

WILSON Excuse me, sir.

MAINWARING What is it?

WILSON Have you got a match?

MAINWARING (**Handing him a box**) Oh here... (**Tapping map and instructions**) I thought so, Wilson... it's all pretty straightforward.

WILSON Oh, really, sir?

MAINWARING Yes. (**Pointing to map**) We are here at X railway halt... map reference (**Mumble, mumble**) (**Points**) There's that hill over there – and the battle school is here... map reference (**Mumble, mumble**). It's only about a mile away – we should be there by tea time.

WILSON That's good, sir.

They both march back to the platoon.

JONES (**Saluting**) Platoon ready to march off, sir.

MAINWARING (**Returning salute**) Thank you, Corporal... Just a minute. Where's Godfrey?

JONES He's er... he won't be a minute, sir.

MAINWARING He'll just have to catch up, that's all. Now pay attention, men. As I know the way, I shall keep well in front. Sergeant, you will bring up the rear.

WILSON Yes, sir.

MAINWARING Platoon attention! Left turn, by the right, quick march. (**They march off. Mainwaring gestures with his stick**) Right wheel. Forward. (**They march out of the station. Godfrey appears and runs to catch up. Wilson helps him**)

TELECINE: COUNTRY LANE. DAY

Platoon marching along narrow country lane, Mainwaring well in front. They come to a signpost. All the names are painted out.

MAINWARING Platoon, mark time. (**He looks at signpost, then looks at his map. He gestures to the left with his stick**) Platoon forward! (**They all follow him**)

TELECINE: COUNTRY LANE. DAY

Platoon marching along. They come to small crossroads.

MAINWARING Platoon... mark time! (**He looks at his map – then gestures to the left with his stick**) Forward!

TELECINE: RAILWAY PLATFORM. DAY

The platoon march in through the gate.

MAINWARING Platoon... halt!

Wilson hurries up to him.

WILSON I thought you said we'd be there by tea time, sir.

MAINWARING There's no need for sarcasm, Wilson. I must have taken the wrong turning. Platoon, about turn! By the right, quick march!

They march off.

TELECINE: COUNTRY LANE. DAY

The platoon are marching along. They come to a fork in the road.

MAINWARING (**Pointing with his stick**) Left wheel!

They all turn left and pile up against a brick wall.

TELECINE: COUNTRY LANE. DAY

The platoon are marching. Close up of terrible face peering through the hedgerow. It is Captain Rodrigues.

Mainwaring is now well in front. As he rounds a bend, two figures spring out and pull him into the hedgerow. The platoon march past. Suddenly fire crackers are thrown from each side of the road. They all scatter in panic.

WALKER Blimey, an ambush!

JONES (Rushing about) Don't panic! Don't panic! (He tries to fix his bayonet) Where are they...? I'll get 'em!

WILSON Where's Captain Mainwaring?

FRAZER Look!

They all turn round. Mainwaring staggers out of the hedge in terrible disarray.

HUT AT BATTLE SCHOOL. NIGHT

The hut is bare except for a pile of straw... some empty palliasses... and a pile of blankets. The platoon Staggers in through the door. Walker and Pike are carrying Godfrey between them in a chair grip.

FRAZER This is it. It's empty.

WALKER Blimey, what a dump.

They all sink down on their equipment. Frazer, Walker and Jones form a little group on their own.

FRAZER Did you see this place as we marched in? It looks just like a prisoner-of-war camp.

WALKER I wonder if the Red Cross send food parcels?

FRAZER Just look at the time... 11 o'clock. It's taken us five hours to get here from the station, and it's only a mile away.

JONES You know, I don't think Mr Mainwaring really knew the way at all.

FRAZER It's a disgrace... yon's not fit to be in charge of men.

MAINWARING (Crossing over to them with forced cheerfulness) Well, men, we got here.

He is greeted with hostile looks.

FRAZER Aye, we did.

JONES Better late than never, eh?

WALKER Does this weekend course include map reading, Mr Mainwaring?

WILSON Now, now, Walker.

Major Smith and Captain Rodrigues enter. Major Smith is dressed in baggy cord slacks, desert boots, long khaki jersey nearly down to his knees – his shirt epaulettes are drawn through holes in his jersey and they have cloth insignias on them. He is also wearing an officer's peaked hat with all the stuffing knocked out – the two sides hang down and the front is pushed up. He is about 40-ish.

Captain Rodrigues is Spanish, dressed in a similar style, with an officer's forage cap worn straight on the head Spanish style – also about 40.

SMITH Good evening, Captain Mainwaring.

MAINWARING (Saluting) Good evening, sir.

SMITH You got here at last then – I'm afraid you've missed your evening meal – supper finished four hours ago.

MAINWARING Er... yes, sir... Fall them in, Sergeant.

WILSON Fall in, you men.

The platoon fall in.

SMITH All right, at ease. You can all relax – we don't go in for a lot of formalities here. Now, as you chaps know, this is a special H.G. battle school... and we only have the weekend to try and initiate you into some of the secrets of guerrilla warfare. (On turn) Now the man who will be in charge of you during the next two days is Captain Rodrigues. He is an expert in all forms of guerrilla tactics. He fought in Spain during the Civil War and, as you all know, that was a pretty dirty business.

WALKER (Out of the corner of his mouth) Yes, and it doesn't look as if he's had a wash since.

SMITH My job here is to keep a paternal eye on you... and make sure you don't get knocked about too much...

GODFREY Oh, thank you very much.

SMITH After all, some of us aren't getting any younger, are we?

JONES Permission to speak, sir?

SMITH Certainly.

JONES You don't want to worry about us senior soldiers, sir... you can knock us about as much as you like... we can take it... and dish it out. Give 'em the old cold steel – they don't like it up 'em, you know, sir, they don't like it up 'em.

SMITH That's the spirit. Well, I'll leave you in the capable hands of Captain Rodrigues. Carry on.

MAINWARING Platoon, attention. (He salutes)

SMITH What! (Returns salute) Oh, jolly good. (He goes)

MAINWARING Stand at ease.

RODRIGUES You can cut all that business out – we don't do any of that 'shunning and arm waving here – all we do is teach you how to kill Nazis – that's all I'm interested in, killing! (He draws his fingers across his throat) Is that clear?

MAINWARING Er... oh yes, very clear, isn't it, Sergeant?

WILSON As clear as crystal, sir.

RODRIGUES Now, are there any questions?

MAINWARING **(To Wilson)** Have you any questions?

WILSON Ask him about food, sir.

MAINWARING Yes, Captain, what about a meal?

RODRIGUES Cantina closed four hours ago. Never mind, I always think of my men… here. **(He throws Mainwaring a small sack he has been carrying)** Some carrots and onions.

MAINWARING Carrots and onions!

RODRIGUES It's what you would eat if you were living off the land.

WILSON Onions!

RODRIGUES **(Breathing in his face)** What's wrong with onions…? I eat them all the time.

WILSON **(Staggering back)** I'd never have guessed.

RODRIGUES You'd better eat them while you can – they're getting very scarce. Right, you got your food. **(Pointing to pile of straw, says to Jones)** You! Old man!

JONES Yes, sir.

RODRIGUES You see that pile of straw over there.

JONES Yes, sir, yes, sir.

RODRIGUES With it, you stuff your palliasse.

JONES I beg your pardon?

RODRIGUES Put it in your palliasse.

He moves down to Mainwaring and Wilson.

JONES A bit Continental, ain't he?

RODRIGUES Right, Captain, you've got a palliasse to lie on… and a blanket each to cover you… not to mention carrots and onions to eat… what more could you want?

WILSON I've really no idea.

RODRIGUES You'd better get some sleep. In this place we start early in the morning. **(He goes)**

MAINWARING **(To Wilson)** I never heard anything like it in all my life, Wilson. To think that… that… brigand is a Captain in the British Army. He looks like an anarchist to me.

WILSON Thank goodness he's on our side, sir.

MAINWARING Now men… we've got a pretty busy weekend ahead of us – so on the command 'fall out' I want you to start filling your palliasses with straw. Platoon, fall out!

The platoon fall out and gather in a surly mob round the straw.

FRAZER Look at this, sleeping on straw, with one blanket each – we shall freeze to death.

PIKE **(His eyes are running and he is blowing his nose)** I've been looking forward to this weekend for ages, Uncle Arthur, and then it goes and turns out like this. **(He sniffs)** It's rotten, that's what it is.

WILSON All right, Frank, there's no need to blub.

PIKE I'm not blubbing, it's this straw, it's brought on my hay fever.

GODFREY I can't eat raw carrots – they give me shocking indigestion.

JONES Me too, you know, Mr Godfrey – still, lucky I've got me old bicarbonate with me.

Mainwaring can stand it no longer. He picks up the sack and moves over to the group.

MAINWARING Well, men, I'd better dish these out. **(He hands out the carrots and onions)** Now, I know we've only got one blanket each, so, as usual, we must improvise.

JONES Permission to speak, sir?

MAINWARING Yes, Jones.

JONES Why don't we all huddle together, sir, that will keep us warm. We used to do a lot of huddling in the Sudan.

MAINWARING I'm not too sure about that, Jones. It might be bad for discipline. All the same, in a case like this, I think we might stretch a point.

FRAZER **(With a terrible glare at Mainwaring)** I'm very particular who I huddle together with.

MAINWARING I'm sure we all are. I think we shall all feel much better after a good night's sleep.

The men are all making their beds up. Mainwaring crosses to them. Wilson hands him a palliasse.

WILSON Your palliasse, sir.

MAINWARING Thank you, Wilson.

Godfrey gives Mainwaring some straw. Mainwaring turns out light and takes down blackout. Moonlight streams in. Mainwaring lies down.

THE HUT. NIGHT

Sleeping figures on floor. Cut to Pike and Wilson who are lying side by side.

PIKE Uncle Arthur.

WILSON Yes, what is it?

PIKE I ain't half hungry.

WILSON Have the rest of my carrot.

PIKE Uncle Arthur, I'm so cold. Do you mind if I cuddle up to you?

WILSON Certainly not.

PIKE I shall tell mum.

WILSON Oh, all right.

Pike sticks his thumb in his mouth and closes his eyes. Jones creeps over to Mainwaring and shakes him.

JONES Mr Mainwaring.

MAINWARING Who's that?

JONES Permission to whisper, sir.

MAINWARING Oh, it's you Jones. What is it?

JONES I'm sorry everything went wrong today, sir.

MAINWARING Thank you, Jones.

JONES It wasn't your fault, sir – it was the fortunes of war. After all, you've been a good officer to us – you've led us through thick and thin.

MAINWARING It's a lonely task being a commander you know, Jones. One must take the rough with the smooth.

JONES Yes, well, I just wanted you to know, sir, that I've still got faith in you.

MAINWARING **(Touched)** Thank you, Jones.

JONES Even if no one else has. Good night, sir.

MAINWARING Good night, Jones. **(Jones crawls away)**

There is a silence followed by a rustling of straw.

WALKER **(In loud voice)** Crawler!

THE HUT. DAY

The platoon are all asleep in various positions. The sun is streaming in through the windows and we can hear birds singing. Suddenly the door opens and Captain Rodrigues creeps in and throws a thunder flash on the floor. He stands and waits, with his arms folded. There is a bang – everyone wakes up in a panic and starts shouting at once. Mainwaring has been sleeping with his head under a table – he sits up quickly and hits his head. He falls back and gropes for his glasses . EXPLOSION.

WALKER Blimey! The Germans have landed.

JONES **(Jumping up)** They're here, they're here.

SPONGE Where are my teeth? Who's got my teeth?

Jones rushes forward, steps on Frazer and falls headlong.

FRAZER Ow! You stupid Sassenach! You've ruined me.

JONES **(Picking himself up)** Don't panic. Don't panic. **(He is rushing about, trying to fix his bayonet)** Don't panic. Don't... **(He suddenly stops as he realises who it is. The panic dies down. Mainwaring dazed, staggers over to the Captain)**

MAINWARING Er, good morning, Captain. You certainly gave us a start. It's a bit early in the morning for that sort of thing, isn't it?

RODRIGUES **(Poking his face into Mainwaring's)** It is not early in the morning, Captain, it is ten minutes to nine. **(He points to his watch)** The rest of the camp has been up for two hours.

MAINWARING Good gracious – we must have overslept.

RODRIGUES You certainly did. You'd better hurry up, I want you and your men outside ready to start training in ten minutes.

MAINWARING But what about breakfast?

RODRIGUES Breakfast finished one hour ago. Now, Captain, listen to this. During the time you are here, every platoon is given the chance to capture my headquarters. So far, no one has succeeded.

JONES We'll have a go, Mr Mainwaring, sir. We'll go through them like a dose of salts, won't we, sir?

RODRIGUES It used to be a prisoner-of-war camp. It is surrounded by two fences. One is a barbed wire fence – the other is electrified. And the space in between is patrolled by dogs.

GODFREY Er... what sort of dogs, sir?

RODRIGUES Alsatians.

GODFREY Oh.

RODRIGUES And they don't get much to eat.

GODFREY Oh dear.

JONES Never mind, Mr Godfrey, I've still got my bicarb – that's good for hydrophobia, you know.

Rodrigues goes.

MAINWARING All right, men, fall in outside as soon as you're dressed.

WALKER **(Taking Jones on one side)** 'Ere, Jonesey, I've had enough of this. I'm starving.

JONES So am I, Joe, but what can we do?

WALKER Look – as soon as I can, I'm going to nip off and try and find some grub.

JONES But there's no shops round here.

WALKER No, but there's a farm just at the side of the camp – there's bound to be something to eat there – you leave it to me.

TELECINE: FIELD. DAY

Platoon are all lying in a row, face down. They are all covered in camouflage. A whistle blows and they start to crawl forward. One of the figures detaches itself from the group and crawls rapidly towards a clump of bushes. It is Walker. Mainwaring gives a signal and they all break cover and charge forward between two trees.

Cut to Captain Rodrigues behind tree with two of his men. He gives a signal – one of them pulls on a rope. The whole platoon falls head first.

TELECINE: ANOTHER FIELD. DAY

Platoon are all lying in a row. Cut to close up of Captain Rodrigues with a megaphone.

RODRIGUES Don't forget to keep your heads down – we are using live ammunition. Wave the flag when you're ready.

Cut to Mainwaring and Wilson – he is carrying a flag.

WILSON They're going to use live ammunition, sir.

MAINWARING I shouldn't take too much notice of that, Wilson. I can assure you they wouldn't dare. All right, wave the flag. (Wilson waves flag – there is a burst of machine gun fire which shoots the top off)

RODRIGUES Move those men forward, Captain.

Film speeded up – they all crawl forward at the double.

TELECINE: FARM. DAY

Walker outside farm building, sound of sheep inside. He gives a furtive look around – quickly opens door and goes in.

WALKER (Out of vision) Blimey, it ain't half dark in 'ere. (More sheep sounds) Got you!

The door opens. Walker's head comes round the edge – he looks round and nips out. He is carrying a sheep dog in his arms.

TELECINE: A RIVER CROSSING. DAY

Mainwaring leads his men to the river bank. Thunder flashes are going off all the time. The platoon gather in a group.

RODRIGUES Hurry up – get those men across the river, Captain.

JONES It looks awfully deep to me, Mr Mainwaring.

MAINWARING No, it's all right. We can cross here.

WILSON Do you think that's wise, sir?

MAINWARING Don't argue, I tell you I can see the bottom.

He steps into the river. Cut to faces of platoon. There is a terrific splash.

JONES Mr Mainwaring, sir, are you all right?

Cut to helmet going across river.

TELECINE: FARM. DAY

Walker outside farm building. Sound of pigs inside. He opens door and goes in... pig noises. Comes out with little piglet under his arm. He licks his lips – looks up – does a take – sees a big farmer standing beside him. Gives sickly grin – hands him piglet.

WALKER Want to buy a bacon slicer?

TELECINE: ASSAULT COURSE. DAY

Rope crossing between two trees. Mainwaring climbs up. Cut to double crossing rope. Cut to close up of hand with knife cutting rope. Double falls. Cut to Mainwaring in mud at bottom.

TELECINE: FARM. DAY

Walker outside chicken coop. He goes inside... frantic chicken noises... comes out with chicken under arm... chicken escapes... he catches chicken... licks his lips... looks up... sees farmer... hands him chicken.

WALKER I was just taking it across the road.

TELECINE: ASSAULT COURSE. DAY

Planks across water. Mainwaring leading platoon. Close up of his face – he shouts.

MAINWARING All right, men, follow me.

Cut to close up of rope round plank. Rope tightens and pulls plank away. Double goes headlong into water.

TELECINE: FIELD. DAY

Walker runs across field. He is carrying his forage cap full of eggs. Jones runs up.

JONES Come on, Joe. Where have you been?

WALKER Here, cop hold of these. (He hands him the eggs)

JONES Blimey, eggs! Where did you get 'em?

A thunder flash explodes. They both take a dive. Jones' face goes in the eggs.

TELECINE: FIELD. DAY

Dinner time. Long trestle tables in field. Five filthy looking characters are dishing out the food. The platoon are all in a queue with their mess tins.

RODRIGUES Tea, stew, taters, carrots, rice pudding, jam. All right, make it quick you've only got 15 minutes.

The platoon rush forward to be served. The tea goes in the first tin. All the rest is sloshed in the second tin.

Mainwaring comes through. Second man is smoking a cigarette – it falls in Mainwaring's stew. Captain Rodrigues picks it out and shouts at second man.

RODRIGUES I've told you before – be with the hygiene –clean, clean. Come on, hurry up.

TELECINE: MONTAGE: DAY

Foreground: close up of Captain Rodrigues shouting. Background: men running. Smoke – thunder flashes going off.

Foreground: Captain Mainwaring exhausted. His face is filthy and he is mopping it with handkerchief. Same background.

Cut to Mainwaring running through smoke. He falls in a deep depression that has been covered in old foliage and bushes. He lies panting at the bottom. He grabs a bush to pull himself up – bush comes away and reveals a tunnel. He strikes a match and looks inside.

THE HUT. NIGHT

The platoon are settling down for the night.

JONES **(To Wilson)** I hope Mr Mainwaring's all right, Mr Wilson. I wonder where he could have got to?

WILSON I've really no idea, Jonesey. One minute he was leading us through that smoke screen and the next minute he seemed to disappear off the face of the earth.

The door bursts open and Mainwaring comes in. He is flushed with triumph.

MAINWARING All right, men, on your feet, quick. We've got work to do.

WILSON There you are, sir. Where on earth have you been?

MAINWARING Never mind that now.

JONES What are we going to do, sir?

MAINWARING We're going to capture the camp headquarters tonight.

WILSON But we can't do that, sir – the place is surrounded by a huge barbed wire fence.

MAINWARING I'm well aware of that, Wilson.

JONES Yes and it's also surrounded by a second fence of electrified wire.

GODFREY Yes and in between it's patrolled by those awful dogs.

WALKER How on earth are we going to get through that lot, sir?

MAINWARING Don't worry, men. Leave it all to me. After all, I've never let you down yet, have I?

They all exchange looks.

Mainwaring reacts.

THE TUNNEL. NIGHT

The platoon are crawling along.

SMALL STORE ROOM. NIGHT

Shelves stacked with tins, etc. There is a small, heavily barred window. A trap-door opens in the floor and the platoon climb up into the room.

MAINWARING **(Whispering)** Now, don't make any noise, men. **(He shines a torch round the room)**

WALKER **(Striking a match)** Cor... look at all this... tea – sugar – spam – corned beef. It's a bloomin' treasure house.

MAINWARING This must be the stores. **(He shines his torch on the door and opens it a crack – a thin shaft of light hits their faces. We can hear laughter)**

RODRIGUES **(Out of vision)** What a bunch that platoon from Walmington-on-Sea are – I only hope they never have to face any Germans.

SMITH **(Out of vision)** You know, I think you were a bit hard on that Captain Mainwaring.

RODRIGUES **(Out of vision)** It's about time these amateur soldiers were taught a lesson. He should go back to managing a bank.

MAINWARING **(Whispering)** All right, men, stand by.

WALKER **(Whispering)** Excuse me, Captain Mainwaring. I think I ought to stay behind to cover your rear.

MAINWARING Good idea, Walker. Ready men? Now!

They all burst through the door.

MAINWARING Now, get your hands up – every one of you.

There is the sound of terrific confusion. Close up of Walker as he closes the door and looks round the room.

RAILWAY CARRIAGE. DAY

The men are all laughing and talking.

MAINWARING An excellent weekend's work, Wilson.

WILSON Yes, indeed, sir. I shall never forget the look on that Spanish fellow's face when we burst in the room.

MAINWARING Amateur soldiers indeed.

FRAZER I want to congratulate you, Captain Mainwaring. I never doubted you for one minute.

MAINWARING Thank you, Frazer.

JONES I've said it before and I'll say it again – you're our inspiration, sir.

They all shout 'That's right' etc.

WILSON Is it true, sir, that Major Smith is recommending us to G.H.Q. for being rather good?

MAINWARING Yes, it is, Wilson. All the same, I would have liked the platoon to have had a more tangible reward.

WALKER **(To Jones)** What's tangible mean, Jack?

JONES It means something solid.

Walker reaches under the seat and pulls out a sack.

WALKER Well, how about this then? **(He starts to hand out tins)**

MAINWARING Good heavens – where did you get all this stuff, Walker?

WALKER Well, I was covering the rear, wasn't I?

They dive at tins.

WALKER Two bob a time, all right?

SERIES THREE **EPISODE THREE**

Recorded: Sunday 8/6/69
Original transmission: Thursday 25/9/69, 7.30–8.00pm
Original viewing figures = 11.3 million

ARTHUR LOWE .... CAPTAIN MAINWARING
JOHN LE MESURIER .... SERGEANT WILSON
CLIVE DUNN.................................. LANCE CORPORAL JONES
JOHN LAURIE .... PRIVATE FRAZER
JAMES BECK .... PRIVATE WALKER
ARNOLD RIDLEY .... PRIVATE GODFREY
IAN LAVENDER .... PRIVATE PIKE
JANET DAVIES.. MRS PIKE
BILL PERTWEE .... ARP WARDEN
AVRIL ANGERS .... THE TELEPHONE OPERATOR
TIMOTHY CARLTON .... LIEUTENANT HOPE BRUCE
STANLEY MCGEAGH.................................. SERGEANT WALLER
PAMELA CUNDELL, OLIVE MERCER
& BERNADETTE MILNES .... THE LADIES IN THE QUEUE
GILDA PERRY.. DOREEN
LINDA JAMES.. BETTY
RICHARD JACQUES .... MR CHEESEWRIGHT & MEMBER OF PLATOON
COLIN DANIELS & CARSON GREEN .... THE BOYS
PLATOON .... COLIN BEAN, FRANK GODFREY,
.... HUGH CECIL, VIC TAYLOR, DESMOND CULLUM-JONES,
.... RICHARD KITTERIDGE, MICHAEL MOORE,
.... GEORGE HANCOCK, FREDDIE WILES
BOY OUTSIDE PHONE BOX .... JOHN WATTERS

THE LION HAS 'PHONES

Originally titled, 'Sorry, Wrong Number'

• BILL PERTWEE REMEMBERS •

'I'd done a little television work prior to *Dad's Army* and quite a lot of radio from the end of the 1950s until late '60s. My first impressions upon joining the team at the rehearsal of the very first episode was of a bunch of folk who were slightly laid back in their approach to it all. After two or three hours my thoughts were that the combination of all these talents was going to be something quite unusual.

'At lunch, on that first day, Jimmy Perry, who I'd never met before and seemed a bit edgy, asked what I thought about the show. I told him that I was sure, given a chance to become established, the series would be a success. There was something about the set-up that was different to all the other situation comedies being aired at that time. It wasn't just that it was about the Home Guard and the fact it was a historical piece, but also because the actors and the characters they played seemed to be, even then, sparking off one another – something I was sure would be enhanced even further as the main idea and characterisations developed.

'I think my comments to Jimmy relaxed him a little; he's told me since that I gave his confidence a boost that day. One has to remember this was his first move into writing for television. David Croft's knowledge of writing for theatre and television, as well as his previous successes as a television director, combined with Jimmy's vision of what might develop in the future, was a marvellous combination of enthusiasm and expertise.

'I had no idea at that early stage that it was going to be more than a one-off job for me. Just a couple of lines was very welcome as my long run in the radio shows, *Beyond Our Ken* and *Round the Horne*, had come to an end after nearly nine years, so I was in the market-place for whatever came along next, and that turned out to be *Dad's Army*.

'I think the cast of *Dad's Army* was a little suspicious of me at first with the background I had in variety and revue. So when I got further calls to join the team I know Arthur Lowe asked David Croft: "Where did you get this fellow from?" Of course, he meant me! Early on, I just concentrated on learning lines and giving them as much weight as I thought they needed. David Croft didn't seem to have any worries about this "warden" who rushed in, shouted a bit, pushed people around, made himself objectionable, and swept out again. There was little subtlety about my performance, which I think was the reason for a little antipathy towards me early on. I took no notice of this and was quite happy to be enjoying myself – and being paid for it!

'As time went on I became as much a part of the "family" as anyone else, and friendships were cemented with families and friends as if we'd all known each other years. Actually, when I watch repeats nowadays I think John Laurie was more OTT than I was – and wasn't he just marvellous?

'Everyone turned in good performances. Clive Dunn makes me laugh on and off screen, while John Le Mesurier's eccentric performances were excellent; you just had to admire his style. Ian Lavender always gave a professional performance, particularly as the German officer in "Wake Up, Walmington!". One of my favourite people was dear Teddy Sinclair, the verger. He only had to enter a scene with his cap and yellow duster hanging out of his cassock and you started to laugh. David Croft and Jimmy Perry were quite important to the overall success of the series, too. Our two school masters certainly knew how to get the best from their pupils. And we shouldn't forget Hitler's contribution: if it hadn't been for him, we wouldn't have had the Home Guard. Finally, Bud Flanagan singing, "Who Do You Think You Are Kidding, Mr Hitler?" set the whole tone for the period.'

BILL PERTWEE

The Lion has 'Phones

TELECINE: EDGE OF FIELD. HEDGE BACKING

Mainwaring and Wilson are standing side by side – Mainwaring is looking through his field glasses.

Cut to L.S. of field – we can see stooks of wheat in neat rows.

Cut back to Mainwaring and Wilson.

MAINWARING All right, Sergeant – fall the men in.

WILSON **(Shouting)** Platoon... fall in.

Cut to L.S. of field. The stooks of wheat all get up and fall in – in three ranks. Sheep bleat and run away.

Cut to close up of Wilson.

WILSON Platoon... slope arms.

Cut to stooks sloping arms. Cut back to close up of Mainwaring.

MAINWARING Very sloppy, men – very sloppy.

STOOK Get knotted.

MAINWARING Who said that? Take that man's name, Sergeant.

Wilson walks down the ranks, trying to find out who it is.

TELECINE: STREET. DAY

Rows of dustbins on the edge of the pavement.

Cut to Mainwaring and Wilson.

MAINWARING All right, Sergeant. Fall the men in.

WILSON **(Shouting)** Platoon... fall in.

Cut to L.S. of street – the dustbins fall in.

Cut to close up of Wilson.

WILSON Platoon... slope arms.

Cut to dustbins sloping arms.

MAINWARING Very sloppy, men – very sloppy.

DUSTBIN Get knotted.

MAINWARING Who said that? Take that man's name, Sergeant.

Wilson quickly walks down the ranks, lifting the lids off the dustbins.

TELECINE: CHURCHYARD. DAY

Rows of tombstones.

Cut to Mainwaring and Wilson.

MAINWARING Fall the men in, Sergeant.

WILSON **(Shouting)** Platoon... fall in.

Cut to L.S. of churchyard – the tombstones fall in.

WILSON Platoon... slope arms.

Cut to tombstones sloping arms.

MAINWARING Very sloppy, men.

TOMBSTONE Get knotted.

MAINWARING Take that man's name, Sergeant.

Wilson comes up to tombstone.

WILSON **(Reading)** William Potter, died 1910.

TELECINE: FARMYARD. DAY

Milk churns standing in rows. Behind them is a corrugated iron shed.

MAINWARING Fall the men in, Sergeant.

WILSON Platoon... fall in.

The pieces of corrugated iron detach themselves from the building and fall in.

CHURCH HALL. DAY

Platoon standing in group. Mainwaring and Wilson enter either side of platform.

MAINWARING A good morning's work, men. A first class exercise in the art of camouflage. Now, pay attention, men. The subject of my lecture today is communications. In the event of an invasion, enemy paratroopers will try to seize the following points. **(He points to the diagram on the board)** The gasworks, here... The railway bridge, here... The telephone exchange, here... and the water reservoir, here. With all these points out of action, the town would be crippled. No gas, no trains, no telephones, and no water. After all, not many of us can last very long without water to drink.

FRAZER I've managed it for years.

MAINWARING In short, all these parts of the town are absolutely vital. So the object of the exercise is...

JONES To stop the enemy getting his hands on our vital parts!

MAINWARING Er... well, yes. **(On his turn to board)** Now we shall post two men at each one of these points. In the event of an attack, one of the men will run to the nearest telephone box and phone me at the church hall here.

FRAZER Excuse me, sir. If one of the men is running to phone you, what happens to the man who's left behind?

WALKER He'll be running the other way.

MAINWARING This is not a matter for levity, Walker. No, the man who is left behind will pin the enemy down with constant, withering fire.

JONES It's going to be a bit difficult to keep up a constant, withering fire, sir – we've only got five rounds each.

MAINWARING You'll just have to make every shot tell. Now, you will see on the map here that I have pinpointed the nearest telephone box to all these strategic points (He points) The railway bridge – the nearest phone box is a hundred yards away, here... The gasworks – there's one here, fifty yards away. And the water reservoir, there's one here, just outside the gates. Now the problem is the telephone exchange, unfortunately the nearest phone box is over half a mile away. So there could be a considerable delay in summoning help.

WILSON Perhaps it would save time, sir, if we used one of the phones in the exchange.

MAINWARING What? Oh, yes, of course... Well done, Wilson.

The men exchange looks.

MAINWARING Now, as soon as I get a call – I shall relieve you at the head of a swift mobile attacking force. By the way, make sure that all your bicycles are in good working order.

FRAZER There's only one thing, sir.

MAINWARING What's that, Frazer?

FRAZER What happens if the phone box is out of order?

MAINWARING Well, in that case, as usual, we shall have to improvise. Now, has anybody got any suggestions?

THE PLATOON Yes, sir.

MAINWARING You'd better write all this down, Wilson.

WILSON Yes, sir. (He takes out a notebook and pencil and goes to Mainwaring)

JONES Permission to speak, sir?

MAINWARING Yes, Jones.

JONES Well, sir, one of us could climb to the top of the gasometer – and heliograph down on to the church hall.

WALKER That's a long way for one man to heliograph.

MAINWARING I don't think I quite follow you, Jones.

JONES Heliograph, sir... you reflect the rays of the sun in a mirror – we used to signal like that on the north west frontier of India. That was when we was fighting the Phantoms. They were the boys, you know... they used to come at you with them long knives... (etc. etc.)

MAINWARING Yes, that will do, Jones, thank you.

JONES Well, you could, sir – you could heliograph.

MAINWARING There's only one snag, Jones. We can't see the gasworks from the church hall.

GODFREY Perhaps one of us could be up at the top of the church tower, sir.

MAINWARING That's a good idea – make a note of that, Wilson... Wait a minute, there's a slight snag... all these strategic points are in different directions... the man on the tower might not be looking.

GODFREY Well, he could keep walking round, sir.

MAINWARING Excellent. (On his turn) What have you got so far, Wilson?

WILSON (Reading) Jones on the top of the gasworks flashing his heliograph – and a man on the top of the tower, er... walking round.

MAINWARING I'm not too happy about Jones' heliograph. We can't rely on the sun – after all, it might be raining.

WALKER In that case, sir, we could tic tac.

MAINWARING Tic tac?

WALKER Yes, you know, sir, like on the racecourse, tic tacking the odds. (He does some signals) All you need is a pair of white gloves – and you're away.

GODFREY Well, I've got a rather nice pair of white evening gloves you could have. I used to wear them for the annual Civil Service Stores staff ball. That was a long time ago, of course, people don't bother to wear them nowadays. I always think it's a pity – a gentleman never seems properly dressed without gloves.

Mainwaring reacts.

PIKE You wouldn't be able to signal Sunday lunch time, sir.

MAINWARING Why not?

PIKE With everyone cooking their Sunday dinners – the gasometer would be down.

JONES Permission to speak, sir? Why couldn't we shoot a hole in the top of the gasometer and then set light to it. You'd see that for miles.

MAINWARING I think we're going into the realms of fantasy now, you know, Jones.

JONES (Muttering to Frazer) I don't know what he's

talking about – he asked for suggestions, didn't he? What did he want to ask for them in the first place?

WILSON All right, settle down, Jones.

MAINWARING Now, still assuming that all the phones are out of action – how would we signal – if the enemy tried to capture the water reservoir?

WILSON Well, sir, perhaps we could tip some cochineal in the water – then, when they turned the taps on at G.H.Q., they'd know that the reservoir was being attacked.

WALKER You can't get it in wartime, it's very scarce. Fortunately, I've got a few bottles I could let you have cheap.

FRAZER What about rockets?

WALKER Yeah – I can let you have some of those too – mind you, *they* come a bit expensive.

FRAZER I've got some pre-war stock in my shop.

WALKER You would have.

FRAZER Which type would you prefer, sir? The ones that go bang – or the ones that give off a spray of coloured stars?

GODFREY Can't we have the coloured stars, sir – they're so much prettier.

JONES I know how we can signal from the railway bridge, sir. Just tap on the rails, you can hear that for miles if you put your ear on the line.

PIKE But a train might come along and run your ear over.

JONES Don't be silly... if you had your ear on the line, you'd hear it coming.

They all start to argue.

MAINWARING That will do, men. All this has stimulated a very interesting discussion. But in the meantime, we shall have to assume that the phone isn't out of action.

PIKE I'm not allowed to use a public telephone box, Mr Mainwaring – my mum says it's unhygienic – you can catch 'things' from the receiver.

MAINWARING Well, you could always hold it away from your face.

PIKE I tried that once, sir, but I couldn't hear.

MAINWARING So you've never really used a phone box?

PIKE No, sir.

MAINWARING What do you do when you want to make a phone call, then?

PIKE Uncle Arthur lets me use the one in the bank.

WILSON Frank!

MAINWARING Really?

PIKE Yes, but I don't use it very often, sir.

MAINWARING I'm glad to hear it.

PIKE Only when I phone my Auntie in Scotland.

MAINWARING I'll talk to you later, Wilson.

GODFREY Excuse me, sir – I've never used a phone box either. I did try it once but I got in such a terrible muddle. You see, I'm hopeless with machines.

MAINWARING Well, there's only one thing for it – I shall have to make sure that you all know how to use a phone box.

WALKER You've got to be a right nana not to know how to use a phone.

MAINWARING This is not for you, this is for the benefit of the people that don't know. Now, pay attention.

PIKE **(Aside to Godfrey)** I still don't like it, Mr Godfrey. My mum says you get Mastiffs in your ears.

The men are all gathered round Mainwaring in a semi-circle.

MAINWARING Pike! Now we'd better go through this by numbers. On one, you pick up the phone... on two, you insert twopence... ching ching... ching... ching...

WILSON Excuse me, sir, what is the ching ching?

MAINWARING That is the sound of the coppers dropping into the box. Now don't be put off by this sound – it's quite normal. The operator will then say 'Number please' and you ask for this number, which is Walmington-on-Sea... er...

WILSON Three three three, sir.

MAINWARING I know what the number is, Wilson. Walmington-on-Sea 333. The operator will then say 'I'm connecting you'. Now, when you hear me answer, press button A. Have you got that? **(They all nod)** Right now, we'll just try it. Wilson?

WILSON Yes, sir.

MAINWARING You will be the operator. Are you ready? One... **(They all pick up the phone in their right hands)** Two... **(They all put in two pennies and chant 'Ching-ching, ching-ching')** Come on, Wilson... 'Number please'.

WILSON Number please.

OMNES Walmington-on-Sea 333.

MAINWARING Get on with it, Wilson.

WILSON What, sir?

MAINWARING I'm connecting you.

WILSON What for... oh yes, of course... I'm connecting you.

JONES Permission to speak, sir?

MAINWARING Yes, Jones.

JONES You don't put the coppers in until the operator tells you.

FRAZER You're wrong… you put them in first.

WALKER No, no. Jonesey is right… you put them in when the operator tells you.

MAINWARING All right, men… all right. There's only one way to settle this, we must try it out under actual combat conditions. We will all proceed to the phone box near the reservoir. Right, fall them in, Sergeant.

WILSON Right, men, fall in, in three ranks.

TELECINE: RESERVOIR. DAY

Long shot showing how large reservoir is. Platoon appear in single file, marching along edge. Mainwaring is at the head of it. Suddenly he sees something.

MAINWARING Platoon, halt! Sergeant Wilson – Corporal Jones – come with me at once.

They all run down to the edge of the water. Two small boys are drying their feet.

MAINWARING How dare you boys swim in the reservoir. Do you realise we have to drink that water?

FIRST BOY We're not doing any harm. 'Sides, we had our costumes on. Why can't we swim in it?

MAINWARING You've no right to be doing anything in it. Clear off at once!

SECOND BOY **(To first boy)** We'd better do what the soldiers say.

FIRST BOY They're not soldiers, they're Home Guards. It's old Jones the butcher… and old frosty-face from the bank.

MAINWARING **(Waving his walking stick)** That will do… clear off! **(He gestures with his stick)** Platoon, forward!

OUTSIDE THE RESERVOIR. DAY.

Small boy runs past reservoir gates and phone box, chasing a ball.

OUTSIDE THE RESERVOIR. DAY.

Brick wall – telephone box. There is a small gate in the wall and a note which reads '——— water board'. The platoon file through the gate on to the pavement. It is on the main road, we can hear traffic passing.

WILSON Platoon, halt!

MAINWARING Now, men, I'm going to take you into the telephone box two at a time and make sure you all know how to use it. Pike, Godfrey – you'd better come in with me first. Corporal Jones, form the rest up in a queue outside.

JONES Right, form up in a queue outside the gate.

Mainwaring goes into box with Pike and Godfrey. Mainwaring is in the middle, Pike is facing the wall.

MAINWARING Now, the first thing we… **(He sees Pike)** For goodness sake, turn round, boy. How can I talk to you with your back to me?

PIKE Sorry, sir – this is how I got in. **(He starts to turn round and ends up in the middle with Mainwaring against the wall)**

MAINWARING This is no good, we'd better go outside again.

They all go out and come in again. Mainwaring is in the middle, Pike is on his left, Godfrey on his right. Godfrey has his arm round Mainwaring's shoulder.

MAINWARING Now you pick up the… **(He notices Godfrey's arm)** Godfrey.

GODFREY Yes, sir?

MAINWARING Would you mind removing your arm from my shoulder.

GODFREY I'm sorry, I can't, sir… this is how I came in.

MAINWARING Well, go out and come in again.

GODFREY Yes, sir. **(He does so)**

MAINWARING Now, first of all, you lift the receiver. **(He picks up the receiver but can't get it up to his ear because Godfrey's arm is in the way)** It's no use, I shall just have to take you one at a time. You wait outside, Godfrey. **(Godfrey goes)**

MAINWARING Now then, Pike, take these two pennies. **(He gives him the coppers)** Now, lift the receiver. **(Pike picks it up – and holds it away from his face)** Put it to your ear – it won't bite you. **(He looks up and sees a small boy with his nose pressed flat against the glass. He knocks at the window and signals him to go away)** Now, Pike, I want you to make the call to the church hall – there won't be a reply because there's no one there to answer – so you can press button B and get the money back. Now, are you ready? **(He sees the boy's face again. He pushes open the door)** Wilson.

WILSON **(Out of vision)** Yes, sir.

MAINWARING Tell that boy to go away at once. **(To Pike)** Now put the pennies in. **(Pike puts them in)**

PIKE You were right, sir. They went 'ching ching' just as you said.

OPERATOR **(Out of vision – distort)** Number, please!

PIKE Walmington-on-Sea er… I've forgotten the number, sir.

MAINWARING Oh, you stupid boy… it's Walmington-on-Sea er… **(He pushes open the door)** Just checking on the number, Wilson.

WILSON Walmington-on-Sea 333, sir.

MAINWARING Quite correct.

PIKE Walmington-on-Sea 333.

OPERATOR **(Out of vision – distort)** I'm connecting you.

MAINWARING Let the phone ring for a bit… and then press button B and get the money back.

PIKE Yes, sir. **(He presses Button A)**

MAINWARING What did you want to press Button A for?

PIKE Somebody's answered… Oh hullo, mum.

MRS PIKE Is that you, Frank? Where are you phoning from?

PIKE I'm in a call box, outside the waterworks.

MRS PIKE I thought I told you never to use a public phone box!

PIKE It's not my fault, mum, Mr Mainwaring made me do it.

MRS PIKE Did he indeed! Well, I'll have a few words to say to him next time I see him.

PIKE He's here now.

MRS PIKE Well, let me speak to him.

PIKE Mum wants to speak to you, sir.

MAINWARING **(He takes phone)** Mrs Pike? May I ask what you're doing in my office?

MRS PIKE I brought Frank's scarf down for him to wear – he'll catch his death without it. I heard the phone ring.

MAINWARING All the same, Mrs Pike, you've no right to… **(Mrs Pike's voice cuts in and chatters on at a high speed)** Oh really… **(Mainwaring pushes door open and calls)** Wilson!

MRS PIKE **(Ouf of vision – distort)** Now look here, Mr Mainwaring, what's the idea of letting my Frank use a public phone box? I've never let him use one before in his life.

WILSON Yes, sir?

MAINWARING Come in and sort this out, will you? It's Mrs Pike.

Wilson comes into the box and he hands him the phone.

WILSON Hullo, Mavis.

MRS PIKE Oh, it's you, Arthur. I'd have thought you'd have known better than to let Frank use a public phone box.

WILSON It's not my fault, Mavis.

MRS PIKE Of course it's your fault.

WILSON You molly-coddle that boy far too much, Mavis. I think you're being very silly.

MRS PIKE Oh, I'm silly am I? Well, you're silly if you think that I'm only here to administer to all your little comforts every evening.

WILSON Oh really, Mavis.

MRS PIKE You think that you've only got to knock at my door, and I'll come running.

WILSON I've never asked you to run, Mavis.

MRS PIKE You take me for granted, Arthur – and you always have taken me for granted. And I'm not going to stand for it any longer. **(She hangs up)**

WILSON She's hung up, sir – what am I going to do?

MAINWARING I don't know, Wilson. I've got a platoon to run – I can't be involved in your little domestic squabbles. Get the next man in.

OUTSIDE TELEPHONE BOX. DAY

Two queues of men are outside the box. Jones, Frazer and Walker are on the end of one queue.

FRAZER Of all the absurd ideas – showing us how to use a phone box.

JONES We never had no telephone in the Sudan, you know. If we had done those Fuzzie Wuzzies would have had their long knives out and cut it off before you could say Matagataba.

FRAZER If it wasn't for that stupid boy Pike – and that old fool Godfrey, we wouldn't be here wasting our time.

Two women join the end of the queue.

FIRST WOMAN **(To Frazer)** What are you queuing up for?

FRAZER We're all waiting to make stupid phone calls.

SECOND WOMAN **(To First Woman)** What did he say?

FIRST WOMAN He says they're all queuing up for phone calls.

Third woman joins the queue.

THIRD WOMAN What's at the top? What are they waiting for?

SECOND WOMAN Phone calls.

Walker overhears this, and pushes Frazer in front of him.

WALKER 'Ere you are, Taff, you can take my place – I'm in no hurry.

FIRST WOMAN Why are you queuing up for phone calls?

WALKER Haven't you heard?

FIRST WOMAN No, what?

WALKER They're going on ration tomorrow.

FIRST WOMAN **(To Second Woman)** Did you hear that? They're going to ration phone calls.

SECOND WOMAN **(To Third Woman)** They're going to ration phone calls.

THIRD WOMAN When?

FIRST WOMAN Tomorrow.

WALKER If you ladies take my tip – you'll make as many as you can – after today you'll only be allowed one a month.

FIRST WOMAN **(To Third Woman)** Did you hear that? They're going to ration to one a month.

THIRD WOMAN Good job we joined the queue – I said there was something going on.

WALKER I'll tell you what I'll do ladies – as a special favour – when this lot have finished – I'll stand guard outside the box – and you can make as many as you like. A tanner a time, how's that?

FIRST WOMAN That is kind of you.

WALKER Right, I'll take the bookings now.

FIRST WOMAN Here's half a crown, I'll have five.

SECOND WOMAN I'll have ten. **(Gives him five shillings)**

WALKER There you go then, any more?

THIRD WOMAN **(Handing him ten shillings)** I'll have 20.

SECOND WOMAN In that case, I'd better have some more.

Walker collects the money.

OUTSIDE RESERVOIR. NIGHT

Frazer is standing on guard outside the gate. We can hear planes overhead and ack ack fire. He looks up at the sky, stamps his feet and blows on his hands. He walks over and knocks on the phone box. It opens and Walker pokes his head out.

WALKER What's the matter?

FRAZER It's your turn to keep watch.

WALKER **(Coming out)** Oh, all right. It ain't half cold out here.

FRAZER I'm afraid there's going to be a heavy raid on London tonight – just listen to all those planes going over.

WALKER Well, let's hope a few less come back.

Suddenly there is a terrific roar of a plane – followed by a huge splash.

FRAZER One's come down in the reservoir. Remember what the Captain said – one of us has to phone him and the other keeps up a withering fire.

WALKER Right, here's my five rounds, Taffy. Have you got tuppence? Don't worry, I'll reverse the charges.

Frazer goes through gates as Walker makes for the phone box.

EDGE OF RESERVOIR. NIGHT

Mainwaring comes into picture, followed by Wilson, Jones, Godfrey and Pike.

MAINWARING Well done, Frazer. What's happened?

FRAZER Nothing, sir, I've been keeping the plane under observation. It's a Dornier.

MAINWARING Are you sure?

WILSON Yes, sir, you can tell by the outline – you see the way the fuselage slopes back, and the way the tip of the tail…

MAINWARING All right, Wilson, we all know you came top in aircraft recognition.

FRAZER No, sir, I came top – he came second.

MAINWARING Where's Walker?

FRAZER He went off to phone you.

MAINWARING That was half an hour ago.

FRAZER He'll have run away. I always knew he was no good.

JONES Cowardice in the face of the enemy. That's No.1 Field Punishment – tied to the wheel of a gun carriage.

PIKE We haven't got a gun carriage, Mr Jones.

FRAZER Well, we'll just have to improvise.

MAINWARING Oh, be quiet. I can't understand why it hasn't sunk.

WILSON That's because the reservoir's only half full, sir – the aircraft's sitting on the bottom. When it's full, the water's ten feet deep.

MAINWARING I want to know how we're going to tackle the plane, Wilson, I'm not interested in details of the waterworks.

GODFREY Excuse me, sir, do you mind if I…

MAINWARING All right, Godfrey, only hurry up.

Godfrey goes.

MAINWARING There's no sign of anybody in the plane, they must have all jumped out by parachute.

JONES Permission to speak, sir?

MAINWARING Yes, Jones.

JONES Why don't we call on them to surrender in official tones. And then if they do not answer, we will be cognisant of the fact that they are not there, and have sprung off, previous.

MAINWARING **(Reacts)** What's the German for surrender?

JONES I don't know, sir – but Handy hoch is the German for hands up.

MAINWARING Yes, Jones, you've told us that before. Well, we might as well try it. **(He shouts)** Handy hoch! **(No answer)** Handy hoch! **(No answer)** It's too dark... they probably can't see us. We need something white to wave. A shirt will do. Who's wearing a white shirt? **(They all shake their heads)** Pike, that white scarf you're wearing, that'll do. Take it off.

PIKE But I can't take it off – I'll catch cold.

MAINWARING Don't argue, boy, take it off at once!

WILSON Yes, take it off!

PIKE **(Taking his scarf off)** My mum will be furious about this, Uncle Arthur – she hasn't forgiven you yet, for what you said to her over the phone.

MAINWARING Now, Jones, I want you to wave this, and I think it would have more effect if we all shouted at once. Now, are you ready? **(They all nod)** Right.

They all shout 'Handy hoch' – Jones waves the scarf. Suddenly there is a terrific burst of machine gun fire – they all throw themselves on the ground.

JONES Permission to speak, sir? There *is* somebody in the plane.

PIKE Look at my scarf, Uncle Arthur – it's full of bullet holes.

MAINWARING Bloody cheek!

WILSON I've never heard you swear before, sir.

MAINWARING I've never felt like this before, Wilson. Damn foreigners! Coming over here – and then having the cheek to fire on us – well it's about time they were taught a lesson. We'll show them! They're up against us, now! People with guts! Jones, go and phone G.H.Q. for help.

Jones starts to go – Mainwaring stops him.

MAINWARING Wait a minute, Jones – you don't know the number.

JONES Yes, I do, sir – it's Walmington-on-Sea 333.

MAINWARING Don't be absurd – that's the church hall – it's no good phoning there – we're all here! **(He starts to write the number on paper)** That will do, Jones. Now this is the number – 166. **(He hands him the paper)** Commit that number to memory, and after you've used the phone, destroy it.

JONES Destroy the phone?

MAINWARING No, the paper, you idiot. **(Jones goes)** All right, men, spread out and keep down.

INSIDE PHONE BOX. NIGHT

Jones scrambles into the box and closes the door. There is no light in the box. There is just enough moonlight outside for him to see. He has a small torch.

JONES **(Picking up phone)** Now, let me see, Walmington-on-Sea 991. That's it – 991.

He puts twopence in the box.

CINEMA CASH DESK. NIGHT

Doreen and Betty are sitting inside – Betty is painting her nails.

DOREEN Did you say he was a Free French Pilot?

BETTY That's right.

DOREEN So, what did you say?

BETTY I told him straight – I said a Free French Pilot you may be – but it's still going to cost you 1s 9d to see it.

MR CHEESEWRIGHT You'd better cash up now, Doreen – the main picture's just started – and don't forget to put down all the servicemen who got in half price.

DOREEN Very well, Mr Cheesewright. How many halves have we got in tonight, Betty?

BETTY Two sailors, 12 soldiers, no, 13 counting that nice Major who comes every week.

Phone rings.

DOREEN **(Picking up phone)** Oh, you mean **(The phone is level with her mouth)** – Major Brooks.

INSIDE TELEPHONE BOX. NIGHT

JONES Major Brooks?

DOREEN **(With puzzled look at receiver)** Yes, that's right.

JONES Can you help me?

DOREEN Certainly, sir... 'One of our Aircraft is Missing'.

JONES That's funny, I thought it was one of theirs.

DOREEN No... it's 'One of *Our* Aircraft is Missing'. It went up five minutes ago.

JONES Well, it's come down now.

DOREEN No, sir... it doesn't come down till 10.30... If you hurry you'll just catch it. Eric Portman and Googie Withers are in it.

JONES Well, why are they shooting at us?

DOREEN No, sir... they're not still shooting it... it's finished.

JONES Of course they're shooting... can't you hear 'em? **(More gun fire)**

DOREEN It's one of *them*, Betty. If you don't hang up at once I'll send a policeman round to that box. **(She hangs up)** Some people!

JONES **(Rattling the hook)** Wait a minute, Major – don't hang up. Major! Major... Now, what am I going to do...? I haven't got any more pennies. **(He shines his torch on a button above phone... reads)** In the event of an emergency, lift phone and press button. **(He does so)**

OPERATOR Emergency! Which service do you require? Fire, police or ambulance?

JONES There's an enemy plane in the reservoir. I want G.H.Q. Area Command.

OPERATOR I'm sorry, I can only get you fire, police or ambulance. Is the plane on fire?

JONES No, it's not.

OPERATOR Well, you don't want the fire service, do you? What about an ambulance? Is anybody hurt?

JONES No, not yet. **(Another burst of fire)** On the other hand, they might be by now.

OPERATOR I don't think they'll send an ambulance just on the off chance. What about the police... is the plane causing an obstruction?

JONES Not really, no.

OPERATOR Well, what's it doing?

JONES It's shooting at us.

OPERATOR Oh, shame... I'm sorry... I wish I could help you but I only deal with emergencies. Ta-ta.

JONES Ta-ta. What do you mean ta-ta. Hello, hello. **(Jones has been flashing his torch during this conversation. Suddenly a voice shouts 'Put that light out' and the door bursts open)**

WARDEN Who's in...? **(He breaks off)** Oh, it's you... What do you think you're doing, flashing your torch like that? Do you realise there are enemy planes overhead?

JONES Yes, and there's one down in the reservoir.

WARDEN What are you talking about?

JONES There's an enemy plane crashed in the reservoir.

WARDEN Well, you're a Home Guard... why aren't you dealing with it? What are you doing hiding in this phone box?

JONES I'm not hiding, I'm trying to get on to G.H.Q. for help. I haven't got any more coppers.

WARDEN Oh blimey! Shift over, I'll do it.

EDGE OF RESERVOIR. NIGHT

Mainwaring and Wilson are lying side by side.

MAINWARING They're taking long enough to get here from G.H.Q., Wilson.

WILSON Perhaps they've got held up, sir.

MAINWARING I don't know how we're going to get these Germans to surrender. They could hold out for days.

A young Guards Lieutenant crawls into the picture – he and Mainwaring salute.

LIEUTENANT I'm from G.H.Q. – Lieutenant Hope Bruce, Coldstream Guards.

MAINWARING Captain Mainwaring, Home Guard. This is Sergeant Wilson.

WILSON How do you do. **(They both salute)**

LIEUTENANT Are they still shooting out there?

MAINWARING Yes, sir, they've been keeping it up for the past hour.

A Sergeant crawls in and salutes.

LIEUTENANT Are the men in position, Sergeant?

SERGEANT Yes, sir... I've got the reservoir completely surrounded.

There is another burst of fire from the plane.

LIEUTENANT You'd better get your men back out of the way, Captain – we can't expect Home Guards to tackle a situation like this... it's a job for the regular army.

MAINWARING Well we've managed all right up to now.

LIEUTENANT Managed what? They haven't surrendered yet, have they? I can't understand why the damn plane hasn't sunk.

WILSON That's because the reservoir's only half full. The plane's sitting on the bottom.

LIEUTENANT I can see that, Sergeant... I'm not a complete fool you know. Sergeant Waller, there's only one thing for it. We'll just have to lob a few mortar bombs on to that plane... that'll soon fetch 'em out.

SERGEANT Yes, sir... I'll get the men to stand by.

MAINWARING You can't do that, sir.

LIEUTENANT I beg your pardon!

MAINWARING That's the whole town's water supply – you might crack the bottom of the reservoir.

LIEUTENANT When I want your opinion, Captain, I'll ask for it. **(To Sergeant)** Cancel those mortars. **(He crawls out) Walker comes into picture.**

MAINWARING Where have you been, Walker?

WALKER I've been to have a word with the bloke in charge of the reservoir. I had to slip him five bob but he did it.

MAINWARING Did what?

WALKER Opened the sluices. The water will be up to the top in a couple of hours and they'll have to swim for it unless they want to sit on the aerial.

MAINWARING Well done, Walker.

Lieutenant returns.

LIEUTENANT I've decided what to do, Mainwaring. We're going to sit here till we starve them out.

MAINWARING I don't think that will be necessary, sir. I think they'll be surrendering in about a couple of hours from now.

LIEUTENANT Oh, why?

WILSON Well you see, the fact is they just don't like it up 'em. They can't stand it.

JONES You're right, you know, Mr Wilson – they don't like it up 'em etc. etc.

MAINWARING Well, I think we can safely leave the Coldstream Guards to mop up.

SERIES THREE **EPISODE FOUR**

Recorded: Sunday 22/6/69

Original transmission: Thursday 2/10/69, 7.30–8.00pm

Original viewing figures = 11.8 million

ARTHUR LOWE .... CAPTAIN MAINWARING
JOHN LE MESURIER .... SERGEANT WILSON
CLIVE DUNN .... LANCE CORPORAL JONES
JOHN LAURIE .... PRIVATE FRAZER
JAMES BECK .... PRIVATE WALKER
ARNOLD RIDLEY .... PRIVATE GODFREY
IAN LAVENDER .... PRIVATE PIKE
JANET DAVIES .... MRS PIKE
FRANK WILLIAMS .... VICAR
TIM BARRETT .... CAPTAIN PRINGLE
MICHAEL KNOWLES .... CAPTAIN CUTTS
EDWARD SINCLAIR .... VERGER
HAROLD BENNETT .... MR BLEWITT
MAY WARDEN .... MRS DOWDING

THE CHOIR .... FRED TOMLINSON, KATE FORGE, EILIDH MCNAB, ANDREW DAYE, ARTHUR LEWIS

PLATOON .... COLIN BEAN, FRANK GODFREY, HUGH CECIL, DESMOND CULLUM-JONES, RICHARD KITTERIDGE, VIC TAYLOR, MICHAEL MOORE, GEORGE HANCOCK, FREDDIE WILES, LESLIE NOYES

BOYS (IN CHURCH CHOIR) .... TONY CARPENTER, THOMAS MCCADE, FREDDY SHAKESPEARE

NOTE: IN THE ORIGINAL SCRIPT, CAPTAIN PRINGLE WAS CALLED CAPTAIN MARSH.

The Bullet is Not for Firing

• STEPHEN LOWE REMEMBERS •

'I was used to seeing Dad in a frame from an early age. I had two dads: the one in the frame, and the one that everybody else has. In the beginning, when I was still very small and had to hide under the seat during the scary bits, an ornate proscenium arch held my dad captive. He was very far away then, and by no stretch of a young imagination could one reach out and touch him. His voice ran thinly around the gallery, as if coming to you down a long tube.

'It was no surprise for me, then, the day that we went across the road to the Forge Café to see Dad in a frame again. Television held him captive in a different way: fake walnut contained a small tube with a strongly radiused screen which, in its turn, contained an image of my father. He played Sydney Barker, a steward on a passenger ship. His voice came thinly to my ears through an inadequate speaker, turned down low so as not to disturb the neighbours. As my dad was not a steward on a passenger ship, but a man in a frame, I soon worked out that he was an actor. This held no mystery for me, since it had been so since my first realisations.

'When, later in life, now a boy, people said to me: "Is it odd having an actor for a father?" I would reply succinctly: "No!" And they would assume that to be the end of our conversation on that topic. Of course it wasn't strange. It is the most natural thing on earth for a child that its father does what its father does.

'When further grown to the difficult age of 14, my father started on *Dad's Army*. I remember now how excited he was at the prospect of working with the team that has since become immortalised, fossilised in an unlikely suspension of time and videotape. He had a great enthusiasm for his work, and entered into the spirit of everything he did. Until it was over, when he would discard it with a cold heart and not another thought.

'If people asked me was Dad like Mainwaring at home, I would look at them as if to say: "Bugger off!" But maybe I was like that because he was, and I didn't want it to be that way. He was fixated by unimportant detail, had an inflated sense of his own importance, tripped over things and banged his head. But he was brave, too, and I saw him once put his fists up to a man half his height again.

'Arthur was a quick study: if he chose he could learn his lines in the taxi on his way to work. In many cases, he knew what the line would be without ever reading it. Unfortunately, he didn't always choose to exercise his unique ability. This annoyed some of the other players, so he saw a chink in their armour and would fiddle with it for his own amusement. This made some of them very cross.

'In the end, he burnt himself out. It took the form of narcolepsy, a condition where you can't sleep when you want to, and you can't stay awake when you need to. Unwisely, in a career marked by wise decisions, he took a part in a play called *Caught Napping*. But nobody ever really caught Arthur napping – he was far too sharp.'

STEPHEN LOWE *Arthur's son*

The Bullet is not for Firing

SIDE OFFICE. CHURCH HALL. DAY

Mainwaring is asleep behind the desk. Wilson is dozing opposite, with his feet up. The All Clear sounds.

MAINWARING (**Waking**) What's that?

WILSON The All Clear, sir.

MAINWARING Good heavens! What time is it?

WILSON About six o'clock, sir.

MAINWARING Ah, 18.00 hours, eh?

WILSON No sir, that's at night.

MAINWARING Isn't it night?

WILSON No sir, it's the morning.

MAINWARING Oh, is it? Why haven't you taken the blackout down?

Wilson gets up to remove the screens.

WILSON Did you drop off, sir?

MAINWARING Oh no, no.

WILSON I thought you did, your eyes were closed.

MAINWARING I was just resting them, Wilson. I wasn't asleep – far from it.

WILSON With all the responsibilities you have, sir, I wouldn't blame you for taking forty winks.

MAINWARING I did not take forty winks, Wilson.

WILSON I'm sure you were a hundred per cent alert all the time, sir.

MAINWARING I was, Wilson.

WILSON Even if you *were* snoring.

MAINWARING Perhaps you'd better go and put the kettle on, Sergeant.

WILSON Yes, sir.

They both move to the hall to light the kettle.

CHURCH HALL. DAY

MAINWARING They'll need a hot drink, poor devils, after being out all night.

WILSON I think it's a bit absurd the way they stand us to, just because someone reports seeing a parachute. Who's to say it wasn't one of our pilots anyway.

MAINWARING That's hardly likely is it, Wilson? We shot down literally hundreds of theirs, but you very rarely read about one of ours being shot down, do you?

WILSON We don't read about it – no, but surely common sense tells you it must happen sometimes.

MAINWARING I don't want any of that sort of talk, Wilson. Some of those Nazi planes on their way back were obviously stricken. One was practically touching the roof tops. The one that was loosing off his machine gun.

WILSON (**He sniffs**) I think they must have hit the gas works.

MAINWARING (**Indicating gas ring**) You haven't lit it.

JONES (**Out of vision**) Left, right, left, right.

MAINWARING Here they are, we must get our hats, Wilson. Can't let the men see us improperly dressed.

They rush off to the office to get their hats. Jones appears at the door. The platoon file in, in single file and form up in threes.

JONES Right wheel, right wheel, mark time. (**He marks time himself**) Pick 'em up there, put some guts into it. Pick 'em up there, Godfrey.

GODFREY They don't go much higher, I'm afraid.

JONES Squad, halt.

Jones goes on marking time himself, he suddenly notices that he is the only one and stops. Mainwaring and Wilson enter.

JONES Right turn! (**This faces the squad to the back of the hall**) As you were, left turn! Sorry, Captain Mainwaring, sir, I got a little bit muddled there.

MAINWARING Never mind, Jones, just carry on.

JONES Very good, sir. Order arms! (**They start**) As you were. Now, I know we've been up all night, but when I give the order to order arms, I want to see you snap to it like one man. Order arms!

They execute the move a little raggedly.

JONES (**Chest swelling with pride**) That's more like it. (**Confidently to Mainwaring**) We mustn't let the men get slack, sir, must we, sir? The worst thing you can do with men is to let them get slack.

MAINWARING Thank you, Jones. Just hand back the ammunition.

JONES Ah, we haven't got none, sir.

MAINWARING Haven't got none. What have you done with it?

JONES I have to report, sir, that we engaged enemy plane with rapid fire, sir.

MAINWARING You did what?

FRAZER It was so low, you could almost touch it. Jonesey here was fixing his bayonet.

WILSON Are you sure it was one of theirs?

PIKE I saw it. It was a plain as the nose on your face, it was a Heinkel, Uncle.

WALKER He loosed off with his machine gun at Marks and Spencer's – Jewish firm you see.

FRAZER I never knew that.

WALKER 'Course it is.

JONES So we let 'em have it right up, sir. And, sir, I have to report, he did not like it, sir. They don't, you know. He weaved from side to side, then disappeared with black smoke coming from his engine nascels, sir.

WILSON You mean, you think you shot him down?

WALKER Either us or those two Spitfires on his tail.

MAINWARING This is very serious, Jones. You know perfectly well we only have five rounds each. If the enemy flings himself upon us tonight, this platoon will have to stay indoors, won't it?

JONES No, sir, we still have the bayonets, sir.

GODFREY And I still have my rounds, sir. I put them in a little pocket in my camel hair cardigan. By the time I'd undone all the buttons on my overcoat and battledress blouse er… the plane had passed out of sight.

WILSON One hardly knows whether to be pleased or sorry about that, does one, sir?

GODFREY The buttonholes are awfully small on those greatcoats. I don't know whether anything can be done about it.

WALKER I know a geyser what will fix that for you in a jiffy. Charge you a bob each.

GODFREY That seems very reasonable to me for new buttonholes.

WALKER He doesn't do that, he files down the buttons.

MAINWARING That'll do, Walker. We will have to report this to H.Q., Wilson. Meanwhile, attend to your rifles. The kettle's boiling.

GODFREY That's good news. I'm absolutely dying for a cup of tea.

PIKE Me too.

General assent from the platoon.

MAINWARING That comes later, Godfrey. Our first thought must be for our weapons. They need pulling through and boiling out.

FRAZER Here, just a minute. We're all gasping. We've been on guard all night.

MAINWARING We've all been on our toes all night, haven't we, Sergeant?

WILSON Yes, sir – in a manner of speaking.

MAINWARING But we're a front-line fighting unit. Our first thought must be for our weapons, they get the first water. Pull them through and boil them out.

Sounds of dissent from the troops.

MAINWARING Right then, that will be all. Carry on, Sergeant.

Mainwaring goes hastily into the office.

WILSON Yes, sir, er, em… fall out, you chaps.

FRAZER What a lot of bull. The inside of that rifle can wait, the inside of me can't.

OFFICE. DAY

Wilson enters.

MAINWARING I don't know what H.Q. are going to say about this, Wilson.

WILSON Do we have to tell them?

MAINWARING Of course we do. Otherwise, how are we going to replace the ammunition, it's like gold.

There is a knock on the door, Walker puts his head round the door and salutes.

WALKER Ah, excuse me, sir. This ammo, I think I can get it for you, sir, under the counter like.

MAINWARING No, Walker, thank you very much. It is quite out of the question.

WILSON How much will it cost?

WALKER Ah, it'll come out about a bob a round.

MAINWARING No, we couldn't possibly do it.

WILSON Where does it come from?

WALKER Oh, that's easy. There's an Irish Battalion at Galshead.

MAINWARING Surely, they don't sell their ammunition.

WALKER Get up the boozer, ten o'clock on a Saturday night and they'd sell the Pope.

MAINWARING That'll be all, Walker. Go and boil your rifle.

WALKER Sorry I spoke. **(Walker goes)**

WILSON If it's the money you're worried about, sir, I expect we could have a whip round.

MAINWARING I won't hear of it, Wilson. It's dishonest – it's my duty to report this to H.Q. and that's exactly what I'm going to do.

HALL

Jones amongst group of the platoon.

JONES Look, I don't like none of that Bolshie talk. We'll do what Captain Mainwaring says even if it is a lot a bull. Start pulling through yer rifles.

They turn their rifles over to get the pull throughs from their flaps.

WALKER He could've let us have a cup of char first, you know, Jonesey. I mean it's not as if we were regular soldiers, they can fall into kip after being on stand-by all night. We've got to go and do a day's work.

FRAZER You don't call what you do a day's work?

WALKER That whisky you get every week don't fall off a lorry of its own accord you know, it has to be pushed.

JONES It comes very hard when you have to work with the brain, like I do.

WALKER Come off it, Jonesey. All you have to do is give a couple of good wallops with your chopper and keep your fingers out of the way.

JONES That's all you know, Joe. You want to try it some time. Here I am with a long roll of boned rib. 'I'll have three books', she says. That's three 1s 8ds at 2s 2d a pound. Now, where do you slice it, that's the point, where do you slice it?

WALKER Go on, do what you always do, give 'em short weight and put your hand on the scales.

JONES That's libel, that is libel.

WALKER **(Indicating the pull through and the barrel)** Go on, bung it in the hole.

Jones makes a few attempts to put the pull through into the foresight end.

JONES You shouldn't make charges you can't substan... substan... substanti... these barrels are smaller than what they used to be, aren't they?

WALKER It goes in the other end, you silly old sirloin slicer.

Cut to Frazer, he is trying to pour hot water down the barrel. The fire bucket stands below to receive the water. He misses.

FRAZER That's a damn silly arrangement. Have yer no got a funnel?

GODFREY May I help?

FRAZER What makes you think you'd do any better?

GODFREY Well, I get quite a lot of practice. You see I have to fill my sisters' hot water bottles every night.

FRAZER All right. I'll hold and you pour.

PIKE That's right Mr Godfrey, you be mother.

Cut to Jones and Walker. Jones is struggling to pull through the pull through.

WALKER What's the matter, Jonesey?

JONES It's a bit stuck, Joe.

WALKER What have you shoved on the end? One of your old nightshirts?

OFFICE

Mainwaring puts down the phone.

MAINWARING That's done anyway.

WILSON What did they say?

MAINWARING It was only a sergeant clerk, he's taken the details.

WILSON Are we going to get the ammunition?

MAINWARING I'm sure they'll do their best.

WILSON Would you object, if I got Walker to er... sort of hire it?

MAINWARING What are you talking about, Wilson?

WILSON Well, perhaps he could get it on sale or return. What we don't use, we could send back.

MAINWARING This is war, Wilson, not the Rotary Club Dance. Well, I'd better see how the men are getting on. They seemed a bit truculent.

WILSON I think they're just a bit tired and thirsty, sir.

MAINWARING I'd better go in and boost their morale.

WILSON I wouldn't if I were you, sir.

MAINWARING You know, Wilson, I sometimes wonder if you have the stomach for this job.

WILSON Yes, there you have the advantage of me, sir.

Mainwaring turns and goes into the hall.

INTERIOR HALL

MAINWARING How are we getting on, men? Are those barrels all bright and shining? Ah, having trouble, Jones?

JONES It's a bit sticky, sir.

MAINWARING Let me try. **(He takes the rifle)**

JONES Mind you, sir, my right arm is not as powerful as it was of yesteryear, sir, through not having the quantity of joints to chop.

MAINWARING You know you get a better purchase if you wrap it round the hand. **(Mainwaring tries unsuccessfully)** What have you got on the end here?

JONES I think there's just a possibility it's got knotted, sir.

MAINWARING Ah, we must try other means, mustn't we? **(He goes to the banister – the Verger is polishing it)** A little wrinkle I learned in the last conflict. We tie the end to some immovable object... so... **(He twists the pull through round the banister)**

PIKE Just like Roy Rogers ties his horse.

GODFREY Trigger.

MAINWARING Then, all that's needed is a sharp jerk. (**He gives a sharp jerk, the banister breaks away**)

VERGER I just polished that.

MAINWARING I'm sorry, Verger, we'll have it mended for you.

VERGER The Vicar's going to play merry hell about this when I tell him.

MAINWARING Yes, all right, Verger. I'll talk to His Reverence in person.

VERGER He still hasn't got over you doing bayonet practice during evensong. Bloodcurdling it was, right in the middle of his responses.

MAINWARING We must evidently attach it to some more substantial object. (**He crosses to an upright supporting the gallery**) Ah, this will do.

PIKE If that comes away, sir, the whole hall will fall down.

MAINWARING Hardly likely to come away is it, Pike?

PIKE I suppose not, sir. (**Mainwaring tests it all the same and looks up in some trepidation**)

MAINWARING Here goes. (**He gives a very hard tug, the pull through breaks off short. Mainwaring looks at the top and the bottom**)

WILSON Poses a bit of a problem, doesn't it, sir?

MAINWARING I know that, Wilson.

WILSON Perhaps there's an armourer at Area Command.

MAINWARING Jones is not taking this to Area Command. He'd look a right fool, wouldn't he?

PIKE How about making the barrel red hot, that would burn it away.

MAINWARING This is a precision instrument, Pike.

GODFREY There's millions of red ants in one of our window boxes. If you pour a drop of honey down, they might eat it away – er – given time.

MAINWARING I don't think we have that much time, Godfrey.

WALKER I could get you the honey.

FRAZER Some powerful spirit's what you need.

WALKER What about a teaspoonful of Harpic, that clears most things.

MAINWARING Bring me that stair rod. (**He indicates the stair rods on the stairs leading to the stage**)

Pike goes to get it.

VERGER 'Ere, that's parish property, you know.

Pike goes with the stair rod, taking no notice.

VERGER Vandals!

PIKE Here you are, sir.

MAINWARING Shove that down. Now, give it a tap or two.

Frazer bangs it with the butt of his rifle, it jams. Mainwaring tries to move it but to no avail.

WILSON Oh that's much better, Frazer.

MAINWARING It should be all right now, Jones, we've got it started.

Mrs Pike enters.

MRS PIKE Where's my Frank?

PIKE Here I am, Mum.

MRS PIKE Where have you been? I've been worried sick about you.

PIKE We've been shooting at aeroplanes. We think we shot one down.

MRS PIKE Have you washed your face?

PIKE No, Mum. We've only just got back from shooting at aeroplanes.

MRS PIKE It's a disgrace. You're coming straight home with me and we're going to give it a good go with the flannel. Come along!

PIKE But, Mum, I've got to boil out my rifle.

MRS PIKE I'll soon see about that. Mr Mainwaring, he's coming straight home with me. It's a perfect disgrace keeping him out all night like this with a dirty face.

MAINWARING Mrs Pike, you must not keep barging in here, interfering with the running of my platoon.

MRS PIKE Then you want to run it better. Look at his hands. Show Mr Mainwaring your hands, Frank.

PIKE No, Mum.

MRS PIKE Show Mr Mainwaring your hands. (**He does so reluctantly**) There, do you go around with hands like that, Mr Mainwaring?

Mainwaring accidentally shows his hands.

MAINWARING No, of course I don't. It's not the point, Mrs Pike.

MRS PIKE (**Seeing rifle**) What are you trying to do with that?

MAINWARING He got it jammed.

MRS PIKE Come here with it. (**She ferrets in her handbag. Pike hands the rifle to her. She fishes inside the magazine with a button hook and pulls out the pull through. She hands it back**) No wonder it's jammed – there's a bit of string stuck in it. Come along, Frank.

TELECINE: FIELD. DAY

The platoon are on their hands and knees in line, crawling forward and searching.

PIKE I've found another one, Mr Jones.

GODFREY So have I, that makes seven.

JONES Keep at it, we need every cartridge case we can find, otherwise they won't replace them. Come on, Joe, give a hand.

WALKER I've got my five. I picked them up as I fired them.

JONES Now why didn't you hand 'em in?

WALKER I couldn't very well, could I? Want a light?

Close up of Walker's hand. Five cartridge cases made into lighters.

MAINWARING'S OFFICE. DAY

Close up of pile of empty ammunition on Mainwaring's desk.

MAINWARING That's good, Wilson, very good. Well worth the trouble.

WILSON I've been having a word with the lads. Between us, we'd be more than happy to buy the stuff from Walker.

MAINWARING I've told you, I will not be a party to that, Wilson. Besides, it's too late. Put those empty cases in the cupboard as evidence.

WILSON Evidence?

MAINWARING At the Court of Inquiry.

WILSON The what, sir?

MAINWARING **(Waving the letter)** Area have ordered us to have a Court of Inquiry, to enquire into the loss of 75 rounds of 300 ammunition.

WILSON Oh dear, oh dear, oh dear. Oh dear – oh dear – oh dear.

MAINWARING What on earth's the matter with you?

WILSON Nothing, sir, it's just that for a few paltry bob, we could have hushed it all up.

MAINWARING My motto is, and always has been 'honesty is the best policy'.

WILSON I would have thought that one about using a steam roller to crack a walnut would have been more suitable to the occasion, sir.

SECTION OF RAILWAY COMPARTMENT

Two Captains are sitting opposite each other. Captains Cutts and Pringle.

CUTTS I say, Pringle, it doesn't seem quite like the General to convene a Court of Inquiry about a little thing like this, does it?

PRINGLE He didn't want it. It was this pompous little Captain fellow – Mainwaring. We just asked, quite politely, why he needed more ammo. He started to get all regimental – saying he didn't want to cover anything up.

CUTTS Damn nuisance! I've got two tickets for that Leslie Henson show tonight – taking a Wren.

PRINGLE Commissioned?

CUTTS Not really. She's a sort of Midshipwoman.

PRINGLE Trust the Navy to think up something like that.

CUTTS We'll cut it short then, eh?

PRINGLE You bet. I'm having a five shilling utility dinner at the Ritz. I'm taking a F.A.N.Y.

CUTTS Commissioned?

PRINGLE I don't know, they all look alike to me.

INTERIOR HALL

A trestle table is drawn up camera left, with three chairs. Jones and Walker are at each end of a large Union Jack. Wilson is reluctantly directing operations.

PIKE Where does he want this, Uncle Arthur?

WILSON Don't ask silly questions, Frank.

PIKE It'd look very nice over the wall here like this – only you wouldn't be able to use the door. **(He drapes it over the entrance to the office)**

WALKER Perhaps Captain Mainwaring would like to drape it round himself like Britannia.

MAINWARING **(Entering for the last speech through folds of the Union Jack)** I don't think that's very funny, Walker. Put it over the table. We have two officers coming down from Area – show them we can do it properly.

WALKER Tell you what, I can get you half a dozen Coronation beer mugs. Each one has a picture of George VI with his crown on his bonce. Six bob each – very regal.

MAINWARING No, thank you, Walker, this is a Court of Inquiry. We won't have time for swilling beer.

Enter Jones in full dress uniform.

JONES Lance Corporal Jones reporting, sir.

MAINWARING Good heavens, what's that?

JONES Full dress uniform, sir. Lord Kitchener always liked to see us wearing it, sir, when we were on a fizzer. You'll notice the red coat, sir, worn by the British Army for over 200 years. Trouble was it used to show up and lots of soldiers got killed. They got fed up with this and one day in India they covered themselves in dust, and they didn't get shot any more. So hence the expression 'khaki'. That's an Urdu word, sir, it means dust. Hence the other expression 'not so dusty', you see…

MAINWARING That will do, Jones.

Enter Frazer with a sword wrapped in paper.

FRAZER I've brought ye my sword, sir.

MAINWARING What's that for?

FRAZER In the Navy, it has to go on the table in front of the Senior Officer.

WILSON Do we really need that, Frazer?

FRAZER We should no be having all this palaver at all, but if ye going to do it, do it properly.

JONES Frazer's right, sir. We used to have lots of swords on the table in the Sudan, sir. We always used to give them Fuzzie Wuzzies a fair trial, sir – before shooting them.

FRAZER You point it at the man if he's guilty.

Mainwaring has unwrapped the sword. The end of it bends at an angle of 45 degrees.

MAINWARING That's going to be a bit difficult.

FRAZER I used it to make toast at the fire.

MAINWARING It was a kind thought, Frazer. We'll keep it in reserve. Now, pay attention, men! I know some of you think I'm letting you down by calling in Area Command, but consider this. To fight for our homes and loved ones we must have ammunition. I know the way the Army works and this is the only way we'll get it.

Pike enters carrying an ammunition box.

PIKE Excuse me, sir. This has just arrived from Area H.Q. I think it's the ammunition.

MAINWARING Later, Pike. Ah well, obviously, they were impressed by the fact that we tackled the problem in the correct manner. Issue it at once, Sergeant Wilson.

Enter Godfrey.

GODFREY Excuse me, sir. Two offices from H.Q. are outside. They seem rather pleasant gentlemen, quite young.

MAINWARING Right, Sergeant, parade the witnesses outside. Bring them in here, Godfrey.

GODFREY Yes, sir.

Enter the Vicar and Verger. The Verger is carrying the banister.

VICAR Ah, Captain Mainwaring. Mr Yeatman here tells me there was an incident this morning.

VERGER Wanton vandalism it was.

VICAR Thank you, Mr Yeatman.

MAINWARING I've already told the Verger that we will be responsible for the repair.

VICAR Does seem a pity that you can't show more consideration for our property.

MAINWARING I'm sorry, but there is a war on you know. **(He sees the officers entering and salutes)** Good afternoon, gentlemen, it is all ready for you.

VERGER If you ask me, most of the damage is being done by the ones who are supposed to be on our side.

VICAR That'll do, Mr Yeatman.

JONES **(To Verger)** You've been a troublemaker for years, you have.

MAINWARING All right, Jones, we don't want to go into that now.

JONES Why do you always take the collection home to count it?

MAINWARING That'll do, Jones.

JONES It ought to be counted in the church.

MAINWARING Jones! Fall the men in outside. **(To Officers)** It's all ready for you, gentlemen. Do you mind, Vicar, I have a Court of Inquiry starting here.

VICAR And I have a meeting in my office, if I could see it for maps and guns. We'd better discuss this later.

VERGER Vandals!

VICAR **(As they go into the office)** Why do you take the collection home?

MAINWARING Sorry about that, gentlemen. Slight trouble in dealing with the civil power. **(To Officers)** Captain Mainwaring.

PRINGLE Captain Pringle.

CUTTS Captain Cutts. We're pretty keen to bash on, Captain Mainwaring, so may we start?

MAINWARING Of course.

PRINGLE We both have some pretty urgent affairs to attend to.

MAINWARING Right, sit down, we'll start right away.

Jones returns.

JONES Permission to speak, sir?

MAINWARING Yes, Jones.

JONES The men have fallen in, sir.

MAINWARING Good. You stand by to call in the witnesses. Sergeant Wilson will take down the evidence. I will now read the order convening the Court of Inquiry. **(He clears**

his throat) The Court of Inquiry will assemble at St Aldhelm's church hall, Walmington-on-Sea at 17.30 hours on Monday 12th May to enquire into the loss of 75 rounds of 300 ammunition.

An old man enters and walks tentatively to the centre.

MAINWARING By No.1 Platoon, B company, Walmington-on-Sea Home Guard. Er... do you mind? This is a private military Court of Inquiry.

MR BLEWITT Oh sorry. **(He turns to go out and sees Jones)** Has the Vicar's meeting been cancelled?

JONES No, Mr Blewitt, I think he's in the office.

Mr Blewitt starts towards the office, hobbling.

MR BLEWITT Ah, I thought it was funny if he cancelled it without telling me. Do you mind if I come through?

MAINWARING No, no of course not. Help him, Sergeant Wilson.

SIDE OFFICE CHURCH HALL

Jones and Wilson help Mr Blewitt as he hobbles across.

JONES It's good to see you getting about again, Mr Blewitt.

BLEWITT Oh, I'm much better now.

WILSON We missed seeing you in the bank.

BLEWITT Well I was 16 weeks with my leg up, you know.

CUTTS May we continue?

MAINWARING As quick as you can, Sergeant.

JONES You can't flash about at Mr Blewitt's time of life you know, Mr Mainwaring.

BLEWITT I'll be younger than you are.

CUTTS Shall we carry on?

MAINWARING Certainly. **(He reads)** A Court of Inquiry will assemble...

PRINGLE Shall we take that notice as read?

CUTTS Yes let's.

MAINWARING Oh, very well, gentlemen.

CUTTS Can we call the first witness?

JONES Permission to speak, sir?

MAINWARING Yes, Jones.

JONES I would like to volunteer to call first witness.

MAINWARING Get Private Walker, Jones.

JONES Call Private Walker! **(Moves to another position)** Call Private Walker! **(Moves again)** Call Private Walker! **(Returns to Mainwaring and Salutes)** I've called Private Walker, sir.

An old lady enters.

MAINWARING Now, Walker.

MRS DOWDING Is this the Vicar's meeting?

Walker enters behind.

MAINWARING **(Testily)** No. It's through there.

MRS DOWDING I thought it was funny, cancelling it without telling me.

WALKER Come on, darling. I'll walk you there.

CUTTS Is this going to happen throughout the entire proceedings?

MAINWARING No, I – I'll put a man on the door at once. Sergeant Wilson.

Wilson is on his feet ferreting through his pockets.

MAINWARING What's the matter, Wilson?

WILSON I seem to have mislaid my pencil, sir.

MAINWARING Great Scott, borrow this. **(He hands him one)** Jones! Stop anyone else coming in.

JONES Stop anyone else coming in! **(Moves)** Stop anyone else coming in! **(Moves again)** Stop anyone else coming in!

MAINWARING Now, Walker, we're enquiring into the loss of 75 rounds of 300 ammunition.

JONES **(Returns and salutes)** I've stopped anyone else coming in, sir.

MAINWARING Start your evidence, Walker.

PRINGLE **(Taking notes)** Name?

JONES Jones.

MAINWARING Not you.

WALKER **(Salutes)** Joe Walker. Wholesale supplier, scrap dealer and Private.

PRINGLE Now, what happened?

MAINWARING Shouldn't he be on oath?

PRINGLE He doesn't *have* to be, but I suppose if you want it that way, you can swear him.

MAINWARING It's my experience, gentlemen, that if you do a thing the right way, there are no comebacks. Where's the Bible, Wilson?

WILSON I haven't got one, sir.

MAINWARING I told you to provide one.

WILSON You never said a word about a bible.

MAINWARING Oh yes, I did – when I told you to order the extra milk.

WALKER I know where I could lay my hands on one. A quid – gold letters on the back – authorised version – no rubbish.

MAINWARING Stand to attention, Walker. There's no time

for that now. There must be a bible somewhere – get one from the church.

WILSON It's chained up, sir… for some extraordinary reason.

WALKER No bother, just nip in there, do the swearing, nip back here and do the chat.

JONES Permission to speak, sir?

MAINWARING Yes, Jones.

JONES In the office, sir, there's a book by Baden Powell – a fine man, sir, and very religious. He wore a boy scout hat, sir. Couldn't we use that, sir?

MAINWARING What the boy scout hat?

JONES No, sir, he wrote a book called 'Scouting for Boys'.

MAINWARING Don't be ridiculous.

PRINGLE Look, we're allowed to take evidence without oath, why don't we just get on with it?

MAINWARING Well, under the circumstances, I think perhaps we should.

WALKER **(Confidentially)** Look, if you want to play it my way I can lay my hands on 75 rounds at eight o'clock tonight. Two pounds ten.

MAINWARING Continue with your evidence, Private Walker.

WALKER Ah well, we were swanning around by the waterworks like, minding our own business, when out comes this dirty great Heinkel. 'Look at that, Jones', I says. Jones is the Corporal, you see.

WILSON Excuse me.

MAINWARING What is it now, Wilson?

WILSON I've only got as far as 'swanning around'.

PRINGLE But I've got the gist of it. Carry on.

WALKER Well, 'Look at that', I says. 'What?', says Jonesey. 'A big Heinkel', I says. 'Where?', he says. 'There', I says. 'I can't see it', he says, his eyes being on the blink, of course, he being the age he is. Course, he's over 70 and a bit deaf.

JONES I heard that.

MAINWARING All right, Jones. Go outside.

JONES I'm outside, sir.

PRINGLE Look, could we stick to the point?

MAINWARING Yes, Walker – just tell us about the shooting as quick as you can.

WALKER Yes, sir. Sorry, sir. So we shot at him.

CUTTS We'll need a teeny weeny bit more detail than that, won't we?

WALKER I was giving him more detail, wasn't I?

WILSON Suppose we take it from the point where you loaded your rifles.

PRINGLE What's far more important, who gave you the order to fire?

WALKER Ah, Jonesey. Corporal Jones.

MAINWARING Get that down, Wilson. Jones gave the order to fire. I think we're getting somewhere now, gentlemen.

From the side office comes the sound of the choir 'O Be Joyful in the Lord All Ye Lambs', etc.

PRINGLE What in heaven's name's that?

MAINWARING Excuse me, I'll soon attend to *this*. **(Crosses to the door)**

SIDE OFFICE. CHURCH HALL

Cut to the choir who are singing under the Vicar's direction. Mainwaring tries to get the Vicar's attention.

MAINWARING Excuse me, Vicar, Vicar.

The Vicar finally stops them.

VICAR What's the matter?

MAINWARING I've a very important Court of Inquiry, and I can't have all this.

VICAR I beg your pardon, Mr Mainwaring, but it is the church's hall, you know.

MAINWARING No it isn't. It's been requisitioned.

VICAR Not this room. This room is still church property.

MAINWARING But we can't carry on in there with all this noise.

VICAR If you can do your bloodcurdling bayonet practice during my responses, I can do my Jubilate during your Inquiry.

MAINWARING You and I are standing shoulder to shoulder, facing a common enemy. Can't we co-operate?

VICAR Oh, very well. We'll do something quiet – the 'Nunc Dimitis'. Lord, now lettest thou thy servant depart in peace. Nothing personal, Mr Mainwaring.

They start to sing softly. Mainwaring returns to the main hall.

INTERIOR HALL

MAINWARING I've dealt with that. I don't think there will be any more interruptions.

There is a flash of lightning and crash of thunder. Heavy rain is heard.

MAINWARING Right, Wilson, stand the men to. Stand by the sandbags, stirrup pump. Stretcher party fall in behind the scout hut.

Mainwaring exits.

In office – Mainwaring puts on tin hat.

Mainwaring returns to hall and goes to table.

WILSON It's not a bomb, sir, it was thunder.

MAINWARING Oh, I'm sorry. Let's continue, gentlemen.

The men start to pile into the hall led by Frazer.

MAINWARING What are all these men doing?

FRAZER We're not stopping out there, we're getting soaked to the skin.

GODFREY Perhaps you would allow us to fall in with an umbrella, sir. I have one extra that someone could borrow.

MAINWARING Oh, really.

PIKE If I get wet again, my mum will play hell.

MAINWARING Should we adjourn for half an hour gentlemen?

PRINGLE Great Scott, no!

CUTTS I definitely think we should continue.

MAINWARING But we can't have all the witnesses listening to each other.

PRINGLE Why don't Corporal Jones and the platoon demonstrate to us precisely what took place.

CUTTS I say, what a wizard idea.

MAINWARING Very well. Corporal Jones, show them what happened.

JONES Well, sir, when I saw the plane, sir, I remembered all you taught us about engaging enemy aircraft. You remember, sir, how you told us to camouflage our faces with khaki handkerchiefs.

MAINWARING That's right, Jones.

JONES Well we didn't have no time for that rubbish for a start. Then you said we was to scatter, well we did that all right. Then I gave the order. **(He listens)** I gave the order. **(He listens again)** Then I gave the order. **(He takes off his hat)**

MAINWARING Well, go on, Jones.

JONES Captain Mainwaring, I think I'm going... I can hear the voices of angels.

MAINWARING It's all right, Jones, it's not angels, it's the choir in the side office.

JONES Ah, I thought the harmony was a bit ropey.

WILSON Am I supposed to be taking all this down?

CUTTS For God's sake, no. What happens next?

FRAZER We remembered what you taught us, sir.

PLATOON That's right, sir.

General assent.

JONES 'Cock', I said. Go on lads, show them. **(They all cock their rifles)** 'Plane right', I said, just like you said, sir. **(They aim)** 'Swing with the plane' lads, swing with the plane, aim in front of it.' Just like you said – then I gave the order, 'shoot!'

MAINWARING Not shoot, fire!

There is a deafening report as the whole platoon fires. They all look up in awestruck silence. The Vicar appears in the doorway.

VERGER Vandals!

Something Nasty in the Vault

Originally titled, 'Don't Let Go'

SERIES THREE **EPISODE FIVE**

Recorded: Sunday 15/6/69

Original transmission: Thursday 9/10/69, 7.30–8.00pm

Original viewing figures = 11.1 million

ARTHUR LOWE .... CAPTAIN MAINWARING
JOHN LE MESURIER .... SERGEANT WILSON
CLIVE DUNN .... LANCE CORPORAL JONES
JOHN LAURIE .... PRIVATE FRAZER
JAMES BECK .... PRIVATE WALKER
ARNOLD RIDLEY .... PRIVATE GODFREY
IAN LAVENDER .... PRIVATE PIKE
JANET DAVIES .... MRS PIKE
BILL PERTWEE .... ARP WARDEN
ROBERT DORNING .... BANK INSPECTOR
NORMAN MITCHELL .... CAPTAIN ROGERS

OTHER MEMBERS OF HOME GUARD .... COLIN BEAN, FRANK GODFREY, DESMOND CULLUM-JONES

GIRL CLERK IN BANK .... YVONNE ARMITAGE

ATS GIRL .... CHRISTINE COLE

OLD LADY IN BANK .... EVE DEWHURST

• PETER DAY REMEMBERS •

'The bomb was a real one! A 50kg German unexploded bomb dropped on Petersham. It was made safe, then buried again, and rediscovered when drains were being dug in 1967.

'My son, Rupert, who was eight at the time, spotted it on his way home from school. The workman said he could have it, so he asked my wife if that was okay. She agreed, gave him her string bag and told him to go and get it. He replied: "Oh no, it's too big for that!" My brother was home at the time, so he and my wife went with Rupert to collect it. On the way back, he said to my brother: "Drive very slowly, you never know." But, of course, it was safe.

'It was some time later that *Dad's Army* needed a bomb, so my son's seemed the obvious choice. I copied the fuse and detonator from a replica in the Imperial War Museum, and fitted some twisted aluminium tail fins – the whole thing was heavy. It had to look right sitting on Mainwaring and Wilson's lap, so it was painted the appropriate colour, with correct German markings. It now resides in Richmond Museum.'

PETER DAY
Visual Effects Designer

Something Nasty in the Vault

MANAGER'S OFFICE. BANK. DAY

Mainwaring is sitting at his desk. There is a knock on the door.

MAINWARING **(Reading)** A-ha, the rats deserting the sinking ship – **(Knock)** Come in.

Pike enters with tea tray and Wilson.

PIKE Your tea, sir.

MAINWARING Thank you, Pike – I hope it's nice and hot.

PIKE Yes, sir.

MAINWARING Do you realise what the date is? **(He taps calendar)** It's exactly a year since we first heard that stirring call from Anthony Eden for Local Defence Volunteers.

WILSON So it is.

MAINWARING Exactly a year, Wilson, since we stood in this office, ready to fight to the last man – exactly a year since I was appointed leader of the platoon.

PIKE Many happy returns, sir.

WILSON If I remember rightly, sir, you appointed yourself leader.

MAINWARING Why must you always spoil everything, Wilson.

MAIN SECTION OF BANK

There are two grills. A clerk is behind one. Pike is behind the other. Jones comes in and goes up to Pike's section.

PIKE Morning, Mr Jones.

JONES Morning, Frank, how's Mr Mainwaring this morning?

PIKE I think he's a bit tired.

JONES All these night patrols getting him down, are they?

PIKE They're certainly getting my mum down – she says she's fed up with me and Uncle Arthur coming in at all hours.

JONES Well, none of us are getting enough sleep these days – still, with a war on, we've all got to get used to going a bit short.

PIKE That's what Uncle Arthur told my mum. **(Pointing to cheque in Jones' hand)** That your wages cheque for the staff, Mr Jones?

JONES Yes, here you are. **(He hands him the cheque)** It's a bit more this week. £2 12s 6d all together. That's 30s for Miss Mortimer in the cash desk. And 22s 6d for the boy, Raymond. He used to get a pound, but I'm giving him a rise this week.

PIKE I see. **(He starts to make the money up)**

JONES If you want to keep good staff these days, you've got to pay 'em, you know.

PIKE **(Counting it out)** That's two pound notes, one ten shilling note – and a half a crown £2 12s 6d. **(He puts it in a silver bag)**

JONES I'll put it in this old carrier. **(He puts it in a paper carrier)** I don't want everybody to know I'm carrying the wages – I might get knocked on the head. So long. **(Turns to go, and sees Walker)**

WALKER **(In a loud voice)** Hullo Jonesey – getting the wages are you?

JONES Ssssh, not so loud, Joe. **(He hurries out)**

WALKER Hullo, Pikey **(He pushes a huge bundle of filthy notes and a paying-in book across the counter)**

PIKE Morning, Mr Walker. You paying in again? It's the third time this week.

WALKER Well, I can't keep it all under the mattress, can I? It gets so lumpy! **(He laughs)**

Pike is counting the notes – he pulls out a fiver and holds it up to the light.

PIKE This five pound note looks a bit funny to me, Mr Walker.

WALKER Blimey, don't say it's a dud.

A sharp man in a bowler hat and pince-nez glasses stands behind Walker.

PIKE I'd better show it to Mr Mainwaring.

WALKER All right, hurry up – I'll mind the shop and see nobody takes anything. **(He nudges man in bowler hat and laughs – man stares hard and says nothing)** You putting it in, or taking it out?

Man stares.

Walker lowers his voice.

WALKER Want to buy some clothing coupons – shilling each?

WEST No, thank you.

WALKER Tell you what, to you, a special price – 10s a dozen.

WEST No, thank you.

WALKER Petrol coupons?

WEST No, I don't have a car.

WALKER Ah, I can help you there.

Mainwaring comes back with Pike.

MAINWARING Now, look here, Walker – this five pound note is a forgery.

WALKER Wait a minute – wait a minute – what's all this Walker business – I'm not on parade now you know. I'm a customer.

Pike laughs.

MAINWARING **(To Pike)** All right, Pike, I'll attend to this. The point is, I cannot accept this, er… Mr Walker.

WALKER Are you sure it's a fake?

MAINWARING Of course it's a fake – and a very clumsy one, too – only a fool would be taken in by it . Who gave it to you?

WALKER You did.

MAINWARING When? **(Ad lib)**

WALKER Last week – don't you remember, those two bottles of whisky I got you?

MAINWARING Oh, I see. **(He lowers his voice and leans across)** All right, I'd better give you five more. **(He takes out his wallet, counts out five ones – and puts the fake fiver back in his wallet)**

Man behind looks very suspicious and tries to overhear what is being said.

WALKER You want to be a bit more careful with your money, Mr Mainwaring.

MAINWARING **(Feeling his chin)** Listen, can you get me some razor blades?

WALKER They're a bit scarce – but I can let you have a dozen – ten bob.

MAINWARING That's a bit steep.

WALKER Well, I said they were scarce – give me the money now, and I'll let you have them tonight.

MAINWARING All right – **(He takes a pound out of his wallet)** Have you got change? Don't bother, I'll take two ten shilling notes from your money. **(He puts his own pound note on top of Walker's money – takes two ten shilling notes – business with notes)**

PIKE One, two, three…

WALKER You're a financial wizard, Mr Mainwaring. No wonder they made you bank manager. **(He laughs)**

MAINWARING I shall see you on parade tonight then, *Mr Walker.*

WALKER I shall be there, *Mr Mainwaring* – meanwhile, don't take any more dud fivers, will you? **(He laughs)**

Mainwaring turns to go.

MR WEST Mr Mainwaring?

MAINWARING Yes, sir.

MR WEST May I have a word with you, please?

Mainwaring lifts up flap and comes through.

MAINWARING Certainly, sir.

MR WEST My name's West.

MAINWARING How do you do, Mr West. Do you want to open an account?

WEST No, I'm an inspector from the head branch.

MAINWARING Yes, well er… Perhaps we'd better go into my office.

WEST Yes, perhaps we had.

Mainwaring opens door to West, but West goes through flap.

MAINWARING Are you there?

WALKER **(To Pike)** Blimey, a bank inspector – what has Mr Mainwaring been up to?

MAINWARING'S OFFICE. BANK

Mainwaring and West come into office – Mainwaring closes the door.

MAINWARING Let me take your hat and gas mask, sir. **(He takes hat, umbrella and gas mask. He hangs it up on the coat rack – on the rack are three steel helmets, gas masks, two bayonets and frogs – and Wilson and Pike's rifles, propped against the wall. He takes his revolver holster down from the rack – crosses to his desk and sits down, putting the revolver on the desk. He points to chair)** Please sit down, sir.

WEST Thank you. **(Points to revolver)** Do you always interview people with a revolver on your desk, Mainwaring?

MAINWARING Oh yes, sir – especially in the spring.

WEST What's the spring got to do with it?

MAINWARING Surely you realise, sir – that Hitler's only been waiting for the spring to invade.

WEST And I suppose you think that you're going to stop him, with that pop gun.

MAINWARING Not only me, sir – there's the rest of my platoon as well – we're all fully armed and trained to kill.

WEST Really? Well, I'll get to the point, Mainwaring – your monthly reports to Head Office have been getting very irregular lately.

MAINWARING May I remind you, sir – that I not only have the bank to look after, **(on rise)** but also the security of this entire stretch of coast, from Stone's Amusement Arcade to the Novelty Rock Emporium.

WEST You know, a lot of you chaps are going to be heartbroken when this war's over, Mainwaring – you love being in the Home Guard – it gives you all the opportunity you want to dress up and strut about in uniform.

Mainwaring gets up – puffs himself up and struts around the desk.

MAINWARING For your information, Mr West – I never strut about.

For the first time, West notices the Lewis gun propped up against the sandbags at the window.

WEST Good heavens, what's this great gun doing here?

MAINWARING That is a Lewis Machine Gun Mark I – we keep it there in the day time – it covers the entire High Street from Stead and Simpson to Timothy White's.

WEST Do you mean to say that you'd use it to shoot at Germans?

MAINWARING If they came out of Timothy White's, yes.

WEST But they might shoot back.

MAINWARING Quite probably.

WEST But the bank would get damaged – really, Mainwaring, this is highly irregular. You realise I shall have to report this to Head Office.

The sirens go.

MAINWARING Excuse me, sir. **(He opens the door and shouts)** Sergeant Wilson – Private Pike!

He takes off his jacket – puts on his uniform blouse.

Wilson and Pike come into the office – take off their coats and start to put on their uniform jackets. From now on the scene is played at terrific pace.

MAINWARING **(Strapping on his revolver)** This is Mr West from Head Office. Sergeant Wilson, my Chief Clerk.

WILSON How do you do?

MAINWARING And Private Pike – one of my cashiers.

Pike nods – he and Wilson are putting on their tin hats and the rest of their equipment.

MAINWARING What day is it today, Pike?

PIKE **(Coming to attention)** Thursday, sir.

MAINWARING And what plan do we use on Thursday, Sergeant?

WILSON Plan 'B', sir.

MAINWARING All right, Sergeant, put it into operation.

WILSON Yes, sir. **(He moves to door)**

PIKE Excuse me, sir – can I put plan 'B' into operation – you promised me I could last week.

MAINWARING That's what I like to hear, keenness – you don't mind do you, Wilson?

WILSON **(Standing back)** Not at all, sir.

MAINWARING Go ahead, Pike.

PIKE **(Moves to the door – opens it smartly and shouts in clear efficient voice)** Attention all staff – attention all staff. Plan 'B' will be put into operation at once – all non-combatant members of the staff will proceed at once to shelter 'A' – Captain Mainwaring, Sergeant Wilson and Private Pike will proceed to shelter 'C'.

MAINWARING Well done, Pike – there's good potential N.C.O. material there, Wilson.

WILSON Yes, sir. Awfully good.

MAINWARING **(To West)** You see, sir – it all works just like a well oiled – smooth – precision machine – no panic – no fuss.

WEST Very good, Mainwaring. There's just one little thing you've forgotten.

MAINWARING What's that?

WEST Today happens to be Friday.

MAINWARING What? **(To Pike)** You stupid boy – go and stop the staff at once.

BANK MANAGER'S OFFICE

The All Clear is going. We can hear the office door being unlocked. It opens – in comes West, Mainwaring, Wilson and Pike. Wilson and Pike put their rifles down and quickly change.

WEST Really, Mainwaring, what a waste of time – two hours we've been sitting in that shelter doing nothing. All we heard was one plane – for all we know it might have been one of ours.

PIKE Oh no, sir, it was definitely a Dornier – you could tell by the noise of the engines – it went. **(He does engine noise)**

MAINWARING That will do, Pike.

WILSON He's quite right, you know, sir. It's a sort of high-pitched whine. **(He does engine noise)** Now, if it was one of ours it would be much lower – like this. **(He does the noise)**

MAINWARING Yes, you can always tell a Jerry plane – it's a sort of nasty, high, foreign sound. **(He does the noise)**

They are all standing in a circle just below the glass roof of the office.

WEST This is no time for a lecture on enemy aircraft.

MAINWARING Pike, go and get on with your work.

WILSON Yes, get out Frank.

WEST I shall have to… **(Suddenly he looks up and sees a large hole in the glass fanlight)** Good Lord, look at that. How did that hole get there?

MAINWARING That's strange, I've never noticed that before, have you, Wilson?

WILSON No, I haven't.

WEST **(Hopping mad)** You fools – you fools – while you've been sitting in that shelter, playing soldiers – someone's broken into the bank. Quick, call the police.

MAINWARING Now, don't panic, sir. All the money's downstairs in the strong room.

WEST What's this then? **(He picks up a pound note off the floor)** And this and this... **(He picks up more notes)**

MAINWARING All right, sir, I'll phone the police. **(He crosses round to behind his desk)** I must say I think you're taking a very high handed...

Suddenly he disappears.

WEST Good gracious – where did he go to?

WILSON I've really no idea, sir – most extraordinary. **(He crosses round behind the desk)** Mr Mainwaring are you... **(He disappears)**

WEST This is absurd – what are they playing at? **(He crosses round behind the desk – he sees a large hole in the floor – there are one pound notes lying round the edge of it)** Someone's broken into the strong room! **(He frantically picks them up. Then shouting down the hole)** They've broken through the floor into the strong room, Mainwaring – Mainwaring are you down there?

MAINWARING Look out, Wilson, it's slipping – don't let it hit the ground... get hold of it, man.

WILSON I am getting hold of it – it's heavy.

MAINWARING All right, I've got my end, lower it down – easy – don't jog it, whatever you do. Easy...

WEST **(Out of vision)** What's going on down there, Mainwaring...? Can you hear me, Mainwaring...? Mainwaring.

THE STRONG ROOM

Mainwaring and Wilson are sitting on the floor with a medium-sized bomb in their arms. The main weight of the bomb is taken by a broken beam. The place is in chaos, shelves broken – deed boxes scattered – broken bags of silver – and notes are lying everywhere.

WILSON If you could sort of lower your end, sir – we might be able to squeeze out.

MAINWARING Stop it, Wilson... the slightest movement and it could go off.

WILSON But we can't sit here all day holding this thing, sir.

MAINWARING If you don't stop joggling it, Wilson, we'll be sitting on a cloud holding a harp.

WEST **(Shouting down hole)** Why don't you answer me, Mainwaring – have they taken much? Mainwaring! **(He forces his head through the hole – and we can see it upside down)** Mainwaring – Wilson – why are you sitting there like that – what's that thing you're holding?

WILSON I think it fell out of that plane, that you thought was one of ours.

WEST You fools! You fools! My God, it's a bomb – a bomb! **(He panics)** I'm stuck, I can't get out! **(He tries to wriggle free)** That thing could go off any minute – what would Head Office think! **(At last he pulls himself free)** I'll go and get help – don't go away!

West rushes out of office, nearly knocking Jones over.

Jones comes in and closes door.

JONES That was Shell that was. I've got your sausages, Mr Mainwaring, they've just come in and I thought – that's funny... **(He shouts)** ... Mr Mainwaring!

• BILL HARMAN REMEMBERS •

'This is my favourite episode. I remember as a young man, new to television, being privileged to watch the performances close-up of Arthur Lowe and John Le Mesurier in that cramped set of the bank vault, with the bomb on their lap. Just two men, their dialogue and their reactions. A triumph of comedy writing, casting and performance.'

MAINWARING **(Out of vision)** Is that you, Jones?

JONES Yes, I've brought your sausages. Where are you?

MAINWARING **(Out of vision)** I'm here.

JONES Where? Oh, I get it, you're doing a camouflage... that's good that is, I can't see you at all.

MAINWARING I'm here.

JONES I give up, Mr Mainwaring, you're too good for me – I tell you what – you give me a clue. **(He moves away from the desk)** Am I getting warmer?

Jones crosses to behind desk.

JONES Am I getting any warmer now?

WILSON You're very warm indeed, Jones.

Jones sees the hole in the floor and goes down on his knees.

JONES **(Shouting down through the hole)** You'd no need to go to all that trouble, Mr Mainwaring, just to hide from me. I've brought you some sausages. I know you like a nice banger.

WILSON We've got one of our own, Jones.

Jones puts his head right through the hole.

MAINWARING Now, listen to me very carefully, Jones. Go and get *help.*

JONES Blimey, is that a bomb you and Mr Wilson are holding?

MAINWARING Of course it's a bomb, man, go and get help.

Jones quickly pulls his head back and straightens up.

JONES Don't worry, Mr Mainwaring. **(He rushes about and shouts down the hole)** Don't panic, don't panic. I'm in charge of things now. **(He opens the door and shouts)** Private Pike, in here at the double. **(Shouting down hole)** All right, Mr Mainwaring, Mr Wilson – hang on.

Pike comes in.

PIKE What is it, Mr Jones?

• DAVID CROFT REMEMBERS •

'The set for this episode was on two levels: we had the basement where the bomb was and the office upstairs. Two cameras were positioned up on top and the rest down below; cameras in those days were extremely heavy so you couldn't keep moving them between the two sets.'

JONES I'm putting this bank under martial law. There's an unexploded bomb down in the strong room.

PIKE Well, what are we doing here? We'd better get everyone out of the bank – it might go off.

JONES It won't go off – Mr Mainwaring and Mr Wilson are holding it.

PIKE Oh, that's all right then... What?

JONES Now, listen, I'm going to clear everyone out of the bank – then I'm going over to my shop to phone up the bomb disposal people, and they will do that... then I'll get as many of the platoon together as I can and come back here –

PIKE What shall I do, Mr Jones?

JONES Put your tin hat on – get your rifle and bayonet – and don't let anyone in this room, except me.

PIKE But supposing the bomb goes off – what shall I do then?

JONES You'll just have to use your initiative. Shan't be long. **(He goes out – then returns)** Don't panic! **(He exits again)**

Pike puts on his tin hat – gets his rifle from the corner and fixes his bayonet. He crosses to the hole and looks down.

PIKE Mr Mainwaring – Uncle Arthur, are you down there? **(He is now right in the hole and his head is upside down)** Uncle Arthur, are you down there?

STRONG ROOM

Pike's head is upside down in the hole.

PIKE Is that *the* bomb you're holding?

MAINWARING What's happening up there, Pike?

PIKE Mr Jones has taken charge of everything – so you've no need to worry, sir.

MAINWARING We've every need to worry. Has he sent for the bomb disposal people?

PIKE Yes, sir, he's phoning them.

MAINWARING Well, that's some comfort, Wilson. We shan't have long to wait now.

WILSON There's only one problem, sir. How's he going to get into the strong room? There's only two keys and we've got them both in our pockets.

MAINWARING He'll just have to come down through the hole, won't he?

PIKE Uncle Arthur?

WILSON Oh, what is it, Frank?

PIKE Do you think I ought to phone mum and tell her you're holding a bomb.

WILSON NO!

PIKE But she might get cross if she found out that you'd been holding a bomb and she wasn't told about it.

MAINWARING Listen, Pike – have you cleared everyone out of the bank?

PIKE Mr Jones was doing it, sir.

MAINWARING Well, go and make sure – just get the staff out of the bank.

Pike gets up, moves to the door, stops and goes back to the hole.

PIKE What plan shall I tell them to put into operation sir? A, B, C, D or E?

MAINWARING **(Frantic)** Any bloody plan!

PIKE Oh! **(He crosses to door, opens it and shouts)** Attention all staff – attention all staff – put – er... plan 'A' into operation. – All non-combatant members of the staff will...

Warden comes into picture.

WARDEN Who are you shouting at, lad?

PIKE The staff. I'm putting plan 'A' into operation.

WARDEN What are you talking about? There's nobody there. Now, look here, what's going on? Some wild-eyed lunatic came charging into the A.R.P. post saying there was an unexploded bomb in the bank. Is it true?

He comes into the office. Pike leaps back and points his rifle and bayonet at him.

PIKE Get back – get back.

WARDEN You gone barmy or something?

PIKE No, get back – Mr Jones said I wasn't to let anyone into this office except him. This bank is under martial law.

They are both circling around the desk.

WARDEN Put that thing down – I'm only trying to help.

PIKE I don't care – I've got my orders and nothing's going to stop me from carrying them out. (**Suddenly he disappears**)

Mainwaring and Wilson are showered with debris.

WARDEN Blimey! (**He goes round behind the desk. Pike has fallen through the hole up to his arms**) What are you playing at? (**He pulls Pike out and pushes his head through into the hole**) S'truth – is that a bomb you're holding, Mr Mainwaring?

MAINWARING If someone says that again, Wilson – I shall go mad!

WARDEN Do you realise that bomb could blow up half the High Street? Now look, this is an A.R.P. matter and I'm taking charge of the situation – now, just stay where you are…

He draws his head back.

STRONG ROOM

MAINWARING I don't know which gives me the greater comfort, Wilson – to know that he's in charge – or Jones.

WILSON I think Jones has our interest more at heart, sir.

Pause.

MAINWARING Are you frightened, Wilson?

WILSON Well, now that you've brought it up, sir, I must confess that I am.

MAINWARING So am I.

WILSON Not only that, sir, I've got this terrible itching on the end of my nose.

MAINWARING I tell you what, Wilson – if you bring your right hand round to the top of the bomb – and I take my right hand away for a minute – I can scratch your nose.

WILSON That's awfully good of you, sir.

They change their hands round – Mainwaring scratches Wilson's nose.

MAINWARING How's that, Wilson?

WILSON Much better, sir.

MAINWARING (**Goes to scratch it again**) Any more?

WILSON No thank you, sir. That's just right.

MAINWARING'S OFFICE

Frazer, Walker, Godfrey, Pike and Jones and three other members of the platoon are standing round the hole, they all have their steel helmets and their H.G. jackets on. The desk has been moved.

FRAZER (**To Jones**) How long since you phoned the bomb disposal people?

JONES About 20 minutes – they said they'd get here as soon as they could.

FRAZER (**Shouting down hole**) Are you all right, Captain Mainwaring – is there anything you need?

WALKER (**Trying to comfort them**) By the way, I've got your razor blades, Mr Mainwaring.

FRAZER That's a stupid remark, that is – I mean he's not going to want to shave at a time like this.

WALKER I'm just trying to comfort him. When you're under stress it helps to talk about normal everyday things.

GODFREY Yes, I think we really ought to try and keep things as normal as possible.

MAINWARING'S VOICE Corporal Jones!

JONES Yes, sir.

MAINWARING'S VOICE Now, listen to me. Get the men out of the bank… You can't do anything and there's no point in you risking your lives for nothing.

WALKER He's right you know. I don't think there's any point in hanging about either. I mean, after all, what can *we* do?

JONES I see, it's like that is it? Anybody else want to go?

WALKER Look, I didn't say I wanted to go, did I? I just said there's not very much we *can* do if we stay.

FRAZER I don't care about that – I'm staying here with the Captain and Mr Wilson.

JONES What about you, Mr Godfrey?

GODFREY I'd rather stay if you don't mind – I know we can't do very much, but I'm sure it's a comfort for them to know that we're here. After all, Mr Mainwaring wouldn't leave us, would he?

PIKE And I couldn't leave my Uncle Arthur – my mum wouldn't like it.

JONES **(To the three other members of the platoon)** Are you blokes staying? **(They all nod)** All right, Joe – if you want to go – you'd better go.

WALKER Who said anything about going – you silly old duffer. All I said was...

The door opens and in comes the A.R.P. Warden and with Captain Rogers – he is a very large man.

WARDEN What do you lot think you're doing? No one's allowed in here – I've cleared the street.

JONES Well you're not clearing us out – I happen to be in charge.

WARDEN Oh no you're not – this is an A.R.P. matter – and I'm in charge.

JONES Now don't you come it with me, mate – I tell you I'm in command.

FRAZER Aye, that's right, and I'm second in command.

ROGERS **(Shouting)** Look, I'm Captain Rogers, Bomb Disposal and I'm in command. Now, where's the bomb?

JONES **(Coming to attention)** Oh yes, sorry, sir – **(Pointing down hole)** It's down there.

Captain Rogers goes down on his knees and looks down hole.

ROGERS You chaps all right?

MAINWARING Yes, thank you, sir.

ROGERS We'll soon get you out of that mess, I expect. Who keeps the key to the strong room door?

MAINWARING We do, sir – there are only two, and we've got them both on us. Can't you come down through the hole?

ROGERS I wouldn't like to jump down there with my weight – it might set the thing off. Hold on. **(He stands up)** Hmm... tricky – very tricky. There are only two keys – and they've got them both.

JONES **(Coming to attention)** Permission to speak, sir?

ROGERS I beg your pardon?

JONES Let me go down and get the keys, sir – let me go down. I'm thin enough to get through the hole.

FRAZER No, sir – let me go down. I'm much more wiry than he is.

JONES Oh no you're not – I'm more wiry than you are.

ROGERS I can't risk anybody going down there – there's only a bit of wreckage holding that bomb. Someone jumping down could easily dislodge it – and the whole lot would go sky high!

WARDEN Well, if you don't want me anymore – I'll just make sure the street's clear.

He goes.

FRAZER You leave it to me, sir – I think I've got something in my shop that will do the trick.

MAINWARING'S OFFICE

Frazer is sitting on a chair beside the hole. Rogers and the rest of the platoon are gathered round him – Frazer has a fishing rod and the line goes through the hole. The picture is held for a beat of four.

ROGERS **(Shouting down hole)** Are you ready, Mainwaring?

MAINWARING Ready.

ROGERS **(To Frazer)** All right – start to swing it.

FRAZER Aye, sir. **(He starts to swing the line)**

STRONG ROOM

We can see the fishing line swinging through the hole. Instead of a float, it has a weight on it and a fairly large hook underneath.

MAINWARING All right, Wilson – keep your end steady – I'm going to try and catch it. Once more. Try again.

Wilson now has his left arm underneath the bomb and his right arm over the top.

Mainwaring makes several attempts to catch the line.

MAINWARING'S OFFICE

Frazer has the rod which is bending – the line is very tight.

ROGERS All right – take it easy now.

FRAZER I've got a bite!

STRONG ROOM

Wilson's end of the bomb is shaking up and down.

MAINWARING What are you doing, Wilson – for Gawd's sake, don't pull it – hold it steady, man.

WILSON I can't help it, sir – it's this fishing line.

We now see that the hook is caught in his sleeve. As the line pulls, it jerks his arm up and down.

MAINWARING **(Shouting)** Stop pulling – the line's caught. **(Frazer stops pulling)** Now, keep very still, Wilson and I'll try and creep my hand across and unhook you.

Mainwaring slowly passes his hand across Wilson's chest and unhooks the line. He brings it back, holds it in his teeth.

MAINWARING Keep it still – don't pull now, whatever you do. **(He gets the keys from his pocket and puts them on the hook and then holds the line)** All right, haul away slowly.

The line goes out of shot.

WILSON Just look at that tear, sir – this is my best jacket.

MAINWARING Really, Wilson, fancy worrying about a little tear at a time like this.

WILSON It's not me, sir – what's Mrs Pike going to say?

JONES **(Through hole)** All right, sir – we've got the keys. The Captain's on his way down now.

MAINWARING Thank goodness for that.

There is the sound of the strong room door being unlocked. It opens and Rogers comes in with a Gladstone bag – he puts on his best bedside manner.

ROGERS How are we today then, all right?

MAINWARING As well as can be expected.

ROGERS **(He kneels down beside the bomb and opens his bag and takes out a stethoscope. He looks at the bomb)** Hmmm… I thought so – it's an S.c.50 – at least I think it is. **(He hums to himself and runs a tape measure over the bomb)** Hmmm… Let me see now, circumference 630 mm, length 1,095 mm. Yes, it's a 50 kilogramme all right. Just one more check. **(Takes out notebook and thumbs through it)** We want to know what we're tackling, don't we?

MAINWARING It would be as well.

ROGERS Yes, this is the boy – contains 25 kilogrammes of High Explosive – makes a crater six metres in diameter and three metres deep. I thought they'd stopped dropping these.

MAINWARING Is this a small bomb then?

ROGERS Oh – Good Lord – yes! They're dropping mostly 100 kilogramme ones now. This Johnny shifts about 37 cubic metres of stuff.

WILSON Er… what sort of stuff?

ROGERS Anything that's near it. Mind you, I have a pet theory that with these bombs – there is a dead area. And if you're standing in the right position all you get is a slight concussion. Wouldn't want to put it to the test though – would you – har!

Mainwaring and Wilson exchange looks. Rogers puts his stethoscope to his ears and starts to listen to the bomb. We can hear the sound of Mainwaring and Wilson's heartbeats.

ROGERS Can't hear a damn thing – your heartbeats are vibrating against the casing – would you mind holding your breaths please? Right – deep breath in – hold it – out – another please – hold it – out. That's all right.

WILSON Can we let it out now?

ROGERS Oh yes, all right. Nothing to worry about there – I think we can penetrate.

He unscrews the small plate on the side of the bomb and looks inside.

ROGERS Hm… nasty, very nasty – we've got a trembler.

MAINWARING That makes three of us – is that bad?

ROGERS **(Starts to screw cap back on)** I shall need a special tool to deal with that. I'm afraid I'll have to nip back to H.Q. Now, whatever you do, don't tip it – keep it level – do you understand? Keep it absolutely level.

They both nod their heads in misery.

ROGERS Shan't be long. **(He goes. He turns at the door)** I'd better close the door, we don't want anyone to pinch anything.

WILSON I don't think I can stand very much more of this, sir.

MAINWARING Come on, Wilson, you must cheer up. There's a destiny that shapes our ends – rough hew them how we may. **(Wilson gives him a look – pause – Mainwaring clears his throat)** I'm reminded of the story of the Australian soldier, who arrived at the front line and he was greeted by a British officer who said – 'Ah! My man, have you come here to die?' And the Australian soldier replied – 'No – I came here yesterday' D'you get it? Wilson? – It's a play on words – die – day. **(He looks at Wilson with a terrible forced smile)**

WILSON Yes, sir, I think I get it.

He forces a smile – they both look down at the bomb – the smiles freeze on their faces.

THE STRONG ROOM

Mainwaring and Wilson have got their eyes closed – there is the sound of terrific hammering and sawing from the office above, and voices all talking at once.

FRAZER **(His head coming through the hole)** All right, Mr Mainwaring, Mr Wilson – hold on, we're going to get you out of there.

His head goes and Walker's takes his place.

WALKER You've got nothing to worry about – we've got everything organised up here.

His head goes and Godfrey's takes its place.

GODFREY Excuse me, Mr Mainwaring, Mr Wilson – would you care for a cup of coffee?

WILSON How awfully nice.

MAINWARING Thank you, Godfrey, that would be very welcome.

Godfrey's head goes and then comes back.

GODFREY One lump or two, sir?

MAINWARING Two please.

GODFREY What about Mr Wilson?

WILSON No sugar for me, thank you.

His head goes – Jones takes his place.

JONES We're nearly ready now, sir.

MAINWARING What's going on up there, Jones?

JONES You'd be surprised, sir.

MAINWARING'S OFFICE

They have rigged up a derrick which consists of three wooden uprights lashed to the desk – at one side of the hole. Across the top of the upright, stretched to and resting on the sandbags at the window, is a steel bar from Jones' shop. Tied under the bar is a block and tackle. Jones is testing the rope. The rope has a large hook at the end, is threaded through the block, and stretches out through the office door into the main bank. Pike, Sponge and the other two Privates are holding it.

JONES Right, lower away, when I give the signal.

They lower Jones through the hole.

THE STRONG ROOM

Jones appears through ceiling and is lowered down.

JONES **(Getting off rope)** I didn't give you the signal. You've got nothing to worry about now, sir.

MAINWARING What on earth are you going to do, Jones?

JONES We're going to get that bomb off you, sir.

MAINWARING I think we'd better wait until Captain Rogers gets back.

JONES He's gone back to H.Q., sir – he may be ages and there's no time to lose.

WILSON I think he's right, sir – it's worth a try.

The door opens. Frazer, Godfrey and Walker come in. Frazer is carrying some rope – Godfrey has a tray and two cups of coffee.

GODFREY Here's the coffee, sir.

He holds a cup to Mainwaring's mouth – Walker holds the other cup to Wilson's mouth. Frazer starts tying the rope to one end of the bomb.

JONES All right, a bit lower...

GODFREY Coffee, sir.

MAINWARING That's the one without the sugar.

Godfrey gives them a drink.

Frazer throws a piece of rope to Godfrey.

FRAZER Here – tie this on the end.

Godfrey puts down the cup and ties the rope round the end of the bomb.

GODFREY **(To Walker)** Would you mind putting your finger there, please?

Walker has a five pound note in his hand.

MAINWARING Put that money down at once, Walker!

WALKER Sorry, sir, it stuck to me hand. All this money lying about, keeps getting in the way.

He sticks his finger on the knot. Godfrey ties a very nice bow.

FRAZER What kind of knot do you call that?

GODFREY I used to use it on the Christmas parcels in the Civil Service Stores. I think it's called a cupid's bow.

Frazer pulls the bow and it comes undone.

FRAZER It's a good job I didn't have you with me in the Navy.

GODFREY Oh, I don't know – I might have quite enjoyed it. I always fancied the idea of being a sailor.

JONES Are you ready, Jock?

FRAZER **(Giving the rope a tug)** Aye, this should do the trick.

Jones brings the hook over and attaches it to the rope.

JONES Right, I'll stay here – you other three get up top and help pull.

GODFREY **(Taking cups)** Don't worry about the cups, sir. I'll wash them up later.

Godfrey, Frazer and Walker go.

JONES Now, what we're going to do, sir, is to pull this bomb up out of the way and then tie it off. I should think you'll get a mention for this, sir. **(He shouts)**

MAINWARING I shouldn't think so.

JONES Never mind, sir. I'll give you half a pound of liver when it's all over. **(He shouts)** All right – take the strain. **(The rope tightens)** Are you ready? **(Shouts of 'yes')** Right – heave!

The bomb flies up in the air – Jones, who has been holding the rope, goes up with it. He hits his head on the ceiling.

JONES Bring it down! Bring it down!

The bomb comes down a few feet and starts to spin.

MAINWARING Hold it, Wilson! It's spinning!

WILSON You all right, Jonesey?

JONES Yes, thank you, sir.

Mainwaring and Wilson jump to their feet.

MAINWARING My legs have gone to sleep.

WILSON Perhaps if you rubbed them, sir, it might help.

MAINWARING Don't bother about me – stop that bomb spinning.

Wilson drops Mainwaring – reaches up to bomb and stops it spinning.

WILSON Are you all right, Jonesey?

JONES Yes, thank you, Mr Wilson. **(He climbs up through the hole and he shouts at the men)** What do you think you're playing at? Tie it off. **(His legs disappear through the hole)**

WILSON **(Helping Mainwaring to his feet)** Let me give you a hand, sir.

MAINWARING Thank you, Wilson.

WILSON I think there's only one thing we can do now, sir.

MAINWARING What?

WILSON Run!

He gets Mainwaring's arm round his shoulders and they hobble through the door.

THE ROSE AND CROWN

A corner of the bar. Mainwaring and Wilson are surrounded by the other members of the platoon and Mr West.

MAINWARING Men, as I remarked to Sergeant Wilson earlier on – all the members of our platoon are part of a close-knit, integral unit – and today that unit played its part to the full.

WEST I think I can speak for Head Office, Mainwaring, when I say that we're very proud of you all for saving the bank.

PIKE Excuse me, sir. We had eleven pints and Mr Godfrey's port and lemon. It come to 10s 6d.

WEST Just a moment, Mainwaring. Under the circumstances I'm sure Head Office will like to show their gratitude.

Mrs Pike rushes in.

MRS PIKE There you are, Arthur, are you all right?

She flings her arms round Wilson.

WILSON Yes, of course I am. There's no need to fuss.

MRS PIKE Just to think of you holding that bomb like that.

WILSON Oh really, Mavis, don't be embarrassing.

MRS PIKE You're so brave, you really are – and you, Mr Mainwaring – you're brave too!

Rogers comes in and puts the fuse on the table.

ROGERS I was right after all. All that time you were holding a trembler.

MAINWARING A what, sir?

ROGERS When that bomb went through the concrete ceiling of the strong room, the shock broke the wiring in the fuse and turned it into a trembler fuse. By keeping it horizontal you stopped it from going off – if you had tipped it by as much as a few inches the whole lot would have gone up. The bank should be very grateful to you two. You certainly saved their bacon.

PIKE **(Handing back note)** Excuse me, sir. She won't take it.

WEST Oh, that's very generous of her.

PIKE No, she says it's a dud.

WALKER Don't worry – use one of these. **(Taking notes from each pocket)**

MAINWARING Walker! Those belong to the bank!

WALKER Ah – but they're bomb-damaged, aren't they?

SERIES THREE **EPISODE SIX**

Recorded: Sunday 29/6/69

Original transmission: Thursday 16/10/69, 8.00–8.30pm

Original viewing figures = 12.4 million

Note: Although the episode was recorded in colour it only exists in black and white in the BBC archives.

ARTHUR LOWE .... CAPTAIN MAINWARING
JOHN LE MESURIER .... SERGEANT WILSON
CLIVE DUNN .... LANCE CORPORAL JONES
JOHN LAURIE .... PRIVATE FRAZER
JAMES BECK .... PRIVATE WALKER
ARNOLD RIDLEY .... PRIVATE GODFREY
IAN LAVENDER .... PRIVATE PIKE
ANTHONY SAGAR .... DRILL SERGEANT GREGORY
JOHN RINGHAM .... CAPTAIN BAILEY
EDWARD SINCLAIR .... VERGER
COLIN BEAN .... PRIVATE SPONGE

PLATOON ..... FRANK GODFREY, HUGH CECIL, DESMOND CULLUM-JONES, ... RICHARD KITTERIDGE, VIC TAYLOR, MICHAEL MOORE, ... GEORGE HANCOCK, FREDDIE WILES, LESLIE NOYES

ROOM AT THE BOTTOM

• ARTHUR FUNGE REMEMBERS •

'As a dresser you're more or less a nursemaid; you have to look after them and see they get everything they want. On *Dad's Army* there would have been about three dressers, perhaps four if there were any women in the cast.

'I mainly looked after Clive Dunn, John Le Mesurier and Ian Lavender; I got to know them all well and would occasionally spend time with them away from work. Sometimes John Le Mesurier would send a car round to pick me up at nights and I'd go over to his home in Baron's Court; while John played the piano I'd pour him drinks until it got so late I'd have to say: "Look, John, I've got to go home." I felt he was a very lonely, sad man, but a lovely person – I was extremely fond of him. He was always good to work for, I never had any trouble with him, and we became good friends. He always gave me the impression that he needed someone to look after him, but that was just him, it's easier if you've got someone to do it for you!

'One episode I particularly remember was "The Big Parade", in which Pike gets stuck in a bog. The platoon all get muddy and have to walk back into town before the parade, where they see the Warden and Verger who take the mickey out of them. We were shooting the parade the next day so I got all the costumes and put them into black plastic bags; when I brought them out next day they were all wet and muddy, which was necessary. But no one was going to put them on, so I said to Ian: "Look, I'm going to dress you first. I'm going to put you in plastic underneath, then put the uniforms on and you won't be touched by any of the wet at all." He agreed, and once I'd got Ian completed and everyone saw the clothes clung to him realistically, but that he wasn't feeling wet, they agreed to do it. When the scene was filmed everything looked great. I learnt in my job that sometimes you have to pick the person who will do things for you, then the others will follow!'

ARTHUR FUNGE
Senior Dresser

Room at the Bottom

CHURCH HALL. DAY

Wilson is there. Captain Bailey comes in.

WILSON Good evening, sir.

BAILEY Where's Captain Mainwaring?

WILSON We have the auditors in at the bank, so Captain Mainwaring had to stay behind to clear up a few points.

BAILEY I'm afraid I can't wait for him. I've got to call on two other units. Perhaps you could give him a message for me.

WILSON Certainly, sir.

BAILEY It's a bit awkward really. I don't quite know how to start.

WILSON Do sit down, sir.

BAILEY Thank you. Tell me, how long has Mr Mainwaring been a Captain?

WILSON Ever since we started, sir.

BAILEY You mean when you were Local Defence Volunteers?

WILSON That's right, sir.

BAILEY But there were no commissions in the L.D.V.

WILSON Weren't there, sir?

BAILEY No, of course not. After all, it was only in February this year that officers in the Home Guard were granted a commission. How did he get to be a Captain in the first place?

WILSON Well he, er... sort of made himself one, sir.

BAILEY Oh, did he? You know, I could never quite fathom out why, as a Captain, he was only in charge of a platoon.

WILSON Why – is that wrong, sir?

BAILEY Well, it is usual to have a Lieutenant in charge of a platoon. Mind you, there've been all sorts of rum ranks in the Home Guard and we're only just starting to sort it all out. I'm very sorry and all that, but he never was a Captain and he can't walk around with three pips on his shoulder. He'll just have to take one of them off. You must tell him as soon as he gets here.

WILSON Yes, sir. I'll er... do that.

BAILEY You can also tell him I'll confirm it in writing in the next few days.

WILSON Very well, sir. **(He salutes and Bailey goes)** Only a Lieutenant, eh! **(He smirks)** Fancy that.

The door opens and Walker comes in with a mug of tea.

WALKER Cup of char, Sarge.

WILSON Oh how awfully nice. Thank you, Walker.

WALKER What's up, Sarge? You look like the cat who's just got at the cream.

WILSON Oh... nothing.

WALKER By the way, I got your whatsname. Twenty five bob, right. **(He hands him a small tissue paper parcel)**

WILSON Oh thanks.

WALKER You do look happy tonight, Sarge. **(He goes)**

Wilson opens parcel. Takes out a rather smart officer's beret. He puts it on, tries it at various angles. At last, gets one he likes. He picks up his mug of tea and starts to sip it. The whole thing is done with an Errol Flynn, rakish air.

WILSON **(Looking in mirror)** I'm afraid I've got some bad news for you, Mainwaring. **(He starts again)** Now, look here, Mainwaring, you'd better brace yourself for a shock. **(Pause)** Mainwaring –I'm afraid one of those pips has got to come off. **(Pause)** Good evening, *Lieutenant* Mainwaring. Hmmm.

He stands looking in the mirror, lost in a dream. The door opens. Mainwaring comes in – he is dressed up to the nines. Officer's peaked hat – the top of his denim jacket has been well pressed back and scrubbed white. He is wearing a smart khaki collar and tie. He has a white lanyard on his revolver and his trousers have a knife-edge crease.

MAINWARING Hullo, Wilson – everything all right?

WILSON Yes, thank you, sir.

MAINWARING By the way, you'll be pleased to hear that I managed to get that Drill Sergeant.

WILSON What Drill Sergeant, sir?

MAINWARING Oh really, Wilson – don't you remember? I said the platoon was getting a bit sloppy. Anyhow this chap's coming on Friday to give the men an hour's drill. He should be pretty good, he's from the Coldstream Guards. **(He notices Wilson's beret)** What on earth's that you've got on your head?

WILSON It's a beret, sir – rather nice, don't you think?

MAINWARING You've no right to be wearing that.

WILSON Haven't I, sir.

MAINWARING Of course not. Only Officers can wear those. You can't go walking around wearing things you're not entitled to, you know, Wilson. The Home Guard is now a properly organised fighting unit. The days of people promoting themselves to all sorts of fancy ranks is over.

WILSON It's funny you should say that, sir. That's what Captain Bailey said earlier on.

MAINWARING Oh he's been in, has he?

WILSON Yes, sir, but he couldn't wait.

MAINWARING What did he want? The usual red tape nonsense, I suppose.

WILSON Yes, sir, he says you've got to take a pip off.

MAINWARING Oh is that all… What?

WILSON He says you're not really a Captain, sir. You should only be a Lieutenant.

MAINWARING Are you trying to be funny, Wilson?

WILSON No, sir.

MAINWARING Well, we'll soon settle this. **(He picks up the phone).** Young upstart. Eastgate 166 please. Pity he's got nothing better to do. You know, Wilson, sometimes I think that… 'Oh G.H.Q., Mainwaring, Walmington-on-Sea Platoon here. I'm sorry to bother you but there seems to be some mistake. Captain Bailey was here earlier on this evening and he left some peculiar garbled message. **(Staring hard at Wilson)** Of course, it's just possible that my Sergeant could have got it wrong. **(Wilson stares back)** It's quite absurd of course, something about taking a pip down. Yes… yes… I thought so, thank you.' **(He hangs up)**

MAINWARING **(His eyes narrowing)** What's the game, Wilson?

WILSON Game, sir?

MAINWARING Yes, game, man. What's the idea of saying I wasn't a Captain. Making me ring up G.H.Q. like that. What sort of fool do you think I look?

WILSON Who did you speak to, sir?

MAINWARING The Sergeant in the office – of course he didn't know what I was talking about.

WILSON Oh.

MAINWARING Well, I'm waiting for your explanation. **(There is a pause)** You know, I'm forced to say that you have confirmed a suspicion that's been in my mind for some weeks now.

WILSON What's that, sir?

MAINWARING That you are jealous of me, Wilson.

WILSON Jealous, sir?

MAINWARING Don't think I haven't noticed the way that you keep looking at my hat. That's why you bought that beret, you had to try and keep up with me. You don't fool me for one minute, Wilson. You'd give anything to be in my shoes.

WILSON I can assure you you're wrong, sir.

MAINWARING I'm not in the Home Guard for the glory I can get out of it. **(Tapping his shoulder)** These three pips mean nothing to me. I'd be just as happy to be a Sergeant, or even a simple Private. Being a Captain doesn't mean **(snaps his fingers)** that much to me.

The phone rings – Wilson picks it up.

WILSON 'Walmington-on-Sea Home Guard. Just a moment please.' **(To Mainwaring)** It's for you, sir. **(Hands phone to Mainwaring)**

MAINWARING 'Mainwaring here. Oh, hello, sir, how are you? Yes, I did ring earlier, sir. I spoke to the Sergeant there. He'd only just come on duty? He didn't know what, sir? **(Long pause)** Yes, sir… I er… I… Yes, sir.'

The phone clicks the other end. Mainwaring is still holding it – staring into space.

WILSON I'm sorry, sir, I really am. **(He goes)**

Mainwaring is cutting off his pip with a pen knife. Godfrey enters. Mainwaring does not hear him come in. He comes up to the desk.

GODFREY Excuse me, sir. **(Mainwaring puts his jacket behind his back)** Can I help in any way?

MAINWARING No thank you, Godfrey.

GODFREY Tailoring is my line, sir. Don't forget I was 35 years in the men's outfitting at the Civil Service Stores.

MAINWARING I doubt if that can be of much help to me, Godfrey.

GODFREY Well, at least let me try, sir. **(He takes the jacket)** What seems to be the trouble?

MAINWARING **(Giving up)** I'm taking a pip off each shoulder.

He starts to cut the other pip off. Godfrey puts on his glasses and pulls the bits of cotton off the other epaulette.

GODFREY I'll just pull these little bits of cotton off. The trouble is, you can always see the mark where the pips have been.

MAINWARING Yes, I know.

GODFREY Why *are* you taking them off, sir?

MAINWARING I can't go into it now, it's a long story. But I don't want you to say anything to the men about this.

GODFREY About what, sir? **(Wilson comes in)**

MAINWARING Never mind. All right, you can go.

Godfrey goes.

WILSON It's nearly time to dismiss the parade, sir. **(Mainwaring has now got his jacket on)** Oh, I see you've taken them off.

MAINWARING Yes, Wilson, I've taken them off. Look, I'd rather not say anything to the men about this just yet.

WILSON But they're bound to notice.

MAINWARING Well, I shall just have to think of something, so that they don't notice.

WILSON But Godfrey knows.

MAINWARING Oh don't worry about him, Wilson – he doesn't even know what time of day it is.

YARD. DAY

Frazer, Jones, Walker and Pike are gathered round Godfrey.

FRAZER You say he was taking one of his pips off?

GODFREY Yes, that's right.

JONES You must have been seeing things, Mr Godfrey.

GODFREY Oh no, I helped him.

FRAZER Perhaps he's been promoted.

JONES Yes – that must be it – the next step up is a Major – and he'd have to take his three pips off, to put a Crown on.

WALKER Oh blimey, don't say that – he's pompous enough as a Captain.

Wilson enters.

WILSON Okay. Properly at ease.

They fall in.

WALKER **(To Jones)** I can't wait to see what he's wearing on his shoulders.

WILSON Platoon, attention.

Mainwaring enters. He is wearing his steel helmet and a shoulder protector – half a rubber tyre. Wilson salutes.

MAINWARING Thank you, Sergeant. **(He walks down the ranks. They all try to see what's under the tyre)** Look to your front, Frazer.

JONES **(Coming to attention)** Permission to speak, sir?

MAINWARING What is it, Jones?

JONES Why are you wearing your shoulder protector, sir? Is that the standard dress from now on?

MAINWARING No, it isn't, Jones. I'm just testing it. Anything wrong with that?

JONES No, sir. I like it, I like it.

MAINWARING Stand at ease. I just want to say a few words about the exercise on Sunday.

FRAZER **(Coming to attention)** Excuse me, sir – you canna take the parade with your badges of rank covered up. You've told us many times it's not the man that we salute – but the King's commission.

WALKER That's right, sir. I mean how can we salute you if we can't see your rank. You'll have to take it off.

They all stare at Mainwaring. There is a terrible hush – Mainwaring looks at Wilson.

MAINWARING All right, men, I may as well tell you now… **(Suddenly the Verger rushes into the yard)**

VERGER Mr Mainwaring, sir… Mr Mainwaring, sir.

MAINWARING What is it, Verger?

VERGER The Bismarck's been sunk, sir.

MAINWARING What?

VERGER The German battleship Bismarck – it's been sunk. It's just come through on the wireless.

The platoon all cheer.

MAINWARING **(Shouting above the din)** All right, men, dismiss.

The platoon break off – talking excitedly.

MAINWARING **(Mopping his brow)** This is excellent news, Wilson.

WILSON Yes, sir. Once again the Navy's saved your bacon.

CHURCH HALL OFFICE. DAY

Wilson is sitting at Mainwaring's desk. Captain Bailey enters. Wilson gets up and salutes.

WILSON Good evening, sir.

BAILEY Evening – Mr Mainwaring not here yet?

WILSON No, sir – we've still got the auditors in.

BAILEY Hmm – pity. How did he take it last night?

WILSON Take what, sir?

BAILEY His pips off, man.

WILSON He cut them off, with a pen-knife, sir.

BAILEY No, I mean how did it affect him?

WILSON I think he was pretty cut up about it. You see, sir, he just lives for the Home Guard.

BAILEY Yes, I realise that, Sergeant, and that only makes my task more difficult.

WILSON What task is that, sir?

BAILEY The trouble is, when Mainwaring rang up G.H.Q. yesterday, they started looking into things and it appears that he hasn't even been granted a commission as a Lieutenant.

WILSON I don't think I quite understand.

BAILEY It's perfectly simple. Mainwaring hasn't got any rank at all. Therefore he's got no authority to be in charge of this platoon. **(He hands Wilson a letter)** It's all in that letter. Give it to him as soon as he arrives. By the way, you're in command until I can make other arrangements. **(He goes to the door and turns)** Good news about sinking the Bismarck, wasn't it?

WILSON **(In a daze)** Awfully good news, sir. **(Bailey goes)**

JONES **(Out of vision)** Platoon, attention. Evening, Mr Mainwaring.

Bailey comes straight back in again.

BAILEY I think I'll go out the other door. Don't forget to give Mainwaring that letter, will you? **(He goes out of the other door)**

The door opens – Mainwaring comes in. He is wearing a belted army officer's mackintosh with no badges of rank on the shoulders.

MAINWARING Hello, Wilson.

WILSON Hello, sir.

Mainwaring takes off his 'mac' and hangs it up. He has only got two pips on each shoulder.

MAINWARING You'd better get the men together, Sergeant. I want to talk to them.

WILSON Before you do that, sir. I think...

MAINWARING It's no good putting it off, Wilson. The platoon has got to be told that I'm only a Lieutenant, and that's that. After all 'ours is not to reason why'.

WILSON Before you do anything, sir, I think you ought to read this letter. Captain Bailey left it for you.

MAINWARING Oh, he's been in again has he?

WILSON Yes sir, he couldn't stop.

MAINWARING I don't know what's the matter with that man. **(He takes letter)** Anyone would think he didn't want to see me.

WILSON **(Backing towards the door leading out into the hall)** Well... if you don't mind... I'll do something else... **(He quickly goes out of the door)**

OUTSIDE OFFICE DOOR. DAY

Wilson closes the door and stands listening. He takes a cigarette packet out and lights up. He goes down on one knee and looks through the keyhole. Suddenly there is a loud bang.

WILSON My God – he's shot himself!

He quickly opens door and goes in.

OFFICE. DAY

Wilson comes in. Mainwaring is standing by the desk, holding the letter and staring into space.

WILSON Are you all right, sir?

Mainwaring doesn't answer – the door bursts open – Jones comes in.

JONES **(To Mainwaring)** I'm sorry about that, sir. Mr Godfrey had one up the spout and it went off. It's all right, no one's hurt. **(Mainwaring still stares into space)** I said it's all right, Mr Mainwaring. What's the matter with him, Mr Wilson?

WILSON I'm afraid he's had a bit of a shock.

They put Mainwaring into his chair.

YARD OUTSIDE CHURCH HALL. DAY

JONES I can't get over it – fancy Mr Mainwaring not being an officer after all. He's not an officer at all. He's not an officer at all. I wonder how he's taking it.

PIKE It was terrible at the bank today. He never came out of his office once. Mr Wilson had to put his letters under the door.

WALKER Poor old Mainwaring – we're going to miss him, you know.

FRAZER Its his own fault, if you ask me. He's been tempting providence for a long time – strutting about the place like a peacock.

GODFREY Well, I like Mr Mainwaring, he was always so considerate, never unkind or anything like that, not even to me.

PIKE I wonder who we'll get to take his place.

JONES That's a point, Pikey, I hadn't thought of that.

GODFREY Whoever it is, I hope he doesn't shout. I can't stand people who shout.

FRAZER You're too soft, the lot of you. You need somebody to shout a bit.

WALKER I wouldn't like to think what would happen if you were in charge, Taff. You'd have us running around from what's-its-name till breakfast time.

FRAZER Aye – I would – I would. I'd knock spots off you.

JONES They told Mr Wilson he was in charge, until the new officer takes over.

GODFREY Well, I don't suppose we shall see Mr Mainwaring on this parade ground again.

Wilson enters and goes over to platoon.

WILSON All right, fall in, you chaps. I thing I ought to tell you that I have been put in charge of the platoon until a new officer can be appointed.

WALKER Does that mean you'll be leading us in the exercise on Sunday?

WILSON Yes, I'm afraid it does.

PIKE What's going to happen to Mr Mainwaring?

WILSON Well, he's no longer a member of this platoon.

MAINWARING That's not strictly true, Sergeant. When I was told that I was no longer your commanding officer,

I must admit that my first reaction was to leave quietly. Then I said to myself: the defence of this town must come first. This country needs every able-bodied man it can get, and no man can be an island unto himself. I was proud to march at your head as Captain Mainwaring – I am even prouder to march in your ranks as Private Mainwaring. That's all.

JONES You'll always be a Captain as far as I'm concerned, Mr Mainwaring. Come on, sir, fall in beside me. Move over, Mr Godfrey.

They all move down and make a space for Mainwaring. Mainwaring comes smartly to attention, marches into the space, does an about turn, puts his arm out and dresses off. He stands at ease.

JONES Very good, Mr Mainwaring, very good indeed.

GODFREY **(Smiles at Mainwaring)** Yes it was, sir, very good.

FRAZER Sycophants!

JONES You haven't got a bandook, have you, Mr Mainwaring? He hasn't got a bandook, Mr Wilson.

WILSON Could one of you chaps lend Mr Mainwaring a rifle? **(A rifle is passed to him) (Wilson goes up to Mainwaring)** You're quite sure you want to go on with this, sir?

MAINWARING I thought I'd made that quite clear.

WILSON Right. Platoon.... Platoon... **(To Mainwaring)** Are you ready, sir?

MAINWARING Get on with it, Wilson.

WILSON Platoon... attention. **(They all come smartly to attention except Mainwaring who is just a beat behind)** Stand at ease! **(The same thing happens again – Mainwaring is just a beat behind)**

JONES **(To Mainwaring)** I used to have that trouble, Mr Mainwaring. Mind you, I practised and I'm all right now.

WILSON Platoon, attention.

They all come smartly to attention except Mainwaring who is just a beat behind and Jones who is two beats behind.

JONES I think you're putting me off, Mr Mainwaring.

WILSON That was better, sir.

MAINWARING No, it wasn't better, Wilson, it was wrong. Let's have it again.

WILSON Platoon, stand... **(Mainwaring starts to move)** stand... **(He starts to move again)** stand at ease! **(Mainwaring stands at ease, the rest of the squad stands at ease after him very raggedly)**

WILSON Platoon... attention! **(They are all together except Jones)**

FRAZER **(To Walker)** It's taken Jones a year to get it right – and now Mainwaring's put him back where he started.

Sergeant Gregory enters. Marches up to Wilson.

GREGORY Evening, Sergeant. Name's Gregory... Drill Sergeant. Is the platoon ready?

WILSON Er... ready for what?

GREGORY Drill – I'm supposed to give you an hour's drill tonight.

MAINWARING **(Hissing to Wilson)** Don't you remember, Wilson. I told you last night he was coming.

GREGORY **(Pointing his stick at Mainwaring)** What are you doing? Stop talking in the ranks – stop talking. Now let's have a look at yer. **(He turns his back on Wilson and looks down the platoon)**

WILSON **(Whispering to Mainwaring)** Are you sure you wouldn't like to slip away quietly, sir?

MAINWARING I don't think I have anything to fear, Sergeant.

WILSON But it's so awkward, sir.

GREGORY **(Wheeling round)** What are you doing talking again. **(To Wilson)** Why are you calling him, sir?

WILSON Well er...

GREGORY Well, what is he then, a knight or something? Looks like a rough night to me. **(He gives a terrible laugh)** What's the matter wiv you lot – ain't you got no sense of humour. **(He glares at them – they all laugh feebly)** That's better – 'ave a good larf – git plenty of air in yer lungs. I do a lot of larfin I do. In my job I git plenty to larf about. I should think you lot will give me a few chuckles before the evening's over. **(Godfrey gives a half smile)** What are you larfin at then, lad?

GODFREY I'm not really laughing – that's my normal expression.

GREGORY Looking at you – I should think that's about the only thing that is normal. **(Pike turns and laughs)** Look to yer front, lad. **(Pike looks down)** Git your 'ead up. Who do you think you are? One of the Bisto kids. Don't go looking on the ground, there's nothing there. I should know, I've been all over it. What an 'orrible lot. **(He crosses to Jones)** You an old soljer, are yer?

JONES That's right, Sergeant. I went all through.

GREGORY I'll bet you did, I spect you bin through more than I've had 'ot dinners. Kitchener may need you, but I don't. I mean, I don't know what I'm doin' 'ere tonight. I could have been doin' something useful, like drilling soljers. **(He turns on Wilson)** Where yer git that 'at?

WILSON I beg your pardon?

GREGORY That 'at.

WILSON What hat?

GREGORY That 'at on your 'ead.

WILSON I bought it, actually.

GREGORY **(Imitating Wilson's voice)** Ho, you actually bought it, did yer. That's an officer's 'at, that is – you got no right to be wearin' officer's 'at. Talk about Fred Karno's. What are you, the boys of the old brigade. **(Crossing to Walker)** Why aren't you in the Army?

WALKER I was, I got my ticket.

GREGORY What for?

WALKER I was allergic to corned beef.

GREGORY I thought so – you've got malingerer stamped all over you. **(Crossing to Pike)** You're due for the army soon, ain't yer?

PIKE I want to go into the Navy – but my mum says I'm too delicate.

GREGORY Oh dear, oh dear. I am sorry. What is wrong with you, lad?

PIKE I've got a chest.

GREGORY Oh really – you'd look bloody funny without one, wouldn't you? Well I know a good cure for that – start running on the spot, go. **(Pike starts running)** Come on, pick 'em up – you're like some foreign nancy boy treadin' grapes. Hup! Hup! Hup! Hup! **(Pointing to Walker)** And you, come on. Hup! Hup! Hup! Hup! **(Jones starts to run on the spot as well – Gregory crosses to him)** Not you – not you – only the young ones. I don't want to be had up for manslaughter, do I?

JONES But I'd like to do it, Sergeant.

GREGORY No, you'd better not. I wouldn't want anything to happen to you, you're such a nice old gentleman, you remind me of my Granddad.

JONES Oh, really.

GREGORY He died ten years ago. We dug him up last week – he looks better than you do now.

MAINWARING Now look here – you're going too far.

GREGORY **(Eyes narrowing)** I beg your pardon?

MAINWARING I said you're going too far.

GREGORY **(To platoon)** Did you hear that? It's 'is Lordship – he says I'm going too far. Well you're going too far, but you're not going to git anywhere. All right, start running. Hup! Hup! Hup!

Mainwaring starts running.

WILSON I think you ought to know, Mr Mainwaring used to be our officer.

GREGORY Officers! I hate 'em. Pick 'em up. I'll give you a wet shirt. Hup! Hup! Hup! Hup! Halt. All right, at ease. Platoon – wait for it. Attenshun!

Mainwaring is behind.

GREGORY You're a bit behind, ain't yer... you 'orrible knight. **(To platoon)** Right, hold that... now, when you're at attention, I want to see **(He rattles this off at terrific speed)** You stand up straight, chins in – chests out, stomachs in – thumbs in line with the seams of your trousers.

GODFREY I wonder if you'd mind repeating that. **(Gregory glares at him)**

GREGORY Slope arms **(They all slope without counting – they do it quite well, except Jones)** Oh, give it here. **(He snatches rifle)** Right, watch me – and when I've done it – I want you to do it exactly the same – j'understand. Slope Arms – 1 2 3 – 1 2 3 – 1. Right. **(He throws the rifle back to Jones)**

JONES **(Doing the drill)** 1 2 3 – 1 2 3 – 1. Right. **(He throws the rifle at Gregory – it lands on his foot)**

TELECINE: WOODS. DAY

Jones and Walker and Godfrey are sitting by some bushes – Wilson joins.

WILSON Any sign of the enemy, Jones?

JONES Not so far, Mr Wilson.

WILSON I think before we go any further we'd better send out a scout. We don't want to run into an ambush.

JONES I'd like to volunteer for that, Mr Wilson – let me be a scout.

WILSON Must you? Oh, very well. Now, I want you to run over to that rise – have a good look and if you can't see any of the Eastgate platoon...

WALKER Excuse me, Sarge, it's not the Eastgate platoon – it's the Southgate platoon.

WILSON Is it? – oh well, whatever it is. If it's all clear give us a signal and we'll come on.

JONES Very well, Mr Wilson – if it's all clear and I don't see the enemy, I'll give you the signal – and you'll come. **(He dashes off)**

WALKER **(To Wilson)** I don't think you ought to have sent him, you know, Sergeant.

WILSON But he's so keen all the time, I couldn't stop him.

WALKER Mr Mainwaring wouldn't have done that.

WILSON Wouldn't he? Oh Lord!

Cut to long shot of Jones running.

Cut to close up of two Home Guards looking through bushes. The first one puts his fingers to his lips, the second one gives the thumbs up sign. They draw out of sight as Jones dashes past.

Jones reaches the top of the rise, goes down on his hands and knees. He peers over the top and looks round. He is now flat on his stomach.

Cut to close up of his leg, he is not wearing any gaiters. His boot is sticking in an anthill. Suddenly the ants start to swarm out, they go over his boot and up his trousers.

Cut to close up of Jones' face. Suddenly he jumps up, starts to beat at his trousers. He rips them off and waves them up and down to try and get the ants out.

Cut to Wilson, Walker and Godfrey.

GODFREY It's all clear, Mr Wilson. Look. (He points)

WALKER Why has he taken his trousers off to signal, Sarge?

WILSON You know what he is – he always overdoes everything. All right, come on. (He blows a whistle and signals the platoon on)

They all break cover and move off at a trot down the slope. Suddenly thunder flashes are hurled amongst them.

Cut to long shot showing enemy from rear view, standing up and shooting at them. There is the sound of rattles, shouts of 'bang, bang, bang'.

YARD OUTSIDE CHURCH. DAY

The platoon file in, very dejected. Walker, Frazer, Godfrey, Jones and Pike gather in a group.

FRAZER Terrible, terrible disgrace. Fancy being wiped out like that.

Private Sponge and another pass by.

PRIVATE SPONGE I tell you, if things go on like this, there won't be any platoon left for the new officer to take charge of. The whole thing's falling to pieces, if you ask me.

The Privates go.

FRAZER (To Jones) Did you hear that – did you hear that, Jonesey?

JONES I certainly did – the men are absolutely at rock bottom.

GODFREY If only we could get Mr Mainwaring back as an officer.

JONES (Looking at Walker) What about it, Joe?

WALKER It's no good looking at me, Jonesey – this time I'm stumped.

PIKE Wait a minute – I think I've got an idea. Well, why shouldn't I have one?

They all look at him in amazement.

CORNER OF CHURCH HALL. NIGHT

Jones, Walker, Godfrey and Pike are all sitting in a group, writing letters. Frazer is smoking his pipe – he is the only one not writing.

Cut to Jones.

VOICE OVER Dear Sir. Permission to write. As an old soldier of 30 years' service, and a member of the Royal Antediluvian Order of Buffalos, may I put in a good word for our late Captain. His reduction in rank has had a shattering effect on our morales and... (Voice fades)

Cut to Pike

VOICE OVER Dear Sir. As the youngest member of the platoon, I would like to say what a fine soldier – officer and gentleman, Mr Mainwaring is – are – was. My mum says... (Voice fades)

Cut to Godfrey

VOICE OVER Dear Sir. May I most humbly and respectfully beg to place before you the following facts for consideration at your convenience. To whom it may concern, Mr Mainwaring has always carried out his duties in a conscientious and diligent manner... (Voice fades)

Cut to Walker

VOICE OVER Dear Sir. If you ask yours truly, this caper of slashing our officer, Captain Mainwaring, down to size is not much bottle. Fair do's is what I say. Hoping this finds you as it leaves me. J. Walker Esq. P.S. If a couple of bottles of Scotch would tip the balance – you're on.

JONES Here, Jock, aren't you going to write a letter?

FRAZER I'll do it when I get home. I'm not illiterate, you know. I'm quite capable of writing a letter on my own.

FRAZER'S HOME. NIGHT

Frazer is standing at a high Victorian clerk's desk, writing by the light of a flickering candle. He is wearing his dressing gown – all around him is pitch black.

VOICE OVER Dear Sirs. Now that the post of Commanding Officer for the platoon is vacant, I would like you to consider a Private who served with distinction during the last conflict. Unfortunately, some understandable jealousy has caused him to be passed by whenever promotion was due in the past. In spite of all this, I feel I must speak and reveal his name, which is Private Frazer. Signed, A Well Wisher.

YARD. CHURCH HALL. DAY

The men are drawn up on parade. Captain Bailey is addressing them.

BAILEY **(Holding bundle of letters)** After receiving all these letters from the platoon – G.H.Q. felt duty bound to grant Mr Mainwaring his commission. **(There is a cheer from the platoon)** In future, the three platoons – Eastgate, Southgate and Walmington-on-Sea – will be formed into a company and Mr Mainwaring will be second in command and have his rank of Captain confirmed. **(More cheers)**

WALKER **(Out of the corner of his mouth to Jones)** Blimey, there's no need for them to overdo it.

BAILEY **(To Wilson)** Good news, eh, Sergeant?

WILSON Yes awfully good, sir.

BAILEY The letters we received from the platoon were unanimous in their praise for Captain Mainwaring – or perhaps I should say practically unanimous. **(Terrible glance from Frazer. Mainwaring enters in Captain's uniform)** Congratulations, Captain Mainwaring. **(He shakes his hand)**

MAINWARING Thank you, sir. **(To platoon)** And I want to thank you, men, for your trust and confidence in me.

FRAZER Aye, we have that, sir.

MAINWARING And to assure you that I shall continue to lead you for as long as my country has need of me.

FRAZER That's good news, sir.

MAINWARING That's all. Dismiss.

They all crowd round Mainwaring.

JONES Well done, sir – well done.

GODFREY Welcome back, Mr Mainwaring. Welcome back.

WALKER Any time you want anything, don't forget to let me know.

PIKE My mum won't half be pleased, Mr Mainwaring.

FRAZER Don't forget, sir – if you're thinking of making up another Lance Corporal, I'd be proud to serve under you.

MAINWARING I'll bear that in mind, Frazer. **(To Wilson)** A pretty nasty business, Wilson – still all's well that ends well.

WILSON I must say, it did have its funny side. You know, when I got home, I laughed and laughed.

MAINWARING Did you really?

WILSON Oh yes – to think all that time you were running things – you really had no authority, did you, sir?

MAINWARING No, you're right. I mean, I'd no power to promote you to Sergeant, had I?

WILSON Er... no, sir.

MAINWARING I'm sure we'll sort it all out in time, Wilson – meanwhile perhaps you'd like to borrow my pen-knife.

He offers him his pen-knife. Wilson takes it and looks down at his stripes.

SERIES THREE **EPISODE SEVEN**

Recorded: Sunday 6/7/69

Original transmission: Thursday 23/10/69, 7.30–8.00pm

Original viewing figures = 13.2 million

ARTHUR LOWE .... CAPTAIN MAINWARING
JOHN LE MESURIER .... SERGEANT WILSON
CLIVE DUNN .... LANCE CORPORAL JONES
JOHN LAURIE .... PRIVATE FRAZER
JAMES BECK .... PRIVATE WALKER
ARNOLD RIDLEY .... PRIVATE GODFREY
IAN LAVENDER .... PRIVATE PIKE

EDWARD EVANS .... MR REES
EDWARD SINCLAIR .... VERGER
DON ESTELLE .... MAN FROM PICKFORDS
ROY DENTON .... MR BENNETT

PLATOON .... COLIN BEAN, RICHARD JACQUES, FRANK GODFREY, ... HUGH CECIL, VIC TAYLOR, RICHARD KITTERIDGE, ... MICHAEL MOORE, GEORGE HANCOCK, FREDDIE WILES, LESLIE NOYES

REMOVAL MEN .... EDWARD WESTERN, CHARLES ADEY-GRAY, ... COLIN CUNNINGHAM

COMMITTEE MEMBERS .... EILEEN WINTERTON, DAVID J GRAHAME

NOTE: IN THE ORIGINAL SCRIPT, THE TOWN CLERK WAS A SMALL, SHARP YORKSHIREMAN WITH GLASSES CALLED MR PENDLETON.

BIG GUNS

• BILL HARMAN REMEMBERS •

'Don Estelle's first appearance in *Dad's Army* was in "Big Guns". This delightful little man played the driver of the Pickford's van delivering the field gun. Pickford's motto was "The Gentle Giant" so David couldn't resist casting Don in the part.

'When the field gun arrives at Walmington, the platoon all rush out to see it. Pike asks Wilson: "Is this ours, Uncle Sergeant?" to which Wilson replies, in his usual gentle way, something along the lines of "Yes, of course it's ours, of course." John Le Mesurier was uncomfortable with this line at rehearsals, thinking it a little far fetched but David was reluctant to change it. So, all week, Pike asked the obvious question and Wilson gave the obvious answer, each time seemingly more uncomfortable saying it.

'At the final studio dress rehearsal, everyone in costume, with make-up, wardrobe, full technical lighting, camera and sound crew present, the gun arrived, the platoon rushed out to see it and Pike said: "Is this ours, Uncle Sergeant?" The normally affable John who I'd never heard raise his voice, suddenly yelled back: "Of course it is, you #@$*!" There was a stunned silence for a second then the entire cast and crew collapsed in heaps of laughter. The original line went back in for the recording of course, but it took willpower on everyone's part to get past that section without giggling.'

BILL HARMAN
Assistant Floor Manager

BIG GUNS

OFFICE. CHURCH HALL. DAY

The hall is empty. We can hear the platoon marking time.

WILSON **(Out of vision)** Platoon, halt! Left turn. All right, fall out for ten minutes. **(They fall out)**

Mainwaring comes in, followed by Wilson. Mainwaring crosses and sits.

MAINWARING Splendid church parade. I thought the men looked very smart.

WILSON What I can't understand, sir, is why you marched us all round the town first. After all, the church is only next door.

MAINWARING Well, we couldn't very well nip over the back wall, could we? I mean, what's the use of having a church parade if you don't parade?

WILSON But surely it was hardly necessary to go round the town twice?

MAINWARING It was well worth it. The men marched extremely well.

WILSON Pity Godfrey had to fall out.

MAINWARING Never mind, he caught up with us on the second time round.

There is the sound of voices outside.

VERGER **(Out of vision)** I don't care who told you to deliver it, you can't leave it there.

MAN **(Out of vision)** I'm sorry. I've got my orders and that's that. Someone's got to sign for it.

VERGER Well, I'm not signing for it.

MAINWARING What on earth's going on out there?

He crosses to the door and bumps into the Verger coming in with a little Pickford man.

MAINWARING What is the matter, Verger?

VERGER You might well ask. The Vicar's not going to like this, you know. **(Hands Wilson a paper and points to the little man)** He wants someone to sign it.

MAINWARING **(To Wilson)** What's it say, Wilson?

WILSON **(Reading)** A note from you. A call from us. A date is fixed – no worry or fuss. A Pickford van, a gentle giant. The work is done – a satisfied client.

MAINWARING **(Looking at little man)** A gentle giant.

PICKFORD MAN Well, there's a war on, isn't there? Look, just sign for it, I can't hang about. We've got six more to deliver today.

Jones and Walker enter.

MAINWARING **(To Pickford man)** What is it you want me to sign for?

PICKFORD MAN It's got it on the chitty. One 13-pounder.

MAINWARING What's that?

JONES There's a huge firing piece out in the yard, sir.

WALKER It's a ruddy great gun out in the yard.

MAINWARING What! **(He rushes out)**

VERGER **(Following him)** The Vicar's going to be furious about this you know, Mr Mainwaring.

PICKFORD MAN **(To Wilson)** Just sign, will you, sir?

WILSON Yes, of course.

YARD OF CHURCH HALL. DAY

There is a large 13-pounder, quick-firing Naval gun on a mounting in the yard.

MAINWARING Good heavens, Wilson! Look at that!

WILSON I say, it's rather big, isn't it?

MAINWARING Wilson, if Hitler comes now, we'll blast him right into kingdom come. How does it work do you think?

WILSON I haven't the foggiest notion. Have you ever handled one of these, Jonesey?

JONES No, sir – we used to use the Gatling Gun in the Sudan – you turned a handle. It was invented by an American dentist named Mr Gatling. In the Sudan we used to form up into a square with the gun in the middle and when those Fuzzie Wuzzies came towards us with their bloodcurdling cries we waited till the last minute and then we used to bob down and the blokes behind us would let 'em have it. Rat-tat-tat-tat! Mind you, if you didn't bob down quick enough, you got the top of your helmet shot off, hence the expression 'Get your head down'.

WILSON It says on this: '13-pounder Naval gun on special wheel mounting'.

MAINWARING If it is, we're in luck. Frazer was in the Navy.

WILSON That's right, sir. Chief Petty Officer.

MAINWARING Walker! Get Frazer and the rest of the platoon.

WALKER Yes, sir. **(He goes calling)** Here, Taffy, come and see what Father Christmas brought.

Jones is now looking through the telescopic sights.

JONES Here, there's a telescope thing here.

WILSON I think they're sights, Jones.

JONES Oh yes, I can see some sights. I can see that haystack clearer than your face. There's a couple of people there and they're... Here, come and have a look, Sarge. **(Wilson looks through sights)**

WILSON Hm... rather unusual.

MAINWARING There's no time for that now.

PIKE Cor! Is that ours, Uncle Sergeant?

WILSON It would appear so, Pike.

GODFREY Does it make a very big bang?

WALKER Let's face it, it's not a peashooter, is it?

GODFREY Bangs give me an awful headache – that's why I dread Guy Fawkes night so.

MAINWARING Ah, Frazer. I expect you've seen one of these before, eh?

FRAZER Aye, aye I have that.

MAINWARING Well, to us it's a very mysterious piece of mechanism. To you, it's probably like meeting an old friend.

PIKE Yes, how do you shoot it, Mr Frazer?

FRAZER Well, I can't say that I am familiar with this particular weapon.

MAINWARING But surely one gun is very like another. I mean you must know the principle of the thing.

FRAZER Aye, I daresay the principle is the same.

JONES Then, come on, Frazer, show us what to do.

WALKER Yeh, let's get cracking.

FRAZER Well, it's not as simple as it looks. The bullets come out that end and go in there somewhere.

WALKER Don't get too technical.

MAINWARING You, you were a Chief Petty Officer, weren't you?

FRAZER Aye, I was.

WILSON Perhaps Frazer didn't have too much to do with guns.

FRAZER Aye, that's right.

MAINWARING What did you do?

FRAZER Well, I did all sorts of things.

MAINWARING Such as?

FRAZER Well, I was mostly a cook.

MAINWARING A cook?

JONES A cook! And all the time I thought you was something important.

FRAZER If you were on a ship, would you think your food was not important?

MAINWARING You – you said you fought at Jutland.

FRAZER No I didn't. I said I was at Jutland. Sailors eat, you know, even in battle. When the shells are flying, it takes a strong man to stay below and make shepherd's pie.

GODFREY I think you have to be strong to do anything with boats. I used to feel queasy on the Serpentine.

MAINWARING Well, that's a disappointment, but I'm sure we'll manage somehow.

FRAZER Sorry if I've let you down, sir.

MAINWARING Of course you haven't let us down, Frazer.

WALKER Never mind, Taffy, next time there's an air raid you can do us a plum duff.

The Pickford man re-enters.

PICKFORD MAN I nearly drove away and forgot. This book come with it, I think it tells you how to make it go off. **(To the other removal men)** Come along, don't hang about, quick sharp, in the van. **(They follow him off. Mainwaring takes the book)**

MAINWARING It's all here, Wilson. **(He opens it)** The gun crew consists of G.L., S.S., trainer, breech worker and two loaders.

JONES Permission to speak, sir?

MAINWARING Yes, Jones.

JONES I would like to volunteer to be the S.S., trainer and breeches.

MAINWARING Thank you, Corporal, but I believe that is the entire crew.

WILSON Perhaps they explain it in a later chapter, sir.

MAINWARING Well, I'll read on. Position for close up.

JONES We used to do that in the Vicar's pantomime, sir – in the funny drill scene. 'Close up', the man used to say and we all lifted our clothes up.

WALKER I bet that was hilarious.

MAINWARING Thank you, Jones. Let's concentrate on the matter in hand. Number 1 – the gun layer. Oh, G.L. ... the gun layer. Number 1 – the gun layer sits at the elevating wheel on the left.

JONES Permission to speak, sir? I would like to volunteer to be the gun layer, sir.

GODFREY If it's a sitting job, it might rather suit me.

MAINWARING Very well, Godfrey – sit down.

WALKER Now you've got him in, sir, he'll have to stay there till the end of the war.

Mainwaring reads again.

MAINWARING Number two – the breech worker – sits on the right in line with the breech.

JONES I would like to volunteer to be the breech worker on right in line with the breech, sir.

MAINWARING Oh very well, Jones. **(Jones stands as directed)**

JONES Shall I sit side-saddle or astride, sir? **(He sits and turns to Walker)** Here! Watch it, Joe.

MAINWARING **(Reads again)** Number three – the loader – stands to the rear of number 1 – that's you, Pike. **(Pike stands behind Godfrey)** Number four – the trainer – sits at the training wheel on the right. That's you, Frazer. **(Frazer sits at the wheel on the right)** Number five – the loader – stands in the rear of three. You be number five, Walker. Stand behind Pike. **(Walker goes to his position)**

MAINWARING **(Reads)** S.S. at the sights. I wonder what S.S. stands for?

WILSON Sights Superintendent?

MAINWARING Well, it had better be you, Wilson. Now, are we all clear so far?

GODFREY **(Shifting on seat)** It's not very luxurious.

MAINWARING It's not meant to be – this is war. Now, what's next? **(He reads)** Action. Clear away obstructions to the working of the gun.

WALKER Well, you'd better get rid of Jones here, for a start.

JONES I heard that.

MAINWARING That'll do, Walker.

MAINWARING Next, open the breech. Open the breech, Jones. **(Jones tries to open the breech)**

JONES It won't shift, sir.

MAINWARING Give him a hand, Pike.

Jones, Walker and Pike try to open the breech.

JONES I think it's rusted up, sir.

MAINWARING Let me have a go.

He tries to open the breech with no success.

VERGER Excuse me. **(He steps forward and flicks a switch)** You had the safety catch on.

MAINWARING Why do people always have to interfere?

PIKE It's our gun.

JONES Troublemaker.

MAINWARING Breech worker reports bore clear. Call out the bit about the bore, Jones.

JONES Bore clear! Bore clear! Bore clear!

MAINWARING All right, Jones, all right. **(He reads)** Loader loads the gun and calls 'Gun loaded' to breech worker.

PIKE Gun loaded to breech worker.

MAINWARING Just 'Gun loaded', boy. **(Reads)** The loader should take extreme caution to ensure that his fingers are out of the breech when the breech worker works the breech. As soon as his fingers are clear he calls to the breech worker – the corner of the page is torn away.

PIKE Why should I say that, sir?

Mainwaring shows Pike that the corner of the page of the book of instructions is torn away.

WILSON We'll never know what he calls, will we, sir?

FRAZER How about, 'Hands away!'

WALKER If he doesn't get his hands away, how about 'Ouch'?

MAINWARING Now, I've warned you once, Walker. No, we want something brief and to the point.

WILSON How about 'Fingers out'?

MAINWARING That'll do. Go on Pike.

PIKE Fingers out!

MAINWARING Breech worker closes the breech.

Jones does so.

JONES **(Calls out)** Shut up, sir!

MAINWARING I beg your pardon.

JONES Shut up, sir. The breech is shut.

MAINWARING It doesn't say anything about you saying that.

JONES Well, it sounds military, doesn't it?

WILSON I think it sounds rather rude.

GODFREY How about 'Once more into the breech'?

MAINWARING Don't be ridiculous. **(Reads again)** On the order 'Fire', the gun layer pulls his lanyard. Go on, Godfrey.

GODFREY Yes, sir.

MAINWARING What are you doing?

GODFREY Pulling my lanyard.

MAINWARING Not that one, this one.

GODFREY Do you mean to say I actually make it go off?

MAINWARING That's what it says here.

GODFREY Oh, I really don't think I'm suited to the post.

JONES Please, sir, I should like to pull the lanyard. Let me pull it, sir, let me pull it.

MAINWARING You can't reach across and pull it, what about the kick?

JONES I should like to do that as well, sir.

MAINWARING The recoil, man! Pike, you pull it.

PIKE I'm putting the shells in, I can't pull it and push it.

WILSON I'm not exactly over-employed, sir. Perhaps I could oblige.

MAINWARING Right, you pull it, Wilson.

WILSON Do you think you could move just a tiny bit forward, Godfrey?

MAINWARING Now, we all understand how the thing… er… the gun works, don't we? (**Cut to their blank faces**) So we'll have a practice.

FRAZER That's all very well, but what are we aiming at?

MAINWARING Quite right, Frazer. Now, let's imagine that that milk van over there on the coast road is a tank. Aim at that and I will work out the range and inclination. Range – 700 yards. Inclination – two degrees.

JONES (**To Godfrey**) Have you got the inclination?

GODFREY No, I'm quite all right, thank you very much.

WILSON No, no, Godfrey, my dear fellow. Turn your little handle till that little dial shows two degrees.

MAINWARING Left, 20 degrees. Now, keep it in your sights. Steady! Fire!

JONES I shouldn't if I was you, sir.

Mainwaring looks to his right. The barrel is pointing right at him.

SIDE OFFICE CHURCH HALL. DAY

Mainwaring in office. Mainwaring is firing a toy gun. Wilson enters.

WILSON That's much more your size, sir.

Jones and Walker come in.

JONES Evening, Captain Mainwaring. Evening, Sergeant Wilson. (**Puts down the sack he is carrying**) I got the sawdust for the T.E.W.T.

MAINWARING Well done, Jones.

WALKER And I've got the tins for the T.E.W.T. (**He empties some battered Spam tins on the desk**)

MAINWARING And I've got the toy gun.

JONES Good, sir, now we've got something to shoot for the T.E.W.T.

Wilson is looking very puzzled.

MAINWARING Now we need something to put the T.E.W.T. on.

JONES What about that big blackout screen in the hall, sir?

MAINWARING Very good idea, Jones. Go and get it. (**Jones goes**) Give me a hand, Walker.

WILSON Excuse me, sir. What is a T.E.W.T.?

MAINWARING Really, Wilson. Fancy not knowing what a T.E.W.T. is.

WILSON I wasn't here last night when you fixed it up, sir.

MAINWARING Well T.E.W.T. stands for Tactical Exercise Without Troops. I told the men to bring various items to make a model of the town.

Frazer and Godfrey enter. Frazer has a sack and Godfrey is carrying a cardboard box.

FRAZER Good evening, Mr Mainwaring. I've brought as much stuff as I could.

GODFREY (**Putting down box**) And I've brought a few things that might help, sir.

MAINWARING Well done, men.

Jones comes in with blackout screen.

JONES Here you are, Mr Mainwaring.

MAINWARING (**Clearing the desk**) Right, put it on the desk, Jones. (**They put the screen on the desk**) Now the sawdust. **Jones tips the sack of sawdust on the screen and they spread it out evenly.**

JONES (**Picking out a bit of suet**) What's this bit of suet doing here? That boy Raymond's getting very careless. Can't use it now, it's covered in sawdust. Never mind, it can go in the sausages. (**He blows it and puts it in his pocket**)

MAINWARING (**Aside to Wilson**) Make a note, we don't want any sausages this week, Wilson. Now, we need something to represent the church – there's a mess tin behind there, Walker, get that.

Mainwaring puts down a mess tin.

FRAZER (**Taking an empty square whisky bottle out of his sack**) How about this for the tower, sir?

MAINWARING Haven't you got something a little more reverent?

FRAZER (**Taking a large tin of fruit salts out of his sack**) Only this tin of fruit salts.

MAINWARING That'll do. (**He takes it and puts it down beside the mess tin**)

Pike enters with cardboard box.

PIKE Evening, Mr Mainwaring. I think I've got everything.

MAINWARING Well done, Pike. Now, the High Street. Lay out the Spam tins, Walker. (**Walker lays out the tins in a row**) And we want something for the promenade, get some hymn books, Wilson.

WILSON I don't think the Vicar would like that very much, sir.

MAINWARING This is war, Wilson. Get them. Now, we need something for a bandstand.

GODFREY (**Taking out a powder puff**) How about this little puff, sir? (**He puts it in position upside down. By now Wilson has finished laying out all the hymn books for the promenade**)

MAINWARING Now the allotments.

FRAZER **(Holding up a loofah)** Will this do?

MAINWARING Excellent. **(He takes it and puts it in position)** Now something for the gas works.

WALKER How about this tin of bicarbonate of soda. **(He hands him the tin)** One and fourpence.

MAINWARING Thank you. **(He puts it in position)** The cricket pitch. **(He takes a hanky out of his pocket and lays it in position)**

WILSON The scoreboard. **(Puts box of matches down)**

MAINWARING Now we need something for the pier.

PIKE Here you are, Mr Mainwaring. **(Hands him a bath brush)**

MAINWARING Fine. **(Puts it in position)**

WILSON Don't forget the pier's been blown up in the middle, sir.

FRAZER Well, that's simple enough. **(He picks up the brush and breaks it in the middle)**

WILSON That's my bath brush, Frazer.

FRAZER Then what was it doing in Mrs Pike's bathroom?

WILSON Well 'em – er. What I meant to say was, it was mine. That is, before I gave it to Mavis.

MAINWARING Now our gun is here. **(Puts toy gun in front of the church)** Have you got the soldiers, Pike?

PIKE Yes, sir. **(Gives Mainwaring box with seven soldiers in it)**

MAINWARING **(Setting the soldiers up behind the gun)** This knight in armour is you, Jones. **(Puts down a knight in armour)**

JONES Oh thank you, sir.

MAINWARING And this Highlander is you, Frazer. **(He puts down a Highland soldier)**

FRAZER Aye.

MAINWARING Walker and Godfrey. **(He puts down two guardsmen)** And this is you, Pike. **(He puts down a soldier without a head on)**

PIKE Why should I be the one without a head? After all, they are my soldiers.

MAINWARING You'll do what you're told, Pike.

PIKE It's not fair.

GODFREY Well, I don't mind being the one without the head, sir.

MAINWARING Oh, very well. **(He changes them over)** Let me see, we've got an Indian and a cowboy. I shall be the cowboy. **(Puts down the cowboy)** And you will be the Indian, Wilson. **(He puts down the Indian)**

WILSON I rather thought I'd be the Indian, sir.

MAINWARING All right, Wilson. We're all ready, call the men in.

WILSON **(Going to the door)** Will you all come into the office for the… er… TWIT.

They all file into the office and gather round the board.

MAINWARING **(Holding his stick)** Good evening, gentlemen. Will you all gather round the table. Now, pay attention, please. **(He clears his throat)** As you must realise, our fighting potential is now enormously increased by the addition of a 13-pounder gun. In the light of this, we must now conceive our whole form of tactics on a much broader scale. **(Pike is leaning on the table)** Don't lean on the gasworks, boy! Now, with our main armament here **(He taps the gun)** we can command this whole stretch of coast. However, there are certain obstacles in our way. For a start this puff, I mean this bandstand will have to go. Not only is it in direct line of fire, there is nothing to stop the enemy using it as cover for one of their invasion barges. That's just the sort of shabby trick the Nazis would use. Anyhow, I have written to the Town Clerk telling him it's got to come down in 48 hours.

WILSON Isn't that a bit high-handed, sir?

MAINWARING No, not at all. Believe me, I know these local officials. It's the only sort of language they understand.

WILSON But they'll never be able to get it down in 48 hours. It's made of solid iron.

WALKER War weapons! I'll take it down for nothing, Mr Mainwaring. Just so long as I can keep the iron.

MAINWARING I think we'd better leave it in official hands, Walker. Now, the next thing that gets in the line of fire are those allotments. They've all got to be flattened. **(He sweeps aside the loofah with his stick)**

FRAZER But those are my runner beans and my tomatoes. Ye canna interfere with those. What about the 'Dig for Victory' campaign?

MAINWARING It can't be helped, Frazer. Guns before vegetables.

GODFREY I've got an idea, sir. Couldn't we leave them for the moment, and if there's an invasion signal we could all run out and pick them, very quickly.

Mainwaring reacts.

MAINWARING Now the next thing that is in line of fire is the cricket pitch. The scoreboard will have to come down.

WILSON But, sir… not the scoreboard!

MAINWARING I know you're Captain of the cricket team, Wilson, but we can't make any exceptions.

WILSON Couldn't we possibly leave it until the cricket season's over, sir?

MAINWARING Unfortunately, Wilson, the Nazis don't play

cricket. If they did, we wouldn't be on opposite sides. All right, now, in the event of the balloon going up, this will be our new plan of action. Pike –have you got the armoured van?

PIKE Yes, sir. (**He produces a toy car**)

MAINWARING Right, put it behind Jones' shop. (**Pike puts the car behind a tin**) Now, we will all take up our positions as we would be during a normal working day. (**He hands a soldier to Jones**) All right, Jones, get in your shop.

JONES I beg your pardon, sir.

MAINWARING You are the solider. Put it on the tin.

JONES Oh, I understand now, sir. (**He puts the soldier on top of the tin**) I'm in my shop, sir.

MAINWARING Thank you, Jones. Now, you, Frazer will be in your shop. (**He hands him the soldier**) And you, Walker will be in your… er… business premises. (**He hands him the soldier**) Sergeant Wilson, Private Pike and myself will be in the bank. (**He puts the Indian, soldier and cowboy on a tin**)

GODFREY Where shall I be, sir?

MAINWARING Oh yes, Godfrey, you'd better be in… er… the… er.

WALKER He'll either be in the one on the front or the one in the town. (**Mainwaring hands him the headless soldier**)

MAINWARING That'll do, Walker. Now let's imagine the church bells have just gone. You, Jones, will run out of your shop.

JONES Yes, sir. (**He picks up his soldier and drops it in the sawdust**) Just a minute, sir, I lost myself in the sawdust.

MAINWARING Oh hurry up, Jones.

JONES (**Finding his soldier**) It's all right, sir, I've got hold of myself now.

MAINWARING Now, you will run round the back of your shop and start up the van. Quickly drive down the High Street and pick up Frazer, who will be waiting outside his shop. (**Jones is moving the car**) Then pick up Walker, who will be waiting at the bottom of the Slope Alley. You will then drive down to the bottom of the High Street, turn sharp left at the bottom and proceed up the Eastgate Road to the church hall.

WALKER He can't do that, Mr Mainwaring – one way street.

MAINWARING Not in an emergency, Walker. Meanwhile, we will run from the bank to the church hall. (**He jumps his figure through the sawdust**) Come on, Wilson, move yourself! (**He and Pike jump their figures through the sawdust**)

GODFREY Can't I get a lift in the van, sir?

MAINWARING We can't be sure where you'll be at any one time, Godfrey. So you'll have to make your own way to the hall. The rest of the platoon will get there as quickly as they can. Now let's assume that enemy invasion barges are trying to land troops. We are manning the gun and keeping up a constant fire. They're also dropping parachute troops so Private Sponge will take Jones' place at the gun and you, Jones, will take the rest of the platoon in the armoured van to deal with the parachute troops. Right, now we'll just try that. Are you ready, Jones?

JONES Yes, sir, all ready.

MAINWARING Fire! (**He fires the gun**) All right, Jones, move the van. Fire!

Mainwaring is firing the gun and Jones is moving the van up and down the screen. The rest of the platoon are getting very excited. The door opens. The Town Clerk, Mr Rees, comes in followed by Mr Bennett, the Borough Engineer.

REES (**Tapping Mainwaring on the shoulder**) Good evening, Mainwaring.

MAINWARING (**Turning round**) Good evening.

REES You know me, Mr Rees, Town Clerk. This is Mr Bennett, the Borough Engineer. (**Mr Bennett grunts**)

MAINWARING How do you do? (**Mr Jones, carried away, is still moving the van**) All right, Jones, you can stop now.

JONES Is the war over now, sir?

MAINWARING Yes, just for now. (**To Rees**) We were just having a T.E.W.T.

REES Really?

MAINWARING Tactical Exercise Without Troops. (**Pointing**) This is Walmington-on-Sea.

REES You could have fooled me. Now look, Mainwaring, I'm not going to beat about the bush. What's the idea of sending me an ultimatum, I'm not used to getting ultimatums.

MAINWARING The point is that the bandstand has got to come down.

REES Why?

MAINWARING Because it is directly in the line of fire.

REES But that bandstand is a rare example of Victorian artwork. It was erected to commemorate Queen Victoria's visit to this town in 1891.

JONES I remember it well… I was given special leave to take part in the Guard of Honour and as the old Queen came down our ranks she stopped in front of me and she said, 'You remind me of my dear Albert' and I looked at her with tears in my eyes and I said, 'And you, Your Majesty, remind me of my dear old Mum', and she walked away. Hence the expression, 'We are not amused'.

MAINWARING Neither are we.

REES As I was about to say… you can't say that bandstand's got to come down like that, Mainwaring. Before a decision is taken it's got to go before the Town Council.

MAINWARING Well, put it before the Council then.

REES I can't do that, it's got to be discussed in Committee first.

MAINWARING There's no time for all that red tape. Isn't there any other way we can do it?

REES We could have an emergency meeting. That's if it were considered urgent enough.

MAINWARING Of course it's urgent. The whole defence of this town rests on that gun.

REES You'd better try to convince the Committee of that.

MAINWARING I'll do better, I'll lay on a full demonstration.

The Verger enters.

VERGER Excuse me, sir.

MAINWARING Not now, Verger.

REES All right then, if you think you can pull it off, I'll get the Committee along.

MAINWARING Very well then. Sunday morning at 10.30.

WILSON Do you think that's wise, sir?

MAINWARING I know what I'm doing, Wilson.

VERGER Excuse me, sir.

MAINWARING Go away, man.

REES All right then, 10.30 Sunday. I wouldn't miss this for the world.

VERGER Excuse me, sir, I've got to put this blackout up.

MAINWARING Come back later.

VERGER It's got to go up now and that's that.

He picks up the screen and the whole contents of the sand table slide on the floor.

SIDE OFFICE

Mainwaring is at the desk. There is a knock on the door.

MAINWARING Come in.

Again there is a knock.

MAINWARING Come in.

The knocking is resumed. Mainwaring leaves his desk and opens the door. The whole space is filled with a camouflage net. Jones gets his head round half-way up.

JONES This has arrived, sir. I think it's a camouflage net so that our firing position will not be perceived from the air.

MAINWARING Excellent, Jones, excellent. Get someone to help you throw it over the gun. **(The net falls forward with Pike on top)**

JONES Private Pike is helping me, sir. **(Pike sneezes)**

PIKE Blimey, it isn't half dusty.

MAINWARING Never mind, Pike, get it out of here and over the gun. Spread it well out and hold it down with sandbags. Off you go. **(Jones and Pike struggle off with the net)**

There is a knock at the door.

MAINWARING Come in. **(Enter the Town Clerk)** Ah, Mr Rees, come in. We'll be ready for the demonstration in five minutes. You're a little early.

REES Five minutes, eh? What would happen if I was the invasion, eh? Would you have five minutes then, eh?

MAINWARING If you were the invasion, Mr Rees, you wouldn't knock on the door. You would be heralded by a peal of bells followed by a hail of high explosive shells from our gun.

REES Well, we'll see about that, won't we?

MAINWARING Follow me, Mr Rees. I think you might be quite impressed.

They go outside.

CHURCH YARD

The camouflage net is now covering the gun completely.

MAINWARING Well done, Jones. You've made a good job of that camouflage net. **(He turns to the Town Clerk and salutes rather pompously)** Permission to carry on, sir?

REES Carry on should be the right name for it, I should think.

MAINWARING Detachments rear! **(The principals fall in, except Godfrey)** Private Godfrey, Private Godfrey, what's the matter with you, Godfrey? **(Godfrey takes two pieces of cotton wool out of his ears)**

GODFREY I'm sorry, sir. I took precautions, in case you let it off.

MAINWARING Fall in with the gun detachment. Now on the command 'Action', I want to see you all move like greased lightning and get that gun ready for action. S-Q-U-A-D.

WILSON **(Interrupting)** Wouldn't it be better if we removed the camouflage net before we start.

MAINWARING I don't consider that very good thinking.

WILSON Why not, sir?

MAINWARING What is the point, Wilson, in camouflaging our gun when the enemy is elsewhere, and uncamouflaging it as soon as he is likely to see it? The men will get the gun ready for action and then at the very last minute they'll fling aside the net and pour forth our deadly fire.

REES Deadly – who to?

MAINWARING I'll soon show you. **(He calls)** Enemy tank right, action!

Jones, Frazer and Godfrey struggle to get under the camouflage net. Walker and Pike go for the ammunition. They struggle ineffectually for some moments.

MAINWARING Hurry up, Jones. **(He turns to Rees)** They're very keen, you know. **(He shouts)** Range 500 yards.

REES It'll be range ten yards by the time they're ready.

WALKER Here you are, Jonesey, I've got a shell for you. Where are you? **(He prods a body)**

GODFREY I'm not Mr Jones.

VOICE OF FRAZER Somebody's in my place.

MAINWARING Come along now. Enemy tank right, range 500.

REES Standing still, is it?

MAINWARING Four hundred and fifty yards. Come along, Jones, is the gun ready for action?

JONES I don't know, sir, I can't find it.

MAINWARING **(Going to rear)** Where are you, Jones? **(He gets his feet tangled in the net and falls)** Oh, Walker, try to find him.

WALKER Right. Here you are. **(He gives Mainwaring the shell. He lifts the net)** And cop hold of this. **(He dives under)** Where are you, Jonesey?

MAINWARING **(Calling to Rees)** Won't be a moment now. Where are you, Jones? Are you there, Frazer?

FRAZER I can't turn this handle for this blasted net.

VOICE OF GODFREY I think I've found my place.

MAINWARING Right, Pike, Wilson... er... take this net off. Enemy tank right, range 400 yards.

Pike and Wilson grab the barrel end of the net. Jones scrambles out from under the net and comes up to Wilson.

JONES Don't worry, sir, I'm not going to let it beat me.

MAINWARING Stay where you are, Jones. We're taking the net off. Hurry up, Wilson. Have you set the range?

Wilson and Pike take the net off the barrel end of the gun and in doing so throw it over Mainwaring and Jones.

MAINWARING Take that damn thing off. **(To Rees)** We'll have them any minute now. Enemy tank right, range... er... 300 yards.

REES Here, Mainwaring. I think I've seen enough. I'll report to my sub-committee.

MAINWARING Good, well I'm sure you understand that we'll soon sort out these minor details of our drill.

REES I'm sure you will. I'm going to tell my committee they can sleep sound in their beds.

MAINWARING You can rest assured of that.

REES Provided they make them inside that enemy tank.

He goes, as Mainwaring and the rest struggle to free themselves.

SERIES THREE **EPISODE EIGHT**

Recorded: Thursday 23/10/69

Original transmission: Thursday 30/10/69, 7.30–8.00pm

Original viewing figures = 12.5 million

ARTHUR LOWE .... CAPTAIN MAINWARING
JOHN LE MESURIER .... SERGEANT WILSON
CLIVE DUNN .... LANCE CORPORAL JONES
JOHN LAURIE .... PRIVATE FRAZER
JAMES BECK .... PRIVATE WALKER
ARNOLD RIDLEY .... PRIVATE GODFREY
IAN LAVENDER .... PRIVATE PIKE
BILL PERTWEE .... ARP WARDEN
FRANK WILLIAMS .... VICAR
EDWARD SINCLAIR .... VERGER
NAN BRAUNTON .... MISS GODFREY
JENNIFER BROWNE .... WAAF SGT.
ANDREW CARR .... OPERATIONS ROOM OFFICER
THÉRÈSE MCMURRAY .... THE GIRL IN THE HAYSTACK
KENNETH WATSON .... RAF OFFICER
VICKI LANE .... THE GIRL ON THE TANDEM
HAROLD BENNETT .... MR BLEWITT
JACK HAIG .... THE GARDENER

PLATOON ...... HUGH HASTINGS, DESMOND CULLUM-JONES, VIC TAYLOR, ... FREDDIE WILES, GEORGE HANCOCK, MARTIN DUNN, ... LESLIE NOYES, ROGER BOURNE, FREDDIE WHITE, JIMMY MAC

EXTRAS .. BRIAN NOLAN (RAF OFFICER), CHRISTINE COLE (WAAF PRIVATE), ... JEAN FADGROVE (WAAF CORPORAL), IONA MACRAE (WAAF SGT) .... SANDY STEIN (WING COMMANDER)

STUNTMAN .... JOHNNY SCRIPPS

THE DAY THE BALLOON WENT UP

• HAROLD SNOAD REMEMBERS •

'The first problem with the location work on this episode began when I was woken in my hotel room at four-thirty in the morning by a telephone call. It was the people providing the balloon saying they thought it extremely unlikely that we would be able to film because the wind was far too strong. Being an optimist, I suggested delaying going out to the army training area for an hour. We actually waited a further two hours once we were there but the wind did die down sufficiently to enable us to film the sequence.

'There was another unplanned event in this episode: there is a point when Mainwaring is rescued from the balloon when he gets caught up on a railway bridge. I'd tracked down a suitable bridge over a virtually unused railway line and had it confirmed that there would be no trains on the day of filming. We were halfway through the sequence with the camera being held on a crane 15 feet or so above the line when the cameraman suddenly called out in panic: "There's a train coming!" I dashed along the line waving my arms and, thankfully, the driver stopped. It wasn't the normal goods' train that occasionally used the line, it was an engine towing a truck dispensing weedkiller on to the track. Apparently, someone had decided to do it that day because there were no other trains scheduled to run!'

HAROLD SNOAD

The Day the Balloon Went Up

THE YARD. DAY

The men are lounging around – waiting for parade. They are without rifles. Mainwaring enters with a paper in his hand.

WALKER Listen – I'll bring the van round to the back of your shop as soon as it's dark – then you can help me load the meat on – it's for this friend of mine who's got this restaurant. He'll see you right.

JONES Now look, Joe – I've told you before, I don't want anything to do with your black market activities.

WALKER It's not black market, you silly old duffer – he's got a Chinese restaurant.

JONES Well, yellow market then – I don't want anything to do with it.

MAINWARING Sergeant Wilson! Why aren't the men fallen in?

WILSON Well, probably because I haven't told them, sir.

MAINWARING Well, would you mind telling them now?

WILSON Right, fall in you chaps. Squad... Squad, 'shun! **(Jones is late)** That wasn't awfully good, was it? Stand at... ease! **(Jones is again late)** Try to do it when the others do it, Jones.

JONES I'm sorry, Sergeant.

WILSON You see, it makes the whole squad look so slovenly.

JONES Sorry, Sergeant.

WILSON It could be the way I give the command, I suppose.

JONES **(Coming to attention)** You give a beautiful word of command, Mr Wilson – though if I may say so, you're a bit refined. The sergeants I served under used to bark it out, very fiercely – being mostly of a savage nature. Bark it out, Sergeant, and I'll not be found lacking.

WALKER You don't want a sergeant, you want an Alsatian.

MAINWARING That's enough, Walker.

WILSON Perhaps if I shout a bit louder, sir, it might make Jones feel more at home.

MAINWARING Get on with it, Wilson.

WILSON Squad... 'shun! **(He barks it)**

Jones is on time but – being to attention – now stands at ease. The rest of the squad come to attention.

WILSON Remarkable, don't you think so, sir?

MAINWARING The only slight criticism I have is that the rest of the squad is at attention, and Jones is standing at ease.

WILSON By Jove, so he is. Jones, do you think you could put your legs together?

MAINWARING What do you mean – 'put your legs together'? You're supposed to be a sergeant, not headmistress at a girls' school. Jones – 'shun!

Jones comes to attention – the rest of the platoon obey the command and stand at ease.

MAINWARING That's the way to do it, Sergeant.

WILSON The only slight criticism I have, sir, is that the rest of them seem to be standing at ease.

MAINWARING Stand at attention, all of you! **(He goes to Jones)** Very smart, Jones.

JONES Thank you, sir. I've got some nice kidneys for Mrs Mainwaring.

MAINWARING Don't talk on parade, Corporal. Bring them to the office after inspection. **(Mainwaring passes to Walker, who has something large in each jacket pocket)**

MAINWARING Walker – what have you got in those pockets?

WALKER There's a pound of granulated there, and a pound of sultanas there.

MAINWARING Wilson, you really must check this sort of thing before I inspect the men.

WILSON Yes, sir. It's disgraceful, Walker. If you do that again, I'll make you throw the stuff in the dustbin.

WALKER Makes no odds to me –you've already paid for it.

WILSON It's not for me, it's for Mrs Pike.

GODFREY May I be of assistance?

MAINWARING Look to your front, Godfrey! Don't wear your hat straight like that – you look like George Formby.

GODFREY I'm sorry, sir – would you mind holding this? **(He hands Mainwaring a walking stick, in order to adjust his hat)** Is that better?

MAINWARING What's this? **(Indicating stick)**

GODFREY I get a little twinge of gout when there's a damp spell – only in one foot fortunately.

Mainwaring looks down – Godfrey is wearing one carpet slipper.

MAINWARING You can't come on parade like that – fall out! Now, pay attention, all of you. It is quite clear to me that this platoon is getting very lax in the matter of personal appearance and discipline, and this is borne out by the signal I have received from the C.O. It appears that he came through here yesterday and didn't receive a single salute. Furthermore – a Lance Corporal even had his hands in his pockets, which he did not remove.

JONES Permission to confess, sir.

MAINWARING Yes, Jones.

JONES I was that Lance Corporal, sir.

MAINWARING I'm surprised at you, Jones – I've always found you most punctilious about saluting.

JONES It was a case of forgetfulness, sir.

MAINWARING Forgetfulness? But surely you haven't forgotten what an officer looks like.

JONES No, sir, I had forgotten my braces, sir. I thought if I took my hands out of my pockets to salute him – it would not be seemly, sir.

MAINWARING I see. Well, we're going to spend the next five minutes saluting. You give the order, Jones, and remember – it's the longest way up – one – shortest way down – two. And pay special attention to this: palm to the front, so! Forefinger in line with the right eyebrow, so. Carry on, Corporal.

JONES Squad, hup!

ALL Longest way up – one

JONES Shortest way down – two

ALL Shortest way down – two.

Enter the Vicar.

JONES Squad, hup!

ALL Shortest way up – one…

The Vicar sees that he is being saluted.

VICAR Oh! Oh – er, er – bless you. That's rather taken the wind out of my sails. I came here to be very cross with you, Mr Mainwaring. Someone has written something very rude on the back of the spare harmonium.

MAINWARING I don't see how that concerns my platoon.

VICAR Well, it's in the tower room. Your men sleep in there on fire-watch.

MAINWARING They wouldn't do a thing like that.

VICAR Well, they have. Come and see for yourself.

MAINWARING Wilson, come with me. Jones – carry on with the saluting.

Mainwaring, Wilson and the Vicar go.

JONES Squad, hup!

ALL Longest way up – one – shortest way down – two.

JONES Squad… hup!

ROOM IN THE TOWER. DAY

It is quite a small room. There is a steep stair approach and a ladder going to the tower above. There is a good-sized window in one wall. We see the front of the harmonium. The Vicar enters, followed by Mainwaring. They are both breathless.

MAINWARING Double up, Wilson.

VICAR **(Pointing to the back of the harmonium)** There! What have you to say to that?

MAINWARING Ah. Well, my men don't do that sort of thing and I'm going to prove it. Wilson!

Wilson arrives – leaning up against the entrance, completely out of breath.

WILSON By Jove, sir, it's a jolly long way up, isn't it?

MAINWARING Go down and get Jones' section up here.

WILSON What, all the way down again?

MAINWARING At the double.

WILSON Can I go home then, sir?

MAINWARING No, I want you up here – a witness. You can get the rest of them. **(Wilson turns and goes)** Now – where's the instrument?

VICAR I beg your pardon?

MAINWARING The instrument – that the culprit used.

VICAR Oh. **(He picks something off the harmonium)** Here it is – it's a wax crayon. What's more, it won't rub off.

THE YARD. DAY

JONES Squad… hup!

ALL Longest way up – one – shortest way down – two.

JONES That's better. Now, when you get it up – with the forefinger in line with the eyebrow – I want you to give it a little wiggle – like that. Squad… hup!

Enter Wilson – breathless.

WILSON All right, Jones – that's enough of that. Bring your section, single file – up to the top of the church tower – at the double. The rest of you can go.

JONES **(Leading the way)** Right – follow me. Left, right, left, right, left…

ROOM IN THE TOWER. DAY

MAINWARING **(Putting his head in the entrance)** Hurry up, Wilson! I want to dispose of this matter once and for all.

VICAR Really, Mainwaring, I don't see the point of having the whole platoon round in here with their great big ugly boots.

MAINWARING I'm not having a slur like this hanging over my troops. Every one of my men is going to write that word, and you can compare the handwriting.

VICAR Mr Mainwaring – I am here to take care of the spiritual needs of my parish –not to play 'Inspector Hornleigh investigates'.

Jones enters.

JONES The Sergeant is lagging behind, breathless, sir.

MAINWARING Jones – come here! I've brought your section up here because you were the last on duty in the tower. Now, do you see that word?

JONES Yes, sir.

MAINWARING Did you do that?

Jones looks.

JONES I don't understand the question, sir.

MAINWARING Did you write that?

JONES Mr Mainwaring – I'm shocked… shocked that you should think me capable of such improper conduct.

MAINWARING It's nothing personal, Jones. I want you to take this crayon and copy those letters underneath.

JONES What, now, sir?

MAINWARING Now.

JONES In public?

MAINWARING Yes, in public.

JONES With His Reverence looking on?

MAINWARING Get on with it, Jones.

Jones takes the crayon and approaches the harmonium.

JONES I can't do it, sir.

MAINWARING It's an order, Jones.

WALKER I expect he'd rather do one of his limericks, wouldn't you, Jonesey?

WALKER What about 'There was a young lady called Vickers'?

JONES I told you that in confidence.

MAINWARING Get on with it, Jones.

Jones writes. The Vicar is pained. Walker is amused.

MAINWARING Hah. Well, that clears Jones.

JONES **(To Vicar)** I want you to know, sir, that I did not enjoy that.

VICAR Neither did I.

MAINWARING You next, Walker.

Walker takes the crayon.

WALKER **(Impersonating Pike)** My mum wouldn't like it, Mr Mainwaring.

MAINWARING Hurry up, Walker.

WALKER Shall I sign it?

MAINWARING I don't think there's any similarity, do you, Vicar?

VICAR Don't drag me into it.

We see the Verger outside the window, suspended from a cable. He is swinging from side to side and up and down. He has a duster in his hand.

MAINWARING You next, Pike.

Jones notices the Verger.

PIKE What's it mean, Mr Mainwaring?

MAINWARING All in good time, Pike.

JONES Permission to speak, sir?

MAINWARING Not now, Jones. Go along, Pike.

VICAR Has it occurred to you that somebody has got to remove all this?

JONES Permission to interrupt, sir?

MAINWARING Not now, Jones.

Sponge goes to write.

MAINWARING You next, Frazer.

FRAZER I'm refusing to obey.

MAINWARING Did I hear you right, Frazer?

FRAZER You canna touch pitch without being defiled.

JONES Sir, permission to report that the Verger is outside?

VICAR Oh, tell him to come in. I'm five minutes late.

JONES He's outside the window.

VICAR I beg your pardon?

JONES He's going up and down and… and… side to side.

VICAR **(Looking at his watch)** There's no need for him to be that impatient. **(He goes to the window)** Verger! Oh, my sainted aunt.

They all look out of the window.

MAINWARING What are you doing out there?

VICAR I told him to clean the windows, but I didn't expect him to go to that length.

MAINWARING **(Looks up)** It… it's a barrage balloon. He's caught in the cable of a barrage balloon.

Wilson enters out of breath.

WILSON I've come back, sir… the whole platoon's… queuing up… ready for you, sir.

MAINWARING Quick, Wilson, into the yard!

WILSON Oh, not again.

MAINWARING Jones – follow me with the rest of the platoon.

JONES Yes, sir. Don't panic. Don't panic anyone! Don't panic.

THE YARD. DAY

Godfrey is in the centre of the yard, looking up.

GODFREY Er… if you could manage to hold on a little longer, Mr Yeatman, I'll summon assistance.

TOWER DOOR AT SIDE OF YARD. DAY

Mainwaring appears at the bottom of the stairs. Mrs Dowding is waiting there.

MRS DOWDING Mr Mainwaring, the Verger has been taken from us.

MAINWARING Don't worry, madam, we'll soon have him under control.

Mainwaring joins Godfrey.

GODFREY I'm glad you're here, sir. Er… something rather odd has happened to the Verger.

JONES Don't panic, sir. Don't panic.

MAINWARING I've no intention of panicking, Jones. I'm just thinking out what to do.

They go out of shot towards the centre of the yard, leaving Mrs Dowding. The Vicar arrives at the bottom of the stairs.

MRS DOWDING I heard a voice from above, Vicar.

VICAR Yes – very distressing for you, Mrs Dowding.

MRS DOWDING I thought an angel from on high had visited me.

VICAR You would, naturally.

MRS DOWDING It cried out to me: 'Help! I am caught in this ruddy string!'

CENTRE OF YARD. DAY

MAINWARING Come on, all of you – grab this cable and heave. Come on, Godfrey.

GODFREY Er… would you mind holding this? **(He hands his stick to Mainwaring)**

MAINWARING Throw it away, man! Come on! Walker… Frazer… Jones!

JONES Don't panic. Don't panic.

VERGER **(Voice from above)** Somebody'd better panic – this is killing me.

MAINWARING Hold on, Verger! Help is at hand. Heave! **(The rope sticks)**

WALKER Hang on – it's stuck round the weathercock on the steeple.

MAINWARING So it is, Wilson!

Wilson enters from the tower.

WILSON Yes, sir?

MAINWARING You and Pike run to the top of the tower and scramble up the steeple!

WILSON Oh my God.

FRAZER There's no time for all that palaver – one good heave and it will carry away. Heave.

WILSON That's done it.

WALKER Look out, Vicar!

There is the sound of a breaking weathercock and falling masonry.

TOWER ROOM AT SIDE OF YARD. DAY

Vicar and Mrs Dowding in doorway.

MRS DOWDING Vicar, do you think this is a judgement on us?

VICAR I think it's most unlikely.

CENTRE OF YARD. DAY

Party at cable as before.

MAINWARING Easy does it – grab him.

The Verger comes down.

MAINWARING Untie him, Pike. Hang on, the rest of you.

PIKE How did it happen, Mr Yeatman?

VERGER Well I saw this cable thing wrapped round the lamppost.

JONES There you are, you see, you shouldn't touch things what don't concern you. You're a trouble maker.

MAINWARING Never mind that, Jones.

WALKER What are we going to do now?

MAINWARING Hang on for a moment while we think.

GODFREY I think we should all let go rather quickly and let it float away.

MAINWARING We can't do that – if those cables drift across high tension wires, they can black out whole counties.

FRAZER Well we can't hang on here for the rest of our ruddy lives.

WILSON If we brought it down a little further we could grab all those ropes dangling from the balloon itself.

MAINWARING Good idea. Heave away when I tell you.

JONES I think, sir – if we pulled it down a bit – we could hold on to those string things from the balloon itself.

MAINWARING Thank you, Jones. One, two, three, heave! A bit more – one more heave – go! Grab one, Pike. Keep it steady, all of you. **(Pike goes for a line)** Go on, Walker. Well done, Sponge. **(Walker and Sponge go for a line)**

JONES I'm going to hold on to one of these ropes.

MAINWARING Well done, Jones.

One by one they all take a line. Enter the Warden.

WARDEN Here! Who's in charge here? Where's Mainwaring?

WALKER He's the pig in the middle.

Mainwaring is still hanging on to the main cable.

WARDEN Now, just exactly what sort of game do you think you're playing?

MAINWARING One of these days, I'm going to have you suspended.

WARDEN Don't stand there muttering threats. Get that thing shifted. You should never have been allowed to bring it here in the first place.

MAINWARING This, Warden, is a run-away barrage balloon – and we have been struggling to bring it under control to prevent further damage.

WARDEN Then why don't you get on the phone to the R.A.F. instead of hanging on there like Winnie the Pooh?

MAINWARING That is precisely what I aim to do.

WARDEN Well, get on with it, then.

MAINWARING Right. Come on, Wilson.

Mainwaring, Warden and Wilson go towards the office. There is a yell from the men as their feet gently leave the ground. Wilson, Mainwaring and Warden rush back and grab the ropes.

MAINWARING Vicar! Come and hang on here while I phone for help.

VICAR Come along, Mr Yeatman.

VERGER No, Vicar. I'm not going up for a second time.

WALKER Don't worry, Verger, lightning never strikes twice.

VERGER It does in our family. I was one of twins.

VICAR Come along, Mr Yeatman.

Verger and the Vicar grab a dangling line.

MAINWARING Right – everyone hold steady – and we'll phone for help.

GODFREY Er... before you go, do you think I could absent myself for a few moments?

MAINWARING Certainly not – come on, Wilson. **(They both go)**

WARDEN 'Ere! If you think I'm standing 'ere holding this, you're mistaken.

WALKER Go on... pretend you're the Statue of Liberty.

WARDEN Oh no. This is a military matter. My duty is to make sure he phones properly. 'Ere – Miss Godfrey – cop hold.

She goes.

JONES There's not much weight in her, you know.

WARDEN Don't worry – she's got big bones. **(He hands the rope to Mrs Dowding)**

GODFREY Hold on Cissy, remember Joan of Arc.

SIDE OFFICE. DAY

Mainwaring is just dialling the last number.

MAINWARING Wilson. Double round and collect as many of the platoon as you can find... Hullo...

Inlay a split screen. A W.A.A.F. telephone operator answers the phone with operations room in the background, containing large scale map of the coast.

W.A.A.F. Operations?

MAINWARING Ah. Mainwaring here – Walmington-on-Sea Home Guard. I have to report that my men and I have captured one of your balloons.

W.A.A.F. Just a moment. **(She turns to the Squadron Leader)** Anyone lost a balloon?

SOLDIER **(At indicator)** There's one adrift from 'E' Sector.

W.A.A.F. Would you speak?

SOLDIER Not now. There's some bandits coming in over 26. Take the details and notify Barrage Commander.

W.A.A.F. Very good, sir. **(To phone)** Could I have the address?

MAINWARING St Aldhelm's church hall, Walmington-on-Sea.

W.A.A.F. Is the balloon attached to anything?

MAINWARING No, not now. It was wrapped round the Verger.

W.A.A.F. On her way to choir practice, was she?

WARDEN Now, look here. This is no time for all this rubbish. Give it here. **(He grabs the phone)** The point is this. Is it dangerous?

W.A.A.F. Well, not unless it catches fire.

WARDEN Not unless it catches fire – do you hear that? It can catch fire!

W.A.A.F. Don't let anyone smoke near it and we'll get someone round before nightfall.

MAINWARING Give me that phone. **(Into phone)** My men can't hang on to it all that time.

W.A.A.F. Couldn't you tie it to something?

MAINWARING What do you suggest we tie it to?

WARDEN Here – give me that phone. **(He takes phone)** They're not tying it up to anything. It can't stop here and that's final.

W.A.A.F. Perhaps the A.R.P. people could help you.

WARDEN **(To Mainwaring)** That's a good idea – get in touch with the A.R.P. people… I *am* the A.R.P. people.

SQUADRON LEADER Bandits 18 – scramble seven.

W.A.A.F. Sorry, I have to go now. We'll send help as soon as possible. **(She hangs up)**

WARDEN Now look here. You're in charge and it's your responsibility; That thing must be shifted, and shifted sharp. So what are you going to do about it?

MAINWARING Don't worry, Warden. I am well capable of handling the situation. Follow me.

THE YARD

They are all holding on to their individual piece of rope. Mainwaring enters.

MAINWARING Listen to me, men. I have a few words to say to you.

FRAZER Surely he's not going to make a ruddy speech.

MAINWARING The R.A.F. are coming to help us.

FRAZER He is!

MAINWARING But naturally they have a lot of things keeping them busy at the moment. Hitler is still poised across the water, and our lads can't relax their vigilance for a solitary second.

WARDEN Look here! I don't want to stand here listening to you making a speech. Get it shifted.

WALKER Couldn't we walk it into the fields and sort of tie it to a tree or something?

WARDEN Now that's the first sensible thing anyone's said for the last half hour – why didn't you think of that?

MAINWARING I was just about to suggest it.

JONES If we was to bring my van along, sir – we could tie it to that – as an extra precaution against it being wafted away by an unfavourable wind.

MAINWARING Good idea, Jones. I'll take your place – you get your van – and then we'll walk it out by the crossroads into Pinner fields. Off you go, Jones.

JONES I'll be back by six o'clock, sir.

He goes.

MRS DOWDING If I were you, Vicar, I'd cancel the confirmation class today.

TELECINE: COUNTRY LANE

Long shot of the balloon floating over hedgerows at about 20 feet.

Long shot of crossroads. The balloon – with the platoon holding the guy ropes – rounds a corner.

Long shot of the cavalcade, the balloon, followed by Jones' van, followed by Warden on an old motorbike.

MAINWARING Keep it up, men! Left, right, left, right!

Mid shot of Frazer.

Mid shot of Godfrey. Close up of Godfrey's feet – he wears one boot and one carpet slipper.

Medium length shot of the cable tied to the van – Jones driving.

Long shot of the cavalcade turning into a field.

Medium length shot of group of cows looking over hedge in amazement.

TELECINE: FIELD

Long shot of the cavalcade approaching an old fallen tree trunk lying in the field.

MAINWARING Hold it down, men, and I'll secure the cable. Untie your end, Jones.

Mainwaring winds the cable round substantial branch about ten inches thick and three foot long.

JONES All clear this end, sir.

Mainwaring steps over the branch to supervise the next stage. He has the slack in his hand – the cable from the line to the balloon is slack and between his legs with the line behind him.

MAINWARING That's it. Now all of you get round the tree and raise it – and I'll take a couple of turns round that main trunk for safety.

JONES Right – jump to it – hup!

They all release their guy ropes. The slack to the balloon is taken up abruptly, throwing Mainwaring back on the line. The line breaks off. Mainwaring is whisked into the air, sitting on it.

• BILL HARMAN REMEMBERS •

'A lot of exciting location stunt filming was provided by "The Day the Balloon Went Up", and it gave me my first taste of helicopter flying. The episode featured a runaway barrage balloon and the platoon's attempts to get it under control. Whilst tying the balloon to a tree, Mainwaring straddles a low branch, the branch snaps off and our hero sets off on a hair-raising balloon ride. For the filming of the flight sequence, we had a rope and branch suspended from a helicopter with stuntman Johnny Scripps doubling for Arthur Lowe for the flying sequences.

'Johnny was about the same height as Arthur but quite a bit thinner. Consequently, the costume department had to pad him out significantly. Johnny didn't say a lot during filming and smiled even less. He just went about his dangerous task in a quiet, professional and workmanlike manner. David Croft wanted the helicopter to ascend and descend throughout the sequence to give the impression that the balloon was alternately rising and falling as it got tossed around by gusts of wind. This meant that one moment Johnny might be carried up over the tree tops, the next we'd see him skimming across a field at a rate of knots with his legs and bottom only a foot or so above the ground.

'For this kind of high-flying stunt, it was normal for the stunt artist to wear a concealed safety harness and one was provided for Johnny. However, he chose not to wear it, preferring to risk falling off rather than not being able to bale out should he be dragged along the ground. It was frightening for us just watching the sequence being filmed, especially as it took a few takes to cover all the camera angles. Stunt artists certainly earn their fees and the good ones are much admired and respected by everyone in the industry. For them, being a consummate professional can literally be a matter of life and death. In the end Johnny's talents contributed enormously to a very funny and effective sequence.

'One of the angles needed for the stunt sequence was Mainwaring's point of view as he sailed through the air. For this a Tyler mount was used. This is a small seat for the camera operator, with a cantilevered arm above it to hold the camera. The whole apparatus is fitted to the side of the helicopter and the camera operator sits on the Tyler seat, half in and half out of the chopper with his feet on the helicopter skids. James Balfour, the film cameraman, shot the POV footage from this mount and at the end of the first sequence it was necessary to move to another location some 15 miles away. As I had never ridden in a helicopter at that time, I cheekily asked the pilot if I could hitch a ride with him. He was happy to oblige but the only spare seat was the Tyler mount. So I was strapped in and we took off on a relatively short but very memorable trip during which the only thing between me and the ground, two thousand feet below, was a rather thin lap safety belt

BILL HARMAN
Assistant Floor Manager

JONES Come back, Mr Mainwaring, come back.

They all dive for the rest of the cable. Jones has hold of the end which was attached to the van. Medium length shot of Jones holding on to the cable – running, and occasionally suspended into air from the ground.

The rest of the platoon pick themselves up and give chase.

The wind is blowing them across the field.

Finally Jones drops off.

The group close up to him, looking upwards.

JONES Don't panic, Mr Mainwaring, don't panic!

The Warden runs up and joins them.

WARDEN Right mess you made of that, didn't you? Well, don't all stand there gawping. You've got a van, haven't you – come on!

WILSON Er – come on, lads – into the van.

They all run to the van. Jones gets into the driving seat, Wilson beside him – the Vicar and the Verger beside Wilson.

WILSON Er – quick, Jones – er, follow that balloon.

Cut to back of van.

Frazer, Walker and Pike help Godfrey aboard.

Long shot of van moving off.

Medium length shot of Warden trying to start his bike in a cloud of exhaust from the van. He is practically obscured.

WARDEN Ruddy hooligans!

Cut to long shot of Mainwaring sailing along between two lines of trees – not too fast – at about 30 feet.

Long shot of van coming into road.

Long shot of Warden still trying to start bike.

Mid shot of Mainwaring hanging on to cable.

Trees and the road below are seen from about 30–50 feet level. See the van if possible.

Medium length shot of the Warden throwing down his bike.

WARDEN Ruddy useless thing!

He runs towards the road. Medium length shot of the Warden reaching the road by the field entrance. He runs a step or two, stops and looks at the receding van.

WARDEN Here – wait for me!

An old man rides up on a tricycle.

WARDEN Get off, Granddad, I'm commandeering this.

He climbs on the tricycle and rides off.

DRIVING COMPARTMENT OF VAN

Walker and Frazer put their heads through the trap behind Jones' driving seat.

WALKER Can you see him, Mr Wilson?

WILSON It… it seems to be getting higher and higher.

VICAR It'll go up each time it encounters hot air.

FRAZER He's never been short of that.

OPERATIONS ROOM, R.A.F

W.A.A.F. Unidentified object in 'C' Sector.

SQUAD LEADER Great Scott! Where did that come from?

W.A.A.F. Perhaps it sneaked in at wave level.

SQUAD LEADER (Grabbing phone) Scramble seven squadron.

TELECINE: COUNTRY LANE

Long shot of van driving along.

Medium length shot of Warden on tricycle.

STUDIO

WILSON He's above the cabin, I can't see him.

JONES Use the observation drill, Joe.

WALKER Right. Come along, Taffy.

BACK OF VAN

Shot from the top of the cabin. Voice of Walker – inside van leading the rest of the voices.

WALKER Open, two, three – up, two, three.

Frazer, Pike, Godfrey and Walker's heads come up through individual trap doors beside the rifle doors.

STUDIO

Mid shot of Mainwaring still – but spinning.

BACK OF VAN

WALKER (Looking right above him) Blimey! (His head comes down)

CABIN

Walker puts his head in the trap behind Jones.

WALKER Turn round, Jonesey, the wind's changing.

TELECINE: COUNTRY LANE

Long shot of van turning round.

Mid shot of Warden from the front – the van passes him, going the other way.

WARDEN Here! Where are you going?

He turns round and pedals after the van.

CABIN

FRAZER This is ridiculous. We can't go back and forward like this for the rest of our lives.

JONES I've got it, Mr Wilson. We must shoot holes in it so as the gases can expire.

WILSON Oh dear – do you think that's wise, Jonesey?

WALKER Blimey, we've got to do something, haven't we?

WILSON Oh all right, but aim carefully.

VICAR Surely even your lot couldn't miss a barrage balloon.

WILSON Yes… but can they miss Captain Mainwaring?

ROOF OF VAN

Walker, Frazer and Godfrey put their heads through the traps. Pike's rifle emerges.

WALKER Keep her steady, Jonesey. Go on, Pike.

The rifle fires.

STUDIO

Mid shot of Mainwaring reacting to bullet going past.

ROOF OF VAN

Pike's head comes through.

PIKE How was that?

WALKER Must be all right – he's still kicking. Let's give him three rounds each.

GODFREY I won't, if you don't mind.

WALKER No. You fix your bayonet in case he comes down low.

STUDIO

Mid shot of Mainwaring – more shots going past.

TELECINE: COUNTRY LANE

Long shot of Warden on tricycle. Sounds of shots in the background.

WARDEN Ruddy hooligans! What do you think you're playing at – cowboys and Indians?

OPERATIONS ROOM

W.A.A.F. and Squadron Leader are gazing at the board intently.

W.A.A.F. Whatever it is, it's moved to eight now.

VOICE OVER TANNOY Charlie Leader here. I've spotted it, it's a ruddy balloon. Hey wait a minute – there's a little fat round thing on the other end. Let's have a look, chaps.

Sounds of engines diving.

STUDIO

Mid shot of Mainwaring. Squadron of Spitfires whizz past him. He holds on to his hat.

ROOF OF VAN

PIKE We winged him – he's coming lower.

FRAZER He'd better come down fast – the way the wind's blowing he'll finish up in Belgium.

TELECINE: COUNTRY LANE

Medium length shot of couple on tandem. The boy behind – girl in front. Warden rides up on his tricycle.

WARDEN Here – I'm commandeering that.

He leaps on the back seat – he pedals off with the girl.

CABIN

JONES He's getting much lower.

WILSON Try to catch him before we get to the bend, Jonesey.

TELECINE: COUNTRY LANE

Long shot of van.

CABIN

JONES It's no good – he's way across the fields now.

TELECINE: HAYSTACK

View of haystacks as seen from Mainwaring's point of view.

STUDIO

Long shot of Mainwaring climbing the stack.

TELECINE: HAYSTACK

Long shot of haystack. Mainwaring breaks through. Shot of girl and boy.

GIRL Oh, Fred… that was wonderful… the whole world seemed to shake like.

CABIN

JONES He's off towards…

GODFREY Er, take the first on the right, Mr Jones – it's a short cut. Such a pretty walk in the summer.

TELECINE: HAYSTACK

Long shot of Mainwaring – hay sticking to him.

Medium length shot of field gentleman clipping single standing bush, shaped like a chicken or some such piece of topiary.

He turns away to put down the clippers – to pick up the secateurs. Mainwaring sweeps past, taking the bush with him.

The old man turns back and the bush is gone.

CABIN

WALKER Can't we go any faster, Jonesey?

JONES What are you talking about? I'm doing over 20 now.

TELECINE: COUNTRY LANE

WARDEN (On tandem to girl) Come on… you'd pedal quicker than that if you had a great big ugly Nazi chasing you.

GIRL You're not exactly Ronald Coleman, you know.

TELECINE: GARDEN

Long shot of line of washing – Mainwaring sweeps through.

TELECINE: RAILWAY LINE

Medium length shot of Mainwaring double on helicopter line – about six foot high – speeding along a railway line.

Medium length shot of tunnel bridge with a road over it. It is approaching from Mainwaring's point of view.

CABIN

FRAZER There's a balloon ahead – by the bridge!

TELECINE: RAILWAY TUNNEL

Medium length shot through the tunnel – Mainwaring suspended.

Medium length shot of rail by signal dropping to clear.

Long shot of van driving up at bridge – platoon de-bus.

Platoon start to retrieve Mainwaring by hauling him up on the cable up on the road. Train whistle is heard. Mainwaring's head appears over the parapet.

WALKER Blimey! Look out!

JONES Open your legs, Mr Mainwaring!

Intense noise of train going under the bridge. Cloud of steam from below enveloping them. Steam blacks out the picture.

Mid shot of Mainwaring lying against the bridge – coming round from a faint.

Pull back to see rest of group.

WALKER He's coming round.

WILSON For heaven's sake, give him air.

GODFREY Er… couldn't we burn some feathers under his nose?

MAINWARING All right… I'm all right – just a few scratches. Where's the balloon?

WILSON We've got it under control, sir.

R.A. F. officer approaches on motorbike.

R.A.F. OFFICER Well done, you chaps.

JONES Platoon, hup!

They all salute, balloon rises.

MAINWARING Quick – follow that balloon!

Long shot of all clambering back into the van.

SERIES THREE **EPISODE NINE**

Recorded: Thursday 30/10/69
Original transmission: Thursday 6/11/69, 7.30–8.00pm
Original viewing figures = 12.6 million

ARTHUR LOWE .... CAPTAIN MAINWARING
JOHN LE MESURIER .... SERGEANT WILSON
CLIVE DUNN .... LANCE CORPORAL JONES
JOHN LAURIE .... PRIVATE FRAZER
JAMES BECK .... PRIVATE WALKER
ARNOLD RIDLEY .... PRIVATE GODFREY
IAN LAVENDER .... PRIVATE PIKE
FRANK WILLIAMS .... VICAR
EDWARD SINCLAIR .... VERGER
JANET DAVIES .... MRS PIKE
NAN BRAUNTON .... MISS GODFREY
SALLY DOUGLAS .... BLODWEN
THE GRAHAM TWINS (VICKI & CATHY) .... DORIS & DORA
OLIVE MERCER .... MRS YEATMAN
HUGH HASTINGS .... THE PIANIST
ELEANOR SMALE .... MRS PROSSER
JENNY THOMAS .... VIOLET GIBBONS
PLATOON .... DESMOND CULLUM-JONES, VIC TAYLOR, FREDDIE WILES, GEORGE HANCOCK, MARTIN DUNN, FREDDIE WHITE, ARTHUR MCGUIRE, LESLIE NOYES, ROGER BOURNE
DRUMMER .... MICHAEL PULLEN
SAXOPHONE PLAYER .... JACK WHITEFORD
HOME GUARD GIRLFRIENDS .... JOANNA LAWRENCE, JULIE CASTELL, LELA FORD, MARY STEWART, MARY MAXSTEAD, CONSTANCE CARLING, CHEROKEE BURTON

War Dance

• BILL HARMAN REMEMBERS •

'My job was to set up the rehearsal room, with the outline of the studio set marked out on the studio floor. I would then attend all the rehearsals, making notes of special props and costume requirements, prompting actors and noting any script changes.

'On location and studio recording days, I would set all the action props for the actors, cue actors when required and generally assist Harold, who managed the smooth running of the studio or location days. Harold was a meticulous planner. He found the locations we would film at, organised the logistics of the shoot and structured the shooting day. These days, his many roles would be filled by a Production Manager, Assistant Director, Location Manager and Unit Manager but at that time, we did it all as a tight, well disciplined team. The Producer's Assistant would type up the camera scripts, call the shot numbers to the cameramen (they were all men at that time) and ensure that continuity was accurate and that the scenes ran to time.

'By the time I joined *Dad's Army*, I'd already worked on a number of other programmes, and came to the series after a six month stint on *Top of the Pops*. It was a strange progression and very different from the youthful buzz of a pop music show, but I was excited about the opportunity of working on a series that had already established itself as a major comedy institution. At 23, I had a huge amount to learn, and this was a fantastic vehicle in which to further my television apprenticeship.

'The production office atmosphere was very focused. David was generally quiet, not flamboyant in his approach to directing but always pleasant and seldom annoyed about anything. I saw him take a phone call from his wife one day as she explained that she'd seriously smashed up a new car he'd bought. Once he had established that she hadn't been hurt, he simply shrugged his shoulders and went back to his writing, seemingly completely unaffected by the costly accident.

'David was an excellent foil for Jimmy Perry whose approach was very different. Jimmy didn't work in the production office but would make regular visits and was always on set or location at rehearsals and on shoot days. This was unusual for scriptwriters, who would normally only be present at the first read-through of an episode, or when a major piece of rewriting was required.

'Where David would quietly giggle or simply smile at cast antics, Jimmy was given to huge grins and loud guffaws. He moved at a lightning pace and would never use lifts, preferring to charge up the many flights of stairs at Television Centre two steps at a time. He loved being one of the troupe, presumably a leftover of his theatre days, and obviously revelled in being present at the "coalface" during the recordings.'

BILL HARMAN
Assistant Floor Manager

War Dance

MAIN OFFICE IN BANK. EARLY MORNING

Pike is dusting. Love has struck him forcibly in the teeth in the last few days. He sings.

PIKE There is a lady sweet and kind.

Was never face so pleased my mind.

I did but see her passing by.

Yet will I love her till I die.

Mainwaring enters and hears the last line or so. Pike resumes.

PIKE Her gestures, motions…

MAINWARING I don't think we want any more of that stuff, Pike.

PIKE Sorry, Mr Mainwaring.

MAINWARING (**Hanging up his hat**) You will learn, as you grow older, Pike, that a bank manager's office is no place for singing.

PIKE Sorry, Mr Mainwaring.

Enter Wilson.

WILSON Morning, Frank. Morning, sir.

PIKE It was good news about the Home Guard dance, sir.

MAINWARING Well – all work and no play you know, Pike. Besides, it will make the wives and sweethearts feel that they're part of the grand effort. It makes them feel that we're all pulling in the same direction. (**To desk**)

PIKE Will we be able to bring a friend then, sir?

MAINWARING Of course. Who did you have in mind – one of your old boy scout friends?

PIKE No, sir – a girl.

MAINWARING A girl? Oh well, that's what dances are for, I suppose. Discuss it with Corporal Jones – he'll be in charge of the invitations.

PIKE I'll bring the coffee in a minute, sir. (**He goes out singing towards the door**) There is a lady sweet and fair…

MAINWARING Pike!

PIKE Sorry, sir, I forgot. (**He goes**)

MAINWARING (**Sits**) I'm far from satisfied with that boy's work lately, Wilson. He never stops humming.

WILSON I think perhaps he's letting his thoughts dwell too much on his private life.

MAINWARING Don't be absurd, Wilson – he doesn't have a private life. He's just a boy.

WILSON He's going on 19. He's walking out with an A.T.S.

MAINWARING With a what?

WILSON An A.T.S. girl.

MAINWARING Good heavens. You want to put a stop to that, Wilson. You never know where they come from.

WILSON She's a local girl, actually. She's on leave. Her name's Violet Gibbons.

MAINWARING Violet Gibbons? I know the girl. Her mother used to clean for us twice a week. Obliging us, she used to call it.

WILSON Well now her daughter's obliging Frank.

MAINWARING The girl used to work at the fish shop, didn't she?

WILSON That's the one, sir.

MAINWARING Not the right sort of background at all, Wilson. The Bank doesn't like that sort of thing.

WILSON What sort of thing?

MAINWARING You know perfectly well what sort of thing. The wrong sort of girl could ruin his whole career in the Bank.

MAINWARING What does his mother say?

WILSON She doesn't know.

MAINWARING You'll have to speak to him, Wilson.

WILSON Why me?

MAINWARING Well – the boy hasn't got a father. You've known his mother a long time – you're the next best thing.

WILSON Just because I'm rather friendly with Mrs Pike – I don't see why I have to act like a Dutch uncle to Frank.

MAINWARING You worry me sometimes, Wilson. You'd do anything rather than face your responsibilities. You just won't grow up, will you? You're not a middle-aged Chief Clerk at all – you're Peter Pan. I don't know how you ever expect to get your own branch.

WILSON Be that as it may – Frank Pike is *not* my responsibility.

MAINWARING I'm sure a lot of people will be very pleased to hear it.

WILSON What do you mean by that?

MAINWARING Well – it's none of my business – but this is a very small town, Wilson. Tongues wag. People put two and two together. You and Mrs Pike arrived in the town at about the same time – both from Weston-Super-Mare… and you look at Pike, in certain light, there are resemblances – the line of the hair, the way he pulls his right ear.

WILSON The whole idea's outrageous. I mean, Mavis would have mentioned it.

MAINWARING I'm sure it's just idle gossip. But at the same time, I think a word to the boy would come best from you.

WILSON I suppose I could chat to him.

Pike enters.

PIKE I've brought your coffee, Mr Mainwaring – Mr Wilson.

WILSON Thank you, Frank. (**He tries to look at Frank's hairline**)

PIKE Anything the matter, Mr Wilson?

WILSON No… no… nothing at all.

Wilson goes quickly out.

PIKE Is anything the matter with Mr Wilson?

MAINWARING No – it's just that his responsibilities weigh a little heavily upon him from time to time. (**Pike goes to door**) Oh… er… Pike – don't take any appointments for me after three o'clock. I have a meeting at the church hall with the Dance Committee.

SIDE OFFICE. CHURCH HALL

Jones, Godfrey, Frazer and Walker are sitting with Mainwaring. They are all in their civilian clothes.

MAINWARING Right, now, since this dance is in the nature of a recreation – I thought it best that we should meet in this friendly, relaxed way rather than in a more formal atmosphere. Pay attention, Walker! – and take your arm off my desk. Now – we're all busy men – going about our essential work as well as being ever alert to defend our beloved land – and I have therefore thought it best – and you can correct me if I'm wrong – that we should each be responsible for one aspect of Operation Dance.

JONES Mr Mainwaring, I think that's a good idea.

MAINWARING Thank you, Jones. Now, what – I ask myself – what are the essential ingredients? What do we need for a successful dance?

WALKER A floor.

MAINWARING I am not asking for suggestions at this stage, Walker. As I see it, there are three requirements. We need music to dance to, food for the inner man and drink for conviviality.

JONES There's one other thing we need, sir.

MAINWARING What's that, Jones?

JONES Women.

MAINWARING Yes – well I think that goes without saying, Jones.

WALKER About the booze, sir. That's very difficult these days – nearly impossible.

FRAZER Aye – but you can get it for us, can't you, Joe?

WALKER Well – I have contacts.

FRAZER At what price?

WALKER Well – a thing costs what it's worth, doesn't it?

FRAZER Mr Mainwaring, I would like to propose that we don't get it from Walker at his fancy profiteering prices.

WALKER Look, there's no need to be insulting – I don't make much out of it.

MAINWARING On this occasion there's no need to trouble, Walker. A very good friend of mine – the secretary of the golf club – is going to stand by us over the matter of the drink.

FRAZER One in the eye for you, Joe Walker.

WALKER Is it? Where do you think the golf club gets it from?

MAINWARING That brings us to food.

GODFREY If it's any help – I'm rather good at making Maids of Honour.

WALKER Blimey – that's a relief all round.

GODFREY They're little buns, actually – with bits of icing on.

MAINWARING I'm sure they'd be very welcome, Godfrey. Can you do anything for us, Jones?

JONES I have earmarked six pounds of sausages for you, sir. More than that, I cannot do.

MAINWARING I'm sure we're all very grateful to you, Jones.

JONES I can also allocate a bit of dripping to fry 'em in.

FRAZER Why don't we cut them up into quarters and put them in sausage rolls?

MAINWARING I think that's a very stimulating suggestion. For my part, I'm sure Mrs Mainwaring could throw a case around them – she's very ingenious in that sort of way. So – we have sausage rolls, Maids of Honour and the liquid refreshment. That brings us to the question of a band. Now, Miss Rowlands has offered her services, and that of her colleagues. You may recall that they used to play in the afternoons at the Marigold Tea Rooms.

GODFREY I don't think we ought to have too much of that Jazz music.

WALKER Not much chance with Miss Rowlands – blimey, talk about Nat Gonella.

JONES Let's have some real good tunes.

GODFREY 'Tell Me Pretty Maiden' is a delightful tune.

JONES And 'Any Old Iron'.

WALKER You can't dance to 'Any Old Iron', can you?

JONES Harry Champion does.

WALKER Look, Mr Mainwaring, if you don't mind me saying so, if you get old Miss Rowlands and her friend with buns on her earholes and a cello between her legs, and that old cow from the library on the 'arp, we might as well all go home.

FRAZER I don't often agree with you, Joe, but you're right.

WALKER Of course I'm right.

MAINWARING Yes, I think there is some force in what Walker is saying. The question is – where do we find the musicians?

JONES There's the Salvation Army, sir – a fine body of righteous men.

WALKER Oh, that'll be great – take your partners for 'What a friend we have in Jesus'.

MAINWARING Walker! May I remind you that we are on Church property.

WALKER I'm sorry, sir – but blimey, the Salvation Army. Look, tell you what. There's an R.A.F. holding unit at Godalston. I'll pop down there and see what they've got.

MAINWARING Good. Well done, Walker. So, we have the food, the wine and the song. Operation Dance has been well and truly launched. I feel sure that we will bring it safely and successfully to harbour.

WALKER Barring torpedoes.

CHURCH HALL

The hall is half decorated with paper streamers and various improvised and borrowed decorations. Pike is on a ladder being steadied by Wilson. He is putting up a large cut-out portrait of King George in the centre of the proscenium. Queen Mary has already been fixed facing away from George.

PIKE Can you hang on to the ladder a bit tighter, Uncle, it's ever so wobbly.

WILSON It's quite safe, Frank.

Enter Mainwaring. He carries a small box containing three or four rosettes.

MAINWARING Here we are, Wilson. Rosettes for the officials – secretary for you, M.C. for Jones, chairman for myself.

WILSON That's very good, sir. (**He picks up the fourth rosette**) Who wears the wine one?

MAINWARING I... I'm giving that to Walker.

WILSON I thought the secretary of the golf club was taking care of it all.

MAINWARING Yes... well he found he couldn't get his extra supplies. But it's quite all right – I've told Walker we won't be able to pay any of his fancy prices and he's assured me that he's hardly going to make anything out of it at all.

Pike comes down the ladder.

PIKE I think that'll stay up, sir.

MAINWARING (**Looking at the heads**) Shouldn't they be facing each other, Wilson?

WILSON I hadn't thought about it, sir.

MAINWARING Back to back like that makes them look as if they've quarrelled. Fix it later. Take these and put them on my desk, Pike. (**Pike takes the box**)

PIKE Very good, Mr Mainwaring. (**He goes**)

MAINWARING Wilson – have you spoken to him yet?

WILSON Er, no sir – not yet.

MAINWARING Well, why not?

WILSON The opportunity hasn't presented itself.

MAINWARING It's presented itself now – he's in my office.

WILSON One can't just dive head-first into a personal discussion on a delicate matter like this – I mean... one needs the right atmosphere... a log fire, a cosy chair... a pipe... a glass of port...

MAINWARING Peter Pan.

WILSON My God, Mainwaring – you can hit pretty low when it suits you. (**He goes**)

Jones comes up to Mainwaring.

JONES Mr Mainwaring, sir, while I was in bed last night I had a sudden thought.

MAINWARING Really.

JONES Why don't we have a cabaret? I know several humorous monologues and I also do impersonations, and Private Frazer's been practising his Highland Sword Dance.

MAINWARING Ah, yes – well, er – we'll put it before the Committee, Jones.

JONES Thank you, Mr Mainwaring, sir. (**He crosses to the centre door and meets Frazer**) Here, Jock – I've had a word with Mr Mainwaring about the sword dance.

FRAZER I've gone right off the idea. (**He limps towards the stage**)

SIDE OFFICE. CHURCH HALL

PIKE I'll go and see what Captain Mainwaring wants me to do next.

WILSON Now don't rush away, Frank. By Jove, you and I don't often get a chance to be alone and have a cosy little chat.

Pike surveys the uncosy surroundings.

PIKE Don't we, Uncle?

WILSON Are you looking forward to this dance, Frank?

PIKE Yes, thank you, Uncle.

WILSON You don't have to keep calling me Uncle.

PIKE No, Sergeant.

WILSON Not that either. We're both grown up – men of the world. You're Frank – I'm Arthur.

PIKE Oh. How do you do?

WILSON Yes – you're… you're not a boy now – we can look each other in the eye and… talk man to man. (**He gives Pike a quick glance and looks away**)

PIKE That's nice, isn't it?

WILSON Yes. There are… heaps of things that we can talk about that we've… never talked about before.

PIKE That's nice, isn't it?

WILSON Don't keep saying 'That's nice', Frank. It's terribly irritating.

PIKE I'm sorry, Uncle… Sergeant… Arthur.

WILSON I… I didn't mean to snap like that, Frank – I… I'm sorry.

PIKE That's all right.

There is an awkward pause.

PIKE It's good being able to talk man to man, isn't it?

WILSON Yes… yes, it's nice.

PIKE What shall we talk about then?

WILSON Well, I've never chatted to you about, um… girls, for instance.

PIKE Oh that. I know all about the birds and bees and things.

WILSON I didn't mean that.

PIKE Miss Beckworth told me.

WILSON Good.

PIKE She knows a lot about girls.

WILSON I'm sure she does.

PIKE She knows a fair amount about boys, too.

WILSON Frank, the point is – who are you taking to the dance?

PIKE Oh. I thought I'd take my girlfriend, Violet Gibbons.

WILSON That's precisely what I wanted to talk to you about.

PIKE Why? You don't want to take her, do you?

WILSON No, certainly not – I don't even know her.

PIKE I didn't think you did. Oh, she's beautiful – she's the most wonderful person in the whole wide world. I love her, Uncle Arthur. When I woke up this morning, I wanted to run to the top of the church tower and shout it to the winds. 'I love Violet Gibbons', I wanted to shout. I didn't though.

WILSON I think you were very wise… er, one mustn't be hasty… there are so many things to consider… I mean – is she suitable, Frank?

PIKE Suitable? What for?

WILSON The Bank.

PIKE She can't go into the Bank – she's in the A.T.S.

WILSON No, Frank… I'm talking about… after the war – when all this is over – when you come back.

PIKE Oh she won't go into the Bank then – she'll be married to me.

WILSON Married!

PIKE Can you keep a secret, Uncle Arthur? I'm going to surprise everyone – I'm going to announce our engagement in the middle of the dance, like Jack Oakie did with ZaSu Pitts.

WILSON Frank, I… I wouldn't do that, if I were you… I, I, I mean, think of your mother – it could be an awful shock to her.

PIKE Oh no, Uncle, she'll like it. When Jack Oakie and ZaSu Pitts did it, she said it was the best part of the film.

WILSON I think it just possible that this may be different, Frank.

BANK OFFICE

Mainwaring behind desk.

MAINWARING It sounds to me as if you made a complete mess of it, Wilson.

WILSON Perhaps if you spoke to him now, sir.

MAINWARING No, it wouldn't be at all a good idea. You need someone nearer to his own age group. Try Walker.

CHURCH HALL

WALKER I don't think it would be much good me talking to him. If the mood takes him, he can be very pig-headed. What about his mum? Has she washed her hands of the whole business?

WILSON Well, that's the point, Joe – she doesn't even know the girl exists. If he, if he blurts it out like that at the dance, she'll... she'll make the most awful scene.

WALKER Tell you what – I might have a word with Violet.

WILSON Violet? Do you... do you know her?

WALKER Well, you know how it is. I was a bit keen on her when she was at Woolworths. Then when she went to the fish shop it sort of somehow... wasn't the same. I mean she was – all right out in the open watching football, but when she got hot in the pictures, people would shift their seats. Well, a man finds that humiliating, doesn't he?

WILSON Have a word with her, Joe. Perhaps she might persuade him not to do anything too hasty.

WALKER Yeah – she tried to persuade me that way once. Mind you, I never was a good listener.

CHURCH HALL

The hall is decorated ready for the dance. The side office is being used for a cloakroom with a table across the door for tickets. Three musicians are getting ready on the stage. There is a period microphone on a stand with the amplifier, camera right. The bar is under the camera right balcony. Jones is on the stage, talking to the musicians.

Vicar enters.

JONES You arrange yourselves here – and point your music out that way. I'll announce each dance – and before I do so, I would like you to give me a ta-ra.

The Vicar comes up to Jones.

VICAR Ah – Corporal Jones.

JONES I'm very busy with my last minute preparations, sir.

VICAR Where's Mr Mainwaring?

JONES He'll be here any minute, sir, he's bringing the sausage rolls – and he wishes to be here first with his good lady so as to greet all the guests personally – whom I shall announce, sir.

VICAR Funny – I've never met Mrs Mainwaring.

JONES Neither have I, sir – I understand they're a very devoted couple – only she don't get about much.

VICAR I wanted to impress on Mr Mainwaring that I'm most anxious that there should be no drunkenness or hooliganism.

JONES Mr Mainwaring is a fine, upright man and a gentleman, and he wouldn't permit any of that sort of thing, not in front of his good lady, sir.

VICAR **(Pointing to bar)** All this lot isn't for gargling, is it?

Walker joins Jones.

WALKER The microphone's ready, Jonesey. All you have to do is switch on. 'Ere Vicar, that Joanna's murder. There's a note missing.

VICAR Oh dear – is it an important one?

WALKER It is if you play 'In the Mood'. It goes Da Di Thump Di Da Thump Da Di Thump Di Da Thump.

VICAR I think it's rather catchy. **(He goes)**

WALKER Look, Jonesey – whatever you do, don't let Pikey near that mike.

JONES He's not still going to announce his engagement, is he?

WALKER Well we've all talked to him – but what can you say? He wants to do it in public like Wallace Beery did and Marie Dressler.

JONES I thought it was Adolphe Menjou and Shirley Temple.

WALKER They didn't get engaged, did they?

JONES Whoever it was, he sees too many pictures, Joe, that's his trouble.

WALKER Look, I've got to rush now – I left my birds in the Horse and Groom.

JONES Joe – you haven't seen Captain Mainwaring, have you? He's bringing the sausage rolls.

WALKER He's over there, taking his coat off.

JONES Ah... **(He crosses)** ...Captain Mainwaring, sir, if you could let me have the sausage rolls, sir, I will display them.

MAINWARING **(With his back to camera)** I'm sorry, Jones, but I'm afraid there was a mishap. Mrs Mainwaring made a slight miscalculation. Half of them were burnt to a cinder.

JONES Oh dear. I'm distressed to hear that, Mr Mainwaring.

MAINWARING I'm very sorry, Jones.

JONES Never mind, sir, you must not upset yourself.

MAINWARING Naturally, I was very... very vexed and I... I gave her a... a good dressing down. **(He turns – he has a large black eye. His glasses are mended on one side with sticking plaster)**

JONES That's a very nasty eye you have there, sir.

MAINWARING I walked into the door of the linen cupboard.

JONES Later on, sir, I'll fetch you two ounces of top-side to put on it.

MAINWARING You needn't trouble yourself, Jones.

JONES It won't come off your ration, sir. Now if you and your good lady will stand over there by the stage, I'll announce the guests as they arrive.

MAINWARING I… I'm afraid Mrs Mainwaring won't be joining us, Jones.

JONES Oh dear – she's not poorly I hope, sir.

MAINWARING I don't want to go into it, Jones. I… I'll greet the guests alone.

JONES They've started arriving, sir. Now keep calm, sir. You stand there… er… in your 'greeting the guests' position, sir.

MAINWARING We ought to have some music, Jones.

JONES Yes, sir. (**To band**) Play some quiet music to greet guests by.

MUSICIAN How about 'Trees'?

JONES Would 'Trees' suit you, sir?

MAINWARING Perfectly. You announce the names as they arrive.

JONES Yes, sir. Keep calm, sir. (**He crosses to the bar**) Stand by to serve the drinks. (**He crosses to the cloakroom**) Stand by for the hats and coats. (**He crosses to the first two guests. They are Mr and Mrs Yeatman, the Verger and his wife**) Blimey – you got here early enough.

VERGER Eight o'clock it says on the ticket.

JONES I never give you a ticket. How did you get a ticket?

VERGER The Vicar gave it to me.

JONES Well, you lay off the meat paste sandwiches until our lads have arrived.

VERGER I don't want your meat paste sandwiches.

MRS YEATMAN Don't take any notice of him – he always was a trouble-maker.

JONES I'm not a trouble-maker. He's the one who's a trouble-maker. We never did find out who wrote those rude words on the spare harmonium.

VERGER Are you insinuating that I have something to do with it?

JONES I'm not insinuating nothing – but why are you blushing, answer me that?

MAINWARING Jones, I'm waiting.

JONES I'm sorry, sir. Mr and Mrs Henry Yeatman. Go on – go and shake hands with the Captain.

VERGER What, with me hat on?

JONES There – I said you was a trouble-maker… put it over there.

Walker has unloaded his coat, hat, etc. and has with him his two girlfriends, they are twins.

WALKER What's the matter, Jonesey, having trouble?

JONES His joint'll be all gristle this week.

MRS YEATMAN It was all gristle last week –that's all you sell!

VERGER Come away, Anthea.

WALKER Now then, ladies, what's your pleasure? Or, failing that, what're you going to have to drink?

JONES 'Ere, wait a minute, I have to announce you first. What are the names of the young ladies?

WALKER Doris and Dora – they're twins.

JONES Blimey – I thought I was seeing double. Which is which?

WALKER I never know – but one bites and the other kicks, so what's the odds?

JONES I'd better announce you as Mr Walker and party.

WALKER No, the party comes later.

JONES Mr Joe Walker – and parties.

Walker crosses to Mainwaring.

WALKER Evening, Mr Mainwaring. (**He sees his eye**) Blimey, how'd that happen?

MAINWARING It was the door of the linen cupboard, Walker.

WALKER What's the matter then, hasn't your old woman got a rolling pin?

JONES (**Off**) Mr and Mrs Sponge.

Cut to Jones.

JONES Mr and Mrs Eccles.

Godfrey enters with his sister, he wears a top hat and a coat and full evening dress with stick and gloves.

JONES Evening, Mr Godfrey – my, you do look smart.

GODFREY Oh dear – some people aren't even in dinner jackets.

JONES Never you mind, Mr Godfrey, you've done us proud.

CISSY Our dear father used to say that one was never embarrassed by being too well dressed.

GODFREY I'm not sure he was right, mind you.

They pass to the cloakroom. Another couple are ready, and Jones announces them.

JONES Mr and Mrs Forkus.

Enter Frazer in full Highland regalia. He is with a very curvaceous land girl.

FRAZER Evening, Jonesey.

JONES Evening, Mr Frazer.

FRAZER This is ma wee niece. Her name is Blodwen.

JONES How do you do, Miss Blodwen?

FRAZER (Quite pleasantly) I think it only fair to tell you, that if you say one word about my kilt – I'll bash your face in.

JONES I… I think it looks very lovely. (He calls) Mr Frazer and Miss Blodwen.

MAINWARING (As Frazer and Blodwen cross to him) Delighted that you could be with us Miss… Miss Blodwen. Evening Frazer. I see this young lady is a land girl.

BLODWEN I'm sorry, I didn't have time to put on a dress.

MAINWARING Never mind, my dear, your partner made up for it.

FRAZER I don't know how you got that black eye, Captain Mainwaring, but I know fine how you're going to get the other one.

Cut to Jones.

JONES Mr Godfrey and Miss Godfrey.

GODFREY Take my arm, Cissy.

CISSY It's just like old times, Charles.

Enter Wilson and Mrs Pike.

MRS PIKE Hullo, Mr Jones. Have you seen Frank?

JONES Not yet, Mrs Pike.

MRS PIKE Arthur, where can he have got to?

WILSON Don't worry so much, Mavis.

JONES Sergeant Wilson and Mrs Pike.

Cut to Mainwaring.

GODFREY Er… you remember my sister, Mr Mainwaring? By Jove, that eye looks nasty.

MAINWARING I rather stupidly walked into the door of the linen cupboard.

CISSY A little bit of folded Christmas card is awfully good for that.

MAINWARING For a black eye?

CISSY No, for keeping the linen cupboard door shut.

GODFREY What you need, Mr Mainwaring, is a hot onion.

MAINWARING On the eye?

CISSY No, Charles, that's for earache.

GODFREY No, dear, it's a mustard plaster for earache.

CISSY No, Charles, that's for backache.

GODFREY It's all rather muddling, isn't it?

WALKER (To Mainwaring) Isn't it time we had a dance?

MAINWARING Quite right, Walker. (He moves through the crowd to Jones) Jones, start the dancing.

JONES Yes, sir. One moment, sir, in one moment. My partner's just arrived, sir. (He calls) Lance Corporal Jones and Mrs Prosser. How do you do, sir? (To Mrs Prosser) Excuse me a moment, my dear. (He pushes across the floor to the band and climbs on to the stage) Come on, play my ta-ra. (The band play a chord. He takes the microphone, switches it on, blows into it and taps it) Is it working? (It howls)

WALKER (Rushing to the control box of the amplifier) Here, don't do that, Jonesey, it's a microphone, not a ruddy barometer.

JONES Ladies and gentlemen, take your partners for a fox-trot. (He comes to the side to Walker) Was that all right, Joe?

The band starts.

WALKER Blimey, now the fun starts. Here comes Pikey.

Cut to Pike, who is entering with his fiancée.

PIKE Mr Mainwaring, this is my fiancée – Violet Gibbons.

MAINWARING How do you do, Miss Gibbons. I know your mother.

Cut to Wilson and Mrs Pike.

MRS PIKE Arthur! Who's that come in with Frank?

WILSON Why bother about them – tonight… is for us, Mavis. We have the wine, we have the music, we have each other.

MRS PIKE I'm having none of that – you wait till you're asked. (He grabs her to his chest and dances off)

WALKER Well done, Mr Wilson.

Fade as the dance continues.

Fade up on Mrs Pike and Wilson still dancing.

MRS PIKE Arthur, I've just got to sit down. That's ten dances without a single break.

WILSON I could go on all night, Mavis.

MRS PIKE That's not like you at all, Arthur.

Cut to Pike with Walker by the public address system.

PIKE I want to make my announcement now, Mr Walker.

WALKER Sorry, Pikey, the amplifier just packed up.

DORIS No it hasn't, you switched it off.

WALKER Why don't you belt up.

PIKE Turn it up nice and loud, Mr Walker.

WALKER You can't do it now, Pikey.

PIKE Why not?

WALKER 'Cos Mr Jones is going to do an announcement, aren't you, Jonesey?

PIKE What's he going to announce? The band are just going to take a break.

WALKER He's announcing his cabaret.

JONES No I'm not, Joe. Mr Mainwaring said I wasn't to do it.

WALKER Well, he's changed his mind.

PIKE I'll do my announcement first.

He grabs the microphone – Walker grabs it back from him.

WALKER Ladies and gentleman. It's cabaret time at Walmington-on-Sea and here, with his impersonations of stars of stage, screen and radio – Corporal Jones.

There is applause as he pulls Jones to the microphone.

JONES **(Sings)** It's Corporal Jones at eight o'clock,

Oh can't you hear the chimes?

They're telling you to take an easy chair,

To settle in the dance hall,

Look at your Radio Times,

Corporal Jones at eight is on the air.

Good evening listeners. Why, who's this? I do believe it's big-hearted Arthur Askey. **(He puts on some glasses)** Hullo playmates. I thank you. And who is this coming this way with his bicycle? Why, it's Jack Warner. Little gel, little gel, mind my bike. **(He makes an incomprehensible American noise with a cigar in his mouth)** And now, by way of a grand finale – George Arliss. **(He puts a curtain ring in his eye. Applause. Ad Lib)**

WALKER Get back on and do Charles Laughton.

JONES I don't do Charles Laughton.

WALKER All right, then, Freddie Bartholomew. Never mind, it's too late.

Pike is at the mike.

PIKE Ladies and gentlemen. I have a very important announcement to make.

Fade down the voice of Pike. Fade up Bing Crosby singing 'Love in Bloom' as we cut to the various faces of Wilson, Godfrey, Frazer – back again to Pike introducing his fiancée – and to Mainwaring, Walker and Jones – all of them listening to Pike, knowing of the impending explosion. Finally cut to Mrs Pike. Silently she screams, she faints and is tended by Wilson, as the final notes of 'Love in Bloom' sing out.

SIDE OFFICE

Wilson is trying to settle himself in Mainwaring's chair, wrapped in a fire blanket.

The door to the hall opens – enter Mainwaring. Also wrapped in fire blanket.

MAINWARING Ah, hullo, Wilson. I didn't know you were here.

WILSON Were you locked out too, sir?

MAINWARING No, no, not at all. Elizabeth is very absent-minded – she must have put the catch on the door, forgetting that I was out.

Enter Pike, wrapped in a fire blanket.

PIKE Oh! Hullo, Mr Mainwaring. Hullo, Uncle.

WILSON Good heavens, Frank – you've been licking those stamps again. Couldn't you get in?

PIKE No, mum threw a bucket of water over me. That's what she does to the cat.

WILSON It's supposed to cool the ardour, Frank.

PIKE It does that all right. Uncle, I don't think I'll get married.

WILSON You're very wise, Frank, I never did.

Mainwaring reacts.

PIKE **(Settling down)** It was a wizard dance, Mr Mainwaring.

MAINWARING It was a pity that Frazer had to hit the Verger with that altar candle.

WILSON Well, Jones started it, of course, by pushing that Maid of Honour down Mrs Verger's dress, shouting 'Coals to Newcastle'.

MAINWARING And Walker had no business to take those two girls down into the crypt. The Vicar was most distressed. That sort of thing lets down the side very badly.

WILSON Still, it was a good dance.

MAINWARING Oh yes. It's a good idea to have these little get-togethers occasionally – makes the wives and sweethearts feel that we're all pulling… er pulling….

WILSON In separate directions?

SERIES THREE **EPISODE TEN**

Recorded: Friday 7/11/69
Original transmission: Thursday 13/11/69, 7.30–8.00pm
Original viewing figures = 13.3 million

ARTHUR LOWE .... CAPTAIN MAINWARING
JOHN LE MESURIER .... SERGEANT WILSON
CLIVE DUNN.................................. LANCE CORPORAL JONES
JOHN LAURIE .... PRIVATE FRAZER
JAMES BECK .... PRIVATE WALKER
ARNOLD RIDLEY .... PRIVATE GODFREY
IAN LAVENDER .... PRIVATE PIKE
BILL PERTWEE .... ARP WARDEN
STUART SHERWIN .... SECOND ARP WARDEN
BILL TREACHER .... FIRST SAILOR
LARRY MARTYN.................................. SECOND SAILOR

NO OTHER MEMBERS OF THE PLATOON APPEARED IN THIS EPISODE.

MENACE FROM THE DEEP

• BILL HARMAN REMEMBERS •

'One of my first and lasting impressions of the core cast, which proved to be generally accurate, was how much like their characters they were in real life. The exception to this was Clive Dunn who, in butcher Jack Jones, was, of course, portraying a character many years older than himself.

'Arthur Lowe always assumed command at rehearsals, on location or in the studio. He epitomised the image of the short man in a supervisory role. And rather than attempt to dispel that image, he seemed to be at pains to live up to the nickname of Napoleon given to his character by Warden Hodges. A fantastic character actor, it was nevertheless hardly a quantum leap from Arthur Lowe to Leonard Swindley or George Mainwaring, although Arthur had a much greater sense of fun than either of those characters and, unlike them, was a master at what he did.

'Arthur's politics seemed to a young, idealistic but naïve liberal thinker like myself to be somewhat right of Genghis Khan. He was a big fan of Enoch Powell, and claimed to be a prominent contributor to the fund set up to promote Powell into the PM's job. A labour government was in power, and one day at rehearsals, while a national garbage collectors' strike was causing major sanitation problems countrywide, Arthur unfolded his *Daily Express*, tapped his finger on the headline and said "Look at this" and he read out loud – *"Edward Heath says it will be a hard road to victory"*. He put down the paper and said: "I don't want to read that sort of pathetic nonsense. I want to open my morning paper and see: *'Forty dustmen shot this morning'*. Then we'll get this country moving!" Noting my surprise at this outburst he said to me, "Do you know what the eighth deadly sin is?" "No" I replied. "Tolerance" said Arthur. I could see a twinkle in his eye as he said it, obviously tickled at the reaction his statements provoked.

'John Le Mesurier was as languid as Arthur Wilson. I saw him arrive at the Bell Hotel in Thetford and, seeing the stairs, ask make-up assistant Penny Maher (in a totally charming fashion of course) if she "wouldn't mind awfully" carrying his suitcases up the stairs. Legend has it that, during the war, he fell in on the parade ground for the first time as a newly conscripted recruit with a set of golf clubs over his shoulder. When we were filming on location, the cast often had to carry rifles and wear helmets and lots of packs and webbing. When the word "cut" was called at the end of a sequence, most of the actors would keep these things with them so that continuity would not be broken. John, however, had the unique ability of being able to shed all his accoutrements in about two seconds flat, dropping them where he stood and walking away as the wardrobe and props crew moved in to gather them up for the next sequence.'

BILL HARMAN
Assistant Floor Manager

MENACE FROM THE DEEP

MACHINE GUN POST AT END OF PIER. NIGHT

Two sailors are crouched behind a Lewis gun. They are all muffled up and are wearing steel helmets. There is a strong wind blowing.

FIRST SAILOR 'Welcome to Walmington-on-Sea' – blimey, what a dump! I joined the Navy to see the world – I didn't expect to finish up stuck on the end of a ruddy pier.

SECOND SAILOR I don't know what you're grumbling at, mate, you got on for nothing, didn't you? Before the war you'd have had to pay a penny. What's the time?

FIRST SAILOR Four o'clock.

SECOND SAILOR Thank goodness for that – another two hours and then it's ta-ta to sunny Walmington-on-Sea for good.

FIRST SAILOR I wonder who'll be doing this rotten job every night when we've gone.

SECOND SAILOR There's a new detachment of mateloes coming in next week.

FIRST SAILOR In that case, someone had better send a telegram to Hitler telling him not to invade for the next few days – 'cos there won't be anybody here to stop him.

SECOND SAILOR Oh yes there will – the P.O. said the Home Guard are taking over for the week.

FIRST SAILOR The Home Guard – blimey, God help poor old England.

CHURCH HALL. SIDE OFFICE. DAY

Jones, Walker, Godfrey, Pike and Frazer are gathered round a blackboard. Mainwaring is standing on one side of it with a pointer. Wilson is standing on the other side. On the board is a well drawn diagram of the pier, showing the centre section which has been blown up. The platoon are all muffled up – greatcoats, balaclavas, etc.

MAINWARING Now, before we move off, men – I'll just go over the details once again.

WILSON **(Aside)** Oh Lord – not again.

MAINWARING What did you say, Wilson?

WILSON Nothing, sir.

MAINWARING Now, we have been entrusted with the highly responsible task of manning the machine gun post at the end of the pier here, **(He points)** for the next four nights. As you will observe, the centre of the pier here... **(Points)** ...has been blown up to prevent it being used to land enemy troops. So I think you will agree with me that we shall need a boat to get us from this point of the pier, here... **(Points)** to the end of the pier, here.

WALKER Here, here.

MAINWARING Walker! **(Points)** We shall use a dinghy – unfortunately there's only room for three in the boat so we shall have to make several trips. Now, we need someone to row the boat.

JONES Permission to speak, sir? I should like to be the one to row the boat. Let me do it, sir – let me do it.

MAINWARING No, Jones – I think we ought to have someone who's used to it. You're a sailor, Frazer – you can do it.

FRAZER Aye, aye, sir.

MAINWARING Now, the plan is this, we shall proceed to the pier here. **(Points)** And embark into the boat here. **(Points)** You, Frazer, will take Sergeant Wilson and myself across first – then you row back and pick up Walker and Jones – take them across – then row back and pick up Pike and Godfrey – take them across and then...

WALKER Row back and pick up yourself.

MAINWARING I shan't tell you again, Walker. Now, let's check up and see what food we've got. After all, we're going to be stuck on the end of that pier all night.

JONES I've got three pounds of sausages, sir – I cooked them dinner time.

MAINWARING Good.

GODFREY And I've got the mustard, sir – three kinds, French, English and German. Which would you prefer?

MAINWARING I think we'll just take the French and English, Godfrey.

PIKE And my mum's made us a lovely cake. **(He unwraps cake)** Look.

MAINWARING Splendid, Pike.

FRAZER And I've got some apples and tomatoes from my garden, sir.

WALKER And I've got a half a bottle of whisky, sir – it's on the house.

MAINWARING Well, whatever happens, we shan't go short of food, eh, Wilson?

WILSON No, sir, it's positively a gastronomic orgy.

MAINWARING What have you brought?

WILSON Half a pound of acid drops – they're my favourite.

MAINWARING Really, I'd never have guessed. Now, I think that's the lot. Now, before we... **(He notices Pike is wearing**

a huge football scarf on top of his greatcoat and balaclava helmet and muffler) You can't wear a coloured scarf with your uniform, Pike.

PIKE My mum said I've got to wear it – I get croup.

MAINWARING Croup! **(To Wilson)** That's what chickens get.

WILSON He gets it as well, sir.

MAINWARING Does he really – extraordinary. Now come on. Let's get a move on – I want to get settled down on the end of the pier before it gets dark.

TELECINE: THE TOP OF THE PIER. DAY

There is a small boat moored to an iron ladder which reaches down into the water. There are bits of twisted ironwork, broken ends of wire, and barbed wire all round. Frazer is sitting in the boat at the oars. Wilson is sitting in the stern. Mainwaring is at the bottom of the ladder. The rest of the platoon are waiting at the top of the ladder.

MAINWARING **(Shouting up the ladder to the men at the top)** All right, men, pay very careful attention as to how I get into the boat. It's a bit tricky and I don't want any of you falling in the water, do you understand?

Walker, Pike, Godfrey and Jones all nod their heads.

MAINWARING Now, you'll observe that I keep one hand and foot on the ladder, and I put the other foot into the boat. Give me your hand, Wilson.

Mainwaring reaches out and takes Wilson's hand – he puts one foot on the side of the boat, as he does so he pushes the boat away so that he is doing the splits, with one leg and one hand on the ladder and the other leg on the side of the boat.

MAINWARING Stop jogging the boat up and down, Wilson.

WILSON It's not me jogging it up and down, sir – it's the sea.

MAINWARING Turn the boat round, Frazer, turn it round.

FRAZER I wish you'd make up your mind which way you're going to get in.

Frazer turns boat round and brings the stern under the ladder.

Cut to Walker, Jones, Pike and Godfrey watching.

MAINWARING **(Out of vision)** Will you keep the boat still, Frazer.

FRAZER **(Out of vision)** I'm keeping it as still as I can. Ouch! Get your foot out of my face.

WALKER Now watch Mr Mainwaring very carefully – we don't want anyone to fall in, do we?

They all laugh.

WILSON **(Out of vision)** Mind out, sir!

MAINWARING **(Out of vision)** Move over, Frazer – I can't get in.

FRAZER **(Out of vision)** How can I move over – I'm the one who's supposed to be doing the rowing. Ow! You kicked me in the stomach, you stupid Sassenach.

MAINWARING **(Out of vision)** How dare you speak to me like that – take his name, Wilson.

JONES I thought Mr Mainwaring said he wanted to get there before dark.

Cut to the boat. Frazer and Wilson are in the stern – Mainwaring is at the oars. Cut back to platoon.

WALKER **(Shouting)** Come in number 27 – your time is up.

They all laugh.

MAINWARING **(Out of vision)** Corporal Jones, take that man's name.

THE END OF THE PIER. DAY

There is an iron ladder leading up to the broken deck of the pier. Behind is the amusement arcade – it is boarded up. Wilson is on the deck and Mainwaring is climbing up the ladder. The sea is below, out of picture.

WILSON Here we are, sir. **(He reaches down and pulls Mainwaring up on to the deck)**

MAINWARING Thank you, Wilson. **(He shouts down the ladder)** All right, Frazer, now row back and pick up the others. And this time, get them into the boat properly.

We can hear Frazer's voice shouting something rude in Gaelic – there is the sound of the boat moving away.

MAINWARING What did he say, Wilson?

WILSON I don't know, sir – I think it was Gaelic.

MAINWARING Well, whatever it was, it didn't sound very nice. **(Icy)** Yes, well shall we go in, Wilson?

He opens a door with the words 'Monte Carlo Amusement Arcade' over the top. He goes in.

INSIDE AMUSEMENT ARCADE. DAY

There are several slot machines round the walls – a table and bench with a pile of blankets on it in the corner – in the other is slung a hammock. At the far end is a door with a blackout trap. Outside the door is a pile of sandbags. Mainwaring and Wilson enter.

MAINWARING Ah, this looks all right, eh, Wilson?

WILSON Absolutely delightful, sir.

Mainwaring crosses to the far door, opens it and looks out.

MAINWARING We set the Lewis gun up out here – we can take it in turns to keep watch.

Mainwaring crosses over to the hammock.

MAINWARING Good, a hammock – I'll take that.

WILSON Really, sir.

MAINWARING What's the matter?

WILSON I must protest! Just because you're the officer, you take the hammock. You don't say 'May I take the hammock?' or even 'Do you mind if I take the hammock?' – you just cross over to it, put your hand on it, and say 'I'll take that!' and that's the sort of behaviour I just can't stand.

Pause.

MAINWARING I'm sorry, Wilson.

WILSON Eh?

MAINWARING It was most unthinking – and most undemocratic of me. As you know from past experience, I'm the last one to take advantage of my position.

WILSON Really, sir?

MAINWARING Yes. We shall take it in turns to use the hammock.

WILSON Thank you, sir.

MAINWARING I'll go first.

Walker enters with the Lewis gun. Godfrey follows with the magazines.

MAINWARING Ah, there you are, Walker – did you have a good crossing?

WALKER The sea's getting a bit choppy, Mr Mainwaring.

GODFREY Do you mind if I sit down for a minute, sir – I'm feeling a little queer.

Walker turns.

MAINWARING There's no time for that, Godfrey. Set up the Lewis gun in the machine gun post, Walker. (**He points to door**) – and cover it over – we don't want the sea air to get to it. If Hitler kicks off tonight we shall be right in the thick of it.

Walker sets up the Lewis gun – and covers it over with one of the blankets. Godfrey takes off his greatcoat.

MAINWARING You know, Wilson, I almost hope that Hitler does have a go tonight. I'm simply spoiling for a fight.

WILSON Yes, sir.

Walker comes in and crosses to the hammock.

WALKER That hammock looks cosy, Mr Mainwaring. Who's going to have it?

MAINWARING We're going to take it in turns.

WILSON Captain Mainwaring's going first.

WALKER I am surprised.

MAINWARING Put the blackouts up, Sergeant.

Mainwaring turns on the lights. Wilson and Walker put the blackouts up.

Mainwaring crosses to a field telephone in the corner – picks up the receiver and winds the handle.

MAINWARING Hullo, sir – Captain Mainwaring reporting. We've taken up our positions – and we're ready for anything that Hitler can throw at us. We're as snug as a bug in a rug here – you can rest assured that the only way Jerry will get past us is over our dead bodies. Thank you, sir – goodnight. (**Mainwaring puts the phone down**)

MAINWARING (**To Wilson**) That's the sort of fighting talk they like to hear at G.H.Q., Wilson.

Jones and Frazer enter.

JONES Here we are, Mr Mainwaring, sir. Young Pike's just tying the boat up.

There is the sound of wind.

FRAZER Listen! (**There is a pause – they all gather in a little knot round Frazer**) What's that sound?

MAINWARING It's only the wind blowing through the iron girders.

FRAZER Aye! That's what you'd call it – but to someone like me, who's spent his entire life at sea – it's the cry of ancient mariners lost in the deep. Listen! There it is again – can you no hear their tormented cries for help?

Long pause.

FRAZER (**Very brightly**) I did that speech in the dramatic society's production of 'The Lighthouse Keeper'. I was the best thing in it.

MAINWARING I'm very glad we missed it.

Pike enters.

PIKE I've tied the boat up, Mr Mainwaring.

MAINWARING Well done, Pike. All right, gather round and I'll just give you the orders for the night. Now we're on duty till 6.30 in the morning. (**Looking at watch**) The time now is... er... five minutes to 2100...

WILSON Twenty fifty five, sir.

MAINWARING Yes, well, that's what the time is. Now I've drawn up a rota – and it works out at an hour and a half's guard duty each. Godfrey, you will take the first watch... er... 21.00–22.30, Jones 22.30–24.00 hours. Walker 24.00–25.30...

WILSON No, sir, 1.30 – you start again when you get to 24.00.

MAINWARING (Giving him a glare) All right, Wilson.

WILSON I only wanted to explain.

MAINWARING Anyway, Godfrey's next. All right Godfrey, you'd better get outside. Now, we must see about something to eat. I'm starving. (To Pike) Where's the food, Pike?

PIKE I'm sorry, sir – I left it in the boat.

MAINWARING Well, go and get it at once, you stupid boy.

JONES Permission to speak, sir? Who's going to sleep in the hammock?

MAINWARING We'll take it in turns.

WILSON Captain Mainwaring's to be first, fancy that.

MAINWARING I shall relinquish it when I go on duty.

JONES There's nothing like sleeping in a hammock, Mr Mainwaring – they're so cosy, they wrap right round you. You know, during Nelson's time when the sailors were in port they used to have their wives aboard – the trouble was you could never tell who was in what hammock – so they hung one leg over the side – and in the morning the bosun used to come round and run his hand up them to see if they were men's legs or women's legs... hence the expression 'show a leg'.

Pike comes back.

MAINWARING Ah, there you are, Pike. (Pike stands looking pasty) Put the food on the table – I can't wait to get my teeth into one of those succulent sausages of yours, Jones.

JONES I've cooked them just as you like them, Mr Mainwaring – lovely and crisp on the outside and pink in the middle – very tasty, very sweet.

MAINWARING (To Pike who is still standing in the same position) Well, don't just stand there, boy – I told you to put the food on the table.

PIKE I don't know what to say, Mr Mainwaring.

MAINWARING What do you mean?

PIKE I can't put the food on the table, 'cos I haven't got it.

MAINWARING You don't mean to say you left the food behind!

PIKE Oh no, sir – I brought it with me. The food's in the boat all right – there's only one snag.

MAINWARING What's that?

PIKE The boat's gone.

JONES What!

WALKER Blimey, all that lovely grub!

MAINWARING Do you mean you didn't tie the boat up?

PIKE Oh yes, sir, I tied it up – you see there were two cables – a big thick electric one and a thin one. I tied it to the thin one.

MAINWARING Why did you do that?

PIKE I didn't want to touch the thick one – I might have got electricityfied.

MAINWARING You stupid boy – you must have tied it to the telephone wire. (He crosses to the phone, picks up the receiver and winds the handle) It's dead. (Pause) We're marooned – completely cut off from the outside world – no phone... no boat... and no food.

WILSON We've still got my acid drops, sir.

MAINWARING Then suck one.

There is a pause.

PIKE I'm sorry, Mr Mainwaring.

They are all in a tight group, staring at Pike. There is a long pause. Pike starts to shuffle his feet – he goes over to Walker.

PIKE I'm sorry, Joe. (Walker gives him a look – he goes to Jones) I'm sorry, Mr Jones. (Jones stares – he goes to Frazer) I'm sorry, Mr Frazer. (Frazer stares – he goes to Wilson) I'm sorry, Uncle Arthur. (Another pause. He crosses to the door, opens it and puts his head outside) I'm sorry, Mr Godfrey. (He closes the door. There is a pause. The door opens and Godfrey puts his head inside)

GODFREY What about?

MAINWARING Get back on duty, Godfrey.

Godfrey closes the door.

WALKER 'Ere – I've got an idea, Mr Mainwaring. Couldn't we signal for help?

JONES Yes, sir – we could flash a light.

MAINWARING Good idea – get a torch, Wilson.

WILSON I haven't got a torch, sir.

MAINWARING Do you mean to say we didn't bring a torch with us?

WILSON You never said anything about bringing a torch.

MAINWARING I distinctly remember telling you to bring the torch and two loaves when you took our library books back.

WALKER Look, why don't we open and shut the window, Mr Mainwaring – then they'll see the light on the shore.

MAINWARING Excellent idea. (On turn) You haven't heard the last of this, Wilson.

They all move over to a small window shaped like a porthole which is painted over.

JONES Permission to speak, sir? I should like to be the one to open and shut the window – so that they'll see the light on the shore.

MAINWARING Thank you, Jones, but I think Sergeant Wilson ought to do it. We'll use Morse code.

WILSON I don't know Morse code.

MAINWARING Naturally. Frazer, you were in the Navy – how do you spell out 'Help'?

FRAZER Now, let me see… it's H-E-L-P.

JONES It's no good asking him, sir, he was only a cook.

FRAZER What do you mean 'only a cook'… I'll have you know…

MAINWARING All right, Frazer, that will do.

JONES I know the Morse code, sir – what you want is S.O.S. Three dots – three dashes – and three dots.

MAINWARING Excellent. All right, Sergeant, stand over there.

WILSON That's all very well, sir, but I don't see how I can do dots and dashes with a window.

MAINWARING Have you no imagination, Sergeant? You just open and close it at various speeds.

WILSON Oh yes, of course, sir.

MAINWARING Now, what is it again, Jones?

JONES Three dots – three dashes – and three dots, sir. That's dit-dit-dit-dar-dar-dar-dit-dit-dit.

MAINWARING All right, come on, Wilson – start ditting.

WILSON What, sir?

MAINWARING Come on, man… dit-dit-dit.

WILSON Dit… dit…

Wilson starts to open and close the window quickly – he does it twice. On the third one the window gets stuck.

JONES That's no good, Mr Wilson – that last one was a dar instead of a dit – you're 'dar'ing when you should be 'dit'ing.

WILSON I can't help it – the window's stuck.

MAINWARING **(Pushing him out of the way)** Oh – let me do it, Wilson.

THE PROMENADE. NIGHT

The A.R.P. Warden and a second Warden are leaning on the railings. A.R.P. Warden is wearing new uniform. Behind is a shed with the words 'Peter Pan's Children's Boating Pool' on it.

SECOND WARDEN It's chilly tonight, mind you're all right in that new uniform of yours.

WARDEN It's smashing ain't it. I only got it this afternoon.

SECOND WARDEN It's not fair, why should you have one and not me?

WARDEN Look, mate, I've waited a whole year for this uniform.

SECOND WARDEN I'm sorry.

WARDEN **(Pointing)** Look! There's a light flashing.

SECOND WARDEN **(Turning)** Where?

WARDEN At the end of the pier – look! There it is again.

SECOND WARDEN It must be old Mainwaring and his mob – they're on guard out there tonight.

WARDEN I might have guessed it was them. **(Walking up and down)** I must get out there – I must get out there – I've got to… **(Sees shed – starts to open door)** Wait a minute… **(Drags out boat)** …I'll stop 'em.

SECOND WARDEN But you'll never get out there in one of those little boats… they're for kids.

WARDEN I've got to get 'em… I tell you, I've got to get 'em.

• BILL HARMAN REMEMBERS •

'My memories of this episode include an uncomfortable night's filming on the pier at windy Great Yarmouth, and the threats of what the crew would do to Harold Snoad and his loud-hailer (which he was very fond of) if he persisted in giving orders through it at full volume from a distance of six feet!'

END OF THE PIER. NIGHT

The door opens and Walker comes out, followed by Mainwaring, Wilson, Jones, Frazer and Pike.

WALKER **(Pointing)** They've seen us, Mr Mainwaring – there's an object moving towards us.

MAINWARING Good, we shan't be long now.

WALKER It ain't half making a lot of splashing – I wonder what it is?

TELECINE: ON THE SEA. NIGHT

The Warden is furiously paddling the little boat. As it moves along in the water it gets lower and lower until it finally sinks.

END OF THE PIER. NIGHT

WALKER That's funny – whatever it was, it's disappeared.

MAINWARING It can't have disappeared. Can you see anything, Wilson?

WILSON Not a thing – it's all rather eerie.

FRAZER It was making so much noise a minute ago.

JONES Permission to speak, sir? It could be a secret weapon.

WALKER Don't be daft, Jonesey, that thing came from the shore. If it was a secret weapon – it wouldn't be coming at us from our own side, would it?

JONES Perhaps that's what the secret is. **(Suddenly there is a horrible squelchy, sucking noise)** What's that noise?

PIKE **(Pointing with horror)** Mr Mainwaring, look! There's er… there's er… thing! Coming up the ladder. **(He cocks his rifle)** Shall I shoot it?

MAINWARING No, leave it to me, Pike. All right, keep quiet everyone.

Mainwaring draws his revolver. The platoon gather in a tight knot round him and wait. The squelching sound gets nearer. A head comes to the top of the ladder – and we see a figure like a drowned rat. It is the Warden – he steps on to the deck.

WARDEN **(Purple with rage)** You… you stupid load of hooligans.

AMUSEMENT ARCADE. NIGHT

The Warden is sitting on a box with no clothes on and a blanket wrapped round him. He still has his tin hat on. He has a half bottle of whisky in his hand.

WARDEN **(Shivering)** You… you… her… jer… just wait till I ger… ger… get back on dry ler… ler… land. I'm going to rer… rer… report you for…

WALKER Oh shut up, I don't know what you're grumbling at, I gave you my bottle of whisky, didn't I?

MAINWARING All right, men, gather round. **(They all gather round him except Pike)** I'm sorry things have turned out like this, but we shall just have to make the best of a bad job and stick it out till morning. Walker, go and see if Godfrey's all right.

Walker goes.

WILSON If only we had something to eat, sir. I'm starving.

MAINWARING You're not the only one, Wilson, we're all starving.

WILSON Yes, sir, I know – but…

MAINWARING Oh, suck one of your acid drops.

PIKE **(Calling)** Mr Mainwaring, quick, come here.

They move over to Pike who is standing beside a slot machine. It has a glass dome on the top. Inside is a little crane with a claw on the end. Underneath is a pile of chocolate bars.

PIKE Look at all these bars of chocolate.

MAINWARING By Jove, that's a bit of luck.

Wilson raises his rifle butt.

MAINWARING Wilson – what do you think you're doing?

WILSON I'm going to smash the glass, sir, to get the chocolate out.

MAINWARING Smash the glass – have you taken leave of your senses. We're not savages, you know – we are a properly disciplined army of fair-minded, sporting Britishers – not a lot of Nazis – that's just the sort of thing they'd do. No, we shall get the chocolate by fair means. Now we want someone to volunteer to work the crane.

JONES I should like to volunteer to work the crane – let me do it.

MAINWARING All right, Jones – I shall navigate. Now let's have some pennies. **(He takes some change out of his pocket)** That's a pity, I haven't got any. What about you, Sergeant?

WILSON I'm afraid I haven't got any either, sir.

PIKE Neither have I, sir.

JONES **(Giving him a penny)** I've got one, sir.

MAINWARING One's no good. What about you, Frazer?

FRAZER Did you speak?

MAINWARING Have you got any pennies?

FRAZER Aye, I have thank you.

MAINWARING Hand them over then.

FRAZER Well, I er….

MAINWARING It's for the good of the platoon, Frazer. **(Frazer hands over a pile of pennies)** Stand by, Jones.

JONES Standing by, sir.

MAINWARING **(Puts penny in slot)** Right – left a bit – right hand down – **(The faces of the platoon are gathered in a tense circle)** Left –left. **(The claws close round the chocolate and the crane lifts up)**

JONES I've got it, sir – I've got it!

The bar of chocolate drops back again.

FRAZER **(Pushing Jones out of the way and taking over the controls)** Here, let me do it.

JONES That's not fair, Mr Mainwaring – I was working the controls.

FRAZER They're my pennies, aren't they?

MAINWARING All right, Frazer **(He puts a penny in)** Now – right – right.

FRAZER I don't want any interference – I can manage on my own, thank you.

Fade down and up.

Close up of claws with a bar of chocolate, it lifts a few inches and the chocolate drops out.

MAINWARING I'm afraid that's the last of the pennies, Frazer.

FRAZER Oh no! That's one and six I've spent. Do you hear me – one and six!

MAINWARING All right, Frazer, there's no need to make all that fuss.

FRAZER It wasn't your money, was it?

MAINWARING That will do, Frazer.

Walker comes in.

MAINWARING Where have you been, Walker?

WALKER Godfrey was asleep on duty, so I shot him.

MAINWARING Good.

WALKER What's the trouble?

JONES We're trying to get some chocolate out of this machine.

WALKER Oh, is that all. Stand back. **(He pushes a button on the side of the machine – gives it a kick and a little door on the side flies open. He puts his arm in and takes a bar of chocolate)** Here you are. **(He hands the bar to Mainwaring)**

MAINWARING We can't take that – it's stealing.

WILSON Not really, sir. After all, we've put 1s 7d in the machine – and there is a war on.

MAINWARING Perhaps you're right. **(He hands the bar to Frazer)** As it was your money we put in, Frazer, you can have the first one.

FRAZER Aye.

He takes the chocolate, tears off the wrapper and wolfs it in three bites. Walker, by now, has got all the rest of the bars out.

MAINWARING These bars of chocolate must be two years old – what's it taste like, Frazer?

FRAZER All right – a wee bit soapy perhaps, but not bad – not bad at all.

MAINWARING **(Taking the bars from Walker and handing them round)** All right, men, tuck in.

They all tear the wrappers off and start to eat.

PIKE It's cardboard!

They all protest in chorus.

JONES They're all dummies, Mr Mainwaring.

FRAZER **(Licking his lips)** Mine was all right.

AMUSEMENT ARCADE. NIGHT

The platoon are all asleep. Mainwaring is in the hammock – the rest are lying on the floor, wrapped in blankets. The Warden is propped up in the corner with the whisky bottle in his hand – staring.

Suddenly there is a terrific burst of drunken singing from the Warden.

Mainwaring wakes.

MAINWARING **(Getting up from the table and crossing to the Warden)** How dare you wake us up like that – shut up and go to sleep at once.

WARDEN **(Staggering to his feet – as he does so the blanket drops from round his shoulders)** Don't tell me to shut up!

MAINWARING **(To Wilson)** Cover him up, he looks revolting.

Wilson drapes the blanket round the Warden.

WARDEN Oh, I'm revolting, am I? Come on, put 'em up.

Warden squares up to Mainwaring – the blanket drops off – he still has his tin hat on.

WARDEN I've had enough of you, Fatso! We're going to have this out here and now. **(He squares up to Mainwaring)**

WILSON **(Aside to Mainwaring)** Don't upset him too much, sir – he's the best bowler I've got in the cricket team.

MAINWARING I can't help that, Wilson. **(To Warden)** For goodness' sake, control yourself. **(The platoon grab him and wrap the blanket round him)** Put him in the hammock.

WARDEN **(Crying)** Nobody likes me.

WILSON Yes they do.

WARDEN I'm the most unpopular person in Walmington-on-Sea. Just because I tell them to put their lights out – somebody's got to do it – somebody's got to do it.

MAINWARING What a disgusting scene.

They bundle him in the hammock – he instantly falls asleep with loud snores.

MAINWARING What do you expect from a tradesman.

AMUSEMENT ARCADE. EARLY MORNING

Everyone is asleep. The blackouts are still up.

Close up of Jones – a little jet of water springs up just in front of his face. This happens several times – Jones opens his eyes and watches the jet.

JONES **(Looking down between the boards)** Blimey, the tide's come up high. Hullo, that's funny. I wonder what that is. **(Jones gets up and crosses to Mainwaring. Shakes him and whispers in his ear)** Permission to speak, sir?

MAINWARING (**Opening his eyes**) Oh, it's you, Jones – what's the matter?

JONES There's something under the pier I don't like the look of, sir.

MAINWARING What's the time?

JONES Quarter to six, sir.

Mainwaring, getting down off the table and putting his glasses on. Mainwaring falls.

JONES That's right, sir, down there.

MAINWARING All right, now, what is it?

JONES (**Taking him over to his place – he points**) Look down between the boards.

Mainwaring goes down on his hands and knees and looks between the crack – a jet of water spurts up in his face.

MAINWARING (**Wiping his face**) I'm in no mood for jokes at this time of the morning, Jones.

JONES No, sir – it's not a joke – look at that big, black thing floating in the water.

MAINWARING Where? (**He looks again**) Good Lord, it can't be – it is – it's a mine.

JONES A what, sir?

MAINWARING There's a mine trapped under the pier, man – quick! There's not a moment to lose – grab a boat-hook and follow me. (**He rushes over to some boat-hooks hanging on the wall – takes one and rushes to the door. He shouts over his shoulder to Jones**) Wake the men up, Jones. (**He goes**)

JONES (**Grabs a boat-hook and rushes about**) Don't panic – don't panic – there's a mine under the pier – grab a boat-hook and follow me. (**He rushes out**)

TELECINE: UNDER THE PIER. DAY

Mainwaring and Jones are running along the girders with their boat-hooks.

MAINWARING Now listen, Jones – whatever you do, don't let the mine touch the girders or we shall all be blown sky high. (**He pushes the mine away with his boat-hook – it drifts towards Jones**) Push it away, Jones, push it away.

JONES (**Pushes the mine with his hook**) I am pushing it away, sir.

The rest of the platoon come down the ladder.

MAINWARING All right, men, spread out – and keep pushing it away.

The Warden comes down the ladder.

WARDEN (**To Mainwaring**) Here, what do you think you're doing?

MAINWARING We're trying to stop this mine from blowing up.

WARDEN This is an A.R.P. matter – I'll take charge. Give me that. (**He tries to grab Mainwaring's boat-hook**)

MAINWARING Get out of the way.

Mainwaring and Warden struggle – the boat-hook gets caught in the Warden's blanket – he slips and falls in the water, leaving the blanket behind. The Warden comes to the surface close to the mine – the mine starts to follow him as he swims away.

WARDEN (**Swimming wildly**) Get it off – get it off!

WALKER Blimey, it's following him.

MAINWARING It must be a magnetic mine – it's his tin hat that's doing it. (**Shouting to Warden**) Take your helmet off!

The Warden takes his helmet off. He swims towards the girder and they pull him out of the water.

JONES (**Pointing**) Look, sir, it's drifting out to sea.

MAINWARING Quick everyone, up on deck. We must blow it up before it does any damage.

TELECINE: THE MACHINE GUN POST. DAY

They all rush out of the door.

MAINWARING Frazer – you take the Lewis gun – the rest of you, take aim – in your own time, fire!

They all blaze away.

FRAZER Look, sir – it's drifting towards the shore.

MAINWARING Don't talk, keep firing. (**He draws his revolver and blazes away**)

JONES It's going towards the Novelty Rock Emporium.

MAINWARING Keep firing, men!

WALKER We haven't got any more ammo, sir.

Warden comes into the picture – he has no clothes on.

WARDEN You'll never hit it like that. (**Starts to unscrew an iron knob on the top of the railing**)

MAINWARING We've had just about enough of you – now clear off!

WARDEN Stand back. (**He takes a run and bowls the knob – they all watch – there is a terrific explosion. They all duck**)

MAINWARING By Jove, you were right, Wilson – he is a good bowler.

WILSON Yes, sir – he does even better with his clothes on.

SERIES THREE **EPISODE ELEVEN**

Recorded: Friday 14/11/69

Original transmission: Thursday 20/11/69, 7.30–8.00pm

Original viewing figures = 11.1 million

ARTHUR LOWE .... CAPTAIN MAINWARING
JOHN LE MESURIER .... SERGEANT WILSON
CLIVE DUNN .... LANCE CORPORAL JONES
JOHN LAURIE .... PRIVATE FRAZER
JAMES BECK .... PRIVATE WALKER
ARNOLD RIDLEY .... PRIVATE GODFREY
IAN LAVENDER .... PRIVATE PIKE
BILL PERTWEE .... CHIEF WARDEN
NAN BRAUNTON .... MISS GODFREY
STUART SHERWIN .... BILL (SECOND ARP WARDEN)
ROGER AVON .... THE DOCTOR

PLATOON .... HUGH HASTINGS, DESMOND CULLUM-JONES,
.... VIC TAYLOR, GEORGE HANCOCK, FREDDIE WILES,
.... MARTIN DUNN, FREDDIE WHITE, LESLIE NOYES,
.... JIMMY MAC, ROGER BOURNE

BRANDED

• JIMMY PERRY REMEMBERS •

'The focus of "Branded" was on conscientious objecting and Godfrey always seemed the most obvious character to concentrate on, partly because of the reaction we could extract from Frazer. In many ways, it's a sad episode – comedy and tears are always close together.

'I wouldn't dare be a conscientious objector, it's easier to go with the flow. I was lucky to be in the Royal Artillery because if you were a gunner you didn't get close to the enemy, unless they overran you, of course. During the Second World War, conscientious objectors attended a tribunal and often ended up serving as stretcher-bearers or some other similar role.'

JIMMY PERRY

BRANDED

YARD OUTSIDE CHURCH HALL. DAY

The platoon are standing in a group – Wilson enters.

WILSON Captain Mainwaring will be a little late this evening – so he's asked me to carry on with the training programme.

WALKER Can't we just fall out for a smoke till he gets here, Sarge?

WILSON I'd rather you didn't, if you don't mind.

WALKER Oh, all right.

WILSON Now, pay attention. Today Mr Mainwaring was going to do some stalking – in other words, how to creep up behind an enemy sentry in the dark.

WALKER **(Pointing to Frazer)** Old Taff here can show us how to do that – he's the biggest creeper of the lot.

They all laugh.

WILSON Now, now, settle down please.

FRAZER You can laugh, Joe – it may interest you to know that I'm an expert stalker. In fact at one time I was considered one of the finest stalkers in the Highlands.

WALKER Yes, and you're quite a chatterbox in the Lowlands.

WILSON Now, we want someone to creep up on.

JONES I'd like to volunteer for that, Sergeant Wilson. I'd like to be the someone you creep up upon.

WILSON No, no, you're always volunteering, Jones – we'd better have someone else, to take the enemy sentry's part.

JONES I'd like to do it, Sergeant – I'd like to do it – I'd like to take the enemy sentry's part.

WILSON We must give some of the others a chance. Godfrey.

GODFREY Yes, Sergeant.

WILSON You can be the enemy sentry – you'll need something to sit on.

JONES I'd like to volunteer to be the something to sit on.

WILSON Oh, Jones – please. **(To Godfrey)** Go and get Mr Mainwaring's chair out of his office. **(Godfrey goes)**

WILSON Frazer, you seem to know more about this than most of us, so perhaps you could er... sort of put us in the picture.

FRAZER **(Taking charge)** Aye – I'll do that. Now, pay attention. Now, you approach your quarry from behind. And all the time keep down wind of him.

PIKE Why do you have to do that, Mr Frazer?

FRAZER So that he doesn't get your scent.

JONES Don't be silly Jock – humans can't smell humans.

WALKER You're not standing where I am, mate.

JONES Now then, Joe, I don't want any insubordination.

FRAZER Pay attention in the ranks. Right, just watch me – I'm creeping up behind the sentry. **(He creeps forward, picking his feet up and putting them down very carefully)** Yer notice the way I'm picking my feet up – and putting them down very carefully. It's most important that you watch where you're putting your feet.

WALKER Especially if you're crossing a field of cows.

WILSON Oh, Walker, please.

FRAZER **(Glaring at Walker)** As I've just said – you have to be very careful where you're putting your feet – you could step on a dry twig – snap – and the sentry would be at your throat in a second. **(He wheels round and grabs Walker by the throat and starts to shake him)**

WALKER **(Breaking loose)** Hold on – hold on – have you gone stark raving mad or something?

FRAZER So, always watch where you're putting your feet.

WALKER I will, mate, I will.

Godfrey comes out with a swivel chair.

WILSON All right, Godfrey – just put it down.

Godfrey puts the chair down.

WILSON Now, sit down. Somebody blindfold him, will you?

JONES I'd like to volunteer for that, Sergeant Wilson – I'd like to blindfold Mr Godfrey.

WILSON There's no need to make all that fuss, Jones.

JONES I know, but I keep getting left out all the time.

WILSON Just do it. **(Jones blindfolds Godfrey)** And then spin him round. **(Jones and Walker spin the chair round)**

GODFREY You know, this puts me in mind of when I was a child. My sisters and I used to play 'Putting the tail on the Donkey'.

JONES We used to play that game as well, Mr Godfrey. They were real games in them days.

WILSON Now, spread out . When I blow the whistle – I want you all to creep forward and take him by surprise. As soon as you hear anything Godfrey – swing round – point your finger and pretend to shoot him. You'd better try it.

Godfrey swings right round in a full circle – points his finger and shouts.

GODFREY Pop! Was that all right, Sergeant?

WILSON Not quite – but it will do. Now are you ready? **(He blows whistle)**

Frazer, Jones, Walker and Pike are in a line. Wilson blows his whistle and they all start to creep forward slowly – lifting their feet right up in the air. They reach Godfrey and gather in a group round him.

JONES **(Tapping Godfrey on shoulder)** We've arrived, Mr Godfrey. **(Godfrey does not move – Wilson crosses to him and shakes him)**

GODFREY **(Waking up and taking off blindfold)** I'm sorry, Sergeant – I must have dozed off. It was being in the dark, you see. And I've had rather a tiring day, waiting at the clinic.

WILSON All right, we'll try it again, and this time I'll be the enemy.

JONES **(Grabbing whistle from round Wilson's neck)** I'll take the whistle, Sergeant, I'll take the whistle.

WILSON **(Giving him the whistle)** All right, Jones, don't strangle me. **(He sits in chair and blindfolds himself)**

They all line up – Jones blows he whistle. They start to move forward. Mainwaring enters. They all come to attention. Mainwaring sees Wilson and walks towards him. Wilson spins round in the chair, points his finger and goes 'bang'.

MAINWARING All right, Wilson. I know I'm dead.

WILSON **(Taking off blindfold)** Oh, it's you, sir. I'm sorry, I thought you were the platoon.

MAINWARING Really – I didn't know I was that heavy footed. I want to see you in the office – it's very important.

WILSON Very well, sir. Carry on, Jones.

JONES Yes, Sergeant. **(Grabbing blindfold)** I'll go in the chair – I'll go in the chair.

Wilson and Mainwaring go. Jones gets in the chair and blindfolds himself.

WALKER **(To others)** Come on, let's go and make a cup of tea.

FRAZER That's the first sensible idea you've had tonight, Joe.

They all go.

JONES **(Blowing whistle)** All right, off you go.

Close up on Jones' face – he twitches his head from side as he listens. Pan back to show him sitting all alone in the yard.

SIDE OFFICE. DAY

Mainwaring comes in the door, followed by Wilson – Mainwaring crosses to his desk.

MAINWARING Close the door, Wilson. **(Wilson closes the door and crosses to desk. Mainwaring hands him a letter)** Read that.

WILSON But it's addressed to you, sir.

MAINWARING I know that – read it.

WILSON **(Looking at it)** That's funny, it's from Godfrey – why should he write you a letter?

MAINWARING You'll soon find out.

WILSON **(Reading)** 'To Captain George Mainwaring, Officer Commanding 1st Platoon, Walmington-on-Sea Home Guard. Dear Sir, It is with much regret that I must tender to you my resignation. Owing to personal reasons, I feel that I can no longer remain as a member of the platoon. Therefore I must ask you to accept my two weeks' notice, as from the end of the week. I remain, dear sir, your obedient servant, Charles Godfrey.' Hmm, it's a pity he's going, sir, we shall miss him.

MAINWARING What do you mean, pity he's going – he can't leave just like that.

WILSON I don't see how you can stop him, sir. He's given you two weeks' notice.

MAINWARING This is war, Wilson – not Sainsbury's. You'd better go and get him, we'll find out what all this is about.

WILSON Yes, sir. **(He goes)**

Mainwaring crosses to a board with lists of names on.

MAINWARING Now let's have a look at the rota. *Monday* – Number one section on patrol, gasworks – railway bridge – telephone exchange – 22.50 Godfrey puts on kettle – 22.58 Godfrey makes tea ready for return of patrol at 23.00 hours. *Tuesday* – Number three section – patrol to Novelty Rock Emporium – Godfrey leaves here 23.30, arrives Novelty Rock Emporium 23.50, makes tea ready for arrival of patrol at 24.00 hours. No, I couldn't possibly let him go, he's far too valuable. **(There is a knock on the door)** Come in. **(Godfrey and Wilson enter)**

GODFREY You wanted to see me, sir.

MAINWARING Yes, Godfrey – sit down, will you? **(Wilson starts to go)** Don't go, Wilson, I shall need you. **(Picking up letter)** Now then, Godfrey, what's the idea of this letter?

GODFREY I'm afraid it means that I've got to leave, sir.

MAINWARING You mean you feel that you're a little too old for active service, is that it?

GODFREY Well no, not really, sir.

MAINWARING Then, what's the matter?

GODFREY Well, I got up the other morning slightly earlier than usual. *Mind you*, I usually get up at around 7.30 – you see I always make the early morning tea, then I take a cup up to my two sisters, Dolly and Cissy – up until quite recently we've always had a special brand of tea from the Army and Navy stores – but of course it's on such short ration nowadays that we have to put up with anything we can get.

WILSON I quite agree with you, my dear fellow, some of the stuff we've been getting lately is terrible – all those nasty little bits of tea dust floating on the top.

MAINWARING **(Glaring at Wilson)** Wilson! **(To Godfrey)** I don't quite see what this has got to do with leaving the platoon, Godfrey.

GODFREY I'm coming to that, sir – let me see, where was I?

WILSON You were just going to make the early morning tea.

GODFREY Oh yes – well, I went into the larder to get the milk, then I saw something that made me realise that I just couldn't carry on.

MAINWARING What on earth was it?

GODFREY A mouse.

MAINWARING A mouse?

GODFREY Yes, you see in the larder was a great big, empty pudding basin – a mouse had fallen inside and it was running round and round trying to get out. I knew I ought to kill it because we're overrun with mice, so I got hold of it, and as I held it in my hand I could feel its little heart beating under its fur – and I just couldn't bring myself to do it.

MAINWARING So, what did you do?

GODFREY I took it out in the garden and let it go.

MAINWARING Look, Godfrey, I still don't see what this has got to do with you wanting to leave the platoon.

GODFREY Don't you understand, sir – if I couldn't bring myself to kill that mouse – how could I ever kill a German?

MAINWARING But if you felt like that, why did you join the Home Guard in the first place?

GODFREY Well, when the Home Guard was first started, things were so desperate – I somehow felt different from the last time.

MAINWARING Things are still desperate, Godfrey – Hitler could invade at any moment. And we need every man we can get. But what did you mean when you said you felt different from the last time?

GODFREY Well you see, sir – during the last war I was a conscientious objector.

MAINWARING What?

GODFREY A conscientious objector.

MAINWARING **(Half rising)** A con… **(He can't even bring himself to say the word – his voice goes cold)** You mean you didn't *want* to fight?

GODFREY No, not really, sir.

MAINWARING I can't believe it, Godfrey, I really can't. **(Pause)** I think the best thing you can do at the moment is to go home.

GODFREY **(Getting up)** Very good, sir – are you sure you don't want me for anything else this evening?

MAINWARING No, I don't – just go.

Godfrey crosses to the door, opens it and turns.

GODFREY I'm sorry about this, Mr Mainwaring – I really have enjoyed being with you all – I can only hope that during my service I have given every satisfaction.

MAINWARING Oh get out, man.

Godfrey closes door.

WILSON Don't you think you're being a little harsh, sir?

MAINWARING **(Getting up and pacing up and down)** Harsh? Harsh, Wilson – all this time we've been harbouring a damn conchie in our ranks – and you tell me I'm being harsh.

WILSON After all, sir, a man must follow the dictates of his conscience.

MAINWARING Where would the country be today if we all felt like that, eh? Just supposing that you'd finished work at the bank one afternoon and you went round to have tea with Mrs Pike – and when you got there you found a Nazi storm trooper forcing his attentions on her – what would you feel like then, eh?

WILSON Oh really, sir.

MAINWARING Ah, yes, yes – that strikes home doesn't it, Wilson – that really cuts to the bone.

WILSON That's rather an old fashioned argument, don't you think, sir.

MAINWARING Perhaps I am old fashioned, Wilson. I just can't stand cranks – fancy not wanting to fight – I mean, it's just normal. Apart from anything else, what are they going to say at G.H.Q. when they find out?

WILSON Need they find out, sir?

MAINWARING I shall have to put in a report about it, and then what are they going to say? We shall be known as Captain Mainwaring's company of cowards.

WILSON What are you going to do about him then?

MAINWARING I know what I'd like to do. I'd like to give him the rogue's march.

WILSON Oh, what's that?

MAINWARING They used to do it in the British Army many years ago – if a man was a coward and had brought disgrace on his Regiment – they would parade him in front of the men – tear the gold braid off his hat – cut of his epaulettes – tear off his medals – and break his sword.

WILSON It would be a bit difficult to do that to Godfrey, sir – he's only wearing a suit of denims.

MAINWARING All right, Wilson. Get the men on parade.

WILSON What are you going to say to them, sir?

MAINWARING I'm going to tell them the truth. I may not be able to cut off Godfrey's epaulettes in front of the men physically – but I can do it verbally.

THE YARD. DAY

The platoon are drawn up on parade, waiting. They are at ease.

WALKER **(To Jones)** 'Ere, Jonesey, what's all the mystery about?

JONES Don't ask me, Joe. All I know is we were told to fall in for a special parade – Mr Mainwaring has a very important announcement to make. By the way, where's Mr Godfrey?

PIKE He left about half an hour ago. As he passed me, I said, 'Where are you going, Mr Godfrey?' and he didn't even answer. I think he had tears in his eyes.

FRAZER Ach! He's as soft as a cream puff – if I was in Mr Mainwaring's shoes I'd give him something to cry about.

Wilson enters with a small beer box – he puts it down in front of the parade.

WILSON Right, properly at ease **(Mainwaring enters)** Platoon... attention.

Jones is late.

Jones reacts.

Mainwaring reacts.

Mainwaring and Wilson exchange salutes. Mainwaring climbs on the box.

MAINWARING All right, gentlemen, at ease.

They stand at ease – Jones is late.

Jones reacts.

Mainwaring reacts.

MAINWARING During the past 14 months we have been together.

Wilson moves across.

Mainwaring dries up.

Wilson turns.

Jones winks.

MAINWARING During the past 14 months we have been together **(Warden comes into picture and stands beside Mainwaring)** and we have had to put up with many trials and tribulations... **(Warden pulls at Mainwaring's jacket – Mainwaring looks sideways – then looks down)** What is it, Warden?

WARDEN You going to be long?

MAINWARING I don't know. I've got something very...

During Warden's conversation with Wilson, Mainwaring is droning on in the background with his speech...

MAINWARING We have had to put up with many trials and tribulations – shortage of weapons – long hours of duty – going without sleep – working during the day – and doing Home Guard duties in our spare time – giving up everything to guard our homeland against the Nazi threat.

WARDEN **(To Wilson)** What's Napoleon going on about then?

WILSON He's got something very important to say to the men.

WARDEN Why is he standing on a box?

WILSON Well, er...

WARDEN Is that the only way he can get them to look up to him. **(He laughs)**

Mainwaring stops and goes 'shhh!' to Warden. The whole platoon turn their heads as one and go 'shhh!'.

WILSON Yes, shhh!

WARDEN Look, I can't hang about all day, mate – I was asked to come along and explain about the Civil Defence exercise on Saturday afternoon.

WILSON Well, you'll just have to wait.

WARDEN Oh, we'll soon see about that.

Cut back to Mainwaring.

MAINWARING ...which is waiting all the time just across the Channel ready to strike. We do these things freely of our own accord – we do not ask for a reward. **(Warden drags a bigger beer box into position beside Mainwaring and stands on it – he towers over Mainwaring)** The only reward we can hope for is from a higher authority, up above.**(He sees the Warden towering over him)**

A SMALL GUARD HUT. NIGHT

The hut is in deep gloom – just one small, shaded light above a stove – there are some boxes round it – the kettle is boiling and Pike is making the tea – he is singing to himself. The black-out blanket over the door parts and Frazer comes in like a shadow – Pike does not see him.

PIKE **(Singing)** There was a brave old Scotchman at the Battle of Waterloo. The wind blew up his petticoats and showed his... **(Suddenly sees Frazer)** Oh, hullo, Mr Frazer – did you have a nice patrol?

FRAZER For your information, laddie – the word is Scotsman – Scotch is something you drink – I can't understand why you English have such an obsession with what we Scots wear under our kilts.

Jones and Walker enter – all the patrol are wearing their greatcoats.

WALKER Blimey, it ain't half chilly out tonight.

JONES I see you got the tea ready, Pikey – there's a good boy.

Pike pours out and they all sit in a tight circle round the stove.

WALKER Listen to that wind – good job you're not wearing your kilt tonight, Taff – otherwise you might find it a 'wee' bit draughty round…

FRAZER **(Cutting in)** And it's a good job you're not going to mention the word kilt again – otherwise you might find it a 'wee' bit draughty, with my fist round your nose.

WALKER Sorry I spoke.

JONES **(Sipping tea)** 'Ere, Pikey, what did you put in this tea?

PIKE Why, don't you like it, Mr Jones?

JONES Well, it's not as good as Mr Godfrey makes.

FRAZER Don't mention that name to me – just fancy all this time, we've had a conchie in our ranks, without knowing it.

PIKE What's going to happen to him, Mr Jones?

JONES You heard what Mr Mainwaring said at the parade – he's going to make him stay with the platoon until he can find somebody to replace him.

FRAZER It's a downright disgrace, that's what it is – a disgrace.

PIKE My mum thinks men ought to be men – I heard her telling my Uncle Arthur, last night.

WALKER I feel a bit sorry for him meself – he's a nice old boy. What do you think, Jonesey?

JONES I don't know much about conscientious objecting – I've been a soldier all me life – ours is not to reason why – ours is but to do or die. I can remember once when we was on the North West Frontier…

PIKE The North West Frontier of what, Mr Jones?

WALKER Golders Green.

JONES No, the North West Frontier of India… we was surrounded by hundreds of Pathans.

PIKE You mean those black men with turbans?

JONES No, they're not black – they're the same colour as you, Pikey.

WALKER You mean they're green.

JONES Look, let me get on with the story, Joe. They've got hawk-like faces – with hook noses – and cruel, beady eyes.

WALKER **(Pointing to Frazer)** Like old Taff 'ere.

JONES Come to think of it – he does look like a Pathan.

FRAZER Don't talk rubbish – I'm Highlander born and bred.

WALKER Perhaps his father had a bicycle.

JONES Anyhow – there we was surrounded by hundreds of Pathans –

WALKER They're the ones who don't like it up 'em.

JONES Oh, shut up.

Godfrey comes in.

GODFREY Am I too late to make the tea?

PIKE Yes – I made it, Mr Godfrey – we didn't think you were coming.

FRAZER **(Getting up)** All of a sudden there's a very nasty smell in here. Come on, it's time to get back on patrol.

JONES Yes – come on Joe – come on Pikey.

They all get up and pick up their rifles.

GODFREY I brought some upside-down cakes – my sister made them specially – would anybody like one? **(They all stare at him)** What about you, Mr Jones?

JONES No, I'm… er, not hungry thank you.

He offers the tin to Pike who puts his hand to take one.

PIKE Thank you, Mr Godfrey.

Frazer knocks his hand.

FRAZER Come on.

They all go out – Godfrey, left alone, looks down at the tin of cakes and slowly starts to eat one.

CIVIL DEFENCE EXERCISE. DAY

Two A.R.P. Wardens are standing outside a long, low, tin hut. There is a small flap in the side. A large stove with a tin roof over it is standing beside the hut and the pipe from it goes in through the side wall. The Second Warden is putting some rags in the stove.

FIRST WARDEN Don't put too many rags in there, Bill – you know what an old fuss-pot Mainwaring is.

SECOND WARDEN I hope this smoke test isn't too much for them, Mr Hodges.

FIRST WARDEN You needn't worry about that – they're dead keen – anyhow I'll keep an eye on 'em – after all, we don't want them coming out looking like kippers, do we? **(He laughs. There is the sound of marching feet)** Look out, here comes Napoleon.

• BILL HARMAN REMEMBERS •

'The episode "Branded" gave Arnold Ridley another opportunity to show off his fine acting skills. Arnold was quite frail and forgetful. At the end of one filming session in Thetford, the cast were bussed back to London in a large coach. Arthur Lowe and Ian Lavender were appearing in a show in the West End and had to be back in town to get ready for curtain up. Arthur had got a lift back but Ian travelled on the coach. Arnold asked if I'd mind persuading the driver to make a slight detour so that we could drop him off at his home in Highgate.

'By the time we got close to Highgate, we were already running behind schedule and Ian was growing more and more anxious that he might be late for his theatre call. Unfortunately, Arnold was not as familiar with his neighbourhood as he had led us to believe and by the time we'd seen the same streets for the third or fourth time, Ian was about ready to murder me for allowing the farce to continue.

'Finally, when we realised we were still no closer to Arnold's home, Ian stormed off the coach and hailed a taxi. One couldn't blame him. As a professional actor, it would have been unforgivable to arrive late for a live appearance. We eventually found Arnold's home. Throughout the ordeal he'd seemed blissfully unaware of the panic his lack of navigational skills had caused. By the time I saw Ian next he had gracefully forgiven me for my lack of judgment. From then on, all transport went directly to the destination specified on the call sheet.'

BILL HARMAN *Assistant Floor Manager*

WILSON Left, right, left, right, Platoon, halt!

The platoon comes into the picture.

WILSON Platoon… halt. Right turn. Stand at ease.

MAINWARING **(Crosses to Warden)** Good afternoon, Mr Hodges – we're all ready for you.

WARDEN Right, gather round.

Platoon listening.

FIRST WARDEN **(To platoon)** Now, this afternoon we're going to do 'Rescuing an unconscious person from a burning building'. Now, this hut 'ere is full of smoke – we've been burning damp rags in this stove 'ere, and the smoke's going through this pipe 'ere to the hut 'ere. **(They all nod)** Now, when you get inside the hut – you'll find sacks filled with straw – they represent the bodies – you get hold of one and go out of the flap the other side – when you get outside you carry the body up the ladder and over the wall.

WALKER 'Ere, what about the smoke – we shall suffocate.

FIRST WARDEN Not if you do it properly, you won't. I'll just show you – right, Bill. **(Second Warden spreads a groundsheet on the ground)** Now, watch me very carefully. **(He gets down on his knees)**

WALKER Let us pray.

FIRST WARDEN You trying to be funny?

MAINWARING That will do, Walker.

FIRST WARDEN Right, as you all know – smoke always rises – so there is a small area of two inches from the ground which is smoke free. What you do is this, you get your nose flat on the floor, like this… **(He faces the platoon and squashes his nose with his right-hand forefinger)** …and keep your mouth tightly shut. Now, the fresh air goes up through your nostrils, so… **(He gestures with the two fingers of his left hand up his nostrils – all the time he is speaking with his mouth closed)** …now, is that clear? **(Platoon watching)** Whatever you do, don't lift your nose off the floor – you go along like this – watch. **(He crawls along with his nose on the floor)**

WALKER **(Aside to Jones)** You can see by the shape of it – he's done a lot of practising.

JONES Permission to speak, sir?

MAINWARING Yes, Jones.

JONES Well, sir, that's all very well – but supposing your nose is longer than two inches?

MAINWARING For your information, Jones – my nose is not longer than two inches.

WILSON No, no, sir – when Jones said your nose, he wasn't referring to your actual nose – he was talking about a hypothetical nose.

PIKE Excuse me, Mr Hodges, has the hut got a wooden floor?

WARDEN Yes, it has – why?

PIKE My mum wouldn't like the idea of me pushing my nose along the ground – I might get a splinter in it.

FRAZER Damned cissy.

WARDEN Well, don't let that worry you, lad. Don't give it a moment's thought. If you like **(Shouts)** I'll put a bloody carpet down.

MAINWARING I won't have you swearing at my men, Mr Hodges.

WARDEN They're enough to make anyone swear. I'm trying to give a lecture and all they can do is argue about their noses. You don't realise how lucky you are to be allowed to go through a smoke-filled hut. There's plenty of people who just can't wait to go through one.

MAINWARING Get on with it.

WARDEN Now, this can be a bit dangerous, so pay attention. My assistant will go round to the other flap and count you off as you come through, if anyone of you doesn't appear, I shall come straight in and get you out. Okay?

MAINWARING Right! Round we go men.

WARDEN Right, off you go, Bill, and don't forget there's 17 to come through.

SECOND WARDEN Right-oh, Mr Hodges.

MAINWARING I'm going through first. I don't expect my men to do anything that I can't do.

WILSON Do you think that's wise, sir.

MAINWARING Just stand by to send the rest of the men through, Wilson. **(He gets down on his hands and knees and crawls through the flap – as he does so a billow of smoke puffs out)**

WARDEN **(Shouting)** Number one coming through, Bill.

JONES I should like to volunteer to be the next one, to go through the smoke-filled hut, Sergeant.

WILSON Oh, all right then.

Jones gets down and is just going to crawl through the flap, when it opens and Mainwaring comes out again.

WARDEN What are you doing coming back? You'll mess all my counting up.

MAINWARING I can't help that – there's not enough smoke in there.

WARDEN Cancel that, Bill – he's come back. **(He crosses to the stove and starts putting in more rags – shouts to Jones)** All right, Corporal, start taking the men through.

Jones goes through the flap.

WARDEN **(Crossing to Mainwaring)** What are you playing at? You'll asphyxiate them.

MAINWARING If a thing's worth doing – it's worth doing properly.

THE END OF THE HUT. DAY

The Second Warden is there. Two men come out. First Warden comes into picture. Jones enters, then starts to go back.

FIRST WARDEN 'Ere, where are you going?

JONES I've forgotten my body.

FIRST WARDEN Don't worry about that. **(Jones rises)**

JONES Don't tangle with a butcher.

Jones leaves. Frazer appears.

FRAZER Ooh!

FIRST WARDEN What's the matter with you?

FRAZER I've got a splinter up my nose. **(He leaves)**

Clouds of smoke are coming out through the flap.

SECOND WARDEN There's a lot more smoke than usual.

FIRST WARDEN It's that Captain Mainwaring – he's a blooming maniac – keeps putting more rags on the stove. **(Wilson comes through the flap)** Come on, you, hurry up and get over that wall.

WILSON Oh, just clear off will you?

THE TOP OF THE HUT. DAY

MAINWARING Go on, Pike. **(Pike goes)** Walker – no smoking in there. **(Walker goes)** All right, Godfrey, you're not getting out of this.

GODFREY I wasn't trying to get out of it, Mr Mainwaring.

MAINWARING You'd like to, though, wouldn't you – now, you go first – and remember I'm right behind you – so don't try any of your conchie tricks on me. **(He pushes him and Godfrey goes through the flap)**

THE END OF THE HUT. DAY

Walker crawls through the flap, followed by Pike. The two Wardens are watching. The rest of the platoon have come over the wall.

PIKE Which way now?

FIRST WARDEN Oh, that way – over there – 15 – only two more to come. Right, Bill, you follow the others over the wall.

SECOND WARDEN Right you are, Mr Hodges. **(He comes over the wall)**

Godfrey comes through the flap. The Warden helps him up.

FIRST WARDEN Come on, Grandpa – where's Captain Mainwaring?

GODFREY He's just behind me.

FIRST WARDEN Right, I'm going over the wall – you can wait here for him.

GODFREY Er… very well.

The Warden goes over the wall. Godfrey is left alone. Pause.

Godfrey opens the flap – clouds of smoke billow out – he shouts.

GODFREY Mr Mainwaring, are you all right? **(Pause. He shouts over wall)** Mr Hodges, Mr Mainwaring hasn't come out yet. **(No answer. He lifts the flap).** All right, Mr Mainwaring – I'm coming. **(He puts his handkerchief over his face and crawls through the flap)**

GODFREY'S BEDROOM. DAY

Godfrey is propped up in bed. A doctor and Godfrey's sister Cissy, are standing beside the bed.

DOCTOR **(Closing his bag)** He'll be as right as rain in a day or two, Miss Godfrey – just see that he gets plenty of rest.

CISSY Thank you, Doctor. Is it all right for Mr Mainwaring to come in now?

DOCTOR Yes, of course.

CISSY **(Crossing to the door and opening it)** My brother will see you now, Mr Mainwaring.

They all enter.

MAINWARING Thank you, Miss Godfrey… Well Godfrey… er feeling better?

GODFREY Yes. Thank you, sir.

PIKE Some flowers, Mr Godfrey.

GODFREY Thank you.

JONES Some strengthening sweetbreads.

FRAZER I've brought you a bottle of Scotch.

WALKER I've brought you a quarter of tea.

GODFREY From the Army and Navy?

WALKER No, from a fellow I know in the Air Force.

WILSON **(Whispering to Mainwaring)** Well, aren't you going to thank him for saving your life, sir?

MAINWARING **(Hissing back)** Yes, of course I am. **(He clears his throat)** Now, look here, Godfrey – I may have said a few harsh things in the past – but I want you to know that I… deep down **(He shuffles his feet and looks around the room – looks at a photograph above the bed)** What's this photograph of you in uniform, Godfrey?

GODFREY It was in the last war, sir.

MAINWARING You're wearing the Military Medal.

GODFREY Yes, I know.

MAINWARING But you told me you were a damn conchie – I mean a conscientious objector.

GODFREY So I was, sir.

MAINWARING Then how did you win the Military Medal?

CISSY He volunteered as a medical orderly. My brother wouldn't tell you himself, Mr Mainwaring – but during the Battle of the Somme, he went out into no man's land under heavy fire and saved several lives.

GODFREY It wasn't very… **(The men all stare with open mouths)**

Mainwaring dumbfounded.

JONES Sorry, we've all stood upon you in false judgement, Mr Godfrey.

Walker and Pike murmur 'Yes'.

FRAZER Speaking for myself, I never doubted you for a single minute.

WILSON **(To Mainwaring)** Perhaps in future Godfrey could be our medical orderly, sir.

MAINWARING Thank you, Wilson, that's an excellent idea. As from today, Godfrey, you're appointed platoon Medical Orderly – report back as soon as you're fit.

GODFREY Thank you, sir.

MAINWARING Well, we mustn't tire you anymore. Goodbye Godfrey.

GODFREY Goodbye, sir.

They all start to go.

MAINWARING There's still one thing I can't understand, Godfrey.

GODFREY What's that, sir?

MAINWARING Why didn't you wear your medals?

GODFREY Somehow I thought they looked rather ostentatious, sir.

MAINWARING Ostentatious… but good Lord, man – if I'd have won the Military Medal – I'd have worn it proudly on my chest for all the world to see.

GODFREY Yes, sir, and that would have been all right – because somehow you look like a hero.

WILSON It just goes to show, sir – you can never judge by appearances.

Mainwaring gives him a terrible glare.

SERIES THREE **EPISODE TWELVE**

Recorded: Friday 21/11/69
Original transmission: Thursday 27/11/69, 7.30–8.00pm
Original viewing figures = 11.8 million

ARTHUR LOWE .... CAPTAIN MAINWARING
JOHN LE MESURIER .... SERGEANT WILSON
CLIVE DUNN .... LANCE CORPORAL JONES
JOHN LAURIE .... PRIVATE FRAZER
JAMES BECK .... PRIVATE WALKER
ARNOLD RIDLEY .... PRIVATE GODFREY
IAN LAVENDER .... PRIVATE PIKE
BILL PERTWEE .... CHIEF WARDEN
JANET DAVIES .... MRS PIKE
PATRICK TULL .... THE SUSPECT
ROBERT MOORE .... THE LARGE MAN
LEON CORTEZ .... THE SMALL MAN
OLIVE MERCER .... THE FIERCE LADY
MIRANDA HAMPTON .... THE SEXY LADY
ROBERT ALDOUS .... GERMAN PILOT
BRAN .... AS HIMSELF

PLATOON... LESLIE NOYES, JIMMY MAC, HUGH HASTINGS, ROGER BOURNE, ... DESMOND CULLUM-JONES, VIC TAYLOR, GEORGE HANCOCK, ... FREDDIE WILES, MARTIN DUNN, FREDDIE WHITE

MAN HUNT

• DES STEWART REMEMBERS •

'As an armourer for the BBC I was away from home for a great deal of the year. Consequently, when I had the opportuntiy to take one of my sons on location, I jumped at the chance. When I was sent to Brandon, near Thetford, for a week's filming on *Dad's Army*, I took my eldest son, Gary.

'All was well until about five days into the shoot. Gary was sat by me as Arthur Lowe was doing his piece to camera. This was a low angle shot looking up into Arthur's face. When he'd reached midway in his piece it started raining and Gary said, quite naturally: "It's raining!" This interrupted Arthur's flow and he stopped. A few words were bandied around because of Gary's interruption, and being a small lad of nine years old, he started crying. With that Arthur walked over to Gary, ruffled his hair, and said: "Don't cry, lad, it's only a film. We would have had to do it again anyway as there are spots of rain on the camera lens." This caring approach from Arthur Lowe is in direct contrast to his screen persona, as I always thought of him as a rather grumpy fellow. How wrong I was. After the episode was completed, Jimmy Perry also came up to me to make sure Gary was all right, concerned that he was still upset about the incident.

'I worked with David Croft and Jimmy Perry on several of their shows, including *Are You Being Served?* and *You Rang, M'Lord?*, as a health and safety adviser. All the armourers who worked on *Dad's Army* would make sure John Laurie and Arnold Ridley had lightweight dummy rifles. They were made from cast aluminium and quite light compared to the 11 pound weight of the real rifles carried by the rest of the cast. Sometimes the two aluminium rifles were returned to us after use; sometimes we had to fetch them from where they'd been dropped, as the distance from the shoot to the armourer's vehicle was too far for these stalwarts to carry them.

'The role of the armourer on *Dad's Army* would begin with the assistant floor manager visiting us in the armoury and selecting the appropriate weapons. If we had the weapons in stock we'd take them to the studio or location. If not, the buyer would arrange to hire them.

'If the weapons were to be used on location, we had to liaise with the local police for permission to use them in that area, as well as arranging secure storage. Sometimes we'd be allowed to store them in the police station, other times in a registered firearm dealer's premises. Once everything had been sorted we delivered the weapons to the location, issued them to the actors and collected them at the end of every scene if they were no longer required. If there was to be any firing we were responsible for the safety of the artistes and staff, ensuring that not only would the gas discharge not cause any injuries but that people were protected against the noise levels. We would normally issue yellow foam earplugs and if the camera operator could see them through the lens, the make-up girls would disguise them with flesh-coloured make-up cream.'

DES STEWART
Armourer

Man Hunt

CHURCH HALL. DAY

The men are all drawn up on parade – Mainwaring is addressing them.

MAINWARING Pay attention, men. The war has been going on now for over 18 months, and there's no doubt about it – Germany is feeling the pinch. It's true we've been pushed out of Greece and we've been pushed out of Crete. But in each case it's been done by the use of parachute troops. There's no doubt about it, gentlemen, 1941 will go down in history as the year the parachute revolutionised military strategy. Mind you, I saw it coming years ago – but no one would listen to me. I can recall as long ago as 1936 – Elizabeth and I were on holiday at Bognor, and I went up for a 5s-trip in a biplane – and as we soared through the clouds, the wind blowing in my face, I looked down (**Godfrey has his eyes closed**) and then the idea came to me 'Parachute Troops'. As soon as we got back to the boarding… er… hotel where we were staying, I wrote a long letter to the War Office explaining the whole thing – and believe it or not, gentlemen, I never even got a reply. Just like our great leader Winston Churchill I was shouting in the wilderness – 'Wake Up, England!' (**Godfrey quickly opens his eyes**) However, the boot's on the other foot now – and I am in the position where my ideas are no longer ignored. At least – not in Walmington. Now men – I expect you're wondering where all this is leading.

WALKER (**Out of the corner of his mouth to Frazer**) If he doesn't hurry – it's going to lead to us not getting a drink.

FRAZER Blether – blether – blether.

MAINWARING What was that, Frazer?

FRAZER I was just thinking, sir – it's very profound – very profound thinking indeed.

MAINWARING Thank you, Frazer. Today I have received a memo from the War Office that has been sent to all Home Guard Units. I'll read it to you… 'To all ranks of the Home Guard. In order to create alarm and confusion, the enemy has recently been dropping numerous empty parachutes in the southern counties. In future all parachutes found must be reported at once to G.H.Q.'.

JONES Permission to speak, sir?

MAINWARING Yes, Jones.

JONES What happens if one of our airmen jumps out by parachute, and then when he lands he takes it off and walks away – and we come along and see the parachute, but we do not know it is his, because he has walked away previous. How do we know it is a British parachute and not a Nazi one?

MAINWARING That's a very good question, Jones. Now let me see. (**He looks at paper**) Ah, I thought so, it's all here. (**He taps paper**) It's very simple – our parachutes are pure white – Nazi parachutes are a dirty, off-white, creamy colour. One might have guessed, of course. There's your answer, Jones. If it's not white, it's not one of ours. (**To platoon**) Now, men, you know me, you know that I'm not given to making outlandish, sweeping statements that I cannot support. You also know that I never make a move without working everything out from A to Z. However, in my considered opinion, there's more to this memo about empty parachutes than meets the eye. As you know, Hess landed in this country by parachute six weeks ago – and since then we've heard nothing, it's quite obvious that the rats are leaving the sinking ship – for all we know, several Nazi leaders may have landed in this country during the past few weeks.

PIKE Excuse me, Mr Mainwaring. That new commissionaire outside the cinema looks awfully like Hitler.

The platoon laugh.

Pike reacts.

MAINWARING All right, men, I know it sounds absurd but we must check everything. Wilson…

WILSON Sir.

MAINWARING The next time you got to the pictures ask to see his identity card.

FRAZER But supposing we do find an empty parachute, Mr Mainwaring – by the time we've reported it back to G.H.Q., whoever was on the end of it could be miles away. What about using a tracker dog, sir – a good dog could sniff the parachute and lead us to whoever came down in it.

MAINWARING Excellent idea, Frazer… the only snag is, I don't think any of us has got a dog.

WALKER I can get hold of a dog for you, Mr Mainwaring.

MAINWARING Is it a good smeller?

WALKER Eh?

MAINWARING Can it pick up a scent?

WALKER Yes – anything you like.

GODFREY Is it fierce?

WALKER Yes – anything you like.

GODFREY Oh dear.

MAINWARING When can you get it here?

WALKER Tomorrow night if you like.

MAINWARING Good, that's settled then. All right, men, that's all for now. Parade… attention. Dismiss.

Mainwaring crosses to the office, followed by Wilson.

JONES **(To Walker)** You coming for a drink, Joe?

WALKER Er… I've just got to have a word with Mr Mainwaring. See you down there.

SIDE OFFICE. DAY

Mainwaring and Wilson come in. Mainwaring crosses to desk and puts his hat down. Walker enters looking very shifty.

WALKER Excuse me, Mr Mainwaring – can I have a word with you?

MAINWARING Certainly, Walker. What is it?

WALKER **(Looking at Wilson)** Well it's… er, rather intimate.

WILSON I'll be off then, sir.

MAINWARING No you stay, Wilson – you might be able to give some advice, you don't mind do you, Walker?

WALKER Er – no, no.

MAINWARING Intimate, eh. Now you know, Walker, **(Leaning across the desk)** I'm not only your Commanding Officer – **(Dropping his voice)** – but your friend. Now, what is it? Is it a woman?

WALKER Eh?

MAINWARING **(Louder)** Is it a woman?

WILSON Really, I think I should go, sir.

Mainwaring reacts.

WALKER No, no, Mr Mainwaring – it's not a woman. It's a parachute. I found one.

MAINWARING **(Dropping back in his seat – disappointed)** Oh, is that all. **(Jumping up)** What! When was this?

WALKER About two weeks ago in the woods.

MAINWARING Well, why on earth didn't you report it?

WALKER I mean, I didn't know, did I, I mean you only told us today.

MAINWARING But you should have done something about it, Walker.

WALKER I did do something about it.

MAINWARING What!

WALKER I had it made up into eight dozen pairs.

MAINWARING Eight dozen pairs of what?

WALKER **(Dropping his voice and looking down on the floor)** Ladies knickers.

MAINWARING **(Exploding)** Ladies knickers!!! **(Wilson winces)** Ladies knickers. **(Mainwaring comes round the desk quivering with rage)** Here we are, fighting for our lives –with our backs to the wall – living on rations cut down to the bone – going without sleep – the entire German army poised just across the Channel ready to strike – and you had a parachute made up into ladies knickers.

WILSON I do wish you wouldn't keep on using that word, sir.

MAINWARING **(Shouting)** All right then – bloomers.

Wilson reacts.

WALKER I didn't think I was doing any harm, Mr Mainwaring – it was just lying on the ground, I mean, nobody wants an old parachute, do they? I mean, think of all that lovely silk going to waste.

MAINWARING **(Trying to keep his temper)** All right, Walker – all right – was it one of ours, or one of theirs?

WALKER Eh?

MAINWARING Our parachutes are white – German parachutes are cream – was it white or cream?

WALKER I can't remember.

MAINWARING Well, go and get a pair and have a look.

WALKER I can't – I sold them all on my stall in the market last Saturday – they went like hot cakes.

MAINWARING You must have some odd scraps of material left over – get hold of those.

WALKER I can't do that either – you see I gave this bloke the whole parachute to make up for me.

MAINWARING Well, get hold of him.

WALKER I can't – you see he moves around a lot.

MAINWARING **(Sinking into his chair)** We've simply got to get our hands on a pair of those, er – underthings. We must find out if they're white or cream.

WILSON Well, sir, if Walker sold eight dozen pairs – plenty of people must have bought them.

MAINWARING Ah – that's good thinking, Wilson – of course, there's plenty of them about – come round to the bank tomorrow afternoon as soon as we close and make some enquiries and find out if they're white or cream. We must get to the bottom of this.

TELECINE: ROW OF HOUSES. DAY

Mainwaring, Wilson and Walker are marching up the street. They are all dressed in civilian clothes. Mainwaring is leading, carrying his umbrella under his arm. Wilson is on his left – Walker on his right – they are both just a pace behind – all three are carrying gas masks. They stop outside the first house.

MAINWARING All right, now, leave this to me. (He knocks on the door) (To Wilson and Walker) We shouldn't have any trouble here – everybody knows me in Walmington-on-Sea. It goes without saying, as a bank manager I carry a lot of respect.

A large man opens the door – he is wearing a singlet and trousers.

MAINWARING Good afternoon, sir.

LARGE MAN We don't want any. (He slams door)

MAINWARING Perhaps we'd better try the next house.

WALKER You don't want to give up like that, Mr Mainwaring – let me try. (He knocks on door) You've got to be persistent – you've got to have the technique – you know – get the old foot in the door. Watch me, I'll show you. (The door opens) Ah, good day, sir.

The large man goes to shut the door – Walker quickly puts his foot in the door – the large man opens the door wide and slams it on his foot – Walker pulls his foot out quickly and hops up and down in pain. The door shuts.

NEXT HOUSE

Walker knocks on door. A mild little man – with a bald head and glasses, opens the door.

WALKER (Aside to Mainwaring) This should be a pushover. (To man) Ah, good day, sir. Has your wife bought any new underwear lately?

The little man doesn't say a word – he quietly closes the door. There is a pause – they all exchange puzzled looks. Suddenly we hear an enormously loud man's voice.

MAN (Out of vision) Up to your old tricks again, are you?

WOMAN (Out of vision) No, Jim, you've got me all wrong.

MAN (Out of vision) I'll teach you.

There is the sound of a slap – the voices argue very loudly – there is a glass crash – then silence.

MAINWARING (Clearing his throat) Yes, well, I think we'll move on, shall we? (They move on to the next front door. Mainwaring knocks. Door is opened by a large, fierce, middle-aged lady) Ah, good afternoon, madam, that was quick. (He gives a little laugh – lady glares at him) Now you know me, I'm Mainwaring – the manager of the bank. Now this is quite official – I'd like to see your underwear – to find out if it's white or cream. The explanation is quite simple, you see – a parachute...

WOMAN How dare you? (Single shot on woman – her hand reaches out – there is the sound of a loud slap – still on woman, picture goes out of focus – comes back in focus – swings from side to side – door slams)

Cut to Mainwaring on ground. Wilson helps him up.

NEXT HOUSE

MAINWARING All right, Wilson – you try this time.

WILSON Do you think it's wise, sir?

MAINWARING Get on with it, man.

Wilson knocks on door and leaps back.

MAINWARING Nobody's going to bite you.

WILSON I'm not so sure, sir.

The door opens – a very sexy lady is standing there.

LADY (Smiling) Hullo.

WILSON Er... good afternoon.

LADY Well, what can I do for you?

WILSON Well, the fact is er...

LADY Yes?

MAINWARING Get on with it, Wilson.

WILSON Yes, well I wonder if er... (He whispers in her ear – she smiles)

LADY Certainly, come in – won't you? (Mainwaring and Walker step forward) Not you two – just him.

WILSON (Smirking) Excuse me, sir.

He pushes past Mainwaring and goes inside – the door closes. There is a pause – Mainwaring and Walker look at each other.

WALKER (Lighting a cigarette and leaning against the wall) 'Ere, Mr Mainwaring – have you noticed the extraordinary influence Mr Wilson has over women.

MAINWARING I'm getting a little tired of Wilson's sordid little peccadilloes, Walker. And I don't want to discuss them, they bore me.

WALKER Sorry I spoke.

The door opens – Wilson comes out – the lady is smiling.

WILSON Well, good day – and thank you.

LADY You're welcome. T.T.F.N. (She closes the door)

MAINWARING Well, come on man – what are they? Cream or white?

WILSON (Smirking) Actually, sir – they're blue.

NEXT HOUSE

MAINWARING (Knocking on door) Surely we're bound to have luck here.

WILSON There doesn't seem to be anybody at home, sir.

WALKER (Looking through letter box) There's a little boy standing in the hall, Mr Mainwaring. Hullo, little boy –

is your mummy at home? (**To Mainwaring**) He's all alone in the house.

MAINWARING Well, that's no good, is it? Come on.

WALKER Hold on – I've got an idea. (**Speaking through letter box**) Now listen, little boy, put your ear to the letter box – I want to ask you something. Go upstairs to your Mummy's room and…

MAINWARING (**Draws Wilson away**) I don't think I like the look of this, Wilson – you can never tell what Walker's up to.

WALKER It's all right – I've fixed it.

Warden comes into picture with middle-aged woman, large man and several others.

WOMAN That's them, Warden.

WARDEN Oh, it's you, is it – I might have guessed. I've had complaints that you've been knocking at doors asking funny questions.

WOMAN He ought to be put away.

WILSON Will you clear off, this has got nothing to do with you.

LARGE MAN I've read about people like him in the *News of the World.*

WARDEN All right, what's the game?

MAINWARING I can assure you, Warden, that there's a perfectly innocent explanation for all this. (**A pair of black and white check knickers come through the letter box**)

MAINWARING (**Grabbing them**) Oh, they're no good either – we'll never find what we're looking for.

CHURCH HALL. DAY

Jones is standing at one end of the hall – the platoon are lined up at the other end in front of the stage. The front rank consists of Frazer, Pike, Godfrey and Sponge.

JONES All right now, pay attention. I want you to imagine you're marching along – all of a sudden the enemy opens up with machine gun fire. Now what do you do?

GODFREY Er… kneel down.

JONES No, Mr Godfrey, you don't kneel down – you throw yourself flat on your face. As soon as you come under fire – there's four things you've got to remember. Down – Crawl – Observe – Fire. Watch me – I'm marching along. Now, Pike, you be the Nazi machine gunner – and when I come round the corner let me have it, all right?

PIKE Yes, Mr Jones.

JONES The rest of you back him up by making machine gun noises. Now, I'm marching along, it's a lovely day – the sun's shining and the birds are singing.

GODFREY Would you like me to do the bird noises?

JONES No thank you, Mr Godfrey, we'll just imagine them.

GODFREY (**To Pike**) Pity, I'm rather good at bird noises.

JONES Now, I'm marching along. (**He starts to march on the spot**)

FRAZER So you keep saying – get on with it.

JONES All right, Jock, all right. Now, I'm marching along.

PIKE (**Backed up by the rest of the platoon**) Rat – tat – tat – tat – tat. You're dead, Mr Jones, we got you, we got you.

JONES I hadn't come round the corner yet, had I? You've got to wait till I come round the corner – now, I'm marching along – now I'm marching round the corner. All right, let me have it.

Jones starts to go down in slow motion.

JONES I'm doing it in slow motion, now, so that you can see exactly what's happening –

FRAZER What's the difference?

JONES You'll notice that my left elbow takes the weight of my body – keep the tip of the rifle clear of the ground – otherwise you'll get your foresight bunged up with mud.

PIKE They don't like it up 'em.

JONES That was the *down* bit. Next, the *crawl.* (**He crawls**) Now, the *observe.* (**He shades his eyes with his hand and looks round**) Ah, there he is. Now the *fire.* Bang – bang – bang.

PIKE But, Mr Jones why do you crawl away from the spot where you got down before you start firing?

JONES That's a very good question, Pike. And the answer is very simple really. You see – as soon as you get down, the enemy is watching the spot where you got down. So, if you was to start firing without crawling away from the spot where you got down, he'd know where you was – 'cos he's watching the spot where you got down. On the other hand, if you crawl away from the spot where you got down, and then start firing – you'll take him by surprise, 'cos you're not where he thought you were when you got down – the reason being that you have crawled away previous. Now, is that clear?

PIKE Up to where you said it was simple.

JONES Pike, go and fetch Mr Mainwaring – and then we can show him what we've learnt. (**Pike crosses to office**) Now, don't forget – Down – Crawl – Observe – Fire.

Walker comes in with a dog on the end of a long piece of string.

JONES All right, Mr Godfrey, I can manage.

WALKER 'Ere he is, what do you think of him?

JONES Blimey Joe, what's this?

WALKER What do you mean – it's the tracker dog Mr Mainwaring asked me to get.

Mainwaring, Wilson and Pike come out of the office.

WALKER Here you are, Mr Mainwaring. One tracker dog as ordered.

MAINWARING A very nice looking animal, Walker. (**He draws Walker on one side – Wilson follows**) By the way, did you manage to track down any of those er... you know?

WALKER No, I'm sorry, not a single pair.

WILSON It looks as if we shall never know if they were cream or white, sir.

MAINWARING We've got to find out – it's very important. We shall just have to discuss this later. Now, let's have a look at this dog. He looks all right, but do you think he's got the stamina to track across miles of country?

WALKER Of course he's got the stamina – this dog could keep going for days.

The dog collapses on the floor – wags his tail violently.

MAINWARING The best thing we can do is to try him out under actual combat conditions – to see what he's like as a tracker. Now, we want someone to be the Nazi parachutist – so that the dog can pick up his scent.

JONES Permission to speak, sir? I should like to volunteer to be the Nazi parachutist so that the dog can pick up my scent.

MAINWARING Very well, Jones. Right, Walker, take the dog and the rest of the platoon outside and as soon as Jones has laid the scent, I'll blow the whistle.

Walker and the platoon go outside. Wilson, Mainwaring and Jones remain behind.

MAINWARING If that dog can do the job, Wilson, he's going to be a great asset to the platoon.

WILSON I hope he can, sir – he's an awfully nice dog.

MAINWARING Right now, Jones, I want you to imagine that you have just dropped by parachute. Now what do you think he ought to be, Wilson, a Nazi war leader who's come to give himself up – a spy – or a saboteur?

WILSON I think he'd better be a saboteur, sir. I mean, if it was a Nazi leader coming to give himself up, he'd hardly be running away, would he?

MAINWARING Good thinking, Wilson. You'd better be a saboteur, Jones – and you've landed by parachute to blow up a key position.

JONES Very well, sir.

MAINWARING Now, take your jacket off.

JONES What for, sir?

MAINWARING So that the dog can pick up your scent.

JONES Right, sir. (**Taking off his jacket**) Ah, so this is Walmington-on-Sea. I will blow up a key position – I think I will blow up the bank.

MAINWARING You'd better make it the town hall, Jones.

JONES Very well, I think I will blow up the town hall. (**Hands Mainwaring his jacket**) I must be off quickly before someone spots me.

He runs across the hall to the office – opens the door – goes in.

Jones re-enters.

JONES I've made a smell, sir.

MAINWARING I've laid a scent!

JONES That's very kind of you, sir. (**He goes up bell tower**)

MAINWARING (**Blows**) Right, there's the parachute, Walker, let's see if he can pick up the scent.

Walker shoves the jacket under the dog's nose – and the dog rushes towards the office. They all go into the office and the door closes – immediately it opens again and the dog rushes across the hall and up the tower stairs.

FRAZER He's gone up the bell tower. Come on.

They all clatter up the stairs.

MAINWARING By Jove, he's picking up the scent well, Wilson.

WILSON Awfully good, sir.

They are both looking up the stairs.

Mrs Pike enters and comes up behind them. Mrs Pike taps Wilson on the shoulder.

WILSON (**Turning**) Oh, it's you, Mavis – I wish you wouldn't creep up on me like that.

MRS PIKE Don't be silly – I wasn't creeping up on you. How much longer are you going to be? (**Whispering to Wilson**) Don't forget it's our little tête-à-tête supper tonight.

MAINWARING (**Pricking up his ears**) Potato supper?

MRS PIKE You see, Mr Mainwaring – tonight it's the anniversary of when we first met – and we always have a tête-à-tête supper every year. (**Glaring at Wilson**) And I don't want it ruined by him being late.

WILSON Oh really, Mavis.

MAINWARING Now look, Mrs Pike, I cannot allow your domestic affairs to interfere with the efficient running of my platoon.

Jones comes running down the stairs – comes round the front of them and stops. There is the sound of barking and the men's feet clattering down the stairs.

JONES I have to report that they are hot on my trail.

He rushes out through the door. Walker and the dog – followed by the rest of the platoon – come down the stairs. The dog is on a long piece of string – he turns sharply in front of Mrs Pike – the string wraps round her legs and she falls.

WALKER (Covers his eyes and looks between his fingers) I've just remembered, Mr Mainwaring – I sold Mrs Pike the last pair. The parachute was a British one. (Pointing)

MAINWARING I do think you might have told us, Wilson.

TELECINE: ROAD. DAY

Warden is riding along on his bike. He sees something and stops.

WARDEN Blimey.

He quickly turns off the road and rides across the grass – a parachute is hanging from a tree. He gets off his bike and tries to pull it free.

TELECINE: ROAD. DAY

Van is moving along road.

TELECINE: BESIDE THE ROAD. DAY

Warden is still trying to free the parachute. Small man comes into the picture – he is wearing a German hunting outfit – double-breasted leather coat – Tyrolean hat with shaving brush – gaiters and boots.

SMALL MAN (Tapping Warden on shoulder. He speaks with a thick German accent and is holding a map) Excuse please?

WARDEN Not now, mate, can't you see I'm busy?

SMALL MAN Please, I just want to know the way to Downsend Woods.

WARDEN Where?

SMALL MAN Downsend Woods. (Pointing to map) See, it is marked here on the map.

WARDEN Oh, it's about a mile over in that direction – you can't miss it. (He turns back to parachute)

SMALL MAN Thank you. (He runs off)

WARDEN Give me a hand to pull this thing down will you, mate? (He turns) Blimey, where did he go? (He starts to pull again) Flippin' thing. (He gives an extra tug, and the parachute comes down on top of him – completely covering him)

TELECINE: ROAD. VAN

Van is going along road. It pulls up.

Jones is driving – Mainwaring is sitting beside him. Mainwaring jumps down.

MAINWARING (Calling) Sergeant Wilson! (Wilson comes round from the back of the van with the rest of the platoon) (Points) Look!

WILSON Good heavens.

MAINWARING (Drawing his revolver) All right, men, follow me, at the double. (He leads them over to the parachute and they surround it – the figure is still struggling under it) We've caught him red-handed – keep him covered, men. All right, come out with your hands up. (The figure still struggles) Still got some fight in him, has he? Right, grab him, men!

They all jump on the figure and start to clobber it – the figure stops struggling.

MAINWARING Now, let's see what we've caught. Jones, get your bayonet out.

JONES Yes sir, yes sir.

MAINWARING Now, slit it open.

Jones rips open the silk – the Warden's head comes through the slit.

WARDEN (Purple with rage) (Hisses) You… you stupid load of hooligans.

WALKER Mr Mainwaring – look! Look what the dog's doing!

They all drop the Warden and turn – the dog is sniffing the parachute harness.

MAINWARING I do believe he's picking up the scent… (The dog makes off, dragging Walker with him) Yes, he's got it – come on! (They all follow)

WARDEN (Struggling) Oi, come back!

TELECINE: EDGE OF FIELD. DAY

The dog is in front, pulling Walker. Mainwaring and the rest of the platoon are following.

MAINWARING Come on, men, keep up!

TELECINE: A RATHER NICE HOUSE. DAY

The dog goes through the gates and up the drive. They all follow. They all go round the side of the house on to the lawn at the back. An elderly gentleman is asleep in a deckchair with *The Times* over his face.

MAINWARING (As he goes by, he lifts up paper) Sorry to disturb you, sir. (He puts paper back again)

TELECINE: BOTTOM OF THE GARDEN. DAY

The dog leads them to a small tool shed – he starts to scratch on the bottom of the door.

MAINWARING (Drawing his revolver) We've got him – all right, Jones, tell him to come out with his hands up.

JONES Yes, sir. Come on – ze here mit your handies hoch.

The platoon are in a half circle round the door with their rifles pointed. There is a pause – the door starts to open. A little Pekinese comes round the edge. The dog goes up to it and licks its face. The Warden comes running across the lawn.

WARDEN (Breathless) Mr Mainwaring.

MAINWARING Oh, what is it?

WARDEN You wouldn't be looking for a man with a German accent, would you?

MAINWARING Well, of course we're looking for a man with a German accent.

WARDEN Well, one came up to me while I was trying to get that parachute out of the tree.

MAINWARING That was his parachute, you fool.

WARDEN He asked me the way to Downsend Woods.

MAINWARING Downsend Woods! Quick men, follow me – there's no time to lose.

TELECINE: A RISE. DAY

The platoon come over the rise and halt.

WILSON (Pointing) Well, there is Downsend Woods, sir.

MAINWARING (To platoon) Can any of you men see anything?

FRAZER Aye, sir, look! There's someone up that tree!

He points to a tree about 300 yards away. Mainwaring looks through his field glasses. We can see through the glasses – he brings them into focus – we see the small man looking back through field glasses.

MAINWARING (Out of vision) It's him all right.

The man starts to scramble down the tree.

MAINWARING Come on, quick.

They all make off.

TELECINE: BOTTOM OF THE TREE. DAY

They reach the bottom of the tree. The dog stops – sniffs – and then makes off, followed by the platoon.

TELECINE: WOODS. DAY

Small man running – he stops – mops brow – hears barking and shouts – starts to run again.

TELECINE: WOODS. DAY

Platoon runs by

TELECINE: BOMBED BUILDING. DAY

Small man staggers into picture. Sound of dog and shouts – he runs into door at the side. Platoon come into the picture. They halt.

JONES He must be a saboteur, Mr Mainwaring. Look, he's blown the building up.

MAINWARING Don't be absurd, Jones – it was bombed in an air raid last year.

JONES Oh. No wonder we didn't hear the bang.

Dog leads them up to door.

FRAZER He's gone inside, sir.

MAINWARING Right, men. House clearing drill.

WARDEN If you don't mind, Mr Mainwaring, I'll wait outside.

They divide into two sections and flatten themselves against the wall – each side of the door. Mainwaring fires his revolver at the lock and hinges – Walker is on the other side.

MAINWARING Ready, Walker?

WALKER Yes, Mr Mainwaring.

MAINWARING Now.

Walker kicks in the door – it falls in. Mainwaring, crouched low, dashes in.

INSIDE BOMBED BUILDING. DAY

The small man is crouching in terror in the corner. Mainwaring comes in door, throws himself flat on the ground – points his revolver at man.

MAINWARING (**Standing up**) Right – the game's up.

The rest of the platoon crowd in behind him.

SMALL MAN (**Hysterical**) Get back – get back! You're not going to get it – do you understand – you're not going to get it. I've waited years for this, schemed and planned for it and I'm not going to give it up.

He reaches inside his coat and pulls out a small black egg-shaped object.

WALKER Look out, he's got a bomb!

Walker dives for the man's feet to bring him down. The man throws the object towards the door. The Warden comes through the door and catches it.

WALKER Throw it away, it's a bomb!

WARDEN Blimey! (**He throws it to Wilson – Wilson throws it to Pike – Pike to Jones – Jones to Frazer**)

FRAZER It's not a bomb at all – it's too light. (**He shakes it and opens it – inside is a small white spotted egg in a bed of cotton wool**) It's an egg.

SMALL MAN Give it to me, it's mine.

MAINWARING Aren't you a Nazi war leader?

SMALL MAN No, I'm a Viennese ornithologist.

MAINWARING A what?

WILSON A bird-watcher, sir.

SMALL MAN You see – I read in the papers that a Golden Oriole had been spotted in this area – it's a very, very rare bird – all my life I had wanted one of the eggs – and I was determined to get one.

WALKER Why didn't you ask me?

MAINWARING Why on earth did you run away?

SMALL MAN It's a protected bird – it's against the law to take the eggs.

MAINWARING Good Lord, man – we might have shot you out of hand.

JONES Hence the expression, sir – a bird in the hand is worth two in the bush.

WALKER Never mind, old son.

He bangs man on shoulder – and breaks the egg.

SERIES THREE **EPISODE THIRTEEN**

Recorded: Friday 28/11/69
Original transmission: Thursday 4/12/69, 7.30–8.00pm
Original viewing figures = 13.6 million

ARTHUR LOWE .... CAPTAIN MAINWARING
JOHN LE MESURIER .... SERGEANT WILSON
CLIVE DUNN .... LANCE CORPORAL JONES
JOHN LAURIE .... PRIVATE FRAZER
JAMES BECK .... PRIVATE WALKER
ARNOLD RIDLEY .... PRIVATE GODFREY
IAN LAVENDER .... PRIVATE PIKE
FRANK WILLIAMS .... VICAR
EDWARD SINCLAIR .... VERGER
HAROLD BENNETT .... MR BLEWITT
JOAN COOPER .... MISS BAKER
RONNIE BRANDON .... MR DRURY

EXTRAS .... JAY NEIL, BRIAN JOHN, ROY HATTERWAY, WALTER TURNER

NO OTHER MEMBERS OF THE PLATOON APPEARED IN THIS EPISODE.

No Spring for Frazer

No Spring for Frazer

SIDE OFFICE. CHURCH HALL. DAY

Mainwaring is preparing some papers, Wilson enters.

MAINWARING Are the men ready for the field craft lecture, Wilson?

WILSON Yes, sir, they've fallen in.

MAINWARING Right, march them over to the recreation ground. I'll join you there. Did the Town Clerk give us permission?

WILSON Yes, sir, but he said would we try to keep away from the children's swings and the Donald Duck sandpit.

MAINWARING You can tell him that I'm giving instruction on the use of cover in infantry warfare, not playing ring a ring of roses.

WILSON Oh yes, and would you keep off the rose beds. He doesn't seem to take us very seriously.

MAINWARING He'll change his tune when he hears the tramp, tramp of Nazi jackboots pounding across the bowling green.

WILSON Pike and Jones are outside waiting for you to inspect their rifles again – oh and Frazer with the Lewis gun.

MAINWARING Right, wheel them in.

Wilson goes to the door.

WILSON Er… Captain Mainwaring will see you now.

MAINWARING Wilson, make it an order.

WILSON Captain Mainwaring will see you *now*!

MAINWARING Oh good Lord.

Pike, Frazer, Jones enter, Pike with the bolt of his rifle in his hand.

JONES Sorry, sir. They made a bit of a mistake then.

MAINWARING They made…?

JONES Under my orders.

MAINWARING Let's have a look at it, Pike.

PIKE I've polished most of the marks off, sir.

MAINWARING Ah yes, that's much better. Always bear in mind, Pike, this is a precision instrument. Now you must promise me that you will never again let your mother clean it with a bath brick.

PIKE Yes, sir.

MAINWARING Let's see it, Jones. I must say I'm very surprised at you allowing your rifle to get into such a state.

JONES I'm sorry, sir. You see, I cleaned it with mutton cloth, and I think there must have been a bit of mutton left on it.

MAINWARING That doesn't quite excuse the piece of sausage skin in the magazine does it?

JONES I'm sorry, I won't take it into the shop anymore.

MAINWARING Right. Bring it over here, Frazer.

Frazer places the Lewis gun on the table.

FRAZER Thank heavens it's not my turn to clean this again for three weeks.

MAINWARING That's not the right attitude at all, Frazer. The cleaning of this gun should be regarded as an honour and a privilege.

FRAZER If it were a privilege, we'd never get a look in. You and the Sergeant would be doing it all the time.

MAINWARING That's enough of that, Frazer. (**He examines the gun**) The butterfly spring is missing. Where is it?

FRAZER Oh aye, I must have left it in my workshop. I took the bits home to buff 'em up on my polisher.

MAINWARING Now, look here, Frazer. In the first place you had no business taking any part of this weapon off the premises. And in the second place, it's quite useless without the butterfly spring. If a Nazi parachutist came bursting through that door, all you could do would be to hit him with it.

JONES Permission to speak, sir?

MAINWARING Yes, Jones.

JONES It could inflict a very nasty wound, sir, in the hands of a desperate man.

MAINWARING Well, I'm not taking any chances. Sergeant Wilson, march the men to the recreation ground and we'll stop at Frazer's place on the way.

FRAZER'S WORKSHOP

It is a lean-to affair against the side of his house, with a door, a dirty window, a bench with an electric grinder/polisher cum lathe hooked up to an old electric motor. It is mainly used for wood working. In the centre or to one side is an old table. In the background are one or two objects covered in sacking.

Frazer enters, holds open the door for Mainwaring and Wilson.

FRAZER This is my little den, sir.

MAINWARING Right, bring the gun in here, Jones, and we'll reassemble it.

Jones brings in the gun. Frazer crosses to the bench.

FRAZER That's funny.

MAINWARING What's the matter, Frazer?

FRAZER The box has gone.

MAINWARING What box?

FRAZER The box I put the parts in.

MAINWARING Frazer, just keep quite calm and tell us precisely what you did.

FRAZER I cleaned the gun parts on this. (**He indicates the electric buffer**) And I put them in the box here, and then I put on the lid to stop them getting dirty while I sanded down that box. (**He crosses to a box in the corner covered with sacking**)

MAINWARING What sort of a box was the one here? (**He indicates the bench**)

FRAZER (**Reluctantly**) Well, just a box – like the one here.

MAINWARING I'm not interested in that one there, what did this one here look like, Frazer?

FRAZER Well, it looked like this one here. (**He takes off the sheet to reveal a coffin – newly made**)

MAINWARING Good heavens.

WILSON What an extraordinary thing to collect.

FRAZER I'm no collecting 'em, I make 'em.

WILSON I'm sorry, Frazer – we had no idea.

FRAZER Well, you don't go around broadcasting it, do you?

JONES It's morbid, if you ask me.

FRAZER It's just a skill I have with my hands. I learnt it as a wee boy.

MAINWARING You told me you were a fisherman in the Hebrides.

FRAZER Aye, I did that. A wild, lonely place, you understand. You needed to do everything yourself.

MAINWARING Even this?

FRAZER Aye, that and dentistry. (**He handles the pliers**) One tool does pretty well for both functions.

MAINWARING The point is, where is it now?

FRAZER As like as not, Mr Drury will have taken it.

JONES Mr Drury wouldn't do a thing like that. I've know him since he was a lad in short trousers pinching my dad's apples.

FRAZER He's the undertaker, you old fool, he ordered it.

MAINWARING Right. Every second this weapon is out of action places the whole security of our island home in jeopardy. Round to Mr Drury's at the double.

DRURY'S SHOP OR PARLOUR

There are two desks, funeral flowers, urns, etc. Miss Baker, his secretary, is at one desk, she is middle-aged with earphones. She is on the telephone.

MISS BAKER Mr Drury will be round right away. Please don't apologise, Mrs Parkinson. There was no need to make a reservation, we're quite accustomed to dealing with these matters as they arise.

Enter Mainwaring and Frazer.

MAINWARING Ah, good evening, Miss Baker.

MISS BAKER Good evening, Mr Mainwaring. What brings you here?

MAINWARING I wish to see Mr Drury on the matter of the utmost gravity.

MISS BAKER Oh dear, you don't mean to tell me it's poor Mr Jones.

JONES (**Entering**) I heard that.

MISS BAKER (**In confusion**) I'll tell him. (**She goes into the door which leads to the interior of the shop**)

JONES He always was a money-grabbing old cuss. (**He calls to Miss Baker**) I'll go when my time's come, not before.

MAINWARING That'll do, Jones.

WILSON You don't really need me here, do you, sir?

MAINWARING Yes, I do. (**He notices Wilson's expression**) What's the matter with you, Wilson?

WILSON Me? Nothing. What makes you ask?

MAINWARING Shall we say you're not your usual laughing self.

WILSON Maybe it's just that I find the whole situation a little bizarre.

MAINWARING I don't see why. We've simply come to a funeral parlour to ask the undertaker if we can look in one of his coffins to find the spare part for a Lewis gun.

WILSON Yes, I suppose it could happen to anyone.

Enter Mr Drury on his way out with a small bag.

MAINWARING Oh, Mr Drury.

DRURY Sorry, can't stop. (**He hurries straight out**)

JONES Blimey, he was in a hurry.

MAINWARING After him, Wilson.

WILSON Yes, sir. (**He goes out, calling at the door**) Walker, follow that undertaker.

Mainwaring follows after Wilson, Jones is about to follow as well.

FRAZER Wait a minute, Jonesey. Er... Miss Baker, d'ye mind that Mr Drury ordered a box from me on Wednesday?

JONES Why should she mind, she works here?

FRAZER I'm asking her if she remembers.

MISS BAKER Yes, I remember it quite distinctly. (**She starts to look at an order book**)

FRAZER Well, you see, it's not quite finished to my satisfaction. I would like to examine it.

MISS BAKER I see – (**She turns the pages**) 5'9" elm, wasn't it?

FRAZER That's the one. With inset name plates and brass handles.

MISS BAKER I'm afraid it's gone. It was for Mr Horace Blewitt.

JONES Horace Blewitt. Not old Horace. Why, I served him two books' worth of best end of neck only two days ago.

MISS BAKER He's passed away.

JONES Poor old Horace, he never even had this week's ration.

FRAZER Could I go and pay my last respects? He's likely in the Chapel of Rest, I shouldn't wonder.

MISS BAKER No, he's still at home. His brother wanted him to Rest in Peace overnight – on the dining room table.

FRAZER Oh, aye indeed. Well, we're sorry to have troubled you, Miss Baker. Come on, Jonesey.

At the door they meet Mainwaring who is out of breath.

MAINWARING It's 21, Marigold Avenue.

JONES On the dining room table.

FRAZER Mr Mainwaring if you could excuse me from the field craft lecture, Jonesey and I feel we ought to pay our last respects.

MAINWARING Ah, well, yes in the circumstances you're excused. (**He goes**)

FRAZER You keep his brother talking. I'll... (**He indicates feeling around**)

They go out.

MR BLEWITT'S HOUSE

Set consists of dining room with door and exterior window, fireplace and mantelpiece and small section of the hall and stairs on the other side of the door. Also included in the set is a portion of the area outside the window.

MR BLEWITT Come through here, Mr Jones.

FRAZER In my calling, Mr Blewitt, I'm no stranger to sorrow, but had I known that box was for my old and trusted friend, tears would have mixed with the varnish.

MR BLEWITT I didn't think you knew him.

FRAZER Intimately.

JONES Just think, Sydney, he was in my shop only on Wednesday. I give him two books of best end of neck.

Frazer is in the foreground, trying to spot the spring in the box while Jones talks.

MR BLEWITT Well, he come home here and he put the shopping down here on this very table and he unwrapped that very meat you served him.

JONES You never know, do you?

MR BLEWITT Never, and do you know what his very last words were he ever said?

JONES What were they?

MR BLEWITT He stood there, where Mr Frazer's standing now, with the meat in his hand. 'Look at that', he said, 'all bloody bone'. The second after that he was gone.

JONES You've got to have bones with best end of neck.

MR BLEWITT Ah, but this was all bone. There wasn't a bit of meat on it.

JONES What would happen to the sheep if there was no bone with best end of neck. His head would flop about, wouldn't it?

MR BLEWITT There should be some meat as well.

JONES There must have been some meat, that's what keeps the bones from falling apart, isn't it?

MR BLEWITT There was plenty of gristle.

JONES There was meat an' all.

MR BLEWITT If there'd been any meat he'd still be with us. It was the shock.

JONES You're as good as saying I done him in.

MR BLEWITT I'm not. I'm just saying it was all bone and gristle.

JONES That's done it. You've insulted me. Come on, Jock.

FRAZER (**Still looking**) Er... bide a wee while. I've just a few more respects to pay.

JONES We're not stopping in this house one second longer. (**He drags Frazer away, Frazer stops him just outside the door**)

FRAZER You old fool. D'ye not mind what we come for?

JONES I don't mind what we come for. Oh... well, it's too late now, isn't it?

FRAZER Yon Captain'll have me shot at dawn.

SIDE OFFICE. CHURCH HALL

Mainwaring is on the telephone. Pull back to reveal Frazer, Jones, Wilson and Walker.

MAINWARING Ah, Captain Rogers. Mainwaring here. I was wondering what the position is... Captain

Mainwaring – Home Guard… I was wondering what the position is… Walmington-on-Sea Home Guard, Captain Mainwaring. I was wondering what the position is regarding spares for the Lewis machine gun. What have you got in stores? What all? Oh I see, rather as I expected. No, no, no, just a routine enquiry. **(He puts down the phone)** Not a single nut.

JONES Couldn't we get a piece manufactured, sir, by some skilled person.

WILSON Yes, Walker, you have a friend who's rather good at metalwork.

WALKER You mean Albert?

WILSON Yes, doesn't he make spare parts for things?

WALKER Yeh, well, he did but he's taking a holiday at the moment.

MAINWARING Well, when will he be back?

WALKER Ah, well, he'll be some time. He was caught making a spare part for a safe.

JONES Mr Frazer here, sir, would like to express his regret for losing this very important mechanical contrivance, sir.

MAINWARING I think it's a vital lesson to us all. For the want of a nail, the shoe was lost, for the want of a shoe the horse was lost, for the want of a horse the battle was lost.

JONES Hence the saying 'Keep your hair on'.

MAINWARING Precisely, but we are not going to be beaten. We are going to… I don't think that's got anything to do with it, Jones.

JONES Come to think of it, neither do I, sir.

MAINWARING These continual interruptions of yours make it very difficult for me to follow a clear line of action, Jones. Where was I?

WILSON You weren't going to be beaten, sir.

MAINWARING That's right. That gun must be made battleworthy without delay. Get the rest of your section, Jones, and I'll outline the plan of action.

EXTERIOR. MR BLEWITT'S HOUSE. BY THE WINDOW

It is night – faint moonlight. Mainwaring approaches with a torch. He checks that all is clear and then flashes his torch once. The whole scene is conducted in whispers. Wilson creeps up to him.

MAINWARING Right, Wilson, you know the part you have to play.

WILSON Yes, sir, I go to the far corner of the terrace. If anyone approaches I signal.

MAINWARING Right, off you go.

Wilson goes. Mainwaring turns and gives two flashes. Wilson returns.

WILSON What sort of signal?

MAINWARING Give a cuckoo whistle.

WILSON A what, sir?

MAINWARING A cuckoo whistle.

WILSON How?

MAINWARING Oh, you blow through your cupped hands. Hold this. **(He hands him the torch)** You cup your hands thus and then make a cuckoo sound like this. **(He tries to do it. Wilson imitates. We just hear a blowing sound. Walker enters and watches them for a second)**

WALKER Here, if you're that cold you can have these gloves, 12s 6d a pair – virgin wool – that's from the sheep that…

MAINWARING Shut up, Walker. Wilson, if you can't do it, you'd better cough.

WILSON Yes, sir. **(He goes)**

WALKER Have you got the torch, sir?

Mainwaring realises that Wilson has the torch.

MAINWARING Wilson!

Off stage, out of vision there is a blowing noise.

MAINWARING Bring back the torch.

Enter Wilson with the torch.

WILSON What d'you say, sir?

MAINWARING Give me that torch.

WILSON Yes, sir. **(He hands it over and goes)**

MAINWARING Right, Walker, go to work.

Walker examines the window.

MAINWARING Can you do it?

WALKER It's an open invitation.

MAINWARING I'll hold the light.

Walker produces a thin chisel and hammer.

WALKER Er, would you mind looking the other way, sir, I promised the bloke what showed me I wouldn't pass it on.

MAINWARING Aha, honour among thieves, eh?

WALKER No, he was a copper.

Mainwaring looks away. Walker inserts the chisel, gives a sharp tap.

WALKER That's it.

MAINWARING Well done, Walker.

He flashes the torch three times. Walker opens the window. Pike and Godfrey enter.

MAINWARING Godfrey, you know your allotted task.

GODFREY Yes, sir. I watch the side and if Mr Blewitt's light goes on, I give you the signal.

MAINWARING Good. Off you go at the double. (**Godfrey gives an unbelieving look**) Well, well, off you go.

MAINWARING Right, now you, Pike.

PIKE I go straight into the hall and keep cavey at the bottom of the stairs.

MAINWARING Right, in you go. (**He flashes the torch four times. Walker has opened the window**)

PIKE (**Climbing in**) I saw William Powell do this once in a picture called *Raffles.*

MAINWARING Never mind that now, Pike.

PIKE No it wasn't, it was Ronald Coleman.

Jones enters with Frazer.

JONES Corporal Jones and Private Frazer reporting, sir, in answer to your flash.

MAINWARING Ssssh. You know your task.

JONES Yes, sir. I will hold the torch and Mr Frazer will do the looking. Should it be so necessary I will do the lifting and Private Frazer will do the ferreting.

MAINWARING Right, in you go.

Frazer and Jones go to the window. Frazer goes in.

JONES Here, I'm supposed to be first.

FRAZER Then why don't you wake your ideas up and jump to it.

JONES I'm awake enough not to leave butterfly springs in coffins.

MAINWARING Jones! Frazer! You're taking desperate measures to protect the security of our homes. Stop quarrelling.

JONES I'm sorry, sir.

MAINWARING Everybody, no more talking.

JONES Yes, sir.

Jones climbs in. There is a thud.

MAINWARING What's that?

JONES I dropped the torch.

MAINWARING Well, pick it up.

JONES I've found it, sir.

FRAZER Give it here. (**There is the sound of a switch going on and off**) It's bust.

JONES It's bust, sir.

MAINWARING Give it to me. (**Mainwaring takes the torch through the window and starts to bang it in order to make it work**)

FRAZER There's candles here. Have you got a match?

Wilson coughs, out of vision.

MAINWARING Down everyone!

Jones' head appears.

JONES There's a match in the pocket of my coat hanging in the...

Frazer's hand comes round and gags him. Someone approaches.

WILSON (**Out of vision**) Excuse me, sir.

MAINWARING What the devil's the matter? (**Enter Wilson**)

WILSON I just came to explain that I wasn't signalling. I just a sort of... rather irritating tickle in my throat.

MAINWARING Get back to your post.

WILSON I think I'd better signal by blowing my nose.

MAINWARING Yes, good idea.

FRAZER Where's the matches?

WALKER Here you are. Here's a lighter, 25 bob.

JONES You nearly shoved my teeth down my throat then.

FRAZER Stop blathering.

INSIDE OF DINING ROOM

Frazer lights the match. Two candles are in candlesticks on the mantelpiece. He lights them and gives one to Jones.

JONES I don't like this, Mr Frazer.

FRAZER Aye, it's a wicked business but it has to be done.

They approach the coffin. They suddenly freeze as they see it.

FRAZER The Captain will have to know about this.

JONES Come on.

They creep to the window.

EXTERIOR OF WINDOW

Frazer's head comes through.

MAINWARING Have you got it?

FRAZER Bad news, Mr Mainwaring.

MAINWARING What's the matter?

FRAZER They've screwed him down.

MAINWARING Great Scott.

JONES (**Putting his head through the window**) They've screwed him down, sir.

FRAZER Sssh. I've already told him.

Godfrey enters from the back.

GODFREY Excuse me, sir. It's all clear round the back, I wonder if you could spare me for a few minutes.

MAINWARING Certainly not. What we need is a screwdriver.

WALKER I usually have one but I flogged it to an old age pensioner to tighten his crutches.

MAINWARING We must improvise. Has anyone got a knife?

GODFREY I – I have a fruit knife, if it's any help.

MAINWARING The very thing. Let's have it.

GODFREY It's rather a nice one with a mother-of-pearl handle. My auntie gave it to me when I was 14. I was so proud of it.

MAINWARING **(Taking it)** Right, here you are, Frazer.

GODFREY One treasured these things so much more than the children of today.

INTERIOR. DINING ROOM

Frazer is holding a candle and examining the screws.

FRAZER Here, Jones, hold the candle while I ease the fixing.

JONES I'll be glad when this is over.

FRAZER Hold the light steady.

EXTERIOR OF WINDOW

MAINWARING They're taking too long. We should have found the spring and been away by now.

Frazer's head comes through the curtain.

FRAZER Are you there, Captain?

MAINWARING Yes, have you got it?

FRAZER The blasted knife broke in half, it's no good.

MAINWARING Get Pike's scout knife.

Jones' head comes through.

JONES Mr Mainwaring, the knife's broken in half. **(Frazer pulls him back in)**

GODFREY What a shame, I shall miss it terribly on picnics.

MAINWARING Back to your post, Godfrey.

GODFREY Do you think I could be…

MAINWARING No, you could not.

INTERIOR HALL. FOOT OF STAIRS

Pike is in the foreground looking up stairs. We see Frazer and Jones open the door and creep up to him. Frazer taps him on the shoulder. Pike lets out a yell.

FRAZER AND JONES Ssshh.

FRAZER Give us yer scout knife.

PIKE What do you want it for?

FRAZER **(Taking it)** To unscrew the coffin. **(He goes into the room)**

PIKE I'm not having it used for that.

JONES Now, don't be difficult, Frank.

PIKE My mum would have a fit.

FRAZER Jones, bring the candle.

JONES Coming, Mr Frazer. **(To Pike)** You stop here on guard.

Jones goes in to the room with candle. Frazer starts to work on the screw. Pike approaches from behind and taps them both on the shoulder. Frazer and Jones let out a yell.

PIKE Sshh. His light's gone on upstairs.

BLEWITT **(Out of vision)** Is anyone there?

FRAZER Quick.

JONES Don't panic, don't panic.

EXTERIOR OF WINDOW

MAINWARING What's the matter?

FRAZER Blewitt's coming.

JONES He's coming. Don't panic. Help me out.

They scramble out.

MAINWARING Quick, this way.

They go.

Mr Blewitt comes to the window.

MR BLEWITT Anyone there?

Godfrey comes round from the back.

GODFREY There's a light in the window at the back. I think the gentleman… **(He sees Blewitt)** Ah, good evening.

MR BLEWITT It's awful. My brother Horace has got a screw loose.

GODFREY Ah, ah well, there's one in every family. Good night.

INTERIOR SIDE OFFICE. NIGHT

MAINWARING Right, are we all here? Frazer, Jones, Walker, Pike, Godfrey. Where's Godfrey? (**We see they are all standing round, bar Godfrey**)

WILSON I think he ran all the way home, sir.

MAINWARING I take it that in all this confusion you failed to retrieve the butterfly spring, Frazer?

FRAZER Aye. I'm sorry, Captain.

MAINWARING Tonight, no doubt Goering will loose his devilish weapons on us. And our machine gun is useless. A Junker's 88 could fly up and down the promenade all night at 50 feet picking us off one at a time and we couldn't lift a finger to stop him.

WALKER We're not allowed to fire at enemy aeroplanes anyway.

MAINWARING That's not the point, Walker.

FRAZER I'm very sorry, sir.

JONES Yes, sir, Mr Frazer is very sorry, sir.

FRAZER I've a tongue in my head. I don't need to have you to speak for me.

MAINWARING Well, it's a lesson to us all.

PIKE For the want of a horse, a shoe was lost.

WALKER Couldn't we go back later and have another go?

MAINWARING Not now, Walker, there's a raid on. We all have our duties to do.

PIKE Will Mr Frazer get court martialled, sir?

MAINWARING (**Rather washing his hands of the whole affair**) It's a possibility.

FRAZER But the funeral's tomorrow. What chance have I got to get it back?

MAINWARING What indeed, Frazer?

JONES Don't worry, Mr Frazer, the Captain will take care of everything. You're our inspiration in times of trouble, sir. Even at this moment I don't mind betting that an ingenious plan is forming in your mind.

Fade on Mainwaring's face.

TELECINE: WALL OR HEDGE ADJOINING A CHURCHYARD

Wilson, Pike, Walker and Mainwaring are crouched there out of sight.

WILSON It seems rather a desperate thing to do, sir.

MAINWARING It may not be necessary. Frazer was officiating at the funeral all morning. He may have managed to retrieve the spring.

WILSON Well, how shall we know?

MAINWARING He's going to signal to me.

Mainwaring looks over the wall. Cut to funeral party approaching the graveside.

MAINWARING Here they come. Give me those glasses.

Cut to shot through the glasses. The party has stopped at the graveside. It consists of the Vicar, the Verger, Frazer, Jones, Mr Blewitt, three funeral directors and a couple of mourners. Frazer shakes his head from side to side rather obviously. The Vicar sees him. Frazer realises that the Vicar has seen him and tries to cover up his action.

MAINWARING It's not good. Right, Pike stick the notice up. Don't let anyone in.

Pike puts up the notice which reads 'Unexploded bomb: keep out'. Walker bangs it in with a sledgehammer.

WILSON I'm sure there must be some law against this.

MAINWARING (**Handing Wilson the glasses**) Keep your eye on me, if they seem reluctant to go, run across and tell them the bomb is ticking and about to go off any minute.

WALKER What do we do, sir?

MAINWARING Keep everyone out until darkness. Then we're going to leave it to Frazer, he's the one who'll get court-martialled.

Mainwaring leaves the party.

PIKE Here, Uncle Sergeant. There is a law against grave robbing. It's called habeas corpus.

We see Mainwaring cross to the funeral party. The coffin is being lowered. We see him mime to Jones that a plane came over during the night and dropped a bomb. It is somewhere in the churchyard and at any moment it will blow them to smithereens. Jones passes on the message in mime to the Vicar. The Vicar passes it on to Blewitt and the Verger. They all scamper off.

Cut to Wilson and Pike and Walker.

WILSON Well... er... do what the Captain said and I might well see you tonight. (**He slinks off**)

SIDE OFFICE. NIGHT

VERGER Ah, working on next Sunday's sermon, sir?

VICAR Oh just making a few notes. Where are you off to with that spade, Mr Yeatman?

VERGER St Matthew's church.

VICAR Have they disposed of the bomb?

• BILL HARMAN REMEMBERS •

'At the end of filming in the graveyard near Thetford, the quick-witted Jimmy Beck turned to Arnold Ridley and said: "Hardly worth you leaving is it, Arnold?" On paper, that might sound an insensitive remark to make to a senior citizen, but it was said and received in good humour, typical of the friendly banter exchanged between cast and crew. The irony, of course, was that Jimmy would be the first of the ensemble to die, while Arnold went on for quite a few more years after Jimmy's untimely death.'

BILL HARMAN
Assistant Floor Manager

VERGER I'm going whether they have or not, sir. I couldn't sleep tonight if I hadn't done something about poor old Mr Blewitt. He needs filling in.

VICAR I'm sure it will wait until morning.

VERGER But it might rain, sir, and that would be an abomination in the sight of the Lord.

VICAR I'm sure it would be more of an abomination if you were blown all over the churchyard.

VERGER Don't you worry, sir. I'll be all right.

VICAR Well, go if you must. I must say that you're a much braver man than I am, Mr Yeatman.

VERGER There's different sorts of courage, sir. I don't know how you have the nerve to get up and give those sermons every Sunday. **(He goes)**

GRAVE SIDE. NIGHT

Pike, Frazer, Godfrey, Walker and Jones are gathered round.

PIKE I'm not going down there and that's all there is to it.

FRAZER I'm sorry to hear that, Frank. I'd go myself only my shoulder's playing up. I was counting on you because you're young and strong.

PIKE I'm not. I'm ever so weak, feel my muscles – there's nothing there.

GODFREY I'm a little too portly I'm afraid. Perhaps Mr Walker could do it.

PIKE Yes, go on, Joe. You've got the muscles.

WALKER Yeah, but I haven't got the guts. Natural born coward, that's me. Jonesey will volunteer, won't you, Jonesey?

JONES What, to go down there?

FRAZER He won't do it. He doesn't volunteer unless Captain Mainwaring is listening.

JONES That's a very hurtful thing to say, I'm not like that at all. I will volunteer to perform the task.

FRAZER Aye, and tell Captain Mainwaring afterwards.

JONES If I were a younger man, I'd punch your head in. As it is, I'm giving you formal notice that I will no longer honour your meat coupon.

WALKER Come on, we don't want to be here all night arguing, do we? Here's the screwdriver, Jonesey. Come on Pike, give an 'and to lower him.

They start to help Jones down.

PIKE You hold on to me, Mr Godfrey, in case he pulls me in an' all.

FRAZER Jonesey, are you all right?

JONES What do you care?

FRAZER I take back what I said. You're doing this for me. I've no call to insult you.

JONES **(Head up)** I accept your apology.

WALKER Here, grab hold of the shovel.

GODFREY I think somebody is approaching.

JONES Quick, help me out.

There is a brief struggle to get Jones out, without success.

WALKER I can see him coming. Stay where you are, we'll hide behind the gravestones until he's past.

Jones ducks down, the others disappear. The Verger approaches and starts shovelling in the earth. After a few spadefuls, Jones starts to throw it back. The Verger tries one shovel more. Another shovelful is returned. Verger yells and runs off.

SIDE OFFICE. NIGHT

Mainwaring, Wilson and Verger are talking.

MAINWARING I assure you, Verger, that none of my men would be a party to such a childish prank and I speak not only as their commander but as a life-long student of human nature. **(We see his fingers are crossed)**

VERGER But I recognised them running off. There was that tall, rude Scots one, the mummy's boy, Granddad and the clever dick one.

MAINWARING They've all been in the hall doing weapon maintenance.

VERGER All right then, send for them.

MAINWARING Right. **(He crosses to the door)** Frazer, Pike, Godfrey. Who else did you say?

VERGER The clever dick one.

MAINWARING Walker.

They all enter, puffing.

MAINWARING There you are, Verger. Satisfied?

VERGER Why are they all out of breath?

WALKER We've been doing P.T.

FRAZER Aye, press-ups.

VERGER **(Indicating Godfrey)** What? He's been doing press-ups!

GODFREY Just little, teeny-weeny ones.

VERGER It seems very fishy to me. I think they've been running. And there was another one as well – down below.

Enter Jones covered in earth.

JONES That was a terrible experience, sir.

VERGER **(He sees Jones)** There, what did I say?

MAINWARING You're late, Jones. Where have you been?

JONES Digging for victory, sir.

MAINWARING There you are, he's been digging for victory.

VERGER Who digs for victory at night?

JONES I do.

VERGER There's evil doings afoot and the Vicar will have to be informed. **(He goes to the door)** I wouldn't be surprised if you find yourselves embroiled with the Bishop. **(He goes)**

MAINWARING Well, I hope you're all satisfied with your night's work.

WILSON I rather thought it might turn out this way.

MAINWARING I explained to you, Frazer, the conditions under which you undertook this venture. I obviously could not be a party to such a hair-brained scheme and now you've been caught, you'll have to face the consequences. Grave robbery is probably quite a serious matter.

FRAZER I don't think it's any worse than housebreaking.

MAINWARING I'm now going to report this matter to headquarters. No doubt you will be court-martialled for putting the Lewis gun out of action. **(He picks up the phone. There is an ominous silence)**

WALKER Never mind, Jock, they won't shoot you. Have a fag. **(He hands them round)**

MAINWARING Two seven nine two, please.

WILSON I said this would happen.

MAINWARING Shut up, Wilson.

JONES I'm very sorry the outcome is like this, Mr Frazer.

PIKE What happens when you become embroiled with the Bishop?

GODFREY He withholds from you the benefits of the Church.

PIKE What, like collections and hymns?

WALKER Who's got a light?

FRAZER Here, I've got one.

MAINWARING Ah, Mainwaring here. Could I speak to... Captain Mainwaring, Walmington-on-Sea Home Guard. Could I speak to Major Rogers please?

Frazer produces the butterfly spring from his pocket. He shows it to Walker and Jones.

FRAZER Look.

WALKER The butterfly spring.

FRAZER It must have been in my pocket all the time.

WILSON That was rather careless of you now, Frazer.

MAINWARING Ah, Captain Rogers. I have rather a serious matter to report to you.

FRAZER Captain Mainwaring. **(He dangles the spring in front of Mainwaring's nose)**

MAINWARING One of my men has mis... er... mis... **(He stops. He doesn't know whether to put down the receiver or not. He hands it to Wilson)**

MAINWARING Here, Wilson – you deal with it.

VOICE **(On other end)** Hello, hello?

Wilson hands it to Godfrey.

GODFREY Have you an account with us?

SERIES THREE **EPISODE FOURTEEN**

Recorded: Friday 5/12/69

Original transmission: Thursday 11/12/69, 7.30–8.00pm

Original viewing figures = 13.3 million

ARTHUR LOWE .... CAPTAIN MAINWARING
JOHN LE MESURIER .... SERGEANT WILSON
CLIVE DUNN .... LANCE CORPORAL JONES
JOHN LAURIE .... PRIVATE FRAZER
JAMES BECK .... PRIVATE WALKER
ARNOLD RIDLEY .... PRIVATE GODFREY
IAN LAVENDER .... PRIVATE PIKE
MICHAEL BILTON .... MR MAXWELL
RALPH BALL .... MAN ON STATION
JOHN LEESON .... FIRST SOLDIER
JONATHAN HOLT .... SECOND SOLDIER

PLATOON .... DESMOND CULLUM-JONES AS PRIVATE DESMOND

SONS OF THE SEA

• DESMOND CULLUM-JONES REMEMBERS •

'When I arrived for the exterior filming for this episode I was surprised to find that I was the only member of the platoon's back row required for this particular instalment. On discovering the storyline I presumed that the fact that I'd been in the Navy led the management to guess that I could handle an oar.

'Filming was in a boat in Lowestoft harbour, causing much interest with many on-lookers; safety was taken care of by the local lifeboat services, which was just as well because the current caught us and we couldn't complete the shoot; we had to use a studio mock-up to enable us to finish the shot with complete control.

'This was a very interesting episode for me, and I shall never forget the classic spot where Captain Mainwaring opens the door of the goods' wagon door and asks of a *Times*-reading, bowler-hatted gentleman: "Qu'est-ce que c'est la gare?" to which the said gentleman replies: "La gare est Eastbourne"! A very enjoyable episode.'

DESMOND CULLUM-JONES

"Keep
it
unde
your
hat!"

Sons of the Sea

INSIDE OFFICE. DAY

Mainwaring is standing in front of the window with his back to the camera. Mr Maxwell, a solicitor, is sitting in front of Mainwaring's desk. He is a small man in his early 50s.

MAXWELL Well, Mr Mainwaring, I'm afraid it looks as if you've been left holding the baby.

Mainwaring turns – he is folding a bundle in his arms.

MAINWARING It does indeed, Mr Maxwell. You don't mind if I set this Lewis gun while we talk, do you?

He unwraps the bundle – the Lewis gun is inside it – he sets it upon the top of the sandbags.

MAXWELL Not at all.

MAINWARING It's my first job every morning – just in case of a sudden attack, you know.

MAXWELL Quite. Now to return to the problem.

MAINWARING **(Interrupting)** Just a moment. Pike, tell Carter Patterson to move their van. Their horse is blocking the line of fire. You were saying.

MAXWELL Yes – about Mr Johnson. As you know, he had no relatives.

Enter Wilson.

MAINWARING **(Pressing buzzer)** Just a minute – this is my Chief Clerk – he was familiar with Mr Johnson's affairs.

MAXWELL The point is, when Mr Johnson died, the only possessions he had in the world were the clothes he stood up in – and his boat 'The Naughty Jane'. **(Holds paper)** It will have to be sold, of course – but it may not be easy – after all, not many people will want to buy a boat in wartime.

WILSON I'm afraid we've got a bit of a problem here – unfortunately his account was overdrawn to the extent of £32 12s 6d.

MAINWARING Oh really? In which case the boat becomes the Bank's property, and must be sold to offset the overdraft.

WILSON Shall I put an advert in the *Walmington Gazette*?

MAINWARING Good idea, Wilson.

MAXWELL Well. **(Rising)** I'll be off now, Mr Mainwaring. I'll send you my account, just in case you do manage to sell the boat and there's any money left over after paying off the overdraft. **(He hands Mainwaring envelope)** Well, good day, Gentlemen. **(He goes)**

MAINWARING Here are the particulars of the boat. **(Reads from paper – Wilson writes)** Rowing Boat – 15 feet long – fitted with four oars – seaworthy.

WILSON That's not much good, sir – I mean, there's a war on – you can't row about on the sea in wartime.

MAINWARING The boat's not on the sea, Wilson – it's kept on the river about a mile upstream. If they want to see it they can... wait a minute, I've got an idea.

WILSON Oh no, sir!

MAINWARING **(Quivering with excitement)** River patrols – half a dozen determined men – armed to the teeth in that boat could cause havoc if the Nazis got a foothold. Swift silent patrols striking at the enemy where it hurts most – and then disappearing into the night – cutting through the water – silent, deadly, not a sound. Muffled oars, of course.

WILSON Muffled oars.

MAINWARING Yes, that's how General Wolf captured Quebec – rowed up the St Lawrence river with muffled oars. Showed those damned Froggies a thing or two.

WILSON What are muffled oars, sir?

MAINWARING They're... er... er... I don't know – we'll just have to ask someone.

WILSON But, sir – we're already on patrol five nights a week – the Novelty Rock Emporium to Godfrey's cottage – the gasworks – the telephone exchange – the railway bridge – mobile patrols in Jones' van – it's getting too much.

MAINWARING Do I detect a slight lack of enthusiasm in your voice, Wilson?

WILSON But we must get *some* rest, sir.

MAINWARING I realise that, Wilson – I just want to try it – that's all. Now, it's Friday today and the next Home Guard parade is on Sunday morning. So we'll try it out tomorrow afternoon. We need six volunteers – that will be Pike, Sponge, Walker, Jones, Godfrey and Frazer. I'll get a message to them today.

SECTION OF THE CHURCH HALL. DAY

MAINWARING Good afternoon, men. Thank you for coming, and I would like to propose a vote of thanks to Sergeant Wilson for this very excellent mock-up of a boat. Very good, Wilson. It shows a great deal of imagination.

WILSON I learnt it from my nanny in the nursery.

MAINWARING Oh – did you? Take your place.
Now, this afternoon I want to work out some sort of drill – so that when we get on the river, we know what we're doing. There might be people watching, and we don't want to make fools of ourselves in public, do we?

WALKER (**Aside to Jones**) We don't want to – but how can we help it with him in charge.

MAINWARING Believe it or not, men – this time yesterday I knew nothing whatsoever about boats. I was a nautical virgin – and I knew there was only one person who could help me – Miss Beckworth. So I went round to see her and she gave me a little book called 'How to handle your oars' – it is issued to the sea-scouts. I sat up most of the night swotting it up – and I think I can safely say that I have grasped the main points of handling a boat. However, if I do go wrong, I'm sure Frazer will put me right.

FRAZER Aye, I will that.

Godfrey enters.

GODFREY Sorry I'm late, sir. It was rather exciting. I was playing bowls.

MAINWARING That's a good excuse – so was Drake.

GODFREY May I enquire what they are doing?

MAINWARING Sitting in a boat of course. Go and take your place – foreward.

FRAZER Forrard.

MAINWARING Eh?

FRAZER The word is 'forrard'.

MAINWARING Ah, yes – forrard, we must get these things right. Private Frazer will be steering the boat and he will be the cockswain.

FRAZER Cocks'n.

MAINWARING Thank you, Frazer. Now, I will sit beside the er – cocks'n er –

FRAZER Aft.

MAINWARING Eh?

FRAZER Aft.

MAINWARING I shall sit on the aft.

Frazer reacts.

MAINWARING Now – we need some oars.

JONES I would like to volunteer to pass round the oars, since you wouldn't let me be the cockswain.

MAINWARING Oh – all right Jones.

They are all sitting in their positions – including Frazer. Mainwaring crosses over to the corner – collects the four brooms.

MAINWARING (**Handing out the brooms**) These are your oars, men, you will hold them upright like this with the blades in the air. (**He shows them – then takes his place**) Now – on the command 'Ship your oars', you will lower them into the...

FRAZER (**Barking at him**) Rollocks!

MAINWARING I beg your pardon, Frazer?

FRAZER Rollocks.

MAINWARING You lower them into the rollocks. Go on – do it. (**They lower oars**) Now, on the command 'Catch' – you lower the blade in the water. On 'Pull' – you pull. On 'Up' – you up – and on 'Feather'... let's try it, shall we?

FRAZER Catch – Pull – Up – Feather – Catch – Pull – Up – Feather – Catch – Pull – Up – Feather.

MAINWARING Stop, Jones.

Jones continues.

MAINWARING Jones! You're not keeping up.

WALKER He may not be keeping up but he's giving the floor a good polish.

MAINWARING Now, if I want to stop the boat completely, I shall give the command 'Hold water', in which case you will hold the blades of the oars in the water. Have you got that – 'Hold water'?

GODFREY Excuse me, sir.

MAINWARING What is it, Godfrey?

GODFREY I don't mind doing a little rowing if it's needed.

MAINWARING I think we'll stay as we are for the moment, Godfrey. All right – we'll try that again. 'Give way together.'

FRAZER Catch – Pull – Up – Feather – Catch – Pull – Up – Feather – Catch – Pull – Up – Feather.

TELECINE: THE RIVER. DAY

Close up of Frazer in the boat.

FRAZER Catch – pull – up – feather. Catch – pull – up – feather.

Cut to shot of Frazer with Mainwaring sitting beside him.

MAINWARING Excellent, men. Good idea of mine, Frazer, having a practice first. (**Shouting**) There are quite a lot of people watching from the bank, Wilson – I think we're making a good impression.

WILSON (**Out of vision**) Yes, sir – awfully good.

FRAZER (**Barking in Pike's direction**) Keep up – keep up.

MAINWARING Yes, keep up, Pike, you're throwing the whole stroke out.

PIKE (**Out of vision**) I can't help it, sir – I feel sick.

MAINWARING Nonsense, boy – you're only on the river. It's as calm as a millpond.

PIKE (**Out of vision**) I feel sick.

MAINWARING You stupid boy. **(Shouts)** Hold water.

For the first time we see the whole crew, leaning exhausted on their oars.

MAINWARING This is no time for feeling sick – you're showing us up in front of the public.

PIKE I can't help it, Mr Mainwaring.

MAINWARING You'd better lie in the bottom of the boat – I don't want people to see –there's only one thing for it – I shall have to take your place.

WILSON **(From the bow)** Is that wise, sir?

JONES Don't you think we ought to turn back, sir? There's a bit of a mist coming in from the sea.

MAINWARING Nonsense – it's as clear as a bell. Move over, Pike – get in the bottom of the boat. **(He takes Pike's oar)** All right, men – we'll just go up to the mouth of the river – then turn round and come back. Carry on, Frazer.

Cut back to Frazer close up.

FRAZER Aye, aye, sir. Catch – pull – up – feather. Catch – pull – up – feather.

ON RIVER IN BOAT

FRAZER Catch.

JONES Permission to stop rowing, sir? It isn't half coming up foggy.

MAINWARING Nonsense, it's only a little sea mist. It'll soon clear. Believe me, I know this stretch of water like the back of my hand. We'll just row to the mouth of the river – then we'll turn back.

WILSON It's awfully thick, sir – I can hardly see to read.

WALKER Yes, it ain't half coming up.

MAINWARING Oh all right – turn the boat round.

FRAZER Aye, aye, sir. You start rowing. Catch – pull – up – feather. Catch – pull – up – feather.

MAINWARING Are you sure you turned the boat round, Frazer?

FRAZER Of course I turned it round.

MAINWARING Can you see the river bank, Wilson?

WILSON I can't even see you, sir.

MAINWARING You'd better come and take over from me for a bit, so I can concentrate on the navigation.

WILSON All right, sir. **(He starts to clamber towards Mainwaring)**

PIKE Ow! You trod on me, Uncle Arthur.

WILSON I'm sorry, Frank – I forgot you were there.

He reaches Mainwaring and they change places.

MAINWARING **(To Frazer)** All right, Frazer – I'll take over the steering. Move over.

FRAZER You don't know anything about handling a rudder.

MAINWARING Let me be the judge of that, Frazer.

Frazer moves over muttering. Mainwaring takes his place at the tiller.

WILSON Do you think that's wise, sir?

MAINWARING When I want your opinions, I shall ask for them. Now come on – all together 'Pull'. Put your back into it, Wilson. It will be dark soon, and we shan't be able to see a thing.

WILSON It's not exactly crystal clear at the moment, sir.

MAINWARING That will do, Wilson Now come on – all together – pull.

AT SEA. NIGHT

The mist has now almost cleared. It is very dark.

MAINWARING All right, men, rest your oars. **(They all stop rowing)** Thank goodness this mist is clearing. We must be well upstream by now. Can you see the bank, Frazer?

FRAZER I'm having nothing to do with this, I wash my hands of the whole affair.

MAINWARING There's no need to sulk, Frazer.

PIKE **(Dragging himself up to beside Wilson)** I don't half feel awful, Uncle. Can I have a glass of water, please?

WILSON Oh, don't be ridiculous, Frank – I haven't got a glass of water.

WALKER Hold on, Pikey – I'll get you some water. **(He takes his forage cap off – leans over the side of the boat and scoops up some water)**

PIKE My mum wouldn't like me to drink river water, Joe – it's full of germs.

WALKER Look – do you want a drink or don't you?

PIKE Oh, all right. **(He takes the cap and drinks. He instantly spits it out again)** It's salt!!!

JONES Salt!!!

WALKER Give it here. **(He takes a drink – and spits it out again)** It is salt.

JONES If it's salt, that means we're at sea – we're all at sea – don't panic – don't panic.

MAINWARING Quiet, Jones. I thought you were supposed to be a sailor, Frazer – now look at the mess you've landed us in.

FRAZER You were the one who took over the steering.

MAINWARING That will be enough of that, Frazer. Now, quiet, everybody, while I just think what we're going to do.

Pause.

JONES Permission to speak, sir? Why don't we all shout out 'Help'?

MAINWARING Excellent idea, Jones.

WILSON I think 'ahoy' would sound more urgent, sir.

MAINWARING Perhaps you're right, Wilson. All right, men, all together – ready now.

They all shout 'ahoy'.

JONES I don't think anybody heard us, Mr Mainwaring.

WILSON If we could find the north, sir, and row towards it – that would take us back to the shore.

MAINWARING Excellent, Wilson – where's the north, Frazer?

FRAZER Why ask me? You're the one who's supposed to know. Have another look at the back of your hand.

MAINWARING If I may say – I think you're being very childish, Frazer. (**Frazer gives a grunt of disgust and turns away**) Now, has anybody got any suggestions on how to find the north.

GODFREY Moss always grows on the north side of trees, sir – if that's any help.

MAINWARING It isn't, Godfrey.

JONES Permission to speak, sir? If you point the hour hand of your watch at the sun, and then halve the angle between that and 12 o'clock, that points to the south.

MAINWARING It happens to be night, Jones.

WILSON Perhaps it might help if we pointed it at the moon, sir.

JONES No, it's got to be the sun, Sergeant – we used to find our way like that in the Sudan. Mind you, we used to get a lot of sun in the Sudan, 'cept at night, of course, we didn't get it at night.

WILSON If we could find the North Star, that might help, sir.

JONES You've got to find the Great Bear first – that's the group of stars that looks like a milk saucepan – now the stars opposite the handle point to the North Star. In other words, if it was a saucepan – it's where you'd pour the milk.

WALKER Hence the Milky Way. (**There is a pause. They all give a sickly grin. Pause**)

MAINWARING Walker, I know that I have rebuked you many times in the past for making stupid remarks – but this time I'm glad to see that the gravity of the situation hasn't killed your lively Cockney sense of humour. It's people like you who are the backbone of our country.

WALKER (**Embarrassed**) Well, I was only trying to cheer us up like – wasn't I?

MAINWARING Precisely – and I find it a great comfort, the way at a time of crisis like this we're all sticking together. (**There is a long pause – Godfrey blows his nose**)

FRAZER (**Gives a little cough**) Mr Mainwaring, I'd like to apologise – what you've just said has made me realise I've behaved very badly.

MAINWARING Thank you, Frazer. Now perhaps you'll tell us where the north is.

FRAZER I can't.

MAINWARING Why not?

FRAZER 'Cos I don't bloody well know. Do you think I'd be sitting in this stupid boat with you stupid load of Sassenachs if I knew the way?

MAINWARING What about the stars?

FRAZER There's too much cloud.

Pause.

JONES Permission to speak, sir? If you dangle a nail tied to a piece of string over the palm of your hand – it always swings to the north.

WALKER You silly old duffer – that's for pregnant women – to see if it's a boy or a girl.

AT SEA. NIGHT

Several hours later. The platoon have shipped their oars and are huddled together for warmth. They have their forage caps pulled down. Pike is huddled next to Mainwaring and Wilson.

PIKE Uncle Arthur?

WILSON What is it, Frank?

PIKE I read a story in the *Hotspur* once, about some men who were adrift in a boat for days and days. In the end they got so hungry – they decided that one of them had got to be eaten – so they drew lots.

MAINWARING (**Pricking up his ears**) Oh – who lost?

PIKE The Captain.

MAINWARING You stupid boy. (**He turns away**)

PIKE (**Whispering to Wilson**) I wouldn't want to eat Mr Mainwaring – I know him too well.

WILSON Oh, do be quiet, Frank.

Pause.

PIKE Uncle Arthur?

WILSON Oh, what?

PIKE Do you think I'll go blind?

WILSON What are you talking about?

PIKE They say if you do it, you'll go blind.

WILSON Do what?

PIKE Drink sea water.

WILSON You don't go blind through drinking sea water – you go mad.

PIKE Well, do you think I'll go mad?

WILSON Don't be absurd.

PIKE The Ancient Mariner did.

WILSON Yes, but he drank much more than you.

MAINWARING What's the time, Wilson?

WILSON Five o'clock, sir.

MAINWARING Thank goodness for that. All right men, pay attention – it will be light soon – and then we'll be spotted by a boat.

WALKER Supposing we aren't spotted, sir.

MAINWARING We're only in the Channel you know – plenty of boats about.

WILSON Yes, but one of them might be a German boat.

MAINWARING We don't want any of that sort of talk here, Wilson – there are no German boats in the English Channel.

JONES Mr Mainwaring, sir – I heard voices – coming across the water from over there – **(Points)**

They all freeze. We can hear the faint sounds of laughter.

JONES There it is again, sir.

MAINWARING By Jove – you're right, Jones – we can't be very far out from the shore after all – thank goodness for that. Right – now when I give the signal, we all shout 'ahoy'.

WILSON Do you think that's wise, sir?

MAINWARING Oh really, Wilson.

WILSON Well, it's just occurred to me, sir – if we all shout now, they might not hear properly – it's just possible that they might think we're Germans – and start shooting at us.

MAINWARING Good thinking, Wilson. We'll row in – very quietly – then, when we're close to the shore – we'll all shout – then they'll know we're British.

JONES Permission to speak, sir? Why don't we muffle our rollocks – then they won't hear us.

WILSON Good idea. Did you find out about that…

Mainwaring reacts.

WALKER We can use our forage caps, sir – that should do the trick.

WILSON Oh, that's how it's done, sir.

MAINWARING Excellent, Walker. Right, men, take your places.

TELECINE: SMALL HARBOUR. NIGHT

The boat is quietly rowed into the picture. There are some stone steps leading down to the water. The boat gently bumps into the bottom of the steps. Wilson ties the boat to an iron ring which is let into the wall. They quietly ship their oars and put their caps on.

MAINWARING **(Whispering)** Well done, men, we made it. Now listen. **(They all huddle together)** When I say go – we all shout together as loud as we can 'Ahoy – we're British'. Have you got that? **(They all nod)** Are you ready? **(They all nod)** Now!

They all open their mouths to shout. Suddenly there is a burst of applause and a solo voice starts to sing in French, accompanied by an accordion. They all freeze in horror with their mouths open. Several French voices pick up the chorus.

JONES Permission to speak, sir? I don't think we're in England.

MAINWARING My God – we must have drifted across the Channel.

WILSON Do you think perhaps we ought to surrender? After all, we are armed and in uniform – and I don't think the Germans will like that very much.

MAINWARING **(Icy)** I'm going to pretend that I didn't hear that last remark, Wilson.

WILSON It seems the only sensible thing to do, sir – after all we can't fight the entire German army.

WALKER If we shove off again now, Mr Mainwaring – we might be able to get away without being seen.

MAINWARING That's no good, Walker. It will be light soon – they'd spot us in a minute on the open water – and we'd be caught like rats in a trap. There's only one thing for it, we must creep ashore and hide until it gets dark again. Come on, take your boots off.

THE DOORWAY OF A WAREHOUSE. NIGHT

Mainwaring runs into the picture followed by Wilson and the rest of the platoon. They are carrying their rifles and Frazer has the Lewis gun. Their boots are slung round their backs, they all crouch in the doorway. We can still hear the singing.

MAINWARING All right, men, keep well back.

GODFREY Mr Mainwaring.

MAINWARING Oh what is it Godfrey?

GODFREY Do you think I might be excused for a minute?

MAINWARING Certainly not.

GODFREY We were in that boat for an awfully long time, sir.

MAINWARING Well, you should have taken advantage of it.

WILSON We can't stay here very long, sir, we shall be spotted – besides, my feet are killing me.

MAINWARING **(Pointing)** Look, there's a railway siding – we'll hide in one of those trucks. Come on.

They follow him out of the picture, picking their feet up gingerly.

TELECINE: RAILWAY SIDING. NIGHT

Mainwaring is leading the platoon along a line of trucks. They are running in agony.

Mainwaring stops beside a cattle truck. The sliding door is open.

Mainwaring **(Hissing over his shoulder)** All right, men – in here, quick.

He starts to bundle them through the door.

DOORWAY OF WAREHOUSE. NIGHT

A Tommy comes into the doorway. He is wearing a steel helmet, an overcoat, etc. and is carrying a rifle over his shoulder with a fixed bayonet. He lights a cigarette. We can still hear the singing. Another Tommy comes into the picture.

SECOND SOLDIER Give us a light, mate. **(He takes light from the first soldier's cigarette)** Ta. Blimey, listen to that racket – it's been going on all night. Some party, eh?

FIRST SOLDIER They certainly know how to celebrate – those French Canadian Pilots.

SECOND SOLDIER What's it in aid of then?

FIRST SOLDIER The squadron's shot down its 50th Nazi plane. They've hired the room over the pub for the night.

SECOND SOLDIER It's a wonder nobody's complained.

FIRST SOLDIER Who's going to complain, after what they've done?

SECOND SOLDIER You're right there, mate – good luck to 'em.

INSIDE CATTLE TRUCK. NIGHT.

There are piles of straw scattered round. The platoon are all gathered in a group round Mainwaring.

MAINWARING Right –are we all here? **(He glances round)** All right, men – you can put your boots on now.

JONES What are we going to do next, that's the trouble?

MAINWARING We're going to hide here until it gets dark again – and then we're going to try and make it back to the boat.

WALKER Blimey, Mr Mainwaring – it's only just starting to get light – we shall have to be here for a whole day.

PIKE We shall starve, Mr Mainwaring.

MAINWARING Nonsense, Pike – it won't hurt you to go without food for a few hours – you eat far too much as it is. All right, men – make yourselves comfortable – we might as well get what rest we can.

They settle down and pull straw over themselves.

INSIDE CATTLE TRUCK. DAY

Light is streaming through the slits at the side. The truck is moving along. The men are all asleep. Close up of Jones as he opens his eyes – realises they are moving and scrambles over to Mainwaring.

Jones looks through grille.

JONES Wake up, Captain Mainwaring, sir – the truck's moving!

MAINWARING **(Waking up and scrambling to his feet)** What! Good heavens! **(He looks out through a small grille)** We're right out in the country – I can see the tops of trees. **(Looking at his watch)** Good Lord – it's 12 o'clock – we must be somewhere in the middle of France.

JONES Don't panic! Don't panic! We're in the middle of France.

MAINWARING All right, men, settle down. Sergeant!

WILSON Yes, sir?

MAINWARING We must immobilise our weapons – we don't want them to fall into enemy hands. Walker, open that door a few inches. **(Walker opens the door)** Wilson, collect the rifle bolts and throw them out of the door one by one. Frazer!

FRAZER Aye?

MAINWARING Take the Lewis gun to pieces and throw bits out of the door.

Frazer starts to take the Lewis gun to pieces.

WILSON **(Taking the bolts and throwing them out)** It looks as if we're going to have to surrender after all, sir.

MAINWARING Surrender?! We're not going to surrender, Wilson – we're going to drop off one by one and make our way back to the coast.

WALKER But we don't stand a chance in these uniforms, Mr Mainwaring – they'll spot us in a minute.

MAINWARING Oh no they won't, Walker. All take your jackets off – come on, hurry up. **(They take their jackets off)** Good job we're wearing civilian shirts. Now roll your jackets up and stuff them inside your shirts. **(They do so)**

JONES But we'll get shot as spies, Mr Mainwaring.

MAINWARING No we won't, Jones – keep your caps in your pockets and if things look hopeless, put them on. Believe me, they won't be able to touch you.

JONES You're our inspiration, Mr Mainwaring, sir – what would we do without you?

FRAZER We wouldn't be in this mess for a start.

MAINWARING All right, men, line up. **(They line up. By now they have stuffed their jackets inside their shirts and buttoned them up)** As you probably realise, we're in a pretty tight corner – but the situation is not completely hopeless. **(Wilson gives him a look)** Now, every time this train stops, we're going to drop off one by one, and make our own way back to the coast. From there we'll have to try and get across the Channel the best way we can. Now, before we part, I'd like to thank you personally for all you've done, and wish you the best of luck. **(He starts to go down the line)** Good luck, Sponge.

SPONGE Thank you, sir – goodbye. **(They shake hands)**

MAINWARING Good luck, Pike.

PIKE Thank you, sir – goodbye. **(They shake hands)**

MAINWARING Good luck, Walker.

WALKER Thank you, sir – goodbye. **(They shake hands)**

MAINWARING Good luck, Frazer.

FRAZER Aye – goodbye. **(They shake hands)**

MAINWARING Good luck, Godfrey.

Godfrey is overcome – doesn't speak. They shake hands.

MAINWARING Good luck, Jones.

JONES Goodbye, Mr Mainwaring, sir. **(They shake hands – Mainwaring goes across to Wilson)**

MAINWARING Well, Wilson – this is it. Goodbye.

They train stops with a jolt. Mainwaring is thrown forward and puts his arms round Wilson.

WILSON Really, sir – there's no need to overdo it.

MAINWARING Quick, the train's stopped – you go out first, Jones – open the door, Walker.

JONES Wait a minute, Mr Mainwaring, you've still got your cap on. Put it in your pocket.

WALKER That looks a bit suspicious, Mr Mainwaring.

MAINWARING Open the door, Walker.

Walker pulls the door open – there is a man standing on the platform. He is dressed in a dark suit, bowler hat and umbrella. There is a pause. They all stare at him. Mainwaring quickly slams the door shut.

MAINWARING My God – we've stopped at a station.

WILSON Let's hope he didn't see us.

MAINWARING Don't be absurd – of course he saw us. There's only one thing for it – we shall have to bluff our way out of this. What's the French for 'What is this station?', Wilson?

WILSON Qu'est que c'est la gare?

MAINWARING Right – open the door, Walker.

Walker pulls the door back. The man is still standing there.

MAINWARING Bonjour. Qu'est que c'est la gare?

MAN Eh?

MAINWARING **(Shouting)** Qu'est que c'est la gare?

MAN Oh. Er… La gare est Eastbourne – actually – why are you talking French?

MAINWARING Because we're… Eastbourne. Do you hear that, men, we're not in France after all.

The men all laugh and cheer with relief.

MAINWARING **(To man)** What are you doing here?

MAN I'm waiting for the 12.30 to Walmington-on-Sea.

WILSON That's good, sir – if we wait with him we can be home in time for lunch.

MAINWARING We're not getting on any train, Wilson – we're going to walk back down the line and pick up those rifle bolts. Come on. Get dressed.

TELECINE: DAY

Long shot of men walking slowly back along length of railway line.

SERIES FOUR **EPISODE ONE**

Recorded: Friday 17/7/70

Original transmission: Friday 25/9/70, 8.00–8.30pm

Original viewing figures = 14 million

ARTHUR LOWE .... CAPTAIN MAINWARING
JOHN LE MESURIER .... SERGEANT WILSON
CLIVE DUNN .... LANCE CORPORAL JONES
JOHN LAURIE .... PRIVATE FRAZER
JAMES BECK .... PRIVATE WALKER
ARNOLD RIDLEY .... PRIVATE GODFREY
IAN LAVENDER .... PRIVATE PIKE
BILL PERTWEE .... ARP WARDEN
JANET DAVIES .... MRS PIKE
EDWARD SINCLAIR .... THE VERGER
COLIN BEAN .... PRIVATE SPONGE
PAMELA CUNDELL .... MRS FOX

PLATOON .... HUGH HASTINGS, VIC TAYLOR, LESLIE NOYES, FREDDIE WILES, DESMOND CULLUM-JONES, FREDDIE WHITE, GEORGE HANCOCK, FRANK GODFREY, KEN WADE

EXTRAS IN CINEMA .... DAVID MELBOURNE, BILL LEONARD, NINA WEST, ELLISON KEMPE, LESLIE GOLDIE, JEAN WOOLLAND, JULIA STRETTON (CIVILIANS) .... DAVID PIKE, LLOYD GOODE.(ARMY) .... RONNIE LAUGHLIN, ROGER TOLLIDAY (RAF) .... TIM O'SULLIVAN.(SAILOR) .... MAUREEN NEIL, ANNA HILTON.(ATS) .... GYPSY KEMPE (USHERETTE)

OTHER EXTRAS .... ANTHONY HAMILTON, JOHN HOLMES

THE BIG PARADE

• MEMORIES OF HAROLD SNOAD •

'This episode involved a sequence which required Pike to slip into a bog, with the other members of the platoon trying to rescue him as he slowly sank lower and lower – not the easiest thing to achieve safely! I suddenly remembered that the river running through the army training area we used had a sluice gate system, and I worked out that by using this it was possible to raise the level slightly so that the water flooded the surrounding area. Before we did this I had a pit dug – seven foot by five and six foot deep – in which we placed a five-foot high rostrum for Pike to stand on when he first found himself sinking; the plan being that during the sequence we'd progressively reduce the height of the rostrum thereby giving the impression that Pike was sinking deeper and deeper.

'We flooded the river and produced a couple of inches of water over an area the size of a football pitch and, of course, the pit also filled up. Once we'd added some floating weeds, peat and black cork chips we had achieved exactly what was required. At the end of the day's filming we removed the rostrum and returned to the unit hotel.

'The next day, I went to see the very helpful officer in charge of the battle area to tell him that the "rushes" were okay and that the pit could be filled in. He didn't seem to be in quite his usual cheery mood, and the reason soon became obvious. Apparently it was his habit to walk his dog by the river every evening. He was the sort of man who wore tough knee-high boots so the prospect of strolling through an area of what he thought were puddles hadn't worried him in the slightest – until he suddenly disappeared down our specially dug pit! I hastily invited him and his wife to join us for dinner that evening at the unit hotel and all was forgiven.

'Incidentally, it was deliberately planned that Pike's rescue wouldn't involve Wilson. The reason for this was because although John Le Mesurier was a delightful man and a brilliant actor, he was certainly not a practical man and Jimmy Perry and David Croft knew that if John had been called upon to do anything as part of the rescue process his contribution would have been a total disaster. It was for this reason that the script called for Wilson to get caught up on some barbed wire as the others ran to assist Pike.'

HAROLD SNOAD

THE BIG PARADE

BACK TWO ROWS OF CINEMA. NIGHT

We see a large close up of Mainwaring's face – it is dark – we hear a threatening German voice. Cut to a cinema screen. We see Conrad Veidt in a scene from *The Spy in Black.* Cut back to Mainwaring. We pan along to the next seat and we see Wilson – then next to him is Mrs Pike – we hear the loud German voice again. Mrs Pike grips Wilson's hand. Wilson looks sideways at Mainwaring, sees that he's not looking and grips it back. Mrs Pike snuggles up to him – reaction from Wilson. Pan along to the next seat. Pike is sucking his thumb. Back to the screen – a close up of Conrad Veidt. Back to Mrs Pike.

MRS PIKE Oh, Arthur, he's so romantic, don't you think?

WILSON Hmm...

Cut back to Conrad Veidt, then back to Mrs Pike.

MRS PIKE In a way he's rather like you, Arthur. Strong and masterful.

WILSON Hmm – yes.

Cut back to Conrad Veidt, then to Mainwaring.

MAINWARING (To Wilson) What is this chap? Some sort of foreigner?

WILSON Yes, sir.

MAINWARING Disgraceful, having German actors in films. Why couldn't they have got someone British for the part?

Cut back to Conrad Veidt in love scene holding a girl in his arms, then back to Mrs Pike and Wilson.

MRS PIKE Just look at the way he's holding her in his arms, Arthur.

Suddenly she sees Frank with his thumb in his mouth, she slaps his hand.

MRS PIKE Frank - take your thumb out of your mouth.

PIKE Sorry, Mum.

Cut back to Mainwaring. He is being joggled by someone sitting beside him. Mainwaring reacts, the camera pulls back and we see a soldier kissing an A.T.S. girl. The camera pulls right back and we can see the whole picture. Mainwaring, Wilson, Mrs Pike and Frank sitting in a row, surrounded by various service couples all snogging. There is a couple just in front and to the right of Mainwaring. The man is wearing an army greatcoat with the collar turned up so we do not see his face. He almost has his back to the camera as he is kissing the girl with him – he is slightly blocking Mainwaring's view. Mainwaring is moving his head to try and get a clear view of the screen. At last he loses his patience and taps the man on the shoulder.

MAINWARING (Hissing) Would you mind sitting up, please. (The man takes no notice) Would you mind sitting up, please – I can't see the screen.

The man quickly straightens up – it is Jones – he is with Mrs Fox.

MAINWARING Thank you.

Jones is sitting rigid, staring in front.

MRS FOX What's the matter?

JONES (Hissing) It's Mr Mainwaring.

MRS FOX (Starting to turn) Oh. Hello Mr...

JONES (Stopping her) Shhh! Don't turn round.

MAINWARING (To Wilson) I think it's disgraceful the way people behave in the cinema nowadays, Wilson.

Wilson quickly takes his hand away from Mrs Pike and straightens up.

WILSON Yes, sir.

The film ends – the lights go up, the couples all straighten up quickly and adjust themselves.

MAINWARING I find all this very embarrassing, Wilson. I've never sat in the back row before – I always go in the grand circle as a rule.

WILSON You've just got to take what seats you can get in wartime.

MAINWARING The fact that there is a war on is being used as an excuse for everything these days. One can't even go to the cinema without it developing into a bacchanalian orgy.

WILSON Oh, it's not as bad as that, sir.

MAINWARING There's no doubt about it, public morals are going to pieces. There's far too much permissiveness. I shall be glad when the war's over and people stop doing this sort of thing. All I can say is – it's a good job my wife Elizabeth isn't here tonight.

WILSON By the way, why didn't she come, sir?

MAINWARING She doesn't like the talkies.

WILSON Why not?

MAINWARING The moment Al Jolson first opened his mouth and said 'You ain't heard nothing yet' – she complained of a headache – she hasn't been to the cinema since.

WILSON But that was 12 years ago, sir.

MAINWARING Yes, well she's not a great one for changes, you know.

PIKE (To Mrs Pike) Mum – that looks like Mr Jones.

He points to the man sitting in front of Mainwaring with the army greatcoat turned up.

MRS PIKE No, that can't be.

PIKE I tell you it is, Mum. **(He leans across to Mainwaring)** I think that's Mr Jones sitting in front of you, Mr Mainwaring.

MAINWARING What? **(He taps the man on the shoulder)** Is that you, Jones?

JONES **(Purple with embarrassment, turns round)** Oh good evening, Mr Mainwaring.

Mainwaring stares hard. Jones points to Mrs Fox.

JONES This is my friend Mrs er… Mrs Fox.

Mainwaring stares even harder.

JONES **(Hurriedly)** She's a widow, you know.

MAINWARING **(Coldly)** Really.

Jones gives Mainwaring a sickly grin and sinks down into his overcoat. The lights go down and the newsreel starts.

COMMENTATOR This is the Gaumont British News bringing the truth to the free people of the world.

We see some troops being inspected by Winston Churchill.

Cut to a close up of the regimental mascot, it is a beautiful ram. It is between two soldiers and we just see their legs each side of it.

MAINWARING Look at that, Wilson.

WILSON Awfully nice, sir.

MAINWARING By Jove, that gives me an idea.

WILSON Oh no, sir.

Cut back to the screen. Churchill is going down the ranks. Suddenly the words 'Air Raid Alert' appear on the screen. Cut back to Mainwaring.

MAINWARING I'll tell you later. Come on, we'd better report for duty.

They start to get up.

WILSON **(To Pike)** Come on, Frank.

PIKE But we haven't seen the Donald Duck yet, Uncle Arthur.

WILSON Oh, come on.

INTERIOR. CHURCH HALL. DAY

The platoon are drawn up on parade. Mainwaring and Wilson are in front.

MAINWARING Now, pay attention, men – last night I went to the cinema and I saw something there that really made me think.

JONES Permission to speak, sir? The lady and I are just good friends.

MAINWARING I wasn't talking about you, Jones. I was referring to the ram.

WALKER **(Aside)** What's the difference?

MAINWARING The regimental mascot in the newsreel. Now, as you know, there is a parade next Sunday morning of all Civil Defence and Home Guard units, to mark the start of the Spitfire fund week, and we shall, of course, be leading. I thought that it might be a good idea if we had a mascot. I'm not quite sure which sort of mascot it should be – so I'm going to throw this idea at you and then you can kick it about.

JONES Permission to speak, sir? In bygone days, ships of the line used to have a figurehead as a mascot – a painted lady.

MAINWARING I was referring to something live.

WALKER Well, couldn't we have a live painted lady?

WILSON Do be quiet, Walker.

PIKE I've got a white mouse, sir. What about that as a mascot?

MAINWARING Oh, don't be stupid boy.

GODFREY I've got a very large pussy cat, sir.

MAINWARING I appreciate your suggestion, Godfrey – but we'd never get a cat to march along smartly.

WILSON Excuse me, sir, it's just occurred to me. As we saw a ram being used as a mascot in the newsreel, why don't *we* use a ram as well?

FRAZER **(Pointing to Private Sponge)** Private Sponge here is a farmer, perhaps he can help us.

SPONGE Yes, I've got a few – but they're very funny tempered at this time of year.

PIKE **(To Frazer)** Why are they funny tempered, Mr Frazer?

FRAZER Well, as he said, laddy – it's the time of year – the time of year.

PIKE What time of year?

WALKER The time when they're after…

MAINWARING **(Snapping)** Don't you tell this boy anything, Walker! Right then, Sponge, I take it that you don't mind if we borrow one of your rams.

SPONGE If you can catch one, you're welcome to it – but I warn you, it won't be easy.

MAINWARING Nonsense. We'll just take one section along – that should be enough.

The Warden enters and stands looking at the parade.

MAINWARING Wilson!

WILSON Yes, sir.

MAINWARING Go and see what Mr Hodges wants.

WILSON Right, sir. **(He crosses over to the Warden)** Can I help you?

HODGES I want to have a word with Napoleon, is he busy?

WILSON Well, he is rather – he's trying to work out how to catch a ram.

HODGES Oh yes… Well that's going to help the war effort, isn't it?

WILSON We want to march behind it at the parade on Sunday.

HODGES That should make 'em feel at home – they're used to following like a lot of sheep. (**He gives a loud laugh**)

MAINWARING (**Shouting across to him**) What is it, Warden?

HODGES (**Crossing over to him**) It's about the parade on Sunday. Can I have a word with you in private?

MAINWARING You can say anything you want to say in front of my men. I've no secrets from them.

HODGES Right. (**He is carrying a large square of white card with a plan of the parade on it**) This is a plan of the procession and you're at the back – so you'd better tell 'em now.

MAINWARING Don't be absurd – we're not at the back – we're leading the procession.

HODGES Look mate, someone had to make the decision – so I've done it, you're at the back.

MAINWARING But I spoke to the Town Clerk about it on Monday at the Rotary luncheon.

HODGES Don't come that class distinction stuff with me, mate.

MAINWARING But we've got to be in front, I shall be marching with a ram.

HODGES Your personal life's got nothing to do with me.

MAINWARING But we've got a mascot.

HODGES I don't care if you've got a dovecot.

MAINWARING What gives you the right to say that you're going to lead the parade?

HODGES Simple, ain't it? Alphabetical order.

MAINWARING What are you talking about?

HODGES Well, we're A.R.P. and you're Home Guard – 'A' comes before 'H'. I'll show you. (**Points to plan**) First comes the sea-scouts band. Then us 'A' A.R.P., then the Nurses – then the Rescue Service then the Fire Service, 'F', you see. That's A, B, C, D, E, F, G, 'H' Home Guard – you're last.

MAINWARING Don't be absurd, how can the Nurses and Rescue come before us – N and R come after H.

HODGES Oh no, they don't. They're Auxiliary Nurses and Auxiliary Rescue. I keep telling you 'A' comes before 'H'. You want to go back to school, mate.

WILSON It's just occurred to me sir – that we're Army that's 'A'.

HODGES Oh no, you're not – you're not proper Army.

MAINWARING Yes, we are, we're Auxiliary Army, that makes us even further in front.

HODGES How can you be Auxiliary Army?

WILSON Look sir, it's quite simple. We're Army and he's A.R.P. So we're both 'A's, right? That makes us level – so we take the second letter of Army which is 'R' – and the second letter of A.R.P. is 'R', so we're still level. Now we take the third letter of Army.

MAINWARING Which is 'M' and the third letter of A.R.P. which is 'P' – 'M' comes before 'P', so we're first.

MAINWARING Well done, Wilson. (**Turns to Hodges**) There you are – if you're going in alphabetical order, we're first – 'Army'.

HODGES That's what you think!

He marches out. As he goes, the whole platoon whistle the Laurel and Hardy tune in time.

Warden walks. The platoon stop. He moves to door – stops. Platoon stops. Warden goes.

MAINWARING The first round to us, I think, Wilson.

WILSON Yes, sir.

MAINWARING So number one section will parade here tomorrow evening at six o'clock and march to Private Sponge's farm to catch that ram. That's all – dismiss!

They dismiss – Walker draws Jones on one side.

WALKER 'Ere, Jonesey, I've got an idea.

JONES What?

WALKER If we catch that ram – after we've used it in the parade – we can kill it – you can sell it in your shop, then we'll share the money 50 – 50.

JONES But I'm not allowed to sell black market meat – I could go to prison.

WALKER Look, mate – where is that ram doing the best for the war effort? Marching along all ponced up in a parade – or being eaten?

JONES I don't know, you're getting me confused – anyhow I couldn't kill a little animal.

WALKER What are you talking about? You're a butcher – you're cutting 'em up all day long.

JONES Yeah, but that's different – I don't know any of them personally. Anyhow, what about Private Sponge, it's his ram.

They both look at Sponge, who is talking to Pike.

WALKER Look at him – does he look as if he goes short of food? Believe me, these farmers get plenty of meat. Look, mate, if we do this, we shall not only be making some money – but you'll be able to let your lady friend have a bit on the side.

Jones stares at Walker – opens his mouth to speak. Walker pats his cheek.

TELECINE: SOME OPEN GROUND AT SPONGE'S FARM. DAY

Close up of a clump of grass. The grass parts and we see Frazer's face. He is wearing his forage cap with lumps of twigs and grass stuck in for camouflage.

FRAZER Ssshh! Don't make a sound.

Jones' and Walker's faces come up each side of him.

FRAZER What a magnificent animal.

Cut to single shot of ram eating.

Cut to Frazer, Jones and Walker.

FRAZER Keep down.

Their heads go down.

Cut to close up of Mainwaring and Wilson in a clump of bushes. Mainwaring is looking through a pair of field glasses.

WILSON Somehow, I've got the feeling that that ram might not like the idea of being caught very much.

MAINWARING Oh, don't be a pessimist, Wilson. Frazer knows how to do it, he's an expert at fieldcraft.

Cut to Frazer's head peeping up.

FRAZER Right, stand up and reveal yourselves.

Jones, Walker, Pike, Godfrey, Sponge and two others slowly stand up.

FRAZER **(Whispering to Jones and Walker)** Now, what we've got to do is to make the ram think that we're perfectly normal.

WALKER That's going to be a bit difficult.

FRAZER Sshh! He's got to accept us as part of the landscape. Now, spread out and slowly encircle him.

Cut to high angle shot – the section moves forward.

Cut to Mainwaring and Wilson.

MAINWARING We won't interfere unless it's absolutely necessary, Wilson.

Cut to high angle shot of platoon. They have now surrounded the ram and are slowly closing in.

Cut to close up on Jones and Frazer. Single of Godfrey.

GODFREY Oh dear, he looks awfully fierce.

Cut to single of ram pawing ground.

Cut to low angle shot inside circle of section closing in – their faces get nearer.

FRAZER Now!

They all leap on the camera.

Cut to high angle shot. The section are in a heap, the ram is running away. Close up Frazer.

FRAZER After him.

Cut to high angle shot – several of the section are leaping at the ram and trying to bring him down in a rugger tackle.

Cut to Mainwaring and Wilson.

MAINWARING Come on, Wilson.

They run forward.

Cut to the ram being chased by the men. It runs through a gap in the hedge. The men follow. Pause. The men come running out through the gap in the hedge, chased by the ram. The ram runs through the gap in the hedge followed by the men. Godfrey is last, he pauses at the gap, walks a few yards along the hedge and goes through a gate.

TELECINE: EXTERIOR. ANOTHER FIELD. DAY

The men come to a halt, breathless, Mainwaring and Wilson run up.

MAINWARING **(Breathing hard)** Where is it?

FRAZER **(Pointing)** It's gone down by the river, Mr Mainwaring.

MAINWARING Well, get after it then. **(Gasping for breath)** I've never seen men so out of condition. **(They all stare hard at him)** Pike – you're the youngest – run after it and keep it in sight, we'll follow.

PIKE Yes, Mr Mainwaring. **(He runs off)**

TELECINE: EXTERIOR. NEAR THE RIVER. DAY

Pike is running.

TELECINE: EXTERIOR. CLUMP OF BUSHES. DAY

Pike runs up to the bushes, looks around, hears something and crashes through them. There is a pause, we hear a strangled cry.

TELECINE: EXTERIOR. NEAR THE RIVER. DAY

Mainwaring and the men are running. They stop.

MAINWARING We're never going to find it like this – we'd better spread out.

TELECINE: EXTERIOR. CLUMP OF BUSHES. DAY

Wilson runs up to the bushes and pauses for breath.

PIKE **(Out of vision)** Help! Help!

WILSON Good Lord!

He dives through the bushes.

TELECINE: EXTERIOR. SOME MARSHY GROUND. DAY

Pike is up to his waist in a bog, the edge of it is surrounded by barbed wire.

PIKE Help!

Wilson runs into the picture.

PIKE Help! Uncle Arthur, help!

WILSON Yes, all right, now er… keep still, whatever you do, keep still.

Pike continues to struggle.

WILSON Stop struggling, Frank – you'll only sink deeper. Hold on, I'm coming.

TELECINE: EXTERIOR. CLUMP OF BUSHES. DAY

Mainwaring, Jones, Walker, Frazer and Godfrey halt in front of the bushes.

JONES **(Out of breath)** Hold on a minute, Mr Mainwaring, I…

PIKE **(Out of vision)** Help!

WILSON **(Out of vision)** Help!

WALKER What was that, Mr Mainwaring?

PIKE **(Out of vision)** Help!

WILSON **(Out of vision)** Help!

WALKER Listen, there it is again.

PIKE **(Out of vision)** Help!

WILSON **(Out of vision)** Help!

JONES Sounds like an echo.

FRAZER It's coming from the other side of these bushes, sir.

MAINWARING Quick, come on.

They all dash through the bushes.

TELECINE: EXTERIOR. SOME MARSHY GROUND. DAY

Pike is still in the bog, he has sunk a little deeper. Wilson is hopelessly entangled in the barbed wire.

PIKE Help!

WILSON Help!

Mainwaring and co. dash into the picture – they go to Wilson.

WILSON Thank goodness, you've come, sir.

PIKE **(Bleating)** I'm sinking, Mr Mainwaring.

JONES Young Pike's in the bog – he's in the bog. Don't panic, don't panic!

MAINWARING Quiet, Jones – hold on, Pike.

WILSON What about me, sir?

MAINWARING You'll just have to wait. Don't be so selfish. Follow me, men.

Mainwaring leads them round through a gap in the wire.

MAINWARING We need something to pull him out with.

WALKER **(Pointing to a notice board facing away from them)** What about that notice board, sir?

MAINWARING Good idea, get it quick!

Walker dashes over to the board and pulls it out of the ground.

JONES It might be an important notice, Mr Mainwaring.

MAINWARING Nonsense – what's it say, Walker?

WALKER **(Holding it up)** Beware of the Bog.

Mainwaring grabs it and holds it out to Pike.

MAINWARING Grab hold of this, Pike.

Pike tries to reach the notice board, but it is too short.

PIKE I can't reach it, Mr Mainwaring.

MAINWARING **(Throws the board away)** That's no good, we shall have to try something else.

JONES Permission to speak, sir ? Why don't we throw him a rope?

MAINWARING Don't be absurd, Jones. By the time we've got a rope, it will be too late.

PIKE Oh no!

WILSON **(Shouting from the wire)** Excuse me, sir…

MAINWARING **(Crossing to him)** I've told you before, Wilson, you'll have to wait your turn.

WILSON Not me, sir, I was going to suggest a way to help Frank.

MAINWARING What?

WILSON Of course, if you don't want to hear.

MAINWARING This is no time for sulking – the boy's sinking.

WILSON Well, I was going to suggest that if you lay your jackets down, you'll be able to get to him.

MAINWARING Good thinking, Wilson. Right, men, take your jackets off. Hurry up.

They quickly take off their jackets and hand them to Mainwaring who throws them on the bog.

MAINWARING It's not enough.

JONES Permission to speak, sir, I still think a rope would be better.

MAINWARING Oh shut up – take off your trousers.

JONES Yes, sir, yes, sir.

He starts to take his trousers off.

MAINWARING And the rest of you men – take your trousers off.

They quickly take off their trousers.

GODFREY Would you like my flannel binder, sir?

MAINWARING What?

GODFREY It's very absorbent.

MAINWARING Anything – hurry up!

He throws the trousers down on top of the jackets.

MAINWARING **(To Sponge)** Lie down there. **(Pointing to bog)**

SPONGE Well, I dunno...

MAINWARING Do as you're told – if we hadn't been chasing your blasted ram, this would never have happened in the first place.

Sponge lies face downward on the jackets. Mainwaring sits astride him.

MAINWARING Frazer, grab my left hand!

FRAZER Aye, aye, sir.

MAINWARING Walker, hold on to Frazer.

WALKER Right, Mr Mainwaring.

Pike has, by now, sunk in the bog up to his armpits. Mainwaring is sitting astride Sponge, Frazer is holding Mainwaring's left hand, Walker is gripping Frazer.

MAINWARING Grab hold of my hand, Pike.

Pike reaches up and grabs Mainwaring's hand.

MAINWARING **(Shouting to Frazer)** Right, heave, heave.

They all start to pull.

PIKE I saw this happen once in a Tarzan film, Mr Mainwaring – a bloke was trying to get a man out of a swamp and he got eaten by a crocodile.

MAINWARING Shut up, you stupid boy, concentrate. Heave!

Dissolve to Mainwaring, Sponge, Frazer and Walker pulling Pike over the jackets and trousers. Pike gets to his feet covered in mud.

PIKE **(Very formal)** Mr Mainwaring – I should like to thank you for saving m life.

MAINWARING **(Embarrassed)** Oh, nonsense!

WILSON **(From the wire)** Do you think you could possibly spare a minute to get me free now, sir?

MAINWARING All right, Wilson, we'll be with you in a moment.

FRAZER Just a minute, Mr Mainwaring, where's Jones?

Everybody looks around.

MAINWARING I don't know.

WALKER I don't know. He was 'ere when we were getting Pikey out of the bog.

GODFREY Mr Mainwaring, sir, look! **(Pointing towards buoy where the platoon notice a cap floating)**

MAINWARING **(Urgently)** Get down again, Sponge.

SPONGE **(Lying down in mud)** Oh, Lord.

Mainwaring gets down to look for Jones.

FRAZER **(Pulling him out of the way)** Let me try, Mr Mainwaring, my arms aren't as short as yours.

MAINWARING All right, hurry up!

Frazer sits astride Sponge. Walker grips his left hand. Frazer puts his arm in the bog and starts raking around.

MAINWARING Can you feel anything, Frazer?

FRAZER **(In grave tones)** Nothing, sir – nothing at all.

Frazer gets off Sponge and they all stand up on the edge of the bog. They slowly take off their hats.

MAINWARING I can't believe it – I simply can't believe it.

As they are standing in a tight group, Jones pushes his way through with a coil of rope round his shoulders. They all stare at him, aghast.

JONES I've got a rope, Mr Mainwaring.

TELECINE: EXTERIOR. A STREET. DAY

The section are marching back from the bog. Their uniforms are plastered with mud except Wilson's which is in tatters from the barbed wire. Hodges, the A.R.P. Warden, and the Verger come round the corner on their bikes. As they see the marching men, they stop.

WARDEN **(With a delighted grin)** Look at 'em – look at 'em.

MAINWARING **(To the section)** There's the Warden, men. No doubt he'll have some clever, sarcastic comment to make – take no notice.

The section draw near the Verger and Warden, with their heads held high.

MAINWARING Left, right, left, right.

The section look straight ahead. The grin freezes on the Warden's face as they get nearer, he starts to turn purple and stands, gripping his handlebars. The section draws level and passes him.

VERGER Are you all right, Mr Hodges? You look as if you're going to have a heart attack.

HODGES I've waited months for this moment and now it's come I… I… can't think of anything to say.

INTERIOR. CHURCH HALL. DAY

Close up of a large photograph mounted on stiff card of a regimental mascot, it is a beautiful goat – with long white hair and horns.

FRAZER (Out of vision) There's no doubt about it – it's a beautiful animal.

WALKER (Out of vision) There you are – you've only got to leave it to me – I told Mr Mainwaring I'd get him a mascot and I've got him one.

Walker, who has been holding the photograph, lowers it – and we see the real goat – it is nothing like the photo. It is thin and scraggy with very short horns, it stands, looking miserable and is surrounded by Walker, Frazer, Jones, Godfrey and Pike.

PIKE It's not very much like the photo, Joe.

WALKER It will be all right – we'll just tart it up a bit.

JONES You're never going to get away with this, Joe. You promised Mr Mainwaring that you'd get the same goat as the one in the photograph.

WALKER Well, we'll just have to make it look like the goat in the photo, won't we?

FRAZER Rubbish. How are you going to do that? The parade starts in an hour.

WALKER You'll see, mate. Pikey, go and get those horns off the wall of the Vicar's office.

PIKE Right. (He goes)

GODFREY My sister, Dolly, had her handbag eaten by a goat once.

JONES Well, you're not carrying a handbag are you, Mr Godfrey?

GODFREY No – but they eat other things as well.

Pike returns with a pair of twisted antelope horns on a small shield – he hands them to Walker.

WALKER Ta! Now, you watch this.

He pulls the horns off the shield and sticks them on top of the goat's short horns, they hang at odd angles. Walker tries to straighten them several times, but they keep flopping apart.

WALKER What we need here is a bit of fuse wire. See if you can find some – there's a good boy, Pikey.

VERGER (Out of vision) Very well, Vicar. I'll just wait to have a word with Mr Mainwaring first.

WALKER It's the Verger – don't let him see the goat.

They gather in a tight knot round the goat. The Verger enters, he is dressed in a Chief Petty Officer's uniform.

VERGER Where's Mr Mainwaring?

JONES Hello, Verger. Joined up, have you?

VERGER You know perfectly well that this is my uniform as Boson of the sea-scouts. My band is leading the parade this morning. (Pointing to the horns that Walker is wiring together) What are you doing with the Vicar's horns?

WALKER What? Oh, they fell off the wall. I'm just mending them.

VERGER The Vicar's not going to like this, you know – he's very proud of those horns – he got them up the Umbarla-Umbarla when he was a missionary.

WALKER Was that when he was trying to climb out of the pot?

VERGER Where's Captain Mainwaring? I wanted to ask him… What's that smell?

JONES What smell?

VERGER That terrible smell.

JONES I can't smell any smell, can you, boys?

They all chorus 'no'.

VERGER I shall have to report this to the Vicar.

Mainwaring and Wilson come through the main doors. The Verger turns to go and sees them.

VERGER There you are, Mr Mainwaring, I just wanted to tell you that my boys will be at the assembly point in the station yard in half an hour.

MAINWARING Splendid Verger, we shall see you there.

VERGER I must go now – I've got to have a word with the Vicar about a funny smell. (He goes)

Mainwaring crosses to the men. During this time, Walker has put the horns back on the goat.

MAINWARING Good morning, men. As soon as the rest of the platoon arrive, we'll march off to the station yard. Did you get the goat, Walker?

WALKER Well er… yes, I did.

MAINWARING Where is it then?

They break away and reveal the goat. Mainwaring stares at it, unable to believe his eyes. He crosses to Walker, purple with rage.

MAINWARING How dare you?

WALKER Yeah, well I… thought it might work.

MAINWARING You told me you could get a goat, you showed me a photograph of it and I gave you five pounds. And you turn up with this… this thing.

FRAZER (**Aside to Godfrey**) Joe's going to really get what's coming to him now.

GODFREY Oh dear.

MAINWARING I was relying on that goat to lead the parade this morning and now you've ruined everything.

WALKER I'm sorry, Mr Mainwaring. Look, here's your fiver back.

He takes a five pound note out of his pocket and gives it to Mainwaring. Mainwaring takes it and holds it in his left hand down by his side.

MAINWARING You know what this means, don't you? We shall have to go on parade without a mascot.

The goat snatches the note out of Mainwaring's hand and starts to eat it.

MAINWARING How could you ever think that a wretched, miserable, moth-eaten creature like this could possibly… (**He gestures towards the goat with his left hand and suddenly realises that it is empty**)

Close up of goat chewing.

TELECINE: EXTERIOR. STATION YARD. DAY

Hodges, the A.R.P. Warden, is standing in front of a group of 12 other wardens. They are drawn up on parade in three ranks of four. They are wearing civilian suits, respirators, black steel helmets with a white 'W' on, and A.R.P. armbands. Hodges is wearing a white helmet. The sea-scouts drum and bugle band has not fallen in yet, they are gathered in a knot round the Verger.

HODGES Attenshun! Stand at ease, very smart. Right, now, as we are leading this parade – it's up to us to show Captain Mainwaring and his toy soldiers that we can be just as smart as any Home Guards.

We see Mainwaring and his platoon marching into the yard.

HODGES Here they come. Right, attenshun! Right turn.

They are now facing in the direction of the march. Hodges marches round to the front and takes up his position.

HODGES Stand at ease!

Hodges stands and waits with a smug look on his face. Mainwaring marches his platoon right up to Hodges.

MAINWARING Platoon, halt!

Mainwaring is face to face with Hodges.

MAINWARING About turn!

The platoon are now in front of the wardens. Mainwaring ignores Hodges and marches round to the front. Hodges stares, unable to believe his eyes, then quickly follows Mainwaring round to the front.

MAINWARING (**Shouts to Verger**) Right, Mr Harman, fall your boys in.

The Verger blows on his whistle and the sea-scouts fall in.

HODGES (**To Mainwaring**) What do you think you're playing at?

Mainwaring ignores him.

WILSON Look, just clear off, will you?

HODGES I told you the Wardens were leading this parade.

MAINWARING And I told you the Home Guards were leading it and that's that.

HODGES Well, where's your mascot then?

MAINWARING I don't wish to discuss it with you any more – you'd better take up your position.

HODGES We'll soon see about that matter, mate.

He quickly moves round and takes up his position in front of the wardens.

MAINWARING Ready, Mr Harman?

The Verger nods.

MAINWARING (**Shouting**) Parade will move off. Quick… march.

The band starts to play and they all move off.

Cut to Hodges, we hear Mainwaring giving 'left, right'. Hodges picks it up and quickens it. The Wardens start to gain on the Home Guards. Hodges shouts out the time even quicker. Mainwaring realises that the Wardens are trying to quicken, and speeds up his pace. Hodges is now marching beside Mainwaring. The Wardens are starting to push through the ranks of the Home Guards and pass them. The Verger looks round, sees what is happening and quickens the band. The whole parade breaks into a trot. The Wardens by now are pushing through the ranks of the Home Guards, trying to get in front. The band goes even quicker. They are all running, sea-scouts, Home Guards and Wardens – all mixed up.

Fade on chaos.

SERIES FOUR **EPISODE TWO**

Recorded: Friday 24/7/70

Original transmission: Friday 2/10/70, 8.00–8.30pm

Original viewing figures = 12.3 million

ARTHUR LOWE .... CAPTAIN MAINWARING
JOHN LE MESURIER .... SERGEANT WILSON
CLIVE DUNN .... LANCE CORPORAL JONES
JOHN LAURIE .... PRIVATE FRAZER
JAMES BECK .... PRIVATE WALKER
ARNOLD RIDLEY .... PRIVATE GODFREY
IAN LAVENDER .... PRIVATE PIKE
BILL PERTWEE .... ARP WARDEN
EDWARD SINCLAIR .... VERGER
FRANK WILLIAMS .... VICAR
GEOFFREY LUMSDEN .... CAPTAIN SQUARE
ROBERT RAGLAN .... THE HG SERGEANT
COLIN BEAN .... PRIVATE SPONGE
DON ESTELLE .... SECOND ARP WARDEN
VERNE MORGAN .... THE LANDLORD

PLATOON .... DESMOND CULLUM-JONES, FREDDIE WILES, HUGH HASTINGS, VIC TAYLOR, LESLIE NOYES, FRANK GODFREY, FREDDIE WHITE, KEN WADE

EXTRAS .... EILEEN MATTHEWS (WOMAN IN PUB); LEONARD KINGSTON, THOMAS LIARD, GEOFFREY BRIGHTY, FRANCIS BATFONI, BILL LODGE, CHARLES FAYNOR, PAUL BLOMLEY (SOLDIERS)

STUNTMAN .... JOHNNY SCRIPPS

DON'T FORGET THE DIVER

• HAROLD SNOAD REMEMBERS •

'This episode involved Jones getting stuck on the blades of a windmill, which then starts going round and round. During the location recce I had great trouble finding a suitable windmill which, for practical reasons, had to be reasonably near our filming area. Eventually I discovered one that was perfect visually but, unfortunately, the mechanical system hadn't been modernised in any way and still needed a very strong wind to revolve the blades. Since we obviously couldn't rely on there being sufficient wind on the day – and, anyway, it could well have been dangerous filming in those conditions – I had to find another way. Suddenly I hit upon the idea of erecting a small hut on the ground in front of the windmill. From the front – the side facing the camera – the hut looked perfectly normal but it actually had no rear wall, and standing behind the hut were two scene boys who were pushing the four blades of the windmill as each passed them, the end result looking as if the windmill was working in the usual accepted way.'

HAROLD SNOAD

Don't Forget the Diver

INTERIOR. SMALL BAR AT ANCHOR. EVENING

Captain Square is standing at the bar with a Sergeant and Corporal. They are members of the Eastgate platoon and are all wearing H.G. uniform. Captain Square is wearing quite a lot of medal ribbons including 1914–1918 and Arabian Campaign.

SQUARE There we were, stuck out in the desert – no food and, worst of all, no water. And all the time Johnny Turk was sniping at us. My tongue was so swollen it filled my entire mouth. You know, at that moment, I'd have sold my soul to the devil for a drink.

SERGEANT Would you like another, sir?

SQUARE Thank you, Sergeant.

SERGEANT **(To landlord)** Same again, please.

The landlord draws three pints.

LANDLORD We don't see you gentlemen from the Eastgate platoon in this part of the world very often.

SERGEANT No – we're over here to see about the big exercise next Sunday.

LANDLORD What exercise is that?

SERGEANT All the Home Guard units in the area are taking part.

SQUARE That's enough, Sergeant – careless talk remember – careless talk. Let me see – where was I?

SERGEANT Out in the desert, dying of thirst. **(He hands Square a pint)**

SQUARE So I was. Cheers! **(He drinks)** As I was saying, my tongue was black, absolutely black – then I remembered the old trick of sucking a pebble – the only trouble is there are no pebbles in the desert – all sand you know. Then I had an idea, I pulled out my gold hunter. **(He pulls a gold watch out of his top pocket – it is on a long gold chain)** Beautiful watch – belonged to my father – it's even got an alarm, and I popped it in my mouth – kept it there for two days, there's no doubt about it, this watch saved my life.

LANDLORD That's a remarkable story, sir.

SQUARE And what's even more remarkable – when I pulled the watch out of my mouth – it was keeping perfect time – hadn't lost or gained a second. I'll prove it to you. I'll put this watch in my mouth for a few minutes, then you'll see. I'll just set the alarm.

He fiddles with the watch and puts it in his mouth.

Cut to the door of the bar – Mainwaring and Wilson come in.

WILSON I must say, sir – I can do with a glass of beer.

MAINWARING Yes, I always look forward to my pint after parade, Wilson.

WILSON Oh Lord – look, sir – there's that terrible old bore, Captain Square. I wonder what he's doing over here?

MAINWARING Probably come over from Eastgate to see about the exercise on Sunday. Come on, we'll go to the other end of the bar.

They both go to the end of the bar.

LANDLORD Good evening, Mr Mainwaring. Evening, Mr Wilson.

They both nod.

SQUARE **(With his watch in his mouth)** Evening, Mainwaring.

Square drains his glass with his watch in his mouth. Mainwaring and Wilson stare, fascinated – they can see Square's watch chain leading into his mouth.

MAINWARING **(Aside)** Why on earth has he got his watch in his mouth, Wilson?

WILSON **(Sniggering)** Perhaps he's watching his drinking, sir.

MAINWARING **(Staring hard)** Really, Wilson – you know your jokes get more and more childish.

The alarm goes off in Square's mouth. He pulls the watch out and listens to it.

SQUARE There you are – going perfectly. I think this calls for another round. **(To Mainwaring)** Oh, I'm sorry, you were here first, Mainwaring – after you.

MAINWARING That's all right.

SQUARE **(Pushing the mugs across the counter)** Same again.

The landlord starts to draw three pints.

SQUARE **(To Mainwaring – lowering his voice)** Well, Mainwaring. Looking forward to Sunday, eh?

MAINWARING **(Still looking at the beer)** Should prove interesting.

SQUARE You're going to have a bit of a job capturing that mill with us inside. How are you going to get across that open ground – not a scrap of cover.

MAINWARING **(Coldly)** No doubt we shall find a way.

The landlord pushes the three pints over to Square and takes the money.

LANDLORD **(To Mainwaring and Wilson)** Now it's your turn, gentlemen – sorry to keep you waiting. Pints?

MAINWARING Thank you.

The landlord takes a mug – holds it under the tap – pulls the handle. There is a gurgle and a few drops of froth go into the mug.

LANDLORD Sorry, gents – no more beer.

WILSON Well, that's nice, isn't it?

INTERIOR. CHURCH HALL. DAY

Mainwaring is standing in front of the blackboard on which a diagram is drawn. The rest of the platoon are gathered around. The Verger is dusting in the hall.

MAINWARING ...and so, Gentlemen, this is, without a doubt, the most difficult exercise we have ever had to tackle.

Pan round on blank-looking faces.

MAINWARING To sum up then. The Mill here – inside Captain Square and the Eastgate platoon. The river here – wall here – boathouse here – trees and bushes here. All round the mill, open ground – not a scrap of cover – our job is to cross that open ground and place an explosive charge inside the mill. Any suggestions?

Cut to Verger, listening.

JONES Permission to speak, sir? How about a tunnel?

MAINWARING A tunnel?

JONES Yes, sir – if we all get down behind the wall – and then dig a big hole downwards – then, when we are nice and deep downwards, all of a sudden we start to dig sideways – sideways and sideways – and when we are under the mill – we tunnel upwards – and upwards – and we should be inside the mill.

WALKER Or else in Australia.

Cut to Verger jotting in a notebook – he quickly puts it away and disappears at the back of the hall, dusting vigorously.

MAINWARING I think you're going into the realms of fantasy now, Jones.

JONES **(Aside to Walker)** There he goes with his realms of fantasy again. He's playing with fire now. I'm in charge of his meat.

WILSON I've got an idea, sir. In one of Shakespeare's plays – I can't remember which one – some king or other dressed his army up as bushes so that they could move across open ground – in order to attack the castle.

Pause.

MAINWARING Yes, hmm – yes. I must admit that it's a good idea... **(He breaks off as he sees the Verger dusting)** How much longer are you going to be dusting, Verger?

VERGER I don't know, I've got to keep the place clean. The state you leave it in after every parade is a disgrace.

MAINWARING Well, you'll just have to do it some other time – you're getting on my nerves creeping about the place with that miserable look on your face.

VERGER This happens to be my normal expression. You can't be a Verger with a funny face, you know.

JONES Well, you seem to manage all right.

VERGER **(Crossing to office muttering)** Dirt, that's what they treat me like – dirt. **(He goes into office)**

MAINWARING I'm sorry, men, where were we?

WALKER I've got it, sir – what about getting inside a dummy log and drifting down the river? That would do the trick.

MAINWARING That's a good idea, Walker – the only trouble is we'd need someone to push it, and I don't think any of us could stay under that long.

WALKER 'Ere, why don't we get someone in a diving suit to push the log?

MAINWARING Don't be absurd – who would have a diving suit?

FRAZER **(Casually)** I've got a diving suit.

MAINWARING You've got a diving suit! How on earth did you get that?

FRAZER It happened when I was in the South Seas – with a friend of mine, Wally Stewart – we were diving for pearls. Well, one day he was down below and I was standing up on deck – the native boys were working the pumps when, all of a sudden, I felt four pulls on his air pipe – that means 'Haul me up'. I knew that something was wrong – I looked down – the water out there is as clear as crystal, and there was Stewart fighting for his life with a giant squid. I didn't hesitate, I dived down into the depths and I plunged my knife between those two hideous eyes – my lungs were bursting – a red mist was swimming in front of my eyes – the water was black with an inky liquid from the squid. I gave the signal and they quickly pulled Stewart up. When we got him on deck, I unscrewed his helmet and then I realised – they'd pulled him up too quickly – he was dying from the dreaded 'bends' – I cradled him in my arms. He gazed up at me and said, 'Jock, look after my dear mother, see that she gets all my possessions'. **(Pause)** Well, he only had his diving suit – and it was'ner any use to her, so I gave her ten bob and kept it. **(Pause)** Every time after that – whenever I went down in that helmet, I could hear that poor man's voice crying, 'Help – Help!'.

There is a long pause.

MAINWARING So, we'll take it that you have a diving suit, Frazer.

JONES Permission to speak, sir? I will have a word with the Vicar about borrowing his imitation log from 'Babes in the Wood'. He's registered with me for meat – he'll do anything for a bit of kidney.

MAINWARING Oh, very well, Jones. Right, that's all for now. We'll parade here tomorrow night as usual.

INTERIOR. SIDE OFFICE. CHURCH HALL. DAY

VERGER Hello.

SQUARE **(Out of vision – distort)** Hello, who's that?

VERGER It's me here, Captain Square – the Verger, Walmington-on-Sea Parish Church.

SQUARE **(Out of vision – distort)** Any news?

VERGER Yes, sir. I've found out how they're going to get into the mill.

SQUARE **(Out of vision – distort)** How?

VERGER The same way as Shakespeare did it.

SQUARE **(Out of vision– distort)** Shakespeare? What are you talking about, man?

VERGER They're going to dress up as bushes and creep across the open ground.

SQUARE **(Out of vision – distort)** By Jove – that old trick, eh! Mainwaring must be slipping – thanks for your help.

VERGER It's a pleasure, sir – I'd do anything to help you, you're a gentleman – not like Mainwaring's lot – treat me like dirt they do – just like dirt.

INTERIOR. CHURCH HALL. DAY

Frazer is sitting on a bench. He has his diving suit on – the glass on the helmet is open – the pump is a few yards away from him. The rest of the men are gathered round Mainwaring, who is standing beside the plan on the blackboard.

MAINWARING Now, we'll just go through it once more. I shall be in the boathouse here – Frazer will push the log from the inside of the boathouse out into the river – then, keeping under water, he will push the log along the river until it is level with the mill. What do you do then, Frazer?

FRAZER As soon as I'm level with the mill – I give one pull on the life-line.

MAINWARING As soon as Frazer pulls his life-line, I shall give one warble on my bird warbler. Then, what do you do, Wilson?

WILSON As soon as I hear you give a warble on your bird warbler – I shall carry out the first diversion.

MAINWARING Right! Walker?

WALKER As soon as you warble and Sergeant Wilson starts his diversion – I help him with it.

MAINWARING Good. Frazer?

FRAZER While the diversion is attracting the attention of the defenders of the mill – I quickly tip Jones, in the log, on to the bank.

MAINWARING Excellent – Jones? **(There is no answer – he looks round)** Where's Jones?

WALKER He's dressing up as a log.

MAINWARING **(Shouting)** Hurry up, Jones. It shouldn't take you all that time to dress up as a log.

WALKER **(In soothing voice)** And here we have Betty in a natty little one-piece woodland ensemble.

The office door opens – and Jones appears, dressed as a log. The top of it is covered in leaves – his right arm is sticking out as one of the branches – the bottom of the log from the knees down spreads out like a little skirt – he minces towards the centre of the room.

MAINWARING **(Aside to Wilson)** What do you think, Wilson?

WILSON I don't know, sir – I really don't know.

MAINWARING Well, it's too late to change our plans now – we shall just have to go through with it and hope for the best. **(He crosses to the log)** Now listen, Jones – where are you?

JONES **(Opens a little door where his face is)** Here I am, sir. **(He salutes with his right arm which is a branch)**

MAINWARING We've got to the point where you've been tipped on to the bank. What do you do then?

JONES While Sergeant Wilson is creating a diversion, I make my way towards the mill.

MAINWARING Good. I shall then give two warbles on my warbler. What happens then?

GODFREY When I hear you giving two warbles – I carry out the second diversion.

WALKER And I help him carry out the second diversion.

MAINWARING That second diversion should give you enough time to reach the mill, Jones. If you're flat against the side of it, the people inside won't be able to see you. You divest yourself of the tree trunk – climb up the ladder, here and throw the time bomb through the window, here. Wait a minute, where are you going to put the time bomb?

JONES Between me legs, sir.

MAINWARING What?

JONES I'm going to tie it round my waist so that it hangs between my knees, sir. Then, when I want to release it – I just pull on the string and it drops down.

MAINWARING Give him the time bomb, Wilson.

WILSON Right, sir – here you are, Jones.

He holds out an alarm clock – on the end of a bit of string. He looks puzzled.

WILSON It's a bit difficult, sir – I don't see where…

JONES Here you are, Mr Wilson.

Another little door opens half-way down the log. Jones' hand comes out, takes the clock and closes the door.

MAINWARING Right, Jones, tie it on.

The log starts to wriggle about.

MAINWARING Hurry up.

JONES It's a bit difficult, sir. I've only got one pair of hands you know. **(The log wriggles even more)**

MAINWARING Help him, Walker.

Walker goes over to the log. Taps on the little door.

WALKER Open up, Jonesey.

The door opens and Walker puts his hand in.

JONES I'm tying the knot. Put your finger on it – not there, there!

MAINWARING Hurry up, Jones – I want to try this out – to see if you can release the bomb. Are you ready?

JONES Yes, sir.

MAINWARING Off you go.

He moves across the hall with little hops.

MAINWARING Release the bomb.

Jones gives a few more hops and the bomb drops down like a chicken laying an egg. Walker makes clucking noises.

MAINWARING That will be enough of that, Walker. All right, Jones – you can stop hopping about. Seems to work all right, Wilson.

WILSON Yes, sir – shall I put the bomb back inside him.

MAINWARING We can't go through all that again. We'll assume it's there. Right now, stand by men, I want to go through the whole thing from start to finish. **(To Jones)** I want to start... where are you?

The bottom door of log opens.

JONES I'm here, sir.

MAINWARING **(Bending down)** Ah! I want to go from the beginning.

The top door opens.

JONES All right, sir.

MAINWARING Get him on to the raft. Are you ready, Frazer?

FRAZER Aye, sir. **(To the pumps)** Don't forget what I taught you, boys, keep up a nice steady pressure.

SPONGE Don't worry, Mr Frazer, we'll keep pumping.

FRAZER **(To Pike)** Don't forget the signals. If I pull four times on my air pipe, that means I'm coming up – and if you pull four times on my life-line that means you want me to come up.

PIKE I've got it. Two separate signals. Four and four.

MAINWARING Right. **(He screws the glass into place)** Start pumping. Wilson, Godfrey, take up your diversion positions.

Godfrey and Wilson get into position.

MAINWARING **(He and Pike help Frazer to his feet. Mainwaring taps his helmet)** Frazer is now in the water – he pushes the log out of the boathouse and is now in the open river.

JONES **(In log)** Trickle, trickle, trickle.

Mainwaring reacts.

JONES That's the water lapping against the log.

The picture is now as follows: Mainwaring, Pike, Sponge and Hastings working the pumps. Frazer in his diving suit, Jones in the log on the pram and four other members of the platoon are at the far end of the hall in the boathouse. Wilson and Walker with four others are at the back of the hall. Godfrey and two others in the far corner of the hall at the back.

MAINWARING Yes – very good. Now, I am looking through my periscope. **(He holds up a small mirror on the end of a stick)** Frazer has now submerged and is pushing Jones, in the log, up the river.

Frazer is now walking along, pushing Jones, in the log, on the pram.

MAINWARING He reaches the bank level with the windmill. **(He blows his bird warbler)** That's the signal for your diversion Wilson – Wilson!

WILSON **(From the back of the hall)** Yes, sir?

MAINWARING I'm warbling – are you diverting?

WILSON Yes, sir – we're doing it behind the wall.

MAINWARING Well, I can't see you.

WILSON How could you, sir? We're behind the wall.

MAINWARING Start again. **(Shouts)** Frazer, Frazer!

Frazer takes no notice.

PIKE He can't hear you, Mr Mainwaring.

MAINWARING Give him the signal to come up – four pulls on his breast rope.

PIKE Right. Thank you – Mr Mainwaring.

He gives a pull on Frazer's breast rope. Frazer falls flat on his back. He lies there like a beetle trying to get up.

MAINWARING Come on – help him up.

They all rush over and help Frazer up. Close up of Frazer's face inside helmet – he is looking very strange.

PIKE He ain't half looking a funny colour, Mr Mainwaring.

MAINWARING Perhaps he's not getting enough air. Sponge – give him some more air.

SPONGE We're pumping as hard as we can, Mr Mainwaring.

MAINWARING I can't understand it, I...

WALKER Mr Mainwaring...

Pike is on air pipe.

MAINWARING **(Gives Pike a push)** You stupid boy – you're standing on his air pipe. I wonder if he's all right?

WILSON Perhaps we ought to take his helmet off, sir?

PIKE You can't do that, Uncle Arthur – he'll get the bends in his head.

WALKER No one will know the difference.

MAINWARING Oh, this is absurd. **(He mouths the words 'are you all right?'. Frazer nods his head)** He's all right. We've wasted enough time as it is. All right, Frazer? **(Thumbs up)** All right, Jones? **(Door comes up and hits him in the face. Mainwaring falls over cables)**

Frazer is pushing the log. Hodges enters in the background.

Mainwaring **(Sharply)** What is it you want, Warden?

HODGES Well, I er...

He breaks off as he sees Frazer starting to walk slowly across the hall, pushing the pram with Jones in the log on top.

HODGES I er... what's going on?

MAINWARING It needn't concern you, Warden – what we're doing is vital to the war effort.

HODGES Vital to the war effort. A bloke in a diving suit pushing another bloke in a pram, dressed in a log, vital to the war effort?

JONES Trickle, trickle, trickle.

HODGES What's that?

MAINWARING That's the water lapping round the log.

Warden reacts.

HODGES Don't go away, Gerald must see this. **(He quickly goes)**

MAINWARING Right, come on now, let's start again. When Frazer reaches the point level with the windmill – I shall give the signal for the first diversion.

He is looking in the mirror. Hodges returns with a second warden.

HODGES There you are, what did I tell you? A bloke in a diving suit – pushing another bloke in a pram, dressed in a log. Now call me a liar.

SECOND WARDEN **(Aghast)** Well, I never did – you were right. Here you are, here's your five bob. Are they on our side?

Chaos continues.

ESTABLISHING SHOT OF WINDMILL

INTERIOR. INSIDE WINDMILL. DAY

Captain Square, a Sergeant, Corporal and four men all in Home Guard uniform are in the upper part looking out of the windows.

SQUARE **(Calling to Sergeant)** Any sign of Mainwaring's mob yet, Sergeant?

SERGEANT **(Who is looking out of the back window)** No, sir – nothing.

SQUARE **(Looking at his watch)** It's only a quarter to two – they're not due to start till two o'clock.

The Sergeant crosses to Square.

SERGEANT **(Looking at his own watch)** I make it a quarter past, sir.

SQUARE **(Tapping his gold watch)** What? Damn thing must have stopped.

SERGEANT I don't see how the Walmington-on-Sea lot are going to get across that open ground – all the others have failed.

SQUARE Well, keep a look out for a lot of bushes – that's part of their master plan – according to the Verger. **(He laughs)**

SERGEANT Do you think he's reliable, sir?

SQUARE Of course he is – he's my fifth column. I've got him posted in the graveyard now – it's on the side of a hill – he can see everything that's going on. I'll just check up, see if he's okay.

He goes to field telephone.

TELECINE: EXTERIOR. GRAVEYARD. DAY

The Verger is doing some weeding beside a large, old, flat tombstone. At the top of it is a stone urn with a lid on it. He puts down his hoe, looks around to see that no one is looking and pulls out a pair of field glasses from under his cassock. He looks through them. There is the sound of a phone ringing – he crosses to the urn, lifts the lid – inside is a field telephone – he lifts it up.

VERGER Verger here.

SQUARE **(Out of vision)** Anything happening?

VERGER Not yet, Captain Square – but I've got my eyes peeled.

SQUARE **(Out of vision)** Let me know as soon as anything moves.

VERGER Yes, sir.

The Verger puts down the phone, replaces the lid – and squints through the glasses.

INTERIOR. INSIDE BOATHOUSE. DAY

Frazer is standing in his diving suit with his helmet on and the glass open. Mainwaring is standing on one side of him – Pike on the other. Jones is standing beside them, dressed in the log. Sponge and Hastings are at the pumps – three other privates are standing in the background.

MAINWARING (To Jones) Now, we'll just have a quick check before we start. You've got the clock – I mean the bomb – between your legs, Jones?

JONES Yes, sir – I've got it tied quite securely.

MAINWARING I'll just make sure, if you don't mind. (He opens the little door) Yes, that's all right. (He gets hit round head by branch) Right, close the glass. (Pike closes the glass) Start the pumps. (Frazer gives four pulls on his breast rope)

PIKE Mr Mainwaring – Frazer's given four pulls on his rope – that means he wants to come up.

MAINWARING You stupid boy – he's up already – stop pumping. (He opens the glass) What is it, Frazer?

FRAZER I just wanted to scratch my nose.

MAINWARING Well, hurry up then. (Frazer scratches his nose) Have you finished?

FRAZER Aye.

MAINWARING Right. (He closes the glass) Start the pumps.

Sponge starts pumping. There is a ladder leading down into the water, they help Frazer on to it. Mainwaring taps his helmet and Frazer goes down into the water, out of frame. Mainwaring turns to Jones.

MAINWARING All ready, Jones?

JONES Yes, sir.

MAINWARING Well, good luck then.

JONES Thank you, sir.

Jones closes the door in front of his face.

MAINWARING Right, get him on the raft.

JONES Trickle, trickle, trickle.

MAINWARING You don't need to trickle now.

They pick Jones up and start to lower him on to the raft, out of frame.

TELECINE: EXTERIOR. OUTSIDE BOATHOUSE. DAY

We see the diver emerge from the boathouse, pushing the log on a small raft of tyres. As soon as they get out into the river the diver submerges.

TELECINE: EXTERIOR. RIVER. DAY

The log is floating along the river, we can see bubbles coming from behind the raft.

TELECINE: EXTERIOR. OUTSIDE BOATHOUSE. DAY

Close up of mirror on stick, poking through a hole in the side of the boathouse.

INTERIOR. INSIDE BOATHOUSE. DAY

Mainwaring is holding the end of the mirror on the stick.

MAINWARING Jones is level with the windmill. Pike, come and take over the periscope – while I give the signal for the diversion.

PIKE Right-oh, Mr Mainwaring.

Pike comes down and takes hold of the stick. Mainwaring crosses up to the side door of the boathouse and opens it a few inches and blows his bird warbler.

INTERIOR. INSIDE WINDMILL. DAY

The Sergeant is looking out of the window through field glasses. He sees something – shouts to Square who is looking out of one of the other windows.

SERGEANT I think they've started, sir.

Square and the rest of the men cross over to the window.

SERGEANT (Pointing) Look over there, sir – behind that wall. (He hands the glasses to Square)

SQUARE (Taking the glasses and looking through them) What on earth are they up to?

TELECINE: EXTERIOR. WALL. DAY.

We can see a wall about six foot high – at the top of the wall we can see the top of 15 rifles and bayonets. The picture is seen through the circles of Square's field glasses.

WILSON (Out of vision) Left, right – left, right, left, right.

SQUARE (Out of vision) Why the hell are they drilling – they're supposed to be attacking us – that's typical of Mainwaring and his blimp mentality.

SERGEANT (Out of vision) Perhaps it's a trick, sir.

INTERIOR. WINDMILL. DAY

SQUARE It can't be, I can count 15 rifles – that's the whole platoon.

TELECINE: EXTERIOR. RIVER. DAY

The log is level with the windmill. The diver emerges – tips the log on to the bank – and quickly submerges again. Cut in to close up of log getting to its feet. Go right in to big close up of little door in front of Jones' face – inside we can hear a knocking.

JONES (Inside log) I can't get the door open, it's stuck. I can't see – I can't see.

Pull back to long shot of the log walking round in circles – it walks back to the river bank and falls in with a terrific splash.

INTERIOR. BOATHOUSE. DAY

Pike is at the periscope – he shouts to Mainwaring.

PIKE Mr Mainwaring – Jones has fallen back in the water again.

MAINWARING (Out of vision) What? What's the matter with him?

TELECINE: EXTERIOR. RIVER BANK. DAY

The log tries to climb on to the river bank and falls back into the water.

TELECINE: EXTERIOR. WALL. DAY

We can see the wall through the circles of Square's field glasses. We see the tops of the rifles with fixed bayonets marching forwards.

WILSON (Out of vision) About turn.

The rifles start to go backwards.

SQUARE (Out of vision) Why are they marching backwards?

The rifles start to go forwards again.

SQUARE (Out of vision) There's something fishy here – get the Verger on the phone.

TELECINE: EXTERIOR. BEHIND THE WALL

Walker and three other men are carrying long poles on their shoulders. The rifles are tied to the poles, sticking upwards in three ranks of five. Wilson is giving the commands.

WILSON Left, right, left, right, left, right. About turn.

The men about turn and change the poles from one shoulder to another. But the rifles are still pointing in the same direction.

TELECINE: EXTERIOR. RIVER BANK. DAY

The diver is pushing the log back on to the river bank – the log gets to its feet and totters forwards towards the mill.

TELECINE: EXTERIOR. GRAVEYARD. DAY

The Verger is looking through his field glasses – the phone rings – he takes the lid off the urn and picks it up.

VERGER Verger here.

SQUARE (Out of vision) What's going on behind that wall, Verger?

VERGER I can't understand it, sir – they've got a lot of rifles tied to poles.

SQUARE (Out of vision) Have you been drinking? Pull yourself together man.

TELECINE: EXTERIOR. FIELD. DAY

Big close up of Godfrey – in the distance we can hear the bird warbler.

GODFREY Oh dear, that's the signal for the second diversion. Where's Joe got to? (Walker hurries into the picture)

WALKER Haven't you started the diversion yet, Mr Godfrey?

GODFREY I was waiting for you.

WALKER I've been helping Sergeant Wilson with his diversion – I can't be everywhere. Come on, let's get on with it.

For the first time we see that they are with some sheep. They start to put tin hats on the sheep.

WALKER Right, as soon as we've got these tin helmets on the sheep, we drive them towards the mill.

GODFREY Excuse me, why are we putting these helmets on these sheep?

WALKER Simple, as soon as they see these sheep coming towards them – they won't know whether it's us dressed up as sheep or not – and while they're trying to make up their minds, Jonesey will be inside that mill.

TELECINE: EXTERIOR. FIELD. DAY

Close up of the top of the log. It is moving across the open ground. It stops – Jones opens the little door, we can see his face – we hear a dog whimpering. Jones looks down. Cut to close up of mongrel dog looking up and wagging its tail. Cut back to Jones' face.

JONES Go away – clear off.

Cut to long shot of log tottering along. Dog is sniffing at Jones' heels. Jones kicks out to try and get rid of dog – it still follows him. Jones stops. Cut to close up of his face, it changes to a look of horror.

JONES Oh no!

TELECINE: EXTERIOR. GRAVEYARD. DAY

The Verger is looking through his glasses. He gives a start. Through his glasses we can see the sheep in tin hats. He hurries to the urn – lifts the lid – and winds the phone.

SQUARE **(Out of vision)** Yes?

VERGER Captain Square, sir – they're moving towards you, dressed up as sheep with tin hats on.

SQUARE **(Out of vision)** What?

VERGER They're dressed up as sheep, with tin hats on.

SQUARE **(Out of vision)** You *are* drunk – get off the line.

INTERIOR. BOATHOUSE. DAY

Pike is looking through the periscope. Mainwaring and Sponge are helping Frazer out of his diving suit.

PIKE **(To Mainwaring)** Mr Mainwaring, sir, Mr Jones has reached the mill.

MAINWARING Good. **(He moves towards the door)** Come on – we'll go and wait for Sergeant Wilson and the others at the rendezvous – and then move in for the kill. **(He goes out of the door followed by Pike, Frazer – who has got out of his diving suit – and the others)**

PIKE Have you caught the dreaded bends yet?

TELECINE: EXTERIOR. GRAVEYARD. DAY

The Verger is looking through his glasses. The Vicar comes into the picture.

VICAR Ah, there you are, Mr Harman.

VERGER **(Turns, startled)** Oh hello, sir.

VICAR I've been looking for you everywhere. What are you doing?

VERGER Me, I'm er... bird watching, Your Reverence.

VICAR Really, I'd no idea that you were keen on ornithology.

The phone starts to ring – the Vicar looks around – crosses to the urn – lifts the lid and picks up the phone.

VICAR Hello. Vicar, Walmington-on-Sea Parish Church. Just a moment. It's for you, Verger. **(He hands the phone to the Verger)** It's a beautiful day don't you think? **(The Vicar goes)**

TELECINE: EXTERIOR. OUTSIDE MILL. DAY

Jones is standing up against the wall of the mill – he has just finished getting out of his log suit. He starts to climb the ladder. He still has the alarm clock dangling between his knees. As he is half-way up the ladder, the alarm goes off – he reaches down to try and turn it off – but he can't quite reach it.

INTERIOR. MILL. DAY

Square, the Sergeant and his men are looking out of the front window. Suddenly we hear the sound of an alarm clock.

SERGEANT Listen to that, sir – sounds like an alarm clock. **(The sound stops)**

SQUARE What? Must be my gold hunter. **(He pulls out his watch and listens to it)** Yes, it's started again – I knew it was reliable.

SERGEANT Sounded to me as if it came from the back, sir.

SQUARE (Pointing) Look, the Verger was right, they're all dressed up as sheep with tin hats on. How on earth did they do that?

SERGEANT Perhaps they're using midgets, sir.

Suddenly we see Jones' face at the back window behind them.

JONES We've won – we've won.

He throws the clock into the room, the Sergeant quickly picks it up and throws it back.

JONES Hurrah, we've… (As the alarm clock is thrown back – Jones tries to catch it and falls back with a muffled cry)

TELECINE: EXTERIOR. CLUMP OF TREES. DAY

Mainwaring, Wilson, Pike, Frazer, Walker and Godfrey and the rest of the platoon are watching the mill.

WALKER (Pointing) He's done it, sir – he's thrown the bomb in.

WILSON He's jumped on to one of the sails – I wonder why he did that?

MAINWARING Come on, we'll go and accept their surrender.

They all move rapidly out of the trees.

TELECINE: EXTERIOR. SAILS OF WINDMILL. DAY

Close up of Jones clinging to sails.

JONES Help – Mr Mainwaring – Help!

TELECINE: EXTERIOR. MILL. DAY

Mainwaring, Wilson and the rest are approaching the door. Mainwaring looks up.

MAINWARING (Shouting) Hold on, Jones, we'll get you down in a minute. (He knocks on the door with his stick) I'm just going to accept their surrender.

The door is opened by Captain Square.

SQUARE Yes?

MAINWARING We've won – I've come to accept your surrender.

SQUARE What are you talking about – we threw the bomb back.

MAINWARING Don't split hairs with me, sir – I tell you we've won.

Wilson, Frazer, Walker, Godfrey and Pike are standing in a little group slightly away from Mainwaring.

WALKER Blimey, look, the sails are moving.

Cut to long shot of windmill. The sails are moving round. A dummy figure of Jones is on one of the sails. Cut back to Mainwaring and Square at door.

SQUARE I refuse to surrender and that's that.

Wilson comes up to Mainwaring.

WILSON Excuse me, sir, the sails are moving.

MAINWARING (Looking up) What!

We can hear Jones' cries.

WILSON What are we going to do, sir?

MAINWARING Leave this to me, Wilson. (He waves his walking stick) I'll stick something in the machinery. (He goes into the door of the mill)

Cut to long shot of sails going round – we can hear Jones' voice, 'Don't panic – don't panic'. Mainwaring comes out of the door with his walking stick broken off at the hilt. Cut to tight group of the platoon with their heads going round and round watching the sails. Cut to the sails going faster. The dummy figure of Jones falls off.

TELECINE: EXTERIOR. RIVER. DAY

Jones lands in the river with a splash – he wades for the bank and starts to climb up.

SERIES FOUR **EPISODE THREE**

Recorded: Friday 31/7/70

Original transmission: Friday 9/10/70, 8.00–8.30pm

Original viewing figures = 13.2 million

ARTHUR LOWE .... CAPTAIN MAINWARING
JOHN LE MESURIER .... SERGEANT WILSON
CLIVE DUNN .... LANCE CORPORAL JONES
JOHN LAURIE .... PRIVATE FRAZER
JAMES BECK .... PRIVATE WALKER
ARNOLD RIDLEY .... PRIVATE GODFREY
IAN LAVENDER .... PRIVATE PIKE
BILL PERTWEE .... ARP WARDEN
JANET DAVIES .... MRS PIKE
ERIK CHITTY .... MR SEDGEWICK

PLATOON...... COLIN BEAN, HUGH HASTINGS, VIC TAYLOR, LESLIE NOYES, ... FREDDIE WILES, FRANK GODFREY, DESMOND CULLUM-JONES, ... FREDDIE WHITE, GEORGE HANCOCK, KEN WADE

STUNTMAN .... JOHNNY SCRIPPS

Boots, Boots, Boots

• BARBARA KRONIG REMEMBERS •

'It's with much pleasure that I look back at my time with *Dad's Army*. Firstly, it was fun because both the production team and the cast got on so well together. The atmosphere in rehearsal, studio and on location, was always relaxed and truly good-humoured. I'm sure that both Jimmy and David were having kittens at times, but it never showed.

'From a costume point of view, the production afforded me the opportunity for some interesting research, and some of the funniest occasions of my career. The series I costumed called for a change from the early issue of fatigues to one more approximating the universally worn Army uniform.

'Over a period of about three weeks, I spent quite a bit of time at the Imperial War Museum, reading up all sorts of records involving the Home Guard, and came across several amusing items. One was the fact that at some point an error had been made by a manufacturer of general issue forage caps with the result that they buttoned the wrong way; the Army rejected them and they went to the Home Guard, as did a set of experimental puttees tried out for the ATS and found wanting. Area badges used in *Dad's Army* were selected rather ambiguously so as not to tread on regional toes! But individual platoon badges were left to individual choice and I thought CP for Croft/Perry seemed the most apt.

'Army uniform is not the most comfortable, or cool, thing to wear and I can remember most clearly how much of it was taken off and left about between shots, with the poor dressers going around frantically getting everyone back into it again.

'A couple of particular incidents have stuck in my mind. During one of the episodes, Mainwaring wanted a flock of sheep dressed in as much uniform as possible to fool a threatened German invasion. The local farmers provided the sheep and then vanished. This left Brian Willis, Pip Bryce and myself, all sophisticated Londoners who had never been near a sheep in our lives, to round them up and endeavour to costume them! With cries of "Here sheepy-weapy, come to mummy/daddy then", we did our humble best as they shot off in all directions – much to the amusement of a large crowd, the cast and crew. We did it, though, the proof is on film.

'A similar thing happened when the ceremonial "ram" had to be dressed in the outfit designed for it in "The Big Parade". It was the biggest, most stubborn creature and nothing would induce it to stand up. Several hefty farmers solved that problem. Nothing so easy for the make-up artistes, though. They had to eradicate some dark patches on the small goat that Mainwaring had found for his outfit and was supposed to be white. The girls trying to hold it and apply the requisite foundation was a sight not to be forgotten.

'All in all, it was a great time on a great production.'

BARBARA KRONIG
Costume Designer

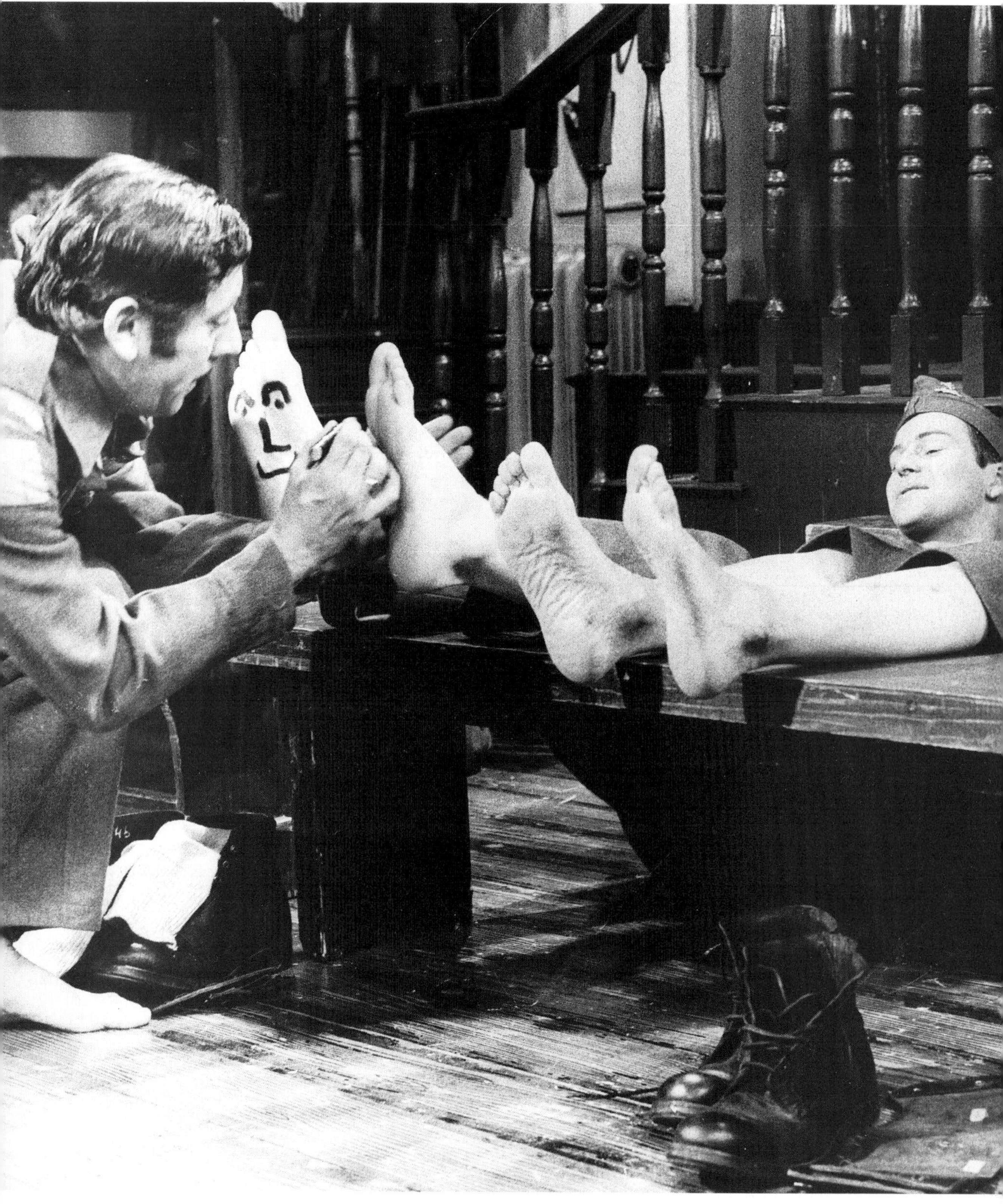

Boots, Boots, Boots

INTERIOR. CHURCH HALL. DAY

The platoon are lined up on parade. Mainwaring is addressing them.

MAINWARING ...so, to sum up – whatever mode of transport we use, bicycles, Jones' van or other forms of vehicular transport, in the end it all boils down to one thing – the three 'F's. (**Walker does a take**) Fast feet – functional feet – and last – fit feet. A soldier without his feet is useless – and therefore, during the next few weeks, we are going to concentrate on getting our feet fighting fit. (**Mainwaring has under his arm two scrolls printed on glazed linen**) Now, I've managed to get hold of two diagrams issued by the Royal Army Medical Corps. This is the first one as a foot should be. (**He takes one of the scrolls from under his arm – unrolls it and holds it in front of him – it is about two foot by one foot, and contains a diagram of the sole of a foot in a boot – he points to the toes**) Now – (**He points to the big toe**) This is the first metatarsal.

JONES Permission to speak, sir? I am not as other men – my feet are different to that chart.

WALKER Don't tell me they're webbed.

Jones reacts.

MAINWARING Quiet, Walker. What do you mean, different, Jones?

JONES Well, sir, that bit you're pointing to, attached to the top of the foot.

MAINWARING The first metatarsal, you mean.

JONES Well, sir – I have not got a first... er... what you called it. I've got a big toe.

MAINWARING Metatarsal's the medical term for toe, Jones.

JONES Oh, thank you, sir.

MAINWARING So, there you have it. (**He points to the toes one by one**) First metatarsal, second metatarsal, third metatarsal, fourth metatarsal. (**Points to little toe**) and last but not least.

WALKER The little piggy who went 'wee, wee' all the way home.

Wilson grins.

MAINWARING It's not a laughing matter, Wilson.

Mainwaring hands Wilson the second scroll.

MAINWARING Hold this. (**He points to his own diagram**) You'll notice the perfect outline of this boot – plenty of room for the feet – no cramping or pinching. Now, in contrast, I'm going to let you see something rather nasty. Right, Wilson, show them your foot.

WILSON I beg your pardon, sir?

MAINWARING Unroll your foot.

WILSON I don't quite…

MAINWARING The chart, Sergeant.

WILSON Oh, I see.

He unrolls the chart and holds it in front of him. The chart contains the outline of a foot pinched in a badly fitting, pointed shoe. The toes are all cramped and there is a large bunion.

MAINWARING Now, you see what can happen to a foot in a badly fitting shoe. **(Coldly)** Now the first thing I want to do is to inspect your feet to see that your boots are fitting. **(He hands his chart to Wilson – who gets rid of them – and starts to go down the line. He stops in front of the first man – Private Sponge – he bends right down and feels his feet)** That's all right, Sponge. **(Mainwaring straightens up and feels a slight pain in his back. He passes on to Pike – bends right down, feels his feet – and has even more trouble straightening up)**

PIKE Are my metatarsals all right, sir?

MAINWARING Yes, very good, Pike – very good. **(Mainwaring's face screws up with pain as he puts his hand on his back)**

WILSON Allow me, sir. **(He helps Mainwaring up)**

MAINWARING Thank you, Sergeant… **(Mainwaring passes on to Godfrey, tries to bend down and finds it too much)** …Lift your foot up, Godfrey. **(Godfrey lifts his foot a few inches)** Right up.

Godfrey tries to lift his foot higher – staggers – and grabs Mainwaring's head and forces him down. Mainwaring gives a cry of agony.

MAINWARING This is absurd – get me a chair, Wilson.

WILSON Yes, sir. Get a chair, Pike.

GODFREY None of us getting any younger – are we, sir?

MAINWARING **(Coldly)** Look to your front, Godfrey.

Pike puts the chair down – Godfrey sinks into it with a sigh.

GODFREY Thank you, Sergeant.

MAINWARING That's to put your foot on, Godfrey.

GODFREY I'm so sorry, sir.

He gets up and puts his foot on the chair – Mainwaring feels his foot.

MAINWARING Very good fit – they'll take you 20 miles.

GODFREY Thank you for your confidence, sir.

Mainwaring passes on to Walker.

MAINWARING Right, Walker – put your foot up.

WALKER No need to worry about me, Mr Mainwaring – my feet are fine.

MAINWARING I said put your foot up.

WALKER Well… I er…

MAINWARING Do as you're told at once, Walker.

Walker very reluctantly puts his foot on the chair.

MAINWARING Those boots look rather big – I've never noticed before that you had such big feet.

WALKER **(With sickly grin)** Well, you know what they say, sir – big feet – big er…

MAINWARING **(To Walker)** Big what? What's he talking about? I asked you a question, Wilson – big what?

Wilson whispers in his ear. Cut to big close up of Mainwaring.

MAINWARING **(Staring hard at Walker)** Really. **(Pause – pointing to boot)** There's something strange here, Wilson.

WILSON Strange, sir?

MAINWARING Yes – strange.

He gets hold of Walker's boot. It has no sole on it and lifts right up. He turns it round to the side. The boot is a false cover, underneath Walker is wearing a very smart pair of black and white correspondent shoes.

MAINWARING What's the meaning of this, Walker?

WALKER Well, they're more comfy.

MAINWARING Those boots are Government property – you've completely ruined them.

WALKER No, Mr Mainwaring – they're not the ones I was issued with. I've got 200 pairs of army boots in stock. Any time you want…

MAINWARING That's enough. See me afterwards.

He passes down the line. Wilson moves the chair. They stop in front of Frazer, who puts his foot on the chair. Mainwaring feels the boot.

MAINWARING That boot feels a little tight to me, Frazer.

FRAZER No, they're fine.

Mainwaring lifts up his gaiter and sees that Frazer has no socks on.

MAINWARING Why aren't you wearing any socks?

FRAZER I never wear socks. A Highlander has no need of such fancy frivolities – up there we never molly-coddle our extremities. **(Turning furiously to Walker)** And if you make a remark about kilts – I shall strike you down where you stand.

MAINWARING All right, Frazer. All right.

He passes on to Jones, who puts his foot up.

JONES No need to worry about my feet, sir – when I was in India my feet were the talk of the continent. One day I was strolling nonchalantly through the peasaw, by way of the bazaar, on my way to the river. I noticed a young native woman doing a bit of dobering so I quickly whipped off my boots and socks, to wash my feet, you understand, when suddenly the native woman started murmuring towards me. 'Son da bahara, son da bahara', she said, then I noticed something that I hadn't noticed before, she was stripped to the waist – they do a lot of that out there, sir.

MAINWARING Yes, all right, Jones. **(Feeling them)** They certainly seem in tiptop condition.

JONES Yes, sir. I bathe them in cold tea.

MAINWARING Cold tea?

JONES Yes, sir, I learnt that in the Sudan – always used to soak our feet in cold tea in the Sudan.

GODFREY What a good idea – Indian or China?

MAINWARING **(Coldly)** Don't be insolent.

He steps back and addresses the men.

MAINWARING Now, it's quite obvious to me that we have got to do a lot of work to bring our feet up to scratch. So, starting next weekend, we are going to do a course of long route marches.

TELECINE: MONTAGE OF MARCHING

Close up of feet and agonised expressions on men's faces.

INTERIOR. CHURCH HALL. DAY

The platoon march into the hall, Wilson and Mainwaring are at the head.

WILSON Mark time – platoon, halt. Left turn – stand at ease.

Jones halts.

MAINWARING Well done, men – well done – that was five miles yesterday – and seven miles today. Now, on the command 'fall out' – I want you to take your boots off and have your feet ready for inspection. Corporal Jones!

JONES Yes, sir?

MAINWARING I'll inspect their feet in five minutes.

Mainwaring and Wilson cross to the office.

JONES **(Stepping out in front of the platoon – looks towards the door – as soon as Mainwaring and Wilson have gone into the office, he addresses the men in the style of Mainwaring)** Well done, men – well done. Well, you heard what he said – fall out. Platoon, fall out.

INTERIOR. SIDE OFFICE. DAY

Mainwaring sits at his desk. Wilson is standing beside it.

MAINWARING That's better – it's good to get the weight off one's feet. Now then, Wilson, I've brought you in here because...

WILSON Excuse me, sir – I wonder if I might be allowed to sit down as well.

MAINWARING Why? Don't you feel well?

WILSON No, I feel fine, sir – a little tired, perhaps.

MAINWARING What's the matter – didn't you sleep well?

WILSON Not for this last two or three hours.

MAINWARING Sit down if you must.

Wilson pulls up a chair and sits beside the desk.

WILSON That's very thoughtful of you, sir.

MAINWARING You and I have a certain position to uphold in this platoon, Wilson.

WILSON Yes, sir?

MAINWARING Now, I regard myself as a pretty shrewd judge of character.

WILSON Yes, sir.

MAINWARING And I think, over the years we've been together – I've got to know your character pretty well. You're not the brash extrovert type who's always bawling and shouting about, you handle the men in a quiet, subtle way.

WILSON Thank you, sir.

MAINWARING I also know that you are a very shy, sensitive man, Wilson – therefore I make a point of never doing anything to embarrass you, or show you up in front of the platoon.

WILSON Thank you, sir.

MAINWARING That's why I didn't ask you to have your feet inspected with the rest of the platoon.

WILSON That's very kind of you, sir.

MAINWARING So, before we go into the hall to inspect the men's feet – I'll inspect yours in here, in private.

WILSON Really, sir, there's no need to inspect my feet – they're perfectly all right.

MAINWARING No doubt they are, but I must make sure. Take your boots off. **(Pause)** Come on, Wilson, it's only me. **(Pause)** Look, we can't have one rule for some, and another rule for others.

WILSON In that case, sir – who's going to inspect your feet?

MAINWARING Well I er... I er... I see your point, Wilson.

Pause – Mainwaring leans across to Wilson and lowers the tone of his voice.

MAINWARING Look, I'll show you mine, if you show me yours.

They both start to remove boots.

INTERIOR. CHURCH HALL. DAY

Three benches are laid in a semi-circle in front of the stage. The platoon are all taking their boots off. Frazer, Godfrey, Walker and Pike are sitting on the bench staring at their bare feet. Jones is standing beside them, also in his bare feet.

PIKE Just look at my feet, all swollen and nasty – my Mum will be furious when she sees them – on top of that – I've got a terrible headache.

WALKER You know why you've got a headache don't you, Frank?

PIKE No – why, Joe?

WALKER Well, you see, when you don't use your brains a lot, they drop down into your feet – and all this marching's sent them rushing back to your head again – that's what makes it ache.

PIKE That's not true, Joe.

WALKER Ain't it?

JONES Now, come on – all lie down on your backs with your feet on the benches.

They all lie on the floor, groaning.

JONES Come on – don't make all that fuss – right, I'm going to tell Mr Mainwaring we're ready.

He crosses the hall in his bare feet.

INTERIOR. SIDE OFFICE. DAY

Mainwaring is sitting in his chair one side of the desk. Wilson is sitting in a chair the other side of the desk. They both have their bare feet on the desk facing each other. Jones comes through the door.

JONES Feet ready for inspection, sir. I... er... (He breaks off as he sees Mainwaring and Wilson) Al Sunda Baham.

INTERIOR. CHURCH HALL. DAY

The platoon are all lying on their backs in a semi-circle in front of the stage. Their feet are raised in the air on benches. Frazer and Pike are lying with their feet away from the audience.

PIKE My feet ain't half sore, Mr Frazer.

FRAZER So are mine, laddy – you'll just have to put up with it.

WALKER (Getting up) I've got the very thing 'ere – it's a stick of foot salve. They're sixpence each.

FRAZER I don't want that rubbish.

WALKER Look, you haven't tried it yet, have you?

PIKE I wish you'd put some on my feet, Joe.

WALKER All right, I will. (Walker draws two little faces on the bottom of Pike's feet. Nobody can see what he is doing) Then, if you don't like it – you don't have to buy it. How's that, Pikey?

PIKE Much better, Joe.

WALKER How about you, Taff?

FRAZER Well I...

PIKE It's very soothing, Mr Frazer.

FRAZER Oh, all right.

WALKER (Starting to draw on Frazer's feet) You won't regret this.

FRAZER Just so long as I don't have to pay for it.

WALKER No, you needn't buy it if you don't want to. I bet that feels better already.

FRAZER Aye – it's not bad – not bad at all.

The office door opens. Jones comes in – and Walker lies down in his place.

JONES Right – attention.

Cut to long shot of row of feet. We see them all except Frazer's and Pike's. The feet are lying at all angles. On the command 'attention' they all straighten up. Mainwaring and Wilson come in.

JONES All ready, sir. Permission to speak, sir?

MAINWARING Yes, Jones?

JONES I should like to volunteer to be the first one to have his feet inspected.

MAINWARING Very well.

Jones lies down at the top of the half circle – his feet up on the bench. Mainwaring runs his stick up the middle of Jones' foot – the toes curl up. Jones jumps up.

MAINWARING Very good reflexes, Jones.

JONES Thank you, sir.

Mainwaring passes down the line, inspecting the feet.

MAINWARING Not bad, men – but we've still got a lot of work to do. From tomorrow I intend to embark on an intensive feet-hardening course. (Groans from men) Even though some of us are not as young as we used to be, I'm sure we shall all put a bold face on it. (He reaches the end of the line – suddenly he sees Pike's and Frazer's feet. Cut to close up of the two pairs of feet. For the first time we see the faces on them)

TELECINE: FOOTBALL FIELD. DAY

Mainwaring, dressed as referee, trots past camera, leading

Wilson, Walker, Jones, Frazer, Godfrey and Pike. They are all dressed in football togs. Picture from waist upwards only. Mainwaring holds the ball above his head – blows the whistle, and throws it in. Cut to their feet, they are not wearing any boots or socks. Close up of bare feet kicking ball and agonised facial expressions.

TELECINE: BEACH. DAY

Low angle shot of platoon in running shorts and singlets – they are all in the 'on your marks' position for a race. Mainwaring has a starting pistol. We do not see the surface on which they are running at this stage.

MAINWARING On your marks – get set – go!

He fires the pistol.

Wide angle shot of platoon attempting to race – with bare feet along pebbles on beach. Close ups of bare feet and agonised expressions.

TELECINE: SEA SHORE: DAY

Close up of Mainwaring

MAINWARING Platoon, 'shun – slope arms – left turn – by the right – quick march!

Cut to platoon marching – we still do not see their feet.

MAINWARING (Out of vision) Pick those feet up – come on, right up.

The platoon does so – water splashes upwards into frame from below. Long shot of platoon. We see that they are drilling in the sea.

MAINWARING (Out of vision) About turn.

The platoon does so. Close up of Mainwaring.

MAINWARING Left, right, left, right, left, right.

Cut to close up of Hodges, the Warden.

HODGES Having a nice paddle?

Cut to close up of Mainwaring.

MAINWARING About turn, left, right, etc.

Cut to close up of Hodges.

HODGES If the Nazis invade now, you'll be able to meet them half-way.

Cut to close up of Mainwaring.

MAINWARING Ignore him, men.

Mainwaring takes his place at the head of the platoon as they draw level. Cut to long shot of platoon marching along in the sea, level with the shore.

• DAVID CROFT REMEMBERS •

'Whenever we needed a double or stuntman for Arthur, we always tried hiring Johnny Scripps. He was marvellous and, in my opinion, looked just like Arthur. He could also fall over in a funny way, again like Arthur.

'In this episode Captain Mainwaring disappears into a great big hole on the beach, and it was Johnny that went down. The scene was very difficult because to dig a hole of any depth at the water's edge is virtually impossible; before you know it, the hole has filled with water again, and the sand around it collapsed; something that was dug to four feet is suddenly back to two-feet deep. To get around the problem I got four blokes to dig like hell, then I filmed the sequence extremely quickly.

'We filmed the beach scenes at Winterton, but had to be careful because you couldn't spend too much time looking out to sea just in case a boat went by.'

MAINWARING Left, right, left, right.

Cut to close up of Hodges.

HODGES I shouldn't go too far that way, Mr Mainwaring.

Cut to platoon – still marching. Cut to close up of Hodges.

HODGES There's a great big…

Cut to Mainwaring at head of platoon. He suddenly disappears under the surface.

HODGES (Out of vision) That's it.

INTERIOR. FRANK PIKE'S BEDROOM. NIGHT

Close up of Pike – he is in bed, asleep. There is a night light burning. Pan up to wall above bed – it is covered with photos of film stars 1939–41. We can hear the music in the background of 'If I had a talking picture of you'. Pan down to Frank's head. He is sleeping peacefully – suddenly we hear the faint sound of marching feet. The sound gets louder. Pike looks worried and starts to toss and turn. The sound of marching feet gets louder and starts to drown the music. We can hear Mainwaring's voice 'Come on, left, right, left, right, pick 'em up'.

PIKE (Calling out faintly in his sleep) Mum – mum.

The sound of the marching is now very loud.

PIKE (Louder – still asleep) Mum – mum.

Suddenly he sits bolt upright in bed and screams – he shouts at the top of his voice. 'Mum – mum.' Cut to long shot of bed – he is wearing a huge pair of rubber clown's feet. Cut to door, Mrs Pike comes in, in her dressing gown and switches on the light.

MRS PIKE What on earth's the matter, Frank?

She crosses over to the bed.

PIKE (Pointing to his feet) Look! (Cut to feet sticking out of the bed clothes – they are now quite normal) My feet!

MRS PIKE There's nothing wrong with your feet, Frank. (She covers them up)

PIKE I had a terrible nightmare, Mum. I dreamt that my feet were all huge and swollen and horrible.

MRS PIKE (Stroking his head) Never mind, it's all over now – you go back to sleep. It's all that marching you've been doing. I'm going to have a few words to say to Captain Mainwaring tomorrow.

PIKE He's only trying to make our feet tough.

MRS PIKE Well, your feet won't take it, you've got sensitive feet – you've always had sensitive feet since you were a child – it runs in the family, your Uncle George had such sensitive feet he didn't know where to put them. (Tucking him in) Now, do you want a hot drink?

PIKE No thanks, mum.

MRS PIKE All right then. (She crosses to the door)

PIKE Mum?

MRS PIKE Yes.

PIKE Good night.

MRS PIKE Good night, Frank.

PIKE Mum?

MRS PIKE Yes, Frank.

PIKE Can I have a glass of water?

MRS PIKE I'll get you one – I'll leave the light on.

PIKE Mum?

MRS PIKE Yes?

PIKE Kitchen water – not bathroom water.

INTERIOR. CHURCH HALL. DAY

Walker, Jones, Frazer and Godfrey are gathered round the notice board outside the office door.

WALKER (Pointing to the notice) Blimey, look at that – another route march on Sunday – 20 miles! This is ridiculous.

JONES We'll never make it, Joe – it will kill us.

GODFREY Oh dear – I don't think I can take any more.

JONES Can't you think of some way to get us out of it, Joe?

WALKER Why do you always expect me to get you out of everything?

FRAZER Because you're the one who always has the 'smart ideas'.

WALKER Well, as a matter of fact I have got an idea – it will cost us a few bob.

JONES That doesn't matter – what is it?

WALKER All we've got to do is to make Mr Mainwaring's feet uncomfortable, so that he can't march very far.

JONES How can we do that?

WALKER Simple – get hold of a... Look out!

Mrs Pike comes into the hall and pushes Frank towards the office door.

MRS PIKE Come on, Frank – I'm going to have this out with Mr Mainwaring – here and now.

PIKE Oh Mum! I feel such a fool.

MRS PIKE I can't help that. (She nods to Jones and the others) Good evening. (They all chorus 'good evening'. Mrs Pike opens the office door and pushes Pike in front of her and they both go in – the door closes)

INTERIOR. OFFICE. DAY

Wilson is in the office alone – he looks up as Mrs Pike and Frank enter.

WILSON Oh, hello, Mavis.

MRS PIKE I want to speak to Mr Mainwaring, Arthur.

WILSON He hasn't arrived yet.

MRS PIKE Have you seen Frank's feet?

WILSON (Smirking) Why, has he lost them?

MRS PIKE Really, Arthur, this is no time for stupid jokes. Have you looked at Frank's feet.

WILSON Er no... not lately.

MRS PIKE They're in a terrible state – he woke up screaming in the night.

WILSON I never heard him... oh.

MRS PIKE Arthur!

There is an embarrassed pause.

PIKE Mum, Uncle Arthur lives miles away – how could he hear me in the night?

MRS PIKE Never mind about that – stand over there. Now

listen, Arthur, you're going to tell Mr Mainwaring that Frank is not going on any more route marches.

WILSON I can't do that, Mavis.

Mrs Pike crosses over to Wilson and hisses in his ear.

MRS PIKE **(Across table)** Well, if you don't – and Frank wakes up in the night again, you won't be there to hear it.

She quickly goes. There is a pause.

PIKE Uncle Arthur – I've got an idea, if Mr Mainwaring's feet hurt – he wouldn't be able to take us on that route march, would he?

WILSON No, no – he wouldn't.

PIKE Why don't we buy another pair of boots exactly like Mr Mainwaring's only a bit smaller and swap them over.

WILSON What a wonderful idea – that's awfully clever. I bet nobody else would think of an idea like that.

INTERIOR. CHURCH HALL. DAY

WALKER All we've got to do is buy another pair of boots exactly like Mr Mainwaring's – only a bit smaller and swap them over.

JONES 'E's bound to rumble it, Joe.

WALKER No, he won't if we go to the same shop where he always buys his boots. We'll just make the new pair look a bit worn and he'll never know the difference.

GODFREY That's awfully clever. I bet nobody else would think of an idea like that.

INTERIOR. SEDGEWICK'S SHOE SHOP. DAY

It is a little old fashioned shoe shop with shoe boxes piled high to the ceiling. The door opens – there is a bell on a spring which rings furiously. Walker, Frazer, Jones and Godfrey troop in.

WALKER **(Whispering to them)** Just leave all the talking to me. **(To Godfrey)** Now don't forget, Charlie, when I give you the signal, say you feel faint and you want a glass of water.

GODFREY Yes, all right. A glass of water.

FRAZER This is going to cost us a fortune.

WALKER Look out.

A little old man comes from the back of the shop – it is Mr Sedgewick.

MR SEDGEWICK Good afternoon, gentlemen.

WALKER Good afternoon – my friend 'ere wants a pair of brown boots. **(He points to Jones)**

MR SEDGEWICK Are you sure you don't want black boots, brown boots are for officers only.

WALKER Well, he's going to be an officer, aren't you?

JONES That's right – I'm going to be an officer.

MR SEDGEWICK **(Looking at Jones' ribbons)** Well, you've certainly got the experience to be an officer. What size?

JONES I think I'm going to be a big officer.

WALKER What size boots?

JONES Eights.

WALKER Mr Mainwaring always buys his boots here, doesn't he?

MR SEDGEWICK That's right.

WALKER He wants the same sort as Mr Mainwaring has. **(Kicking Jones)** Don't you?

JONES Yes I do. I want the same as Mr Mainwaring has.

MR SEDGEWICK Right.

He starts to look through the boxes.

FRAZER How much are they?

MR SEDGEWICK 35s a pair. **(He has his back to them)**

FRAZER **(Hissing to Walker)** That's 7s each! Ask him if he's got anything cheaper.

WALKER Shut up.

Mr Sedgewick takes down a box.

MR SEDGEWICK Here you are.

He takes the boots out of the box. Walker signals to Jones.

JONES Oh, look, Mr Godfrey's not well.

Godfrey has sunk into a chair and is fanning himself.

GODFREY Can I have a glass of water, please?

MR SEDGEWICK I'll get one. **(He goes out of the back of the shop)**

WALKER **(Grabbing the boots)** Quick, change these over for a half a size smaller than Mr Mainwaring takes.

All except Godfrey – they rush to the boxes.

JONES Right. **(He grabs the boots from Walker and runs up the ladder)** What size does Mr Mainwaring take?

WALKER He takes a... I don't know, what size boots does Mr Mainwaring take, Taff?

FRAZER How should I know?

WALKER Do you know, Charlie?

GODFREY Know what?

WALKER Never mind – look, as soon as he comes back with the glass of water, drink it quickly and ask for another. Look out!

Mr Sedgewick returns with the water.

MR SEDGEWICK **(To Godfrey)** Here you are, sir – I'm sorry you're not feeling well.

He drinks.

GODFREY Thank you.

FRAZER That wasn't enough.

He takes the water.

GODFREY Do you think I might have another?

MR SEDGEWICK (Puzzled) Certainly. (He quickly goes)

JONES (To Walker) You didn't ask him what size boots Mr Mainwaring takes.

WALKER I didn't have time, did I… (To Godfrey) Look, as soon as he gives you the glass of water, drink it down and ask for another one.

GODFREY I don't think I can manage any more.

WALKER You'll have to force yourself. While he's drinking the glass of water, Taff, you ask what size boots Mr Mainwaring takes.

Mr Sedgewick returns with the glass of water and a jug.

MR SEDGEWICK I thought I'd bring plenty.

He hands the glass to Godfrey. Godfrey manfully gulps it down.

WALKER Give him some more.

Mr Sedgewick starts to pour more water into Godfrey's glass. His hand is very shaky.

WALKER 'Ere, let me help you.

He gets hold of Mr Sedgewick's hand and shakes it – the water goes everywhere but in the glass.

FRAZER By the way, what size boots does Mr Mainwaring take?

MR SEDGEWICK Mr Mainwaring's got a very small foot. He takes a 6½ – why?

FRAZER Well, I er…

Godfrey is now finishing his third glass.

WALKER You want some more, don't you, Mr Godfrey?

Godfrey reacts.

Mr Sedgewick pours some more water into the glass.

WALKER Steady! Steady! You're spilling it.

Walker grabs Mr Sedgewick's hand and shakes it.

FRAZER (Whispering) You're dicing with death, filling him up with water like this.

GODFREY I think I've had enough, thank you.

WALKER Jonesey, 'ere you want a drink, don't you?

JONES Eh – oh yes, I want a drink – after all those years in the Sudan, I can never get enough water. (He drinks out of the jug)

WALKER He had a terrible time in the Sudan, you know – nearly died of thirst.

JONES I nearly died of thirst in the Sudan you know.

WALKER Oh look, he's drunk it all. I didn't have any – all this drinking's made me thirsty. Go and get some more.

He gives Mr Sedgewick the jug – the old man takes it and goes out of the back.

JONES He's a very nice man.

WALKER Quick, change these. (He thrusts the boots into Jones' hands. Jones runs up the ladder) We want a six.

JONES A six – a six – don't panic – don't panic. (He is pulling boots and shoes out of their boxes, they are falling all over the place) I've got it, I've got it. (He quickly changes the boots over and comes down the ladder)

Mr Sedgewick comes back with the jug. He sees all the boots on the floor.

MR SEDGEWICK What's happened?

FRAZER We saw a mouse.

JONES Yes, it was mostly a mouse.

Walker quickly thrusts the boots into the box. Mr Sedgewick takes them from him.

MR SEDGEWICK Doesn't he want to try them on?

WALKER No, he won't show you his feet – he's sensitive about his toes.

MR SEDGEWICK What's wrong with them?

WALKER He had his toes tortured in the Sudan, didn't you?

JONES Yes, that's right – them Fuzzie Wuzzies tortured my toes terribly – terrible toe torturers they were.

WALKER Right, pay the man, Taff.

FRAZER What?

WALKER Give him his 35s.

Frazer mutters and hands over the money – they all rush for the door.

MR SEDGEWICK Wait a minute, what about the coupons?

WALKER Sure, how many do you want? (He pulls out a huge bundle)

MR SEDGEWICK Where on earth did you get all those clothing coupons?

WALKER I've got a large family – 'ere you are. (He gives Mr Sedgewick a sheet of coupons)

GODFREY May I be excused?

WALKER Not now – come on.

Walker pushes them all out of the shop. Mr Sedgewick looks at the boots and shoes strewn all over the floor.

MR SEDGEWICK (Starting to put the shoes back in the boxes) That's funny, I've never seen mice in here before.

The boxes have all been put back neatly in their place. Mr Sedgewick is just putting the last one in position. The shop bell rings – Wilson and Pike come in.

MR SEDGEWICK **(Turning)** Good afternoon, gentlemen.

WILSON Good afternoon. I'd like a pair of brown boots for er… this young man. **(He points to Pike)**

MR SEDGEWICK Brown, eh – is he going to be an officer as well?

WILSON What?

MR SEDGEWICK Well, only officers are allowed to wear brown boots, you know.

WILSON Oh, are they? I mean yes – he's going to be an officer.

MR SEDGEWICK He's a bit young for an officer.

WILSON Well, he's awfully keen.

MR SEDGEWICK I bet you're a proud father.

WILSON I don't quite follow you.

MR SEDGEWICK Your son, becoming an officer.

WILSON He's er… not my son.

MR SEDGEWICK **(Staring hard at them both)** That's funny, I could have sworn…

WILSON **(Coldly)** Would you mind showing us the boots, please?

MR SEDGEWICK I'm so sorry – what size does the young man take?

PIKE Nines, please.

MR SEDGEWICK Nine – let me see.

He turns his back to them and starts looking at the boxes.

PIKE I want the same sort that Mr Mainwaring always has.

MR SEDGEWICK Don't they all? Here we are.

He pulls out a box and takes out the boots.

WILSON **(Sinking into a chair)** Oh dear.

MR SEDGEWICK Will one glass be sufficient?

WILSON What?

MR SEDGEWICK Water – you are feeling faint, aren't you?

WILSON That's awfully clever of you – how did you guess?

MR SEDGEWICK I'll get it. **(He goes)**

WILSON **(Picking up the boots and handing them to Pike)** Quick, Frank, change these for a six.

Pike takes the boots and runs up the ladder.

PIKE **(Pulling out boots)** Sevens – eights – twelves. I still can't find them.

WILSON Get up higher. **(He pulls out some more boots)**

PIKE Mum will be furious with you, making me go up high – you know I can't stand heights – I get terrible verdigris.

WILSON **(Pulling out a pair of boots)** It's all right – I've found a pair of sixes – you can come down.

Pike on ladder. Sedgewick returns. Sedgewick reacts. Pike reacts.

WILSON We er… saw a mouse.

MR SEDGEWICK That's all right – I've brought the cat.

INTERIOR. CHURCH HALL. DAY

Walker, Jones, Frazer and Godfrey are gathered in a small group in the corner of the hall. Walker has a piece of sticking plaster on his forehead.

JONES Good job Mr Mainwaring's wife makes him sleep with her in the air raid shelter every night – it makes it easy for you to change the boots over.

WALKER What do you mean, easy? **(He feels the bump on his forehead)** I nearly took the top of my head off getting through that low door.

FRAZER **(Lowering his voice)** You know, I've never met Mrs Mainwaring.

JONES It's funny you should mention that – neither have I.

FRAZER What's she look like?

WALKER She was sleeping in the top bunk. It was so dark – I could only see her outline. **(Lowers his voice)** She's a big woman.

FRAZER Big, eh!

WALKER Oh yes – you know, sort of…

GODFREY I think it's very caddish to talk about a lady like that.

JONES Well, we've never seen Mrs Mainwaring.

GODFREY That's no excuse.

Wilson comes through the main door – he has a piece of sticking plaster on his forehead, the same as Walker. Pike, who is talking to a group of men in the corner, hurries over to him.

PIKE Did you manage to change the boots over?

WILSON **(Looking round)** Keep your voice down.

PIKE Well – did you?

WILSON **(Feeling his forehead)** Yes.

PIKE You know, I've never seen Mrs Mainwaring – what's she like?

WILSON It was so dark I could hardly see anything.

PIKE You must have seen something.

WILSON Well she was rather – sort of… **(He gestures vaguely)**

Mainwaring comes in. They all chorus good morning.

MAINWARING Good morning. Fall the men in, Sergeant. I'm going to get the map. **(He crosses to the office door and goes in)**

WILSON Right, fall in – in three ranks.

They start to fall in.

INTERIOR. OFFICE. DAY

Mainwaring crosses to his desk, opens the drawer and takes out a map. He opens it on the table and looks at it. There is a knock on the back door.

MAINWARING Come in.

Mr Sedgewick comes in – he has a pair of boots in his hand.

MR SEDGEWICK Good morning, Mr Mainwaring. I've brought that pair of boots you left for repair last week.

MAINWARING But I thought you said that as leather was in such short supply, I'd have to wait a month.

MR SEDGEWICK I managed to find a bit – it was the least I could do – after all, you sent me all those customers.

MAINWARING **(Puzzled)** Really? **(Taking boots)** Thank you. I think I'll wear them now, these are pinching me a bit. **(He starts to change his boots)**

MR SEDGEWICK I'll put them on your account, Mr Mainwaring. **(He turns to go – stops and turns back)** I er... don't want to speak out of turn, Mr Mainwaring – but I think there's a few things you ought to know about your platoon.

MAINWARING Oh – what?

MR SEDGEWICK Well, they drink a lot. And they all want to be officers – you watch out, Mr Mainwaring – there's a lot of 'em – just can't wait to step into your shoes. Good morning. **(He goes)**

INTERIOR. CHURCH HALL. DAY

The platoon are all drawn up on parade, waiting.

WALKER **(Aside to Jones)** I give him half a mile before those boots start to hurt – and he has to pack up. What do you think, Jonesey?

JONES I think he'll manage longer than that – I give him a mile.

WALKER He'll never make a mile.

JONES And I say he will.

WALKER Ten bob?

JONES You're on.

MAINWARING There, that's better.

Mainwaring comes out of the office.

WILSON Platoon, attention.

MAINWARING Right, men, are we all ready? Fit and keen? Twenty miles is a long march, but if I can do it, so can you.

JONES Permission to speak, sir? As long as you can keep going, we shall be right behind you.

Frazer and Walker wink at each other.

MAINWARING Excellent – excellent. Platoon will move to the left in threes – right turn. **(They do so)** Jones, lead off in single file – and let's start out with a merry heart.

JONES With a merry heart – quick march.

They all whistle as Jones leads them out in single file.

SERIES FOUR **EPISODE FOUR**

Recorded: Saturday 27/6/70

Original transmission: Friday 16/10/70, 8.00–8.30pm

Original viewing figures = 14.5 million

ARTHUR LOWE . . . . CAPTAIN MAINWARING
JOHN LE MESURIER . . . . SERGEANT WILSON
CLIVE DUNN . . . . LANCE CORPORAL JONES
JOHN LAURIE . . . . PRIVATE FRAZER
JAMES BECK . . . . PRIVATE WALKER
ARNOLD RIDLEY . . . . PRIVATE GODFREY
IAN LAVENDER . . . . PRIVATE PIKE
BILL PERTWEE . . . . ARP WARDEN
JANET DAVIES . . . . MRS PIKE
MICHAEL KNOWLES . . . . ENGINEER OFFICER

PLATOON . . . . COLIN BEAN, HUGH HASTINGS, VIC TAYLOR

SGT – SAVE MY BOY!

Originally titled, 'The Mine'

• IAN LAVENDER REMEMBERS •

'The existence of such a young platoon member like Pike was based on Jimmy Perry's own experiences in the Home Guard. I always thought of Frank as sheltered and naïve, never an idiot, and although he'd do some childish things, I tried making everything he did logical.

'One of the main reasons *Dad's Army* became so successful was that everyone could watch it, and still can. The entire family can sit down and enjoy the programme without worrying about whether something should be seen by the kids, or if a scene might offend granny.

'Another reason for the success is the characters. Arthur Lowe and John Le Mesurier worked so well together, complementing each other's style. Arthur and John weren't bosom buddies or natural social companions, but they liked each other and were able to strike up a brilliant working relationship. In the show, meanwhile, the characters weren't the best of friends and had been flung together and couldn't escape – it was inspired casting and writing.

'I was the youngest and least experienced member of the cast but everyone took me under their wings from the very beginning and looked after me. They were wonderful. Arthur gave me my greatest piece of advice: during the first series I had little to do and one day he came over and said: "Look, don't worry if you haven't got much to do at the moment, that will come. Meanwhile, get yourself a funny costume and stand near me." So when I was asked to choose a scarf from the wardrobe department, I picked one with loud, clashing colours. I also ordered this awful garish orange cricketing jumper. I'm colour-blind but I knew the colours didn't go well together.

'Everybody came from a different background within the business, which meant they brought with them a vast range of experiences. I was relatively new to the profession, but eventually started receiving my own fan mail. Nothing really happened until about the third or fourth series, by which time the programme had taken off. I always got letters from young girls and old ladies, never anything in between. Sadly, I was not an idol for nubile 18-year-olds!

'I noticed that the public's reaction as a whole changed around that period; people wanted to talk about it all the time. I was receiving invites to various charity events, along with other comedy actors, but people's reaction to me, as opposed to them, was different – mainly in the words they used. People would approach mates of mine, like Malcolm McFee of *Please, Sir!*, and say: "Oh, that was dead funny last week." But to me it would be: "We do love your show." It was an affection that people had for it, rather than simply regarding it as just a funny show. I don't think it was ever the funniest thing on television, but it was ideal for all the family.

'It's over 20 years since the programme finished. Occasionally people ask if playing Pike held back my career. Essentially I'm offered comedy roles nowadays because that's what people know me for; I don't get many chances to play Hamlet so, yes, I've been held back in some ways. But what about all the work I've done because of playing Pike!'

IAN LAVENDER

SGT – SAVE MY BOY!

THE SIDE OFFICE

Walker, Jones, Godfrey and Frazer are sitting facing the blackboard, where Mainwaring has drawn a map of the town – from the Novelty Rock Emporium to Stones' Amusement Arcade. Mainwaring is lecturing by the board, Wilson standing beside him.

MAINWARING Right, pay attention, all of you. I've brought you in the scouts' dressing room because the Vicar made a special request to hold some function or other in the rest of the hall. Now, I want to review the tactical disposition of our forces in the light of the broader, strategical picture as it now is.

WALKER **(To Frazer)** In other words, 'where do we tell Jonesey to stick his bayonet?'.

MAINWARING That'll do, Walker. Hitler is across the Channel, licking the wounds that we gave him at Dunkirk, but make no mistake about it, desperate and dangerous, and perhaps the more so now that he's enmeshed without ally – the Russian Bear.

GODFREY I always thought they were Communists.

MAINWARING We won't go into that, Godfrey. In times of stress one can't be too choosey about one's bedfellows.

WALKER As Robinson Crusoe said when he met Man Friday.

MAINWARING **(Indicates blackboard)** Now, we stand here – shoulder to shoulder on the shores of dear old Blighty. In the middle there's Jack Tar ruling the waves, while in the skies above us are of course...

WALKER The Brylcream Boys.

MAINWARING The Brylcream... I shan't tell you again, Walker.

Pike enters.

MAINWARING You're late on parade, Pike.

PIKE Sorry, Mr Mainwaring, sir.

MAINWARING There's far too much of this laxity going on.

JONES What's he saying?

GODFREY There's too much laxity.

JONES What a funny thing to be giving a lecture about.

MAINWARING Well, Pike – what have you got to say for yourself?

PIKE My mum wouldn't let me have my tea until I tidied my room.

MAINWARING You should have come without your tea.

PIKE She won't let me come without me tea.

MAINWARING Well, from now on I'm taking a very serious view of absence without leave. Take his name, Sergeant.

WILSON Yes, sir.

MAINWARING Now, as I was saying. The enemy are drawn up in their phalanxes – er... have you taken his name, Sergeant?

WILSON Yes, sir.

MAINWARING I didn't see you write it down.

WILSON I don't have to write it down – I know it.

MAINWARING Wilson – when I tell you to take a man's name you must write it down so you don't forget it.

WILSON I'm hardly likely to forget it, am I? I've know him 19 years.

MAINWARING Sergeant Wilson, I'm not suggesting you're going to forget his name. What you might forget is the fact that you took it – do I make myself clear?

WILSON Yes, sir.

JONES He doesn't make himself clear to me.

MAINWARING Thank you. Now – as I was saying.

Wilson fumbles in his pocket and brings out a hankie. Mainwaring takes map off blackboard.

MAINWARING What are you doing, Wilson?

WILSON I'm – er – tying a knot in my handkerchief.

MAINWARING What for?

WILSON To remind me that I took Pike's name.

MAINWARING Wouldn't it be simpler to write it down?

WILSON I don't have any paper.

MAINWARING I should have thought that as the senior N.C.O., you would have enough initiative to borrow a piece of paper. Would somebody kindly lend Sergeant Wilson a piece of paper.

They all shake their heads.

FRAZER You said you didn't want us to have anything in our pockets when we came on duty – only name, rank and number.

GODFREY That was in case one of us was captured.

JONES You did not wish us to show any intelligence, sir.

WALKER Yes, some of us haven't got much to show.

Jones rises.

JONES I've had just about enough of your sarky remarks, Joe.

MAINWARING Jones, sit down, Walker, come and see me after the parade.

WALKER Blimey. It was only a joke.

MAINWARING War is no joke, Walker. Now – where was I?

FRAZER Why don't you stick it on the board.

MAINWARING Stick what on the board?

FRAZER Pike's name.

MAINWARING Ah, yes. A very good suggestion. Do that, Sergeant Wilson.

WILSON Very good, sir. **(He crosses to the board)** Have you got the chalk?

MAINWARING I haven't got the chalk.

WILSON Well, you did have the chalk when you made the diagram.

MAINWARING I haven't got the chalk.

JONES It's down there, sir. **(He indicates a ridge below the wall)**

WILSON Ah yes – so it is.

He writes the name 'Pike' on the blackboard.

PIKE I find that exceedingly humiliating.

FRAZER Don't be a baby. What's it matter?

PIKE I'll tell me mum and she won't give him his egg.

MAINWARING Now – as I was saying. Hitler and his lackey Mussolini are here – we are here, manning our strong points – which are the Novelty Rock Emporium and Stones' Amusement Arcade – with our advanced H.Q. at the Marigold Tea Rooms. Now, here we come to a very serious tactical point. It is quite on the cards that Adolf will have our positions taped – after all, we've been here for some time. He has air reconnaissance, photographs, espionage reports. He will observe our coming and our going. The point is – what are we going to do about it?

WALKER Don't go so often.

MAINWARING You're being very tedious today, Walker.

JONES When we was in the Sudan, sir, we used to employ a little wrinkle. When the Fuzzie Wuzzies discovered our headquarters, we used to shift to an elsewhere – then when they came at us with their assegais in the place where we wasn't, we used to fire at them from the place where we was. And after that, we used to go in with the cold steel. They couldn't abide that, sir – not up 'em. They didn't like it…

MAINWARING Thank you, Jones.

JONES I haven't finished yet, sir.

MAINWARING I think you made your point, Jones.

JONES **(To Godfrey)** He never lets you finish, you know.

MAINWARING What Jones was suggesting is, of course, standard military practice – always surprise the enemy. That's what I intend we shall do. Hitler thinks we are here – at the Novelty Rock Emporium – and here at Stones' Amusement Arcade. As from tonight, we shall be here. **(He points to a place in the centre)**. Now, **(He draws an oblong with a roof on it)** can anyone tell me what this is?

PIKE A little box with a dunce's cap on, sir.

WALKER No, that's the Harris Orphans' Holiday Home Hut.

MAINWARING Quite right, Walker. The Harris Orphans' Holiday Home Hut. It has a commanding position – good observation, all-round field of fire.

FRAZER And three dozen squealing kids.

MAINWARING No, Frazer, no. The orphans were evacuated to a place of safety after Dunkirk.

GODFREY They used to wear those little blue aprons and straw hats. And they made the most wonderful sandcastles. I always used to want to join them – they had such fun.

MAINWARING You're quite right, Godfrey – that's the place.

GODFREY Cissy and I invited three of them to tea once. We had cream buns. My, they did tuck in.

JONES I'd forgotten about cream buns.

PIKE The Marigold Tea Rooms used to fill them with cream while you waited.

WILSON I always used to lick the sugar off first.

MAINWARING Wilson!

WILSON Otherwise, it was so fine it went up my nose and made me sneeze.

MAINWARING Wilson. May we return to the tactical situation?

WILSON I'm sorry, sir.

MAINWARING As I was saying – it has a commanding position and an all-round field of fire. If Adolf attacks us in the Novelty Rock Emporium – well, from now on, we shall give him everything we've got from the Harris Orphans' Holiday Home Hut.

ALL Hut.

THE HOLIDAY HOME HUT. INTERIOR

It is the usual tongue-and-groove wooden affair on a bolted wooden frame. It was built to provide changing accommodation and shelter for about three dozen orphans and their escorts. Evidence of their occupation still remains in the form of buckets, spades – wooden ones of course – water-wings and swimming rings. There are sandcastle flags, buckets full of shells, old sand shoes – benches, lockers, card tables and deck chairs. The window has been sandbagged inside to provide a

firing slit. A partition – four foot behind the firing slit – provides a light trap so that those on duty can have a hurricane lamp.

There is an entrance back and front. The section are in operation, Frazer is on guard at the slit. Mainwaring enters, Wilson is asleep on the bench.

JONES Guard! Guard – 'shun!

MAINWARING All right, as you were.

JONES As you were.

Walker sits down – Godfrey remains standing.

JONES Godfrey, as you were, as the Officer said, at the double.

MAINWARING I thought Sergeant Wilson was in charge of the guard?

JONES That's right, sir – I'm second in charge.

MAINWARING Then where's Sergeant Wilson?

JONES Well, sir, he was feeling a bit drowsy so I told him to have forty winks.

MAINWARING Forty winks... The All Clear hasn't sounded. He's the guard commander, he should be alert all the time. (**He crosses to Wilson who is asleep on the locker top**)

JONES I promised I'd wake him if there was an invasion, sir.

MAINWARING Wilson. (**He shakes Wilson**) Wilson.

WILSON Oh, Mavis – give it a rest.

MAINWARING Wilson!

WILSON (**Waking**) Oh – ah – anything wrong?

MAINWARING Come outside, Wilson. (**He strides outside into the front of the hut**) Now, understand this, Wilson. (**He turns, Wilson is not with him**) Wilson! (**He strides back into the hut**) Wilson – I told you to come outside.

WILSON I was just putting on my boots, sir. (**He has one on**)

MAINWARING When I give an order, I expect you to jump to it. Follow me.

Mainwaring strides off, Wilson follows with one boot on – his cap is in his epaulette.

MAINWARING Where's your hat?

WILSON Here, sir.

MAINWARING Put it on. (**Wilson tries to put the hat on with one hand**)

WILSON Would you mind holding this, sir? (**He hands Mainwaring the boot**) (**Mainwaring takes it**) It's awfully difficult without a mirror. Is that nice?

MAINWARING Never mind about that. Now look here, Wilson, you're supposed to show an example to the men. How can I expect them to be on their toes during an alert when you're fast asleep.

WILSON Well, nothing was happening – I was just having a little nap. You see I've been having so many disturbed nights lately – what with air raids and one thing and another.

MAINWARING Yes – well I'm not concerned with your excuses – if excuses they be. You're going to have to pull yourself together, Wilson – the others manage to keep awake – you will have to do the same or stand down for somebody who can.

WILSON I'm sure if you're dissatisfied with my services, sir, I wouldn't dream of...

MAINWARING That is all, Sergeant. (**He turns on his heel and walks into the hut. He moves over to Frazer who is on guard at the slit**) Any sign of them, Frazer?

FRAZER Of course not. No Christian soul would venture out on a black night like this – it's too dark for a randy tom cat.

MAINWARING Yes – well be that as it may, don't take any chances. Keep a good look out.

FRAZER Will there be a cup of tea on the way to help clear my eyesight?

MAINWARING Pike will be over with it any moment. (**He moves to the main part of the hut**)

WALKER Any sign of the char, sir?

MAINWARING Pike'll be over soon. Now pay attention, everyone. Sergeant Wilson has just explained he had some difficulty in putting his hat on straight without a mirror. Now, I'll give you all a little wrinkle which you'll find invaluable. Er – lend me your cap, Wilson. (**Wilson hands it over**) Now, the scheme is that you put your hat on roughly – and then you find centre, so to speak, by running your forefingers up your nose and you align the buttons of your hat with that. (**He demonstrates as he speaks**). So, we may not have a mirror, but there's no reason why we shouldn't look well turned out, is there, eh? (**He has his cap on very badly**)

Enter Mrs Pike.

MRS PIKE Ooh, Arthur, it is dark and I swear someone was following me along the prom.

WILSON Oh really, Mavis, it's hardly likely, is it?

MRS PIKE Not everyone finds me unattractive, Arthur.

WILSON I didn't mean that. Anyway, in the dark and with the black-out you look just as attractive as – no, I didn't mean that either.

MRS PIKE Frank forgot the biscuits. Where is he?

WALKER He hasn't arrived yet.

MRS PIKE Hasn't arrived? He left ten minutes before me, with the flask. What's happened to him, Arthur?

WILSON Well, how should I know?

MRS PIKE He's only a baby – you should look after him better. Perhaps that prowler's got him.

WALKER Perhaps he *is* that prowler.

MAINWARING Walker! Don't distress yourself, Mrs Pike – he's probably lost his way in the black-out.

JONES Perhaps he's become entangled with some young lady follower, sir. I often did that when I was a young rip.

MRS PIKE Something's happened to him. I know something's happened to him.

FRAZER **(Out of vision)** Hush a moment.

MAINWARING What is it, Frazer?

FRAZER I thought I heard a faint cry.

PIKE **(Very distant)** Help. Help.

FRAZER It's from over there by the water's edge.

PIKE Help! Help!

Mainwaring goes out to the front of the hut and the rest follow.

MAINWARING Absolute quiet, everybody.

PIKE **(Out of vision)** Help!

MAINWARING It's Pike.

MRS PIKE Oh, Arthur.

WILSON It's all right, Mavis.

MAINWARING **(Shouting)** Are you all right?

PIKE **(Shouting)** I've hurt my leg and I'm caught in the wire.

MAINWARING The stupid boy – what's he doing there?

WALKER He must have missed his way and gone through the gap they open for the swimmers.

MRS PIKE Well, don't leave him there in agony, Arthur, go and help him back.

WILSON Ah – er – yes, yes, of course. I wonder if one of you would be so kind as to help me over the wire.

FRAZER I'd not try that if I was you, Sergeant. You'd be blown to little pieces before you'd taken ten paces.

MAINWARING Good Lord, yes – the minefield.

MRS PIKE Oh, Arthur, he's in a minefield.

MAINWARING Don't worry, Mrs Pike, we'll have him back in no time at all. Wilson, get on the phone to the engineers – tell them we need a path clearing.

WILSON Yes, sir – right away. **(He goes into the hut)**

FRAZER It's a miracle he wasn't blown up getting there.

JONES Permission to shout a short message of encouragement to Private Pike, sir?

MAINWARING Yes, go ahead.

JONES **(Shouting)** Cheer up, Private Pike, and don't move a muscle or you'll be blown to Kingdom Come.

GODFREY Poor boy, he must be awfully cold and wet out there.

MRS PIKE Him with a delicate chest, too. You ought to take more care of him, Mr Mainwaring.

MAINWARING I'm waging war, Mrs Pike, not running a clinic.

He goes into the hut. Wilson is on the phone.

MAINWARING What news of the Sappers, Wilson?

WILSON I'm just on to them, sir. **(Into phone)** It really is terribly kind of you, but if you could manage to come just a teeny-weeny bit sooner, we really would be most awfully grateful. Goodbye. **(He puts the phone down)** They'll come as soon as possible but they're removing a landmine. It'll be about three hours.

MAINWARING Well, he'll just have to wait. Serves him right – it'll teach him to be more careful in future.

FRAZER He'll drown.

MAINWARING What's that, Frazer?

FRAZER If you wait three hours, he'll drown. The tide's coming in fast.

WALKER He's right, you know. At high tide you can't see that wire.

MRS PIKE Arthur, you've got to save him. Save my boy, Arthur. He's too young to go. He's got all his life before him.

WILSON Yes, Mavis, of course. Just – just give me time to think a bit.

MRS PIKE While you're thinking, the water's coming up and he can't swim.

JONES Don't panic, don't panic. **(He rushes out to the front of the hut)** Private Pike, you're not to panic!

Mrs Pike starts towards the door.

MAINWARING Mrs Pike, stop her. Jones, be quiet.

WALKER **(Stopping Mrs Pike)** You'll never get there, Mrs Pike. There's mines everywhere.

WALKER How about getting a boat and rescuing him from the sea?

FRAZER Salthaven's the nearest. By the time we get round to here, he'd be drowned in an hour.

MRS PIKE Oh no!

MAINWARING Frazer, try to choose your words. Somehow we've got to get him across that minefield. Did anyone see it laid?

FRAZER Aye, I did – it was done in a sort of criss-cross pattern. Here, I'll show you. Joe – grab those shells.

They go to the table. Walker tips out a bucket of sea shells.

GODFREY The little orphans used to gather them. Aren't they pretty, and you can hear the sea in them.

MAINWARING Put them down.

FRAZER It was this way – they were in rows – like so – four or five of them. The mines were laid about five yards apart – like so, and they made a pattern like this.

MAINWARING Ah – then let us suppose that Pike is lying here. **(He places a stone)** We could have a clear path from the hut to here. **(He indicates the place)**

WALKER On the other hand if we pick the wrong spot, we'll tread on five of 'em.

WILSON You know, I saw a pamphlet once, a little while ago. I believe it's the done thing to sort of prod the ground and feel for the mines.

MAINWARING Yes, yes, yes. Good thinking, Wilson.

JONES We could use bayonets, sir, and when we felt a mine we could detour ourselves.

WALKER Then there's the scaffolding and the rows of wire.

MAINWARING Scaffolding is for tanks and no obstacle to us. We shall have to cut the wire.

WALKER I've got some big cutters down at the yard.

MAINWARING The very thing. No time to wait for the engineer. We'll start to clear the path and we'll mark a route for you.

WALKER Yes, sir.

GODFREY What about using these little flags.

MAINWARING Ideal. We'll mark a path through the mines with these. Off you go.

GODFREY You see, they used to put them on top of their sandcastles.

MAINWARING Right, now, I know I don't have to ask for volunteers, so follow me.

They go out.

MAINWARING Right, stay close.

Godfrey grabs a blanket and a pair of water wings and goes out a little furtively.

INTERIOR OF HUT

MRS PIKE Arthur, not you.

WILSON What?

MRS PIKE Don't you go, Arthur.

WILSON What are you talking about?

MRS PIKE I couldn't bear to lose you both. Let the others do it, Arthur.

WILSON I can't do that. I mean there are some things one just has to do. Otherwise one isn't a man, is one?

MRS PIKE You've always managed somehow, Arthur.

WATER'S EDGE OF BEACH

Pike is caught in the barbed wire. The sound of the waves lapping is close.

PIKE Oh dear! Help!

MAINWARING **(Out of vision)** Hold on, Pike – we'll soon be with you.

MIDDLE OF BEACH

Mainwaring with Jones and Frazer.

MAINWARING Right, well, we may have to carry him back, so we must clear a path wide enough for two of us.

JONES Captain Mainwaring, sir, I would like to volunteer to clear a path wide enough for the two of us, sir.

MAINWARING Your time will come, Jones.

JONES Let me do the prodding with the bayonet, sir – let me do the prodding.

MAINWARING Sergeant Wilson and I will lead. Wilson! Where are you, Wilson?

WILSON **(Approaching late)** Sorry, sir, I was just having a little chat with Mrs Pike.

MAINWARING There's no time for that sort of thing, Wilson. Now, Sergeant Wilson and I will lead and you, Jones, will help mark our route. Frazer and Godfrey will bring up the rear. Godfrey! Where's Godfrey?

JONES He's not here, sir.

MAINWARING Not here! I don't understand.

FRAZER Don't you? It seems crystal clear to me, sir.

MAINWARING What are you trying to say, Frazer?

FRAZER Ach, it's like I always thought. The first whiff of danger and he's away like a scared weasel.

JONES You've no call to say that, Private Frazer.

FRAZER Well, he's not here, is he?

JONES Mr Mainwaring, sir. Private Godfrey is quite frequently in the habit of not being here on account of he gets caught short.

MAINWARING Yes, of course – he'll catch us up. Now, where's the torch?

WILSON I haven't got the torch.

MAINWARING I distinctly remember telling you to bring the torch.

WILSON The word 'torch' never passed your lips.

MAINWARING You know perfectly well that you're responsible for the torch.

MAINWARING What are you doing, Jones?

JONES Excuse me, sir. **(He gets it from Mainwaring's map pocket)**

MAINWARING Ah, well done, Jones. Now, you shine it, Frazer.

FRAZER Aye, aye, sir.

MAINWARING Grab a bayonet, Wilson.

Mainwaring tries to take Jones' bayonet and they struggle.

MAINWARING What are you doing, Jones?

JONES Don't you touch me there, you've touched my scabbard – reflex action – it's sleeping in the Bush Velt.

MAINWARING Right, good luck, everybody. Here we go.

They lay on the sand in the order prescribed.

MAINWARING **(Prodding)** Now, like this, Wilson, and before you crawl forward, make sure there is nothing there.

WILSON I certainly will, sir. **(They prod the sand)**

MAINWARING It's soft here. **(He prods a couple of feet ahead)** It seems all right. **(He eases his weight gingerly forward)** It is all right. **(He looks at Wilson, who is prodding every grain very carefully)** You needn't prod every inch, Wilson. A mine is at least eight inches across, you know.

WILSON I just thought it might pay to be rather cautious.

MAINWARING Come on – move up!

Wilson eases forward very tentatively.

WILSON Ah, I think it's all right.

JONES Permission to speak, sir?

MAINWARING Yes, Jones.

JONES If it wasn't all right, we'd know by now.

MAINWARING Thank you, Jones. Right, now, let's mark our route. Flags, Jones. **(Jones hands him a Nazi flag)** I don't think we'll use that one, Jones.

JONES How about a French one, sir?

MAINWARING Oh, very well. Right, on we go. Prod away, Wilson!

Mainwaring prods vigorously.

EXTERIOR OF HUT

Mrs Pike is waiting. She hears a noise.

MRS PIKE Who's there?

Walker comes into the picture with the large clippers.

WALKER Hello, Mrs P.

MRS PIKE Oh, my heart. I thought you were the prowler.

WALKER Sorry, better luck next time. Where are they?

MRS PIKE Down there, I think.

WATER'S EDGE

PIKE Mr Mainwaring, sir?

MAINWARING **(Out of vision)** Yes.

PIKE Don't be too long, because the tide's coming in.

MAINWARING **(Out of vision)** We'll be as quick as we can.

BEACH

WILSON Just a moment, sir. I've found something.

MAINWARING Does it feel like a mine?

WILSON Well, to tell the truth, I don't have a great deal of experience of this sort of thing.

MAINWARING Well, is it hard?

WILSON Well, one hardly likes to overplay one's hand, so to speak, in order to find out.

MAINWARING Oh, let me feel. **(He gives it a gentle prod)** Yes, yes, there's something there all right. Move the sand away and uncover it.

Wilson starts to edge away the sand with one finger. Mainwaring can't stand the suspense.

MAINWARING Wilson, there's a boy out there who's going to drown if we don't reach him quickly. Get out of the way!

He brushes the sand off the object – it is a small war office booklet.

WILSON What is it, sir?

MAINWARING **(Reading)** Handbook of Field Engineering and Mine Warfare.

WILSON What's that mean?

MAINWARING **(Opening it)** How to lay a minefield.

WATER'S EDGE

PIKE **(Moving to release himself)** Ooh, blimey!

He tries to ease the wire off him but, as he does so, he hears a noise. Footsteps approach.

PIKE Halt, who goes there? Friend or German?

GODFREY It's only me, Frank.

PIKE How'd you get here?

GODFREY Well, it seemed to me that if you could walk along by the water's edge from the bathing gap then I might be able to. I brought you a pair of water wings in case they took some time getting here. They might help to keep you afloat.

PIKE Here, you can't swim yourself, can you?

GODFREY Oh, it's all right, I've brought two pairs. And I expect you're getting rather cold so I've brought a blanket. **(He hands it to him)**

PIKE Thanks, Mr Godfrey. I don't know what my mum'll say if I get a chill.

GODFREY I think I'd better inflate these just in case.

He starts to blow up the water wings.

THE BEACH

Mainwaring is prodding and easing forward.

MAINWARING Right, Jones.

WALKER **(Out of vision)** Mr Mainwaring!

MAINWARING Yes, Walker, we're here.

JONES I expect Private Pike is getting a bit anxious.

MAINWARING Yes, I expect he is.

Suddenly Jones yells at the top of his voice.

JONES **(Shouting)** Don't panic, Private Pike!

MAINWARING Jones!

WILSON Really, Jones, my nerves won't stand it.

JONES I was just giving Private Pike a word of advice and encouragement, sir.

MAINWARING Well, don't. Just shut up!

Mainwaring prods again, he strikes something.

MAINWARING Hello, there's something there all right.

WILSON **(Also finding an obstruction)** And here.

MAINWARING The damn things must be closer together than Frazer thought.

WILSON It could be a stone, I suppose.

MAINWARING Let's clear this one and have a look. Maybe we can lift it. **(He starts to clear the sand)**

JONES Be very careful, sir. Some of these things have booby trap devices to trap boobys.

MAINWARING Shut up, Jones! **(He clears away some top sand)** It's metal all right – not very large though. **(He starts to clear further down)**

WALKER **(Approaching)** I've got the clippers. What's happening?

JONES Don't ask me. Every time I open my mouth, he tells me to shut up.

MAINWARING It's a mine.

FRAZER Can't we skirt round it?

WILSON No, there's one here as well.

WALKER Mind how you go, sir. Some of them have a booby –

MAINWARING I know!

JONES **(Handing him a wooden spade)** Use this, sir.

WALKER Don't do that, sir.

Mainwaring takes it. He has cleared quite a bit more now.

MAINWARING There's some writing on it. It's not English.

FRAZER **(Reading, he pronounces)** Notgnimlaw ot emoclew. It must be Russian.

WILSON I thought they were on our side.

MAINWARING These are our mines.

WILSON Oh, so they are – one gets so confused, doesn't one?

Walker turns his head upside down to read it.

WALKER No, look it says 'Welcome to Walmington'. It's a kid's bucket.

Mainwaring lifts it out of the way.

MAINWARING Very similar shape.

EXTERIOR OF HUT

Mrs Pike is outside. The Warden approaches.

WARDEN I hear there's a spot of trouble. Where's Napoleon?

MRS PIKE Down there, saving my boy.

WARDEN 'Ere, doesn't he know there's a raid on? **(He shouts)** Stop flashing that light! He'll have the Jerry planes buzzing round here like gnats. Put that light out!

MAINWARING **(Out of vision)** Mind your own business. This is a military emergency.

WARDEN **(Calling)** Everything you touch is an emergency, mate. Ruddy hooligans! I'll take ten to one he blows himself up.

Mrs Pike cries.

WARDEN **(Realising what he's said)** Mind you – your boy will be all right, of course.

BEACH

They are now at the wire and amongst the scaffolding.

MAINWARING **(Prodding)** Nearly through, Pike, stay where you are.

WILSON Yes, that's right, just stay where you are, Pike.

PIKE I can't do anything else, Sergeant, er... Uncle. I've got a piece of rusty barbed wire sticking in my bum.

MAINWARING Don't be coarse, Pike. Give me the clippers, Walker. **(Walker hands them)**

JONES I would like to volunteer to clip with the clippers, sir.

MAINWARING Be quiet, Jones. **(He clips the wire)**

JONES **(To Frazer)** I've never known him like this before.

FRAZER He's worried, you fool.

JONES Has he got trouble at home then?

MAINWARING Nearly there.

PIKE Could you clip the bit that's sticking into my you-know-what, Mr Mainwaring?

MAINWARING Just a minute. **(He clips)** There!

PIKE Oh, you've no idea what a relief that is.

More clips.

MAINWARING Can you crawl back with us now?

PIKE I'll try, but my ankle's terribly painful.

MAINWARING We should have brought a blanket to drag you.

GODFREY **(Offering the cup off the top of the flask)** Would you care for a cup of tea before you start back?

MAINWARING Godfrey! How did you get here?

GODFREY Well, along the beach. I thought he'd be rather frightened on his own.

MAINWARING But you might have been blown to pieces.

GODFREY Yes, I suppose so. I'm afraid there's no sugar – it's back in the hut. Oh, and I've brought a blanket.

MAINWARING A very foolish thing to do. Damned brave all the same.

FRAZER A man of steel. I always knew it.

WILSON The water's getting awfully close.

WALKER Right, you show the way, Taff, and me and the Sergeant will drag him.

MAINWARING Well done – spread your weight in case there's a deep one.

JONES Yes, and I'll keep prodding, sir. In case you've overlooked one.

They start to drag Pike.

WALKER One, two, three, heave!

PIKE Ooh, I'll be glad when my mum's put a poultice on it.

WALKER Heave!

PIKE It was sticking right in.

WALKER Heave!

PIKE And it was all rusty.

WALKER Heave!

PIKE Can you die from rust poisoning?

WILSON Oh, do be quiet, Frank!

JONES Wait a minute – I've struck something.

MAINWARING Let me come through. Give me your bayonet, Frazer. **(He prods)** By Jove, it is something.

Two sets of feet come into the picture. We hear the Warden's voice.

WARDEN What are you doing there then, praying to Mecca?

MAINWARING Stay still you fool, you'll be blown sky high.

We now see the Warden standing with an engineering officer.

WARDEN What're you talking about? This is the engineer officer who laid the mines. He says it's all clear here.

ENGINEER OFFICER That's quite right, we didn't lay them in this part.

WARDEN You don't half look a fool, lying down there, prodding with your little bayonet.

ENGINEER OFFICER Yes, actually you could have marched a regiment across. The mines stop 200 yards up the beach.

JONES In that case, what's this doing here?

He holds up an English mine.

WARDEN Great Scott, it's a mine. **(To engineer officer)** You're a right one, aren't you?

MAINWARING Stay where you are, everybody.

JONES Don't panic, don't panic.

MAINWARING Gently with it, Jones.

WARDEN **(To officer)** You got me into this, now get me out of it!

MAINWARING Yes, what do you suggest we do now?

ENGINEER OFFICER Well – er – could anybody lend me a bayonet?

SERIES FOUR **EPISODE FIVE**

Recorded: Friday 10/7/70

Original transmission: Friday 23/10/70, 8.00–8.30pm

Original viewing figures = 16.4 million

ARTHUR LOWE .... CAPTAIN MAINWARING
JOHN LE MESURIER .... SERGEANT WILSON
CLIVE DUNN .... LANCE CORPORAL JONES
JOHN LAURIE .... PRIVATE FRAZER
JAMES BECK .... PRIVATE WALKER
ARNOLD RIDLEY .... PRIVATE GODFREY
IAN LAVENDER .... PRIVATE PIKE

EDWARD EVANS .... GENERAL MONTEVERDI
JOHN RINGHAM .... CAPTAIN BAILEY
LARRY MARTYN .... ITALIAN POW

PLATOON . . COLIN BEAN, DESMOND CULLUM-JONES, GEORGE HANCOCK, ... HUGH CECIL, HUGH HASTINGS, FREDDIE WILES, VIC TAYLOR, ... LESLIE NOYES, FRANK GODFREY, KEN WADE

MPS .... DEREK SHAFFER, ANTHONY POWELL

ITALIAN POWS .... JEREMY HIGGINS, LEE WARREN, PETER MORRE, ... TREVOR LAWRENCE, MARIO ZOPPELLINI, RONNIE LAUGHLAN, ... M. N. EDDY, ROY KANARIS, TONY CORDELL, STEVE CORNELL, . . . IAN SELMAN, PAUL HOLROY, ROBERT MARSHALL, ANTONIO DI MAGGIO, ... CLIVE ROGERS, ANDREW ANDREAS, STEVE PETERS

Don't Fence Me In

• CLIVE DUNN REMEMBERS •

'Throughout my career I've played a lot of older characters, but I've never minded because it's always worked. You put the right hat on, the right moustache, have the right attitude and hope for the best.

'Playing Jones was certainly my cup of tea, and knowing David Croft, an old friend, wanted me for the part was very pleasing. Everything just clicked. Somehow, I seemed to know the character: in my mind I was clear about how he should act – it must have been instinct. As the weeks went by, David and Jimmy Perry soon realised what all the members of the cast did best and made use of it; this is why each of the characters came across as being so strong on screen.

'But it took a while before I agreed to play the role. David and Jimmy were getting a little fed up waiting for my decision because they wanted to get on with the series. Once I knew John Le Mesurier, who was the only person I knew in the cast, had decided to play Wilson, I accepted my offer. I was keen to know whether he was going to be in it, so we kept speaking about the show; we must have been waiting for each other to decide.

'Of course, there had already been *The Army Game*, and I was a little worried that another series about the Army might be too soon. It depended entirely on how the series was going to be made. Obviously I was keen to work, but still felt unsure about the idea, even after I'd accepted. But as soon as I discovered John wasn't playing the officer, as one might expect, but the sergeant, I was confident the show had promise. The idea of a sophisticated performer like John playing the sergeant was such a different approach, it put the stamp on it for me. Despite the first series being shown in the summer, a poor time of year because everyone's on holiday, it still worked well enough for a second series to be commissioned.'

'I'll always be grateful to Jimmy Perry and David Croft for not just giving me the chance to be in the series, but for taking care of the programme so well.'

CLIVE DUNN

Don't Fence Me In

SIDE OFFICE. CHURCH HALL. DAY

Mainwaring is sitting at his desk talking into the phone. Wilson is standing beside desk, reading *Picture Post.*

MAINWARING Yes… yes… I quite realise that, sir – but I can't ask my men to do a job like this – after all they're front-line fighting troops. They're keen and fit – hardly able to wait to have a go at Jerry. (**He puts his hand over the phone**) Stop rustling that paper, Wilson, I can't hear. What… very well, sir, I'll tell them, but I warn you – they're not going to like it. (**He hangs up**)

WILSON Everything all right, sir?

MAINWARING No, it isn't all right. For the next two weekends we're going to be taken off all active duties.

WILSON Oh good, sir – that means we'll get some time to ourselves.

MAINWARING No, Wilson, we're not going to get any time off. We shall be guarding a prisoner-of-war camp. The regular army camp guards haven't had any leave for months. So we're going to relieve them for two weekends.

WILSON So we shall come face to face with some Nazis at last, sir.

MAINWARING They're not Nazis, Wilson – they're Italians. If Hitler does kick off during the next two weekends – we shan't be there to stop him. We shall be playing nursemaid to a bunch of comic opera soldiers.

TELECINE: EXTERIOR. A COUNTRY LANE. DAY

The platoon is marching along. Mainwaring and Wilson are in front.

MAINWARING All right, Sergeant, we'll stop here.

WILSON Very good, sir. (**He drops to the side**) Platoon, halt – right turn – stand at ease.

MAINWARING Now, pay attention, men. The prisoner-of-war camp is just round the corner. There are 60 Italian prisoners in it, and it goes without saying they'll be a pretty sloppy bunch. So, when we march through those gates, I want them to see what smart British soldiers really look like. Have you got that? (**They all nod**) Now, don't forget – chests out, chins in – marching smartly to attention. Squad, attenshun – slope arms – left turn! By the right, quick march.

TELECINE: EXTERIOR. THE GATES OF THE P.O.W. CAMP. DAY

The platoon approaches the gates, marching very smartly. Mainwaring is in front, they reach the gates.

MAINWARING Platoon – halt. Sergeant Wilson?

Wilson hurries up.

WILSON Yes, sir.

MAINWARING Are you sure this is the place?

WILSON It must be, sir – look. (**He points to a notice which reads 'M.O.W. Prisoner-of-War Camp. Keep out'**)

MAINWARING You'd better fall the men out.

WILSON Right, sir. Platoon, fall out.

The platoon fall out. Jones, Walker, Frazer, Godfrey and Pike gather in a knot behind Captain Mainwaring.

MAINWARING This is absurd – whoever heard of a prisoner-of-war camp with no one on guard? (**Pointing to the watch tower beside the gate**) Is there anyone up there?

WILSON No, sir – er… perhaps if you rang the door bell someone might come.

MAINWARING Don't talk nonsense, Wilson – you don't have door bells on P.O.W. camps.

WILSON (**Pointing to an old petrol tin hanging on a string with a bit of iron beside it**) Why not try that, sir – if you hit it, someone might hear.

MAINWARING Good thinking, Wilson. (**He crosses to the tin and hits it, the string breaks and it falls on the ground with a clatter**) Oh really, this is absurd. (**He shouts**) I say – anybody there? (**No answer. He repeats it. Still no answer**)

PIKE I don't like the look of this, Mr Mainwaring, it's just like *Beau Geste.*

MAINWARING What do you mean?

PIKE Where the relief column reached the fort in the desert – and they looked up and all the walls were lined with Legionnaires – and they were all dead – and the Captain shouted 'Anybody there?' – just like you did. The next minute he was flat on his face in the sand with a bullet in his brain.

MAINWARING You stupid boy.

WALKER That wasn't *Beau Geste* – it was Bow-Legs.

WILSON Walker – please.

FRAZER Look, sir – let me climb over the wire – it's not very high.

PIKE I shouldn't do that, Mr Frazer – it could be electrified – and you might get a shock.

WALKER If he was to climb over that wire wearing his kilt – we'd all get a shock.

Frazer gives him a glare.

WILSON (Pointing) Look, sir – there's someone coming out of that hut.

A dirty, scruffy looking P.O.W. comes out of one of the huts and slouches across the parade ground with his hands in his pockets.

MAINWARING (Shouting) Hey, you!

The camera zooms into close up of P.O.W. – he stops – and points to himself.

MAINWARING (Out of vision) Yes, you.

The P.O.W. slouches over to the wire – he is eating an apple, spitting out the pips, he presses his face against the wire.

MAINWARING Now, look here – what's going on?

P.O.W. (Shrugging his shoulders) Hur?

MAINWARING This whole thing looks very fishy to me, Wilson. (Shouting) Who's in charge here? (The P.O.W. shrugs and grunts. Mainwaring turns to the men) Does anybody here speak Italian?

GODFREY I speak a little, sir. (He speaks to the P.O.W.) Vostro piccolo mano e ghiacciato. Permesso e caldo ancora a vita. (The P.O.W. looks shocked)

MAINWARING What did you say to him, Godfrey?

GODFREY Your tiny hands are frozen.

MAINWARING What on earth did you say that for?

GODFREY It's the only Italian I know, sir – you see, I'm a very keen opera fan.

MAINWARING Oh, this is absurd. (Shouting to P.O.W.) Open – open! (The P.O.W. opens the gate and Mainwaring storms through, followed by Wilson) I'm going to get to the bottom of this, Wilson. (He strides towards one of the huts) Watch that man – don't let him escape.

INTERIOR. P.O.W. HUT. DAY

There are several bunks along the wall with P.O.W.s asleep in them. By the door is a small desk. A fattish, bald, middle aged Italian General is sitting at the desk with his feet up reading. On the desk is an old wind-up portable gramophone player.

EXTERIOR. P.O.W. HUT

Mainwaring and platoon go into hut.

INTERIOR. P.O.W. HUT

Platoon enters hut. Mainwaring barges through the door, followed by Wilson – he stops, unable to believe his eyes. The General looks up and beams.

GENERAL Salute!

MAINWARING Who on earth are you?

GENERAL Franco – Bruno – Othello – Monteverdi.

MAINWARING I'm not interested in all that rubbish. Don't you know you should stand up when an Officer comes into the room?

GENERAL Why should I stand up? You are only a Capitan – you should get up for me. I am a General.

MAINWARING I am up… I mean… I er… a General?

GENERAL That's right, Generale – Franco – Bruno – Othello – Monteverdi.

MAINWARING Oh, don't start all that again. Where are the troops who are supposed to be guarding the camp?

GENERAL They go.

MAINWARING Go!

GENERAL Yes, the Capitan left you a note. (He hands Wilson a note)

MAINWARING What's it say, Wilson?

WILSON (Reading) Forgive please we go. We catch 1.30 train to London. Otherwise we miss our endweek leave. Don't worry at Italian prisoners – they quite tame – they work on farms in week. See you Sunday night at 2000 hrs. (Looking up) Eight o'clock, sir.

MAINWARING All right, Wilson. Who's it signed by?

WILSON Captain Shodski – Free Polish Forces.

MAINWARING I've never heard anything like it in all my life. Well, I suppose if you set one lot of foreigners to guard another lot of foreigners, what can you expect? It's outrageous – I shall report this Captain Shodski to G.H.Q. at once. (To General) Where's the phone?

GENERAL In the Guard Room. But don't worry, Capitan, it's okay. I looked after things until you arrived.

MAINWARING But that's not the point. You're supposed to be prisoners of war. Don't you understand? We're enemies.

GENERAL (Getting up and crossing to Mainwaring) What do you mean, enemies? I refused to fight against the British. In the desert I put up my hands and surrendered.

MAINWARING (To General) Now, look – personal feelings don't come into this. You are a P.O.W. and I am here as a representative of His Majesty's Government – and I am going to see that this camp is run properly without any familiarity.

The door opens and Walker and Jones come in.

JONES Shall I fall the men out, sir?

General rushing across the room and flinging his arms round Walker's neck.

GENERAL Hey, Joe – how are you?

WALKER Knock it off – you don't know me.

GENERAL What do you mean? You are my best friend.

MAINWARING What's going on here?

JONES **(Pointing)** That's the Continental method, sir.

MAINWARING Do you know this man, Walker?

WALKER No, I've never seen him before in my life.

GENERAL No, I never seen him before either, I make a mistake.

WILSON **(Aside to Mainwaring)** It all looks rather queer to me, sir.

MAINWARING And me, Wilson. **(To the General)** Now look here, we've had enough of all this foreign business. From now on we're going to run things my way – by the book – do you understand? **(Points to the men in the bunks)** What are all these men doing in bed?

GENERAL Siesta.

MAINWARING We'll soon see about that. **(He runs his stick along the bunks)** Come on, up! Up!

WILSON Do get up, etc.

MAINWARING Jones, get Frazer, Godfrey and Pike in here. **(Poking the P.O.W.s with his stick)** Up, up, up.

JONES Yes, sir. **(He goes)**

GENERAL Don't wake them up – they work hard all the week on the farm.

MAINWARING I have to work hard all the week at the bank, but I don't spend my spare time lounging about in bed. I'm up and about defending my country.

GENERAL They'd be up and about defending their country – but it's too far away.

MAINWARING Poppycock. **(Poking the men with his stick)** Come on, get up – get up!

GENERAL **(Putting his arm on Wilson's shoulder)** Hey, Sargenti, can't you stop him?

MAINWARING **(Turning on General)** Take your hands off my Sergeant at once. **(By now the men are up and standing by their bunks – they look a pretty scruffy bunch)** I've never seen such a shambles in all my life. **(To General)** Just look at them. Why aren't they wearing their P.O.W. uniforms?

GENERAL They very proud, these own uniforms – they are most smart.

Mainwaring looks them up and down. Jones comes in with Frazer, Pike and Godfrey. They line up very smartly – Walker joins on the end of the line.

JONES **(Saluting very smartly)** All present and correct, sir!

MAINWARING **(Pointing to his men)** There you see, that's what real soldiers look like.

GENERAL But I keep telling you, we don't want to be real soldiers – we are not enemies.

MAINWARING Until I get orders to the contrary, we *are* enemies. So you'd better do something about it – I mean you're not even trying – at least make some effort.

GENERAL Ah, Capitan – you are a very hard man.

MAINWARING I have to be hard, General – otherwise we would all be under the Nazi jackboot by now. Well, if you won't do anything about your men – I will. I'll soon lick 'em into shape. Frazer, Godfrey, Pike, Walker. Go round all the other huts and get the men on the parade ground at the double.

FRAZER/GODFREY/PIKE/WALKER Right, sir!

They all double out smartly.

General and Mainwaring offered tomato by P.O.W.

MAINWARING Oh, don't be disgusting. Corporal Jones?

JONES Sir.

MAINWARING Get these men outside and then count them. With the others there should be 60 all together.

JONES Right, you lot – outside – come on, move – move! **(The P.O.W.s don't move)** Oh, it's like that, is it? Well, I'll soon show you. **(He whips out his bayonet and fixes)** Now, come on! **(He gestures to them. They all move towards the door)** That's the only language they understand, sir. They don't like it up 'em, you know, sir – they do not like it up 'em. **(To P.O.W.s)** Come on. Hup-hup-hup. **(They move towards the door with Jones prodding them)**

MAINWARING **(With relish)** That's the stuff, Jones – keep 'em on the move. Excellent, eh, Sergeant?

WILSON Yes, sir.

GENERAL You are a cruel man, Capitan.

MAINWARING **(Still with a look of pleasure on his face)** You don't think I'm enjoying this, do you?

The P.O.W.s have now gone, we can hear Frazer and Jones shouting outside and feet running. Mainwaring opens the window.

MAINWARING All right, Jones, get them into three lines and start counting them.

JONES **(Out of vision)** Right, sir. Come on, you lot, get in line. **(Starts counting)**

MAINWARING Jones will soon find out if there are any missing.

WILSON He's going to have a bit of a job, sir – they all look alike to me.

MAINWARING It's Chinese that look alike, like Chinese.

WILSON Yes, sir, and these all look alike, like Italians.

JONES **(Out of vision)** 28, 29, 30, 31, 32.

FRAZER **(Out of vision)** 46, 47, 48, 49, 50.

JONES **(Out of vision)** 33, 34, 35, 36, 37.

Frazer and Jones together.

FRAZER **(Out of vision)** 56, 57, 58, 59, 60.

JONES **(Out of vision)** 38, 39, 40, 59, 60.

JONES **(Out of vision)** Shut up, Jock – you're getting me all mixed up. Look, we'll start again.

JONES **(Out of vision)** 1, 2, 3, 4, 5, 6, 7, 16, 18, 20.

FRAZER **(Out of vision)** 2, 4, 6, 8, 10, 12, 14, 16, 18, 20.

JONES Look, I'm doing the counting, not you, stop messing me up.

FRAZER **(Out of vision)** It's not my fault if you're illiterate. Anyhow I've counted them – 60, they're all there.

JONES **(Out of vision)** I'm not taking your word for it. I'll start again. 1, 2, 3, 4, 5.

MAINWARING All right, Jones – all right. Now, I want you to give them some drill – smarten them up a bit.

JONES **(Out of vision)** Right, sir – yes, sir.

MAINWARING **(To General)** Here's your chance to see a first class British N.C.O. at work – he'll soon lick your men into shape.

JONES **(Out of vision)** Squad, attention! **(Sound effects)** Quick march. **(Nothing happens)** Quick march **(Still nothing)** Oh yes! Avante! **(Sounds of men marching)** Left – right – left – right. Squad, halt. **(Nothing happens)** Squad, halt! **(Still nothing)** Halt. **(The men are still marching)**

Mainwaring turns back into room, the door bursts open.

JONES Mr Mainwaring, sir – what's Italian for halt! **(There is a loud crash)** Never mind – too late.

THE WATCH TOWER. NIGHT

The tower, which is just beside the main gate, is very small. Walker, Frazer, Godfrey, Pike and Jones are jammed in it very tight. There is hardly room for them to move. They are all facing front.

FRAZER I never heard anything so damn silly in all my life, squashing us all in here like this.

JONES I can't help that – it's Captain Mainwaring's orders. He wants us where he can lay his hands on us, in case of trouble.

WALKER I've had enough of this – I'm going down below.

JONES I've got orders to keep you here until we're relieved.

WALKER Well, I've got to be relieved now, I can't wait.

JONES Oh, all right – but don't be long.

Walker goes down the ladder.

GODFREY I wonder if I might be excused as well, Mr Jones?

JONES All right, Mr Godfrey. Help him down the ladder.

EXTERIOR. SIDE OF A HUT AND SOME BUSHES. NIGHT

It is very dark – the General is standing, smoking a cigarette. Walker comes into the picture.

WALKER There you are. I've been looking for you everywhere. I'm going to get your blokes out tonight as arranged, okay?

GENERAL No, it's too risky. That Captain Mainwaring is a nuisance – he is watching us all the time.

WALKER Don't worry about him – we'll get them out through the tunnel.

GENERAL I still say it's too dangerous. I could get shot for this.

WALKER You're not the only one, mate. If I don't fulfil my orders, it will be the end of me.

GENERAL I suppose you are right – without you, our cause would be lost.

WALKER Right – so don't forget it. Now, listen, as soon as I come off duty I'm going to nip into Walmington on the bike – collect the van – bring it back here and park it just off the road by the wire. Then, when the time comes – we'll get out through the tunnel – into the van and we're away.

GENERAL I still don't like it, Joe.

WALKER Look, mate – all you've got to worry about is getting those radios working by the morning. See you later – ciao.

Walker goes. The General shrugs his shoulders – stamps out his cigarette and goes off in another direction. There is a pause, the bushes part. Cut into close up of Godfrey's little face.

GODFREY Oh dear, oh dear, oh dear.

EXTERIOR. THE WATCH TOWER. NIGHT

Mainwaring, Wilson, Jones, Frazer, Godfrey and Pike are looking out over the top of the tower.

MAINWARING What's the time, Wilson?

WILSON **(Looking at his watch)** Five to twelve, sir.

MAINWARING Twenty-three fifty-five,eh!

WILSON We've been up here for two hours watching, sir, and nothing's happened. Perhaps he's not going to try it tonight after all.

MAINWARING Believe me, Wilson, I know the criminal mind. Walker's bound to show his hand sooner or later. (To Godfrey) Are you sure, Godfrey, that you heard him say that he was going to help the prisoners escape tonight?

GODFREY Oh yes, Mr Mainwaring. He said that he'd got to fulfil his orders, to get them out through the tunnel and away in the van. Then they've got to get the radio working by dawn.

WILSON I still can't believe, sir, that Walker's a fifth columnist.

FRAZER Oh I can, I can. I always said that 'spiv' fellow was no good. There's no doubt about it – no doubt at all.

JONES Joe and I have been pals for years, Mr Mainwaring. To think that all this time I have been harbouring a viper between my bosoms.

MAINWARING I should have suspected something when that General flung his arms round Walker's neck. A true blue Britisher would have pushed him away – instantly!

WILSON If only we knew where that escape tunnel was, sir.

JONES Permission to speak, sir? I've got an idea. Why don't I go into one of the huts and disguise myself as a prisoner, then – when I am crawling through the tunnel with the others – all of a sudden I will stick my bayonet upwards and then you will come along and you will see it sticking up in the ground, and you will know the whereabouts of the tunnel.

Mainwaring gives him an exasperated look and says nothing. Jones pulls at his sleeve.

JONES Didn't you hear what I said, sir?

WILSON **(Pointing)** Look, sir, what's that?

MAINWARING **(Peering into the darkness)** It's Walker – keep down – he might see us! Come on, we'll follow him, don't make a noise.

TELECINE: EXTERIOR. THE CAMP. NIGHT

Long shot of open space with huts on either side. Walker is nipping across the space from hut to hut à la Tom and Jerry. He pauses for a second look round – opens the door of one of the huts and goes in. Mainwaring's face appears round the edge of one of the huts. He signals the men forward. Wilson, Godfrey, Jones, Pike and Frazer nip across the space and gather round Mainwaring in the shadow of one of the huts.

MAINWARING **(To Wilson)** Right, Wilson. **(He draws his revolver)** When I give the word, we'll rush in and catch him red handed.

WILSON All right, sir. **(To the others)** Stand by.

MAINWARING Now!!

They all rush across the open ground. Mainwaring opens the door of the hut and goes in.

INTERIOR. INSIDE THE HUT. NIGHT

The hut is empty. Mainwaring crashes through the door, followed by Wilson and the rest.

MAINWARING All right, Walker, the game's up. Get you... There's no one here, Wilson. The tunnel! They must have got out through the tunnel. It's underneath these floorboards somewhere. We've got to find it.

Group stamping about. Mainwaring and Wilson bump into each other and apologise.

PIKE Here it is, sir. **(He crosses to the stove in the middle of the room, gets hold of it and swings it back. It is on top of a trap door)**

MAINWARING How on earth did you know where it was?

PIKE We saw it in that film, *Escape from Stalag 9*, didn't we, Uncle Arthur?

WILSON Yes, that's right, Frank – not one of my favourite films. Now, let's see – who was in that?

MAINWARING Wilson, take Frazer and Godfrey and cover the other end of the tunnel – if it follows a straight line it should be about a hundred yards from the left of the gate. **(The platoon leave)** Jones, Pike, come with me.

Jones, Pike and Mainwaring all dive down into the hole at the same time.

TELECINE: EXTERIOR. OUTSIDE THE WIRE. NIGHT

Walker is standing by the back of the van. One of the doors is open. He is pushing a P.O.W. in. He drags another one out of the bushes and pushes him in.

WALKER Come on, hurry up – we haven't got all night. **(He bangs the door and shuts it)** Right, we'll soon have you away.

Suddenly there is a terrible yell. Walker turns, terrified, with his back to the van. Frazer comes into the picture, brandishing his bayonet – he is wild eyed with rage.

FRAZER Traitor! Traitor! **(He cocks his rifle)**

WALKER Have you gone barmy ? Don't shoot.

FRAZER No, I'm not going to shoot – shooting's too good

for you. We're going to string you up on the hanging tree. (Away) To the hanging tree!

WILSON Walker, this is really – well, it is, isn't it – it's really too bad.

WALKER What are you talking about, have you all gone mad or something?

FRAZER Don't try and lie your way out of it.

Godfrey comes into the picture.

GODFREY Oh, Mr Walker – why did you do it?

WALKER Do what?

WILSON It's no use, Walker, we know you were trying to help these prisoners to escape.

WALKER Escape! I'm not trying to help 'em escape. I'm taking 'em on night shift.

WILSON Night shift!

WALKER Yes, I've got 'em working in one of my sheds. I collect 'em at night and bring them back early in the morning. They're assembling radios for me.

WILSON How long has this been going on?

WALKER Months. Well, you can't get labour these days, you know – and I'll go broke if I don't fulfil my orders.

GODFREY Oh, those sort of orders.

WILSON We'd better go and tell Captain Mainwaring – he's still in the tunnel.

INTERIOR. INSIDE THE TUNNEL. NIGHT

Mainwaring is stuck – behind him, Jones and Pike are trying to free him.

MAINWARING Push harder, Jones.

JONES I am pushing, Mr Mainwaring. Come on, Pikey, put your back into it.

PIKE I can't, Mr Jones. I'm not in the right position. I can only use my head.

Pike has his head up against Jones' behind. Wilson crawls into the picture and comes face to face with Mainwaring.

MAINWARING Who's that?

WILSON It's me, sir.

MAINWARING Did you catch Walker?

WILSON Yes, sir, but he's not a fifth columnist – he was taking the prisoners out to repair radios for him.

MAINWARING What! I'll have him court martialled for this. Look, I'm stuck – give me a hand.

WILSON Right, sir.

He starts to pull him – bits of earth fall down.

MAINWARING Now, when I say pull – pull. Pull!

Wilson, Frazer and Walker are pulling – Jones and Pike are pulling the other way.

MAINWARING Pull! Ow – what are you doing, Jones?

JONES I'm pulling, sir – you said pull.

MAINWARING No – no – you don't pull, you push. Now, come on – push – push – push!

Wilson, Frazer and Walker are pushing as well as Jones and Pike.

MAINWARING No, no, not you, Wilson – you pull. Jones pushes.

WILSON I'm sorry, sir.

MAINWARING Now, come on. Push, pull, push, pull. Rest, rest.

JONES Permission to speak ? Why don't we do it the same way as you unblock a drain.

WILSON (To Mainwaring) Shall we try that, sir?

MAINWARING Anything – only get on with it.

JONES (Shouting) Now, listen carefully. Captain Mainwaring is the obstruction – what we've got to do is to work him backwards and forwards until he becomes unblocked. Right, Pikey catch hold. Are you ready, Mr Wilson?

WILSON Yes, we're ready.

Walker is holding Frazer, who is holding Wilson, who is gripping Mainwaring's arms. Pike is holding Jones, who is gripping Mainwaring.

JONES Right – forward, back – forward, back.

They rock backwards and forwards, trying to shift him.

MAINWARING Stop! Stop! I must have a rest.

Wilson starts to snigger.

MAINWARING Why are you laughing, Wilson?

WILSON I was just thinking, sir – Winnie-the-Pooh.

MAINWARING What are your talking about?

WILSON Don't you remember, sir? He got stuck in a hole because he'd eaten too much honey – and they had to wait a week for him to get thin enough to free himself.

MAINWARING (Furious) Very funny. Now, pull again.

JONES Permission to do something to you, sir…

MAINWARING What?

JONES This.

There is a terrible cry from Mainwaring and he jerks forward free. Cut to Jones with a bayonet in his hand.

JONES Sorry, sir – sometimes you have to be cruel to be kind.

TELECINE: OUTSIDE THE WIRE. NIGHT

Walker and Wilson are helping Mainwaring out of the bushes. Godfrey, Pike, Frazer and Jones are standing beside the van.

WALKER **(Dusting Mainwaring)** There you are, sir, how do you feel now?

MAINWARING Take your hands off me, Walker, I shall deal with you later.

There is a sound of a car.

WILSON Look, sir, there's a car drawing up at the gates.

Sound of car door banging.

VOICE **(Out of vision)** Halt, who goes there?

BAILEY **(Out of vision)** Captain Bailey from G.H.Q.

WILSON Did you hear that, sir – it's Captain Bailey.

MAINWARING What on earth does he want?

WILSON He must have come about your call to G.H.Q. earlier on.

MAINWARING Good Lord, I'd forgotten all about that. Wilson, get the prisoners out of that van and back through the tunnel and into the hut. I'll try and keep Captain Bailey from going in there as long as possible. Jones, Frazer, Pike, come with me.

TELECINE: EXTERIOR. THE GATES OF THE CAMP. NIGHT

Captain Bailey is standing with two M.P's. A Home Guard is standing behind the closed gate.

BAILEY **(To Home Guard)** Look, open the gate. I want to see Captain Mainwaring.

Mainwaring comes into the picture with Jones, Frazer and Pike.

MAINWARING Good evening, sir. **(He salutes)**

BAILEY Look here, Mainwaring – what's all this about Captain Shodski clearing off and leaving no one on guard.

MAINWARING Nothing, sir. Storm in a teacup. I've sorted it all out.

BAILEY Have you checked all the prisoners?

MAINWARING Yes, sir, I've counted them – there are exactly 60.

JONES I counted them too, sir.

FRAZER Aye and I counted them as well – 60.

BAILEY Well, I want to count them now – come on.

He pushes open the gate and strides towards the hut where the tunnel is. Jones rushes after him and tries to stop him. Mainwaring, Pike and Frazer follow.

JONES I shouldn't go in that hut if I were you, sir.

BAILEY Why not?

JONES Well, it's not a very nice hut, sir. Why don't you go in one of the other huts.

BAILEY I don't want to go in one of the other huts. Come on, Mainwaring.

INTERIOR. INSIDE HUT. NIGHT

It is completely empty. Bailey comes through the black out trap, followed by the two M.P.s, Mainwaring, Jones, Pike and Frazer.

BAILEY The place is empty. Where is everybody?

MAINWARING Well, er...

JONES They're sleeping in one of the other huts. I told you, sir – this isn't a very nice hut.

BAILEY What's wrong with it?

MAINWARING The roof leaks – snow comes in.

BAILEY What, in July?

JONES Well, what I mean is – it would come in if it was winter.

Cut to close up of stove – the trapdoor underneath lifts a few inches. Jones sees it, pushes Bailey out of the way, rushes across the room and sits on the stove.

JONES I hope you'll excuse me sitting down in the presence of officers, sir – but I'm not as young as I used to be.

BAILEY I quite understand.

JONES **(Shouting)** Isn't it nice to see *Captain Bailey* again, Mr Mainwaring – and I see *Captain Bailey* has brought two *Military Policemen* with him.

BAILEY Why are you shouting, Corporal?

JONES I'm so used to shouting at the men, sir – you know, keep 'em on their toes.

BAILEY I see. Now, I want you to go and get all the P.O.W.s – line them up outside the door and send them through. I want to count them.

JONES Right, sir. **(He gets up and pushes Mainwaring down on the stove)** You'd better sit down, Mr Mainwaring, you look tired. And I will go and get the P.O.W.s, **(Winks)** and I will send them though. **(Winks)** And there will be exactly 60 of them, sir. **(Winks)**

JONES **(Out of vision)** Private Frazer, Private Pike, come with me.

Mainwaring winks at Captain Bailey. Captain Bailey reacts.

EXTERIOR. OUTSIDE HUT DOOR. NIGHT

FRAZER That was a stupid thing to say, how are we going to send 60 prisoners through – 20 are missing.

JONES Didn't you ever go to the pantomime when you was a kid?

PIKE **(Laughing)** Oh – I've got it, Mr Jones. Ali Ba Ba and the Forty Thieves.

JONES Yeah, that's right.

FRAZER What are you talking about?

JONES Ali Ba Ba and the Forty Thieves – we keep sending the same lot of prisoners round and round again.

FRAZER It will never work, I tell you – it will never work.

JONES Oh shut up – go and get 'em lined up.

INTERIOR. TUNNEL UNDER THE STOVE. NIGHT

Wilson and Walker are underneath the trapdoor. We can see a couple of P.O.W.s in the background. Walker is trying to push up the trap door.

WALKER It's no use, Sarge, I can't shift it. Let's have a rest for a minute, I'm tired out.

WILSON If it hadn't been for you, Walker, we wouldn't be in this mess in the first place.

WALKER Stop worrying – it will be all right, we'll have a rest and then we'll have another try. Got a fag?

Wilson takes out a packet of cigarettes and they both light up.

INTERIOR. INSIDE HUT. NIGHT

Mainwaring is sitting on the stove. Captain Bailey and the two M.P.s are standing beside him. Jones is standing behind Mainwaring with a clipboard and pencil.

BAILEY I want to get this over with, Mainwaring, and get back to bed. I don't like being called out in the middle of the night.

MAINWARING It won't be long now, sir, I…

Jones suddenly notices cigarette smoke curling up between the floorboards beside the stove.

JONES **(Shouting)** *No smoking* in here, if you don't mind, sir. *No smoking.*

BAILEY What are you talking about, Corporal? I'm not smoking.

JONES **(Shouting)** No, sir. I just wanted to remind you, in case you felt like smoking.

BAILEY I wish you wouldn't keep shouting all the time.

Pike comes in.

PIKE Prisoners all ready for counting, sir.

BAILEY All right, send them through.

JONES Send the prisoners through. At the double! **(He winks at Mainwaring)**

The P.O.W.s start to trot through and go out the end door.

JONES **(Counting)** 1, 2, 3, 4, 5, 6, 7, 8, 9, 10, 11, 12, 13, 14, 15, 16, 17, 18, 19, 20. Twenty, sir. **(Winks at Mainwaring)**

BAILEY Correct. Send the next lot through.

JONES **(Shouting)** Private Pike – send the next lot through.

EXTERIOR. OUTSIDE HUT DOOR. NIGHT

Pike starts to push the next lot of P.O.W.s through the door.

PIKE Right, round again – Chop, chop.

INTERIOR. INSIDE HUT. NIGHT

The P.O.W.s trot through.

JONES 21, 22, 23, 24, 25, 26, 27, 28, 29, 30, 31, 32, 33, 34, 35, 36, 37, 38, 39, 40. Forty, sir.

BAILEY Correct – twenty to come.

JONES Right – Private Pike, next lot.

EXTERIOR. HUT. NIGHT

Pike is pushing the P.O.W.s through the door.

PIKE Come on, Encore – Encore.

INTERIOR. HUT. NIGHT

The P.O.W.s are filing through, Jones is counting.

BAILEY You know, Mainwaring, it's a funny thing but all these Italians seem to look alike.

MAINWARING Yes, sir, I know – it's the same with Chinese.

JONES 58, 59, 60.

BAILEY Sixty. Good, they're all accounted for.

Suddenly the trapdoor crashes open. Mainwaring falls off the stove and P.O.W.s start coming out of the hole.

JONES **(Counting)** 61, 62, 63, 64, 65…

SERIES FOUR **EPISODE SIX**

Recorded: Friday, 7/8/70

Original transmission: Friday 30/10/70, 8.00–8.30pm

Original viewing figures = 13.9 million

ARTHUR LOWE .... CAPTAIN MAINWARING
JOHN LE MESURIER .... SERGEANT WILSON
CLIVE DUNN .... LANCE CORPORAL JONES
JOHN LAURIE .... PRIVATE FRAZER
JAMES BECK .... PRIVATE WALKER
ARNOLD RIDLEY .... PRIVATE GODFREY
IAN LAVENDER .... PRIVATE PIKE
BILL PERTWEE .... ARP WARDEN
JANET DAVIES .... MRS PIKE
EDWARD SINCLAIR .... VERGER
J. G. DEVLIN .... REGAN
ARTHUR ENGLISH .... THE POLICEMAN
PATRICK CONNOR .... SHAMUS
VERNE MORGAN .... THE LANDLORD
MICHAEL LOMAX .... SECOND ARP WARDEN
PLATOON .... HUGH HASTINGS, COLIN BEAN, FREDDIE WILES, VIC TAYLOR, LESLIE NOYES, FRANK GODFREY, DESMOND CULLUM-JONES, FREDDIE WHITE, GEORGE HANCOCK, EMMETT HENNESSY
ATS GIRLS .... DIANA HOLT, BETTY GOULDING
ARP WARDENS .... VICTOR CROXFORD, RON GREGORY
IRISHMEN .... RAY EMMINS, FRED DAVIES

ABSENT FRIENDS

• DAVID TAYLOR REMEMBERS •

'As the assistant floor manager on the series you were the junior of the production team. In the case of *Dad's Army* the team consisted of producer/director, production assistant (now called production manager), producer's assistant (now production assistant) and AFM.

'The fact that the producer/director was a co-writer, and the series had been going some time when I joined the team, made my life as a very new AFM a little easier. The planning for the pre-filming took a while, but a lot of the major locations and dates had been finalised before I joined.

'Now, when I think about it, it seems as if we were away filming for quite a long time, but it was only about a month. Filming was complex and usually involved all of the platoon. The design effort to get the period feel correct was immense; it was imperative to get the correct props, especially vehicles.

'As we were using film, every morning we had a rushes report of the previous day's filming which gave us the opportunity to do retakes if required. Because of the actors' retainer fees we started rehearsals immediately upon returning from filming in Norfolk. Our weekly rehearsal pattern was to read-through and plot on Monday, rehearse on Tuesday and Wednesday, carry out the technical run and attend a planning meeting on Thursday. Camera rehearsals would start at 10.30 on Friday, and then we'd record in front of a live audience at 8pm. By 9.30, we were normally in the bar!

'One of my enduring memories of *Dad's Army* was of Arnold Ridley, who was quite an elderly gentleman. He would always bring with him his own folding canvas chair; when he wasn't on set he'd drop off to sleep in it and I would have to go up to him, gently tap his arm and say: "Excuse me but we're just coming up to your scene." He'd wake up and, in character, always apologise, replying: "I'm terribly sorry, David."

'As the new member of the team I found Arthur Lowe a little daunting as an actor. I tried very hard to do everything right. As part of my duties I had to prompt if anyone forgot their lines. You would try and prompt only when you were sure the actor had definitely forgotten his words. On one occasion I waited for what I thought was long enough before prompting. Immediately Arthur retorted: "I have not forgotten my lines – it was a dramatic pause. Please make a note in your script, my boy, not to prompt too early." The following day, because I had marked the point in my script, I waited and Arthur shouted: "Prompt!" As the AFM you could never win.

'We rehearsed the series I worked on at the North Acton Rehearsal Rooms – a purpose-built block of about 18 rooms where you could leave your set mark-up on the floor for the whole series. As an AFM this was luxury, particularly on *Dad's Army* because the Walmington church hall was such a large set and was used most weeks. If you rehearsed at other places, such as church halls or boys' clubs, you had to mark up every week. Also the rehearsal rooms had a restaurant and most of the cast would eat there at lunchtime. There were a few notable exceptions, however, who preferred the atmosphere of the pub next door. One day we broke for lunch and the cast went off to the restaurant, while the production team sorted out a few things before going upstairs. When we arrived there was no sign of the cast. It transpired that they had all got stuck in the lift. It took over an hour for them to be released. Luckily, although it was a nasty experience, none of them had any ill effects.'

DAVID TAYLOR
Assistant Floor Manager

Absent Friends

SIDE OFFICE. CHURCH HALL

WILSON A room with a view – and you
And no one to worry us
No one to hurry us through
The dream we've found
We'll bill and we'll coo oo oo (**Mainwaring enters**)
Hello, sir – I didn't expect you until tomorrow morning.

MAINWARING I didn't go to London after all.

WILSON Oh – was the lodge meeting cancelled?

MAINWARING No. Elizabeth didn't like the idea of being left alone over night. These raids worry the womenfolk a lot, you know. Is it time for the parade?

WILSON Just about, sir. (**He is rather keen that Mainwaring doesn't stay**) Well, there is no reason for you to stay, sir – after all, we weren't expecting you.

MAINWARING That's all right, Wilson – you give them half an hour's map reading – and I will give them 15 minutes on the future conduct of the war.

WILSON I can do that for you, sir.

MAINWARING What do you know about the future conduct of the war?

WILSON Well – I'll manage. Why don't you go home?

MAINWARING Are you trying to get rid of me, Wilson?

WILSON Of course not, sir.

Pike enters, he is in his grey flannels, blazer – with boots – gaiters equipment and hat.

PIKE Oh – hello, Mr Mainwaring. I didn't expect to see you.

MAINWARING So it would seem – where's your uniform?

PIKE My mum's put it in the wash tub.

MAINWARING She's what?

PIKE She said it smelled of bleach.

MAINWARING Of course it smells of bleach. That's the anti-mustard-gas treatment.

PIKE Well – she said it wasn't fit to be seen and she's giving it a good go with the dolly.

MAINWARING This is disgraceful. Can't you do anything to stop her, Wilson?

WILSON Well – it is awfully difficult.

PIKE She's in one of her cleaning moods, Uncle Arthur – I'd go and grab your bowler hat or she'll have that in the tub an' all.

WILSON Oh, Lord.

MAINWARING Never mind that now – get that uniform back by tomorrow.

PIKE Yes, sir.

He goes. The phone rings.

MAINWARING Answer that, Wilson.

Wilson picks up the phone.

WILSON Hello?

MAINWARING Wilson.

WILSON **(Covering the mouthpiece)** Yes – sir.

MAINWARING How many times have I told you not to say 'Hello'? Announce yourself. We're H.Q. No.1 Platoon, B Company, Walmington-on-Sea Home Guard and you are Platoon Sergeant Wilson.

WILSON **(To phone)** H.Q. No.1 Platoon, B Company, Walmington-on-Sea Home Guard and I am Platoon Sergeant Wilson. Hmm? – Hmm? – Oh hello!

Mainwaring reacts.

WILSON How awfully nice to hear your voice after all this time. Yes – it is ages isn't it – yes, we really must get together again –

MAINWARING **(Containing his patience no longer)** Who is it, Wilson?

WILSON Your wife – sir.

MAINWARING Oh! **(He takes the receiver)** Hello, Elizabeth – but I did give Empress her milk and I put her out of the back door just before I left… No, I am not mistaken, my dear. I remember it quite distinctly because she didn't want to go. **(He looks at his hand – with a handkerchief wound round it)** But I did say goodbye to you, dear – I called from the kitchen door …but, Elizabeth, dear – you know you don't like me crossing the parquet in my military boots.

Wilson reacts.

MAINWARING Wilson, fall the men in.

Wilson leaves.

MAINWARING No, it hasn't slipped my memory, dear, but I haven't seen Corporal Jones yet and you must appreciate that it is very difficult for me to ask him for under-the-counter oxtail when I am trying to maintain the discipline of the platoon… I don't think you are being very reasonable – if I may say so.

The receiver is very obviously banged down. Mainwaring replaces his receiver. He takes off his glasses and starts to clean them.

MAINWARING Are the men ready for inspection, Sergeant?

MAIN HALL. NIGHT

Mainwaring enters, not seeing the platoon which consists of Jones, Pike and two men – one in each of the other corners.

WILSON Well – er – there, there are one or two missing.

MAINWARING **(Still concentrating on his glasses)** Well, call the roll then.

WILSON Yes, sir… Jones.

JONES Very good, Sergeant. **(He reads the roll)** Agnew… not here, Bailey… not here, Godfrey… not here. Hardcastle… not here. Hope… not here. Jones… not here – oh yes he is – it's me. Jones… sir. Lovekin… not here… Macey… not here.

MAINWARING Jones, Jones – what is going on? What is all this?

JONES We've got a little bit of absenteeism without leave, sir.

MAINWARING I should think we have. All right, Sergeant Wilson, what's the explanation, where is everyone?

WILSON I'd rather not say, sir.

MAINWARING What are you talking about?

WILSON Well – well it's sneaking.

MAINWARING **(He nods him to one side)** Now, see here, Wilson, I don't want any of this public school rubbish. I order you to tell me the whereabouts of my troops.

WILSON They are in a pub, sir – playing darts.

MAINWARING They're what?

WILSON Against the A.R.P. Wardens.

MAINWARING Did you give them permission?

WILSON Oh, yes… and I said I didn't think it was an awfully good idea and if it was all the same to them I would rather they didn't.

JONES They thought they might get away with it, sir, but I knew your suspicions would be aroused when you said 'Fall in'.

MAINWARING Back to your place, Jones. This is ridiculous, Wilson. As soon as my back is turned, men come on parade like scarecrows and most of them don't come on parade at all. It's your slack discipline that's causing all this, you know.

WILSON Well, I do get quite cross with them at times.

MAINWARING Well – I'll tell you what I am going to do. I am going to pretend that this parade was called in ten minutes' time – that's 12 er… 16…

WILSON Twenty fifteen, sir.

MAINWARING I know, Wilson. You have ten minutes to round them up and get 'em here – so you had better get cracking.

WILSON Yes, sir.

MAINWARING Right – move! I said move!

WILSON **(He goes out)** I am moving.

MAINWARING I'm very glad to see that you are here, Pike.

PIKE My mum won't let me go into pubs.

MAINWARING Quite right, too. And Jones – I'm very glad to see that as ever you placed your duty first and didn't join the team.

JONES I wasn't picked.

MAINWARING Hmm?

JONES They said I couldn't see the board, sir.

Mainwaring reacts.

PUBLIC BAR OF PUB. NIGHT

The Warden is just throwing a couple of darts.

WARDEN There you are, 47 – chalk it up, Mr Godfrey.

Godfrey has the chalk and the blackboard.

GODFREY That leaves the A.R.P. with 58 and the Home Guard still with 301.

WARDEN Cor blimey – isn't it about time your lot started? **(Frazer takes the darts)**

WALKER Now come on, Taff – let's see that double or they're going to whitewash us.

FRAZER Whist man – you're putting me off. **(He throws)**

WALKER Oh, hell.

FRAZER Well, you didn't do any better.

WARDEN Shall I move the board a bit nearer for you?

Frazer throws two more darts and they both miss. Frazer looks at Walker.

WALKER I didn't say a word. **(He collects the darts)**

Enter Mrs Pike.

WARDEN Blimey, you're late, Mave.

MRS PIKE I had to get Frank off to his parade. Arthur isn't here, is he?

WARDEN No, of course not – he is minding the shop up at the drill hall. What are you having?

MRS PIKE The usual please, Bill.

WARDEN Shan't be a minute, lads. **(He goes to the bar)**

WALKER Hey – see that – Pikey's mum and the Warden. How long has that been going on?

FRAZER Dissipation is eating its way through the land like worms in a coffin lid.

WALKER Yeah – the beer is getting expensive, too. Same again all round, Mr Thurson.

GODFREY Only a small one for me – or I'll be getting tipsy.

THURSON It'll be mild only after this. You've had your bitter for tonight.

Sergeant Wilson enters the pub.

WALKER **(Seeing Wilson)** Aye, aye, this is going to be interesting.

WILSON Ah. Walker, Frazer, I think possibly that it wasn't quite such a good idea to miss the parade tonight because... **(He sees Mrs Pike)** Mavis, I say, what a surprise.

MRS PIKE Yes, isn't it.

WILSON I thought you were at home... w... w... washing things.

MRS PIKE Well, I just popped out for a bit.

WILSON Mavis – I don't really think you ought to come to a place like this all on your own.

The Warden brings back her drink without seeing Wilson.

WARDEN There you are, Mave – one double gin and tonic. **(He kisses her on the forehead)** And don't get all Nelly Dean like you did last week. **(He turns to the Sergeant in order to go to the dartboard)** Excuse me, mate – cor blimey – how d'yer do? **(He goes to the board)**

WILSON How do you do? **(To Mavis)** Does he know you?

MRS PIKE Well – he looks after me from time to time.

WILSON Looks after you?

Cut to Warden and Walker.

WARDEN 'Ere, Joe – tell him that drink was from you.

WALKER What for?

WARDEN When he finds out I have been going with her, he'll half kill me.

FRAZER Yon Sergeant? He couldn't punch a hole in a new laid egg.

WARDEN Couldn't he? Here you, what did you come here for? You ought to be back in the hall, playing soldiers.

WILSON Well... actually I came to get the men back on parade.

WARDEN They're not coming – there's two pints riding on this match and us wardens is winning, so go and present your arms somewhere else.

WILSON I don't think I like your tone.

WARDEN Oh don't you – well try this one. **(He blows a raspberry. Wilson is surprised and shocked)**

Warden triumphant.

WILSON I think that was rather vulgar. **(He turns to Mrs Pike)** Mavis, let me take you away from all this.

MRS PIKE This gentleman has bought me a drink and I think I would like to finish it if you don't mind.

WILSON Oh – oh yes, of course. **(He looks round, he doesn't know how to handle the situation – he decides to go. He turns)** Well, er… come as soon as you can, you chaps.

WALKER Yeh – okay, Sarge. **(Sergeant goes, Walker turns to Frazer)** That was exciting, wasn't it?

FRAZER Yon Sergeant makes me sick. To hell with the man who won't fight for his woman.

WARDEN **(Coming up to them)** I saw him off all right, didn't I?

FRAZER Aye – and we'll continue the game when your hands stop shaking.

CHURCH HALL. NIGHT

The platoon is drawn up for arms drill.

MAINWARING Order… arms!

MEN One two three… one two three, one.

PIKE Oh!

Jones annoyed.

MAINWARING Now, you were late that time, Pike.

Jones delighted.

PIKE I didn't want to tear my pocket, Mr Mainwaring.

MAINWARING Well the others will be here in a moment and then we can carry on with our normal training. **(The phone rings)** Right – carry on, Jones. **(He goes towards the small office)**

JONES Right, on the command – fall out. Carry on with maintenance of your firearms. Fall out.

They fall out.

SIDE OFFICE. CHURCH HALL. NIGHT

Mainwaring comes into small office and answers the phone.

MAINWARING No.1 Platoon, B Company Walmington-on-Sea Home Guard, Captain Mainwaring speaking. Oh yes, Elizabeth – I was about to explain about that when you slammed the receiver down. Very well – when you *put* the receiver down. Yes, yes, dear – I'll ask him in good time, but not now, I have a slight disciplinary crisis on my shoulders and it's very….

She obviously slams it down again.

JONES How long do you want all the two men to carry on?

MAINWARING Don't bother about that, Jones.

JONES No, sir. **(He turns)**

MAINWARING Er – Jones.

JONES Yes, sir.

MAINWARING May I have a word with you?

JONES Yes, sir.

MAINWARING Jones – er – I realise that your professional life must be very difficult at the moment.

JONES Yes it is, sir. Everyone wants a bit under the counter, sir.

MAINWARING I'm sure they do.

JONES If I was to tell you some of the things I have been offered for a bit on the side, sir – it'd make your hair stand on end.

MAINWARING Yes, I'm sure it would.

JONES I couldn't take advantage of half of them – even if I was that way inclined, sir.

MAINWARING Yes – well, as you know, I never ask for any – er – favours, Jones.

JONES I don't think I follow you, sir.

MAINWARING It's just that Mrs Mainwaring has conceived some ridiculous urge for some oxtail. You know how women are from time to time.

JONES You mean like pickles, sir?

MAINWARING Pickles?

JONES Yes, sir – pickles.

MAINWARING I don't think I quite follow you, Jones.

JONES At certain times, sir, women like pickles.

MAINWARING Do they?

JONES Yes, sir.

MAINWARING Oh, well, Mrs Mainwaring doesn't want pickles – she wants oxtail.

JONES And she shall have it, sir. The finest in the fridge. I shall take it round to her personal.

MAINWARING Thank you, Jones.

JONES I must say – it's most exciting news, sir.

MAINWARING What is?

JONES Mrs Mainwaring wanting oxtail, sir – so so to speak.

MAINWARING Is it? – er – I wouldn't have thought it exciting.

JONES Well – at all events – it must have been most unexpected, sir.

MAINWARING Hardly unexpected, Jones. Mrs Mainwaring gets this way from time to time.

JONES How come – you never actually had one, sir?

MAINWARING Well – er – I didn't like to ask for your help. **(The phone rings)** Hello? Look, you have no cause to worry any further my dear. Corporal Jones is going to deliver it personally. **(Jones reacts)** I think I ought to get back to parade now, my dear. Well, I don't think this is the time to go into that sort of thing, my dear – both are very important. **(She obviously slams the phone down again)** That'll be all, Jones, and I would be grateful if you would refrain from mentioning this to the men.

JONES Of course not, sir. I don't think I have the necessary skill, sir, but I was present at the confinement of a cow.

MAINWARING I don't know what you are talking about, Jones, but we will discuss it afterwards.

Jones goes.

Wilson enters.

MAINWARING Now, Wilson – get the men on parade.

WILSON What was that, sir?

MAINWARING Get the men on parade.

WILSON Oh – oh the men – I – I don't think they are here yet.

MAINWARING Not here? You mean to tell me you left without them.

WILSON Well, I suppose I must have done.

MAINWARING Did you tell them?

WILSON I think so.

MAINWARING You think so! But that is what you went for.

WILSON Well, that Warden fellow Hodges, was buying drinks for Mavis and he said last week she was Nelly Dean.

MAINWARING I beg your pardon?

WILSON Then he made a rude noise.

MAINWARING I think your mind is wandering, Wilson. You let it dwell on unhealthy things. Well, I'll tell you what. I'll give you one more chance to redeem yourself. I'm coming with you this time and if those men don't return – you can consider yourself relieved of your command and under open arrest. **(He goes to the door)** Corporal Jones – you are coming with us to that public house. It could be that destiny is moving in your direction.

Jones looks over shoulder.

THE PUB. NIGHT

Frazer is aiming with great deliberation and accuracy. He throws. There is a shout of approval from the Home Guard.

WALKER You've done it. **(General congratulations)**

GODFREY That makes one game all.

WARDEN **(Crosses to Mavis)** Drink up, Mave – you're going slow tonight.

MRS PIKE I mustn't have any more. I shan't be able to stand.

WARDEN I wouldn't let that worry you. You'll be in good hands.

Mainwaring enters – followed by Wilson and Jones.

MRS PIKE **(Seeing Mainwaring)** Oh dear – look who is coming.

WARDEN I'm just about in the mood for him. **(Mainwaring is about to approach the men and the Warden intercepts)** Now see here, Napoleon – if you've come to break up the game, you can think again, because they're not coming.

MAINWARING I've nothing to say to you, so kindly mind your own business. Walker – do your collar up – you are a disgrace to the platoon. **(Walker starts to do his collar up)**

WALKER Blimey – we thought you was in London.

WARDEN That's right – do as daddy says.

MAINWARING Will you be quiet. Now listen to me, men. I don't know whether this is deliberate disobedience or a misunderstanding, but you are all absent off parade. Now double up and fall in outside.

Walker moves.

WARDEN 'Ere – now steady on. It's one game all. You're not leaving now.

MAINWARING Oh yes they are.

WALKER Look – it is a bit awkward, sir. We promised them a game, you see.

MAINWARING War is more important than your game, Walker.

WALKER Yeh, but the Germans aren't actually coming now, are they? I mean – not for the next half hour or so.

FRAZER We're going to finish the game.

WALKER Like Drake.

WARDEN Tell you what, Napoleon, if the bells ring – I'll send them round in time for the battle.

WALKER We'll bring our darts.

MAINWARING Now look here, men.

FRAZER We're not coming, Mr Mainwaring.

MAINWARING Don't talk to me like that. Frazer, outside.

FRAZER You can't make us.

Mainwaring reacts.

MAINWARING Private Godfrey.

GODFREY Eh – yes, sir?

WARDEN He's not coming either.

GODFREY Well… I.

FRAZER Don't you rat on us, black leg.

MAINWARING I think you've all taken leave of your senses, but if you all go up to the hall in five minutes – I'll say no more about it.

WARDEN Go on – get off your high horse and have a pint.

FRAZER Aye – have a pint.

WALKER Yeh, have a couple of jars and we'll all go back together.

MAINWARING Come on, Wilson. They're evidently the worse for drink or they wouldn't behave like this. Come on, Jones.

JONES Well, I've just got a pint coming up, Mr Mainwaring.

MAINWARING Jones!

JONES (**Thinking better of it**) I'm coming.

MAINWARING Come on, Wilson.

WILSON Yes, sir. Mavis – I do think it would be much better if you left with me now.

MRS PIKE What would I do then – come and watch you play soldiers?

MAINWARING Wilson!

WILSON Yes, sir.

They all go.

WARDEN Well, that's got rid of 'im. Now then, last game coming up. My turn to shoot for double. (**He starts to play**)

GODFREY I somehow don't think we are doing the right thing.

WALKER (**Weakening a little**) He looked a bit put out, didn't he?

FRAZER Ach – the man is nothing but a bag of wind.

GODFREY I don't like to let him down. I know he wouldn't let me down. I think I would rather like to go.

FRAZER Oh no you don't – we are in this together and we'll see it through together. I'll not stand by and see the namby pamby weaklings go crawling back.

WALKER Yeh, I think we ought to stick together.

GODFREY I'm sorry, Mr Frazer, I've never been impressed by that sort of talk. I shall do what I think is right. (**He turns**)

FRAZER (**Calling after him**) Black leg.

WALKER Let 'im go.

WARDEN Look, are you playing darts or are you going to stand there blathering all night?

WALKER Yeh, let's play darts.

SIDE OFFICE. CHURCH HALL. NIGHT

Mainwaring is seated opposite Wilson.

MAINWARING The whole thing is beyond my comprehension, Wilson. I mean… fancy not wanting to come on parade. It's the highlight of my day. Do you know, while I'm having my tea I feel a sort of excitement mounting inside me. Then I put on my uniform and I march here to the parade and, do you know, I feel an enormous sense of pride in what we have achieved and what we stand for. We are doing something for England, and now… to see the platoon we've trained for all those months into a highly disciplined body of… fighting men, in the saloon bar – drunk, wenching… ugh. And Walker with a cigarette dangling out of the corner of his mouth… like some lounge lizard. (**Sigh**) I just don't understand it at all, do you?

WILSON Erm?

MAINWARING I said I don't understand it at all.

WILSON No, neither do I, sir. What can she see in him? He's such a coarse sort of man.

MAINWARING I don't think you've heard a word I've been saying.

Jones enters from the side hall with Pike.

JONES I'm afraid I have some bad news, sir.

MAINWARING Yes, Jones.

JONES The absentees still ain't present.

MAINWARING They'll have to be taught a lesson, Wilson.

JONES I would like to volunteer to teach them a lesson, sir. Let me put them all on a fizzer.

MAINWARING We can't do that, Jones.

JONES Give 'em field punishments, sir. Tie them to a wheel of a gun carriage.

MAINWARING We haven't got a gun carriage.

JONES Well, there's my butcher's van, sir. We could tie them to that.

MAINWARING Oh, do be sensible, Jones.

PIKE You can't dock their pay 'cos we don't get none.

JONES You could take away all their privileges, sir.

PIKE We haven't got any privileges.

JONES Then give us some – then you can take them away.

The phone rings.

MAINWARING Answer that, Wilson.

WILSON It's probably your wife again, sir.

MAINWARING Oh, this is the last straw. (**He picks up the phone**) Now look here, Elizabeth... er... oh – I'm sorry, sir. No.1 Platoon, B Company, Walmington-on-Sea. Home Guard – Captain Mainwaring speaking.

WILSON H.G. No. 1 Platoon....

MAINWARING Yes, Colonel?.... Great Scott!... You can rely on us to give the police all the support they need, sir. We'll go round there at once... Yes, sir, I'll take every available man – leave it in my hands. (**He puts the receiver down**) This would come at a time like this. An I.R.A. suspect has been located in Ivy Crescent.

WILSON Well, surely it is up to the police to deal with it.

MAINWARING Normally, yes, but the man is armed – the police have no weapons and have asked for our support.

JONES And they shall have it, sir – they shall have it – we will be there, sir.

PIKE Shall I go to the pub and tell the others, sir?

MAINWARING No – three loyal men are better than a hundred backsliders. Come on, men – we march alone. (**He goes quickly to the door. The others follow**)

JONES (**To Pike as they go**) What did he say about his backside?

MAIN HALL. NIGHT

Godfrey enters. The Verger is polishing the wooden struts to the balustrade with liquid from a large bottle.

GODFREY Oh – still working, Mr Yeatman?

VERGER I'm afraid so – I have to be at it all the time. I'm a fool to myself in that way you know.

Godfrey goes to the side office.

GODFREY Captain Mainwaring, sir – I've returned to duty... I... oh. (**He sees that nobody is there**)

FRONT DOOR OF SMALL TERRACED HOUSE. NIGHT

Mainwaring comes into shot with Wilson, Jones and Pike.

MAINWARING Twenty-seven – this is the one.

WILSON Where's the squad of police?

MAINWARING They're supposed to meet us here.

JONES Perhaps they're hiding behind the bushes. They do a lot of hiding behind bushes – when they're knocking people off.

MAINWARING I don't think that is very likely, Jones.

PIKE In *Public Enemy No.1* they hid behind cars, but there aren't any.

Policeman approaches.

POLICE CONSTABLE Oh – good evening. Are you the man from the Home Guard?

MAINWARING That's right – Captain Mainwaring

POLICE CONSTABLE Well, I'm the policeman.

MAINWARING Where's your squad?

POLICE CONSTABLE I'm the only one the Sergeant could spare.

MAINWARING But there is no raid on – what are the others doing?

POLICE CONSTABLE Playing darts.

MAINWARING Darts?

POLICE CONSTABLE Against the Free French. Oh, the Sergeant would have called it off – only he didn't know the French for cancelled.

MAINWARING Right – we will have to take care of this ourselves.

POLICE CONSTABLE We'd best be careful – they can be pretty ugly customers and he's armed an' all.

MAINWARING That won't worry us – we'll use Ju Jitsu. When he opens the door, I'll grab his arm and pull. Jones... you kneel down and trip him. Pike... you jump on top of him, and get his arm in a lock.

PIKE What sort of a lock?

JONES You want one like this. (**He demonstrates on Mainwaring**)

MAINWARING All right, Jones. (**Mainwaring extricates himself**) Lucky for you I didn't encounter that or you'd be flat on your back. Right – here we go. (**He rings the bell**)

MAINWARING Wilson. (**He hands Wilson a pistol**) Take this and stand over there. Only use it as a last resort – after all he is British – basically.

JONES I think I should knock as well, sir – he's probably listening to Lord 'awhaw.

MAINWARING Quiet, Jones.

PIKE Here he comes.

MAINWARING Right – ready everyone.

POLICE CONSTABLE Here, what am I supposed to do?

MAINWARING Arrest him, of course.

The door opens – Mainwaring steps in front of it to grab the man's arm. Jones kneels behind Mainwaring. Mainwaring pulls the man towards him and falls back over Jones, who is behind his knees. Jones goes for Mainwaring. Jones goes for Pike.

REGAN There, there, it's an awful mischief you'll be doing to yourself if you're not more careful – and you at your time of life and all.

MAINWARING Grab him, Jones – before he goes for his gun.

JONES I've got 'im, sir. **(Hugs the man from behind)**

MAINWARING Right. I'd advise you not to try any more of your tricks.

REGAN What tricks would I be trying? Me a God-fearing man and faithful servant of the Pope.

POLICE CONSTABLE Is your name Patrick Regan?

REGAN Sure 'tis my twin brother you'd be after. Is he in trouble again?

MAINWARING He's bluffing, Constable. Right, off to the station with him.

POLICE CONSTABLE He can't go there – it was bombed the night before last.

MAINWARING Damn – so it was. Where can we take him?

JONES Put him in my fridge, sir – let me put him in my fridge.

POLICE CONSTABLE They're picking him up from your headquarters.

MAINWARING Very well – we'll take him there. Stay right behind him, Wilson. **(To Regan)** If you try anything, it will be the worse for you.

REGAN You're quite right to be cautious, sir. Me twin brother is a terrible rough man. If I was him, you'd be in mortal danger.

MAINWARING I don't want any more of your blarney. Quick march.

THE PUB. NIGHT

The Warden is about to throw his darts.

WARDEN Now what do we need – 17? Right – one and a double eight. **(He throws)** There's the one. **(He throws again)** Whoops – eight. We'll have the double four then. **(He throws)** That's it. That's two pints all round you owe us. I'm going to enjoy this.

WALKER **(Going to the bar)** Come on, Taff – where's your share?

EDNA Sorry, the beer's off.

WARDEN What? After beating the living daylights out of them?

FRAZER Ah – that's bad luck. **(He puts his money back in his pocket)**

WALKER Never mind – some other time.

FRAZER No – gambling debts must be paid on the spot or not at all.

WARDEN There must be a drop in it. Take the barrel in the kitchen, love, and put it through the mangle.

WALKER 'Ere, Captain Mainwaring seemed a bit upset – what say we pop back and finish off the parade for him, eh?

FRAZER You're weakening, Joe – you've a heart of a coward.

WALKER I'm not – it's just that I don't like to upset him.

WARDEN Well, if you're going, I'm coming with you. I can't wait to see his face when I tell him the wardens beat his precious troops. Come on, Mave.

MRS PIKE But Arthur will be there.

WARDEN Who cares about him?

SIDE OFFICE. CHURCH HALL

Enter Mainwaring followed by Regan, Jones and Pike. Wilson brings up the rear.

MAINWARING Bring him in here. Right, you sit down there and behave yourself.

PIKE Yeh – one false move, buddy, and you'll be wearing a wooden overcoat.

MAINWARING Pike?

PIKE Yes?

MAINWARING Don't be silly.

REGAN It's a desperate band of men you have under you, General.

MAINWARING They can give a pretty good account of themselves when it comes to a scrap.

REGAN I'd not like to tangle with them and that's a fact.

WILSON Do you know – on the way here, I had a funny feeling we were being followed.

MAINWARING Don't be neurotic, Wilson. Constable... go and look out for the wagon.

THE MAIN HALL. NIGHT

Godfrey is dozing in a chair. The door bursts open. In come three large men. The Verger is still polishing in the background.

SEAMUS Where is he, then? Where is he?

Godfrey wakes suddenly. Seamus comes up to Godfrey in a threatening manner.

SEAMUS Where is he, then?

GODFREY Where – where is who?

SEAMUS The military man who has laid hands on Pat O'Regan. I'll split his head open and paper the walls with his guts.

GODFREY Oh, oh, I see – well you might find him round behind the stage in one of the dressing rooms.

SEAMUS Come on, boys, and if one of you hits him before me – I'll hit you before him.

Godfrey lets them go, then nips into the office.

SIDE OFFICE. NIGHT

GODFREY Oh, good evening, Captain Mainwaring.

MAINWARING Where have you been, Godfrey?

GODFREY Well, before I go into that, sir – I think I ought to explain that there are three large Irish gentlemen in the hall who say they are going to do awful things to you.

REGAN **(Shouting)** Seamus – I'm in here. **(He rises)**

MAINWARING Stop him, Pike.

Pike jumps on Regan. Jones whips out his bayonet.

JONES If you move a single muscle, you will have it up you and you will not like it.

MAINWARING Right – I'll soon settle this little lot. Give me my gun, Wilson.

WILSON I haven't got your gun.

MAINWARING I gave you my gun in the garden.

WILSON Well, I must have given it back to you.

SEAMUS **(From the hall)** His voice came from over here. He'll be in that room.

MAINWARING Shut the door, Godfrey.

GODFREY I already have, sir.

MAINWARING Where's the key, Wilson?

WILSON I haven't got the key.

MAINWARING You had the key.

GODFREY **(Showing key)** I've locked it, sir.

MAINWARING Right – Pike – run like the wind and get the others.

PIKE Yes, sir. **(He goes)**. But surely, sir, three loyal men are better than a hundred on their backside.

MAINWARING Don't talk rubbish, man. Run.

Pike goes. Three men start banging on the door.

SEAMUS Open up – open up you unbegotten sons of Britannia.

MAINWARING That's enough of that – I call on you to surrender in the name of the King.

SEAMUS Stuff the King. **(There is battering from the outside door)**

MAINWARING One of them has come round. Lock it, Wilson.

WILSON Where's the key?

MAINWARING Well, you are responsible for the key.

WILSON Why should I be responsible for the key?

VERGER Open up – it's me – the Verger.

MAINWARING Oh, come in, Verger.

VERGER I've locked them in – I've locked them in. **(He brandishes the key of the main hall)**

MAINWARING Quick thinking, Verger.

VERGER If I hadn't locked them in, they'd have done for you.

MAINWARING I'm most grateful – I can assure you.

VERGER When the Vicar learns of this – there's going to be a rumpus. It's a misuse of the 'all.

MAINWARING We can't go into all that.

VERGER You said it was for holding parades.

MAINWARING Never mind that now.

VERGER You're 'arbouring desperadoes.

JONES Don't start that sort of talk – you're a troublemaker.

VERGER I'm not a troublemaker – you're the troublemaker.

REGAN If you ask me – you're both troublemakers.

VERGER You mind your own business. **(Hits him over the head with the polish bottle. There is a knock on the door)**

MAINWARING Look out.

WALKER **(Outside)** It's all right, Captain Mainwaring – it's us. **(He enters)** Sorry we're late.

PIKE They was on the way 'ere, Mr Mainwaring – they was on the way.

FRAZER I told them all to report for duty, sir.

Three other members of the squad enter.

MAINWARING Right – now we can do something. Godfrey, you open the door and we'll rush in and overpower them. Are we all ready?

ALL Yes, sir.

WILSON I'll go first.

JONES I'd like to volunteer to go first.

MAINWARING Ready, Godfrey? Right.

Phone rings.

WILSON **(Lifting receiver)** Hello, I'm afraid it's not awfully convenient at the moment.

The Warden enters with Mrs Pike. All hell is let loose in the large hall, but the camera stays in the small hall. We hear blows and grunts.

WARDEN 'Ere, what's all the noise about?

One by one the platoon stagger back into the side office – nursing various wounds.

JONES Mr Mainwaring, they've taken my bayonet.

MAINWARING **(Out of vision)** Jones, let me in.

JONES They took my bayonet.

SEAMUS Is there any more of you after trying?

MAINWARING Quick – shut the door, Wilson. Right – soften 'em up a bit.

MRS PIKE Arthur – they've hit my little Frank. Well, what are you going to do about it?

WILSON Stand out of the way. Ah – yes – well – open the door.

MAINWARING Wilson – what are you doing?

Wilson goes into the hall. There are more blows and grunts. We hold on Mainwaring and the Warden who can see through the door. Wilson re-enters.

MRS PIKE Arthur.

MAINWARING Wilson! Where did you learn to do that?

WILSON Well as a matter of fact – at my public school.

WARDEN I'd never have believed it.

WILSON I think it is about time you cleared off.

WARDEN You're right, mate. I could do with an early night. **(He goes)**

MRS PIKE We could all do with an early night. Come along, Arthur.

POLICE CONSTABLE The van's outside.

MAINWARING Right, everybody get them into the van.

MAIN HALL. NIGHT

Platoon is lined up – black eyes, split heads, arms in slings, cheeks with plasters, etc.

MAINWARING Well, we've all had a good early night and, as a result, none of us seem very much worse for our experiences. I must say I'm very proud of the way you tackled an extremely dangerous task. As for your earlier lapse – well – I'm prepared to forget it because I'm sure it won't happen again.

ALL It won't, sir – you can rely on us.

FRAZER I was against it from the very start.

MAINWARING Now there is only one other thing I have to mention. As a result of a misunderstanding between Corporal Jones and myself... certain rumours are circulating round the town regarding Mrs Mainwaring's condition. They are quite untrue. Mrs Mainwaring and I have never been blessed in that manner, although – in all other respects our marriage has been a most happy one – in fact – quite blissful.

Phone rings.

WILSON Er... the phone is ringing, sir – shall I answer it?

MAINWARING No. **(Sadly)** It's probably for me.

SERIES FOUR **EPISODE SEVEN**

Recorded: Friday 30/10/70

Original transmission: Friday 6/11/70, 8.00–8.30pm

Original viewing figures = 13 million

ARTHUR LOWE .... CAPTAIN MAINWARING
JOHN LE MESURIER .... SERGEANT WILSON
CLIVE DUNN .... LANCE CORPORAL JONES
JOHN LAURIE .... PRIVATE FRAZER
JAMES BECK .... PRIVATE WALKER
ARNOLD RIDLEY .... PRIVATE GODFREY
IAN LAVENDER .... PRIVATE PIKE
BILL PERTWEE .... ARP WARDEN
STUART SHERWIN .... MR ALBERTS (SECOND ARP WARDEN)
GORDON PETERS .... LIGHTHOUSE KEEPER
AVRIL ANGERS .... FREDA, THE TELEPHONE OPERATOR

PLATOON .... COLIN BEAN, HUGH HASTINGS, VIC TAYLOR

Put That Light Out!

• BILL McLEAN REMEMBERS •

'In the mid-1960s I joined a theatrical agency to represent their clients. Almost immediately I was asked to cover a performance of a play at Golders Green Hippodrome in which Arnold Ridley was appearing. He was in his late sixties, what is now known as an "actor of the old school", and, at that time, best known as author of *The Ghost Train*.

'I met him with some trepidation but my worries were groundless, he couldn't have been easier to work with, saying: "You do your job and tell me where to do mine". This working relationship continued happily until his death. However, he didn't suffer incompetence easily, "an advantage of growing old", he told me, "gives you the opportunity to say what you think". I heard him say to the director of a production of *The Ghost Train* that perhaps one day he (the director) would write a play and then he could "bugger it up"!

'Together we found a supply of work, including the role of the Vicar in *Crossroads*. Whilst working on a television production he passed on the information that the director, David Croft, was planning a series using "a lot of old men" and could I follow it up? David was not convinced Arnold would live long enough to complete the first series – Eric Morecambe had referred to him as "the crumbling ruin" – and I think Arnold felt the same as he told me he always had his birthdays early in case he didn't make it!

'However, he survived and was in every single episode, in spite of his leg being in a plaster cast from ankle to hip during the making of one series. By the time of his death he was best known for *Dad's Army* and he and/or Private Godfrey was a household name.'

BILL McLEAN
Agent and Friend

Put That Light Out!

SIDE OFFICE

Jones, Mainwaring and Wilson are in attendance. Mainwaring is lecturing at the blackboard.

MAINWARING Now, to be successful at waging war, every Commander in the field must place himself in the enemy's shoes and see the situation from that point of view. So, what I ask myself, if I were in Adolf's shoes, what would Adolf be thinking?

WALKER He'll probably be wondering what you're doing with his shoes on.

MAINWARING That may be quite amusing, Walker, but it doesn't help very much.

JONES Sir, he'll probably be wondering what we're up to.

MAINWARING Quite right, Jones. What have we been doing since Dunkirk?

PIKE Or perhaps Herr Hitler is putting himself in your shoes, wondering what you're wondering.

MAINWARING Don't be silly, Pike. No, Hitler is saying to himself, what the devil have we been up to since Dunkirk. What are you smiling at, Wilson?

WILSON I was thinking it was an awfully good question, isn't it?

MAINWARING **(Kills him with a look)** Well, of course, the only way for Hitler to find out for certain is to come here and have a look.

PIKE That new Air Raid Warden in Gardenia Gardens looks like Herr Hitler.

MAINWARING No, Pike. I don't think Hitler will come here in person. What he might do is send recce parties by submarine or by fast, silent surface craft.

FRAZER Canoes.

MAINWARING I beg your pardon, Frazer?

FRAZER Canoes. They might come in canoes.

WALKER Blimey, it's Nazis we're talking about not Apache Indians.

GODFREY I thought Apaches were French dancers where the man treats the woman rather roughly. I never liked them very much.

JONES They had a couple on the bill once with Nellie Wallace. He treated her with disdain and threw her at the trombone player. She was a haughty young miss with very big thighs and long black stockings.

FRAZER Big thighs, did you say?

MAINWARING I think we're wandering from the point a little.

WALKER Yeah, let Captain Mainwaring get back into Hitler's shoes.

MAINWARING Now, the most likely place for the recce party to come ashore would, of course, be the estuary, here. **(Shows point on the board)**

PIKE Captain Mainwaring, sir, can I ask a question? Are you saying it is the most likely from 'standing in Hitler's shoes' or from 'standing in your shoes'?

MAINWARING We will leave that aside for the moment, Pike.

JONES Yes, we've passed that bit.

MAINWARING Now, I have secured permission for us to establish an observation post in the lighthouse, here.

JONES Permission to interfere, sir. They don't use the lighthouse now, sir, so it will be shut and not open.

FRAZER They used it when yon convoy came through.

MAINWARING Quite right, Frazer, it is used on special occasions and they're perfectly happy for us to mount guard there from time to time. This evening, Corporal Jones, you will take your section and rendezvous at the A.R.P. post at the Jolly Roger Ice Cream Parlour, here on the jetty. At low tide you will cross the causeway, here. Now, once in the lighthouse, you will open these sealed orders. **(He gives him a package)** At dawn, when the tide goes out, and the causeway's passable, you will return. Is that understood?

JONES Yes, sir. Just one question, sir. What shall I do after I've opened the sealed orders?

MAINWARING Read the sealed orders, Jones. Right – dismiss!

They start to go. Walker hangs behind.

WALKER Excuse me, sir. I shan't be able to go with them this evening. You see, I'm delivering essential supplies.

MAINWARING I've heard about your essential supplies before, Walker.

WALKER Ah, yeah, well this is vital, you see – it's for the hospital, for the nurses.

MAINWARING Not elastic again?

WALKER No – hairpins.

MAINWARING Oh, really, Walker.

WALKER Straight up, sir. Their hair keeps dropping in the operations, see, and the surgeon's a bit of a fusspot. Tell you what, I'll report back here as soon as I've delivered.

MAINWARING This isn't good enough you know, Walker. A parade is a parade.

WALKER I think I'll have that bottle of Scotch you asked

me for.

MAINWARING Yes, well, never mind about that. You just get here as soon as you possibly can. You understand?

WALKER Yes, sir. Oh – and Bert's fixed the Lewis gun – 15 bob and no questions asked. I'll bring it round – and the whisky.

MAINWARING Splendid. Right, off you go.

Walker salutes and goes.

MAINWARING My – he's a rough diamond. Good-hearted though.

WILSON So it seems. But if you don't mind my saying so, sir, this expedition to the lighthouse and all this business of looking out for Nazi recce parties, seems awfully far-fetched.

MAINWARING Do you think I'm a fool, Wilson?

WILSON Well, I wouldn't... er... be quite so sweeping as that, sir.

MAINWARING I'm only using it as a pretext. It's about time we gave Jones a real feeling of command. I can't wet nurse him all the time. Let him handle men, let him deal with this strange mixture of temperaments and learn to lead them. There's always method in my madness you know, Wilson.

WILSON It's most comforting to know that, sir.

Mainwaring reacts.

THE LAMPHOUSE

We see it as a cross section of the optic including the lens, the inner gallery, a wall with switch gear and some controls for the fog signals and distress signals, fire extinguishers, etc. This wall also incorporates the door to the lower part of the lighthouse.

JONES (Out of vision) Left, right, left, right, mark time. Open – door.

Pike, leading the section, opens the door and enters.

JONES Forward!

They enter carrying rifles, slung, and a couple of blankets, rolled.

JONES Mark time! Halt! Right turn.

Jones is very keyed up and shouting pretty loudly.

JONES Right, pay attention. (He shouts again) I am now going to take out the sealed orders and unseal them. (Jones, with some difficulty, balances his rifle while opening the envelope) Now, when I have opened the sealed orders, I will read them to you and you will pay attention.

• PETER DAY REMEMBERS •

'This episode finds members of the platoon inside a lighthouse. To make our replica as accurate as possible we took measurements at Beachy Head lighthouse. I made up some formers, and together with some plastic sections to represent the lenses, formed the lamp housing. The electricians put in a bulb and when it went round and round it looked just like the real thing.

'The rest of the structure was made out of painted plywood, and for the rivets we used wooden circles, stuck them on and painted over the whole thing. It worked well.'

PETER DAY
Visual Effects Designer

GODFREY I wonder if I could be excused while you're opening the orders.

JONES No, you can't, you have to wait. Now, pay attention.

GODFREY It's an awfully long way down.

JONES Here we are, orders for section on watch from the lighthouse. 1. You will commence duty at two thousand hours.

FRAZER Twenty hundred hours.

JONES Silence in the ranks. You will commence duty at twenty hundred hours. 2. You will keep strict look out for any fifth columnists, spies or saboteurs infiltrating up the estuary. Right, do you understand that? Pike, you will watch for fifth columnists. Frazer, you will watch for spies, and Godfrey, you will watch for saboteurs.

PIKE What do we do if we see any?

JONES You tell me. I'm your commander, then I tell Captain Mainwaring, he's my commander and he will tell his commander. Is that understood?

GODFREY May I be excused now?

JONES Not yet, Godfrey. 3. Guards will not be relieved until 08.00 hours. Right, do you all understand the sealed orders?

FRAZER Of course we do. Stop blathering and let's make ourselves comfortable.

JONES I don't want any of that sort of talk. Right, fall out!

They fall out.

FRAZER **(To Pike)** If he goes on like that, I'll chuck him over the side.

JONES I don't want any of that dumb insolence. Right, it's getting dark, so make your beds ready. Pike, you're on guard. Mr Godfrey, it's down at the bottom of the stairs.

Godfrey goes through the door.

PIKE Mr Jones – now I'm on guard alone, do you want me to look out for spies, fifth columnists and saboteurs or just for fifth columnists?

JONES **(Thinks he's being got at)** I'll give you a word of advice, young Pike. Never try to old soldier an old soldier.

Pike looks very mystified.

MAINWARING'S OFFICE

Mainwaring is preparing a schedule.

MAINWARING Right, so we'll revise platoon advance to contact and on Wednesday platoon in the attack.

WILSON Isn't it about time we did platoon in retreat?

MAINWARING We're not going to do any retreating.

WILSON I think we ought to know.

Warden enters.

MAINWARING I don't care for that sort of talk.

WARDEN Ah, glad I caught you. **(To Wilson)** And you.

MAINWARING We're very busy, Mr Hodges, what is it?

WARDEN I'll tell you what it is. **(He takes out a notebook)** For the last two weeks I've been having serious reports from my warden on this street. You've been flashing lights from this hall on 27 separate occasions. That's three more than 17 Pembroke Gardens, and they turned out to be enemy aliens.

MAINWARING No, I'm sorry. I can't accept that at all.

WARDEN Look, it's all down here. On the night before last you opened and shut this door here so many times that my men lost count.

WILSON That's when Jones had been cooking sausages, sir, and the pan caught fire and you were trying to get rid of the smoke before the Vicar came in, so you opened and shut the door to make a sort of draught.

MAINWARING Yes all right, Wilson.

WARDEN There you are – convicted out of your own mouth. Well, I'm not putting up with this any longer. One more infringement from your premises and I'm having you up before the magistrate.

MAINWARING I think you're being very high-handed about this... er... very trivial affair and what's more you have no authority over the Military.

WARDEN Military! That's a laugh for a start. Now look here, Mainwaring. You think you can strut around here like Lord Muck – well you can't. **(He shakes his finger in Mainwaring's face)** I'm in charge of this sector and I'm warning you.

MAINWARING Put your finger down and leave my headquarters.

WARDEN I'm going, but you've had your last chance. **(He moves to the door)** One more flash out of you and you'll have a policeman feeling your collar. **(He goes)**

MAINWARING What a common man he is.

WILSON All the same, I think we should be a little more careful until he cools off.

MAINWARING Oh, there's no need for us to worry about him.

WILSON Well, I daresay he could bring some sort of prosecution.

MAINWARING I doubt it. The Chief Constable is a member of the Bridge Club, you know. That reminds me, I must take you along there some time. You do like a game of bridge, I suppose?

WILSON No, not very much.

MAINWARING I don't know how you think you're ever going to get your own branch.

LIGHTHOUSE

PIKE **(Sitting eating sandwich)** Corporal Jones, Mr Godfrey's rather a long time down there. Do you think he's all right?

JONES I expect he is. There's a lot of steps you know, they always have a lot of steps in lighthouses.

PIKE But he's been gone about 15 minutes.

FRAZER By the time he gets half-way up he'll probably have to go down again.

JONES Perhaps you'd better pop and see if he's all right.

FRAZER Did you lock and bar the door to the rock when you came up?

PIKE No, I left it open, I think.

FRAZER Then wild horses will not drag me down there before dawn.

PIKE Why not, Mr Frazer?

FRAZER It happened to my old schoolfriend – Wally Reagan. He was keeper of the light on the Fairloch Rock. 'Tis a wild, lonely, storm-battered crag, you ken, and many a ship has gone to a cold, watery grave pounding on the granite boulders. One night, such as this, when the wind was wailing dolefully in the rigging.

PIKE Mr Frazer, lighthouses don't have rigging.

FRAZER **(Definitely)** This one did. Wally started down the stairs to bring up a new wick for the lamp. Near the bottom something made him stop. Suddenly, below in the gloom he could hear a low, painful moan and a slithering. Something was moving in the dark. Wally started back upstairs – 20 steps up he stopped and turned – he could see nothing but the dark was darker and the moan was moaning louder, the slithering grew nearer and nearer and nearer. Wally didn't hesitate, he started up the stairs, up and up he climbed, on and on until his lungs were gasping and his heart was bursting out of his chest. He daren't stop because he knew the thing was behind him. He opened his mouth to cry 'help', but no sound would come from his lips. He reached the top and with one last heave he flung himself into the lamphouse and threw his weight against the door. Holding his breath, he listened – there it was, unmistakeable, the thing was on the other side trying to get in, trying to get in.

There is a knock on the door. Pike yells and Jones joins in.

PIKE Aaaahh!

JONES Aaaahh! Don't panic, don't panic! It can't get in, it can't get in!

FRAZER Quiet all of you, quiet! And listen! **(They pause to listen)**

GODFREY **(On the other side of the door)** Would somebody mind opening the door?

THE JOLLY ROGER ICE CREAM KIOSK AT THE END OF THE JETTY

The Warden parks his bike and enters. The second warden is there, making tea.

WARDEN Oh, I didn't expect to see you. Since the siren hasn't gone I was going to leave a note.

SECOND WARDEN Oh, anything important?

WARDEN Well, there's a bit of a blitz on blackouts. The police have been complaining to the big-wigs at Area H.Q. They've sent a note down to me.

SECOND WARDEN We don't have much bother here, being on the harbour front. Fancy a cup?

WARDEN Wouldn't say no. Anyway, watch it. Two lumps please.

THE LAMPHOUSE

PIKE Corporal Jones?

JONES Yes, Pikey.

PIKE You won't leave me and go downstairs without telling me, will you?

JONES No, I won't.

PIKE Corporal Jones, if we went downstairs we wouldn't see Wally's slithering thing, would we?

JONES No, of course not.

PIKE I mean, it's a different lighthouse, isn't it?

JONES Different altogether.

PIKE All the same, I'm stopping up here, aren't you?

JONES As long as possible. When we go, we go together.

PIKE That'll be nice and we'll take our rifles and a candle, and if we see Wally's slithering thing, we'll shoot it.

JONES And we'll fix our bayonets an' all.

PIKE Yeah, I don't suppose slithery things like it up 'em any better than Fuzzie Wuzzies.

JONES You can't beat cold steel, Pikey.

PIKE I wish Uncle Arthur was with us, don't you?

JONES No, I wish we was with him.

Pause.

GODFREY I say.

JONES **(Jumping up in panic)** What's the matter? Where is it?

GODFREY It's nothing, I was just wondering, if we see any spies, how do we tell Captain Mainwaring?

JONES Ah, yes er yes, well, I expect we've got to use our initiative.

FRAZER Failing that, there's a telephone on the wall.

JONES That's right, that's what I said, we use our initiative and use the telephone.

GODFREY How do we know it's working?

JONES We'd better try it, that's the best thing to do. **(Lifting the receiver)** Hello, Jack Jones, the butcher. **(He shakes it)** It's dead.

GODFREY Dead?

FRAZER Then we're cut off.

JONES Everybody keep calm, we're cut off. **(He jiggles the hook)**

PIKE I know what's happened, that slithery thing has wrapped itself round the wire.

FRAZER 'Course it hasn't, you young fool.

GODFREY Perhaps they haven't paid the bill.

FRAZER Lighthouses don't have bills. **(He takes the phone and tries it)**

GODFREY My sister forgot to pay the bill and they cut it off. We didn't know for two weeks, not many people ring us up, you see.

JONES There's some writing here. Perhaps it's operating instructions. Bring your torch, Pikey.

PIKE The battery's not very good.

JONES They print these things so small these days – can't read them.

PIKE There's a light just there.

JONES You can't use that, we're not blacked out.

FRAZER Well, shade it, you can use it long enough for a quick look.

Jones tries the switch below the bracket lamp – nothing happens.

JONES That's cut off an 'all. Everybody keep calm, the electricity is cut off.

PIKE Do you think the slithery thing…

FRAZER **(Interrupting)** Shut up!

JONES Wait a minute – there's a main switch here. **(He pushes a plunger on an electric box, from down below there's a low moan which rises in pitch. They listen)**

PIKE It's the slithery thing. Aaahh, aaahh!

JONES Shut the door, bar the door. **(He rushes to the door with Pike)**

GODFREY Oh dear, I think I'm rather frightened.

PIKE Look. **(He points to the lamp which is beginning to revolve slowly)**

FRAZER It's no slithery thing, it's the generator.

JONES Ah, that's all right then. **(Shouting)** There's no need to panic, lads, it's only the generator, it is only the generator. **(The lamp bursts into brightness)** Oh, blimey!

PIKE We can see the telephone instructions all right now, Mr Jones.

FRAZER Aye, but what about the blackout?

PIKE I think you'd better switch it off, Mr Jones.

JONES You're right, Pikey. **(He goes to the switch)** Keep calm, I'm going to switch it off. **(He pushes at the plunger – nothing happens)** It don't seem to work, that's funny.

PIKE It just says start, it doesn't say stop.

FRAZER Maybe, there's another switch somewhere.

JONES I don't see one.

PIKE They had a time switch in *The Phantom Light with Gordon.*

FRAZER We can't spend all night looking for switches while that thing's lighting up the whole coast. You've got to act, man.

JONES Right, yes, we've got to act. You keep looking for switches, Pikey and we'll do – something else. I know, fix bayonets.

FRAZER You're not going to charge the damn thing, are you?

JONES Do as I say. I'm in command here. Fix bayonets!

GODFREY My sister broke a 40-watt bulb once by accident and there was an awful bang. I think if we were to break that one it would blow us into the sea.

JONES Now, Private Godfrey, hook your blanket on the two bayonets. Hurry up, go on. **(Godfrey takes the corner of his blanket and hooks it on Frazer's bayonet)** Give me the other corner. **(Jones does likewise on his own bayonet)** Right, now follow me. **(He holds up his rifle, Frazer does likewise, they start to run round screening the beam as it circles)**

MAINWARING'S OFFICE

MAINWARING Good, well that's got rid of the bumph for the time being. They love their red tape, these brass hats at the War Office. It makes it very hard for the front-line fighting troops.

WILSON **(Rising)** Well, this front-line fighting troop will make an early night of it I think, sir.

MAINWARING Yes, why not.

Wilson steps out of the office.

WILSON May I put the light out for a while?

MAINWARING Yes, I suppose so.

WILSON I… Hello, that's funny.

MAINWARING **(Inside)** I don't find it very funny, put on the light.

WILSON What do you make of this, sir?

Mainwaring appears.

MAINWARING Oh, it's only the lighthouse. Probably a special convoy or something. Great Scott! Jones' section.

WILSON Do you think it's just possible, sir, they might have meddled with something that didn't concern them?

MAINWARING Come on, Wilson, down to the harbour!

They go quickly.

INTERIOR. JOLLY ROGER ICE CREAM KIOSK

WARDEN **(Finishing cup of tea)** That was just what I call a real good cup of tea.

SECOND WARDEN That fellow Walker from the Home Guard got a couple of extra pounds for us.

WARDEN Did he? I wouldn't have touched it if I'd known. Well, since the Luftwaffe haven't honoured us with their presence I think I'll pop off home. Night, night, Mr Alberts.

He goes out.

EXTERIOR. JOLLY ROGER ICE CREAM KIOSK

He is being illuminated by the light.

WARDEN Here, Mr Alberts, I didn't know they were flashing tonight. I haven't been notified.

SECOND WARDEN I saw the Home Guard lot going across at low tide.

WARDEN What? Not Mainwaring's mob?

SECOND WARDEN Well, that old Lance Corporal anyway.

WARDEN Those bloody hooligans. Put that light out, put that ruddy light out!

SECOND WARDEN They can't hear you, Mr Hodges.

WARDEN I'll make 'em hear me. Put that light out! Where's that phone? **(He goes inside)** I'll get on to Mainwaring, I'll tell him, I'll tell headquarters. I'll have him busted.

THE LAMPHOUSE

Godfrey and Pike are running round with their rifles and blankets keeping up with the beam.

GODFREY I don't think I can keep this up much longer.

JONES Right, Private Frazer, stand by to take over with me next time round.

FRAZER It's like the ruddy Olympic relay race.

JONES Right, left, right, left, right. **(Jones and Frazer take the guns and blankets from Godfrey and Pike)** Pick 'em up, pick 'em up.

FRAZER Don't go so fast, you fool. You're gaining on the light. Pull back, pull back. **(In trying to ease Jones' pace by pulling back on his bayonet, Frazer drops his end of the blanket)**

JONES **(Turning)** What are you playing at, Private Frazer? When I say 'left, right, left, right, pick 'em up'. I mean 'left, right, left, right'. **(In turning, Jones has draped the blanket into the turning track of the lamp. He tries to pull it out)** It's stuck.

PIKE Mr Jones, I think you've clogged the cogs.

The lamp now stops.

FRAZER Well, at least we don't have to run round in circles like squirrels in a cage.

GODFREY Doesn't Walmington look pretty all lit up?

JONES Oh, heck, the light's stuck over the town.

PIKE It's a good job the siren hasn't gone, eh, Mr Jones?

The siren starts.

JONES Captain Mainwaring isn't going to be very pleased with us.

THE JOLLY ROGER ICE CREAM KIOSK

Wilson and Mainwaring arrive and look out to sea brightly illuminated by the beam.

WILSON It seems to have stopped going round and round, sir.

MAINWARING This is damn serious, Wilson, it's lighting up the whole town. We're a sitting target for every Jerry plane within 50 miles.

The Warden emerges.

WARDEN That fool Mainwaring, isn't even in his headquarters. **(He sees him)** Here, look, look. Your lot have done that! The whole town lit up like Blackpool illuminations and now Jerry's arrived.

MAINWARING I'm well aware of the situation, thank you, Warden.

WARDEN I want to know what you're going to do about it? I want to be informed.

MAINWARING You and I have got to get out there, Wilson.

WILSON We can't, sir, the tide's in. The causeway will be under six foot of water.

MAINWARING Then we must get a boat.

SECOND WARDEN You can't, you'd be dashed to pieces on the rocks.

MAINWARING At all events, we can try. **(He goes for one of the circular lifebelts that is hanging outside the kiosk)** Grab those lifebelts, Wilson. **(He starts to put one on himself)**

SECOND WARDEN You can't do it.

WARDEN Don't stop 'em. Let 'em go, let 'em be dashed to pieces. Serve 'em right.

SECOND WARDEN You can't do it, I tell you.

Mainwaring putting on his lifebelt.

MAINWARING There's no such thing as can't. If the spirit is there, nothing can stop us.

SECOND WARDEN There isn't a boat.

MAINWARING Ah, that is an obstacle. We shall have to think of something else.

WARDEN A pound to a penny, he'll try and walk on the water.

Enter Walker, in uniform and with Lewis gun.

WALKER Blimey, this is a bit of a lark, ain't it? Old Jonesey's up the creek without a paddle, and no mistake.

MAINWARING We've got to get that light out somehow, Walker.

WARDEN Shoot it out.

MAINWARING I beg your pardon?

WARDEN He's got a gun, shoot it out.

MAINWARING Oh no, no, no. We can't do that.

WARDEN You mean you couldn't hit it.

MAINWARING We might hit one of my men.

WARDEN Well, what about the town? What about all those women and children? And all those bombs raining down on them?

MAINWARING The bombs are not raining down on them.

WARDEN They will be any minute. Right, if you won't take a decision, I will. Give it here. (**He grabs at the rifle**)

MAINWARING Take your hands off that gun.

WARDEN Don't you handle me, Mainwaring.

MAINWARING Give me back that gun.

There is a brief struggle.

WARDEN Oh, I'm going dizzy. Get me a chair, I'm going to have one of my turns.

They move him to bench. The Warden is sat on a bench. Mainwaring collects himself, Walker takes him on one side.

WALKER Here, Mr Mainwaring, I know a bloke at the Power Station. Now, if I saw him right he'd black out the county. Mind you, the aircraft factory would have to stop.

MAINWARING Don't be ridiculous, Walker.

WALKER Tell you what, there's a transformer round the back here. We could have a go at that.

WILSON Look, if you can't be sensible, Walker, keep quiet.

MAINWARING It seems quite sensible to me, Wilson. Lead on, Walker.

THE LIGHTHOUSE

They have rigged another blanket on bayonets.

JONES Right, lads, lift it up and that will stop the light falling on the town.

They raise the blanket.

PIKE (**Looking out**) That's quite good.

GODFREY Yes, it doesn't stop it entirely. It's a much gentler light. The other was awfully harsh.

Smoke is coming from the centre of the blanket.

PIKE Mr Jones, there's smoke coming from the middle of the blanket.

JONES I expect it's a bit damp, it'll air it for us.

PIKE When my mum puts clothes in front of the fire to air them, they steam white and this is steaming black.

The blanket bursts into flame.

JONES It's on fire, it's on fire. Don't panic, don't panic.

Pike grabs the fire extinguisher.

PIKE I've got it, I'll do it.

Pike sprays everything liberally with foam.

JUNCTION BOX BEHIND THE HUT

WALKER There you are.

WILSON Unfortunately, it seems to be locked.

WALKER That's easy. (**To Mainwaring**) Got a hairpin?

MAINWARING Am I likely to have a hairpin?

WILSON I thought you sold them.

WALKER Well, I don't want to open a new packet, do I? I mean I stand to lose, don't I?

MAINWARING Here, take this paper clip.

WALKER That'll do the trick. (**He turns to operate on the lock**) Look, do you mind looking the other way? It's sort of professional etiquette, do you understand?

WILSON Oh, get on with it, Walker.

Walker opens the door.

WALKER There we are.

MAINWARING Now, all we need is the right switch.

WILSON (**Shining a torch**) I don't see many switches.

WALKER There's plenty of wires though, and insulators.

MAINWARING Lend me your steel helmet, Walker.

WILSON Don't do anything foolhardy, sir.

MAINWARING Right, stand back.

Mainwaring takes the steel helmet and throws it into the box. There is a flash and a lot of smoke.

WALKER Blimey, that should have done the trick.

Mainwaring stands up. His face is blackened and the brim of his hat is charred away.

MAINWARING Right, now walk away slowly as if nothing has happened.

THE JOLLY ROGER ICE CREAM KIOSK

The second warden comes out.

SECOND WARDEN The lights have fused.

WARDEN **(Pointing at the lighthouse)** Pity that one hasn't. Get the hurricane lamps. **(Second warden goes back into hut)**

THE LIGHTHOUSE

Pike is behind the switches.

PIKE Mr Jones, I think I've found the switch.

JONES Then switch it, Pikey. That's what you must do lad, switch it.

Pike switches it. The fog signal starts. It is deep and very loud. They react.

THE JOLLY ROGER ICE CREAM KIOSK

WARDEN Blimey, if they can't see us, they'll be able to hear us. I can't stand it, I shall have to have my pill... **(Mainwaring appears)** Cor blimey, it's Hutch.

MAINWARING Dammit, the light's still on.

WARDEN Of course it is still on. It's gone inside there though. **(He indicates the hut. The lighthouse keeper enters)**

KEEPER Who's been flashing without my authority?

MAINWARING Who are you?

KEEPER I'm the keeper. They've no business to flash without my authority.

MAINWARING Can you switch it off from the mainland?

KEEPER Of course not. It's powered by its own generator.

WALKER Here, why don't we get through on the phone.

KEEPER It's cut off. It's not manned, you see.

WILSON Maybe we could get the exchange to reconnect.

MAINWARING Good thinking, Wilson.

They go swiftly into the hut.

MAINWARING **(Picking up phone and jiggling the hook)** Hello, hello.

KEEPER I used to live there, you see. But my lungs couldn't stand it anymore, the salt got in them, you see. I used to cough something awful, pitiful it was.

MAINWARING Will you please put me on to the supervisor.

OPERATOR Ooh, I can't do that, she goes off at six, there's only me here.

MAINWARING I see, then you will have to deal with it. Now, please listen very carefully.

OPERATOR Yes.

MAINWARING I'm Captain Mainwaring of the Home Guard.

OPERATOR Who?

MAINWARING Captain Mainwaring. M A I N W A R I N G.

OPERATOR Do you want me to write it down?

MAINWARING No, no. Just listen.

OPERATOR Yes, I'm listening.

MAINWARING Now, I'm speaking from the Jolly Roger Ice Cream Parlour.

OPERATOR That's been shut since the war.

MAINWARING I know, it is an Air Raid Warden's post and I'm speaking from there at this moment.

OPERATOR Captain Mainwaring?

MAINWARING That's right.

OPERATOR Of the Home Guard?

MAINWARING Yes.

OPERATOR Are you an Air Raid Warden as well, then?

MAINWARING Look, don't worry about that for now. I want you to connect me to the lighthouse.

OPERATOR I can't, it's cut off.

MAINWARING I know, I want you to reconnect it.

OPERATOR Ooh, I can't do that, you'll have to talk to the supervisor.

MAINWARING That's who I asked for in the first place.

OPERATOR Here, wait a minute. There's an address here that takes messages for the lighthouse.

MAINWARING Good, that's the ticket. Give it to me. **(He turns to Wilson)** Pencil, Wilson, take this down.

OPERATOR It's the Jolly Roger Ice Cream Kiosk.

MAINWARING The Jolly Roger Ice – look, I'm speaking from there.

OPERATOR Can't you give the message, then?

WALKER Here, just a minute, sir. (He takes the phone) Hello, Freda.

OPERATOR Yes.

WALKER This is Joe Walker

OPERATOR Hello, Joe.

WALKER Put 71 into 23 will you?

OPERATOR What you up to, then? Oh, all right, Joe, just a minute.

WALKER (Handing back the receiver) She's putting you through. (To Wilson) We used to run the brandy in from France on the motor boats, see – before the war, and this bent coastguard used to tip me off when they was rounding the bay.

THE LAMPHOUSE

The phone rings, Jones answers it.

JONES Jack Jones, butcher, here.

MAINWARING Now, look here, Jones. This is Captain Mainwaring.

JONES Yes, sir.

MAINWARING I am going to pass instructions to you on how to switch off. You'll have to go down to the generator room.

JONES The generator room? Yes, sir.

KEEPER Wait a minute, it's locked.

MAINWARING Jones, wait a minute. It's locked. (To Keeper) Can you tell me where the key is?

KEEPER Yes, sir. (He starts to fish in his pocket)

MAINWARING Jones, can you hear me?

JONES Yes, sir.

MAINWARING I'm going to tell you where the key is.

KEEPER It's here. (He has it in his hand)

MAINWARING It's here. Er, look, Jones, break the door down and stop the generator.

JONES Yes, sir. (Turning to the men) Now listen, lads, we've got to go downstairs and find the generator room, and when we are there, we must find the door, and when we find it we must break it down and then we must stop the generator.

PIKE Corporal Jones, what about the slithery thing?

JONES We'll stop that an' all. Come on, lads. You stay here, Mr Godfrey.

EXTERIOR. ICE CREAM KIOSK

WARDEN I can hear 'em. Listen, I can hear 'em. Mainwaring! (Mainwaring appears) Listen, there's hundreds of them.

MAINWARING They won't be coming here, they'll be going over somewhere else.

WARDEN Yes, but when they see this, they'll change their minds, won't they? I mean, they'll never have another chance like this in the whole war.

MAINWARING Jones will have it out any minute now.

WARDEN You'll have to shoot, you can't take the risk.

WILSON They'll all be down below now, sir, perhaps you could.

MAINWARING We'll wait for the last possible second. Give me the gun, Walker.

THE LAMPHOUSE

Godfrey is there alone. Suddenly he gets an idea. He makes a rabbit shape with his hand and looks over towards Walmington at the result. He is delighted.

GODFREY Mr Jones, do come and see. I've made a rabbit, it must be the biggest one there's ever been. It's all over Walmington.

JOLLY ROGER ICE CREAM KIOSK

WARDEN They're practically overhead. For Gawd's sake, shoot it out.

Mainwaring operates the bolt.

THE LAMPHOUSE

Godfrey is now doing a bird. He is delirious with delight.

GODFREY Look, I'm doing a bird. It's flying right down the High Street. Oh, what a pity there's no one here to see it.

JOLLY ROGER ICE CREAM KIOSK

WARDEN Look, there's one in the searchlight right overhead. Shoot, you bloody fool, or it'll be murder.

WILSON I think perhaps you should, sir.

MAINWARING Right, here goes.

The light goes out.

THE LAMPHOUSE

Godfrey is in absolute ecstasy. The lamp goes out.

GODFREY Oh dear, I was enjoying that.

JOLLY ROGER ICE CREAM KIOSK

WALKER Blimey, that was a near thing.

WILSON You know, sir, I really do think we ought to concentrate on just guarding things, and give up these sort of exercises.

MAINWARING Nonsense, by doing this, we've encountered difficulties. We've triumphed over them and it's made us better soldiers, richer for the experience.

WILSON I can't help thinking that by the time the bills have come in for that transformer we shall be a lot poorer.

MAINWARING Oh no, there's not a shred of evidence to connect us with that. (**He wipes the back of his hand over his face and sees the result**)

Walker shows his steel helmet which has a bit burnt out of it.

SERIES FOUR **EPISODE EIGHT**

Recorded: Friday 6/11/70

Original transmission: Friday 13/11/70, 8.00–8.30pm

Original viewing figures = 15.6 million

ARTHUR LOWE .... CAPTAIN MAINWARING
JOHN LE MESURIER .... SERGEANT WILSON
CLIVE DUNN .... LANCE CORPORAL JONES
JOHN LAURIE .... PRIVATE FRAZER
JAMES BECK .... PRIVATE WALKER
ARNOLD RIDLEY .... PRIVATE GODFREY
IAN LAVENDER .... PRIVATE PIKE
BILL PERTWEE .... ARP WARDEN
JOHN CATER .... PRIVATE CLARKE
WENDY RICHARD .... EDITH
QUEENIE WATTS .... EDNA
GILDA PERRY .... DOREEN
LINDA JAMES .... BETTY
PARNELL MCGARRY .... ELIZABETH
JOHN ASH .... RAYMOND

PLATOON .... COLIN BEAN, HUGH HASTINGS, VIC TAYLOR

CUSTOMERS .... CHARLES FISHER, REG TURNER, PAT DONOGUE, ... EDDIE CONNOR, HARRY DOUGLAS, CLIFFORD HEMSLEY, ... CARRIE LAMBERT, ROSA GOLD, PAT ORR, TESSA LANDERS

ELDERLY CASHIER .... MARGARET BOHT
WASHER UPPER .... BARBARA SHACKLETON

THE TWO AND A HALF FEATHERS

• ROGER SINGLETON-TURNER REMEMBERS •

'This episode was the only time we saw members of the platoon eating in Walmington's British Restaurant. The austerity of the situation was reflected in the diet, with two principal dishes being toad-in-the-hole and snoek pie. The serving ladies were fearsome creatures, led by the late Queenie Watts, a well-known cockney character actress. The blackboard menu was not always seen in close-up, which is just as well because Paul Joel, the designer, had made various amendments to it, like "Snoad-in-the-hole", a passing reference to Harold Snoad!

'I worked on one series of *Dad's Army* as an assistant floor manager. A lot of the location scenes were recorded at King's Lynn, but before we even got there I was struggling. Arnold Ridley and his wife were both concerned that I should find the folding chair that he'd brought to the previous series' location filming. I guess it had been slung on to the props wagon. In any event, it failed to turn up, though I did have a good look round the BBC Props' Store and made a few phone calls.

'Then, on the journey, I was on the coach with the cast. Unfortunately, I had reckoned without everybody wanting to stop for a tea-break. Looking back, this was not unreasonable on such a long journey, but finding a suitable tea-shop big enough for us all at such short notice on a Sunday afternoon proved a problem.

'Eventually we arrived at King's Lynn and booked into two hotels in the main square. After dinner, Clive Dunn visited the other hotel. When he returned, he told how he'd been much amused by a local man who'd approached him and said: "I know you, don't I? From the telly." Clive had replied that it was possible. The man said: "Yes, I do know you. You're him, aren't you?" Clive had smiled modestly, and said that he thought he might be: *Dad's Army* was already a popular programme. "Yes," said the local. "You're him: you're Mr Pastry!"

'Throughout the filming the wind was blowing straight in off the North Sea. It picked up sand and stung our faces: at the end of each day we were all bright red and cold. One of the problems I encountered involved a frozen skinned hare I brought along to stand in for the roasting kid in the desert sequence. We chose a hare because it's reputed to look very similar to a kid (a young goat) once skinned. The hotel kindly agreed to store it overnight in one of their larders. The next morning, we set off early for the desert, and I nearly forgot the hare. It was sitting in its polythene bag in the larder, completely thawed. In fact the bag had leaked and there was a considerable pool of water and blood left on the larder floor. The staff at the hotel were quite tolerant, though.

'This was one of the few occasions in my life when I regret never having been a boy scout. I had to build a fire and set up the hare on the makeshift spit. I still don't know how people manage to cook things on camp fires with wooden spits without burning the said spit! By the time we'd finished the sequence, the hare was part charred, part raw and thoroughly seasoned with sand. Fortunately, no one had to eat it, but I've never liked barbecues since!

'We took about two days to shoot the material for this episode. The sand pit was extensive and every bit as convincing as North Africa. We used horses instead of camels, of course. Naturally, the horses needed Arab saddles. Authentic saddles weren't available, so the design team had a couple of English saddles modified with wooden pommels covered in red velvet. This meant there was a delay while chunks of wood were carefully removed to make the saddles comfortable for the horses and safe for the riders: Bill Pertwee and John Laurie. It was a memorable episode.'

ROGER SINGLETON-TURNER
Assistant Floor Manager

The Two and a Half Feathers

INTERIOR. BRITISH RESTAURANT. DAY

Note: the British Restaurant was a wartime institution – it was run by the local authorities and W.V.S. to give cheap, nourishing meals to office and factory workers. Open on close up of menu chalked on blackboard – the words British Restaurant are printed at the top.

MENU

Soup 2d

Toad-in-the-hole 8d

Fish & potato pie 7d

Swedes & carrots 2d

Bread pudding & custard 3d

Tea 1d

One slice of bread only with each meal ½d

(N.B. No meal must cost more than 1s 8d)

Pull back to reveal Mainwaring and Wilson standing on each side of the board. They are dressed in their bank clothes.

MAINWARING What are you going to have today, Wilson?

WILSON I think I'm going to have the toad-in-the-hole, sir.

MAINWARING Fish and potato pie for me, I think. Come on, let's get in the queue before the rush starts.

They each get a tray and join in at the end of the small queue at the counter. Serving behind it are three women: Edna – large, middle aged, fierce – and Doreen and Betty. They are all dressed in white turbans and overalls.

EDNA (To Wilson) Soup?

WILSON No, thank you. Toad-in-the-hole, please.

EDNA One toad. (She puts a portion on a plate)

Wilson looks at it – it has one small piece of sausage in it.

WILSON Er... I wonder if I might have another bit of toad?

EDNA Sorry – only half a toad – per portion – per customer. There's a war on, you know. Next.

MAINWARING Fish pie, please.

Edna dishes up a portion of pie.

MAINWARING Er... what sort of fish is it?

EDNA Snoek.

MAINWARING I beg your pardon?

EDNA Snoek.

MAINWARING In that case, I think I'll have the toad-in-the-hole.

EDNA I wish you'd make up your mind.

She dishes up a portion of toad.

BETTY (To Wilson) Carrots and swedes?

WILSON Yes, please.

Pike joins the queue beside Mainwaring.

EDNA Yes?

PIKE Fish pie, please.

Edna dishes up a portion of pie. Three more people join the queue behind Pike.

PIKE What sort of fish is it?

EDNA Snoek.

PIKE I think I'll have the toad-in-the-hole.

EDNA Blimey, another one, I'm not having this. (She shouts down the queue, right in Mainwaring's ear) Listen. The fish pie is snoek – snoek, got it? Next!

DOREEN (To Wilson) Bread pudding?

WILSON Yes, please.

DOREEN With or without?

WILSON With, please.

Doreen swamps the pudding in custard. Wilson reaches over and takes two pieces of bread.

EDNA (Shouting) Hey, I saw that.

WILSON I beg your pardon?

EDNA Don't come all la-di-da with me – put one of those bits of bread back – you're only allowed one slice. (Pointing to board) It says so up there. Don't forget, there's a war on.

WILSON I'm hardly likely to forget, am I?

He puts the piece of bread back.

EDNA And don't forget to take your dirties back to the hatch.

WILSON I always do.

EDNA Oh no you don't – yesterday you left your dirties on the table. I've got enough to do without clearing up your dirties.

WILSON Now, look here.

MAINWARING For goodness sake, go and sit down, Wilson. You're making an exhibition of yourself.

Wilson crosses over to the pay desk.

DOREEN Bread pudding?

MAINWARING Just custard, my dear – have to watch the figure, you know.

DOREEN You've got a nice figure, sir – my friend and I think you're like a big teddy bear, don't we, Betty?

BETTY Yes, just like a teddy bear.

MAINWARING (Beaming) Oh, do you really think so. (He turns, and sees Pike sniggering)

Walker comes in, grabs a tray – and pushes in at the head of the queue in front of Mainwaring.

WALKER Hello, Mr Mainwaring, excuse me – my steak ready, Doreen?

DOREEN Get Mr Walker's steak, Betty.

BETTY (Calls) Mr Walker's steak.

She gets a large, beautifully cooked steak from the hot plate. Mainwaring stares, amazed at all this.

MAINWARING What are you doing with that steak, Walker?

WALKER I'm going to eat it, of course.

MAINWARING But there's two weeks' meat ration there. I've got a toad-in-the-hole.

WALKER Well, you want to watch it, that can be nasty.

MAINWARING Why are they serving you with a steak?

WALKER They're not – I brought it in earlier for them to cook for me. (He hands over a packet) Here's the elastic I promised you, girls. (To Mainwaring) Can't have them falling down on the job. (He crosses over to the cash desk with his tray. Mainwaring follows) Just take for the tea, love.

MAINWARING Now, look here, Walker – flaunting your black market food all over the place can give the platoon a bad name.

WALKER I don't want to be rude, Mr Mainwaring – but I'm not wearing uniform and I'm not on parade – moreover I'm a customer at your bank with over 1,500 nicker in a deposit account. So, if you don't mind, I'll eat my dinner.

By now they have both paid. Mainwaring moves over to a corner table and sits with Wilson. Walker sits down at a table beside them. Pike comes over to Mainwaring and Wilson's table.

PIKE Fifteen hundred and forty-two, actually.

MAINWARING Sit at another table will you, Pike?

PIKE Yes, Mr Mainwaring. (He sits beside Walker)

MAINWARING Can't have the ranks and file eating with us, Wilson – it's bad for discipline.

WILSON In the German army all the ranks eat together, sir.

MAINWARING (Coldly) That doesn't impress me very much.

Walker opens his case and takes out two bottles of sauce, and a jar of pickle. He puts them on the table in front of him.

WALKER Drop of pickle, Pikey?

PIKE Thanks, Joe. (He helps himself) I haven't seen this since before the war.

WALKER (Across to Mainwaring) Pickle, Mr Mainwaring?

MAINWARING No, thank you, not with toad-in-the-hole.

WALKER It's free.

MAINWARING (He prods the toad with his fork) Look at it, Wilson, there's scarcely more than a mouthful here.

WILSON It's awfully difficult. I don't know whether to eat my bit of toad first – or save it till the end.

Jones comes through the door, he is wearing a dress uniform of an infantry regiment 1890. Red coat, blue trousers, spiked helmet. He crosses over to Mainwaring's table. (N.B. Jones was in the Warwickshire Regiment)

JONES Hello, Joe – hello, Pikey. Hello, Mr Mainwaring, I called over at the bank but I just missed you. I've come to say goodbye.

WALKER Got your calling up papers at last, Jonesey – give those Boers hell for me. In case you don't come back, you'd better let me have that ten bob you borrowed.

JONES There's no call to be funny, Joe. If you want your ten bob you can have it. (He starts to fish in his trouser pocket. As his uniform is rather tight he has a bit of difficulty)

WALKER I was only joking.

MAINWARING Sit down, Jones – everybody's staring at you.

JONES Let them stare, Mr Mainwaring. (Still fishing in his pocket, he moves over to Walker's table) I'm not ashamed – I wear this uniform with pride. (He pulls a ten shilling note out of his pocket. A handful of mothballs come out with it and shower all over Walker's table)

PIKE Look out, Mr Jones – one of those mothballs nearly went in my dinner.

WALKER Keep your voice down, Pikey, or they'll all want one. (He takes the 10s note from Jones)

MAINWARING Will you sit down, Jones – you're showing us up. Where exactly are you going?

JONES Up to London, sir. Tonight is the 42nd annual reunion of the veterans of the Battle of Omdurman.

MAINWARING Really?

JONES I served with distinction in that campaign, Mr Mainwaring. I should have been mentioned in dispatches, but they seemed to have run out of paper. Our great leader Winston Churchill took part in that battle, you know, sir. He was a young Lieutenant with the 21st Lancers – that was the last great cavalry charge ever made by the British Army – I'll show you. (He reaches round and grabs the pickle and sauce bottles off Walker's table)

WALKER 'Ere, just a minute, Jonesey.

JONES All right, I'm only going to borrow 'em. There we were between two huge rocks. (**He puts down the salt and pepper pots**) General Kitchener was here. (**He puts down a sauce bottle**) The Mad Mahadi was here, at the head of his army. (**He puts down the other sauce bottle**) And I was here. (**He puts down the pickle jar**) I wasn't alone, of course – there were other troops all round me. Suddenly a trumpet blew. (**He blows**) And thousands of screaming Dervishes and Fuzzie Wuzzies charged straight at us. And there was General Kitchener, sitting on his horse as cool as a cucumber. 'Steady boys', he said – 'don't fire until you see the red of their eyes'.

WILSON I always thought he said it was the whites of their eyes.

JONES Yes, he did, but he shouldn't have. You see, all that sand flying about makes 'em very bloodshot – you get a lot of bloodshot eyes in the desert. I don't mean lying around in the sand on their own – they're attached to the people.

WALKER (**Calling across**) Have you finished with my pickle, Jonesey?

JONES No, I haven't. All day long they charged us and every time we beat 'em back. Those Fuzzie Wuzzies kept coming at us with their great big choppers – chopping heads off right, left and centre. You never saw anything like it, blood everywhere. (**Wilson and Mainwaring are starting to look a bit sick**) The corpses were piled eight foot high – you don't get battles like that now – they were real battles in them days. (**He gets up**) Well, I'll leave you to enjoy your dinner, Mr Mainwaring. See you tomorrow – cheerio. (**He goes**)

WILSON (**Pushing his plate away**) Somehow, I seem to have lost my appetite.

MAINWARING So have I – still can't waste food in wartime – do you mind if I have a little of your pickle, Mr Walker?

WALKER Help yourself.

Mainwaring takes a spoonful of pickle and hands it back to Walker.

MAINWARING It might make it a little more palatable.

He eats – suddenly he stops – sucks in his breath – his face goes red and his eyes pop.

WILSON Are you all right, sir?

Mainwaring jumps up and rushes out of the restaurant.

WILSON Good heavens. (**To Walker**) I wonder what's the matter?

WALKER (**Sniffing the pickle jar**) I don't want to worry you, Mr Wilson, but I think one of Jonesey's mothballs went in the pickle – and Mr Mainwaring's eaten it.

WILSON What!

He gets up and rushes for the door. He is stopped by Edna – who stands in front of him – arms akimbo.

EDNA What about your dirties?

WILSON My what?

EDNA (**Pointing**) Go and take your dirties back.

WILSON Look, just clear off. (**He goes out of the door**) Captain Mainwaring, are you all right, sir.

EDNA Capitalist lackey.

INTERIOR. SIDE OFFICE. NIGHT

Mainwaring is sitting at his desk, writing – there is a knock at the door. Wilson enters.

WILSON Excuse me, sir – Frazer's waiting outside with the new recruit he's recommended.

MAINWARING Right, get them in.

WILSON Yes, sir. (**He opens the door and calls**) Right, Frazer, you can bring your friend in now.

Mainwaring crosses back to the desk and sits. Frazer enters with the new recruit – he is a short, wiry man in his early 60s. He speaks with a cockney accent.

FRAZER I should like to introduce Mr George Clark. He wants to join our ranks.

MAINWARING Good evening, Mr Clark.

CLARK (**Coming smartly to attention**) Good evening, sir.

MAINWARING I'd hazard a guess, Mr Clark – that you've served in the army before.

CLARK That's correct, sir.

MAINWARING Now, Frazer, you know Mr Clark well?

FRAZER Aye, sir – I do that, sir.

MAINWARING And you've known him for some time?

FRAZER Aye, I have, sir.

MAINWARING You'd say he was a man of integrity?

FRAZER And very generous, sir – he stood me several drinks in the bar of The Anchor last Thursday night.

MAINWARING When did you first meet him?

FRAZER In the bar of The Anchor last Thursday night.

MAINWARING Perhaps you'd like to tell us something about yourself, Mr Clark.

CLARK Yes, sir. (**Coughs**) Well, as you guessed, sir – I've been a regular soldier all my life – retired about ten years ago. I've only been living in Walmington-on-Sea a few weeks.

MAINWARING When did you first join the army?

CLARK Forty-four years ago, sir, 1897 – a year later, in

1898, I served in the Sudan under General Kitchener at the Battle of Omdurman.

WILSON Good gracious, sir – that's a coincidence.

MAINWARING Yes, it is. **(Laughs)** You didn't by any chance come across a Lance Corporal Jones, did you?

CLARK You can't expect me to remember that, sir – thousands of men took part in that battle.

MAINWARING I realise that – I was only joking.

CLARK I was in the Warwickshire Regiment.

WILSON Jones was in the Warwickshire Regiment, wasn't he, sir?

MAINWARING Yes, he was.

CLARK Well, it was a long time ago, sir. As a matter of fact, come to think of it, I do remember one Jones – he was always a bit behind everyone else with his drill.

FRAZER That's him.

CLARK He wasn't a Lance Corporal, though.

FRAZER Ah, he wasn't a Lance Corporal, you say.

CLARK No, just an ordinary private.

FRAZER Do you hear that, Mr Mainwaring – just an ordinary private? Not a Lance Corporal at all. I always knew it – I always knew it.

MAINWARING All right, Frazer – all right. Well, we'll just have to wait until tomorrow to find out if it's the same man. I want you here half an hour before parade starts, then we can fit you with your uniform. Now, I'll just swear you in. Hand me the bible, Wilson.

WILSON What bible, sir?

MAINWARING The bible to swear him in, of course.

WILSON I haven't got a bible, sir.

MAINWARING I distinctly remember telling you to bring the bible.

WILSON The word bible never passed your lips, sir.

MAINWARING How can we possibly swear him in without a bible…

INTERIOR. SIDE OFFICE. DAY

Clark is standing in a battledress, the jacket is open. Godfrey, with a tape measure round his neck, is fussing round them. Mainwaring and Wilson are looking on.

MAINWARING Hurry up, Godfrey, the parade starts in 20 minutes.

GODFREY I've nearly finished, sir. **(To Clark)** Haven't you got a pair of braces?

CLARK No, I always wear a belt to keep my trousers up.

GODFREY You should wear braces – otherwise you're not dressed right.

CLARK If I wear braces, I certainly won't be able to dress right.

MAINWARING Can't you find a better blouse for him than that, Godfrey?

GODFREY That's the best I can do, I'm afraid – the customer is rather an awkward size.

MAINWARING Well, you'll just have to alter it – we must have you smartly dressed, Clark – this is a highly efficient unit.

CLARK When do I start training?

MAINWARING We haven't got time for all that, you'll just have to pick it up as you go along.

INTERIOR. A VERY SMALL CORNER OF THE CHURCH HALL JUST OUTSIDE OFFICE DOOR. DAY

Frazer, Pike and Walker are standing in a group, chatting. Several other members of the platoon are standing around.

FRAZER I tell you, this new chap said he knew Jones in the Sudan.

WALKER Blimey – that was in eighteen hundred and frozen stiff – how can he be sure after all these years?

FRAZER This chap said that the Jones he knew was always a beat behind everybody else when they were drilling.

PIKE That still doesn't prove anything, Mr Frazer.

Jones enters, looking the worse for wear – he comes over to them.

WALKER Hello, Jonesey – you look a bit rough. How did the reunion of the Battle of Om-de-bum-bum go?

JONES The Battle of Omdurman.

WALKER I bet you and your mates were fighting those Fuzzie Wuzzies all over again, eh?

JONES **(Weakly)** I had a very nice time, thanks.

FRAZER You were drunk, were you – drunk?

JONES No, I wasn't drunk – we just had a convivial evening, that's all.

FRAZER Mr Mainwaring wants to see you in the office.

JONES Right.

He moves towards the office.

FRAZER **(To Pike and Walker)** Come on, boys. I don't want to miss this.

They all follow Jones.

INTERIOR. SIDE OFFICE. DAY

There is a knock on the door.

MAINWARING Come in.

The door opens, Frazer comes in.

FRAZER Lance Corporal Jones to see you, sir.

Jones comes in, followed by Pike and Walker.

JONES All right, Jock, I don't need to be shown into the office. Good evening, sir. (**He salutes**)

MAINWARING Good evening, Jones – I've got someone here I want you to meet. Private Clark – he's a new recruit.

JONES How do you do?

There is a long pause.

CLARK (**Slowly**) Hello, Jonesey – you remember me?

JONES No, I don't think I do.

CLARK Course you do – 14789 Private Clark?

Pause.

JONES Oh, hello, Nobby.

CLARK Hello, mate – long time no see, eh?

JONES Yeah – long time.

CLARK Remember me now, don't you?

JONES Yeah – I remember.

CLARK And I remember you, mate. I remember you very very well.

The atmosphere has now become decidedly chilly.

WILSON (**Brightly**) Well, it's time for the parade, sir – I'll go and fall the men in. Come along, Jones. (**He crosses to the door**)

MAINWARING Right, Sergeant – then I can introduce Private Clark to the rest of the platoon. Come along, Clark and you, Corporal.

They all go except Frazer, Walker, Godfrey and Pike.

FRAZER Did you see that – did you see that?

PIKE See what, Mr Frazer?

FRAZER I don't think Clark and Jones like each other very much.

WALKER You're a right old mixer, you are, Jock.

FRAZER Maybe – but there's something between those two that Jones doesn't want us to know about.

GODFREY I can't believe that, Mr Frazer.

FRAZER Can't you? I can. There's no smoke without fire – no smoke without fire.

INTERIOR. A TINY SECTION OF A ROOM IN FRAZER'S HOUSE. NIGHT

Close up of Frazer on phone – he is wearing a roll-neck fisherman's jersey.

FRAZER ...you see, after parade, I took this chap Clark for a drink... well, when he'd bought me a couple of pints I asked him straight out. I said, 'What happened between you and Jones?' He was very evasive about the whole thing, but from what I could gather – reading between the lines and putting two and two together – it seems that the two of them were on patrol and somehow they got captured – well, Jones managed to escape and left this chap Clark in the desert to die... mind you there may not be any truth in it, but as I always say – there's no smoke without fire, no smoke...

TINY SECTION OF INTERIOR. GODFREY'S COTTAGE. NIGHT

Close up of Godfrey sitting in armchair with large tortoiseshell cat on his knee. He is talking to his sister, Dolly, who is out of picture.

GODFREY ...you see, Dolly, there's this awful rumour going around about Mr Jones. (**A hand comes into picture with a cup of tea. Godfrey takes it**) Thank you, dear. I just can't believe that Mr Jones would run away and leave this man in the desert to die – I mean, I've known him for such a long time – and, after all, he has won all those medals – and he couldn't have won them if he was a coward, could he, Dolly? I mean he couldn't... could he?

EXTERIOR. A SEASIDE SHELTER ON THE FRONT. NIGHT

Walker is sitting on a park bench with a girl – he is wearing an overcoat and scarf and hat. He has his arm round the girl.

GIRL Look at that lovely moon, Joe.

JOE (**Without much enthusiasm**) Yes, very nice.

GIRL What's the matter with you tonight?

WALKER Well, I've got a lot of things on me mind.

GIRL That's a change – you've usually only got *one* thing on your mind. Come on, give us a kiss.

WALKER Look, there's a time and a place for everything.

GIRL This is the time and the place. Don't you love me any more?

WALKER Eh, 'course I do – I'm mad about you, I don't

know what I'm going to do about Jonesey – I mean I asked him straight out, 'is there any truth in this rumour about you leaving this bloke in the lurch?' – and he refuses to talk about it. Why won't he deny it?

GIRL Are you going to give me a kiss or not?

WALKER I might as well, I suppose – I'm sitting 'ere. **(He kisses her)**

INTERIOR. SITTING ROOM. PIKE'S HOUSE. DAY

Wilson and Pike are sitting on the sofa together. They are both in uniform. Wilson is reading the paper – he is very much on edge. Pike is listening to the wireless, 'Happidrome' is on – we hear a few seconds of it – then we hear Enoch's voice saying, 'Let me tell you'.

PIKE There he goes again – 'Let me tell you'. I love that Enoch, don't you, Uncle Arthur?

WILSON **(Rustling the paper)** What?

PIKE That girl Jean in the bank thinks I'm just like him. Have you heard me do my impersonation of him?

WILSON No, I haven't.

PIKE **(Right in his ear)** 'Let me tell you.'

WILSON Oh really, Frank. **(He reaches up and turns the radio off)**

PIKE What did you want to do that for, Uncle Arthur? That's my favourite programme.

Wilson lights a cigarette.

WILSON I'm sorry, Frank, it was getting on my nerves.

PIKE What's the matter – don't you feel well?

WILSON It's this business with Jones – all these rumours flying about – the atmosphere on parade tonight was terrible.

PIKE Do you think it's true that Mr Jones left this chap in the desert to die?

WILSON I don't know, Frank – I just don't know. **(He gets up)** I'm going home.

PIKE Mum won't like that, she's just getting the supper.

WILSON Yes, tell her to – oh, tell her I want to be alone.

PIKE I can do an impersonation of Greta Garbo too – would you like to hear it?

WILSON No, I wouldn't. **(He goes)**

Frank turns the radio on again and settles down on the sofa.

INTERIOR. AIR RAID SHELTER. NIGHT

Mainwaring is lying in the bottom bunk. The top bunk is occupied by his wife, Elizabeth. All we can see of her is her outline, which is just about six inches above Mainwaring. Mainwaring cannot sleep, tosses and turns – then lights a candle beside his bunk, puts his glasses on and looks at his watch.

MAINWARING Two o'clock. **(He croons softly to the outline above)** Elizabeth – are you awake?

ELIZABETH Mmmmmmmm.

MAINWARING You know, dear, I really think it would be better if we slept in the house when there wasn't a raid on – this shelter is very damp.

ELIZABETH Mmmmmmmm.

MAINWARING I just can't sleep – I think I'll read for a while. **(He picks up a small Home Guard manual – props himself upon his elbow and starts to read – Elizabeth turns in her sleep – her outline changes and knocks him back on his pillow)** I think you'd be much more comfortable if I slept in the top bunk, dear.

ELIZABETH Mmmmmmmm.

MAINWARING I just can't get this Jones business out of my mind. The whole platoon is falling to pieces. You know how I used to look forward to going on duty every evening – the comradeship – the cheerful banter – the wonderful feeling of us all being banded together for a common purpose – now it's all turned to ashes in my mouth. I mean, I had Jones in the office, I said to him, 'Why don't you deny this rumour that you left this chap Clark in the desert to die?'. And he refused to say anything. Why? That's what I want to know. Why won't he speak? **(He is fiddling with a safety pin that is holding together the top of his pyjama jacket – it comes undone)** I wish you'd sew this button on for me, Elizabeth – I keep telling you about it – it's very uncomfortable. **(He is now holding the safety pin open)** Elizabeth, are you listening?

There is a loud snore from Elizabeth, she shifts in the bunk. Mainwaring looks up at the huge outline just above him – he looks at the safety pin in his hand – looks up at the outline – thinks better of it.

MAINWARING Goodnight, dear.

INTERIOR. A VERY SMALL CORNER OF JONES' BUTCHER'S SHOP. DAY

Jones is cutting up some meat. Raymond the boy comes into the picture.

RAYMOND **(Handing Jones three letters)** The post, Mr Jones.

JONES Thank you, Raymond.

He opens the first letter. Inside is a single sheet of notepaper and a white feather. We hear Jones' voice as he reads.

JONES Why did you leave your friend in the desert to die?

Jones opens the second letter. Inside is another sheet of notepaper and a white feather.

JONES There's no room in Walmington-on-Sea for a coward.

Jones quickly opens the third letter. Inside there is a half a feather. He reads the note.

JONES A coward like you is not even worth a whole white feather, so I am sending you half a one.

Jones looks down at the feathers in a daze – he pulls himself together and quickly puts them back in the envelope – he calls.

JONES Raymond!

Raymond comes into the picture.

RAYMOND Yes, Mr Jones.

JONES **(Taking off his apron)** I want you to look after the shop. There's something I've got to do.

RAYMOND What's that, Mr Jones?

JONES Something I should have done a long time ago – I'm afraid it's the only way – the only way.

INTERIOR. SIDE OFFICE. DAY

Mainwaring is sitting at his desk. Wilson is standing beside him. In front of the desk, Walker, Frazer, Pike, Godfrey, Clark and several other members of the platoon are gathered in a group.

MAINWARING Now, gentlemen, I'm going to get to the bottom of this once and for all. All right, Clark, suppose you tell us exactly what did happen in the desert between you and Jones?

CLARK Well, we were on patrol and we were captured by the Dervishes – they pegged me out in the sand. Jones begged for mercy and they took him with them – somehow he managed to escape, but he never came back for me – he left me to die. I must have passed out – I can just remember a native bending over me, going through my pockets. When I came round I was in hospital – that native must have saved my life, even if he did pinch my wallet.

During this speech, Jones comes quietly through the door and stands at the back of the group. He is wearing his civilian clothes.

MAINWARING I find it very difficult to believe that Jones would have left you to die.

CLARK Then why has he cleared off?

JONES **(Pushing his way to the front)** I'll tell you why I cleared off.

MAINWARING Where have you been, Jones?

JONES Permission to speak, sir? I should like to thank you for having faith in me. Up till this moment, my lips have been sealed, but I can now reveal myself and tell you what really happened. You see, sir, it all took place a few days before the Battle of Omdurman.

TELECINE: THE DESERT. DAY

ACTION SILENT: **Long shot of patrol in desert. Two figures on horseback are leading, followed by ten men in single file.**

JONES **(Out of vision) (Pause of ten seconds before monologue)** Private Clark and I were part of a patrol sent out by General Kitchener to find out the strength of the Mahadi's army. **(Close up of Wilson as Colonel Smithe on the leading horse)** ...the patrol was under the command of Colonel Smithe – a tall, resolute man of iron, who scarcely spoke a word. **(Close up of Pike as the Second Lieutenant also on a horse)** ...the other officer was a young, green Second Lieutenant, just out of Sandhurst. He was the Colonel's nephew. **(Close up of Walker as Private Green doing jokes and merry quips)** ...there was also a young cockney, Private Green, who kept our spirits up with jokes and merry quips.

(Close up of Mainwaring as Sergeant Ironside – giving them the rough side of his tongue) ...the Sergeant was Sergeant Ironside, a nasty, coarse fellow who kept giving us the rough side of his tongue. **(Close up of Jones marching. He looks up to the sky)** ...I knew that patrol was doomed from the start. As I looked up... **(Stock shot of vultures wheeling in sky)** ...I could see vultures wheeling overhead, waiting to pick our bones... **(Close up of Jones marching)** ...then, as we rounded a corner, there was an old Farker... **(Single of Godfrey dressed in biblical costume as the Fakir)** ...standing in our path. **(Single of Fakir mouthing words and gesturing)** ... 'Turn back – turn back', said the old Farker – 'it is written in the sand that before the sun sinks, all of you will be dead'. **(Single of Colonel shouting)** 'Rubbish!' said the Colonel. 'Clear out of the way, you old fool.' **(Close up of Fakir gesturing)** ...'Do not go against the will of Allah,' said the old Farker – 'what is written in the sand is written in the sand'. None of us took much notice of him as we all marched past. **(Close up of Sergeant mouthing coarse abuse)** ...however, as he drew level with him, the Sergeant gave him a mouthful of coarse abuse. **(Close up of Fakir looking startled)** ...this seemed to upset the old Farker. **(Close up of Fakir cursing)** ...who said something to the Sergeant in Arabic. I didn't understand what it was at the time, but later I learned it was a curse on us all. **(Close up of Jones marching, mopping brow, etc.)** ...well, we didn't have long to wait before the words of the Farker came true. About midday, when the sun was scorching down like a great big, burning, brass ball, suddenly, without a word of warning, a fusillade of shots rang out. **(As the shots ring out the film now changes to sound and action)**

Cut to close up of Colonel.

COLONEL Take cover!

Cut to close up of Sergeant.

SERGEANT Take cover!

Cut to close up of Second Lieutenant.

LIEUTENANT Take...

He falls from his horse. Jones rushes over and cradles him in his arms.

JONES **(Out of vision)** I rushed over to the Lieutenant – and cradled him in my arms. To think of this young boy, dying out here in this foreign, burning desert – it was too much to bear. **(Putting his water bottle to the Lieutenant's lips)** Here you are, young sir.

LIEUTENANT Thank you, Jones, you're a good chap. Dashed hard lines it happening like this. I want you to promise me something, Jones.

JONES Yes, sir, anything.

LIEUTENANT When you get back to England – go and see my mater... tell her... tell her I couldn't help it.

JONES Help what, sir?

LIEUTENANT Falling off my horse.

Cut to stock shot of Dervishes firing.

Cut to the patrol, all crouched in a sand dune – the horses have run off. Shots ring out.

SERGEANT Keep your *** 'eads down.

Cut to Dervishes firing.

Several bullets hit the sand near them. The Colonel and Lieutenant are crouched side by side.

LIEUTENANT Uncle Arthur?

COLONEL Yes, Franklin.

LIEUTENANT In case we don't get out of this alive – there's something I must ask you.

COLONEL What is it?

LIEUTENANT It's about you and Mater.

COLONEL I'd rather you didn't ask.

LIEUTENANT All right then, I won't.

More shots ring out.

Cut to stock shot of Dervishes charging.

GREEN Blimey, look at that, Sarge – there's thousands of 'em.

SERGEANT Shut up – keep your *** 'ead down. **(To Colonel)** I don't like the look of this, sir – those *** Dervishes mean *** business.

COLONEL You're right, Sergeant – as soon as it's dark we'll have to send someone for help.

JONES Permission to speak, sir?

COLONEL Yes, Jones?

JONES I should like to volunteer to be the one to go and get help as soon as it's dark, sir.

COLONEL Very well, Jones – you'd better take Private Clark with you.

ACTION SILENT: Clark and Jones are staggering along – it is very hot.

JONES **(Out of vision)** We managed to creep out during the night – and the next morning we were on our way for help.

Two Dervishes are on the skyline – they are mounted on horses. It is Frazer and Hodges.

JONES **(Out of vision)** Little did we realise that at that moment, nasty, savage eyes were watching our every move. **(Jones and Clark lay their rifles down – unscrew their water bottles and shake them)** ...all the time the sun was beating down on us and we had to stop for a rest. It was then we realised that our water bottles were empty. **(They both look up)** ...suddenly, we looked up. **(The two Dervishes are pointing their rifles at them)** ...there were two horrible Dervishes looking down at us. It was too late to pick up our rifles – we were trapped, caught by the Dervishes, we knew what we were in for.

Close up of Jones looking heroic.

JONES **(Out of vision)** I was ready to take my medicine like a man. **(Single of Clark grovelling)** ...when all of a sudden Private Clark flung himself down in the sand and grovelled and begged for mercy. **(Close up of Jones looking away)** ...I couldn't stand it, I had to look away. **(The Dervishes are pegging Clark out in the sand)** ...those Dervishes didn't know the meaning of mercy. They pegged Clark out in the sand and left him there to die. **(The Dervishes are riding along – they are pulling Jones behind them, tied to a rope)** ...they dragged me behind them for miles – what fate was in store for me I had no means of knowing. **(Jones is lying beside a camp fire – his hands are tied behind his back. The two Dervishes are cooking a piece of meat on a spit)** After hours of this torture we stopped and they started to cook a meal. **(One of the Dervishes pulls out a dagger and they start to fight)** Suddenly, one of them said something. The other pulled out a dagger – and the next minute they were at each other's throats. **(The two Dervishes are rolling over and over in the sand)** ...they fought like demons. **(Jones rolls to the fire)** ...I realised that this was my chance. They weren't taking any notice of me – so I rolled over to the fire. **(Close up of Jones with look of agony on face)** ...and I burnt through the ropes – it was agony, but I managed to stick it. **(One of the Dervishes breaks away – gets on horse and canters off)** ...suddenly, one of the Dervishes broke away – jumped on his horse and made off. He'd had enough. **(Close up of Dervish shouting something)** ...the other Dervish shouted something after him. **(Close up of Jones' face remembering)** ...then I remembered that Dervishes can't stand fire, they just can't stand it. **(Jones picks up brand and creeps up behind Dervish)** ...I quickly seized a burning brand from the fire and crept up behind the Dervish. **(Dervish turns – Jones thrusts brand in front of his face. Dervish looks horrified)** Suddenly the Dervish turned and saw it. I thrust it right in front of his face, the effect was amazing – he turned from proud warrior into a jibbering idiot. **(Big close up of Dervish's nostrils distending with fear)** ...his nostrils distended with fear. **(Close up of Dervish shouting)** ...then he shouted, 'Om kar yar kar kar. Om kar yar kar kar', which, translated literally means – 'put that light out, put that light out'. **(Dervish starts to take off robes)** ...I had him at my mercy – I made him take his robes off. **(Jones is galloping along with robes on)** ...I quickly put them on over my uniform, took the horse – and before you could say 'knife' – was on my way back to rescue Private Clark. **(Jones is kneeling over Clark – he cuts ropes, takes his wallet out of his tunic)** ...when I got back I thought Clark was a goner. I cut the ropes – and took his wallet out of his tunic to send home with his personal effects. **(Jones opens wallet, takes out a photo and stares at it)** ... I opened it and inside I saw something that, in spite of the heat, made my blood run cold. There was a photograph of the Colonel's lady – the Colonel, sir, was a very upstanding gentleman, but his wife was not quite so upstanding. To think that she and this Private Clark had been... I couldn't believe it. **(Close up of Clark groaning)** ...while I was kneeling there, in a daze of misery, I hear a groan – Clark wasn't dead after all. **(Jones is leading the horse with Clark slung over it)** Well, Mr Mainwaring, I got him on the horse and, after a nightmare journey through the desert, **(Stock shot of patrol in desert)** we came across the relief column. **(Close up of Jones waving)**

INTERIOR. SIDE OFFICE. NIGHT

Big close up of Jones.

JONES Clark was taken back to headquarters – and I never saw him again until last week. I led the column back to relieve the Colonel and my brave comrades. All these years I've kept that secret locked in my bosom – the secret that nobody knew, except the Colonel's lady – Private Clark and myself.

MAINWARING But why on earth didn't you tell us all this before, Jones?

JONES I couldn't, sir – not while there was a chance that the Colonel and his lady were still alive – that's where I've been for the past two days, up in London at Somerset House, going through the records. I'm pleased to say that the Colonel and his lady are now in that great big parade ground somewhere in the sky, where the breath of scandal can no longer touch them. All these years, I've carried the photograph and some letters from her that I found in Private Clark's wallet. **(He pulls out a package of letters)** Now, at last, I can burn them.

MAINWARING I'm sorry, Jones. And I'm going to deal with Private Clark.

WILSON I think he slipped out a few minutes ago, sir.

MAINWARING Why didn't you stop him? He's not going to get away with this – come on, Wilson.

Mainwaring makes for the door, followed by Wilson, Jones, Walker, Frazer, Pike and Godfrey.

EXTERIOR. OUTSIDE CHURCH HALL. NIGHT

As they pour out of the hall they bump into the Warden.

WARDEN You're in a hurry, aren't you?

MAINWARING Did you see a man come out of here about two minutes ago?

WARDEN Yeah – he was rushing towards the station – said he had a train to catch.

MAINWARING We'll get him – come on.

WARDEN I shouldn't bother – he gave me a message for you. I'm to tell you he's very sorry he's had to resign, he'll post the uniform back to you.

MAINWARING He can't do that.

WARDEN Desertion's a serious crime, ain't it – what will you do with him? Put him up against a wall and shoot at him with water pistols – or thrash him with a wet lettuce leaf. **(Laughs)**

WILSON Look, just clear off, will you?

MAINWARING Pike, jump on your bike and see if you can stop him.

JONES He's not worth bothering about, Mr Mainwaring – let him go.

PIKE I didn't like him – my Mum says never trust anyone with eyes too close together.

GODFREY The moving finger writes – and having writ, moves on.

MAINWARING What's that got to do with it, Godfrey?

GODFREY I don't know, sir.

WALKER Look, Jonesey, just burn that photo – and all those letters – then we can forget about the whole thing. 'Ere you are. **(He flicks his lighter)**

Jones holds up the bundle of letters and they burn up.

WARDEN Have you gone mad? What do you think you're doing? An enemy plane could see that miles away.

JONES Oh, shut up.

He waves the burning bundle in front of the Warden's face. Close up of Warden with nostrils distended.

WARDEN Put that light out! Put that light out!

SERIES FOUR **EPISODE NINE**

Recorded: Friday 13/11/70
Original transmission: Friday 20/11/70, 8.00–8.30pm
Original viewing figures = 16.4 million

ARTHUR LOWE .... CAPTAIN MAINWARING
JOHN LE MESURIER .... SERGEANT WILSON
CLIVE DUNN .... LANCE CORPORAL JONES
JOHN LAURIE .... PRIVATE FRAZER
JAMES BECK .... PRIVATE WALKER
ARNOLD RIDLEY .... PRIVATE GODFREY
IAN LAVENDER .... PRIVATE PIKE
CARMEN SILVERA .... MRS GRAY
WENDY RICHARD .... EDITH PARISH
JANET DAVIES .... MRS PIKE
PAMELA CUNDELL .... MRS FOX
JULIA BURBURY .... MISS IRONSIDE
ROSEMARY FAITH .... IVY SAMWAYS
MELITA MANGER .... THE WAITRESS
DEIRDRE COSTELLO .... BUFFET ATTENDANT
DAVID GILCHRIST .... THE SERVICEMAN
ELEANOR SMALE .... MRS PROSSER
JACK LE WHITE .... THE PORTER

PLATOON ...... COLIN BEAN, HUGH HASTINGS, VIC TAYLOR, HUGH CECIL, DESMOND CULLUM-JONES, LESLIE NOYES, FREDDIE WILES, GEORGE HANCOCK, FRANK GODFREY, FREDDIE WHITE

SERVICEMEN .... ERIC STARK, LES CONRAD, DAVID MELBOURNE, PETER WILSON

SERVICE GIRLS .... HILARY MARTIN, ANN DOWNS, CAROL BRETT

CUSTOMERS .... CLIFFORD HEMSLEY, MARIA COPE

MUM'S ARMY

• CARMEN SILVERA REMEMBERS •

'I'd worked with David Croft on two previous occasions: *Hugh and I*, which he directed, and four episodes of *Beggar My Neighbour*, with Peter Jones and June Whitfield. I got on very well with him and one day he phoned and said he'd written a part for me in "Mum's Army" called Fiona Gray. I was absolutely thrilled.

'We met, I saw the script and before long we began rehearsing the episode. I was slightly in awe of the team because they'd all been together so long, but without exception they were very welcoming – it was an enjoyable experience.

'David later told me it was his favourite episode, which was really thrilling. Most of the television I'd done before then had been dramas; I'd never appeared in light entertainment before, and it was a shock when I discovered it was to be recorded in front of an audience. But David's such a wonderful director, so calm and reassuring, that everything worked out well.

'The episode was based on the classic film, *Brief Encounter*, and there was one moment during the dress rehearsal when David began thinking that I looked a bit too young to match Arthur, so he sent me back to the make-up department with instructions on what to do with my hair and overall appearance.

'When it was transmitted some of the critics panned it a bit, claiming it was out of character with the rest of the show. But later repeats soon attracted rave notices. Mrs Gray was a lovely part to play and I'll never forget David presenting me with my own copy of the episode on video tape when I was the subject for *This Is Your Life*. It had been transferred from the original recording on film and included a final scene not shown now on television repeats. When the train bound for London pulls out of the station after Arthur has finished pleading with Fiona not to go, there's a tremendous cloud of steam. In the original recording, as the steam clears, Mainwaring stares towards the other end of the platform, where we see his platoon.

'I've only watched the episode a few times in recent years, perhaps when I've got friends over. I don't really like watching myself on television because I get a little embarrassed. But it was a wonderful episode to make.'

CARMEN SILVERA

Mum's Army

MAIN HALL. NIGHT

Unit is on parade. Mainwaring and Wilson are in their usual positions. Jones is at the far end, away from them.

MAINWARING Platoon – stand at ease.

Jones is late.

MAINWARING Platoon – 'shun!

Jones is late.

WILSON Try to do it with the others, Jones.

JONES Sorry, sir.

MAINWARING Thank you, Wilson. Platoon – stand at ease.

Jones is late yet again.

JONES I think what is causing it, sir, is that – you being at the end of the line – the sound of your command is taking longer to cross the air to reach me, sir.

MAINWARING Yes – it must be something like that.

WALKER Perhaps, if you was to nod your head, sir, he would catch on a bit quicker.

JONES That's right, sir, you nod yer head, sir, and I'll not be found wanting.

MAINWARING I don't think we'll get involved with that, Jones. Now, pay attention. Some of your uniforms are looking pretty shoddy and one or two badges could do with brassing up a bit. Now, this brings me to a little scheme that we have been discussing – haven't we, Wilson?

WILSON That's right, sir.

JONES **(Coming suddenly to attention)** H'up.

MAINWARING What's the matter, Jones?

JONES You nodded, sir, so I sprung to it.

MAINWARING We're not doing that, Jones.

JONES I'm sorry, sir.

MAINWARING Now, we've been approached by several of the womenfolk.

JONES Ay 'up. **(He stands at ease)**

MAINWARING What's the matter now, Jones?

JONES I was standing at attention. sir. Now I'm easing myself.

MAINWARING We have been approached by several of the womenfolk, who would like to join with us in our fight against the common foe. Wilson and I think this is quite a good scheme – don't we, Wilson?

WILSON Yes, sir. Don't nod, will you, sir.

MAINWARING I'll watch it. They could take over some of the paperwork and the making of tea and cocoa, etc...

FRAZER Buttons!

MAINWARING I beg your pardon, Frazer?

FRAZER Buttons, sir. They could sew on buttons.

MAINWARING Precisely – a very good point. Make a note of that, Wilson.

WILSON Yes, sir.

MAINWARING **(Nodding)** A very good point, indeed.

JONES **(Jumping to attention)** Ay 'up.

MAINWARING Jones!

JONES You nodded, sir. Oh – sorry, sir – I forgot we wasn't doing it.

MAINWARING **(To Wilson)** We're going to have to let him go.

GODFREY My sister is very good at sewing – petit point and all that sort of thing – providing someone else will thread the needle.

MAINWARING I think perhaps we should concentrate on rather a younger age group, Godfrey.

PIKE There's a new girl at the sweet shop – she's very obliging.

MAINWARING That sounds more like the girl we need.

WALKER That's right – comforts for the troops.

MAINWARING We don't want any of that sort of talk, Walker.

FRAZER There's a lassie works for the Gaslight and Coke Company. She's a good weight-bearing sonsie girl with a firm body and big strong thighs.

JONES They're very strong – the ones with big thighs.

MAINWARING Well, I'm sure between us, we can round up the right sort of material. What does sonsie mean?

WILSON An obscure Scottish term.

MAINWARING Anyway, bring them along to the office tomorrow. We only need a handful. Properly trained, they'll release us – the frontline troops – so that we can grapple with the enemy.

WALKER I don't suppose Taffy and Jones 'ere will have much energy left after grappling with those big thighs.

MAINWARING Walker, I shan't tell you again.

SIDE OFFICE. NIGHT

Wilson is at the desk doing some work. Mainwaring enters.

MAINWARING Ah, good evening, Wilson. How goes the recruiting?

WILSON The men seem to have brought quite a few along.

MAINWARING Right, we'd better bash on. Get them in – one at a time.

Wilson crosses to the door.

Group standing in hall.

WILSON Ah, now, who's first?

MAIN HALL. NIGHT

Jones is waiting in the hall with Mrs Fox. Also present are Pike with Ivy Samways – a very quiet, retiring girl; Frazer is without his girl. Walker has brought Edith Parrish who is a blonde, forthcoming cockney.

JONES This is Mrs Fox, Sergeant.

WILSON Ah, yes, Mrs Fox. I wonder if you would be so kind as to come in.

MRS FOX Oo – thanks ever so.

She comes into the office with Jones.

SIDE OFFICE. NIGHT

WILSON What an awfully humid day it's been.

MRS FOX Yes, hasn't it.

WILSON Still – you're looking marvellously cool. This is Mrs Fox, sir.

MAINWARING **(He stands and salutes)** How do you do, Mrs Fox?

MRS FOX Nicely, thank you.

JONES She's one of my best customers, sir. I think you will find she will give every satisfaction.

MAINWARING Thank you, Jones.

WILSON By Jove, how rude of me – please have a chair. **(He draws up a chair)** Now, is there anything we can get you? Would you like a nice cup of tea or something?

MRS FOX Oh, I don't think so.

MAINWARING Wilson.

WILSON The kettle's on, it won't take a moment.

MRS FOX Well...

MAINWARING Wilson, I would like a word with you outside for a moment. Please excuse me, Mrs Fox.

He takes Wilson out to main hall.

MAIN HALL. NIGHT

MAINWARING Wilson, I know you are something of a lady's man, but these women are going to be subject to discipline like the rest of our force. Let's start as we mean to go on, shall we?

WILSON Well, surely we can be polite!

MAINWARING I quite agree, but we don't have to have all this Jack Buchanan stuff. We'll just stick to the business in hand, if you don't mind.

WILSON Whatever you say, sir.

They return.

SIDE OFFICE. NIGHT

MAINWARING Sorry about that, Mrs Fox. Name – Fox. Christian name?

MRS FOX Marcia.

MAINWARING **(Writing)** Marcia.

WILSON What a pretty name.

MRS FOX Do you think so?

WILSON It's one of my favourites.

MAINWARING Wilson!

MRS FOX **(Handing over a card)** Oh, there's my address. **(Confidentially)** I've written my age on the bottom.

MAINWARING Thank you.

MRS FOX **(Turning to Jones)** I was just telling Mr Mainwaring – I've written my age on the bottom.

Close up of Jones, who thinks this is a very strange thing to have done.

MAINWARING Occupation?

MRS FOX Widow.

MAINWARING Is that an occupation?

WILSON **(Being charming again)** In Mrs Fox's case, I would say it was almost a calling.

MAINWARING **(Throwing down the pencil)** Wilson!

WILSON Sorry, sir.

JONES Mrs Fox is a very fine cooking lady, sir – and a most understanding and warm female person.

MAINWARING Well, I'm sure that will be most useful. Would you like to join us?

MRS FOX I didn't know you'd come apart.

Wilson laughs cordially. Mainwaring is deadpanned.

WILSON Awfully good – don't you think so, sir?

MAINWARING I'll take that as an affirmative answer. Thank you, Mrs Fox. Next one please, Wilson.

WILSON This way, Mrs Fox.

He shows Mrs Fox out.

MRS FOX **(As she goes)** Thank you, Mr Mainwaring.

JONES **(Leaning over the desk)** She's a very dry wit, sir, is Mrs Fox.

MAINWARING Yes, I'm sure. Thank you, Jones.

Pike and Ivy Samways enter.

PIKE Oh, this is the young lady I was telling you about, sir. Ivy Samways.

MAINWARING Ivy Samways.

WILSON You may remember, sir – she was the one who was very obliging.

MAINWARING Thank you, Wilson.

Jones looks at Ivy.

MAINWARING There's no need for you to stay, Jones.

JONES Thank you, sir. **(Jones goes out with elaborate about turns, left turns, right turns, etc.)**

MAINWARING Now, you're a shop assistant, aren't you?

Jones salutes.

MAINWARING Get out, Jones.

Jones goes.

MAINWARING You're a shop assistant, aren't you?

She nods.

MAINWARING Address?

IVY **(Completely inaudibly)** Twenty-seven, Jutland Drive.

MAINWARING I beg your pardon?

IVY **(Inaudible again)** Twenty-seven, Jutland Drive.

MAINWARING I... I'm afraid I didn't quite catch that.

PIKE Jutland Drive, sir.

MAINWARING Oh, Jutland Drive. **(He writes)** What number?

IVY **(Inaudible)** Twenty-seven.

MAINWARING Umh?

IVY **(Inaudible again)** Twenty-seven.

PIKE Twenty-seven... sir.

MAINWARING Ah... now I wonder what sort of task we can find to fit Miss Samways.

WILSON Answering the telephone, sir?

MAINWARING You're trying my patience rather far today, Wilson.

WILSON She can look after the secrets file, sir, most admirably.

MAINWARING Right... thank you, Miss Samways.

Frazer pops in before they go.

FRAZER A word, sir?

MAINWARING Yes, Frazer.

FRAZER The lassie from the Gaslight and Coke Company cannot be here tonight, sir, but I have asked her, and she wants to join. She's just the sort we want, sir. A fine, firmly built girl – you know – strong... with big thighs.

MAINWARING Yes... thank you, Frazer. Bring her tomorrow.

Walker is in front of the desk – with Edith Parrish.

WALKER Er, Mr Mainwaring, this is Edith Parish – she's a friend of mine.

MAINWARING I see... do you have an occupation, Miss Parish?

EDITH Yeh – I'm an usherette.

WALKER That's right – the Tivoli Cinema – you know – with the torch.

MAINWARING Ah... I expect you see a lot of pictures.

EDITH Yeah... I see a lot of other things an' all.

WALKER **(Confidentially)** Any time you want to see a film... knock three times on the fire exit round the side alley and she'll fit you in.

MAINWARING Y-e-s, well, I don't think I shall be taking advantage of your hospitality, Miss Parish. Now, where do you live?

EDITH Down Berwick Road – 35 – I live with my dad and he's six foot three – so you needn't get any ideas.

MAINWARING I think that will be all, Miss Parish.

WALKER I'll see that she's here tomorrow, sir. **(Talking to her as they go out)** You shouldn't have said that to 'im – he don't get ideas.

MAINWARING **(When she has gone)** I don't think that is the right class of girl for us at all, Wilson. Are there any more?

WILSON No, that's all, sir.

MAINWARING Send the men home then, Wilson. They were very late last night. I'll sort some of this out.

WILSON Very good, sir. **(He goes into main hall)**

MAIN HALL. NIGHT

WILSON Er, right – that's all for tonight, ladies and gentlemen. I hope you've enjoyed it, and we'll look forward to seeing you at the same time tomorrow.

SIDE OFFICE. NIGHT

WILSON **(O.O.V., continues to speak)** Off you go then.

Mainwaring reacts. There's a knock on the outside door.

MAINWARING Come in.

Mrs Gray enters. She is a good-looking, middle-aged woman with great charm, very neatly dressed.

MRS GRAY Captain Mainwaring?

MAINWARING That's right.

MRS GRAY I heard you were needing women helpers for the Home Guard – is that right?

MAINWARING Yes, yes, quite correct. Do sit down.

MRS GRAY I've heard about this platoon since its very beginning. I think you've done a wonderful job.

MAINWARING Well, we just try to do our best for old England in her hour of need.

MRS GRAY I'd love to help. Just to feel that I was doing something.

MAINWARING Your face seems vaguely familiar. Have I seen you at the Golf Club?

MRS GRAY No… I've not been in Walmington long. I had to bring my mother away from London because of the bombing.

MAINWARING I see.

MRS GRAY I'd loved to have stayed – not that there was much that I could have done, but just being there would have shown that wretched little Hitler that we're not going to give in.

MAINWARING By Jove – that's the sort of talk I like to hear. **(Getting down to business)** Now, what's the name?

MRS GRAY Gray.

MAINWARING And the Christian name?

MRS GRAY Fiona.

MAINWARING Fiona – what a pretty name.

MRS GRAY Do you think so?

MAINWARING It has always been one of my favourites.

MRS GRAY Thank you.

MAINWARING Occupation?

MRS GRAY Well… widow, I suppose – if you can call that an occupation.

MAINWARING Well, in your case I would say it was almost a… **(He decides not to say it, and instead writes)** Widow – and the address?

MRS GRAY Thirty-one, Wilton Gardens.

MAINWARING Wilton Gardens! That's quite near me.

MRS GRAY I know… I see you go to the bank every morning.

MAINWARING I say, do you really?

MRS GRAY And how marvellously punctual you are. We thought you were three minutes late the other day.

MAINWARING Was I?

MRS GRAY No. The clock was wrong.

MAINWARING Oh well… in my position one must set an example to the youngsters.

MRS GRAY Oh, I agree. All the old standards are declining so rapidly.

MAINWARING They are – indeed they are.

She looks at him. He looks at her.

MRS GRAY Well, I mustn't keep you.

MAINWARING Shall we see you tomorrow night, then? We usually parade about seven o'clock.

MRS GRAY I can't wait to start. At the moment my life consists of morning coffee at Ann's Pantry and making the dahlias grow.

MAINWARING I'm very fond of dahlias.

MRS GRAY Really? Do you grow them, too?

MAINWARING No… no, unfortunately. My wife says they attract earwigs.

MRS GRAY What a shame, but she's quite right. **(She gathers her bag and gloves)** Captain Mainwaring, may I say something awfully personal?

MAINWARING Well, of course.

MRS GRAY Do you always wear spectacles?

MAINWARING Well, yes I do.

MRS GRAY Would you take them off for a moment?

MAINWARING Well, er, yes, if you wish. **(He takes them off)**

MRS GRAY That's so much better – I always think they act as a sort of… well… they cut off the warmth in a person's eyes – just as a fireguard takes away so much of the heat.

MAINWARING Yes, I suppose you're right. I… I've never thought of it that way.

Wilson enters, Mainwaring hastily replaces his glasses.

WILSON Oh… still here, sir?

MAINWARING Ah… Sergeant Wilson… this is a new recruit… Mrs Fiona Gray.

WILSON Fiona! I say, what a pretty…

MAINWARING **(Interrupting)** Yes… well… I have all the details, Mrs Gray, and I'll see you tomorrow at 7.30.

MRS GRAY I shall look forward to it. **(She goes)**

MAINWARING Most charming woman that, Wilson.

WILSON Is she, sir?

MAINWARING Just the sort of material we need.

WILSON Well, you're such a good judge as a rule, it will be most interesting to see how they all shape up.

MAIN HALL. NIGHT

The section and the girls are there. Frazer's girl is apart from the rest. Frazer crosses to Jones.

FRAZER There she is, Jones, over there.

Jones looks.

JONES I don't think she's got big thighs, Mr Frazer. Long ones maybe.

FRAZER What's the matter with your eyes, man. They're like tree trunks.

SIDE OFFICE. NIGHT

There are dahlias on Mainwaring's desk and the whole place is neater than usual. Mainwaring enters. He goes to the desk and puts down his stick and gloves. He sees the dahlias. He is pleased. He crosses to the mirror, he removes his glasses and admires the result with some difficulty. He puts them in his top pocket. Wilson calls to Mrs Pike outside.

WILSON **(Out of vision)** Go through the main door, Mavis, and we'll be with you in a moment.

Wilson enters.

WILSON Ah, good evening, sir.

MAINWARING Good evening, Wilson.

WILSON Dear, dear, have you broken your glasses, sir?

MAINWARING No, Wilson, I just left them off for a moment. **(He puts them on again)** Right, let's get on with it. **(He goes into the hall)**

MAIN HALL. NIGHT

WILSON Platoon – 'shun!

MAINWARING Now, welcome, ladies.

LADIES Good evening, etc.

MAINWARING Since sooner or later we will be getting you uniforms, I thought it best today to teach you just the rudiments of foot drill, so that we can look like a disciplined body of men and… er women. Now, first of all… the 'at ease' position. The legs should be comfortably apart – about 18 inches or so. **(They do so)** They hands are placed right over left – just over your bot… over your beh… at the back. Have you all got that?

MRS PIKE A lot of red tape nonsense.

PIKE No talking in the ranks, Mum.

MAINWARING Pike. No talking in the ranks. Now, to come to attention… you transfer your weight on to your right foot. **(They lean)** You raise your left foot. I'm doing it in slow motion, of course, and… then place your left foot beside your right. **(He totters – Wilson steadies him)** …thus. Now, here's the tricky bit. At the same time, bring your hands to your sides, with thumbs in line with the seams of your trousers.

JONES Permission to speak, sir? These ladies are not wearing trousers, sir… them being ladies.

WALKER They can put their thumbs in line with the seams of their knickers.

MAINWARING Walker, fall out and stand over there. You will take no further part in this parade.

WALKER **(As he moves to the side)** Blimey, what have I said?

EDITH If we wasn't wearing 'em, he'd have something to go on about.

GODFREY **(To the ladies behind him)** He's very coarse, but very good hearted.

MAINWARING Right, now, let's try it. Give the command, Wilson.

WILSON Squad – 'shun.

They come to attention.

MAINWARING Oh, no… that was very sloppy. Not you, Mrs Gray, that was very good. You must all stand up straight. Stomachs in, chests out.

JONES Not you, Mrs Fox, that's very good.

MAINWARING Right, now, let's go once more. Stand at ease. Squad, 'shun… **(They do so)** Now, come along, Mrs Fox.

JONES Yes, come along, you're all behind.

MRS FOX I was following you.

JONES You mustn't undermine my position, you know.

MAINWARING Stand at ease.

MRS PIKE Silly red tape.

PIKE Mum, no talking in the ranks.

MAINWARING Pike! …I shan't tell you again.

FRAZER Captain Mainwaring. Miss Ironside here is doing it very well. Her legs are going with a very firm, strong action.

MAINWARING Yes, thank you, Frazer. **(To Wilson)** She doesn't seem to have very big thighs to me, Wilson.

WILSON Quite long, though.

MAINWARING Yes, now, let's move on to left and right turn. Now to turn right, you swivel on the right heel and left toe – this. One – two, one – two. **(He demonstrates and totters a little – Wilson helps)**

Walker hums.

MAINWARING Walker! Now brace the rear thigh hard as you go.

FRAZER Aye, that's right. Do as the Captain says – those thighs have to be braced firm and strong.

MAINWARING Yes, thank you, Frazer. Then you lift the rear leg high, and place it beside the front one.

EDITH Blimey – what a way to win the war.

GODFREY You'll find the Captain knows best, if you'd listen to him.

MAINWARING Godfrey, face front and don't keep staring at the ladies.

WALKER Woman mad – woman mad 'e is.

MAINWARING Any more from you and you'll be sent home. **(Walker reacts)** Look to your front. Now, let's try it. Squad – 'shun. Very good, Mrs Gray. **(She reacts)** Squad – left turn. **(They turn different ways)** Ah… face your front.

WILSON There seems to be a little confusion as to which is which, sir.

MAINWARING I know, Wilson.

JONES They had the same trouble, sir, during the American Civil War, when they had to have all sorts of crude, rough, country yokel men as soldiers and they didn't know their left foot from their elbow, sir. So, to overcome this ingeniously, they tied a piece of hay to one foot and a piece of straw to the other, and when they wanted to turn left, the commanding man said 'Hay turn' or 'Straw turn' – according to whether the hay was on the left foot or the straw was on the left foot. Mind you, they had to be careful to get straws on all the left feet or hay, as the case may be. Do you think that would help, sir?

WALKER I think that's a good idea, sir. Then you would be able to come in and say, 'Good evening, ladies, what nice straws you are wearing'.

MAINWARING That's it – go home, Walker.

WALKER I didn't say anything.

MAINWARING I'm not arguing – it's an order.

Fade as Walker is sent home.

ANN'S PANTRY. DAY

We see the window, the door, two or three tables wide by two or three tables deep. Mainwaring enters. He is in his business suit. He selects a table in the foreground, looks round and sits. He removes his spectacles, and takes up his paper. He can't see it, so he puts his specs on again. Godfrey is sitting by the window, concealed by paper. Mrs Gray enters, she is about to sit at the next table when she sees Mainwaring.

MRS GRAY Oh, good morning, Mr Mainwaring.

MAINWARING **(Rising)** Ah, what a surprise. Won't you join me? **(He takes off his spectacles. We see Godfrey drop his newspaper. He reacts to the scene)**

MRS GRAY Thank you. **(She sits)** I haven't seen you here before.

MAINWARING Oh, I come here from time to time, you know – when I get my nose away from the grindstone.

The waitress brings the menu.

WAITRESS Yes, please?

MAINWARING **(Taking it)** Ah, thank you. **(He can't read it – he puts on his spectacles and looks)** Ah, oh no, I don't think I'll bother with any of that. **(He realises that Mrs Gray should have it first)** Oh, I do beg your pardon. **(He hands it to her and takes off his spectacles)**

MRS GRAY No, just coffee for me, as usual.

MAINWARING Yes, that's a capital idea – coffee, please.

Waitress goes.

MAINWARING They used to do the most marvellous Devonshire teas here, you know.

MRS GRAY With jam and cream?

MAINWARING That's right.

The waitress gives Godfrey his bill.

MAINWARING I remember just after the last war. I'd just joined the Guildford branch – a chum and I borrowed a flivver and took a spin down here to Ann's Pantry, just for the Devonshire tea. When I got home, I had the rough end of my governor's tongue, I can tell you. He thought I had toddled off with a bit of fluff.

MRS GRAY Oh, it was all harmless fun, in those days.

MAINWARING Of course it was. Mind you, we used to go the pace now and then. **(He laughs reminiscently)**

MRS GRAY You know, your whole face seems to light up when you laugh. I think you're a very jolly person at heart.

MAINWARING Yes, I think I probably am. Mind you, bank managers don't get much chance of joking and jesting.

The waitress delivers the coffee.

WAITRESS Separate bills?

MRS GRAY Yes, please.

MAINWARING No, no please. Have it with me.

Godfrey passes by to pay the bill.

GODFREY Good morning, Captain Mainwaring.

MAINWARING Godfrey, is it?

GODFREY I haven't seen you in here before.

MAINWARING Oh, I pop in from time to time, you know.

GODFREY I'm just on my way to the clinic. **(He sees Mainwaring properly)** Oh, dear – have you broken your spectacles, Mr Mainwaring?

MAINWARING Oh, no – just giving my eyes a rest, you know.

GODFREY Well, will you excuse me? **(He goes)**

MAINWARING **(To Mrs Gray)** A charming man – one of my most loyal soldiers.

Walker enters.

MRS GRAY They're a wonderful band of men.

MAINWARING I'm very proud of them.

Walker comes to the table.

WALKER 'Allo, Captain Mainwaring – haven't seen you here before.

MAINWARING Well, I come in from time to time.

WALKER 'Ere, if you've bust your specs, I know a bloke that's got 500 frames – hardly used.

MAINWARING No, I haven't broken them, thank you.

WALKER 'Ere, if anyone asks you – you haven't seen me. I'm just delivering a bit of the sweet stuff – savvy?

MAINWARING You mean – sugar?

WALKER Shhh... you haven't seen me. **(He moves off and comes quickly back)** I haven't seen you too, so don't worry. **(He goes)**

She reacts.

MAINWARING Heart of gold that man – do anything for you. What part of London do you come from?

MRS GRAY Oh, just near Regent's Park. Of course it was hopeless for mother. They have the ack ack guns there, you know. Oh dear, was that careless talk?

MAINWARING That's all right – any secret is quite safe with me.

Jones enters with Mrs Prosser.

JONES Hello, Mr Mainwaring, don't often see you 'ere.

MAINWARING I do come in...

JONES This is Mrs Prosser. This is Mr Mainwaring.

MAINWARING How do you do...? Er... this is Mrs Gray.

MRS GRAY How do you do?

JONES **(To Mrs Prosser)** You sit there, my dear. I'll join you in a moment. **(Jones to Mainwaring)** Mrs Prosser is a very good friend of mine, sir, but there is nothing in it.

MAINWARING Oh, I see.

JONES All the same, you won't tell Mrs Fox you've seen me with her, will you, sir? It's just that I give her pieces for her cat and on 'er part she keeps me company from time to time.

MAINWARING Thank you, Jones.

Jones sits.

MAINWARING I'm sorry about all these interruptions. I must say I was looking forward to a nice cup of coffee and a quiet chat.

MRS GRAY So was I.

MAINWARING I have to confess I came here quite deliberately on the chance you'd be here.

MRS GRAY I'd rather hoped you might.

Pike enters and comes to the table.

PIKE Captain Mainwaring, Mr Wilson says he is sorry to spoil your tête-à-tête, but the bank inspectors are here and will you come straight away.

MAINWARING Yes, right – all right, Pike – I'm coming. **(To Mrs Gray)** I'm sorry about this. Let's meet again very soon.

MRS GRAY I'd like that.

MAINWARING I shall see you tonight anyway, on parade.

MRS GRAY Yes, of course, I'll look forward to it.

MAINWARING So will I – sorry, I must go. **(He goes – the waitress approaches)**

WAITRESS Two coffees – that's 1s. 2d.

Mrs Gray realises he hasn't paid, smiles and reaches for her handbag.

THE MAIN HALL. NIGHT

Jones' section are talking amongst themselves.

FRAZER Yon Mainwaring's making an utter fool of himself. There's no other way of putting it.

EDITH Three times they come last week to see *Forty Little Mothers* with Eddie Cantor and they come again last night to see *Shipyard Sally* with Gracie Fields... Shirley shows them in, so they think I don't see, but they're always in the back row – only holding hands, mind. Not like some people I know who seem to have more arms than an octopus. **(This is for Walker's benefit but Jones takes it)**

JONES I've a very possessive nature, Miss Parish.

Wilson enters, and hears some of the gossip.

PIKE They have coffee every morning together.

GODFREY I've not seen them.

PIKE They go to the Dutch Oven now, I have to come and get 'im if there's anything important.

FRAZER Folly, sheer folly – it'll be the ruin of him – somebody should tell him.

GODFREY Well, I think it is none of our business. We shouldn't talk about that sort of thing behind their back.

WALKER Blimey, you're one to talk. It was you what told us about them playing clock golf at the municipal gardens.

GODFREY I thought, I thought it was rather nice.

SIDE OFFICE. NIGHT

Mainwaring is at his desk. Wilson enters.

MAINWARING Ah, good evening, Wilson. It's about time for parade, isn't it?

WILSON Just a few more minutes, I think, sir.

MAINWARING Good. I have rather an important announcement to make concerning the ladies' section.

WILSON Ah, yes – the ladies' section. Er... I did rather want to talk to you about that some time.

MAINWARING Oh, yes?

WILSON I know it is none of my business, but if I don't say something, well... I mean who will?

MAINWARING What are you talking about, Wilson?

WILSON Well, we've know each other a long time – in the bank, with the platoon. You might almost say we're practically friends – nearly.

MAINWARING Wilson – if you have something to say – stop shuffling from one foot to another and cough it up. Are you in some sort of trouble?

WILSON Good Lord, no. It's just that, with the ladies' section, do you think it is just possible that some of us are making tiny little fools of ourselves?

MAINWARING Ah... I see. Well, I appreciate your frankness, Wilson.

WILSON Thank you, sir.

MAINWARING It can't have been easy for you to talk to me on such a delicate matter.

WILSON Well, I only did it for the best, sir.

MAINWARING I'm not insensitive to what people have been saying, so I've decided to dismiss the female section and just hang on to one or two special helpers.

WILSON I see, sir.

MAINWARING So that should solve your problem and get Mrs Pike out of your hair. Come along, I'll make the announcement.

He goes into main hall.

MAIN HALL

MAINWARING Right – pay attention please. Is everybody here, Jones?

JONES Everybody, except Mrs Gray, sir... that is.

MAINWARING Mrs Gray, not here? How strange – perhaps she is a little bit under the weather.

FRAZER Favouritism.

PIKE Ivy says she thinks she is all right, because she saw her carrying two big, heavy cases to the station.

MAINWARING The station!

Ivy whispers to Pike.

PIKE About ten minutes ago.

MAINWARING Ten minutes ago! You saw her go to the station.

WALKER There's only one train, the 8.40 to London.

MAINWARING Take the parade, Wilson. **(Mainwaring hurries out through the office. Wilson calls after him)**

WILSON Do you want me to make the announcement?

Mainwaring has gone.

WILSON Oh, Lord.

STATION WAITING ROOM. NIGHT

It is small and dimly lit by gas. There is one small refreshment counter with a hot-water machine, some tired-looking sandwich cases, etc. Mrs Gray is at the counter getting a cup of tea.

MRS GRAY Not too strong, thank you.

GIRL Not much chance of that, dear. Anything else?

MRS GRAY No, thank you.

GIRL Just tuppence then.

Mrs Gray pays and takes the tea to a table. Mainwaring enters. He sees her and crosses.

MAINWARING What's this then, what's happened?

MRS GRAY Nothing's happened, I'm just going back to London, that's all.

MAINWARING How long for?

MRS GRAY I don't know – a month or two – for good perhaps.

MAINWARING Why? You never mentioned it – you never even hinted.

MRS GRAY I just thought it would be best.

MAINWARING But I don't want you to go. My whole life is completely different. I just live from one meeting to the next.

MRS GRAY I know – I'm just the same, but it's the only thing to do. People are talking.

MAINWARING People always talk – who cares about that?

MRS GRAY But there's your wife.

MAINWARING They won't talk to her. She's not left home since Munich.

MRS GRAY Be sensible, George. You can't afford to have scandal and tittle tattle.

MAINWARING I don't care.

MRS GRAY But there's the bank.

MAINWARING Damn the bloody bank!

MRS GRAY George!

MAINWARING I'm sorry, but don't take that train.

MRS GRAY George, I must.

MAINWARING I implore you – don't take that train; we'll only see each other once a week.

MRS GRAY You're making this very difficult for me, but I've made up my mind – it's the only way.

The sound of a train approaches in the distance.

PORTER **(Out of vision)** Victoria – Victoria train.

MRS GRAY There's my train.

MAINWARING Fiona. I've never begged anyone for anything in my life, but I'm begging you not to go.

Serviceman comes up with a cup of tea. Mainwaring has risen.

SERVICEMAN Finished with those chairs, mate?

MAINWARING Yes, take the damn things.

SERVICEMAN Oh, all right, I only asked.

MRS GRAY I'm sorry, George.

She picks up her cases and moves to the door.

MAINWARING Here, that's heavy, let me.

He helps her with the case. They move on to the platform.

STATION PLATFORM. NIGHT

Mainwaring is separated from Mrs Gray a little.

MAINWARING Look, let's talk about it. Go tomorrow.

The train is heard to stop. She struggles towards a compartment. He follows her.

PORTER'S VOICE Walmington-on-Sea... Walmington-on-Sea. Victoria train.

COMPARTMENT OF TRAIN. NIGHT

Seven people in the compartment. Most of them servicemen with kit bags, equipment, etc. She moves into the compartment. Mainwaring catches up and follows in as well.

MAINWARING Look, do you mind making room for this lady. **(She is trying to put her case on the rack)** Here, let me help you.

PORTER'S VOICE Hurry along please... hurry along.

Mainwaring struggles to get the case on the rack.

MRS GRAY Hurry up, or you'll be coming to London, too.

She bundles him out and shuts the door.

STATION PLATFORM. NIGHT

MAINWARING How do I get in touch with you?

MRS GRAY You won't be able to.

MAINWARING You'll write, won't you?

MRS GRAY Maybe – after a while – I don't know.

PORTER'S VOICE Stand clear, please. **(He whistles. Porter rushes through)**

MAINWARING But, please, you must... promise me you'll write.

MRS GRAY Very well – I promise.

The train whistle blows and there is the sound of the train moving off. Camera remains on Mainwaring.

MAINWARING Please make it soon.

MRS GRAY **(More distant)** Goodbye, George.

MAINWARING Goodbye, Fiona... Bye...

Steam blows across him. Camera moves in for big close up as the sound of the train recedes into the distance.

SERIES FOUR **EPISODE TEN**

Recorded: Friday 20/11/70
Original transmission: Friday 27/11/70, 8.00–8.30pm
Original viewing figures = 16 million

ARTHUR LOWE .... CAPTAIN MAINWARING
JOHN LE MESURIER .... SERGEANT WILSON
CLIVE DUNN.................................. LANCE CORPORAL JONES
JOHN LAURIE .... PRIVATE FRAZER
JAMES BECK .... PRIVATE WALKER
ARNOLD RIDLEY .... PRIVATE GODFREY
IAN LAVENDER .... PRIVATE PIKE
BILL PERTWEE .... ARP WARDEN
FRANK WILLIAMS.. VICAR
EDWARD SINCLAIR... VERGER
DON ESTELLE .... GERALD
HAROLD BENNETT .... MR BLEWITT
FREDDIE TRUEMAN (SPECIAL APPEARANCE) .... E.C. EGAN

PLATOON ...... COLIN BEAN, HUGH HASTINGS, VIC TAYLOR, HUGH CECIL,
.... DESMOND CULLUM-JONES, LESLIE NOYES, FREDDIE WHITE,
.... GEORGE HANCOCK, FRANK GODFREY, FREDDIE WILES

THE TEST

• ROGER SINGLETON-TURNER REMEMBERS •

'We shot the cricket match after the season had finished; we had a real pitch, but the markings had long disappeared. Normally, these days, it would be up to the designer (or possibly the location manager) to organise the preparation of the wicket. In this case, the job fell to me. Recalling all I could of school cricket games, I painted in the crease marks suitably far apart. I guess they were okay because no one complained. It must have been the only time, though, that Freddie Trueman, as guest star, ever bowled on a wicket prepared with a can of cream spray paint!

'Shooting the game took a long time – sports on single camera usually do take a while. One memory I have is of the spent carbon rods from an arc light cooling in the long grass. Not long after this, arc lights were replaced by some of the early halogen lamps.

'Freddie Trueman was a brilliant cricketer, of course, but I'm not aware that he'd tried acting anywhere else. He had to come to Television Centre to record some scenes in the dressing room and I *think* he enjoyed his brief brush with show business.'

ROGER SINGLETON-TURNER
Assistant Floor Manager

The Test

THE YARD

The platoon is lined up – standing at ease. Mainwaring is inspecting them.

MAINWARING Stand at ease. Right, stand easy. I was very disappointed at the turn-out for church parade on Sunday. Now, you may think that it's a waste of time, but I would remind you that during Dunkirk, His Majesty the King called the Nation to a day of prayer. Well, I think you'll have to admit that it worked damn well, and I don't think we should ignore this side of the war effort.

WALKER Sorry I couldn't come, sir. I was delivering essential supplies to a company of A.T.S. girls.

MAINWARING Couldn't you have waited until the afternoon?

WALKER I could, but they couldn't, it was elastic, see.

MAINWARING I see.

WALKER They needed it for their knickers.

MAINWARING Yes, all right, Walker. And Pike, sitting behind you, I notice that your hair is getting very long, it's practically touching your collar. See that you get it cut.

PIKE Yes, Mr Mainwaring.

MAINWARING Yours is getting untidy, too, Wilson, you're not a violin player, you know.

PIKE Mum said it made Uncle Arthur look rather romantic.

WILSON Frank!

MAINWARING Hmm, I don't see it. Now, we have received a letter from the Chief Warden of the A.R.P. Service. Have you got it, Wilson?

WILSON Yes, sir. **(He fumbles in his pockets for it)**

JONES If it's about me and Mrs Prosser being found in the air raid shelter, I would like to say it's not true, sir.

MAINWARING I beg your pardon?

JONES She'd come over all of a sudden faint, sir, and I had to take her to the air raid shelter to pull herself together.

MAINWARING It's nothing to do with that, Jones.

JONES If it was, sir – it wouldn't be true.

WILSON Here it is, sir.

MAINWARING Ah yes. The wardens want to challenge us to a cricket match. Now, I used to be quite a passable opening bat. What about you, Wilson?

WILSON Well, I can bat a bit and bowl a bit.

MAINWARING Good. Now, who else have we got?

JONES I would like to volunteer to keep the wicket, sir. I kept it once to the rear of the great Ranjit Sinhji, who was an Indian gentleman. And he did not like it, sir, because I whipped off his bales.

MAINWARING Good. We'll need a wicket-keeper.

PIKE I'll have a go, sir.

MAINWARING Well done, Pike.

WALKER So will I, sir – I think I can lay my hands on a couple of re-conditioned cricket balls, sir; they're very hard to get, you know.

MAINWARING Thank you, Walker.

GODFREY I'd be delighted to play somewhere that doesn't involve too much walking about.

WALKER Yeh, and not too far from the pavilion.

MAINWARING That'll do, Walker. Who else? What about you, Frazer?

FRAZER I'll have a go if someone will explain the principle of the thing.

MAINWARING Do you mean you don't play cricket?

FRAZER They tried it once on the Isle of Fullach. But it wasn't a success. 'Tis a wild and windy place ye know and the stumps were blown to the ground.

MAINWARING Yes, well it seems to me that we have the nucleus of a team, so shall we play them?

ALL Yes sir, we'll beat 'em, sir.

MAINWARING Good. That's the sort of fighting spirit I like to hear. Well, we'll set up some nets and get a bit of practice, and, Sergeant Wilson, you tell them that we accept the challenge.

WILSON Very good, sir. Er, who'll be captain?

MAINWARING I will.

THE YARD. (LATER)

Nets have been rigged up in the yard, with a coconut matting wicket. Stumps have been put into a wooden block. Walker is batting with cigarette in mouth. Mainwaring is bowling to him, watched by the squad.

MAINWARING Now watch this one very carefully, Walker.

Mainwaring bowls. Walker steps across the wicket and cuts it hard round to leg.

MAINWARING Yes, well that was an easy one, but I want to give you a tip, Walker. **(He goes to the wicket and takes the**

bat) Now, you can all pay attention to this, because you'll all profit by it. Now, whether you play forward to a good-length ball, thus **(He demonstrates)** or play back to – Wilson, pay attention.

WILSON I thought I'd just skip…

MAINWARING This is just as much for your benefit as anybody else's. Or play back a short ball, thus **(He demonstrates)** it is absolutely essential that you play with a straight bat, thus. Do you understand?

WALKER Why?

MAINWARING Why?

WALKER Yeh, why do you have to do that?

MAINWARING Because it's the correct way. If you slash at it in any old ugly fashion, you'll miss the ball.

WALKER Well, I hit it, didn't I?

MAINWARING That was luck. Send me up a good-length, straight one, Pike.

PIKE Very good, Mr Mainwaring. I wouldn't stand there, Walker, that's just about where I shall be putting it.

Pike starts to bowl.

MAINWARING All right, just a minute.

Pike stops.

MAINWARING Now, take particular note how I watch the ball all the way from the bowler's hand, right on to the bat.

Pike bowls – Mainwaring misses.

PIKE Sorry, Mr Mainwaring.

MAINWARING This sun's a damn nuisance, isn't it?

WILSON You seem to lose sight of the ball somewhere between the bowler's arm and the bat, sir.

MAINWARING Let's see you have a go, Godfrey.

Godfrey approaches.

GODFREY Oh, oughtn't I to have pads on?

MAINWARING No, we're not bowling fast ones.

GODFREY It's just that my legs chip awfully easily.

MAINWARING Get on with it. Send him one down.

Pike starts to bowl.

MAINWARING Just a moment.

Pike stops.

MAINWARING Oh no, no, that won't do at all. Haven't you ever played before, Godfrey?

GODFREY Well, when I was at the Civil Service Stores I used to play for the Gentleman's Outfitting Department.

MAINWARING Really?

GODFREY We used to have a match against the Tobacco and Cigarette Department. I christened it the Gentlemen versus the Players.

MAINWARING Indeed.

GODFREY I was quite a wag in those days.

MAINWARING Yes. Now, get your left hand round the front more. Left shoulder more round, head down – look up more. Feet a little more apart, right arm straight. **(Godfrey is now in excruciating position)** Now, relax. Right, bowl him one, Pike.

PIKE **(Walking to his place)** Shall I give him a googly one, or an easy one like I gave to you?

MAINWARING Just bowl, Pike.

Pike runs up a bit, but is stopped just before delivering the ball. Mainwaring falls.

MAINWARING Just a moment, I think we can all learn something from the faults in Pike's bowling action. His arm doesn't go over nearly high enough, the whole action should be as if you are about to turn a cartwheel. Line up and we'll all try it.

GODFREY **(Still crouching)** Shall I remain poised for action, sir?

MAINWARING No, no, no. Just take it easy for a moment, Godfrey. Now, all together – over – and over – and over, come along, Wilson, pretend you're doing a cartwheel.

WILSON I've never done a cartwheel.

MAINWARING What about when you were a child?

WILSON I just didn't do that sort of thing.

MAINWARING Extraordinary. Right, that's enough of that. Now, let's see what happens when we put it into practice.

Enter Jones. He has come straight from the shop in his straw hat, apron, etc.

JONES I'm sorry I'm late, sir, I was in the middle of coupon counting and then the sausages came.

MAINWARING I don't want excuses, Jones, a parade is a parade and you should be here on time.

JONES I've shoved a pound in your left-hand drawer, sir, as usual.

MAINWARING Yes, well, thank you, Jones, but watch it in future. Right, let's resume our batting practice.

JONES I would like to volunteer to do some of that, sir. Let me be the striker, sir.

MAINWARING Oh, yes, all right, get on with it. Take over from Godfrey.

Jones goes to wicket.

MAINWARING Now, notice how I grip the ball, the forefinger is along the seam and slightly to the left. As the ball leaves my hand notice the wrist action so, that's

very good, Godfrey, and the final flick with the finger that will bring the ball in just outside the off stump. This will probably fox you a bit, Jones. **(He bowls)**

Jones clouts it – they watch the ball over the wall and there is a crash of glass.

MAINWARING Pike, go and ask the Vicar if we can have our ball back.

THE CRICKET PAVILION

It is surrounded by benches, lockers and a variety of cricket gear. There is an adjoining room.

G.C. Egan, a professional cricketer in the late 40s, or early 50s is sitting on a locker, lacing up his boots. The Warden enters with Gerald.

WARDEN Ah, there we are. Are you G.C. Egan?

EGAN That's right.

WARDEN **(Shaking him warmly by the hand)** My, this is a great moment for me, I can tell you. My name's Hodges, we spoke on the phone. Gerald, come and meet G.C. Egan.

GERALD How d'you do?

WARDEN **(To Gerald, concerning Egan)** What a cricketer. Last time I saw him, he bowled Len Hutton, Denis Compton and Joe in two overs.

EGAN I nearly had Bill Edrich an' all.

WARDEN He did too. I reckon two overs of him and Mainwaring's lot will be back in the pavilion.

GERALD Are you going to tell 'em?

WARDEN Not until Mainwaring's in his crease, then we can all see his face. 'Ere, sign here, that makes you a warden and it's all official.

EGAN What happens if the siren sounds?

WARDEN You resign.

Enter Mainwaring – he is dressed in white flannels – blue blazer – pullover round his neck and a cricket cap. He carries a small bag and a bat.

MAINWARING Ah, Mr Hodges. Aren't my lot here yet?

WARDEN They probably fell asleep on guard somewhere.

MAINWARING I don't find that very amusing.

WARDEN I hear you lot have been practising in secret.

MAINWARING Oh nothing much, you know, we're just trying to get back in the swing as it were.

WARDEN Yeh, well you won't be back in it long. Send my lot through, will you, if they come in. Come on, Gerald. Ernie, you don't mind if I call you Ernie.

• DAVID CROFT REMEMBERS •

'Around the time we were out filming this episode we travelled to Norwich to visit a factory which made Babycham. As we were leaving, a company representative put several cases of the drink on the bus. John Le Mesurier didn't like Babycham, but the rest enjoyed themselves. I remember Don Estelle, who has a lovely voice, singing all the way back to Thetford, while Freddie Trueman told cricket stories – it was quite an occasion.'

Warden goes into the adjoining room with Gerald and Egan.

Enter Godfrey. He wears white flannels and a pullover and panama.

GODFREY Hello, Mr Mainwaring.

MAINWARING What's that you're wearing on your head, Godfrey?

GODFREY I wear it for bowls. It's nice and shady in the sun.

MAINWARING Oh no, no. I'll lend you a cap.

Mainwaring goes to put his case on the table – Walker enters – he is wearing white flannels, etc. and a dark long overcoat – he sidles up to Mainwaring.

WALKER I got 'em.

MAINWARING You got what?

WALKER Two round things we was discussing.

MAINWARING D'you mean the cricket balls?

WALKER Sshh. **(He brings one out from each pocket)** There you are, two ten each, four for the pair.

MAINWARING Oh no, I'm not paying anything like that. Nobody ever paid two ten for a cricket ball.

WALKER Sshh. Two quid each then, and I'm robbing myself.

Mainwaring hands over some money and takes one ball.

MAINWARING You'd sell your grandmother, wouldn't you?

WALKER There's no market for her.

MAINWARING Here, Godfrey. **(Giving him the cap)** Take this.

Frazer enters – he is fresh from a funeral in his top hat, frock coat, etc. He carries a Gladstone bag.

FRAZER Morning, Mr Mainwaring.

MAINWARING Good grief.

FRAZER It was old Mr Parkinson. I knew him well.

MAINWARING You can't play like that.

FRAZER **(Holding up a bag)** It's all here. I couldn't very well go to that, dressed for this.

Godfrey interrupts with the cap which is too large.

GODFREY Captain Mainwaring, I'm afraid it's a little large.

MAINWARING Stuff it with paper or something, we must all do our best to be properly turned out…

Enter Wilson – he wears a very flamboyant blazer and cap, and carries a large cricket bag – he puts it down. Pike is with him, and he sneaks in quietly. He is dressed in a white shirt, cricket pullover, grey flannels.

WILSON My, that's quite a weight.

Mainwaring sees flamboyant blazer and compares it with his rather work-a-day blue one.

MAINWARING What's that you're wearing, Wilson?

WILSON This, oh, it's a club I used to belong to.

MAINWARING Rather dazzling isn't it.

WILSON Yes, but of course one doesn't wear it while actually at the wicket, you know, sir.

MAINWARING I'm well aware of that, Wilson.

He sees Pike who is also wearing a green coloured, transparent eye shade.

MAINWARING Pike.

PIKE Yes, Mr Mainwaring.

MAINWARING Where are your white flannels, Pike?

PIKE I haven't got any, Mr Mainwaring. Mum put them in the dolly tub and they shrunk up to above my knees.

MAINWARING Come outside. **(Wilson looks. He takes him aside)** Now look here, Pike. Not only are you a member of the platoon, but you're also an employee of the bank. Wearing this sort of thing doesn't do at all, it could set your whole career back. Do you understand?

PIKE Sorry, Mr Mainwaring.

MAINWARING Now, it so happens I have a spare pair, and just this once I'll lend them to you.

PIKE Thank you, Mr Mainwaring.

MAINWARING But it's not the sort of thing I like to do.

PIKE No, Mr Mainwaring.

MAINWARING Trousers are very personal things. One doesn't like to have them bandied about.

PIKE No, Mr Mainwaring.

MAINWARING They're in my case, get 'em.

PIKE Yes, sir.

MAINWARING And take off that dreadful eye shade.

PIKE Edward G. Robinson wears one.

MAINWARING Not on the cricket field.

Enter Warden, Gerald and Egan.

WARDEN Right, how're you getting on, Captain Mainwaring?

MAINWARING My lads are just about ready.

WARDEN Lads, blimey. Shall we toss here or shall we go out on the pitch like they do in the Test Match?

MAINWARING Here will do very well.

WARDEN Right, here we go then. **(He takes out a coin)**

MAINWARING Shouldn't the umpires be here?

WARDEN Oh blimey, it's going to be like that, is it? Where are the umpires, then?

VOICES OFF Umpires, please. Umpires.

The Vicar and the Verger appear.

VICAR Ah, Captain Mainwaring, good afternoon. Shouldn't we have white coats or something?

JONES **(Voice from the back)** Don't panic, sir. **(We see him with large wrap-around pads – wicket keeper's gloves – he wears a white shirt with a stiff collar and tie, and a small cap)** Here's the coats, sir. I'm sorry about the stains, sir, but a small piece of kidney got left in the pocket accidentally.

WARDEN Right, shall we toss then? You call, Captain. Age before beauty. **(He turns to Gerald)** Age before beauty!

VICAR **(About to toss)** I'm not really used to this, you know.

VERGER Don't worry, sir, it's not real gambling.

The Vicar tosses.

MAINWARING Heads.

VERGER It's tails, you've lost.

WARDEN Bad luck, Mainwaring, you're fielding.

OUTSIDE THE PAVILION

The umpires are walking out to the pitch.

VERGER It looks as if the good Lord has sent us a nice day for it.

VICAR Yes, hasn't he indeed. Er, are you in a hurry to get away after the match, Mr Yeatman?

VERGER Not particularly, sir.

VICAR In that case I think you ought to remove your bicycle clips.

The Verger does so, hobbling along beside the Vicar.

VERGER I'm sorry if my appearance is a bit of an embarrassment to you, sir.

VICAR I didn't mean it to sound like that, Mr Yeatman.

MAINWARING We're walking out here as free men, for a friendly British game. That's what we're fighting for you know, Wilson.

WILSON Well, among other things.

MAINWARING **(To Pike)** Ah, managed to get into them all right, Pike?

Pike's trousers are much too big in waist and at least five inches too short above the ankle.

PIKE Yes, Mr Mainwaring, only you're a bit shorter than I am and a bit fatter.

MAINWARING Keep your hands in your pockets until the ball is delivered.

JONES Send them down as fast as you like, sir, I'll catch them, sir, and whip off their bales.

MAINWARING Thank you, Jones. Right, Frazer, Walker, first and second slips. Sponge, mid-on, Godfrey, deep cover.

THE PAVILION

Warden and Gerald are emerging.

WARDEN I'll take the first ball, but go easy for an over or so then we'll start to get on top of the bowling.

GERALD I'm usually better at getting underneath it.

Cut to Mainwaring on pitch. Pike is at silly point.

MAINWARING Pike, come a bit closer. I often get one with a short catch.

PIKE If I come any nearer I'll get me head bashed in.

MAINWARING Just do as you're told, Pike.

The Warden is now at the wicket – he puts the bat up.

WARDEN Is that middle and leg, Mr Yeatman?

VERGER Well, it's just a touch to the leg.

WARDEN Never mind, it's near enough with 'im bowling.

VERGER Are you ready, Vicar?

VICAR Quite ready, Mr Yeatman.

VERGER Will you be saying grace, sir?

VICAR No, thank you, Mr Yeatman, I don't think it's usual.

VERGER Right. Play.

Mainwaring walks to the bowling position.

WARDEN **(To Pike after he's looked round the field)** Are you going to stand there, lad?

PIKE He told me to.

WARDEN You'll get your head bashed in.

PIKE Mr Mainwaring, he says I'll get me head bashed in.

MAINWARING Stay where you are, Pike.

Mainwaring walks to his place – gives his arm a couple of swings.

WARDEN Blimey, I can hear it creaking from here.

Mainwaring reacts and bowls.

The Warden sees that it is a little too wide and doesn't play it – Jones leaps on to the ball, seizes it and launches himself on the wicket, sending the stumps flying.

JONES How's that? How was it, sir? How was it? Just tell me how it was, sir?

VICAR Well it was very spectacular, but it wasn't out.

WARDEN I didn't even move.

JONES Ah, but if you 'ad done, I'd have 'ad you.

VICAR **(Going to wicket to repair damage)** May I borrow your bat?

WILSON **(To Mainwaring)** D'you suppose he's going to do that every time?

MAINWARING He's very keen.

VICAR **(Having completed putting on stumps)** There we are, all ship shape and Bristol fashion, but I'm quite sure it isn't the right expression.

VERGER Right, play.

Jones crouches like a lion. Mainwaring bowls. Warden hooks it soundly for four. Verger signals four.

MAINWARING **(To Wilson)** Just tempting him.

WARDEN I'm going to enjoy this. Don't bother running singles, Gerald.

Mainwaring catches the returned ball and bowls.

We hear a substantial clonk and a grunt as the Warden swipes it.

Mainwaring, Wilson and the Verger watch the ball high into the air and out of the ground. The Verger signals six.

WILSON Are you tempting him again, sir?

The scoreboard moves from four to ten.

PIKE Please, can I stand a bit further away, Mr Mainwaring?

MAINWARING Stay where you are, Pike. Look out for a catch this time, Wilson. **(He receives the ball and goes to his bowling position)**

Warden prepares to demolish it and Jones leaps about in readiness.

FRAZER **(To Walker)** I can hardly bear to look.

Mainwaring bowls wide. Warden watches it go by. Jones launches himself like a goalkeeper. Verger signals wide.

WILSON Bad luck, sir.

MAINWARING (**To Verger**) Personally, I don't think it was wide at all, he could have reached it easily.

VERGER Are you doubting my integrity?

MAINWARING No, just your judgement.

PIKE I felt the wind of that one go past my ear. Can't I move a bit?

MAINWARING Stay there, Pike. (**He receives the ball and turns to bowl**)

WARDEN (**To Jones**) Every ball a new adventure, isn't it? (**Warden sees Jones crouching and leaping**)

WARDEN 'Ere, are you any relation to Tarzan?

Pike cringes, looking over his shoulder. Mainwaring bowls.

VERGER No ball.

The Warden swipes it.

MAINWARING Why did you say 'no ball'?

VERGER Because you didn't bowl it, you chucked it. (**He signals four**) Four.

MAINWARING That was my googly.

VERGER Well, from where I was standing, it was a chuck, and don't argue with the umpire, or you'll be sent off.

MAINWARING You don't send people off in cricket.

VERGER I do.

MAINWARING I suppose I can count myself lucky I wasn't given off-side.

VERGER Right. I'm taking your name for that. (**He writes**) Mainwaring – gross impertinence and sarcasm.

WALKER I wonder what he's got up his sleeve with the next one.

FRAZER I don't know, but I wish I was wearing pads.

Mainwaring bowls. Warden receives it, it is a full toss, he ducks. Jones half catches it, runs behind the wicket to pick it up – and again launches himself at the stumps, which he demolishes.

JONES How's that? How was that? How was it, sir? Just tell me how it was, sir?

WARDEN Not out you fool, any berk can tell you that.

VICAR (**Approaching, to repair damage**) Not out, Mr Jones.

WARDEN There you are, I told you.

JONES Well, you never know, do you?

MAINWARING Jones, come here.

They meet half-way down the pitch.

JONES Don't worry, sir, I'll be quicker than that the next time.

MAINWARING Jones, you must be quite sure that he's gone out of his crease, otherwise the Vicar will spend all day banging the stumps back.

JONES I'm sorry, sir, I'll try to take myself in hand.

VICAR (**Having replaced the stumps**) Right, let's try again, shall we?

Mainwaring catches the ball and moves to bowl.

FRAZER How many more has he got?

WALKER Last one I think.

FRAZER It's as much as I can stand.

Mainwaring bowls. Warden clouts it.

MAINWARING Catch it, Godfrey.

GODFREY Oh dear.

He gazes up – runs forward – backwards – sideways – and finally leaps up as the ball goes over his head into the rough grass near the boundary.

WARDEN Right – Gerald, run.

MAINWARING Quick, Godfrey.

Godfrey is tramping around the rough, looking for the ball.

MAINWARING Hurry up, Godfrey.

GODFREY Sorry, Mr Mainwaring, I seem to have mislaid the ball. I wonder if I could have some assistance?

MAINWARING Walker, Frazer, come on. (**He runs towards Godfrey**)

Walker and Frazer run towards Godfrey.

WARDEN (**Still running**) Keep it up, Gerald.

VERGER (**Counting on fingers**) Five, six, seven.

Mainwaring, Walker, Godfrey and Frazer are searching.

MAINWARING Didn't you keep your eye on it, Godfrey?

GODFREY I could swear it's somewhere here abouts.

WALKER Perhaps it went down a rabbit hole.

FRAZER There are no rabbit holes.

MAINWARING (**Looks up**) Dammit, they're still running.

VERGER Eleven, twelve.

The Warden meets Gerald in the middle of the pitch.

GERALD How much longer do we have to keep this up?

WARDEN Just keep running.

He runs on.

GERALD (**Calling after him**) But my legs are shorter than yours.

WARDEN Keep running.

GERALD (**Running on**) Oh, blimey.

VERGER Fourteen, fifteen.

MAINWARING This is ridiculous.

GODFREY Perhaps we should all join hands and tread the ground systematically.

VERGER Nineteen, twenty.

WALKER Tell you what. **(He produces the second ball from his pocket)** How about having the other one?

MAINWARING **(Feeling in his pocket)** Oh, all right, three pounds d'you say?

WALKER Don't bother; have it on me.

He throws the ball to Mainwaring – Mainwaring throws it to Jones.

JONES **(Demolishing the wicket again)** How's that? How was that, sir? Just tell me how it was.

VERGER **(Calling to scorer)** Twenty-four, Mr Blewitt.

BLEWITT I've bust me point dotting them all down.

MAINWARING This is absurd, you can't run 24, it's a lost ball.

VERGER You just threw it in.

MAINWARING Well, well, yes, we found it.

VERGER Then it's not a lost ball is it? Play on.

WILSON It's over.

VERGER Oh all right, over then.

Long shot of team changing over. Quick shots of scoreboard buzzing up to 48 for 1. Mr Blewitt feverishly scoring. Wilson bowls. Warden swipes. Mainwaring bowls. Gerald is bowled out. Verger gives the 'out' sign. Mainwaring is triumphant. Scoreboard moves to 64 for 2. Frazer bowls. The Warden nicks it. Walker catches it at slips. Scoreboard reads 108 for 3. Pike bowls. Third warden misses it. Jones stumps him. The Vicar gives out. Jones is amazed and delighted. Scoreboard reads 131 for 4. Fourth warden slogs. Godfrey drops a catch. Frazer is exasperated. Blewitt scores. Scoreboard reads 152 for 4.

INTERIOR. CRICKET PAVILION

The Warden is draining a cup of tea into the urn.

WARDEN Well, 152 for 4, not bad, is it, lads? I think we'll declare and let your lot have a bash, Mainwaring.

MAINWARING That gives us three hours to get them. That's a sporting declaration I think, don't you, Wilson?

WILSON Yes, awfully sporting.

WARDEN Good. Right, as soon as you've finished your tea, lads. **(Aside to Egan)** How many overs do you think you'll need to skittle them out, three or four?

EGAN Well, let's say four. Should see this lot off. By the way what number does that little fat chap bat?

WARDEN He'll be opening bat if I know him! Oh, I'm going to enjoy this.

EXTERIOR. FIELD

Wilson and Mainwaring are emerging from the pavilion to bat.

MAINWARING I think I'll take first knock, Wilson.

WILSON Naturally.

Mainwaring looks to see if he's been got at.

WILSON I have heard Mrs Mainwaring might be coming to see the match.

MAINWARING No, no. She's not one for outdoor sports.

WILSON More the indoor type, eh?

MAINWARING No, I wouldn't say that.

They separate to go to their wickets.

WARDEN **(Who is wicket keeper)** Keep well in, lads, we'll be getting a few sitters I expect.

Mainwaring is at the wicket.

MAINWARING Middle and leg, please, Mr Yeatman. **(He puts his bat up)**

The Verger gestures to the off – then to the leg.

Mainwaring gets exasperated and moves. The Verger gestures back to off again.

MAINWARING Can't you make up your mind?

VERGER I'm only trying to do what's right – you can't help some people. Play.

MAINWARING **(Holding up his hand)** Just a moment. **(He looks round the field)**

WARDEN Have a good look then, you won't be there long, that chap would have been bowling for England if the War hadn't started.

Mainwaring looks at bowler. Bowler is walking back for a very long run.

MAINWARING Where's he going?

WARDEN It's where he comes to you want to worry about. That ball leaves his hand at 95 miles an hour. Oh, I'm going to enjoy this.

Mainwaring squares up, frightened. Egan runs with ever increasing speed – he delivers the ball – Mainwaring falls flat on his face to avoid it.

WARDEN Enjoying yourself, Mainwaring?

MAINWARING He wasn't bowling at the stumps, he was bowling at me.

Moans from out of vision.

EGAN **(Holding shoulder)** Oh, oh.

WARDEN What's up?

EGAN The damn thing's gone again. **(Warden joins him for shot)**

WARDEN What are you talking about?

EGAN I'll have to go off – shan't be able to move it for a week. (Egan goes towards pavilion)

WARDEN 'Ere, where are you going?

EGAN Ooh, sorry.

WARDEN Blimey, now we're in trouble. Henry. (He throws the ball) You have a go.

Henry catches the ball and goes to bowl.

MAINWARING Serves you right, Hodges. I'm going to enjoy this.

VERGER Play.

Henry bowls – Mainwaring hits it well – they run.

BLEWITT Blimey, he's hit it.

The scoreboard goes up to 3 – 152 is written at the bottom.

Wilson drives – Mainwaring cuts – squad applauds – Verger signals four – Warden looks very worried. Scoreboard goes up to 20, Mainwaring plays forward. Ball hits pad.

WARDEN How's that?

VERGER Out, you're out. Leg before wicket, plain as the nose on your face, you're out.

MAINWARING Try to control your staff, Vicar. (He goes)

Scoreboard reads 31 for 1 – last player 17. It moves to 46. Pike is batting, having trouble with his trousers. The Warden stumps him. Wilson plays back. Jones hits. Mainwaring applauds. Gerald bowls. Jones' wicket goes down. Scoreboard reads 71 for 3. Wilson cuts. Frazer swipes hard. Verger signals four. Blewitt scores. Gerald catches. Scoreboard reads 98 for 4. Wilson plays to leg. Walker plays with cigarette in his mouth. Vicar signals. Boundary. Walker plays. Ball hits pads. Verger is jubilant. Scoreboard reads 107 for 5. Blewitt scores. Scoreboard reads 125 for 7. Wilson plays. Warden bowls – looking worried. Sponge plays and is bowled. Gerald is keeping wicket. Scoreboard reads 137 for 8. Mainwaring looks worried.

Cut to group outside pavilion.

WALKER Sergeant Wilson's doing well, isn't he? Eighty-one he's made.

MAINWARING Yes, he's had a lot of very narrow escapes.

Hastings plays and is bowled.

MAINWARING That's it, you're in, Godfrey.

GODFREY Oh dear.

MAINWARING Now we only need five to win – just try not to get out, and maybe Wilson will scrape the other six runs.

Godfrey goes.

JONES Let me go in again, sir. Let me go in again.

MAINWARING Don't be silly, Jones, it's not allowed.

JONES I could disguise myself, sir, as an alternative person.

FRAZER He'll be out first ball, I know it.

WALKER Well, suffering the way he does, he won't want to stay out there long anyway.

MAINWARING Here we go.

Godfrey looks terrified. Warden bowls. Godfrey hits it.

MAINWARING He hit it – run!

Godfrey runs one. They run the second. Godfrey drops his bat half-way. Wilson runs back – picks it up for him – escorts him to his crease then runs back to his own place.

MAINWARING Foolish, he should have taken a single and left it to Wilson.

WALKER How many more balls?

MAINWARING Four. If he just blocks them, he might make it.

Warden bowls. Godfrey gives terrific swipe. Warden watches ball into air. Group watch ball into air.

MAINWARING It's going to be a six.

Godfrey is amazed. Verger signals six. Fielders move to congratulate him. Mainwaring and all the squad run towards Godfrey and shake him by the hand.

MAINWARING Marvellous, Godfrey, absolutely marvellous.

WILSON Are you all right, my dear fellow?

FRAZER I knew you could do it, I always had confidence in you.

WARDEN You didn't really win, I should never have declared.

MAINWARING Ah, but you did.

WARDEN All I can say is, you wait until the football season.

MAINWARING We'll be ready. We're prepared for any challenge whether it comes from you or across the Channel, isn't that right, men?

GROUP That's right, sir.

MAINWARING Right then, let's give three hearty cheers for the losers. Hip, hip (They give three cheers) Another one for Godfrey, and Sergeant Wilson. (They give another cheer)

The siren sounds. They stop cheering and look up.

MAINWARING Hullo. Here they come again. Right – off to your posts, men – as quickly as you can.

SERIES FOUR **EPISODE ELEVEN**

Recorded: Friday 27/11/70

Original transmission: Friday 4/12/70, 8.00–8.30pm

Original viewing figures = 15.4 million

ARTHUR LOWE .... CAPTAIN MAINWARING
JOHN LE MESURIER .... SERGEANT WILSON
CLIVE DUNN .... LANCE CORPORAL JONES
JOHN LAURIE .... PRIVATE FRAZER
JAMES BECK .... PRIVATE WALKER
ARNOLD RIDLEY .... PRIVATE GODFREY
IAN LAVENDER .... PRIVATE PIKE
FRANK WILLIAMS .... VICAR
EDWARD SINCLAIR .... VERGER
JANET DAVIES .... MRS PIKE
BLAKE BUTLER .... MR WEST
ROBERT RAGLAN .... CAPTAIN PRITCHARD
ARTHUR BROUGH .... MR BOYLE
COLIN BEAN .... PRIVATE SPONGE
HUGH HASTINGS .... PRIVATE HASTINGS

PLATOON .... VIC TAYLOR, HUGH CECIL, FREDDIE WILES,
.... DESMOND CULLUM-JONES, LESLIE NOYES,
.... GEORGE HANCOCK, FRANK GODFREY, FREDDIE WHITE

MIDDLE-AGED BANK CLERKS .... RICHARD SHEEKEY,
.... JOHN CLEAVEDON, BOB HOOPER

TWO PRETTY GIRL BANK CLERKS ...... HILARY MARTIN, JEANETTE CLARKE

A Wilson (Manager)?

• ROGER SINGLETON-TURNER REMEMBERS •

'In this episode Wilson visits his undamaged new office, which was a set built in the studio: it's hard to imagine building a set these days for such a short sequence. The bombed-out office, meanwhile, had already been filmed on location in a cottage on the army tank range at Buckenham Tofts. At the range there were derelict hamlets and villages, much battered, I presume, by target practice, and we used one of those.

'It had been a long day, dusk had fallen, but the scene where Wilson enters his bombed office was lit to look like day. A few pieces of set dressing, a carefully selected piece of smashed desk and a few smoking blocks of incense-on-charcoal, and the effect was totally convincing.'

ROGER SINGLETON-TURNER
Assistant Floor Manager

A. WILSON (MANAGER)?

INTERIOR. BANK OFFICE. DAY

Mainwaring enters, takes off his hat and gas mask and hangs them up with his umbrella – he crosses to the desk and sits. Pike enters.

PIKE Good morning, Mr Mainwaring.

MAINWARING Good morning, Pike. Any letters?

PIKE Only two, sir – and they're both marked 'delayed by enemy action'.

MAINWARING Do you realise we've had no letters from the Head Office for over two weeks – goodness knows how many important documents have been destroyed in air raids.

PIKE Shall I set up the Lewis gun, sir?

MAINWARING No, that's Wilson's job – where on earth is he? It's nearly a quarter past nine.

PIKE He's not usually late, Mr Mainwaring.

MAINWARING I know he isn't – what's happened to him?

PIKE Perhaps he's been captured.

MAINWARING What?

PIKE Well a Nazi paratrooper could have landed during the night – hidden himself – and then captured Uncle Arthur on his way to work.

MAINWARING Don't be so stupid, Pike – I suppose I'd better set the Lewis gun up myself. (**He picks up the gun and starts to take the cover off – the phone bell rings**) See who that is.

PIKE Yes, sir. (**He picks up the phone**) Hullo, Swallow Bank – no, I'm not the manager – hold on a minute, please. (**He puts his hand over the phone**) Mr Mainwaring – it's a long distance call from London – Head Office.

MAINWARING What – here, hold this. (**He hands the gun to Pike and takes the phone**) Stupid boy. Good morning, sir.

WEST Good morning, Mainwaring – West here – Head Office.

MAINWARING (**Putting his hand over the phone**) Stop fiddling with that gun, boy – put it down.

WEST Hullo, Mainwaring, are you there?

MAINWARING Yes, sir, I'm here.

Pike is still fiddling with the gun.

WEST I'm ringing you up – because I'm afraid a lot of our letters have been destroyed by enemy action.

MAINWARING (**To Pike, losing his temper and shouting**) Put that gun down – put it down!

WEST What's happening? What's happening?!

MAINWARING Nothing, sir.

WEST I thought the bank was being robbed.

MAINWARING Nothing to worry about, sir – everything under control this end.

WEST Well, I won't waste time, Mainwaring, this call is expensive – I just wanted to tell you that I shan't be able to send you anyone to replace Mr Wilson for several weeks – so you'll just have to manage the best you can.

MAINWARING (**Stunned**) What?

WEST I said I can't send you anyone to replace Wilson for several weeks.

MAINWARING (**In weak voice**) Why, where's he going?

WEST What are you talking about – where's he going? You know as well as I do – he's taking over as manager at our Eastgate branch. But he put in for the post months ago. Didn't he tell you?

MAINWARING Well er... I er...

WEST I wrote to you about it weeks ago.

MAINWARING I didn't get it.

WEST It must have been one of the letters that was destroyed in an air raid – anyhow, you'll have to carry on the best you can, don't forget there's a war on – I'll keep in touch. Goodbye. (**Hangs up**)

Mainwaring sits staring into space.

PIKE Are you all right, Mr Mainwaring?

MAINWARING (**In a daze**) Wilson's been made manager of the Eastgate Branch.

PIKE Yes, I know. Mum's awfully proud of him.

Pike goes. The phone rings. Mainwaring picks it up.

MAINWARING Hello.

PRITCHARD Hullo, Captain Pritchard here, G.H.Q., that you, Mainwaring?

MAINWARING Yes, good morning, sir.

PRITCHARD Just wanted to tell you that Sergeant Wilson's commission has come through.

MAINWARING Commission?

PRITCHARD Captain Square wants him to take up his duties with the Eastgate platoon as soon as possible.

MAINWARING The Eastgate platoon?

PRITCHARD I expect you'll miss him – all the same you couldn't expect him to stay with you when he's going to be working over at Eastgate. And it was on Captain Square's recommendation that he was granted his commission. Have you decided who you're going to promote in his place yet?

MAINWARING Er... er...

PRITCHARD Well, let me know as soon as you can – I must say Sergeant Wilson deserves his promotion, he's a good chap – congratulate him for me, will you – cheerio.

Mainwaring drums his fingers on the table and stares into space – he is furious. The phone rings and he picks it up.

MAINWARING Hullo.

VICAR Good morning, Mr Mainwaring – Vicar here.

MAINWARING And what have you got to tell me about Wilson – that he's been made the Archbishop of Canterbury?

VICAR Really, Mr Mainwaring.

MAINWARING I'm sorry, Vicar – I'm not myself this morning.

VICAR Oh dear, aren't you? Well, I'm afraid I've got to make a confession – when I say a confession – I don' t mean that sort of confession, that's mostly for R.C.s. **(He giggles)**

MAINWARING I...?

VICAR What I'm trying to say is – that the whist drive that was supposed to take place in the church hall next Tuesday – is, er... tonight.

MAINWARING Really?

VICAR So would you mind cancelling your parade tonight, otherwise I'm going to look a bit of a fool.

MAINWARING All right, Vicar.

VICAR How sweet of you – thank you very much. Goodbye. **(He hangs up)**

MAINWARING Pike. **(Pike comes in)**

PIKE Oh, Mr Mainwaring, you do look red – shall I open the window?

MAINWARING No, I'm all right – I've just had a bit of a shock that's all – in fact I've had several shocks.

PIKE I've never seen you look like that before, sir.

MAINWARING That will do, Pike – now, look, as soon as you've got time, I want you to get your bicycle and go round to all the members of the platoon and tell them the parade's cancelled tonight.

PIKE Yes, Mr Mainwaring.

Mainwaring picks up two sheets of paper from the 'out' tray.

MAINWARING And get these platoon orders typed out and duplicated, and take them round with you.

We can hear Wilson's voice saying good morning.

MAINWARING **(Hurriedly)** All right, Pike – you can go. **(He drops the orders back in the tray)**

PIKE What about the orders?

MAINWARING You can attend to them later. **(Pike goes – passes Wilson in the doorway – Wilson is carrying several parcels)**

WILSON Good morning, Frank. **(Brightly)** Good morning, sir. **(He hangs up his hat)**

PIKE Good morning, Uncle Arthur – Mr Wilson.

MAINWARING **(Coldly)** What time do you call this, Wilson?

WILSON **(Looking at his watch)** Actually, sir – it's twenty to ten.

MAINWARING Where have you been?

WILSON Doing a spot of shopping. **(He takes an officer's peaked cap out of a paper bag and puts it on)** Do you like it? It's for officers only. **(He takes some cloth and brass pips out of the bag)** And I bought these as well – I don't know which I like best, the cloth ones or the brass ones – only I don't think you're supposed to wear brass ones with battledress, are you?

MAINWARING Judas!

WILSON I beg your pardon, sir?

MAINWARING **(He gets up and comes round the desk to Wilson)** Judas!

WILSON **(Moves away)** I don't think I quite follow you, sir.

MAINWARING You follow me all right, Wilson – you've been following me for years – just waiting to step into my shoes.

WILSON But I'm not stepping into your shoes.

MAINWARING You must have put in for this job as manager of the Eastgate branch weeks ago – and all that time you said nothing.

WILSON I thought you knew, sir.

MAINWARING Rubbish.

WILSON But surely Head Office wrote to you about it?

MAINWARING The letters were destroyed.

WILSON Well that's not my fault, sir.

MAINWARING And what about this commission?

WILSON I'm afraid Captain Square's rather jumped the gun with that – but he was awfully keen to get me – he said he was very impressed with what I've done for the platoon.

MAINWARING **(Exploding)** What you've done.

WILSON Yes he's had his eye on me for sometime.

MAINWARING Just because you've been to some tupenny ha'penny public school.

WILSON I wouldn't call Meadowbridge that, sir.

MAINWARING **(Sneering)** Meadowbridge – you know where I went to school – Eastbourne Grammar.

WILSON Well, what's wrong with that?

MAINWARING Don't be so patronising – I had to fight like hell to get there – and fight even harder to stay there.

WILSON That's all to your credit.

MAINWARING You've never had to fight for anything in your life – brought up by a nanny – Father something in the city – you just had to sit back and let it all come to you.

WILSON It wasn't really as simple as that.

Mainwaring reacts and moves.

MAINWARING Do you realise, I've been manager here for ten years – I should have moved on to better things ages ago – but every time I went for an interview for promotion it was always the same story – 'What school did you go to?' I'd tell them, and that did it.

WILSON I can't believe that that would influence them.

MAINWARING Of course you can't – if you were asked 'What school did you go to?' you just had to say 'Meadowbridge, sir – one of the better public schools – small but good'.

WILSON Actually there were over 300 boys there.

MAINWARING Not only have I made a success of this bank – but I've taken a bunch of shop-keepers, pulled them up by their ankle straps – and made them into a crack platoon.

WILSON I helped a bit, sir.

MAINWARING **(Crossing to phone – picking it up)** I'll show you just how highly I rate your jobs – both as Chief Clerk and Sergeant of the platoon. **(Into phone)** Two five two please – I sat at this desk this morning, Wilson, and I could hardly believe the web of intrigue that was unfolding in front of my eyes. **(Into phone)** Hullo, Jones – I want you to come over here to the bank at once. **(He hangs up, crosses to the door and shouts)** Pike! **(He crosses back to the desk)**

Pike enters.

PIKE Yes, sir.

MAINWARING Until they send someone down from Head Office, you take over the post of Chief Clerk.

PIKE What?

MAINWARING I said you will take over the post of Chief Clerk.

PIKE Do you think I've got the brains for it, Mr Mainwaring?

MAINWARING Of course you have – if Wilson can do it, I'm jolly sure you can.

PIKE But I don't talk posh like Uncle Arthur – I mean, Mr Wilson.

MAINWARING One doesn't judge a book by its cover, Pike.

There is a knock at the door.

MAINWARING Come in.

Jones enters. He is in his butcher's clothes – straw hat – striped apron, etc.

JONES **(Out of breath)** Good morning, Mr Mainwaring – Mr Wilson, Pikey – I came over straight away, sir – I'm afraid I can't stay very long – I've just got the offal in – and there's a queue a mile long – I had to leave the boy, Raymond, in charge.

MAINWARING This won't take a minute – all right, Pike, go and get on with your work.

PIKE Yes, sir. **(He goes)**

MAINWARING Just a minute, Jones. **(He gets up and crosses to Wilson so that he is standing beside him as he says)** Listen to this Wilson, Lance Corporal Jones, I am promoting you to the rank of Sergeant. **(Aside to Wilson)** What do you think of that, Wilson?

WILSON Do you think that's wise, sir?

MAINWARING **(Hissing at Wilson)** And that will be the last time, Wilson, that you look down your nose at me and say in that supercilious voice, 'Do you think that's wise, sir?' What do you say to that, Jones? Jones?

JONES **(Standing in a daze)** I don't know what to say, Mr Mainwaring – promotion to Sergeant – I never dreamed that it would come true – to think that after all these years – I shall finally stand in front of those brave men with three stripes all on my arm. Not just one stripe or two stripes – but three. **(He is quite overcome – he pulls out a large, coloured hanky and blows his nose)**

MAINWARING **(To Wilson)** That's the sort of man I'm promoting to Sergeant – brave – true – and loyal to the last.

JONES **(Recovering)** Just one thing, Mr Mainwaring – what about Mr Wilson? You can't have two Sergeants.

MAINWARING Mr Wilson is leaving us for higher things, Jones – he has been promoted to the rank of second lieutenant and will shortly be joining the Eastgate platoon.

Wilson reacts.

JONES Oh dear – well, I shall miss you, Mr Wilson – but I'm sure no one deserves promotion more than you **(Mainwaring reacts)** – and I want you to know that I shall try to live up to the high ideals and the standards of loyalty that you have put up us.

Mainwaring reacts.

WILSON Thank you, Jonesey.

JONES I wonder, Mr Mainwaring, if you could let me have my appointment in official form, sir – I want to have something to show people in years to come.

MAINWARING Certainly, Jones. **(He sits at his desk and writes on a piece of paper)** This is to confirm that you have been appointed to the rank of Sergeant of the 1st Platoon of the Walmington-on-Sea Home Guard – how's that, Jones?

JONES Thank you, sir – thank you.

MAINWARING I'll get this typed out – then I'll write your name at the top and sign it, that will make it more personal.

He puts the piece of paper in the 'out' tray on top of the platoon orders.

JONES Well, I'll get back to the shop now, sir –

WILSON I'll see you out, Jonesey. (**He crosses and opens the door**)

JONES Thank you, Mr Wilson. Goodbye, Mr Mainwaring.

As they go, they bump into Pike who is coming in.

PIKE Sorry – excuse me – Miss King says will you come at once, Mr Mainwaring – she's got a query with a customer.

MAINWARING Yes, all right – oh and Pike (**Points to the orders in the 'out' tray**) Get those platoon orders typed out and duplicated – and then take a copy round to each member of the platoon, and tell them the parade's cancelled tonight.

Mainwaring goes – Pike crosses to the desk – picks up the platoon orders from the tray. The piece of paper with the confirmation of Jones' promotion is on top of it.

PIKE (**Reading**) This is to confirm that you have been appointed to the rank of Sergeant – I wonder why he's promoted everyone to Sergeant except me – ah well, he's made me Chief Clerk. (**Goes**)

INTERIOR. OFFICE. CHURCH HALL. DAY

The Vicar is standing at the desk looking through the drawers.

VICAR I do wish Mr Mainwaring wouldn't keep using my drawers.

There is a knock on the door.

VICAR Come in.

Mrs Pike enters – she is in tears.

MRS PIKE Is Mr Mainwaring in?

VICAR He hasn't arrived yet. (**He looks up and sees that she is crying – he quickly crosses over to her**) My dear Mrs Pike, what is the matter?

MRS PIKE It's nothing – I want to speak to Mr Mainwaring. (**She cries**)

VICAR Mrs Pike – please tell me what the trouble is.

MRS PIKE It's Arthur, he's deceived me.

VICAR I beg your pardon?

MRS PIKE He's been made manager of the bank at Eastgate – I thought he'd be going over there every day on the train – but he's joined the Eastgate platoon and he's been made an officer and he's going to live over there. (**She cries**) I shall never see him again.

VICAR Of course you'll see him again, Mrs Pike. Eastgate is only ten miles away.

MRS PIKE It might just as well be a hundred miles. (**She bursts into fresh tears – the Vicar puts his arm round her to comfort her**)

VICAR Don't worry, Mrs Pike – after a while he'll come back to you, he'll say (**The Vicar has his back to the door – Mrs Pike's face is buried in his chest the door opens and the Verger comes in**) 'All these weeks I longed for the moment when I could take you in my arms – and tell you how much I've missed you.'

VERGER Ahem... er ahem.

VICAR (**Looking up**) What is it, Verger?

VERGER Well, er, I er... I'm sorry, Vicar.

VICAR What are you sorry about?

VERGER Well, I er...

VICAR What is it you want? This is personal.

VERGER Yes, I can see that.

VICAR State your business.

VERGER It's the harmonium in the bell tower – I can't shift it on my own.

VICAR I only want it moved a few feet, away from the wall where the damp patch is.

VERGER I still can't manage it on my own.

VICAR Mainwaring's men will be here shortly – ask one of them to help you.

VERGER Very well, sir. (**He goes**)

INTERIOR. CHURCH HALL. DAY

The Verger comes through the office door, closes it and pauses.

VERGER I never thought I'd live to see the day when His Reverence would become a victim of wartime immorality.

He crosses to the bell tower.

INTERIOR. OFFICE. CHURCH HALL. DAY

The Vicar is still comforting Mrs Pike.

VICAR You'll see, Mrs Pike, everything will turn out all right in the end.

Mainwaring enters by the back door.

MAINWARING Good evening.

Mrs Pike charges over to him.

MRS PIKE Oh, Mr Mainwaring, can't you do anything about Arthur?

MAINWARING I'm afraid it's out of my hands, Mrs Pike.

MRS PIKE I don't know what's come over him – ambition has turned his head.

INTERIOR. CHURCH HALL. DAY

Jones enters with three stripes on – he is wearing his full equipment and carrying his rifle. He comes to the middle of the hall, looks round, then he looks at his stripes. He comes to attention and slopes arms.

He crosses to the office door – he bumps into door.

Frazer comes through the main door. He also has three stripes on – he comes to the middle of the hall, looks round, then looks at his stripes – he comes to attention and slopes arms.

FRAZER **(In whisper)** Platoon, attention – slope arms – very sloppy – very sloppy indeed. Now, listen to me, there's going to be a few changes around here. Do you understand? I'm in charge now – and you can have it the easy way or you can have it the hard way – the easy way's not so easy – but the hard way is very, very hard – now let's have a look at you. **(He starts to inspect an imaginary line of men)** Stand up straight, Pike! **(He moves on to the next imaginary man)** You'll have to buck your ideas up, Godfrey, otherwise you'll be out on your ears – we can't carry passengers here.

Verger enters.

Frazer moves on – the Verger follows – Frazer still doesn't see him.

FRAZER I'm watching you, Walker – you put one foot wrong and I'll have you, do you understand? **(He moves on)** I shan't warn you again, Jones – unless your drill improves – I shall take that stripe away. So, all of you buck your ideas up – and remember that my name's Sergeant Frazer – Frazer spelt B-A-S-T-A-R-D.

VERGER That's not really how you spell it, is it?

FRAZER **(Turning with eyes blazing)** What?

VERGER The Vicar says you've got to give me a hand with the harmonium.

FRAZER What?

VERGER It's got to be shifted – or perhaps you'd like me to tell the others what you've just been saying.

FRAZER All right – where is it?

VERGER In the bell tower – come on.

As they go, Frazer slips off his gas mask and tin hat and puts them down with his rifle.

VERGER You'd better take your jacket off as well – it's hot work shifting that harmonium.

As they go up the stairs, Frazer starts to unbutton his blouse – as soon as they have gone, Walker enters – he is also wearing Sergeant stripes – he comes to the middle of the hall – looks around, comes to attention and slopes arms.

WALKER **(In whisper)** Platoon, attention – slope arms. Right, now that I've been made Sergeant – I don't want you blokes to worry about being too regimental – you play ball with me and I'll play ball with you. For instance when I call the roll – anyone who is not here and is a regular customer of mine who spends two pounds a week or more buying goods will be marked present. If I find any man has not polished his brass – I will overlook it – provided of course that he buys a new tin of metal polish off me to clean it.

Verger comes down the stairs.

VERGER Excuse me, Mr Walker.

Walker turns, startled.

WALKER Oh hullo, Verger.

Walker pulls his stripes round for the Verger to see.

VERGER Could you give me a hand to shift the harmonium?

WALKER I dunno – now that I'm a *Sergeant.* **(He pulls at his stripes)** I don't think I ought to do that sort of thing. Did you know that I was a *Sergeant*?

VERGER Yes, very nice – it won't take a minute.

WALKER Oh, all right.

He takes off his gas mask and tin hat and puts them down with his rifle.

WALKER **(As they cross)** I'd better take my jacket off – it's dusty up in that bell tower – I don't want to get my stripes dirty.

They go up the stairs – Godfrey and Pike enter – Godfrey has three stripes on.

GODFREY I really can't understand why Mr Mainwaring has made me a Sergeant, I don't think I'm capable – still I'll do my best.

PIKE I'm sure you will, Mr Godfrey.

GODFREY Excuse me, I'm just going to wash my hands.

He crosses to the door beside the stage – opens it and goes in – Sponge enters with three stripes up.

SPONGE Hullo, Pikey – have you seen Mr Godfrey?

PIKE Yes, he's gone to wash his hands.

SPONGE Has he got his first aid kit with him?

PIKE Yes, why?

SPONGE I've cut my finger on my rifle bolt – I want him to put a bandage on it.

He crosses over to the door beside the stage and goes in. Frazer

and Walker come down the stairs – they have their battle dress blouses over their arms – the sleeves are folded inwards so that we cannot see the stripes – they both start to put their blouses on.

WALKER Well, that's a good job done, Taff!

FRAZER We're not here to shift furniture – we're...

Suddenly they notice the stripes.

WALKER Blimey!

The door by the stage opens – Godfrey and Sponge come in.

GODFREY I'm sure there must be some mistake.

SPONGE Of course there must – you can't have two Sergeants.

Suddenly they see Frazer and Walker. Hastings enters with another member of the platoon, they are both wearing Sergeant's stripes.

HASTINGS I'm going to see Mr Mainwaring – there must be some mistake – you can't have two...

There are now six Sergeants – they all register – the office door opens, Jones comes in.

JONES **(Over his shoulder)** Right you are, Mr Mainwaring. **(He turns sees the others)** Blimey. **(Counts)** One – two – three – four – five – six. **(Points to himself)** Seven.

INTERIOR. OFFICE. DAY

The Vicar, Mainwaring and Mrs Pike are standing by the door.

VICAR I really think you ought to talk to Mr Wilson, you know.

MAINWARING I'm having nothing more to do with it, Vicar – I wash my hands of the entire affair.

The door opens, Jones comes in.

JONES I've fallen the Private in, Mr Mainwaring – what shall I do with the Sergeants?

INTERIOR. CHURCH HALL. DAY

Pike is standing on parade alone – the Sergeants are standing in a half circle behind him as Mainwaring comes through the door.

INTERIOR. OFFICE. CHURCH HALL. NIGHT

Mainwaring is sitting at his desk – there is a knock on the door.

MAINWARING Come in.

Wilson enters wearing the uniform of a Second Lieutenant – battle dress – one pip on each shoulder, collar and tie, webbing, gaiters and brown boots, peaked hat and webbing belt. He is carrying gloves, stick and a suitcase.

WILSON I'm, er, going now, sir. I'm catching the 9.30 train to Eastgate.

MAINWARING Why are you going tonight, it's only Wednesday – you don't take over as manager until Monday.

WILSON Well, things are a bit difficult over there, sir – the manager's already been called up – so Mr West from Head Office is going to stay in Eastgate for the rest of the week, showing me the ropes.

MAINWARING Mr West from Head Office, eh? We are honoured. Why are you travelling in your uniform?

WILSON Oh, I don't know – it was just sort of handy.

MAINWARING Rubbish. **(Wilson turns)** You put it on so that you could parade up and down the platform looking for salutes.

WILSON Well, why not? You did.

MAINWARING What do you mean?

WILSON The first day you got your uniform – I followed you.

MAINWARING You followed me?

WILSON Yes, I did. You went up and down the High Street three times looking for a serviceman to salute you. In the end you had to make do with a sea-scout.

MAINWARING That's enough – say what you have to say and go.

WILSON Well, I only came in to say goodbye, sir – aren't you coming down to the station to see me off?

MAINWARING No, I am not – our relationship ends here and now, Wilson.

WILSON Oh, really, sir – after all we've been through together, can't you let bygones be bygones.

MAINWARING Don't try and soft-soap me.

WILSON Well, goodbye, sir.

Wilson holds out his hand. Mainwaring looks at it, stands up, puts on his hat and waits stiffly at attention for a salute – Wilson looks at him, then gives him a sloppy one – Mainwaring returns it very correctly.

WILSON Goodbye, sir.

He goes out of the door into the church hall and closes it behind him – there is a pause – Mainwaring crosses over to the door and opens it.

MAINWARING **(Shouting)** Even if I do go looking for salutes, Wilson – at least I do them properly – that one you gave me just now was rotten.

INTERIOR. CHURCH HALL. DAY

Jones is standing at the blackboard. Frazer, Walker, Godfrey and the rest of the platoon are gathered round.

JONES Right, now, pay attention – Mr Mainwaring will not be with us tonight as he has a lot of work to do at the bank – so I shall be taking tonight's lecture which deals with tactics. (**Points to diagram on board**) Now, can anyone tell me what that is?

WALKER Three bits of Turkish delight.

JONES No it is not, it is ...

Pike enters in his bank clothes.

JONES Hurry up, Private Pike, you're late – and why aren't you wearing your uniform?

PIKE I can't stop, Mr Jones, I'm helping Mr Mainwaring at the bank – he sent me down with a message.

JONES What is it?

PIKE He's expecting a very important call from G.H.Q.

JONES Right-oh.

PIKE As soon as you've taken the message, send someone over to the bank with it straight away. You won't forget, will you?

JONES Of course not.

PIKE I must get back. (**He goes**)

JONES Now, where was I? Oh, yes – now, this is an Impi.

GODFREY Oh, you mean a sort of little elf.

JONES No, Mr Godfrey – an Impi is a Zulu army.

WALKER Blimey, don't tell me you fought the Zulus as well.

JONES No, I did not, but I happen to be a student of military tactics.

FRAZER But we're not fighting Zulus – this is 1941, we're fighting Nazis.

JONES We should not disdain ourselves so that we cannot learn from the past, Private Frazer. Now, the Zulus always attacked in the formation of a fighting bull – the horns, the head and the chest – the horns encircled the enemy first – the head smashed at the front – and the chest surged through the enemy and linked up with the horns. Now, what lesson can we learn from that?

WALKER It's a lot of bull.

JONES One more remark like that, Joe, and I shall... (**The phone rings**) I wonder who that is, giving us a ring?

WALKER Perhaps it's a ring for the bull's nose.

FRAZER It must be the call Mr Mainwaring's expecting from G.H.Q.

JONES Right, Private Godfrey, answer the phone and take the message. (**Godfrey goes into the office**) Now, the King of the Zulus was called Cetewayo and he... What is it, Mr Godfrey?

GODFREY (**Poking his head round the door**) Excuse me, Mr Jones, I can't find the phone.

JONES What are you talking about? Oh right, Frazer – Walker, come with me, the rest of you men stay here.

Jones rushes in followed by Walker and Frazer.

INTERIOR. OFFICE. CHURCH HALL. DAY

Jones comes in with Walker and Frazer. All the time, the phone is ringing.

WALKER (**Holding the end of the phone wire**) Some fool's locked the phone in the drawer of the desk.

JONES I did it for security.

FRAZER What are you talking about, security?

JONES Well, a fifth columnist could have come in here and phoned up Hitler.

WALKER Have you gone completely potty? And who put this ruddy great bar and padlock on?

The three right-hand drawers of the desk have an iron bar running down the length of them secured by a large padlock.

JONES I didn't think the locks were strong enough.

WALKER Quick, give us the key.

Jones tries to open the top left-hand drawer.

FRAZER What are you doing? The phone's not in there.

JONES No, but the key is.

FRAZER Well hurry up and open it.

JONES I can't, I've just remembered I've left the key in my shop.

WALKER Oh, come out of it. (**He picks up a paper knife, pushes Jones out of the way and opens it – Jones pulls the drawer right out and puts it on top of the desk – it is full of papers – he frantically throws them all over the place, looking for the key**)

JONES (**Holding up the key**) I've got it.

WALKER Quick, give it to me.

JONES No, that's not the key for the padlock. No, it's the key for this drawer – that's where I put the key to the padlock. (**Jones opens the bottom left-hand drawer, pulls it out and puts it on the desk, it is full of papers, he pulls them out**) Don't panic – don't panic – I'll find it.

The phone stops ringing.

GODFREY It's all right, Mr Jones, it's stopped ringing.

FRAZER That message could have been an invasion standby – you've really done it now.

The phone starts again.

JONES (Throwing a whole lot of papers in the air) Whoa – it's not here – it's not here. (He tips the drawer up) Right, grab your rifles – we'll have to shoot the lock off – stand back. (He picks up his rifle and shoots at the lock twice – the bullets ricochet round the room. they all dive for cover)

FRAZER You damn fool, those ricochet bullets could have killed us.

JONES There's only one thing for it – we'll smash our way in – I'll go in from the top, you go in from the side.

Jones jumps up on the desk – and starts to smash the top of the desk with his rifle butt – Walker and Frazer start to smash the back – by now the rest of the platoon is gathered in the doorway – the Verger pushes his way through – he stares open-mouthed at them smashing the desk up.

VERGER Vandals – hooligans – they've gone mad – I must tell the Vicar. (He rushes to the back door, shouting) Vicar – Vicar – help – they've all gone mad.

The desk by now is in ruins.

WALKER (Pulling out the phone) All right, I've got it.

JONES (Grabbing it) 'Ere give it to me – Lance Corporal Jones here. (He stops and lowers the phone)

WALKER What's the matter?

JONES Wrong number.

BANK MANAGER'S OFFICE. EASTGATE BANK. DAY

West is sitting at the desk – Wilson is standing in front of it – he is in his bank clothes.

WEST That's the lot, Wilson. I think you've done very well these past three days.

WILSON Thank you, sir.

WEST You know, we have thought of promoting you to manager several times over the last few years.

WILSON I didn't realise that, sir.

WEST Oh yes, if it hadn't been for Mainwaring, you'd have had your own branch ages ago.

WILSON Why, what did he say?

WEST He only said, that in his opinion, you didn't show enough initiative.

WILSON Oh, did he?

WEST You've certainly proved him wrong and, speaking for myself, I think you'll make an excellent manager.

WILSON Thank you, sir.

WEST (Getting up) Well, it's nearly one o'clock, I must close the bank, and get back to London – I expect you're busy with the Home Guard on Saturday afternoons. (He hands him a huge bunch of keys) Here are the keys.

WILSON (Taking them) Thank you, sir.

West comes round the desk.

WEST (Pointing to empty chair) From Monday morning, Wilson, you will be sitting in that chair – at nine o'clock you will enter this office and take your place at that desk as manager. How do you feel about it?

WILSON Awfully nice, sir.

WEST Good luck, Wilson.

WILSON Thank you, sir.

They shake hands.

INTERIOR. MANAGER'S OFFICE. EASTGATE BRANCH. DAY

Close up of clock on office wall at nine o'clock. Camera pans round empty office – we hear several voices chanting 'Good morning, Mr Wilson' – Wilson's voice answers 'Good Morning', the door opens and he comes in – as the door is open we can see his name, A. Wilson – Manager, written on it – he pauses, looks down at it with pride and touches it with his fingers – he closes the door – hangs up his hat and gas mask and sits at the desk – he sits back – swings the chair from side to side – tidies a few objects on the desk – and wallows in being a manager. There is a tap on the door.

WILSON Come in.

Mr Boyle comes in – he is a small man in his late 50s.

BOYLE Good morning, sir.

WILSON Good morning, Mr Boyle.

BOYLE (Who has a handful of papers) I've got several rather important items for you to deal with, sir.

WILSON All in good time – I think I'll have a word with the staff first.

BOYLE Very well, sir. (He crosses to the door, opens it and calls) Mr Wilson would like to have a word with you – will you all come into the office, please.

WILSON I thought it would be rather a good idea for us to get to know each other.

BOYLE Yes of course, sir.

The staff file into the office and line up in front of the desk – there are two young girls and three middle-aged men.

WILSON Before we start work this morning, ladies and gentlemen, I thought we'd have a little chat and get to know each other. First of all, I want you to understand that I like to work in a nice, relaxed atmosphere. (He lights a cigarette) If you have any problems, I don't want you to worry about them – just come along to my office and when you see my name 'A. Wilson – Manager', on the door, I want it to give you a feeling of comfort and security – just tap on the door and come in – as long as my name is outside I shall always be here. Just one more little thing I'd like to say to you…

The siren goes.

BOYLE There go the sirens, Mr Wilson – we'd better go down in the shelter.

WILSON **(Getting up)** Oh, very well – but don't rush – come along everybody – bring those papers with you, Mr Boyle, we can go through them in the shelter. **(To girl)** Come along, my dear, what a pretty dress you're wearing. **(He shepherds his flock through the door and closes it behind him. Pan along to the clock – it is five past nine)**

INTERIOR. AIR RAID SHELTER. DAY

Mainwaring and Pike are sitting side by side.

MAINWARING Confounded nuisance this air raid – we're far enough behind with our work as it is.

PIKE I'm afraid I'm not doing very well as Chief Clerk, Mr Mainwaring.

MAINWARING It's not your fault, you haven't got the experience, Pike – you're doing the best you can.

PIKE I wish Uncle Arthur was still with us.

MAINWARING Mmmmm…

PIKE I never realised how important he was.

MAINWARING No one is indispensable, Pike.

PIKE We certainly miss him in the platoon – I don't think Mr Jones is as good a Sergeant as he was. How much did the Vicar say the new desk was going to cost?

MAINWARING Ten pounds.

PIKE Uncle Arthur wouldn't have locked the phone away like that.

MAINWARING Look, I don't want to discuss it any more.

PIKE All the same, I hope Uncle Arthur's all right.

MAINWARING Don't worry – the devil looks after his own. They haven't had a single bomb drop on Eastgate yet.

FILM. INTERIOR. MANAGER'S OFFICE. EASTGATE BRANCH. DAY

The office is in complete ruins – Wilson comes in, looks round in a daze of misery – he stoops down and picks up something – it is the section of the office door with his name written on it. He throws it down.

INTERIOR. OFFICE. BANK. DAY

Mainwaring is sitting at his desk – he is on the phone to West at Head Office.

WEST Of course, the bank's completely gutted.

MAINWARING How are you going to carry on then?

WEST We're not, we're closing the Eastgate Branch for the duration – and transferring all the business to our branch at Hastings.

MAINWARING That must have been the shortest appointment in history.

WEST How do you mean?

MAINWARING Well, at nine o'clock he was manager of a bank – and at five past there wasn't any bank for him to be manager of.

WEST How's he taking it?

MAINWARING Oh, one never knows with Wilson – he's not given to showing very much emotion.

WEST Well, we've all got to carry on doing our bit, Mainwaring.

MAINWARING Yes, sir, we certainly have. Goodbye.

He hangs up. There is a knock on the door.

MAINWARING Wilson.

Wilson enters.

MAINWARING That was Head Office on the phone, they're very sorry.

WILSON Oh, are they, sir?

MAINWARING And for my part – may I say how sorry I a,m too.

WILSON Yes, it was rather…

MAINWARING Yes – don't sit down, Wilson. I'm rather busy. I've had a word with G.H.Q. – so you can keep your rank. **(He hands him a pair of Sergeant's stripes)**

WILSON Oh – thank you, sir.

MAINWARING Have them sewn on by tonight. That's all.

Wilson goes.

INTERIOR. OUTSIDE OFFICE DOOR. DAY

Wilson closes the door – he looks down and sees 'G. Mainwaring – Manager'. He slowly runs his fingers over the name.

SERIES FOUR **EPISODE TWELVE**

Recorded: Friday 4/12/70

Original transmission: Friday 11/12/70, 8.00–8.30pm

Original viewing figures = 13.1 million

ARTHUR LOWE . . . . CAPTAIN MAINWARING
JOHN LE MESURIER . . . . SERGEANT WILSON
CLIVE DUNN . . . . LANCE CORPORAL JONES
JOHN LAURIE . . . . PRIVATE FRAZER
JAMES BECK . . . . PRIVATE WALKER
ARNOLD RIDLEY . . . . PRIVATE GODFREY
IAN LAVENDER . . . . PRIVATE PIKE
BILL PERTWEE . . . . ARP WARDEN
FRANK WILLIAMS . . . . VICAR
EDWARD SINCLAIR . . . . VERGER
ROSE HILL . . . . MRS COLE
DON ESTELLE . . . . GERALD

PLATOON . . . . COLIN BEAN, HUGH HASTINGS, VIC TAYLOR,
. . . . DESMOND CULLUM-JONES, FREDDIE WILES, GEORGE HANCOCK,
. . . . LESLIE NOYES, FREDDIE WHITE, HUGH CECIL, FRANK GODFREY

ARP WARDENS . . . . ANTHONY LANG, BILL LODGE, CLIFFORD HEMSLEY,
. . . . DOLLY BRENNAN, KIM MCALLEN, JEAN REAVES

UNINVITED GUESTS

• ROGER SINGLETON-TURNER REMEMBERS •

'This episode involved a scene where the church hall chimney catches fire, and it was a really tricky episode to shoot in the studio. Paul Joel, the designer, created the pitched roof of the hall on the floor of the television studio. The ridge of the roof would have been about seven feet above floor level. There was also a chimney stack that had to belch forth smoke.

'The action involved members of the platoon climbing out on to the roof, then they had to straddle the roof and slide across to the chimney. Other members of the team then passed buckets of water up, along the roof ridge so that water could be tipped down the chimney. television studios are full of very expensive electrical equipment and lights, some of which worked off a 415-volt power supply. Sloshing water around in these surroundings is dangerous. The roof was built on a thick waterproof membrane, which was folded over boards to create a shallow tank to catch excess water. This was one of the wettest scenes I've ever experienced at Television Centre.'

ROGER SINGLETON-TURNER
Assistant Floor Manager

Uninvited Guests

THE MAIN HALL. DAY

The platoon is lined up in two files facing each other but running away from camera to the back of the hall. Wilson heads the right-hand column, there is a blank file opposite him ready for Mainwaring. Frazer, Walker and Sponge are behind Wilson, opposite them are Jones, Pike and Godfrey. The rest of the platoon make up pairs behind them. Mainwaring is in the middle, addressing the platoon.

MAINWARING Now, there's no doubt about it at all. In modern warfare, communications are absolutely vital – so I've sent a very firm letter to the War Office demanding wireless sets without further delay.

WILSON What happened about that very firm letter you sent demanding a Bren gun?

MAINWARING We're not discussing guns now, Wilson. Now, should Adolf kick off before these wireless sets arrive, I intend to capture sets from the first wave he sends against us.

JONES I would like to be in charge of the Nazi-wireless-set-capturing party, sir. I should enjoy that.

MAINWARING Yes, well – we'll organise that later, Jones.

JONES We could use bayonets, sir, so as not to damage the wireless machine with bullets.

MAINWARING Thank you, Jones – we'll make a note of your suggestion. Now, once having obtained the sets, the question is how do we go about sending a message.

PIKE They usually say 'calling all cars, calling all cars, there's a stick-up on the corner of seventh and ninety-second'.

MAINWARING I don't think that will be much help to us, Pike.

WALKER Yeah. We don't have any cars…

JONES We could say 'calling all men, calling all men'.

WALKER Yeah, and we'll have plenty of stick-ups once Jonesey gets going with his bayonets.

MAINWARING That'll do, Walker. I have actually studied the correct procedure, so if you will all pick up your wireless sets, we'll get on with it.

They each pick up a tin from in front of their feet. The tins are connected in twos by pieces of string threaded into a hole in the base. The string is knotted inside the tin.

MAINWARING Incidentally, I am very grateful to those of you who supplied us with empty treacle tins, cocoa tins and one or two that used to contain Olde English Humbugs.

GODFREY I once lost a stopping out of a tooth with an Olde English Humbug.

MAINWARING Did you?

JONES Toffees was worse. I broke a whole top set with a toffee.

PIKE I once choked on a gobstopper.

WILSON By Jove, so you did. I'd forgotten that.

PIKE Uncle Arthur banged me on the back. Mum hit him for banging me too hard.

MAINWARING Well, we don't want to go into all that now.

FRAZER Marshmallows.

MAINWARING I beg your pardon!

FRAZER Marshmallows – they are a bit kinder on the teeth.

MAINWARING Good. Now, as you probably recall from your childhood, if you speak into the tin one end, you can hear the voice in the tin the other end. Provided – and this is most important – providing you keep the string tight.

FRAZER **(To Walker)** Turkish delight was nice and soft.

MAINWARING Frazer, what have I just said?

FRAZER I'm sorry, sir – my mind was wandering.

MAINWARING Well, don't let it wander.

FRAZER I'm sorry, sir.

MAINWARING You'll concentrate quick enough if the Nazis start marching down the road, won't you?

FRAZER Yes, sir.

MAINWARING Well, concentrate now. Where was I?

JONES We all have to be tight, sir.

MAINWARING Ah yes, and, like a wireless set, you can't listen and speak at the same time – which is why we have to use correct procedure. Let me show you.

He moves to his place and gets tangled in the strings. When he arrives he picks up the tin.

MAINWARING Now, in the first place, as soon as the set is switched on you are in the listening position, so everybody listen.

They put their tins to their ears. Jones drops his tin.

JONES Sorry, sir. My communication cord's a bit short.

MAINWARING Now, we're all in the listening position.

GODFREY I can hear the sea…

WALKER It must be a Pilchard tin.

Mainwaring sees Wilson. Wilson is trying to get something out of his tin.

MAINWARING Wilson! Wilson – put it to your ear.

WILSON There's a quarter of an Olde English Humbug down at the bottom of the tin.

FRAZER **(Handing him a pencil)** Try this.

MAINWARING Wilson! Leave it there for the time being. Now, to commence proceedings, I place the microphone to my lips and I speak as follows. **(He speaks into the tin)** Hello, all stations, Charlie One. Hello, all stations, Charlie One. Report my signal, all stations, Charlie One. Over. **(They can't understand a word. He takes his mouth from the tin)** Now, is that quite clear?

FRAZER Speaking for myself, sir, I didn't understand one single word.

WILSON I heard you through the tin, it was rather good.

MAINWARING What I said was 'Hello, all stations,Charlie One. Hello, all stations, Charlie One. Report my signal, all stations, Charlie One. Over'.

WALKER What's Charlie One?

MAINWARING Wilson is Charlie One, but I use his call sign.

WALKER How do we know who's who?

MAINWARING Well, it's quite simple really. I'm saying hello to all of you. You Wilson, are Charlie One. You Frazer, are Charlie Two and Walker is Charlie Three, and so on.

FRAZER If you're trying to talk to me, why don't you say 'Hello, Charlie Two'?

MAINWARING Because that's what you say when you talk to me. You say 'Hello, Charlie Two'.

FRAZER You mean, I say hello to me.

MAINWARING No, you say hello to me.

FRAZER Then why don't I say hello, Charlie One?

MAINWARING **(Confused)** Because they don't do it like that.

PIKE Are we all Charlie Ones, too?

MAINWARING For the time being, we will imagine that everyone in this line is headquarters, so we'll all say 'Hello, Charlie One'.

GODFREY Captain Mainwaring, my name really *is* Charlie. Does that make any difference?

MAINWARING No, none at all. Right, now this side will try all together. One, two, three.

Mainwaring's file burble into their tins, 'Hello, all stations, Charlie One. Hello, all stations, Charlie One! Report my signal, all stations, Charlie One. Over'.

MAINWARING That wasn't very good, was it?

JONES Wouldn't it be better, sir, if we had a lot of boy scouts. They can run very fast can boy scouts. They can get through small holes in hedges, they're very good at that, sir.

MAINWARING **(Killing him with a look)** We'll try that once more.

SMALL SET REPRESENTING THE OUTSIDE OF THE HALL AND MAIN DOOR. DAY.

The Verger is clipping a five-foot ornamental bush. The Warden approaches him with Gerald.

WARDEN Hello, Mr Yeatman.

VERGER Hello, Mr Hodges. Sorry to hear about your headquarters last night.

WARDEN Blown to bits it was.

VERGER Did you yourself suffer any loss or injury?

WARDEN Only my spare trousers.

VERGER What a blessing you wasn't in 'em.

WARDEN I'll say. A splinter went right through the seat.

VERGER The good Lord must have been watching over you.

WARDEN He was. I was in the boozer.

VERGER He moves in a mysterious way His wonders to perform.

WARDEN Is Napoleon in?

VERGER Yes, but you're not to let him bother you. The Vicar says you can use his office and anything else you want.

WARDEN I've had a word with the Town Clerk so I shouldn't have any trouble.

VERGER Well, you must have somewhere to do your air raid precautions, mustn't you? Otherwise, where will we all be?

WARDEN **(Moving)** Thank you, Mr Yeatman.

VERGER **(Calling after him)** I'm very glad to have your lot here. It's been all tribulation with Mainwaring.

GERALD **(As they go into the hall)** What's tribulation?

MAIN HALL

Mainwaring is still lecturing.

JONES Mr Mainwaring, if you do this, it is like a chicken passing an egg. **(Business)** Then he passes the egg.

The Warden enters with Gerald and four other Wardens carrying maps, boards, buckets, pumps, etc.

WARDEN Good heavens! What are you teaching them – cat's cradle? Come on then – through here.

He ducks under the strings, followed by Gerald who is carrying a stirrup pump and a bucket.

MAINWARING Just exactly what's going on?

WARDEN I think it would be best if you and me was to talk in the office, private.

MAINWARING I've no wish to talk to you at all.

WARDEN You're going to have to, so let's get cracking. **(He moves into the office)**

MAINWARING Carry on, Wilson, this won't take a moment. **(He moves into the office)**

SIDE OFFICE. DAY

MAINWARING Now, look here, Hodges.

WARDEN No, you look here, Mainwaring. **(He waves a piece of paper)** My headquarters have been put out of action and I have official permission to use this hall here.

MAINWARING On whose authority?

WARDEN See for yourself. **(He hands the paper to Mainwaring)** Now, I'm a reasonable man – we've had our differences in the past, but we're both on the same side and I'm going to be generous. I'm not shutting you out altogether. I'm prepared to go shares with you. **(He moves to the upstage end of the room)** You can keep that half with your chair – I'll have this half. **(He starts to draw a chalk line down on the floor)**

MAINWARING What are you doing?

WARDEN Now, when it comes to the desk, you keep your stuff over there, I'll keep mine over here. **(He draws a line down the centre of the desk top)**

MAINWARING Don't you dare put marks on my desk.

WARDEN I'm only trying to be reasonable and fair. **(Mainwaring starts to rub the marks out)**

MAINWARING I shall rub it out.

WARDEN Well, I'll chalk it again.

Mainwaring rubs again. Warden chalks.

WARDEN I can chalk quicker than you can rub. Look! **(Warden chalks more lines quickly)** Now, you've probably noticed that all these doors are in my half. No, I'm going to be fair. I'll put another mark over here, like this, and over here, like this. **(He puts two lines cutting off the door area)**

WARDEN Now that's Tom Tiddler's ground.

MAINWARING I've had just about enough of this.

He is round by the front corner of the desk.

WARDEN You're standing on my bit, get off!

He shoves Mainwaring into his own half.

WARDEN Now, the only thing I have to insist on is the phone, that has to be in my half. **(He moves the phone to his half of the desk)**

MAINWARING Oh no it doesn't. That is my artery of communication. If Hitler invades some other part of the coast first, that is how I shall be informed.

WARDEN Yeah, well it's my artery every time the siren sounds. If Hitler's coming I'll take a message for you.

MAINWARING It stays there and I give you precisely five seconds to get out of this office.

WARDEN **(Quickly)** One, two, three, four, five. I'm not going.

MAINWARING Wilson! Jones!

Wilson and Jones open the door quickly.

MAINWARING Escort this person from my headquarters.

WARDEN I'm sorry, mate, I'm staying here. This is *my* headquarters.

MAINWARING Wilson, prepare to carry out my orders.

WILSON Yes. Now, would you mind leaving like the Captain says?

WARDEN Look! **(Holding out paper)** I've got authority. There it is in black and white. **(Jones thrusts his bayonet through the paper)**

JONES If you do not leave, you will have this up you and you will not like it.

WARDEN Now look here, Ghandi! **(Jones brandishes the bayonet and makes a savage noise)** Right, I'm going. But you'll hear more of this. **(He goes)**

MAINWARING Well done, Jones.

JONES They do not like cold steel, sir. They cannot countenance it.

MAINWARING Right, let us resume our exercise. **(They move to the door)**

OUTSIDE OF MAIN DOOR. DAY

The Verger is still clipping the bush. The Warden rushes up.

WARDEN He's done it now. He's done it.

VERGER Whatever's up, Mr Hodges? You look as if you're a soul in torment.

WARDEN Get him here! Get the Vicar! It's that Mainwaring. I'll have to sit down or I'll have a turn.

VERGER You come and sit over here. I'll get His Reverence.

WARDEN He threatened me with a bayonet.

VERGER Never!

WARDEN It's true – a bayonet.

The Verger moves him out of camera towards bench.

VERGER He who liveth by the sword shall perish by the sword and that goes for bayonets an' all.

MAIN HALL. DAY

MAINWARING **(At his tin)** You're not going over when I say 'Over'. Try it all together. My side will say 'Over' first. One, two, three.

MAINWARING'S FILE Over.

They transfer their tins from their mouths to their ears. Wilson's line do the opposite.

WILSON'S FILE Over.

MAINWARING'S FILE Over.

WILSON'S FILE Over.

MAINWARING That's better.

JONES I think I've got the hang of it now, sir. Let me do it on my own, sir.

MAINWARING I don't think we're quite ready, Jones.

JONES Let me go solo, sir. I'd like to go solo.

MAINWARING Oh, very well.

WALKER This is going to be good.

JONES Hello, all stations, Charlie One. Hello, all stations, Charlie One. Report my signals, all stations, Charlie One. Over.

MAINWARING That was very good, Jones.

JONES Thank you, sir.

MAINWARING That was absolutely correct. Well done.

JONES Thank you, sir. **(To Pike)** They all thought I was going to get it wrong, didn't they?

PIKE You did it beautifully.

JONES I'm not as big a fool as I look, you know.

MAINWARING Right, let's start again. Tighten your string.

Enter the Warden with Vicar and Verger.

VICAR Mr Mainwaring, I've given Mr Hodges here permission to use my office. I understand he's been molested.

MAINWARING I'm very busy, Vicar, may I suggest you come to my office in 20 minutes.

VICAR It's not your office, it's my office and I've lent it to Mr Hodges here.

WARDEN **(To Gerald)** There, what did I say? I told him, didn't I? I told him.

GERALD You did.

MAINWARING You're interrupting training which is essential to the defence of the realm. Will you kindly leave?

VICAR No, I will not. I want to go to my office, so will you kindly take away all your silly bits of string.

MAINWARING No, I will not.

VICAR Very well, I shall report you to the Bishop and to the police.

MAINWARING Oh, don't be so damn childish.

VERGER Don't you profane His Reverence like that.

MAINWARING I don't want any impertinence from you.

VERGER Oh that's the way it is, is it? Follow me, Vicar. **(With the garden shears in his hands, he clips his way to the office)**

MAIN HALL. NIGHT

Pike, Walker, Jones, Godfrey, Frazer are in a huddle.

PIKE I think it's a cheek, Mr Hodges running his A.R.P. headquarters in here.

WALKER Old Mainwaring won't stand too much pushing around. He's tried to co-operate, but what can you do with a man like Hodges. I mean he's so dead common.

JONES You're right there, Joe. He is common.

WALKER If there's one thing I can't stand, it's common people.

GODFREY I think you're being a little unfair. After all, Mr Hodges runs the Civil Defence very well and it's a very dangerous job.

WALKER I don't say he don't do it well. What I am saying is that he does it so uncouth.

FRAZER If only Mr Mainwaring had put a curse on him.

JONES Don't talk rubbish Jock, how can you put a curse on people?

FRAZER I've seen it done.

JONES When?

FRAZER Over 50 years ago when I was trading coral in the South Seas with a friend of mine.

PIKE Was that the one that got killed by a giant squid, Mr Frazer?

FRAZER No. This was another friend – Jethro, his name was. One day we were anchored off a small island about 20 miles west of Samoa. Jethro told me that he'd heard there was a ruined temple in the centre of the island, with a huge idol that had a ruby the size of a duck's egg set in its forehead. He was determined to get it. Well, as soon as it was dark, we rowed ashore, armed to the teeth, and we set off through the jungle to find the temple. After about two hours cutting our way through the undergrowth, we finally came to a clearing. In the centre was the ruined temple covered with jungle creepers. The place was deserted – we crept inside and there it was – a huge idol with the great ruby in its forehead. The shafts of moonlight that came through the holes in the roof made it glisten like fire. Jethro gave a cry of triumph – jumped up on the idol, dug the ruby out of its forehead with his knife. All the time I could feel eyes, horrible, unseen eyes, staring at us. 'Let's get out', I shouted and we turned to go – then we saw it. Blocking our path in the doorway was a witch doctor. He let out a scream that froze my blood to ice. He shook some bones in Jethro's face and he cursed him. After all these years I can still hear that terrible curse. 'Death,' he screamed, 'death. The ruby will bring you death. Death.'

PIKE Did the curse come true, Mr Frazer?

FRAZER Aye, laddie, it did. He died. **(He pauses and then quickly)** Last year – he was 86.

Mainwaring enters.

MAINWARING Right, on parade all of you.

They line up on the stage-side of the hall.

JONES Yes, sir, on parade like the Captain says. Fall in three ranks and dress smartly by the right and all that.

MAINWARING Yes, thank you, Jones. Now I've been on to Area H.Q., the Civil Defence Authorities and also the Chairman of the Council, who is a fellow Rotarian. I don't mind telling you, I've given them all a piece of my mind. I can assure you that these A.R.P. people will be moved as soon as possible.

WILSON But not this week.

MAINWARING But not this week – I'll tell them, Wilson. In the meantime I think we should all behave like good Christians and, as far as possible, ignore them.

The Warden's voice is heard off.

WARDEN Left, right, left, right.

The Wardens enter the hall.

WARDEN Right wheel. **(They march through the Home Guard ranks)** Right wheel.

The Warden now gives a quick 'right wheel' and 'left wheel' so that they are in line with the Home Guard but near the office side of the hall.

WARDEN Mark time, halt! Left turn – very smart. Right dress.

The Wardens extend their right arms and shuffle to the left in the traditional right dress manner. This squashes the Home Guard up against the stage.

MAINWARING Home Guard. Left dress.

The Home Guard extend their left arms and shuffle right squashing the Wardens back towards the office.

WARDEN All right, all right. That's enough of that, Mainwaring.

MAINWARING You started it.

WARDEN You were taking up more than your half of the hall.

MAINWARING I have twice as many troops as you have.

WARDEN Do you call those troops – that lot. The Bathchair Fusiliers.

The front rank break and advance threateningly. They all speak together.

JONES That's enough of that.

WALKER You can go too far, you know.

FRAZER Let's sort him out.

WALKER How do you fancy a bunch of fives up yer hooter?

FRAZER I think he's already had one.

WARDEN Six to one, that's brave, isn't it?

PIKE This town's not big enough for both of us, buddy.

GERALD **(Pushing Mainwaring)** Don't start anything.

MAINWARING Don't you push me.

The siren sounds.

WARDEN Hello, they're here.

WILSON Saved by the bell.

WARDEN Right, I'll sort you out later. Get your posts manned.

MAINWARING To your duties.

WARDEN Mrs Cole – man the telephone. Mrs Robinson, take charge of the incident map.

MAINWARING Taylor – establish your H.Q. at the Marigold Tea Rooms and patrol from there to Timothy Whites.

WARDEN You get that fire going, Gerald. We may be here all night, it's getting a bit parky. I'm going to my office. **(He goes)**

Mainwaring follows quickly and he turns at the door.

MAINWARING Jones – you keep your sector here in reserve.

INTERIOR. SIDE OFFICE. NIGHT

They get into the office. Mrs Cole is at the phone. Mr Carr at the incident map. Warden sees Mainwaring's map on the desk and chucks it off.

WARDEN Keep that on your side.

MAINWARING Look, I am trying my best to tolerate your presence here, but you're being quite insufferable.

MAIN HALL

Walker crosses the hall to Gerald who is trying to light the fire.

WALKER You'll never light that. The wood's damp and the chimney's cold – what you need is a fire lighter.

GERALD I haven't got any.

WALKER Ah – well, I can help you there. **(He brings out a packet)** This'll have it going before you can say 'gunpowder'. Nine pence to you.

GERALD Oh, thanks.

FRAZER **(Putting his face near Walker)** That's trading with the enemy.

SIDE OFFICE. NIGHT

WARDEN **(On the phone)** Well, make a report and let me have it in the morning. **(He puts down the phone)**

Mainwaring goes to move the phone.

WARDEN Hands off that during an alert. I shall be receiving a constant stream of reports.

MAINWARING And I shall be receiving instructions from the War Office via my Superior Officer.

Phone rings. Mrs Cole takes it.

MAINWARING There you are, they're coming in already.

MRS COLE Walmington A.R.P.

MAINWARING **(Shouting down the receiver)** H.Q. No.1 Platoon, B Company, Walmington-on-Sea Home Guard.

MRS COLE It's for you, Captain Mainwaring.

MAINWARING There – what did I tell you? **(He takes the receiver)** Good evening, sir – Mainwaring here. Oh – oh, hello. Elizabeth.

WARDEN You can pack that in. We've no time for you carrying on chats with your bits of stuff.

MAINWARING Will you be quiet, this happens to be my good lady.

WARDEN Well, cut it short.

MAINWARING Yes, dear. No, I can't possibly come home now. If you're frightened, dear, can't you go and sit in the cupboard under the stairs as usual? Yes, well I would have thought a bomb was more dangerous than a mouse.

WARDEN Cor blimey, hurry up, careless talk costs lives you know.

MAIN HALL. NIGHT

There is smoke coming from the stove.

WALKER Go on, try another one.

JONES There's probably a sparrow's nest in the chimney. They do a lot of that sort of thing – sparrows.

WALKER Then we'll have roast sparrow, very tasty – very sweet.

There is a short whoof and a flash from the stove.

WALKER That's more like it.

JONES What are they made of, Joe?

WALKER Well, they're mostly incendiary bombs that have been damaged by fire.

Verger enters.

VERGER What's this, what's this? That stove is not to be ignited without the consent of the Vicar.

WALKER Oh blimey, it's only a fire.

VERGER It'll have to be notified. There'll be a rumpus. Who lit it?

WALKER The wardens.

VERGER The wardens? Did they? Cheers the place up a nice fire, don't it?

THE OFFICE. NIGHT

MAINWARING Well, perhaps if you made a loud noise, the mouse would go down the hole or something.

WARDEN Cor blimey. **(He seizes the receiver)** Leave the mouse where it is and you jump down the hole. **(He hangs up)**

MAINWARING How dare you?

MRS COLE That's not very kind, Mr Hodges.

WARDEN Don't you start. Look, this raid's been on ten minutes and I haven't received a single manning report.

The bell rings.

WARDEN There you are. Hello. Right, thank you, Mr Yeldan. **(Puts the receiver down. He turns to report girl)** They're standing by in Kyber Road.

Bell rings again.

WARDEN Hello. Chimney on fire? I'll take the details. Get this down, Mrs Cole.

MRS COLE Yes.

WARDEN Well, use the right end of the pen.

MAINWARING Really, do we have to clog up a vital channel of communication with such trivial domestic matters.

WARDEN There's nothing trivial about a fire, mate. It shows up for miles. **(Into phone)** Yes, where is it? Large building next to St Aldhelm's Church, Mortimer Road.

Right – got it. (Puts down receiver) Get on to the fire brigade, Mrs Cole.

The Vicar enters.

VICAR What are you up to now, Mr Mainwaring?

MAINWARING Go away, we're busy.

VICAR Do you realise that you've set the chimney on fire?

Enter Verger.

VERGER The stove in the hall has become a raging, fiery furnace.

MAINWARING Wait a minute. This is a large building next to St Aldhelm's Church.

WARDEN Get out of the way.

Mainwaring and Warden go quickly into the hall.

MAIN HALL. NIGHT

WALKER He lit it. (He points to Gerald)

GERALD It was his fire lighters that did it.

WALKER Well, it never happened before. Generally speaking they won't burn.

MAINWARING What are you doing about it, Wilson?

WILSON When it happened once with the nursery fire – Nanny put salt on it.

WARDEN Blimey, it's a fire not a pigeon.

Mrs Cole pokes her head in from the office.

MRS COLE I've got the brigade on, shall I tell them to come round?

WARDEN What'n us the laughing stock of the neighbourhood? Not likely. Tell them it's a false alarm. Come on, Gerald, up the tower.

GERALD Shall we take the pumps?

WARDEN Good idea.

They go towards the other side of the hall to get the pumps.

MAINWARING Come on, men.

GODFREY Excuse me, sir. If I could have the key to the store cupboard I could get some more bandages.

MAINWARING Yes, here you are.

FRAZER Mr Mainwaring. Bog Turf.

MAINWARING I beg your pardon?

FRAZER A barrel of Bog Turf would douse it in a jiffy.

MAINWARING Be sensible, Frazer.

They run to the tower steps.

THE TOWER ROOM. NIGHT

This is a small room, ten foot square or so, approached by a winding stair. There is a ladder to a trap door in the ceiling. It is not necessary for us to see the trap, but we will use the ladder. There is a window, and outside is a parapet which leads round the exterior of the tower. To get on to the apex of the church roof one must travel along the parapet and then bridge the gap of five or six feet which is supposed to be a sheer drop. The gap is to be bridged by laying the ladder from the parapet across the sill of a small vent window a couple of feet below the apex of the roof.

Jones is sitting on the window-sill with his knees in the room and his bottom out of it. The window is about four foot wide.

JONES Captain Mainwaring, sir. Captain Mainwaring.

Mainwaring enters followed by Pike and Walker.

MAINWARING Jones. Jones, what are you doing?

JONES The chimney's on fire, sir.

MAINWARING I know that.

JONES If you lean out a little, sir, you can see it throwing out sparks like a Roman candle, but you have to be very careful, sir, because there's a sheer drop of about 40 feet down. Aaahhhhhaaahhhhh! (He leans back and overbalances)

Mainwaring and Pike grab him and pull him back.

JONES Thank you, sir. You saved my life then, I'll never forget it, sir. I…?

MAINWARING Get out of the way, Jones. Help me up, Pike.

Helped by Pike and Walker, Mainwaring steps on to a box and endeavours to pass Jones through the upstage end of the window.

MAINWARING Get inside, Jones.

JONES I can't move much, sir. I'm caught on the window by the catch which is made of cold steel, sir, and if I move it goes up me, sir – and I do not like it.

Mainwaring pushes past him.

MAINWARING There's a parapet. I'm going to inch along it and see if I can get to the roof.

The Warden enters, with the Verger, the Vicar and Gerald.

WARDEN Here, what are you doing? This is an A.R.P. matter. Get out of the way.

JONES I'm caught in a very embarrassing situation.

WARDEN What are you talking about?

PIKE His trousers are hooked by the gusset.

WARDEN Well, take them off then.

VERGER Not in front of His Reverence.

WARDEN We can't have him stuck there. Get 'em off. (He dives for Jones' flies, Jones wriggles and protests)

EXTERIOR. BELL TOWER. NIGHT

Mainwaring is at the corner of the tower. He edges back and puts his head inside. Wilson has now joined the group.

MAINWARING What's going on? Leave him alone.

JONES They're trying to take my trousers off, Mr Mainwaring.

MAINWARING Don't be neurotic, Jones! Wilson, there's a gap from the tower to the roof. Get me a plank and I can get across.

WILSON I haven't got a plank. I mean, why should I have a plank?

WALKER There's this ladder, what about that?

MAINWARING Well done, Walker. Hand it out.

Walker and Pike go to get it. Jones gives a shriek.

JONES I am now unhitched, Mr Mainwaring.

MAINWARING Then get out of the way.

JONES He's not very sympathetic, is he?

Jones climbs out on to the parapet.

WALKER Here's the ladder, Captain Mainwaring.

MAINWARING Right, shove it through.

Mainwaring moves to one side of the window, Jones moves a little to the other side. The ladder comes through and takes Jones a little way into the void with it.

JONES Help, put me back, put me back!

MAINWARING Jones, get out of the way. Take the ladder in.

They do. Jones regains his feet.

JONES Mr Mainwaring, you saved my life, I'll never forget that, sir.

MAINWARING Grab the ladder.

WALKER Right, ease it forward so it rests on the sill. (As they do this, we cut inside)

WARDEN Hurry up. Jerry can see that lot for miles.

They take the ladder along the parapet towards the gap. Jones' foot slips en route.

JONES You saved my life, Mr Mainwaring. You keep on saving my life all the time.

The Warden comes outside and helps. Pike and Walker follow through with the pump and the bucket of water.

INTERIOR. TOWER ROOM. NIGHT

The Verger is about to climb through the window.

VICAR Where are you going with that bucket of water, Mr Yeatman?

VERGER I've polished that hall for 30 years, sir. I can't see it go up like a bundle of kindling.

EXTERIOR. TOWER

Mainwaring has got the ladder across the gap.

MAINWARING Right, I think that's firm.

JONES Let me test it, sir, let me test it.

WARDEN (Behind him) Well, get on with it, you old fool. Don't talk so much!

MAINWARING See if you can get along the roof to the chimney, Jones. Pass the word back for some water.

MVOICES Water – water – water.

MAINWARING Pike, Walker! Crawl along the cat walk and see if you can use the pump from there.

INTERIOR. TOWER ROOM. NIGHT

Frazer puts his head inside the window. Wilson, Godfrey and the Vicar are there.

FRAZER We need water.

VICAR (To Wilson) Go on, there's plenty of buckets downstairs.

WILSON Come on, Godfrey. (He turns to Vicar) Aren't you coming?

VICAR No, I'm passing it through.

THE CROWN OF THE ROOF. NIGHT

WARDEN (Behind Jones) Go on, Grandad. Hurry up.

Jones, Warden, Verger and Frazer are now on top of the roof. Pike is near the chimney on a cat walk. Walker has the pump at the tower-end of the catwalk. Mainwaring is on the tower by the ladder, directing operations and ready to pass buckets. The chimney is half-way down the roof between the apex and the catwalk. It is fairly tall and not accessible from either point.

JONES Mr Mainwaring, sir, if I had some water I think I could get it down the chimney.

MAINWARING Pass the water.

INTERIOR. TOWER ROOM. NIGHT

VICAR Hurry up!

Wilson and Godfrey stagger up into the tower with buckets, two buckets each.

VICAR More!

WILSON Oh Lord! (He starts back down the stairs. The Vicar starts to pass the buckets through, if necessary, to one or two other members of the platoon or Gerald)

VICAR Water coming.

The cry 'water coming' is taken up as the buckets are passed to Jones. Jones receives his bucket and chucks it just as Pike is in position by the stack. Pike gets most of the water.

JONES I missed it, Mr Mainwaring. More water!

Pike drowned.

VICAR Water coming.

The cry of 'water coming' is taken up. The empty bucket is passed back, the full ones are passed forward.

VERGER I've still got a bucket of sand here.

WARDEN Well, go and play mud pies then.

The empty bucket and the full bucket arrive to the Verger at about the same time. Liberal quantities are spilt over the Verger.

Jones throws the full bucket, and again Pike gets most of it.

JONES Missed. More water!

The cry 'more water' is taken up. Voices then reply 'water coming'.

PIKE Blimey, how much more? Are you ready, Joe?

WALKER Just about. (Joe has a bucket and is nearly ready to pump)

WARDEN (To Verger) Hurry up.

VERGER Here you are then.

He liberally sloshes contents of the buckets in his hand over the Warden.

WARDEN (To Jones) Here, you're not having this one. I'm doing it. (Warden chucks a bucket. Pike, again, gets most of it)

WARDEN Missed. More water!

The cry 'more water' is taken up.

PIKE Joe, start pumping.

Walker pumps. Using the hose, Pike now starts to try to get his jet down the chimney. In doing so, most of it goes over Jones and the Warden. Jones falls.

JONES You saved my life again...

• PETER DAY REMEMBERS •

'Whilst some of the platoon clambered on to the roof to put out the chimney fire, I sat below feeding smoke canisters and Golden Rain fireworks into the chimney, which produced a kind of sparkly rain effect. It got very hot.

'We normally used a smoke gun to produce such effects. The machine heated up a special vegetable oil, which vaporised into a kind of smoke when it got really hot. We had huge extractor fans in the studio to remove the fumes.

'As we were responsible for health and safety, there was always a fireman on set ready with extinguishers whenever we used such equipment; luckily, he was never called upon.'

PETER DAY
Visual Effects Designer

INTERIOR. TOWER ROOM. NIGHT

Vicar passes the bucket. Wilson and Godfrey arrive with two more buckets each.

VICAR More water!

WILSON (Grabbing the Vicar, exhausted) It's your church – get it yourself.

GODFREY I quite agree.

WILSON (Turning round on Godfrey) More water, Godfrey!

Godfrey meekly goes.

EXTERIOR. THE ROOF. NIGHT

JONES Mr Mainwaring, sir. I'm going to slide down the chimney and I shall stand beside it to my full height – then I shall be able to pour a bucket down.

MAINWARING Don't talk so much, Jones. Get on with it.

JONES Yes, sir, at once, sir.

He toboggans down the roof and finishes astride the chimney.

JONES Ooooh, aaah, ooooh!

MAINWARING What's the matter, Jones?

JONES It's red hot, sir – it's red hot.

MAINWARING Then come back.

JONES I can't, sir. Oooh! Aaah! Oooh! I'm on fire.

PIKE It's all right, Mr Jones, I'll put you out.

He directs the jet on to Jones.

WARD Come on, Verger, he's in trouble, help him!

They both throw buckets over Jones.

JONES Mr Mainwaring, it's gone out!

They look and it has indeed gone out.

VERGER Look, the fire's gone out.

MAINWARING Good heavens, how did that happen?

WILSON **(Putting his head through the window)** Actually, sir, last time I was down there I put some salt on it.

MAINWARING Right, well done, men. Back into the tower and be careful how you go.

Mainwaring, who has come on to the apex of the roof to pass the buckets, now backs towards the ladder bridge.

FRAZER Careful, Captain Mainwaring, that ladder's just on the edge.

Frazer tries to secure it quickly and in doing so, it tumbles and falls out of sight. We hear it crash.

FRAZER It's smashed to little pieces, sir. I'm thinking you'll be there some little time.

MAINWARING Wilson! Take Frazer and go down to the builder's yard and bring back a plank and a ladder.

WARDEN What are you talking about? It'll take half an hour! Send for the fire brigade.

MAINWARING Oh no we don't.

WARDEN It's all right for you. You're dry as a bone, I'm soaked to the skin.

MAINWARING Serves you right for being so damn careless and chucking water about like a kid of six.

WARDEN Bet you wouldn't say that if you was as wet as I was.

MAINWARING Oh yes I would.

There is a clap of thunder and a flash of lightning and the rain pelts down.

WARDEN Ah, well you're going to get a chance, aren't you?

MAINWARING Wilson! Er, perhaps if the brigade aren't doing anything, they wouldn't mind popping round.

SERIES FOUR **EPISODE THIRTEEN**

Recorded: Friday 11/12/70

Original transmission: Friday 18/12/70, 8.00–8.30pm

Original viewing figures = 13.1 million

ARTHUR LOWE .... CAPTAIN MAINWARING
JOHN LE MESURIER .... SERGEANT WILSON
CLIVE DUNN .... LANCE CORPORAL JONES
JOHN LAURIE .... PRIVATE FRAZER
JAMES BECK .... PRIVATE WALKER
ARNOLD RIDLEY .... PRIVATE GODFREY
IAN LAVENDER .... PRIVATE PIKE
GEOFFREY LUMSDEN .... CAPTAIN SQUARE
REX GARNER .... CAPTAIN ASHLEY-JONES
MICHAEL KNOWLES .... CAPTAIN REED
ANTHONY SAGAR .... THE SERGEANT MAJOR
TOM MENNARD .... THE MESS ORDERLY
ROBERT RAGLAN .... CAPTAIN PRITCHARD

PLATOON ..... COLIN BEAN, DESMOND CULLUM-JONES, HUGH HASTINGS, ... VIC TAYLOR, FREDDIE WILES, GEORGE HANCOCK, LESLIE NOYES, ... FREDDIE WHITE, HUGH CECIL, FRANK GODFREY

GIRL IN CANTEEN .... ANITA ARCHDALE

FALLEN IDOL

• ROGER SINGLETON-TURNER REMEMBERS •

'This episode included some long scenes inside a tent, which was erected on turf specially brought into the studio. During one of the scenes, members of the platoon come back to their tent after having a meal which included seed cake. Arnold Ridley had a great dislike of caraway seeds, and said: "I'll sit here and pick the seeds out." I offered to provide some seed-free cake, but he politely refused. He said: "You see, in the War, cake would be such a treat because of rationing that Private Godfrey wouldn't want to waste it." So that's what he did.

'The episode also saw the platoon using sticky bombs. The Visual Effects team made up dummies of these infamously dangerous items. There was no danger for us, of course, but the action required quite a lot of running around in the long grass to stick the bombs on to pretend tanks. Everything had to be done several times to cover each angle necessary for the sequence. The cast was, on the whole, not young and it was an arduous day for us all!'

ROGER SINGLETON-TURNER
Assistant Floor Manager

Fallen Idol

INSIDE MARQUEE AT WEEKEND CAMP. DAY

Interior of large army marquee. There is an opening about eight foot wide. Through it, in the background, we can see the back of another tent and trees and bushes. A regular Army Captain, about 35, is talking to a Warrant Officer. They are both Royal Engineers.

CAPTAIN Captain Mainwaring and the Walmington-on-Sea Platoon are a bit late, aren't they, Sergeant Major?

W.O. I understand they're coming by their own transport, sir. It's a butcher's van – they've converted it into an armoured car and transport vehicle.

CAPTAIN They're very ingenious these Home Guards.

W.O. Oh yes, sir – and they're very keen as well.

CAPTAIN A bit too keen, if you ask me.

Close up of Captain – his cheek starts to twitch.

W.O. Are you all right, sir?

CAPTAIN It's this damn twitch I've developed. I mean, I've been running this school of explosives now for over a year, and it wasn't until we started getting Home Guards here for weekend courses, that I got this confounded twitching.

W.O. If you ask me, you could do with a spot of leave, sir.

CAPTAIN The trouble is they've just got no idea of the danger – they're so mad keen – they charge about all over the place – one of these days they're going to blow themselves sky high. **(He starts to twitch)** I know it – I just know it.

W.O. Never mind, sir. This is the last lot of Home Guards we shall be getting in – the sooner we can put them through the course tomorrow and get rid of them, the better.

There is the sound of Jones' van approaching.

W.O. Then you'll be able to sleep easy in your bed, sir.

CAPTAIN All I can say is – roll on tomorrow night.

Through the opening we can see the van draw up. Mainwaring jumps down from the cab and starts to blow his whistle furiously.

MAINWARING Right, we're here – disembark, men – come on, at the double – at the double. **(He blows his whistle)**

W.O. This lot sound even more keen than the others, sir.

CAPTAIN Oh, Lord – all right, Sergeant Major, go and look after them.

W.O. Right, sir. **(He goes through the opening)** In here, gentlemen, please.

Mainwaring, Wilson and Jones come into tent.

MAINWARING **(Saluting)** Captain Mainwaring, 1st Platoon, Walmington-on-Sea Home Guard, reporting for duty, sir.

CAPTAIN How do you do? I'm Captain Reed.

MAINWARING This is Sergeant Wilson and Lance Corporal Jones.

They both salute. Captain returns the salute.

MAINWARING I must say we're all rather keen to get cracking – we haven't done any practice with live grenades before.

CAPTAIN Haven't you? **(He starts to twitch)**

MAINWARING I can't wait to get my hands on one.

JONES Neither can I, Mr Mainwaring. **(To Captain)** I don't know which I like best, the bomb or the bayonet. I'm fond of both, of course. When I was in France in 1914 – I used to lob those bombs over the top one after another – I used to do a lot of that sort of thing – a lot of lobbing you know – the mad bomber they called me. Of course, I'm not really mad – I'm as sane as you are.

CAPTAIN Oh really. **(He is twitching wildly)** Well, if you'll excuse me – I've got a lot to do – make yourselves comfortable. **(He quickly goes)**

JONES He's a bit… isn't he?

MAINWARING Come on, Wilson, let's go and get our bedding.

WILSON Young Pike's bringing mine in, sir.

MAINWARING We can't have people waiting on us in this platoon, Wilson – we're a democratic unit – we all eat together – we all sleep together – and we all fight together. Rank shouldn't come into it.

Pike staggers in with two large rolls of bedding.

PIKE Here's your bedding, Uncle Arthur.

MAINWARING In future, Pike, you will not wait on Sergeant Wilson. We are all equal here. **(He goes)**

PIKE Shall I take yours out again?

WILSON Don't be absurd, Frank. **(He takes the bedding)**

PIKE Mum says you're not to tread all over the sheets – she doesn't want dirty footmarks all over them.

Walker, Frazer, Godfrey and three others come in with their bedding.

GODFREY **(To Walker)** Oh dear, have we got to sleep on the ground?

WALKER It's either that or stand up all night.

GODFREY It's not going to do my rheumatics any good.

FRAZER Ach! Don't be so namby-pamby – it will make your spine go straight.

GODFREY At my age it's already decided which way it wants to go.

FRAZER **(Muttering)** Silly old fool.

By now all the men have laid their bedding out in a row. Walker, Godfrey, Frazer, Pike and Wilson are together. Jones comes in with his and puts it down beside Walker.

Mainwaring comes in carrying his bedding – he is followed by Sponge with a camp bed and Hastings with a stool and a portable wind-up gramophone. He crosses to the end of the tent where Wilson is laying out his bedding.

MAINWARING All right, Sponge – Hastings, put them down there.

They all dump the stuff down and go.

WILSON I rather got the impression from what you said just now – that we weren't going to have anybody waiting on us this weekend.

MAINWARING **(Icy)** I can hardly be expected to carry a bedding roll – a camp bed – a stool and a portable gramophone on my own – can I? **(He starts to put his bed together)**

PIKE **(Whispering to Wilson)** Uncle Arthur?

WILSON What is it, Frank?

PIKE Have you seen Mr Snuggly?

WILSON Mr who?

PIKE Mr Snuggly, my teddy.

WILSON No, I haven't.

PIKE Mum told me she'd put him in.

WILSON Well, I haven't seen him.

PIKE I must find him – I can't get to sleep without him, you know that.

WILSON I haven't got him.

PIKE Have a look – see if he's in your bed.

WILSON All right. **(He feels down in his bedding and pulls out a teddy bear)** Here he is.

PIKE Put him back – don't let anybody see him.

WILSON I thought you wanted him.

PIKE I don't want anybody to see him – they might laugh at me, wrap him in a towel and pass him over.

Wilson wraps the bear in a towel – Mainwaring sees him.

MAINWARING What have you got there, Wilson?

WILSON Mr Snuggly.

MAINWARING What?

WILSON **(Unwrapping the bear)** My teddy, sir – I just can't get to sleep without him.

MAINWARING Extraordinary. **(He turns back to his bedding)**

PIKE Thanks, Uncle Arthur.

Jones has finished setting up his sleeping bag, it has a wire frame with a mosquito net over it.

WALKER What are you doing, Jonesey?

JONES I'm setting up my bed, of course.

WALKER Are you growing some strawberries in it?

JONES 'Course not.

WALKER What have you got a net on it for?

JONES That's a mosquito net.

WALKER There aren't mosquitoes round here, you silly old duffer.

JONES I know that, it goes with the sleeping bag – I've always had this bag with me – we've been together now for 50 years...

WALKER **(Singing)** ...and it don't seem a day too much. **(He laughs)**

JONES You can laugh, Joe – I was very grateful to have this sleeping bag in the Sudan – as well as keeping out mosquitoes – this net used to keep out the snakes.

WALKER Blimey, don't tell me you had snakes trying to get into bed with you.

JONES It gets very cold out there in the desert at night, and they try to snuggle up to you to keep warm.

WALKER Ugh!

JONES Snakes aren't all cold and slimy, you know – they're quite warm and soft. There was one particular snake I remember – Charlie, I used to call him – he used to come round every night and I could see his face looking at me through the net – he had a pathetic look in his eyes, as much as to say – let me in I'm very cold. I didn't let him in, though. I don't like that sort of thing.

WALKER I had a similar experience when I was a kid and I used to go camping with the boy scouts – this grass snake used to come round the tent. We found him one morning, completely exhausted, lying beside a tent rope.

Captain Square enters.

SQUARE 'Evening, Corporal – Captain Mainwaring about?

JONES Yes, sir – he's down the end. **(He calls)** Mr Mainwaring, Captain Square's here to see you.

WILSON Oh, Lord – it's that terrible old bore again. I'd forgotten that the Eastgate platoon were here with us this weekend.

Square comes over to Mainwaring.

SQUARE Hello, Mainwaring, everything all right?

MAINWARING Yes, thank you. I've got all my chaps settled in.

SQUARE Where are you sleeping?

MAINWARING **(Pointing)** Here.

SQUARE **(Pulling him on one side)** You're not going to sleep with the men are you?

MAINWARING Yes.

SQUARE Can't have that sort of thing, old boy – bad for discipline.

MAINWARING Do you really think so?

SQUARE Definitely – it's not on, old boy – it's just not on – us officers must stick together, you know.

MAINWARING I like to muck in with my chaps as a rule.

SQUARE That's a mistake, old man – I mean, where would it all end? You take a tip from me, rig up some separate quarters for you and your Sergeant. Well, I'm going to get some conner – see you later. **(He goes)**

VOICE **(Out of vision)** Grub up – come and get it.

We hear the sound of a steel triangle.

FRAZER Come on, boys, let's go and get our tea – I'm starving.

They all grab their mess tins and go. Wilson starts to pick up his mess tin. Mainwaring calls him over.

MAINWARING Just a minute, Wilson.

WILSON Yes, sir. **(He comes down)**

MAINWARING **(Looking over his shoulder)** Wait until they've all gone.

WILSON I'd rather like to get something to eat myself.

MAINWARING That can wait – this is important.

WILSON What is?

MAINWARING I er... think you and I ought to sleep together tonight.

WILSON Together?

MAINWARING Yes, away from the others.

WILSON I don't think I quite follow you, sir.

MAINWARING I've been thinking it over and I've come to the conclusion that it's bad for discipline for us to sleep with the O.R.s.

WILSON O.R.s?

MAINWARING Other ranks.

WILSON But you said just now – we all eat together – we all sleep together and we all fight together.

MAINWARING Well, in future we'll just eat and fight together. Now, come on, give me a hand.

INTERIOR. INSIDE MARQUEE. DAY

The marquee is empty – at the far end Mainwaring and Wilson have rigged up some blankets on ropes to make a small cubicle. There is a noticed pinned to the blanket which reads 'Officers and Sergeants only'. We can hear voices – Frazer, Godfrey and Pike enter with several other members of the platoon.

PIKE That was a smashing tea.

FRAZER It wasner bad at all, laddie, they're certainly doing their best to make us feel comfortable.

PIKE The seed cake was lovely.

GODFREY Unfortunately, I can't eat caraway seeds, they give me shocking indigestion.

FRAZER Why did you bring a slice back with you, then?

GODFREY I'm going to eat it later – after I've picked all the seeds out.

Frazer sees the blankets.

FRAZER What's that?

They all cross over to the cubicle.

FRAZER Look! Officers and Sergeants only.

PIKE I wonder why Mr Mainwaring did that?

FRAZER It's obvious – he's getting ideas above his station – he really thinks he's an officer.

GODFREY But he *is* an officer – and after all, he's entitled to his privacy...

FRAZER Snobbish rubbish – we're a civilian army and he's only holding an emergency commission.

Jones and Walker enter with some other members of the platoon.

FRAZER Hey, boys – come and look at this.

WALKER **(Reading notice)** Officers and Sergeants only – that's a bit strong, ain't it?

JONES That's not like Mr Mainwaring – we always muck in together.

Mainwaring and Wilson enter.

MAINWARING Well, men, did you all have a good tea?

The platoon give him a surly look.

MAINWARING You know, I think we're going to be very comfortable here. Now, I'm going to put some gramophone records on. Have any of you any particular requests?

FRAZER How about 'Don't Fence Me In'?

MAINWARING **(Coldly)** I don't think I've got that one, Frazer. **(He goes in the cubicle)**

WALKER **(To Wilson)** Hey, Sarge – why has Mr Mainwaring gone all toffee-nosed?

WILSON He thinks it's bad for discipline for us to sleep with the O.R.s.

WALKER Eh?

WILSON Other ranks.

MAINWARING **(From inside cubicle)** Hurry up, Sergeant, I want you to wind up the gramophone. Go away, boy.

WILSON Right, sir. **(He goes into the cubicle)**

MAINWARING **(Lowering his voice)** What's the matter with Frazer?

WILSON Nothing, as far as I know, sir. **(He starts to wind the gramophone)**

MAINWARING Well, I find his manner distinctly off-hand and rude – what's more, I think he's upset the others.

WILSON How do you mean, sir?

MAINWARING When I came back from tea just now, I noticed there was a change in the atmosphere – the men looked very surly and sullen – I'm very sensitive to these things, you know, Wilson.

WILSON Perhaps you've upset them?

MAINWARING Don't be absurd, I've hardly said a word to them since we've arrived. If anybody's upset them it's Frazer. You don't think he's a communist, do you?

WILSON What on earth makes you say that?

MAINWARING I don't know – he just sort of looks like a communist. And I've noticed that when we're on night duty, he never plays Monopoly with the others.

WILSON Oh really, sir.

MAINWARING You can laugh, Wilson – but I'm a pretty shrewd judge of these things – and I've just got a feeling in my bones that he's a Bolshie.

WILSON Well, they are fighting on our side, sir.

MAINWARING Ah – yes – well, we won't go into that now – all I can say is, it's a pity. I've looked forward to this weekend bombing for ages – it's a comfortable camp – the food's good – and they're doing their best to make us feel at home – then Frazer goes and ruins everything.

WILSON I'm sure you're mistaken, sir.

MAINWARING Well, let's put on some records – perhaps that will boost their morale. **(He picks some records and hands a few to Wilson)**

WILSON Good idea, sir – what about this – Vera Lynn singing 'It's a lovely day tomorrow'?

MAINWARING Oh, no – I think something classical would be better – here, put this on. **(He hands Wilson a record)**

WILSON **(Reading labels)** The Warsaw Concerto. **(He puts it on)**

MAINWARING Wonderful music, Wilson. You can't beat those old masters – they don't make up tunes like that nowadays, you know. Doesn't it make the blood tingle in your veins?

WILSON Yes, sir – awfully nice.

The Sergeant Major enters. The Warsaw Concerto is playing in the background.

W.O. Now, pay attention, gentlemen – you'll be pleased to hear that you're all off duty until lights out at 22.00 hours. Now, there's a free issue of two pints of beer each in the canteen – we're not giving you any more because, for some mysterious reason, Captain Reed wants you to have a steady hand when you throw those bombs about in the morning.

JONES Don't you worry about us, Sergeant Major – you can tell Captain Reed we shall be there first thing, ready and steady.

W.O. That should cheer him up no end.

He goes. Mainwaring and Wilson come out of the cubicle.

MAINWARING What did the Sergeant Major want, Jones?

JONES He says there's a free issue of two pints of beer each in the canteen.

MAINWARING Excellent – we'll have a nice, convivial evening together before we turn in. Come on, let's get ready.

Captain Square enters.

SQUARE Hello, Mainwaring – coming down to the mess for a drink?

MAINWARING What mess?

SQUARE Officer's mess, of course – thought we might have a chota peg or two.

MAINWARING As a matter of fact, we were all on our way to the canteen.

SQUARE Now, look here, Mainwaring. **(He draws Mainwaring to one side and lowers his voice)** There's nothing wrong with the odd drink with the men now and again – but you don't want to overdo it.

MAINWARING Well, we were only going to have a couple of pints together.

SQUARE The other officers are all down in the mess – and if you don't turn up, they might think you were a bit odd.

MAINWARING Really? I wouldn't want them to think that.

SQUARE Of course you wouldn't.

MAINWARING I'll just get my hat. **(He calls)** Wilson!

Mainwaring goes into the cubicle. Wilson follows him. During the whole of this scene, Jones, Walker, Frazer, Godfrey and Pike are standing in a sullen group. The rest of the platoon are standing by their bedding also staring hard.

MAINWARING Look, Wilson, it's a bit of a bore, but I've got to go and have a drink in the officer's mess.

WILSON Oh, I see – then you won't be coming with us?

MAINWARING No, I'm afraid not – I mean, if I don't turn up, the other officers might think I'm a bit odd. You do understand, don't you?

WILSON Oh yes, sir – I mean you don't want to look odd, do you?

MAINWARING Well, I'll er… see you later, Wilson. Sorry I can't take you with me, I'm afraid it's officers only. Look after the men – see that they have a good time. Where's my hat?

He goes out of the cubicle, Wilson follows him. The platoon all stare at him as he comes through the blankets. Square is waiting at the marquee opening. Mainwaring walks down past the platoon, he stops and turns.

MAINWARING **(Tripping over Pike's boots)** You stupid boy. **(With forced bonhomie)** Well, chaps, have a good time tonight. Enjoy yourselves – and er – don't do anything I wouldn't do.

SQUARE Come on, Mainwaring.

Mainwaring crosses quickly to the opening and he and Square go out. Jones, Walker, Frazer, Godfrey and Pike all look at Wilson who is standing at the cubicle. Then they look at each other in disgust.

INTERIOR. OFFICER'S MESS TENT. EVENING

There are a few campstools round a small low table. Two Home Guard officers are sitting round the table: Captain Pritchard and Captain Ashley-Jones. They are both men in their 50s, with quite a few medal ribbons including the 1914–1918 ribbons. The tent is lit by several hurricane lamps. In the background is a table with a few bottles on it. A regular army mess orderly is just finishing lighting the hurricane lamps – the two Captains have large whiskys in their hands. There is a siphon of soda on the table.

PRITCHARD …there it was, hanging out of the window – large as life.

They both roar with laughter. Square and Mainwaring enter.

SQUARE Hello, chaps – this is Mainwaring, Walmington-on-Sea platoon.

They all nod greetings.

SQUARE Pritchard – H.Q., and Ashley-Jones, Dymwych platoon. Take your belt off. What are you going to have? Same again?

The two Captains nod their heads and quickly drain their glasses. The orderly comes over.

SQUARE Three large whiskys – what are you going to have, Mainwaring?

MAINWARING Er… could I have a sweet sherry, please?

They all stare at him, aghast.

SQUARE A sweet sherry!!

ORDERLY I'm sorry, sir, all we've got is a whisky.

SQUARE And damn lucky to get that – make it four large whiskys.

ORDERLY Right, sir.

MAINWARING I don't think I can manage a large one.

SQUARE Don't tell me you don't drink.

MAINWARING Well, I usually have a glass of beer after parade and the odd sherry now and again.

SQUARE Drop of whisky won't hurt you – it's so damned hard to get these days. You want to drink it while you can, you know, Mainwaring – there I go again, must call you Mannering.

ASHLEY-JONES I knew a feller out in India used to call himself Chumleigh – spelt his name Cholmondeley – we always used to call him Chilly Mushrooms. Absolutely silly arse he was.

ORDERLY **(Putting the drinks on the table)** Here you are, sir.

SQUARE Thank you. **(He quickly puts a tiny splash of soda in four glasses and hands them round)** Cheers!

They all drain their glasses. Mainwaring does a take.

MAINWARING Cheers! **(Not wishing to be left out, starts to drink)**

INTERIOR. CANTEEN. NIGHT

A slightly larger tent than the officer's mess. There is a long trestle table – the platoon is sitting at it, à la the last supper. Wilson is in the centre – on his left is Jones, Pike and Godfrey – on his right, Walker and Frazer. In front of them there are two pints of beer each. They are all looking very miserable. In the background are two more tables with the rest of the platoon sitting drinking.

WILSON **(In hollow voice)** Cheers.

ALL Cheers.

They all drink, put their mugs down and stare into space. There is a long silence.

FRAZER This is the end.

JONES Eh?

FRAZER I said, this is the end.

JONES What are you talking about? I've still got a whole bottle left.

FRAZER As soon as we get back, I'm resigning.

WALKER You can't do that, Taff – your country needs you.

FRAZER If the time comes, I shall be there – but I'm not serving under Mainwaring any more.

Pause.

PIKE Uncle Arthur?

WILSON What?

PIKE Would you like to finish my beer?

WILSON No thank you, Frank – I'm afraid I'm not in the mood for drinking.

GODFREY I don't think we ought to blame Mr Mainwaring. I think he's been led astray by Captain Square, and as one of the old members of the platoon, Mr Frazer – I think you ought to give him another chance.

FRAZER (Muttering) Silly old fool.

JONES There's no need to be rude to Mr Godfrey, Jock.

FRAZER Well, he is a silly old fool – calling me old.

JONES Well, you are old.

FRAZER I'm not as old as you are, you old fool.

JONES And I'm not as old as you are, you old fool. I'm not 60 yet.

WALKER You told me you tried to relieve General Gordon when he was bottled up in Khartoum by the Mad Mahdi. Blimey, you must be over 90.

JONES I was a boy soldier.

WALKER What did they do, pin the medal on your napkin?

WILSON Oh, Walker – please.

INTERIOR. OFFICER'S MESS. NIGHT

There are now two bottles of whisky on the table. The three officers are all roaring with laughter. Mainwaring is feeling left out.

SQUARE ...old Bungey rode his polo pony right through the mess – and all through it the punkah wallah was fast asleep – still pulling his punkah – with his foot! (They all roar with laughter) What a night that was. (Square fills the glasses)

MAINWARING No more for me, thank you.

SQUARE Nonsense – you must keep up. (He fills his glass) Cheers!

They all drink.

CONWAY Whatever became of old Bungey?

SQUARE Never saw him after that.

ASHLEY-JONES He was a good chap – only one trouble – couldn't leave the little brown girls alone.

SQUARE I shall never forget one night in the mess in Jubbulpore, when we made him a Cardinal.

ASHLEY-JONES How did he take it?

SQUARE Went through it like a lamb.

CONWAY That takes me back a bit. Haven't seen anybody made a Cardinal for donkey's years.

MAINWARING Er... how can you make somebody a Cardinal?

SQUARE It's a little ceremony we used to perform in the mess years ago.

MAINWARING What do you have to do?

SQUARE Why, do you want to be made one?

They all laugh.

MAINWARING (Feeling reckless) Well, I might.

Mainwaring, by now, is just a little tipsy and is determined to keep up with the others.

SQUARE Us old soldiers are used to it – but I think you'd find it a bit too much.

MAINWARING Oh no, I wouldn't. (Taking the plunge) I want to be made a Cardinal.

SQUARE All right, shall we make him a Cardinal, boys?

ASHLEY-JONES/CONWAY Yes.

SQUARE (Fills his glass) Right, I'll just go through it a few times – so that you can get the hang of it. Here's to the health of Cardinal 'Puff' for the first time. Tap the table with the first finger of your right hand and the first finger of your left hand. Stamp once with your right foot and once with your left foot. Bang the glass on the table once and take one drink. Here's to the health of Cardinal 'Puff-Puff' for the second time. Tap the table with the first and second fingers of your right hand and first and second fingers of your left hand. Stamp your right foot twice, stamp your left foot twice. Bang the glass on the table twice and take two drinks. Here's to the health of Cardinal 'Puff-Puff-Puff' for the third and last time. Tap the table with the first, second and third fingers of your right hand, first, second and third fingers of your left hand. Stamp your right foot three times, left foot three times. Bang the glass on the table three times and take three drinks. Have you got it?

MAINWARING No, not quite.

SQUARE I'll show you again. Here's to the health of Cardinal 'Puff'...

INTERIOR. THE CANTEEN. NIGHT

Wilson, Jones, Walker, Frazer and Godfrey are all sitting silently over their beer. Suddenly, Jones bursts into...

JONES So the commercial traveller said (Laughs) I'm sorry, madam, I only work from Monday to Friday.

They stare at him in stony silence.

JONES Well, I thought it was funny.

PIKE I know some jokes – listen, Uncle Arthur, I've got twopence in one hand and twopence in the other – how much have I got?

WILSON Fourpence.

PIKE Wrong – sixpence – I've got twopence in my pocket. Three tomatoes are running across the desert – which one is the cowboy?

WILSON I've really no idea.

PIKE None of them – there were all redskins. I've got another one – Why did the submarine blush? Give up – Because it saw Queen Mary's bottom.

Pause.

GODFREY I don't think Queen Mary would like that.

PIKE Sorry, Uncle Arthur.

INTERIOR. OFFICER'S MESS. NIGHT

SQUARE ...bang the glass on the table three times and take three drinks. Now, is that clear?

MAINWARING Yes, I think so. **(He stands up)**

Square fills his glass.

SQUARE Now, don't forget. If you go wrong you have to drain the glass and go right back to the start.

MAINWARING Here's to the health of Cardinal 'Puff' for the first time.

He taps with his right and left finger. Stamps with his right and left foot, picks up the glass and drinks.

SQUARE/CONWAY/ASHLEY-JONES Wrong!

SQUARE You forgot to bang the glass on the table. Start again.

MAINWARING Oh sorry. Here's to the health...

SQUARE Must drain the glass first, old boy.

Mainwaring finishes the glass. He tries to get his breath back. Square quickly refills it.

MAINWARING Here's to the health of Cardinal Puff for the first time.

He goes through the first motions and gets them right – bangs the glass on the table and drinks. They all cheer him.

MAINWARING Here's to the health of Cardinal 'Puff-Puff' for the second time. **(He taps the table with one finger)**

ALL Wrong!

Mainwaring reacts.

SQUARE You only tapped with one finger, you should have used two. Start again.

MAINWARING Here's to the health...

SQUARE Don't forget to empty the glass first.

MAINWARING What? Oh, sorry. **(He drains the glass)**

INTERIOR. CANTEEN. NIGHT

In the distance we can hear shouts and cheers from the officer's mess.

FRAZER Just listen to them – a disgrace, that's what it is.

WALKER I can't think what's come over Mr Mainwaring – he's never behaved like this before.

JONES When I was in the Sudan – there used to be right goings on in the officer's mess. Mind you – you had to be careful – if you drank too much in that heat it used to turn you into a jibbering idiot.

WALKER You must have knocked it back a bit then.

INTERIOR. OFFICER'S MESS. NIGHT

Mainwaring is still on his feet and, by now, is quite drunk. The other three are pretty far gone.

MAINWARING Here's to the health of Cardinal 'Puff-Puff-Puff-Puff'.

SQUARE Wrong.

MAINWARING What is?

SQUARE Cardinal 'Puff-Puff-Puff-Puff'.

MAINWARING What's wrong with that?

SQUARE Wrong with what?

MAINWARING 'Puff-Puff' 'Puff-Puff.'

SQUARE Too many 'Puffs'.

MAINWARING What are you talking about – too many 'Puffs'? Yes, you're right – I should have said Cardinal 'Puff-Puff-Puff' and not Cardinal 'Puff-Puff' 'Puff-Puff'.

SQUARE Start again. **(He fills Mainwaring's glass)**

MAINWARING Right. Here's to the health of the Archbishop of Canterbury.

SQUARE What's that got to do with it?

MAINWARING Same thing, it's all religious.

SQUARE It's the wrong denomination.

MAINWARING What's the wrong denom – denom – denomination?

SQUARE One's R.C., the other's C of E.

MAINWARING Oh! Here's to the health of the Archbishop of Canterbury who is a friend of Cardinal 'Puff-Puff' 'Puff-Puff'. How's that?

SQUARE Still too many 'Puffs'.

INTERIOR. MARQUEE. NIGHT

The platoon is all asleep, camera pans along sleeping figures. Suddenly we hear Mainwaring's voice softly chanting 'Puff Puff'. The flap opens and he staggers in and carefully steps over the sleeping figures. He reaches Jones, trips and falls on top of him. Jones wakes.

JONES Yeow! **(He grabs Mainwaring by the throat)** I'm sorry, Mr Mainwaring.

MAINWARING **(Blissfully)** 'Puff-Puff' 'Puff-Puff.'

INTERIOR. MARQUEE. DAY

Captain Reed and the W.O. enter. They are both carrying clipboards. In the distance, we can hear grenades going off.

CAPTAIN Right, that's the Eastgate platoon, Littlebourne-on-Sea platoon and Dymwych platoon – they've all thrown one grenade each. **(There are two bangs, the Captain starts to twitch)** What was that, what was that? I heard two going off at once.

W.O. That's the Walmington-on-Sea Platoon. I think Sergeant Williams is trying to get them finished quickly.

CAPTAIN If he's not careful they'll finish *him* quickly. They're the maddest of the lot. Especially that little old Lance Corporal. **(He twitches)**

Suddenly we hear a groan coming from the cubicle.

CAPTAIN What's that?

There is another groan. The blankets part and Mainwaring stands in the opening, looking terrible. They both hurry over to him.

CAPTAIN Are you all right, Captain Mainwaring? You look ill.

MAINWARING What time is it?

CAPTAIN Eleven thirty.

MAINWARING Where are my men?

CAPTAIN They're all down on the bombing range. I'm giving them a lecture on sticky bombs in ten minutes' time.

MAINWARING I'll come with you.

CAPTAIN Are you sure you feel up to it?

MAINWARING Yes, of course – come on. I don't want to miss the bombing.

The Captain and W.O. exchange looks.

TELECINE: EXTERIOR. FIELD. DAY

The platoon is sitting in a circle on the ground. Captain Reed is holding a sticky bomb. The warrant officer is standing beside him. There is a box of sticky bombs on the ground. Mainwaring is standing with them, looking very odd.

CAPTAIN ...and that covers the nine main points of the sticky bomb – now, before we put it into practical use, are there any questions? **(They all shake their heads)** Right, carry on, Sergeant Major.

WARRANT OFFICER Right, now, pay attention! I want you to imagine that that... **(He points to a mock up of a tank made of corrugated iron and dustbins)** ...is a Nazi tank. Right, line up. **(They all get in a line)** You're first, Sergeant. **(He hands Wilson a bomb)**. Now, you walk smartly up to the tank, don't run, pull the pin out – the cover drops off – and you press the bomb to the side of the tank – to which it will adhere itself. Once the glass breaks inside the bomb – you've got exactly 15 seconds to get clear.

Wilson starts to fiddle with the bomb.

CAPTAIN **(Shouting and twitching)** Don't pull the pin out! Don't pull it out.

WILSON **(Soothingly)** I wasn't going to.

W.O. **(To platoon)** I want you all to go up to the tank with him so that you get the hang of it. Now, whatever you do, don't run – do you understand? Don't run, because a) you don't want to attract the attention of the enemy and b) you don't want to trip and fall flat on your face and blow yourselves up.

Close up of Captain Reed twitching madly.

W.O. Right, off you go. **(He blows his whistle)**

The platoon all walk in a line slowly towards the tank – they reach it. Wilson pulls the pin of his bomb out, the cover drops off. He sticks the bomb on the tank. They all walk away.

W.O. Don't run – don't run. 1-2-3-4-5-6-7-8-9-10, right, down!

They all drop flat on their faces. There is a loud explosion. Close up of Mainwaring's face as he winces.

W.O. Right, Corporal – you're next. **(He hands Jones a bomb)** Now, remember, don't run.

JONES Don't run – right, Sergeant Major.

The platoon all walk in a line towards the tank – they reach it. Jones pulls out the pin – the cover drops off. He sticks the bomb on a dustbin lid. Different angle of platoon without

Jones. They walk away – suddenly they start to run. Close up of Jones.

JONES What are you all running for? You're not supposed to run.

Mid shot of Jones, he looks down at his hand. He is still holding the bomb with the dustbin lid stuck to it. He quickly throws it away. There is a loud explosion. Close up of Mainwaring's face.

TELECINE: EXTERIOR. BOMBING RANGE. DAY

The platoon is sitting a little way from the firing position. Mainwaring and Wilson are standing away from the platoon. Jones' van is parked nearby – the back doors are open. Inside are packed quite a few boxes of grenades, on the ground are four more boxes of grenades. At the firing position, Captain Reed and the W.O. are standing beside Frazer. They are firing grenades from a cup discharger fitted to a P.14 rifle.

W.O. Right, take it steady and don't fire until I say. (He puts a grenade in the cup) Fire!

Frazer pulls the trigger, the grenade soars in the air and explodes.

CAPTAIN Not bad at all.

W.O. (Shouting) Next.

Frazer crosses over to the rest of the platoon and another Private takes his place.

W.O. Only two more to fire, sir.

CAPTAIN (Shouting at Mainwaring) Captain Mainwaring, we shan't need any more grenades – tell your men to load the rest of the boxes on to the van.

MAINWARING Right, sir. (He shouts to the platoon) Walker, Jones, Sponge – put the rest of those boxes back in the van.

They all give Mainwaring a surly look and move over to the van and start to load.

MAINWARING I feel terrible, Wilson. After what happened last night I'm afraid the men will never look up to me again.

WILSON They'll get over it in time, sir.

MAINWARING No they won't – once an officer forfeits the respect of his men, he's done for.

The next man fires.

W.O. Right, last man.

Pike takes his place at the firing point. Mainwaring walks over to the van.

MAINWARING We've nearly finished. Jones, you can drive it away when I give you the signal. I'll bang on the back.

JONES (Getting into the cab) Right, sir.

The W.O. puts the grenade in the cup.

W.O. Are you ready, lad?

PIKE Yes, I'm ready.

W.O. Fire!

Pike presses the trigger, nothing happens.

PIKE I think it's broken, sir.

W.O. You've got the safety catch on, you silly lad. All right, I'll do it.

He reaches down, close up of lots of fingers round safety catch and trigger.

PIKE (Out of vision) It still won't go, sir. Oh!

The rifle goes off and at the same time jerks back. Close up of Mainwaring and Wilson's faces as they follow the grenade flying through the air. Close up of grenade going through roof of van.

JONES There's no need to bang as loud as that, Mr Mainwaring (He drives off)

WALKER Blimey!

They all stand petrified. Mainwaring breaks away, picks up a bike and rides after the van. View from inside van. Mainwaring is pedalling furiously behind the van shouting 'Jones – Jones'. Close up of grenade on top of boxes. It rolls about and falls down in between them. Mainwaring grabs a rope hanging from the back of the van and climbs on. Mainwaring is inside the van, looking for grenade. Long shot of Captain and platoon running after van. The van is now going quite fast. Jones is driving along, singing. Mainwaring's face appears at the hole behind him.

MAINWARING Jones, Jones.

JONES Hello, Mr Mainwaring. Where did you come from?

MAINWARING Quick, stop the van.

JONES Eh!

MAINWARING Stop the van, there's a live grenade in the back.

JONES What! Don't panic. Don't panic.

MAINWARING Get out, man.

JONES Right, sir – right, sir. (He jumps out)

MAINWARING I meant stop the van first, you idiot.

He reaches through and grabs the wheel.

TELECINE: EXTERIOR. POWER STATION. DAY

Close up of large notice which reads 'High tension cables – danger – keep out'. The van is approaching, zigzagging. There are several other notices all round. View from inside van as Mainwaring sees notice. The van slows down and stops. Mainwaring jumps out and runs to Jones.

MAINWARING Quick, Jones, take cover. That whole lot could blow up any minute.

They both dive for cover. Captain Reed, the W.O. and the rest of the platoon run up.

MAINWARING Quick, take cover!

They all dive for cover.

CAPTAIN There are 200 grenades in that van. If that lot goes up it will wreck the power station and put the whole defence of the county out of action.

MAINWARING Are you sure?

CAPTAIN Of course I am.

Mainwaring jumps up and runs to the van.

CAPTAIN Come back, you fool!

Mainwaring climbs into the van, starts to move the boxes. He finds the grenade and jumps out.

MAINWARING I've got it. (He hurls it away and throws himself flat on the ground)

JONES Well done, Mr Mainwaring.

The platoon all cheer. The cheer dies out as a look of horror comes on their faces. Close up of Mainwaring's face. The grenade drops beside him. He looks up, a dog is wagging his tail and panting. Mainwaring jumps to his feet and runs. The dog picks up the grenade in his mouth and runs after him.

SERIES FOUR **CHRISTMAS SPECIAL**

Recorded: Sunday 19/9/71

Original transmission: Monday 27/12/71, 7.00–8.00pm

Original viewing figures = 18.7 million

ARTHUR LOWE .... CAPTAIN MAINWARING
JOHN LE MESURIER .... SERGEANT WILSON
CLIVE DUNN .... LANCE CORPORAL JONES
JOHN LAURIE .... PRIVATE FRAZER
JAMES BECK .... PRIVATE WALKER
ARNOLD RIDLEY .... PRIVATE GODFREY
IAN LAVENDER .... PRIVATE PIKE
BILL PERTWEE .... ARP WARDEN
FRANK WILLIAMS .... VICAR
EDWARD SINCLAIR .... VERGER
GEOFFREY LUMSDEN .... CAPTAIN SQUARE
ROBERT RAGLAN .... THE COLONEL
CHARLES HILL .... SERGEANT PARKINS
COLIN BEAN .... PRIVATE SPONGE
ROSEMARY FAITH .... SHIRLEY, THE BARMAID

PLATOON .... GEORGE HANCOCK, EMMETT HENNESSY, ... LINDSAY HOOPER, MICHAEL MOORE, LESLIE NOYES, ... VIC TAYLOR, FREDDIE WHITE, FREDDIE WILES, HUGH HASTINGS

MESSENGER BOY .... PAUL HUCKIN

OTHER EXTRAS .... DOUGLAS BARTIN, BILL LODGE, ... FRED GAMBIA, WILLIAM CURRAN, JONATHAN KEYS, ... EMMETT HENNESSY, JOHN BELSEY

BATTLE OF THE GIANTS!

• ROSEMARY FAITH REMEMBERS •

'I initially got the part of Ivy Samways in "Mum's Army" because I had worked for David Croft in *Beggar My Neighbour*. Naturally I was a little apprehensive as I didn't know the regulars, but was pleased when I saw Carmen Silvera was in the same episode, as she had been extremely kind to me when I did my very first television part playing her assistant in *Beggar My Neighbour*, before becoming June Whitfield's daughter, Deirdre Garvey, in later series. Pamela Cundell, Janet Davies and Wendy Richard were also very friendly.

'I still recall Ian Lavender sitting beside me and saying in his Pike character: "You're Ivy Samways, you're my girlfriend." In a later episode, when I was not available, Ivy was played by his then wife.

'The men, too, were all very welcoming and many seemed to be quite similar to their characters, although Clive was a lot younger. Another lovely person was Arthur Lowe's wife, actress Joan Cooper. When I

wanted to borrow some sheet music from Arthur for an audition, Joan rehearsed me at their home and my audition for a West End musical was successful.

'John Laurie was another one who was always very sweet to me, and he always called me "his wee pet lamb". In "The Godiva Affair" I kept getting the odd little extra bit and John would sidle up to me and say: "Och, they've given the wee pet lamb a wee bit more to do." As I recall, I did quite well out of "The Godiva Affair" because it was rehearsed and abandoned twice because of strikes or something before it was finally recorded. I got paid three times as, I expect, everyone else did. Only trouble was I had lost a lot of weight for another show and was very proud of my new slim figure in the '40s-style bikini. By the third attempt I had put on some weight, was back in a bathing suit and the little tum was more prominent in the production photos.

'I only ever had bits and pieces to do in "Battle of the Giants!", and my few lines were cut to one or two, so I always feel embarrassed when my name appears on the credits, but you know, the less you have to do, the harder it is.

'The cast were always courteous and kind to me, although Arnold Ridley never remembered me from one episode to the next. "Too many people passing through" he explained at a West End party looking rather bemused when I introduced myself to him again!'

ROSEMARY FAITH

Battle of the Giants!

INTERIOR. CHURCH HALL. DAY

Jones is addressing the platoon who are standing in a group, with Pike, Walker, Frazer and Godfrey in the front. They all have rifles and fixed bayonets with the exception of Godfrey. Behind Jones is a stuffed dummy on a wooden frame directly in line with the office door. Walker has a cigarette in his mouth.

JONES Captain Mainwaring is very busy this evening and he's asked me to give you a lecture on bayonet drill. Now remember, boys, there's no substitute for the old cold steel – they don't like it up 'em, you know – they do not like it up them – which I may have mentioned to you before.

FRAZER Many times – many, many times.

WALKER You can say that again, Taff.

JONES Silence in the ranks – I will not have talking when I'm talking – and put that cigarette out, Private Walker.

Walker stubs cigarette.

JONES Now, a very important item to remember is the scream – this is the thing that really puts the wind up the enemy – now, you fill your lungs up with air and let it out like this. **(Screams)**

Platoon react.

JONES I want you all to try it – deep breath – hold it. **(To Godfrey)** As you're the medical orderly, why don't you go and put the kettle on?

GODFREY I'll stay, if you don't mind, Mr Jones – I should rather like to do some screaming.

JONES Very well. Now, all together – fill up with air and let it out – ready?

They all scream.

INTERIOR. SIDE OFFICE. DAY

Mainwaring and Wilson are sitting each side of the desk, working on papers.

WILSON What a terrible noise! What are they doing out there?

MAINWARING Bayonet practice, of course.

WILSON Well, couldn't they do it a little more quietly?

MAINWARING Of course they can't do it quietly – it's Action – that's what it is, Wilson – Action with a capital 'A'.

WILSON Oh, is it?

MAINWARING I wouldn't mind you showing some Action, Wilson – doing a bit of screaming.

WILSON Somehow I don't think screaming is quite my style, sir.

MAINWARING Sometimes I wonder – just what your style is, Wilson.

There is a knock on the back door.

MAINWARING See who that is.

Wilson crosses to the back door and opens it – a boy is standing outside – he hands Wilson a paper bag.

WILSON For Mr Mainwaring – oh, thank you very much. **(He shuts the door and crosses back to Mainwaring with the bag)** It's for you, sir, from Gills the Tailors.

MAINWARING Good, I've been waiting for this for weeks. **(Mainwaring takes a new hat out of the bag and crosses to the mirror)** It's come just in time for the parade.

WILSON What parade?

MAINWARING The ceremonial church parade on Sunday – we've been discussing it for weeks, Wilson.

WILSON Oh yes, of course.

Mainwaring takes his old hat off and puts on the new one.

MAINWARING What do you think of it?

WILSON What do I think of what?

MAINWARING The hat, of course.

WILSON Awfully nice, sir.

INTERIOR. CHURCH HALL. DAY

JONES Right, Private Pike.

PIKE Yes, Mr Jones?

JONES Now, when you charge that stuffed dummy of Hitler in person – let's hear your scream, lad. **(He screams)** Right – screaming and bayoneting Hitler – in person – in your own time – begin.

Pike gives a blood-curdling scream and charges the dummy – he misses it – the dummy falls off the frame and Pike, unable to stop, charges the office door.

INTERIOR. SIDE OFFICE. DAY

Mainwaring takes his hat off and crosses to the peg on the door. We can hear Pike scream.

MAINWARING I shall wear this for the first time at the parade on Sunday. **(He is still holding the hat as he goes to**

hang it on the peg) I want the whole Battalion to see just how smart we really are.

There is a crash – the bayonet comes through the door and through his hat – he stares at the ruined hat, unable to believe his eyes.

MAINWARING My hat – my hat... who the... **(He tries to open the door but Pike, holding on to his rifle, stops him)** ...Open this door – open it at once – who is that?

PIKE **(Out of vision)** It's me, Mr Mainwaring.

MAINWARING Let go – let go at once.

Pike lets go and Mainwaring jerks at the door – Mainwaring falls back in a heap – Wilson helps him up.

PIKE I'm sorry, Mr Mainwaring, I couldn't stop myself.

MAINWARING You... you stupid boy. **(He holds up his hat)** Look at my hat.

Pike pokes his finger through the tear and wriggles it.

PIKE Oh dear – look at the hole. Was your head in it?

The phone rings. Wilson picks it up.

MAINWARING **(Shouting)** You did that with your bayonet.

WILSON **(On phone)** Oh hullo – how awfully nice to hear your voice.

MAINWARING I shall stop the money for this out of your wages, Pike.

PIKE You can't do that.

WILSON Your wife, sir.

MAINWARING What?

WILSON Your wife, sir.

MAINWARING What... **(He crosses down to Wilson and takes the phone. He puts his hand over the mouthpiece)** Tell her I'm not here, Wilson.

WILSON She heard you shouting, sir.

MAINWARING Oh really. **(Into phone)** Er – hello, Elizabeth – yes, dear, yes, dear – I know, dear, but the fact is I just couldn't stand sleeping with you any longer.

Look from Wilson.

MAINWARING Down in the shelter – but we haven't had any air raids for months, dear, and it's so uncomfortable down there – no – no, dear, I didn't deliberately wait until you'd gone out to move the bedding from the shelter. **(Mainwaring turns and sees Pike grinning in the doorway)** Don't stand there gawping, boy – get out. **(Pike goes)** ...no ...no ...not you, dear ...what? But I can't come and move the bedding back into the shelter now – There's no question of dismissing the parade for another hour... what?... oh, yes... yes... very well... **(He hangs up)** – you'll have to dismiss the parade. **(He picks up his old hat and crosses to the door)**

WILSON I wouldn't take it too much to heart, sir – marriage is an institution in which one has to give and take, you know.

MAINWARING I'll see you at the Bank in the morning, Wilson – good night.

WILSON Good night, sir.

Mainwaring returns and changes hat.

INTERIOR. CHURCH HALL. DAY

JONES **(By dummy)** Right, now – we'll move the dummy up to the other end of the hall so that we don't have any more accidents.

SERGEANT Captain Square.

Captain Square and Sergeant Parkins come through the main doors and crosses to the office.

JONES Platoon, attention. **(Jones salutes Square)** Good evening, sir.

SQUARE Evening, Corporal. **(To men)** Evening, men. **(The men mutter 'evening')**. Captain Mainwaring in?

JONES Yes, sir – I'll tell him you're here.

SQUARE Don't bother – I'll just breeze in. **(He points to Jones' medals)**. You've got an impressive collection of medals there, Corporal.

JONES Yes, sir – I'm very proud of them.

SQUARE So you should be, man – so you should be – don't forget, on your chest, you carry an illuminated history of the British Empire. **(He crosses to the office door)** Very sound – very sound. **(He taps the door and goes in)**

SERGEANT Captain Square to see you, sir.

Wilson salutes.

INTERIOR. SIDE OFFICE. DAY

Wilson is sitting at the desk – Square comes in.

SQUARE Evening, Sergeant.

WILSON **(Getting up)** Good evening, sir.

SQUARE This is Sergeant Parkins – my Butler, rotten Sergeant – damn good Butler.

SQUARE Captain Mainwaring about?

WILSON I'm afraid he's just gone home, sir. Can I help in any way?

SQUARE **(He lowers his voice)** You haven't by any chance got a drop of happy juice, have you?

WILSON Happy juice?

SQUARE Puggle Parni, man – Puggle Parni.

WILSON Puggle Parni?

SQUARE Whisky – where does Mainwaring keep his whisky?

WILSON He doesn't drink it.

SQUARE Extraordinary! In that case I won't stay long. Prepare to sit, Parkins – sit – I just wanted to make sure that Mainwaring had received the orders that I sent last week.

WILSON What orders?

SQUARE About the medals.

WILSON What medals?

SQUARE Why do you keep repeating everything I say, Sergeant – what's the matter with you?

WILSON Nothing, sir – I just can't quite follow your drift.

SQUARE **(Slowly as though talking to an idiot)** When I was acting adjutant – I sent out the Battalion orders which stated – that at the ceremonial church parade on Sunday – all decorations and medals will be worn – and Mainwaring hasn't acknowledged it.

WILSON We didn't get it, sir.

SQUARE You must have got it, man – ten days ago it was. Isn't that right, Sergeant?

SERGEANT Yes – Cook delivered it personally, sir.

WILSON I can assure you, sir, that we didn't get it. Wait a minute, I remember now – we were going through the papers and Captain Mainwaring put one of them in his drawer – when I asked him what it was he said it was nothing important.

SQUARE Have a look in his drawer.

WILSON I can't do that.

SQUARE Of course you can – he's left you in charge.

WILSON I suppose you're right.

He opens the drawer – pulls out some papers and looks through them.

WILSON I wonder why he put it away? I think this is it.

SQUARE **(Snatching paper)** I'll soon tell you – yes – this is it. **(He reads)** At the ceremonial church parade on Sunday August 21st 1941 – all decorations and medals will be worn – signed Captain Square Acting Adjutant – pompous idiot – pompous... **(Rise)** Who wrote this on the bottom?

WILSON It wasn't me, sir.

SQUARE Damned cheek! Wait a minute – wait a minute – the penny's beginning to drop. Now, look here, in the last shindig, I was with Lawrence, in the desert, fighting Johnny Turk. Who were you fighting?

WILSON Just the usual Germans, sir.

SQUARE And what about Mainwaring?

WILSON He wasn't fighting anybody – he was in the army of occupation after the war.

SQUARE I thought so – that's why he didn't read these orders out – hasn't got any medals himself – doesn't want anybody else to wear them – dog in the manger – if everybody else isn't wearing medals – then no one will know that he hasn't got any – doesn't want to be shown up.

WILSON I wonder if you're right?

SQUARE Of course I'm right. Now, look here – when you dismiss the parade tonight, you're to read these orders out – do you understand? That's an order, Sergeant. **(He crosses to the door)** Goodnight. **(He goes)**

WILSON **(Looking at paper)** ...all decorations and medals will be worn – signed Captain Square – pompous idiot – hmmm.

INTERIOR. SIDE OFFICE

Mainwaring is at his desk. Wilson enters from hall.

WILSON The men are sort of lined up if you'd like to run your eye over them.

MAINWARING Run my eye over them! They're not a balance sheet, Wilson. They're a trained fighting unit and you're supposed to be their Sergeant. **(He crosses to door and turns)** For heaven's sake, get a grip on yourself, Wilson. Get your shoulders back and your chin in and stand up like a man.

WILSON Is that better?

MAINWARING No, not really. **(He turns and goes into hall)**

CHURCH HALL. INTERIOR

Mainwaring enters.

JONES Platoon – platoon, attention.

Platoon come to attention.

JONES Platoon ready for inspection, sir.

MAINWARING Thank you, Corporal Jones.

Jones does turning/saluting business.

MAINWARING Very smart, Jones. **(Sees medals)** Who gave you permission to wear those?

JONES Sergeant Wilson, sir. He ordered me to wear them, sir, and in addition he ordered everybody else to wear theirs as well, also.

MAINWARING I see. (He beckons Wilson aside) What are you up to, Wilson?

WILSON I beg your pardon?

MAINWARING Are you trying to undermine my authority?

WILSON It was a battalion order. I merely passed it on, so to speak.

MAINWARING I see. You've not heard the last of this, Wilson. Report to me after parade. (He confronts Jones)

MAINWARING Are you entitled to all that ironmongery, Jones?

JONES Not iron, sir – that one is the Khediv star – given to me personally by the Khediv when we was in Egypt for the first Sudanese Campaign. It wasn't a campaign against the Egyptians you understand, sir. We was on their side and they was against the Mad Mahdi. He was against General Gordon which meant, of course, that we were against the Mad Mahdi also – us being on the side of General Gordon – him being British like us – do you follow so far, sir?

MAINWARING Thank you, Jones. (He is about to move on)

JONES Now, this one is the Queen's Sudan Medal for the second Sudanese Campaign against the Mad Mahdi.

MAINWARING Yes – most interesting, Jones. (He passes on to Frazer – points to medal with a stick)

JONES I was just coming to the exciting bit.

MAINWARING Later, Jones. Is that an authorised decoration, Frazer, or some foreign thing?

FRAZER That's the Polar Medal, sir, for the Shackleton Expedition.

MAINWARING Oh really?

FRAZER 'Twas a wild, lonely place you know, with nothing for the eye to behold but ice and snow – so they made the ribbon white.

MAINWARING Very appropriate.

FRAZER I notice you're not wearing your medals, Captain Mainwaring. Did you leave them at home?

MAINWARING No talking in the ranks, Frazer. (He moves to Godfrey)

JONES Permission to speak, sir?

MAINWARING Yes, Jones.

JONES The Mad Mahdi what we was fighting in the second campaign wasn't the same Mad Mahdi what we fought in the first campaign, but it was his son.

MAINWARING Thank you, Jones.

JONES Now, it's my opinion he wasn't mad at all, but you know what people are, sir, they talk.

MAINWARING Yes, they do.

JONES Mind you, he was mad all right the day he had his horse shot from under him. He was madder than the first Mad Mahdi that day, but I mustn't keep you. You've probably got work to do.

MAINWARING (To Godfrey) I thought you didn't approve of wearing those things, Godfrey.

GODFREY Well, it was an order – and I didn't want to upset you by appearing bare-chested.

MAINWARING You wouldn't have upset me, I assure you.

GODFREY They've come up rather well, haven't they. My sister Dolly had a go at them with powdered chalk and vinegar. Of course lemon juice is even better, but you can't get the lemons.

MAINWARING Thank you, Godfrey – I'll bear it in mind. (To Pike, who is sporting his boy scout badges) What's all this rubbish, boy?

PIKE They're my Scout Badges.

MAINWARING Scout Badges!

PIKE That one's the tenderfoot – that one's for knots and splices – (Points to next) first aid, fire-making and elementary tracking.

MAINWARING You will take those off as soon as this parade is over.

PIKE Well, I didn't want to put 'em on – it was mum. She said if Uncle Arthur – Sergeant Wilson was going to show off – so was I.

MAINWARING Fortunately, Sergeant Wilson has more sense than to... (He turns to Wilson who is attaching his order of medals to his tunic) Wilson! What do you think you're doing?

WILSON Well, I am entitled to them.

MAINWARING You're not entitled to get dressed while I'm inspecting my troops. (Turning to Walker who is wearing an order)

MAINWARING Walker! This is not a musical comedy you know. Take that off at once.

WALKER Here – hang on a minute, Captain Mainwaring. This is the Sacred Order of the Golden Kris of Aba Dhobi.

MAINWARING I suppose it was given to you by the Sheik of Araby.

WALKER Well, it so happens he was a sheik and he had 34 wives and he was stopping in this big hotel in Park Lane and he hadn't brought none with him. Well, I was on the Hall Porters Staff and this sort of Prime Minister geezer who was also an Arab said, 'can you fix him up?', so I said, 'I'll see what I can do', and I got on the blower to a friend and the Sheik was very grateful. He give me this, a kiss on both cheeks and ten quid.

MAINWARING I can't stand any more of this, Wilson.

Dismiss the parade and come in my orderly room. **(He marches to side office)**

WILSON Right now, pay attention. I would like to say on behalf of Captain Mainwaring and myself that we're really awfully grateful for the trouble you've taken over your appearance for this parade. You look really very nice indeed – all of you.

MAINWARING **(Re-entering)** Wilson.

WILSON Right, off you go then and we'll all meet some place – some time – tomorrow – oh – and try to be on time, won't you?

MAINWARING Wilson – in here at the double.

Wilson moves to side office.

INTERIOR. SIDE OFFICE

MAINWARING Shut the door.

He shuts door.

MAINWARING Come here.

Wilson moves.

MAINWARING How dare you?

WILSON I beg your pardon?

MAINWARING How dare you go over my head in this underhand fashion?

WILSON I don't know what all the fuss is about. It was a battalion order. I just passed it on.

MAINWARING It was in my pending drawer – you have no authority to rummage in my pending drawer.

Warden enters in dripping waterproof.

WARDEN Cor blimey – typical English summer.

MAINWARING What the hell do you want?

WARDEN And a merry Christmas to you, too.

MAINWARING Do you mind not dripping all over my part two order.

WARDEN Sorry. **(Starts to take his coat off)**

MAINWARING **(To Wilson)** I do not approve of these medals sprawling all over everyone's chest. It's this war we're concerned with – not the last or the one before that.

WARDEN What's the matter then – didn't they give you any?

MAINWARING We're not discussing me – in fact I'm not discussing anything with you at all. Get out of my orderly room.

WARDEN It's the Vicar's office and he gives me permission to 'ang my 'at 'ere any time I choose. **(To Wilson – indicating his own medals)** He wants to get some service in, doesn't he? **(At door)** I've got a lecture in here, so you keep your voice down.

MAINWARING What a common man he is.

WILSON Still – he was with us in the last lot – wasn't he?

MAINWARING What do you mean?

WILSON He was wearing his 14–18 medals.

MAINWARING That's just the sort of thing I don't approve of. Gallantry is one thing, but to hand out those bits of brass for every tinpot little campaign – just for being there – makes a mockery of the whole thing.

Verger enters – he is wearing his sea-scout uniform and is also wearing one unusual medal.

VERGER Ah. Good afternoon, Mr Mainwaring. Would you have any objection if I had a little ferret in the Vicar's drawers? **(He goes towards the desk)**

MAINWARING I'm very busy. Does it have to be now?

VERGER He wants his medals for Sunday's parade. I think they're in the top left. **(He brings them out)** There we are. Pip, Squeak and Wilfred. **(Mainwaring reacts)** They'll set his surplus off a treat when he's conducting the community hymn singing. **(Exit Verger)**

MAINWARING **(To Wilson)** There – that's precisely what I mean. What can he have done? Two verses of 'Rock of Ages' in a French field and they send him these with the rations.

WILSON Still – it doesn't do much harm, does it – and when we have these parades it is rather marvellous for people like Captain Square – striding out at the head of his platoon with his gongs flapping in the breeze.

MAINWARING He'll love every second of it.

WILSON On the other hand, it's not much fun for those who didn't have any medals.

MAINWARING What do you mean?

WILSON Like Pike, for instance.

MAINWARING Right, you're dismissed now, Wilson. Go and polish your medals for the parade.

WILSON Are you going to polish your cap badge, sir?

MAINWARING I said you were dismissed, Wilson.

INTERIOR. FRAZER'S HOUSE. NIGHT

Frazer is on the phone by the light of a flickering candle – he is wearing a dressing gown – the phone is the old-fashioned kind.

FRAZER Well, we stood there, face to face – my eyes looking at his eyes – and his eyes looking at my eyes – then I saw his eyes flicker and I quickly pressed home my advantage – I asked him quite innocently – 'are you no wearing your medals, Mr Mainwaring?' **(Cackles)** Of course, I knew. **(Cackles)** All the time **(Cackles)** that he had none to wear. **(He brings the cackle to a crescendo and chokes)** I canna wait to see everyone's face when he goes on parade in front of the whole Battalion with no medals – he canna worm out of this. To every man who sins comes Nemesis.

INTERIOR. CHURCH HALL. DAY

Jones, Frazer, Walker and Godfrey are standing in a group – the rest of the platoon are standing around waiting for the parade to start. Wilson is standing on his own, reading a clipboard he is holding – they are all wearing their medals.

WALKER I can't help feeling sorry for old Mainwaring – after all, it's not his fault he hasn't got any medals.

FRAZER It's a disgrace that's what it is, being led by a man with nothing up here. **(He taps his chest)** I mean, he's got nothing up here, either **(Taps his forehead)** but we're used to that.

GODFREY Perhaps we all ought to take our medals off – then Mr Mainwaring won't feel out of place.

JONES We can't do that, Mr Godfrey – it was a battalion order to wear our medals. Mr Mainwaring ought to get some service in.

Mainwaring comes in through the main entrance. He marches smartly to the middle of the hall.

MAINWARING Good morning,everybody. **(He crosses to Wilson)** Fall the men in, Sergeant.

WILSON What... er, sir... right... fall in.

MAINWARING I've got a little announcement to make to the platoon.

WILSON What is it?

MAINWARING All in good time, Wilson – all in good time.

WILSON Platoon, attention. **(They come to attention)** Men all ready for inspection, sir.

MAINWARING Thank you, Sergeant – very smart men – very smart indeed – and this morning I'm sure that you'll all be a credit to the platoon. Unfortunately I have some bad news for you – due to circumstances beyond my control, I am afraid that I shall not be able to be with you this morning. You see my dear wife, Elizabeth – realising that this was a very important parade – sent my uniform to the dry cleaners – she didn't tell me this until we were having lunch on Saturday – I rushed round straight away but unfortunately, as you know, the cleaners always closes at one o'clock on Saturdays – and I'm afraid I was too late. **(Reaction)** If I had another uniform, of course, it would be a different matter... **(Pike comes in with a large parcel)** You're late, Pike – fall in at once.

PIKE I'm sorry, Mr Mainwaring, but I've got something for you.

MAINWARING What?

PIKE Well, you see, yesterday morning, I was coming home from the bank – I popped into the cleaners to collect something – and I saw your uniform hanging there – I knew that you'd want it today, so I picked it up for you. **(He hands him the parcel)**

Mainwaring reacts.

PIKE It was two and three.

MAINWARING Ah... yes... ermmm – thank you, Pike, but unfortunately that won't help. I'm afraid I haven't time to change.

WILSON The parade doesn't start until ten o'clock, sir – you've got 20 minutes. We don't mind waiting. **(To the platoon)** Do we?

PLATOON No.

The platoon all shake their heads. He moves to door. Platoon watch him go.

INTERIOR. SALOON BAR. DAY

We see the drink as from the barmaid's point of view. Bridge music plays as we track along the decorated chests of the men drinking. Square is drinking with the colonel and his sergeant. We arrive at the undecorated chest of Mainwaring.

Jones and Walker are beside him. Three halves of bitter are placed on the bar as we pull back.

BARMAID Three halves of bitter – one and three.

WALKER Thank you, Shirley. **(Feels in pocket)**

MAINWARING No – please – allow me.

WILSON The way you've done your hair is awfully pretty, don't you think so, sir?

MAINWARING Yes – I suppose so.

Verger and Vicar join them. Mainwaring places the money on the counter.

MAINWARING Would you care for a drink, Verger, it's my round.

VERGER That's very civil of you, sir, just a lemonade shandy – and not too much beer please, Shirley. Mustn't forget it's the Lord's Day.

MAINWARING What about you, Vicar?

VICAR Ah – how very kind. Double scotch please.

Mainwaring reacts. Warden joins.

WARDEN If you're in the chair, I'll have a double scotch and all.

MAINWARING I don't think I extended the invitation to you. What about you, Colonel?

Colonel ignores him.

MAINWARING Would you take a drink with No.1 Platoon?

COLONEL No thanks. Square here has lined them up for us.

Mainwaring reacts.

BARMAID One lemonade shandy and one double scotch, sir.

VERGER **(Confidentially)** Make it a single for His Reverence. He's a martyr to it, you know.

MAINWARING Is he?

VERGER We don't want a scene, do we?

MAINWARING No, of course not. Make it a single.

SQUARE Well, Mainwaring – enjoy the parade?

MAINWARING Yes – quite a good turnout, wasn't it?

SQUARE Sorry you lot were behind me. Couldn't see your drill.

SERGEANT We heard them though, didn't we, sir?

SQUARE Yes, late! **(Laughs)**

MAINWARING Yes, well the wind was blowing away from us.

JONES Some of us had difficulty hearing the word of command.

SQUARE Some of you had difficulty walking, too. **(Laugh)**

MAINWARING Ignore him, Wilson.

WILSON I was, actually.

Barmaid delivers money and scotch.

SQUARE I think you should ask the Colonel here if your lot can do the next march past in bath chairs. **(Laughs)**

WARDEN Now that's not fair. Captain Mainwaring was striding out like a two year old.

WILSON Yes, you were awfully smart, sir.

WARDEN Mind you, he didn't have as much weight to carry as you, Captain Square – not having any medals.

MAINWARING When Hitler sets foot on our shores, it's fighting efficiency that'll count, I'll be no good waving medals at 'em.

SQUARE Damn sight better than waving your pension books. **(Laughs)**

MAINWARING My men would wipe the floor with yours any day. They're fitter, and what's more – a damned sight better trained – and better led.

SQUARE I say, I say, I say. These are strong words, eh, Colonel? **(More laughs)**

MAINWARING My platoon can outshoot you – out think you, and in fact, run rings round you – because they haven't been stifled with old-fashioned ideas and a Colonel Blimp mentality.

JONES Quite right, sir – you tell 'em, sir.

SQUARE You'll prove that or apologise, Mainwaring.

MAINWARING I will not apologise – and we can only prove it when the Bosche arrives.

COLONEL We don't have to wait for that, you know. There's the battle course and the field firing range – and we could easily set some initiative tests.

SQUARE I accept. What about it, Mainwaring? Do you accept the challenge – or are you backing down?

JONES We're not backing down.

MAINWARING Of course not – we accept.

WARDEN Oh – I want to see this. Can I be an umpire, Colonel? I'm Civil Defence – I won 't be biased, will I?

VICAR The Verger and I will be umpires, too, and the fact that you've bought me a single scotch will have no effect on my judgement.

JONES Right – we accept – don't we, Mr Mainwaring?

MAINWARING Yes, of course.

SQUARE I make only one condition. Every man who took part in this parade must take part in the test.

MAINWARING Yes – of course – very fair – isn't it, Wilson?

WILSON Yes – very fair. It just means we'll lose, that's all.

INTERIOR. CHURCH HALL

The platoon is seated. Mainwaring and Wilson are at the blackboard.

MAINWARING Right. Pay attention.

JONES **(Shouting)** Pay attention. Pay attention to the Captain. The men are now paying attention, sir.

MAINWARING Thank you, Corporal. The conditions of the test against the Eastgate Platoon have now been forwarded to us and we're able to put you all in the picture – now, you'll probably agree that you hear far too much of my voice.

WALKER Here, here.

MAINWARING Watch it, Walker. So, on this occasion I'm going to let Sergeant Wilson brief you. Carry on, Wilson.

WILSON **(He uses the diagram on board to illustrate his words)** Right then. Both platoons start here in their platoon vans.

MAINWARING Tell them about the map reference.

WILSON Pardon?

MAINWARING I said, tell them about the map reference.

WILSON I was just going to. Just before the start, both platoon commanders will be given a map reference and we have to find the quickest way to it.

MAINWARING Using maps.

WILSON Pardon?

MAINWARING I said, using maps.

WILSON I should have thought that was rather obvious.

MAINWARING Nothing is obvious. Get on with it, Wilson.

WILSON I'm trying to – now – where had I got to?

MAINWARING Practically nowhere.

WILSON Well, if you will keep interrupting, I lose the thread of the thing.

MAINWARING Initiative tests.

WILSON Ah. Yes – we next go to point B – where we will be given initiative tests.

PIKE **(Stands)** Excuse me, Uncle Sergeant. In what type of form will these initiative tests be put? **(He sits)**

WILSON Well –

MAINWARING I think I'd better answer that, Wilson. Obviously we don't know what the tests are – otherwise we couldn't use our initiative, could we?

PIKE **(Rising again)** Thank you.

MAINWARING **(Mutters)** Stupid boy.

WILSON Then we have to cross the river – here – double across the battle course – here – fire five rounds each at the target – here – and then dash across to the building – here.

MAINWARING Using live ammunition.

WILSON Climb to the roof and run the platoon flag, **(Indicates flag with large 'B' in middle)** which Walker has most kindly had made for us.

WALKER By the way, it worked out at three quid.

MAINWARING Three pounds – that's a bit steep.

WALKER You were lucky – I charged the Eastgate platoon five for making theirs.

MAINWARING Now, the first platoon to raise its flag to the top of the pole will be the winner. Now, is all that clear?

ALL Yes **(Etc.)**

FRAZER Captain Mainwaring, I foresee one wee snag. While we're dashing here and there – and running the flag up the pole – old Godfrey will still be trying to climb out of the van.

MAINWARING Oh, come, come. That's an exaggeration, Frazer.

FRAZER It's no exaggeration. It's plain for all to see, the man's decrepit. **(He turns to Godfrey)** No offence, my dear friend.

GODFREY Well – I'm not as sprightly as I was and my feet are rather dicky – but I'm very determined.

WALKER Don't worry – we'll help you along, Mr Godfrey.

ALL Yes – we'll help you.

FRAZER He's a millstone round our necks and you all know it. It's folly to take him with us – sheer folly.

MAINWARING There's nothing we can do about that. He was on the parade, so he must be on the test.

FRAZER Must he? It's my opinion if he had one spark of loyalty to the rest of us – he'd break a leg. **(To Godfrey)** Nothing personal, I'm speaking for the good of the platoon, you understand.

WALKER He can't go breaking legs at his time of life.

PIKE A finger wouldn't be so serious.

FRAZER He could walk with his arm in a sling – no – it would have to be a leg.

GODFREY Well, I'll do anything to help, within reason.

FRAZER Well, there you are – that's it – the question is, how?

JONES Captain Mainwaring, sir. In Victorian times gone by, Mr Livingstone and their exploring gentlemen used to be carried on a chair between two poles – not Poles the people, you understand – they didn't have none of them in Africa. Bamboo poles I'm referring to. Then four strong natives would carry the poles which was carrying Dr Livingstone. I think that four of us should carry Mr Godfrey.

WALKER Who's going to carry you?

MAINWARING I think that's a very good idea – don't you, Wilson?

WILSON Yes – rather quaint.

MAINWARING Good – that solves the Godfrey embarrassment. That's what I like about this platoon – we have agile minds that enable us to triumph over all our difficulties. We're going to lick that Eastgate platoon and send them home with their tails between their legs. Are you all with me?

ALL Yes, sir – you bet – we're with you. We'll win. **(Etc.)**

FRAZER I still think...

MAINWARING Sit down, Frazer.

TELECINE: EXTERIOR. ROAD. DAY

The two vans are drawn up, side by side, with their engines

running – Jones is at the steering wheel of his van – Frazer is standing waiting beside the other door – in the Eastgate van, the Sergeant is sitting in the cab.

The Verger is standing beside the road with a flag on a pole about four foot long.

In front of the two vans, Mainwaring and Square are standing side by side with notebooks and pencils poised.

The Vicar and the Warden are standing in front of them.

The motorbike and side-car is parked behind the van.

Walker joins Warden.

WALKER Here you are, Mr Hodges, here's the flags.

WARDEN Tar. Now listen – the Vicar 'ere will read out the map reference once – you will write it down – run back to your vehicles and, when the Verger gives the signal, you will start. Here's your flags. (Hands over flags) Right, Vicar.

The Vicar opens an envelope and takes out a piece of paper.

VICAR Now, I shall only read this once, so listen very carefully – are you ready?

MAINWARING Oh, get on with it.

WARDEN Now, don't you start, Mainwaring.

VICAR Here goes – the map reference is 629 – 571.

Mainwaring and Square write it down and dash to their vans. Square gets into the driving seat of his van. Mainwaring gets into Jones' van and Frazer gets in beside him – they both 'rev' up in clouds of smoke. The Verger drops the flag and both vans leap forward – Jones' van runs over the flag and the Verger is left holding the end of the stick.

VERGER (To Warden) Look what they've done to my flag, Mr Hodges.

WARDEN Never mind about that, come on.

The Vicar, Warden and Verger run towards the motorbike – the Warden starts the bike – the Verger gets in the side car. Vicar about to mount pillion.

VICAR Oh dear, is it safe?

WARDEN Of course it is. Hurry up.

VICAR (Getting on) Do you mind if I put my arms round you, Mr Hodges?

Warden gives Vicar a look, the bike roars off.

TELECINE: EXTERIOR. CROSSROADS. DAY

The two vans approach the crossroads.

Square's van turns left – Jones' van turns right. The Warden comes up on his motorbike and turns left after Square.

INTERIOR. FRONT OF VAN. DAY

Jones is driving. Mainwaring is sitting next to him and Frazer is beside Mainwaring with the map.

MAINWARING The Eastgate van turned left – are you sure we're going the right way, Frazer?

FRAZER Of course I am – if you think you can do better, you're quite welcome to try.

MAINWARING Can't you go any faster, Jones?

JONES I'm doing 28 miles an hour – what more do you want?

Godfrey pokes his head through the opening at the back of the driving seat.

GODFREY Excuse me, sir.

MAINWARING What is it, Godfrey?

GODFREY I wonder if I might be excused?

MAINWARING Certainly not – get your head back at once. You must be able to go faster than this, Jones – get your foot right down to the floorboards.

JONES I've got it right down now, sir. Oh – arh – oh – arrrh – ah. (He starts to shake)

MAINWARING What's the matter, Jones?

TELECINE: EXTERIOR. ROAD. DAY

Long shot of van weaving all over the road.

INTERIOR. FRONT OF VAN. DAY

MAINWARING What are you doing, Jones? – What are you doing?

JONES (Shaking) Per – per – per – permission to sp – sp – sp – speak, sir?

MAINWARING What is it?

JONES I'm so – so – sorry ter ter ter tell you, si – si – sir – I'm ger – ger – getting my old trouble coming on.

MAINWARING What's that?

JONES Mer – mer – mer.

MAINWARING What?

JONES Mer – mer – malaria, sir.

MAINWARING Oh no – stop – stop the van at once.

TELECINE: EXTERIOR. ROAD. DAY

The van stops – Frazer and Mainwaring jump down and run round to the other side of the van – Mainwaring opens the door of the driving cab.

MAINWARING Stay where you are, Jones.

Mainwaring bangs on the side of the van.

MAINWARING **(Shouting)** Medic! Medics! **(He gives three blasts of his whistle)**

PLATOON **(Out of vision)** Open, two, three.

Flaps open.

PLATOON Out, two, three.

Five rifles come through the slits. They fire – Mainwaring staggers back into Frazer's arms.

MAINWARING Stop! Stop!

Wilson runs into the picture.

MAINWARING What are they doing, Wilson? – What are they doing?

WILSON Well, you gave three blasts on your whistle, sir – that's the signal to open fire.

MAINWARING Nothing of the sort – I wanted the medics – go and get the medic.

WILSON The what, sir?

MAINWARING Godfrey – go and get him, man.

Wilson goes.

Walker and Pike come into the picture, followed by Sponge and several others.

WALKER What's happened, Mr Mainwaring?

MAINWARING It's Jones – he's got an attack of malaria. You and Pike, get him out of the seat. Sponge, you go round the other side.

Sponge goes.

WALKER **(Getting hold of Jones)** You'll be all right, Jonesey. Come on.

Jones is gripping the steering wheel and can't let go.

PIKE He won't let go of the steering wheel, Mr Mainwaring.

MAINWARING Where's Godfrey – **(Blows whistle)** Medics – Medics! Get hold of his wrists. Come on Sponge, push.

Walker and Pike each grab one of Jones' wrists – they pull his hands free and he grips their wrists – they get him down on to the road.

Jones is now standing in the road – he is gripping Pike's right wrist and Walker's left wrist – he is gripping them so hard that as he shakes – he is shaking them as well.

PIKE He dur... dur... dur... doesn't ler... ler... look ter... ter... too good to mer... mer... me.

JONES I der... der... don't fer... fer... feel too ger... ger... good... I... I... I... either.

WALKER Dur... dur... dur... don't wur... wur... worry, son we... we... we... we'll look after you.

MAINWARING Where is Godfrey? **(Blows whistle)** Medics. Medics.

Godfrey runs into the picture.

MAINWARING Where have you been, Godfrey?

GODFREY I'm sorry, sir – as we stopped I took the opportunity to be excused.

MAINWARING Well you'd no right to – as the medic it's your duty to be on hand at all times.

GODFREY Oh dear – what's wrong with Mr Jones?

MAINWARING He's got a bout of malaria – have you got anything we can give him?

GODFREY **(Opening his satchel)** I don't know really, sir.

He takes out some bandages and a bottle of aspirins.

GODFREY I've got some aspirins, some bicarbonate of soda and some ointment for wasp stings.

MAINWARING Wasp stings! This is a fighting unit – not a girl guides' outing. What would you do if one of us was wounded?

FRAZER Quinine – that's what we need, sir, a bottle of quinine – and he should be kept warm.

MAINWARING You're right. **(Shouting at van)** Bring some blankets. Have you got any quinine, Godfrey?

GODFREY No, sir, but I've got a bottle of tonic wine – my sister Dolly swears by it.

MAINWARING **(Taking it)** That will have to do, I suppose. Here, Jones, drink this.

He holds the bottle up to Jones' mouth.

MAINWARING Hold his head, Walker – he's spilling it.

One of the platoon runs up with some blankets.

MAINWARING Now, cover him up – and get him in the back of the van.

JONES Dur... dur... don't worry about me... mur... mur... mur... mur... I've had these er... t – t – t – tacks fer... fer... for forty years. They sur... sur... soon pass.

Wilson comes into the picture.

WILSON What's the matter with Jonesey, Frank?

PIKE He's got an attack of malaria, Uncle Arthur – you know like Leslie Banks in *Sanders of the River.*

WILSON I hated that film, Frank – all those terrible drums.

MAINWARING Wilson! All right, Walker, Pike – get him in the back of the van.

Walker and Pike lead Jones out of the picture.

FRAZER Who's going to drive now, Mr Mainwaring?

MAINWARING I am, of course.

WILSON Do you think that's wise, sir?

MAINWARING Don't argue, get in.

Frazer runs round the other side and gets in – Mainwaring pushes Wilson into the cab.

MAINWARING Hurry up, Wilson – hurry up – we've wasted enough time as it is.

Mainwaring gets in and starts the engine – there is a grinding of gears and the van jerks off.

INTERIOR. FRONT OF VAN. DAY

FRAZER Another half a mile and we turn left, sir.

Pike pokes his head through.

PIKE Mr Mainwaring – Mr Jones has turned all yellow.

MAINWARING Put some more blankets on him.

PIKE More blankets, right.

WILSON Don't you think we ought to get him a doctor, sir?

MAINWARING We can't do that, we shall lose the race – besides you heard what he said – he often gets these attacks – they soon pass.

FRAZER Coming up to the turning very soon now, sir.

WILSON How absolutely sweet.

MAINWARING What?

WILSON A dear little cottage that we just passed – thatched roof and roses around the door – just like Snow White's.

MAINWARING Stop gawping – and keep you eye on the road.

Pike pokes his head through.

PIKE Mr Mainwaring, Mr Jones isn't yellow any more.

MAINWARING Good – good.

PIKE He's turned purple.

MAINWARING What?

PIKE He looks like a beetroot.

MAINWARING Put some more blankets on him.

FRAZER Turn left here, sir.

TELECINE: EXTERIOR. ROAD. DAY

Long shot of van turning left.

INTERIOR. FRONT OF VAN. DAY

Steam is coming through the gap.

FRAZER Where's that steam coming from, sir?

WILSON Perhaps the engine's overheating?

MAINWARING It's not coming from the engine, Wilson. **(He shouts over his shoulder)** What's happening at the back there.

Godfrey pokes his head through.

GODFREY I'm afraid Mr Jones is steaming, sir.

MAINWARING Steaming?

GODFREY Yes, sir, the condensation is running down the walls.

FRAZER Best thing for him, let him sweat it out – give him plenty to drink.

GODFREY There's only the bottle of tonic wine – and he's already drunk half of it.

MAINWARING Well give him the rest – this is an emergency.

GODFREY Very good, sir.

FRAZER Next turning on the left, coming up.

TELECINE: EXTERIOR. ROAD. DAY

Long shot of van turning left.

TELECINE: EXTERIOR. ROAD. DAY

Long shot of Square's van – followed by Warden, Vicar and Verger on motorbike.

INTERIOR. FRONT OF VAN. DAY

WILSON How enchanting.

MAINWARING What are you talking about?

WILSON We've just passed that dear little Snow White cottage again.

MAINWARING What? **(He turns the van)** We've gone round in a circle. What are you playing at, Frazer?

FRAZER Don't shout at me – we can all make mistakes.

Walker pokes his head through.

WALKER Mr Mainwaring – the Eastgate van is coming up behind us. **(He goes back)**

MAINWARING That's your fault, Frazer – thanks to your bungling – they've caught us up.

Mainwaring puts van into gear and jerks off.

FRAZER How do you expect me to read the map properly with your jerky driving?

MAINWARING I don't want any insubordination from you, Frazer – take his name, Wilson.

There is a sound of hooting and shouts from behind. Pike pokes his head through.

PIKE The Eastgate van is trying to pass us, Mr Mainwaring.

MAINWARING Well they won't get past me.

TELECINE: EXTERIOR. ROAD. DAY

Front shot of Mainwaring's van – behind we can see the Eastgate van trying to pass – the road is very narrow – Mainwaring swerves to stop them passing. Behind them, Hodges and the Vicar and Verger in the motorcycle and side car. Hodges passes the Eastgate van and draws level with Mainwaring.

HODGES Pull over – let them pass.

MAINWARING Mind your own business.

HODGES Will you pull over?

MAINWARING Clear off.

Warden overtakes Mainwaring and goes in front of him, forcing him to stop – Eastgate van passes with a cheer. Mainwaring gets down from van and storms up to Warden.

MAINWARING What do you think you're doing?

HODGES It was a good job you stopped otherwise I'd have disqualified you.

MAINWARING It was a good job I stopped – otherwise I'd have run over you.

WARDEN You were obstructing Colonel Square – and more of that bumping and barging and I'll have you out of the race.

MAINWARING **(To Vicar)** This isn't fair, Vicar.

VERGER It's no good appealing to His Reverence – after that foul language you used just now.

MAINWARING I did not use foul language.

VERGER Oh yes you did – I heard you quite plainly – fortunately the noise of the engine stopped it reaching His Reverence's ears.

MAINWARING Let's be reasonable, Vicar.

VICAR I'm sorry, Mr Mainwaring – we're just here as umpires to see fair play – come along, Mr Hodges – Mr Yeatman.

They all go. Mainwaring and co. climb back into van.

TELECINE: EXTERIOR. ROAD. DAY

Square's van is standing by the road with steam coming out of the radiator. Warden and co. are with him.

Square and his Sergeant are standing beside it – one of Square's men has the bonnet up and is poking at the engine. Jones' van comes into sight and passes them with loud cheers – Square shakes his fist.

TELECINE: EXTERIOR. ROAD. DAY.

Jones' van comes along the road and stops. Mainwaring jumps down, followed by Frazer and Wilson.

FRAZER Why have you stopped, sir? – we're well ahead of them.

MAINWARING And we're going to be even further ahead of them – look, Wilson, you see all those sheep in that field?

WILSON Yes, sir.

MAINWARING **(Pointing)** I want you to take Frazer and the rest of the men – and drive all those sheep out of that bottom gate so that they fill the road behind us – I'd like to see Square get through that lot.

TELECINE: EXTERIOR. ROAD. DAY

The Sergeant is closing the bonnet.

SERGEANT It seems to be all right now, sir.

Square is at the wheel – he revs up.

SQUARE Well done – well done – come on, get it – they can't be very far ahead of us.

The Sergeant and Private get in and the van roars off.

TELECINE: EXTERIOR. ROAD. DAY

Mainwaring, Wilson, Pike, Frazer, Godfrey and Sponge are standing singly by the van – the whole road is full of sheep.

MAINWARING **(Shouting across to Wilson)** I distinctly told you to drive them out of the lower gate, Wilson.

WILSON I couldn't help it, sir – they insisted on coming out of the upper gate.

MAINWARING Well, there's one consolation – Square won't be able to get through this lot either.

Cut to shot of road – we see Jones' van completely surrounded by sheep – Square's van appears – turns off into an opening into a field behind the sheep and comes out of another opening in front. It stops.

Cut to close up of Square leaning out of cab and shouting back to Mainwaring.

SQUARE The biter bit, eh, Mainwaring – Har – Har – Har. **(He drives off)**

Cut back to shot of road. The Warden's bike comes up and does exactly the same as Square's van.

Cut to close up of Warden shouting back at Mainwaring.

WARDEN What's the matter, Mainwaring? Why are you looking so sheepish? **(He drives off)**

Cut to close up of Mainwaring purple with rage.

Mainwaring puts van into gear and jerks off.

We later see Mainwaring's van back in front as Square's lorry joins the road at a terrific speed and turns off.

MAINWARING **(Out of vision)** Now they've gone the other way – we'll turn round.

SQUARE **(Out of vision)** Now they've gone the other way – we'll turn round.

Jones' van turns left – Square's van turns right – they both stop.

MAINWARING **(Out of vision)** They're up to something – we'll follow them.

SQUARE **(Out of vision)** They're up to something – we'll follow them.

Square's van turns right – Jones' van turns right – they follow each other round and round in a circle – the Warden arrives on his motorbike.

WARDEN **(Close up)** Blimey, here we go round the mulberry bush.

TELECINE: EXTERIOR. WINNING POST. DAY

The Colonel is standing by a big notice marked 'Finish', he is talking to a Captain. A few Privates are standing around.

COLONEL What on earth's happened to them? They should have been here hours ago.

TELECINE: EXTERIOR. ROAD. DAY

Moving shot from camera car of Square's van.

TELECINE: EXTERIOR. ROAD. DAY

Moving shot from camera car of Jones' van.

TELECINE: EXTERIOR. ROAD. DAY

Moving shot from camera car of Square's van.

TELECINE: EXTERIOR. ROAD. DAY

Moving shot from camera car of Jones' van.

TELECINE: EXTERIOR. NARROW BRIDGE. DAY

Very high-angle shot of bridge across river – the two vans approach each other from opposite sides – they meet in the middle and stop.

Cut to close up of Square looking out of cab.

SQUARE Back up, do you hear? Back up at once.

MAINWARING Don't you tell me to back up – you back up.

SQUARE We'll soon see about that.

He slips the clutch and starts to push Mainwaring back – Mainwaring does the same thing and starts to push Square back.

Close ups of exhaust pipes and wheels moving. Two vans bumper to bumper.

MAINWARING **(Shouting)** Everyone in the back, get out and push.

SQUARE Everyone in the back, get out and push.

The Warden arrives with Vicar and Verger – gets off his bike. Can't reach the front of the van any other way, so starts to climb along the outside of the bridge.

Cut to long shot of bridge – we can see the two vans with men behind each one pushing – clouds of exhaust smoke are pouring out.

Cut to Warden – he has now reached the driving cab of Jones' van – he shouts at Wilson.

WARDEN Back up – back up at once.

WILSON Oh, just clear off.

He pushes the Warden – he falls back and we follow him in close up slow motion until he hits the water.

Cut to long shot of bridge – Jones' van is winning – it pushes Square's van back – Square's men all run back on to the bank followed by the van – Mainwaring drives Jones' van right up on to the bank. The two vans stop a little way apart – Pike runs up to Mainwaring.

PIKE Mr Mainwaring, I think the Warden's drowning.

Mainwaring quickly gets down, followed by Wilson and Frazer.

MAINWARING Come on, Wilson. No, on second thoughts, you stay here – and while they're not looking, let their tyres down.

SERGEANT **(To Square)** There's somebody in trouble in the water, sir – we'd better help.

SQUARE I'll go – you stay here and while they're not looking, let their tyres down.

Everyone rushes down to the river bank except the Sergeant and Private who run over to Jones' van and start to let their tyres down – at the same time Wilson and Frazer run over to Square's van and start to let their tyres down.

Cut to the bank. Mainwaring and Square are pulling the Warden out of the water – the Sergeant and Pike run to Mainwaring and Square.

PIKE/SERGEANT **(To Mainwaring/Square)** They're letting our tyres down, sir.

MAINWARING/SQUARE What!

They let go of the Warden, who falls back in the water. They rush back to the vans – we finish with the two opposite groups lettings down the other's tyres.

TELECINE: EXTERIOR. A FIELD. DAY

Warden is standing near assault course – Mainwaring joins him with Wilson and some of the platoon.

MAINWARING Where's Jones?

WILSON They're bringing him as fast as they can.

Cut to Jones – wrapped in blankets, being carried along on the chair and bamboo by four members of the platoon – Godfrey is hobbling along close to him with the tonic wine bottle and his first aid kit. They approach Mainwaring.

JONES Right – put me down – I'm all right. Put me down. **(He is set down – he gets out of chair and staggers to Mainwaring. He is drunk)** I'm all right now, Mr Mainwaring, my malaria has subsided – one bottle of Mr Godfrey's tonic wine and I'm a new man.

MAINWARING Good heavens – he's drunk.

WARDEN Right now, pay attention. This is your first initiative test. Are you listening, Mainwaring?

MAINWARING Just read it out – that's all you've got to do. Stay with him, Wilson, you're responsible for him.

WILSON Why should I be responsible for him?

MAINWARING Don't argue.

WARDEN The Verger, here, is holding 24 balloons.

Cut to Verger standing with balloons.

WARDEN When I say 'go', he'll release them. You'll fix bayonets and you will burst every one of these balloons before moving on to the next obstacle. Right, go!

Verger releases balloons which are borne away on the gentle breeze.

MAINWARING Fix bayonets and charge.

JONES Don't panic – don't panic. I'll do 'em – I'll get 'em all. **(He can't fix his bayonet)**

Pike hares after balloons and nudges at them. The bayonet pushes the balloon away but doesn't burst it. The platoon all chase balloons.

JONES I'll have 'em. Don't panic – leave it to me.

MAINWARING **(To Wilson, who is watching proceedings)** Are you a member of this platoon, Wilson?

WILSON Well – yes – I suppose so.

MAINWARING Then burst those blasted balloons.

Wilson moves off to burst balloons. Walker is standing – taking it all in – smoking.

Cut to Pike – he fails to burst another balloon.

PIKE They won't go in, Mr Mainwaring. They're not offering any resistance.

WALKER Hang on, Mr Mainwaring – I've got it.

He drags on cigarette – puts it in the end of his barrel and uses it to burst two or three balloons.

Cut to Frazer – he thrusts a couple of times without success and then leaps on one with both feet in sheer frustration.

Cut to Godfrey who is doing rather better than the rest with a safety pin.

GODFREY **(After bursting a balloon)** Mr Mainwaring – a safety pin is quite effective. You have to open it, of course.

JONES **(Bayonet now fixed)** I'll get 'em. Where are they?

He spots a balloon wedged by a fallen tree trunk. Jones dashes at it with a yell and plunges his bayonet in. The balloon bursts – the bayonet goes into the trunk. It sticks. Jones has great difficulty in removing it. It finally comes out suddenly and he falls backwards.

JONES I'll have 'em – who did that?

MAINWARING Right – really – that's the lot. On to the next obstacle.

Warden runs up to him.

WARDEN Oh no it's not – what about that one?

He points to a balloon – it is being carried across a field by the wind – far away.

JONES I'll get it, sir, leave it to me. Where is it?

Cut to Vicar.

VICAR (Putting down binoculars) Hurry up, Mainwaring – Square's lot have finished.

WARDEN He's going to win – I knew he would. Go on – you can't leave till you've burst that one.

JONES I'll get it, sir.

MAINWARING Stay where you are, Jones.

He draws his revolver and fires – the balloon bursts.

WILSON Good heavens.

MAINWARING What do you mean, good heavens? On to the next test, men.

WARDEN Here – no – you're supposed to do it with a bayonet.

FRAZER Another word and I'll do you with a bayonet.

MAINWARING Come on, men – hurry up.

Cut to Godfrey getting into chair – four Home Guards take up the pole.

SPONGE Right. Lift.

They lift and trot off. The arms of the chair come away, leaving Godfrey sitting alone.

Cut to Warden by iron tank about eight foot square and three foot high – full of feathers.

WARDEN Right – pay attention. In this tank are a lot of feathers. You've got to get them feathers into those barrels over there.

Cut to three barrels some 30 yards away.

VERGER Right – Go! (Blows whistle)

MAINWARING Come on, Godfrey – hurry up.

Godfrey's party arrive – the poles have been placed under the chair.

JONES (By tank) Don't worry about this, sir – I'll do it.

He is trying to gather arms full of feathers.

Jones and the other members of the platoon try to run with arms full of feathers. The feathers scatter as they run to the barrel. They reach the barrels without much benefit. Mainwaring arrives with his share of feathers.

MAINWARING This is no good. I've got it. Fill your hats and shove 'em up your jumpers.

PIKE (Who has an idea) Mr Mainwaring?

MAINWARING Not now, Pike.

They turn to the feather bin – Mainwaring meets Godfrey half-way back.

GODFREY At the conclusion of this phase, do you think you could spare me for a moment or two?

MAINWARING Certainly not.

Cut to feather bin – the platoon are shoving feathers in their hats and down their jackets. Mainwaring arrives.

FRAZER You've had some damned silly ideas in the past and this is the damned silliest.

MAINWARING Now, Frazer – none of that. That's no way to talk to an officer. (He puts his hat full of feathers on his head) Come on men – sharp's the word.

They rush to the barrels. Cut to the barrels as they try to unload the feathers from their jackets.

WILSON They're flying everywhere.

PIKE Mr Mainwaring?

MAINWARING Yes, Pike.

Pike sneezes before he can make his suggestion.

MAINWARING Don't waste my time, Pike.

They run back to feather bin. They start to stuff feathers in their jackets.

WILSON If I may say so – this isn't working awfully well.

MAINWARING Have you any better suggestion?

PIKE Mr Mainwaring?

MAINWARING Yes?

Pike sneezes.

MAINWARING Don't keep doing that, Pike.

WILSON Look – if we had some bags.

MAINWARING Good idea – we'll use trousers and tie up the legs. Take your trousers off, Wilson.

WILSON No, I won't.

MAINWARING Take your trousers off.

WILSON Why do *I* always have to take my trousers off?

MAINWARING You have to set an example. Trousers off, everyone.

WILSON Couldn't you set an example?

MAINWARING Just do as you're told, please. (To men) Stuff the feathers in your trousers.

Jones starts to shove feathers down his trousers without taking them off.

JONES Mr Mainwaring. This is not a very hygienic way of going on.

FRAZER You're supposed to take 'em off, tie the bottoms and stuff 'em down the legs.

JONES Do what?

FRAZER Stuff 'em down the legs.

Jones proceeds to stuff feathers even further down his trousers. Frazer and some of the platoon now run with the feather-filled trousers in their hands towards the barrels.

PIKE Mr Mainwaring. Why don't we bring the barrels over here – fill them – and then put them back?

MAINWARING Now look, Pike – one more stupid suggestion from – that's a very good idea. (**Calls to the troops**) Bring the barrels over here.

Cut to Vicar, who is watching Square's lot through binoculars – Warden joins him.

WARDEN How's Square's mob getting on?

VICAR They're still carrying feathers by hand. Mainwaring's lot will win by miles at this rate.

WARDEN Will they? I'll soon see about that.

He moves off towards river.

TELECINE: EXTERIOR. RIVER BANK. DAY

There are two pontoon bridge boats drawn up on the bank – about 20 yards away is a small rowing boat – across the other side of the river is another pontoon boat tied up – the Warden runs down the bank. The Verger hurries into picture.

VERGER Mr Hodges – Mr Hodges – Mainwaring's lot are winning.

0WARDEN What!

VERGER They'll be here in a minute.

WARDEN I'll soon cook his goose.

VERGER What are you going to do?

WARDEN I'm going to pull the plug out – come on, give us a hand.

They both reach down into the bottom of the boat and pull the plug out – the Warden throws it out into the river.

WARDEN That will fix 'em.

Mainwaring runs up with Wilson, Jones, Frazer, Pike, Godfrey on chair, and the rest of the platoon. He goes to the other boat.

MAINWARING Come on, men, hurry up – get in.

WARDEN You can't get in that boat.

MAINWARING Why not?

WARDEN Because it's the wrong boat (**Points to the other boat**) That's your boat.

MAINWARING I shall get in whatever boat I want – now mind your own business.

WARDEN I insist that you get in that other boat.

WILSON You really are being the most frightful bore today.

WARDEN (**Whining**) Please – please, Mr Mainwaring – please get in the other boat.

MAINWARING (**To Wilson**) I don't think he's all there, you know, Wilson.

WILSON Well, he always was a bit strange, sir.

Mainwaring and Wilson get in the boat.

MAINWARING Right, shove off.

They push off and start to paddle across the river. Square, his Sergeant and the rest of his platoon come down to the bank.

SQUARE All right, men, get in.

WARDEN (**Stopping him**) Don't get in that boat, Captain Square – I've pulled the plug out.

SQUARE You damn fool – what did you want to do that for?

The Sergeant runs out of the picture.

WARDEN I'm sorry, sir – but Mainwaring's lot were winning – and I tried to stop them.

SQUARE What!

WARDEN I did it for you, sir – I did it for you.

SQUARE You blithering idiot. (**He points to the boat on the other side of the river**) There's another boat over on the other bank – row over and get it.

WARDEN Yes, sir – yes, sir.

The Warden runs over to the rowing boat and starts to push it in the water.

SQUARE (**To Sergeant who has just appeared**) Where have you been, Sergeant?

SERGEANT (**Holding up a plug**) I took the plug out of that rowing boat – to see if it would fit this boat. (**He leans down to try it**) But I'm afraid it doesn't, sir.

Cut to Warden in boat, rowing like mad.

WARDEN (**Shouting**) Don't you worry, Captain Square, sir – I'll get it for you – I'll… (**The boat starts to sink**) Oh no – oh – no – not again.

The boat sinks.

TELECINE: EXTERIOR. A FIELD. DAY

Mainwaring and the platoon are running across the field – there are explosions all round.

MAINWARING Come on, men, we're nearly there.

Single of Godfrey being carried in chair. The platoon run past a clump of bushes. Cut to Warden crouched in bushes – behind him is a large cardboard box full of thunder flashes. He takes one out. Cut to single of Walker with cigarette in mouth. Cut to single of Mainwaring looking back.

MAINWARING (**Shouting**) Hurry up, Walker – and put that cigarette out.

Cut to single close up of Walker.

WALKER Blimey, a few minutes ago you were only too glad of it. (**He throws the cigarette over the hedge**)

Cut to close up of cigarette landing in box of thunder flashes.

The Warden lights the thunder flash that he is holding – throws it over the hedge – and then crouches down again, grinning, with his fingers in his ears.

Cut to Mainwaring – thunder flash lands at his feet – he kicks it aside. There is a loud explosion inside the bush. Pause. As the smoke clears – close up of Warden's face as it slowly appears over the top of the bush – black.

WARDEN I hate you, Mainwaring!

TELECINE: EXTERIOR. BOTTOM OF THE TOWER. DAY

The platoon are lying down behind some sandbags, firing their five rounds – Mainwaring and Wilson walk over to the Colonel, Captain, Vicar and Verger.

WILSON No sign of Captain Square, sir.

MAINWARING It looks as if we've won, Wilson.

COLONEL As soon as your men have finished, Mainwaring – all you've got to do is run to the top of the tower and haul your flag out.

Mainwaring kneels down beside Jones who is firing wildly.

MAINWARING Hurry up, Jones – we're waiting for you. Why are you shaking – you're not getting another attack of malaria are you?

JONES No, sir, I always fire like this – that's why I prefer the bayonet.

MAINWARING Get on with it. (**To Wilson**) Give me the flag, Wilson.

WILSON What flag, sir?

MAINWARING The platoon flag, of course.

WILSON You never said anything about bringing a flag, sir.

MAINWARING I distinctly told you...

Frazer pulls the flag out of his blouse.

FRAZER I've got it, sir.

MAINWARING Well done. (**He takes it**) Godfrey, you stay here – the rest of you men, follow me.

They all run to the door at the bottom of the tower and go in.

TOP OF TOWER. DAY

Mainwaring heads the party consisting of Pike, Wilson, Jones, Frazer and Walker.

MAINWARING (**Breathless**) Pike, take the flag. (**He runs to the door**) Come on, lads, Square's mob are hot on our heels.

Wilson reaches top.

JONES You've got to get the rhythm you see, Sergeant, it's the rhythm keeps you going.

Jones gets to the top but continues to climb on the spot.

WILSON One more flight and I would quite definitely die.

MAINWARING Do you know how to do that, Pike?

PIKE (**Who is examining the rope carefully**) Yes, Mr Mainwaring. There should be a couple of loops to hold these two toggles on the flag.

MAINWARING (**Starts to pull rope**) If there's a loop it must be here somewhere.

PIKE Mr Mainwaring?

MAINWARING That's the trouble with you, Pike – you lack drive.

PIKE Mr Mainwaring?

MAINWARING Look – there's your blasted loop – now get on with it.

PIKE (**Shouting**) Mr Mainwaring, you've pulled the rope out of the pulley at the end.

MAINWARING Any more insubordination from you, Pike, and I shall complain personally to your mother.

FRAZER Now, how are we supposed to fly the flag?

WALKER We can't, unless we pull the pole in.

JONES (**Still half drunk**) Don't worry, Mr Mainwaring. I'll fix it.

They turn to see Jones climbing over the parapet prior to climbing out on to the pole.

MAINWARING Jones – what are you doing?

JONES I'm going to shin out, Mr Mainwaring – and then I'm going to shin back again.

MAINWARING Stop him, Wilson.

WILSON I can't stop him.

JONES Mr Mainwaring?

MAINWARING What is it Jones?

JONES That tonic wine is wonderful stuff.

MAINWARING Jones, you must come back, it isn't safe.

JONES Don't worry, Mr Mainwaring – agile as a monkey, I am – agile as a monkey.

WILSON The man's a complete fool.

MAINWARING A damned brave one, though.

FRAZER If you ask me – he just does it to create an impression.

JONES I'm at the end, Mr Mainwaring – what do I do?

MAINWARING Thread the rope through the pulley.

JONES What rope?

MAINWARING The rope you attach this flag to.

JONES Where is it?

PIKE It's here. **(Holding it)**

MAINWARING It's here. What's it doing here?

JONES Throw it to me. Whoa. **(He tries to coil rope and makes a mess of it)**

WALKER It's wobbling a lot.

MAINWARING **(Shouts below to ground level)** Godfrey – get a blanket.

JONES I'm not cold, Mr Mainwaring.

MAINWARING It's in case you fall.

JONES I won't be cold then.

WALKER He will be when he hits the ground.

TELECINE: EXTERIOR. BOTTOM OF TOWER. DAY

Godfrey, Verger, Vicar and a helper or two spread the blanket.

EXTERIOR OF TOWER. DAY

MAINWARING Right, here it comes. **(He throws – Jones tries to catch. He becomes attached to the pole. Frazer coils the rope again)**

JONES Try to get it a bit nearer, Mr Mainwaring.

MAINWARING What do you think I was doing?

FRAZER Here – let me have a go. Don't miss this, you silly old fool. **(He throws – Jones catches it but in the effort he starts the pole swinging from side to side)**

TELECINE: EXTERIOR. BOTTOM OF TOWER. DAY

Godfrey's team run either way to meet him.

EXTERIOR. TOP OF TOWER. POLE SWINGING. DAY

JONES Mr Mainwaring, I think that wine is going to my head. I feel just as if I'm swaying from side to side.

MAINWARING Get the rope in the pulley and get back.

Jones is scrambling about, trying to put the rope through the pulley as the pole bends and sways.

JONES **(Licking the end and squinting)** It's like trying to thread a needle.

MAINWARING Hurry up and come back.

JONES That's got it. **(He puts the end of the rope between his teeth and starts to scramble back)**

TELECINE: EXTERIOR. BOTTOM OF TOWER. DAY

Square and his party rush up.

SQUARE Hurry up. They haven't got the flag out yet.

They go into entrance door.

INTERIOR. TOP OF TOWER. DAY

Jones is just being helped over parapet.

MAINWARING Grab him round the waist, someone.

Jones' foot slips – Mainwaring grabs him and steadies him.

JONES You saved my life then, Mr Mainwaring – I'll never forget that as long as I live – I'll never forget you saved my life. **(Starts to shake again with malaria)**. It's come back – it's started again.

MAINWARING Get him away from the edge and cover him up.

They all start to move Jones – Square, his Sergeant and one or two others come out on to the tower.

SQUARE **(Seeing that Mainwaring is not looking)** Quick, get the flag out.

The Sergeant quickly attaches the flag to the rope. Cut to Jones who has all the platoon round him.

MAINWARING Keep him warm – cover him up with your jackets. Wilson – get blankets.

JONES M – M – More t – t – tonic wine.

FRAZER Captain Mainwaring – look.

They look round to see Square pulling his flag to the end of the pole.

MAINWARING Hey – what are you doing?

SQUARE Tough luck, Mainwaring.

• PAUL JOEL REMEMBERS •

'At the end of this episode there's a scene at the top of the tower, which was built in the studio. A camera was then suspended over it, looking down at Jones, who was struggling on the flag-pole. Below him, on the studio floor, was a CSO (colour separation overlay) cloth on which we projected the film of people on the grass at the base of the real tower. This was an electronic method of adding background in behind the actors. The cloth would have been an extremely bright and unnatural blue so that the background didn't overlay on to any of the foreground action.'

PAUL JOEL
Designer

MAINWARING We were first.

SQUARE But you didn't get your flag out did you? It's the flag that counts.

TELECINE: EXTERIOR. BOTTOM OF TOWER. DAY

Group – Vicar, Verger and Colonel. Colonel has binoculars.

COLONEL Yes – he's done it – It's No. 1 Platoon flag – Mainwaring's the winner.

EXTERIOR. TOP OF TOWER. DAY

MAINWARING I'm going to lodge a protest. We were the first.

FRAZER Aye – and it's our flag that's flying.

SQUARE What! **(Runs to Sergeant)** You blithering idiot. You've flown their flag.

SERGEANT It was the one you handed me.

SQUARE What skulduggery is this, Mainwaring?

MAINWARING You've lost, that's all.

SQUARE I'm going to see the Colonel about this. I strongly suspect that you're an absolute bounder. **(He goes)**

MAINWARING He's left his flag behind – chuck it to him, Wilson.

Wilson takes flag and goes to parapet.

WILSON **(Calling)** Excuse me.

WALKER I shouldn't bother about that if I was you, Sergeant.

Wilson has unrolled the flag and is about to throw it down.

MAINWARING Wait a minute – that's our flag. **(Looks to end of pole)** And *that's* our flag.

They all turn to Walker.

WALKER **(Who is plainly lying)** Well, it's like this, Mr Mainwaring – I made one flag for you and it just wasn't up to standard so I made another – which meant I had two of our flags – and I suppose I must have got one of them mixed up with the one I made for Square's platoon. Dear, oh dear. What a terrible mistake to have made.

MAINWARING Walker – I don't believe one word you're saying.

WALKER I didn't think you would somehow. Still – it was an initiative test, wasn't it, sir?

WILSON And Walker *did* use his initiative.

MAINWARING I think you all know me well enough to understand I don't approve of that sort of thing at all. You've behaved very badly indeed, Walker.

WALKER Yes, sir.

MAINWARING And if any of the rest of you were a party to this, you've incurred my most severe displeasure.

ALL Yes, sir.

MAINWARING All the same. I'm glad we won.

HELP! HELP! HELP! HELP! HELP!

LOST *DAD'S ARMY* EPISODES

Your help would be very welcome in trying to find the three 'lost episodes' of *Dad's Army*, which were wiped and are no longer available in the BBC archive.

From series two, 'The Loneliness of the Long-Distance Walker', 'A Stripe for Frazer' and 'Under Fire' are missing.

I, like millions of other *Dad's Army* fans, have never had the chance to watch these episodes, something we might be able to remedy with your help.

Check your attics, your garden sheds, ask your relatives, perhaps somewhere, someone holds an old video recording of these black and white episodes.

If you need to know more, feel free to contact me direct on my email address: rwebber@madasafish.com or write via my publisher at:
Orion Publishing Group, Orion House,
5 Upper St Martin's Lane, London WC2H 9EA.

Many thanks.

RICHARD WEBBER